# Check-*in*
# Check-*out*

## Gary K. Vallen
Northern Arizona University

## Jerome J. Vallen
University of Nevada, Las Vegas, Emeritus

## Gary F. Robinson
Centennial College

Second

Canadian

Edition

PEARSON
Prentice
Hall

Toronto

*.b2303061*
*70111019*

**Library and Archives Canada Cataloguing in Publication**

Vallen, Gary K.
    Check-in check-out / Gary K. Vallen, Jerome J. Vallen, Gary F.
Robinson. -- 2nd Canadian ed.

Includes bibliographical references and index.
ISBN 0-13-204423-4

1. Hotel management.  2. Motel management.  3. Hotel management—Canada.  4. Motel management—Canada.
I. Vallen, Jerome J.  II. Robinson, Gary F., 1945-  III. Title.

TX911.3.M27V34 2008          647.94'068          C2006-905506-8

To fathers and sons who work together.

*Gary K. Vallen and Jerome J. Vallen*

To my wife, Joyce, for her help and understanding, and to our families, friends, and Centennial College for their support.

*Gary F. Robinson*

# Brief Contents

# Contents

# Preface

Change, a dynamic force in all North American business, is the very essence of the lodging industry. New ownership structures, new marketing approaches, new computer applications, new telecommunications media, even new means of managing the human resource continue to alter the field. *Check-In Check-Out* responds to the constantly changing industry by keeping pace with the times and treating these critical topics within the framework of the hotel's front desk and its rooms department.

Sales of guest rooms is the industry's largest income producer as well as its most profitable operating segment. Because the success of this critical department depends on the support of other units, some of which are external to the organization, the discussion focuses on a broad view of lodging management. References throughout the chapters range from human resources to engineering; from accounting to telephone systems; from credit cards to email communications; from legal matters to travel agents; from environmental issues to global distribution systems; from spas to hurdle pricing. Lodging management is an integral part of the world of business. This book's contents provide for that.

The Second Canadian Edition continues to blend the old and the new. While looking ahead to the latest technologies, we have remained grounded in the history and logic that led to the innovations. That strategy remains the focus of our work. It is good pedagogy to examine what has been done and why, even as we step forward toward the innovations promised in this new millennium.

## A Closer Look at the Second Canadian Edition

The Second Canadian Edition continues to build on the successful layout of the American Seventh Edition. However, there are some significant changes.

### Highlights of the Second Canadian Edition

- New Chapter 3, **Housekeeping**, outlines the importance and responsibilities of this department and examines how it interfaces with the front desk.
- New end-of-chapter case studies, based on real situations that hospitality employees encounter, provide excellent practical experience for students.
- New Student CD: A virtual hotel software program provides a demo version for students to practise reservations and front-desk operations.
- Updated technology is discussed in Chapter 14 and throughout the text; this includes the latest information on property management systems and such topics as forecasting.
- Expanded discussions of the increased impact of the Internet on web-based reservations and the benefits of hotel websites.
- Streamlined Part IV on accounting processes to reflect an introduction relevant to front-office operations only
- Increased examination of security in Chapter 2 as part of today's world issues.

# Supplements to the Textbook

**IRCD** *Instructor's Resource CD-ROM (0-13-238393-4):* This resource CD includes the following instructor supplements:

- **Instructor's Manual:** This manual offers a range of helpful materials for both new and experienced teachers: chapter summaries, lecture preparation assistance, overheads, vocabulary, alternative calendars, and guidelines for classroom discussion. Answers to end-of-chapter questions are also provided for instructors to use as discussion, assignments, examinations, or extra credit. Solutions to the new case studies are also provided.

- **Test Item File:** The test item file offers a combination of true/false, multiple choice, and short answer questions. Also available for instructors are sample examination papers for each of the five units that structure the text. Also included is a final examination with objective-type questions, short answer questions, and brief subjective-style essay questions, all with answers.

- **PowerPoints:** The **new** PowerPoint presentations offer instructors a great visual resource.

Most of these instructor supplements are also available for download from a password-protected section of Pearson Education Canada's online catalogue (vig.pearsoned.ca). Navigate to your book's catalogue page to view a list of the supplements that are available. See your local sales representative for details and access.

# Acknowledgements

The authors note with appreciation the contribution of the professional community in making available some of the exhibits used throughout the book. In particular, Gary Robinson would like to thank Tony Pollard, president of the Hotel Association of Canada, and Mary Dempster, hotel manager of the Delta Barrington & Halifax, as well as her team members for their efforts: Scott Davies, Rooms Division Manager; Bruce Rhodenizer; Executive Housekeeper; and Coleen Hatcher, Assistant Executive Housekeeper. Other valued input was received from Fred Lawlor, vice-president and general manager of Avendra, and Chris Lund, Delta Toronto East Regional Vice-President and General Manager.

The authors would also like to thank the following reviewers in Canada for their help in making a great book even better: Mark Elliott, Douglas College; Gabor Forgacs, Ryerson University; Susan Knoop, Northern Alberta Institute of Technology; Donnalu Macdonald, George Brown College; Kerstin Schneider, St. Clair College; Laurie Slater, Red River College; Michael Tarnowski, Algonquin College; Mike Tunnah; and Paul Willie.

Finally, Gary Robinson would like to thank the following people who deserve a lot of credit for the publication of this Canadian edition: Patti Altridge, Developmental Editor, for all of her friendly encouragement; Amanda Wesson, Production Editor; Susan Broadhurst, Production Editor and Copy Editor; and Chris Helsby, Acquisitions Editor.

# About the Authors

**Dr. Gary K. Vallen** is a full professor in the School of Hotel and Restaurant Management at Northern Arizona University. He joined that program in 1988 as one of its founding faculty, bringing 16 years of industry experience to the classroom. Part of that resumé included vice-president and assistant general manager of a casino, hotel sales manager, financial and operational analyst, and associate manager for private clubs.

Dr. Vallen received his undergraduate degree in hotel administration at the University of Nevada, Las Vegas. Despite the long hours of industry, he simultaneously worked and earned an MBA at the University of Nevada, Reno. His Ed.D. degree, with an emphasis in hospitality education (Northern Arizona University), was earned after he began teaching. In addition to *Check-In, Check-Out*, Dr. Vallen co-authored *An Introduction to Hospitality Management* and has published more than three dozen refereed articles and conference proceedings. He is on the editorial boards of six professional journals.

Professor Vallen operates Gary Vallen Hospitality Consultants, which specializes in hosted casino nights for clients of destination management companies and in visitor analyses for festivals, fairs, rodeos, and ski slopes. He has developed and carried out numerous secret-shopper evaluations for both hotels and restaurants. The Southwest location has enabled him to assist many Native American groups, including the Hopi and Navajo, but he is also well known for his rural tourism expertise.

**Dr. Jerome J. Vallen** was the founding dean of the College of Hotel Administration, University of Nevada, Las Vegas, and served in that capacity for 22 years. He is now professor emeritus/dean emeritus. Jerry Vallen returned to the classroom for a short period before taking an assignment as founding dean of the Australian International Hotel School, Canberra.

After earning a baccalaureate degree at Cornell, he entered the hotel industry, carrying with him the food experience gained from the family's small chain of four restaurants. For several years, he taught and worked in industry. Dr. Vallen earned a master's degree in educational administration (St. Lawrence University) and a doctoral degree from Cornell's School of Hotel Administration.

He has co-authored a book on hotel management and edited a work on the legal basis for obtaining a gaming licence in Nevada. Professor Vallen has served as a consulting editor for textbook publishers; a travelling consultant to the U.S. Department of Commerce, which has carried him to more than three dozen countries; an outside examiner for the University of the West Indies; president of a consulting company; member of the board of several private companies and public entities; and president and chairman of the Council on Hotel, Restaurant and Institutional Education (CHRIE).

Such diverse groups as the University Alumni Association, the Educational Foundation of the National Restaurant Association, and the Educational Institute of the American Hotel & Lodging Association have honoured him. So has CHRIE, with its prestigious H.B. Meek Award. Jerome Vallen has been cited in the *Congressional Record* and named among the 100 most important Las Vegans of the twentieth century.

**Gary F. Robinson** embarked on a career in the hotel industry by working with Commonwealth Holiday Inns of Canada in Toronto, Ontario. Beginning as a front-desk clerk in 1966, he worked his way up to the position of innkeeper (general manager) by the age of 27—the youngest person in the company's history to hold this post. Robinson worked in eight different Holiday Inns over a 10-year period before he accepted general manager positions with the Sheridan Inn in St. Thomas, Ontario, and later, with the Highwayman Inn in Orillia, Ontario.

In 1986, Gary was offered a full-time position in the Hospitality and Tourism Administration program at Centennial College in Toronto. He is currently the program's second-year coordinator as well as a Centennial College graduate.

# Part I

# The Hotel Industry

Whatever the title—*lodging, innkeeping, the hotel business*—ours is an amazingly resilient industry. It flourishes because it adopts and adapts easily and quickly to changing circumstances. Associating with it is an exhilarating experience even if one ignores the treasures of its very long history and focuses just on the present. Except for an occasional historical glance, that's what this text does: focuses on managing for the present and the likely future of the lodging industry.

Business and industry experienced three periods of major consolidation during the twentieth century. The era opened with the consolidation of heavy industry, motivated by the economies of scale that were the most evident advantage of mass production. As a result, the giant manufacturers, railroads, and oil producers expanded during this first stage.

The middle of the century witnessed a second period of consolidation, but it was driven by a different need. This time, Canadian business found its economy of size not in the unification of production, but in the consolidation of administrative and financial processes. Through consolidation, the conglomerates of this period were able to span industries and products to build larger and larger enterprises. One of the best-known conglomerates was Canadian Pacific Railway, owners of Canadian Pacific Hotels, who purchased the Canadian National Hotel chain (CN Hotels) in 1988. In 1999, it acquired Princess Hotels and Fairmont Hotels, creating Fairmont Hotels and Resorts. This third wave of consolidation gave our largest owner-operated Canadian **hotelier** an international presence.

The twentieth century closed, and the twenty-first century opened, on still another theme: globalization. As business and industry criss-cross the oceans and enter foreign territories, consumers become more important than producers. Brand names and recognizable logos (for example, McDonald's and Tim Hortons) drive company profits and sales, as did the production and financial issues of previous consolidations 50 or 100 years earlier.

In Part I, we review this need for identification. Since the move toward consolidation is just emerging, contradictions abound. On the one hand, the industry stresses choice and variety. It offers a range of facilities, accommodations, prices, and locations that have spawned an uncountable and confusing number of brands, sub brands, and allied brands. There is simultaneous recognition among hoteliers (and among the heads of other consumer-product industries) that consumers bypass the unknown in favour of brands they recognize and respect. So, even as new concepts and products are announced, a wave of consolidation sweeps over the hotel business. Company 1 merges with company 2 and eventually the weaker brand disappears. Journeys End, a well-known Canadian hotel name, was reflagged as Comfort Inns.

In the first chapter, we identify changes in the industry, trace some of its history, and set the foundation for the operational issues that are treated in the balance of the book. Chapter 2 continues by illustrating the products more specifically and explaining how the industry organizes itself to deliver them. Our new Chapter 3 examines the essential role of housekeeping and the interaction between front office operations and this department. Throughout is the theme of restructuring, by which the hotel industry remains dynamic and competitive.

Changes in society, travel, and business have been matched by new developments in lodging. At one time, hotels served primarily as the storage arm of transportation: locating along travellers' routes, waiting for potential guests to tire and to rest. Today's guests find an array of routes to a variety of destinations for a range of purposes. The hotel industry has had to re-create itself again and again to meet these modern demands. New patterns have appeared, and here we examine four of them: product, market, ownership, and management.

## Chapter 1

# The Hotel Industry: Past and Present

## Learning Objectives

After reading this chapter, you will be able to do the following:

1. **Describe the rich history of hotels in Canada and define "the hotel business."**

2. **Identify traditional methods of classifying hotels.**

3. **Explain new product and market patterns, including product segmentation and marketing to the individual and group guest.**

4. **Describe new ownership and management patterns, including ownership and financing alternatives, chains, management companies, management contracts, and franchises.**

Hotel keeping is one of humankind's oldest professions, tracing its simple beginnings back thousands of years to the prehistoric cave. Tourism, of which hotel keeping is a part, is one of humankind's newest endeavours. So, hotel keeping is an old industry with a young future. It builds on ages of tradition even as it changes with dynamic and often unexpected twists. Hotel keeping, or innkeeping, has flourished through centuries of change, adapting its form and type of service to changing customer demands. The present-day hotel evolved from the relay houses of China, from the khans (roadside stopping places) of the Middle East, from the *tabernas* (taverns) of ancient Rome, from the roadhouses of Europe, from the inns of stagecoach North America, and from the railway hotels of Canada. The lodging industry has emerged from this rich cultural background with a special place in society. Today, hotel keeping is an integral part of tourism's worldwide boom, a major player in the global outreach of business, and a continuing presence in the social, political, and cultural life of every community.

## Scope of the Industry

At first, travel was an individual thing: a solitary traveller on foot or horseback, a loose band of pilgrims, or a small coach full of strangers. Travel was a rare experience because travelling by foot or horse was slow and difficult. Besides, most people were neither politically nor economically free to move about. All three factors have changed dramatically during the past 100 years. Rapid means of transportation have emerged from the industrial and electronic ages, and political and economic freedoms have appeared to help shape the modern travel industry.

▲
**Exhibit 1-1**
One of the newest hotels in Canada is the Trump International Hotel and Tower being built in downtown Toronto. This 70-storey residence and hotel condominium will be the tallest residential building in Canada with 286 luxury rooms and 147 condominium residences.

## A Look Back

For many, many centuries, hotels remained small, rarely exceeding a handful of rooms. Early guests shared their accommodations with strangers and often decided themselves how much to pay their hosts. Small establishments were adequate for the times because the number of travellers was few, and they were housed and fed as part of the innkeeper's own family. All that changed with the Industrial Revolution, which provided the structural steel to build upward. With it came the invention of the corporation, which financed the skyscrapers that housed the new hotels. Creative marketing and amazing developments in transportation such as the commercialization of the jet airplane enticed the world's travellers, completing the circle of forces that created the worldwide tourism phenomenon.

The modern hotel, with its exciting architecture (see Exhibit 1-1), has become a destination in itself, but that wasn't always the case. The historical role of innkeeping has been one of response, of providing services along a traveller's predetermined route. As long as the traveller's course, method of transportation, and travel time were restricted, as long as there were no options, there was no need to differentiate the inn. For nearly two millennia, even the ultimate destination was predetermined. Innkeepers merely located their accommodations along the traveller's known path and waited for the call to service. That was true even as recently as 50 years ago, when roadside motels dominated the Canadian highway segment of the market. The range and quality of accommodations reflected the innkeeper's inclination, not the needs of the guests. Shelter from the elements and an opportunity to rest from bone-wearying travel were the major services that the early inns provided. Food and lodging were basic products then; both were essential since the guest had no alternatives. Lodging is still a basic commodity, but many hotels no longer offer food. Tomorrow may be another story altogether.

## History of Canadian Hotel Development

In Canada, the first inns or roadhouses sprang up along the early stagecoach lines. This was followed by the development of the much larger railway hotels by

Canadian Pacific Railway (CPR) in the late 1800s. The development of roadside motels began post–Second World War as the quality of both roads and cars improved, the middle class became wealthier, and travel by car became the most frequently used method of transportation. The latest changes to the industry occurred with the building of airport hotels beginning in the early 1950s, after the commercialization of jet aircraft. The creation of conference and convention centres in Canada's major cities has further led to the development of large urban properties to fulfill the rooming requirements of these large centres.

**The Canadian Railway Hotels**   Nineteenth-century Canadian Pacific visionary William Cornelius Van Horne dreamed of building lavish rest stops alongside the newly constructed CPR. Noted for his famous quote, "If we can't export the scenery, we'll import the tourists," Van Horne did just that. He built Mount Stephen House high among the wilds of the Canadian Rocky Mountains and began welcoming guests to this first-ever Canadian Pacific Hotels property in 1886. Other grand hotels followed, with the legendary Banff Springs built in 1888, Chateau Lake Louise completed in 1890, and Le Château Frontenac opening its doors in 1893. In the late 1920s, the Château Laurier hotel was expanded; originally owned by the Grand Trunk Railway, by then it belonged to CNR, which had been formed in 1922 out of the Grand Trunk and several other smaller railways. In 1928, the CNR also opened the beautiful Hotel Nova Scotian in Halifax, Nova Scotia. As mentioned earlier—in the introduction to Part I, CP Hotels bought the CN hotel chain in 1988 and then ventured outside of Canada and acquired sun destination Princess Hotels in Mexico, Arizona, Barbados, and Bermuda. Motivated to expand globally, Canadian Pacific Hotels acquired Fairmont Hotels in the fall of 1999, creating Fairmont Hotels and Resorts.

In April 2006, a Canadian company owned by Kingdom Hotels International ("Kingdom"), owners of Raffles Hotels and Colony Capital ("Colony"), acquired Fairmont Hotels & Resorts Inc. (FHR).Their combined portfolios have transformed the companies into a luxury global leader with 120 hotels in 23 countries.

**The Canadian Roadside Hotel/Motel**   Some uniquely Canadian hotel chains were built during the hotel boom of the 1950s and 1960s. On the east coast of Canada, the Llewellyn family created Auberges Wandlyn Inns. Wandlyn now has 21 hotels throughout the Maritimes and Quebec.

In southern Ontario, David Rubinoff purchased an exclusive franchise to build Holiday Inns in Ontario (Commonwealth Holiday Inns), while the Adams family of Montreal created Atlific Hotels and purchased the exclusive franchise rights for Holiday Inns for the rest of Canada. In later years, Atlific did not fulfill its franchise expansion requirements and Holiday Inns Inc. granted Commonwealth Holiday Inns the shared (with Atlific) franchise rights for the rest of Canada. Commonwealth became one of the most successful Canadian hotel companies of the period, with almost 70 hotels in Canada, the United States, the United Kingdom, and the Caribbean. In the 1980s, as economy lodging became popular, Maurice H. Rollins, along with co-founder Joe Basch, and Tom Landers created Journeys End Corporation. They built their first 60-unit Journey's End hotel in Belleville, Ontario, in 1978, and by 1991 had 137 locations. In July 1993, Rollins led Journey's End Corporation into a 50/50 joint venture partnership with Choice Hotels International and stayed on as chairman of Choice Hotels Canada. This economy chain took the Ontario market by storm and has now been reflagged as Comfort Inns, part of the Choice Hotels group.

Of course, who could forget Isadore Sharp, the founder of Four Seasons Hotels and Resorts who built a modest motor hotel in downtown Toronto in 1961. Four

Seasons Hotels and Resorts now operates 69 properties in 31 countries and also manages many Regent hotels worldwide.

In 1935, two Maritime newlyweds, Wally and Sally Rodd, founded Rodd Hotels and Resorts, which now operates 10 hotels in Prince Edward Island, Nova Scotia, and New Brunswick. Atlific Hotels, headquartered in Montreal, also entered the economy market with Venture Inns.

As we move to the west coast, the Gaglardi (current CEO R. Thomas [Tom] Gaglardi) family created Sandman Hotels, Inns & Suites and today operates 31 hotels in British Columbia, Alberta, Saskatchewan, and Montreal. Another large player across Canada is Westmont Hospitality Group, which also operates InnVest REIT Hotels. Westmont Hospitality Group is one of the world's largest privately held hospitality organizations. They own and/or manage more than 400 hotels on three continents, and have formed strategic alliances with many of the world's largest hotel brands, including InterContinental Hotels, Choice Hotels, Hilton, Radisson, Cendant, and Starwood.

**The American Invasion** Since the early 1960s with Holiday Inns and Orangeroof of Canada, which was owned by the Carruthers family of Caterpillar fame (then the Canadian franchise holder for Howard Johnson hotels), almost all of the major American chains have expanded throughout Canada. At the same time, successful Canadian hotel companies such as Fairmont Hotels, Atlific Hotels & Resorts (purchased by Ocean Properties Ltd., Hotels & Resorts in 1997), and Four Seasons Hotels and Resorts began to expand internationally. Today, Canada and Canadians are major players in the national and international hotel scene.

**The Size of the Canadian Hotel Industry** Geographically, Canada is the second-largest country in the world. According to the Hotel Association of Canada, there are presently 6581 hotel properties in Canada with a total of 377 771 rooms, employing 227 000 people and creating $11 billion in national accommodation revenue. Canada is the tenth most popular tourist destination in the world, with 39 million non-resident visitors each year (see Exhibit 1-2).

**Exhibit 1-2** ▶
The Canadian hotel industry fact sheet highlights the importance of the hotel industry to Canada's economy.

- 6581 properties (2004)

- 377 771 rooms (2004)

- 227 000 people employed

- 62.1 percent occupancy rate (2004)

- $117.40 average daily rate (ADR) (2004)

- $72.96 RevPar (revenue per available room) (2004)

- $11 billion national accommodation revenue (2003)

- 41.1 percent of properties with 30 rooms or more are branded (2004)

- 55.3 percent of rooms in properties with 30 rooms or more are branded (2004)

- 66.2 percent of hotels with 100 rooms or more are branded (2004)

Tourism is the world's largest and fastest-growing industry. It includes accommodation, food and beverage, travel trade, adventure tourism and outdoor recreation, attractions, events and conferences, transportation and tourism services. In 2003, tourism spending in Canada reached $52.1 billion and the total tourism gross domestic product (GDP) was $22.6 billion or 1.99 percent of Canada's GDP at market prices. The total tourism sector employs nearly 1.7 million people, or 11 percent of the Canadian labour force.

**The Service Culture** The latter half of the twentieth century and the first part of the twenty-first century have been dubbed the "age of service" or the "service society." This contrasts with the agricultural age of the eighteenth century and the industrial age of the nineteenth century. The hotel industry, along with many other businesses (medicine, banking, retailing), carries this service label. As with many labels, there is sometimes confusion. All hotels do not offer the same level of service and consequently do not charge the same rates. Although we speak of one industry, lodging has many, many parts with but a single commonality: courtesy. The hotel industry has responded rapidly, vigorously, and innovatively to a growing demand for choice. In so doing, it leaves unclear exactly what the hotel business is.

# What Is the Hotel Business?

The lodging industry is so broad an endeavour worldwide, divided into so many pieces, that a single definition is not practical. Nevertheless, many declare lodging to be among the world's largest industries. It is certainly a major segment of international business, but how much so remains an elusive measure. As part of tourism, hotel keeping helps drive the economic engines of developing countries. Because tourism development goes hand in hand with construction, hotels and other elements of tourism (roads, airports, etc.) account for huge investments even in diversified economies. One example is the 5000-room MGM Grand Hotel and Entertainment Park in Las Vegas, which spent $1 billion in construction costs alone! Together, tourism and construction accelerate both the economic rise and the economic downturn of a tourist area. In Canada, one in nine workers is employed in the hospitality industry.

**A Cyclical Industry** The hotel industry is cyclical. It goes through wide swings, from periods of very good times to periods of very bad times. Consequently, the number of hotels and the number of hotel rooms vary over time, shifting up and down as the cycle moves through its loops. That's what happened beginning in the early 1980s. High interest rates, difficulty in getting financing, the beginning of a recession, and the collapse of the real estate market (remember, hotel buildings are pieces of real estate) brought the cycle to a devastating low—a low that lasted for well over a decade. Then came a slow reversal in the cycle. By the mid-1990s, hotel construction began to reappear. That upward momentum accelerated as the 1990s came to an end and continued into the twenty-first century. About three years are needed between planning and opening a hotel, longer if there are special zoning, financing, or environmental issues. Therefore, the building boom that followed the upward cycle of the late 1990s was not readily evident until the close of the century and the beginning of the new millennium.

Recovery was halted suddenly in 2001 by the attack on the World Trade Center in New York City. The entire travel industry experienced a major interruption of the upward trend with those tragic events. Such an abrupt downturn had not occurred since 1973, when the oil embargo brought the travel industry and much of the industrialized world to its knees.

| Monday | 100% |
| Tuesday | 100 |
| Wednesday | 90 |
| Thursday | 90 |
| Friday | 40 |
| Saturday | 20 |
| Sunday | 20 |
| Total | 460% |
| Average per seven days | 66% |

## Special Characteristics of the Hotel Business

The room manager's ability to maximize the number of rooms sold or to increase the average rate per room is limited by several characteristics special to the lodging business. Some of these peculiarities are also found in other industries, chiefly among the airlines.

**Perishability** Even the industry's newest recruit knows that a room left unsold tonight cannot be sold again. Empty hotel rooms, like empty airline seats or unsold television commercials, cannot be shelved, cannot be stored, cannot be saved, and cannot be used again.

**Location** Ellsworth Statler coined the expression "location, location, location" to emphasize its importance to the hotel. Good economic locations are difficult to find in urban Canada. Changing neighbourhoods and shifting markets sometimes doom a hotel whose original location was good. Unlike the airline seat, there is no way to change a hotel's location. So, management has learned to depend less on desirable real estate and more on marketing and sales; less on drive-by or walk-in traffic and more on central reservation systems.

**Fixed Supply** Not only is the location of the hotel fixed but so is its supply of (that is, the number of) rooms. Airlines can adjust the number of seats by adding or removing planes from the route. With hotels, what you see is what you get.

**High Operating Costs** Unlike manufacturing industries, which offset labour with large capital investments, hotels are both capital and labour intensive. The result is high fixed costs (a *large nut* in the jargon of the industry), which continue whether or not the hotel has business. Thus, a high **percentage of occupancy** is needed just to break even.

**Seasonality** Throwing away the key is a traditional practice when a new hotel is opened. The act signifies that the hotel never closes. Yet hotel keeping, even for commercial hotels, is a very seasonal business. The cyclical dip strikes the commercial hotel every seven days as it struggles to offset poor weekend business.

**Occupancy** computations must account for this weekend phenomenon. Especially so since the business traveller—the one who is not in the hotel during the weekends—still accounts for the majority of the lodging industry's business. Given the usual profile of the commercial urban hotel (see Exhibit 1-3), national occupancy percentages in the high 70s and 80s remain an elusive goal.

Annual cycles compound the problem. Commercial business is down even in midweek between Thanksgiving and New Year's Day and from May to Labour Day.

Urban hotels offer special weekend packages for couples and families. They may create weekend spa, theatre, sports, and entertainment packages (to mention only a few) by partnering with activities occurring in the downtown core to create a need for their overnight accommodation.

The resort pattern is the opposite of the commercial pattern. Weekends are busy and midweek less so. The slack period of the commercial hotel is the very season of the resort. At one time, resorts opened on the Victoria Day weekend and closed on Labour Day, or only opened on weekends until Thanksgiving and then closed.

This 100- to 130-day pattern made the hotel's success dependent on the weather. Two weeks of rain are devastating when the break-even point is 80 days of near-full occupancy.

Although the dates of the winter season differ, there are still only 100 days between December 17 and March 15. Both winter and summer resorts have extended their seasons with groups, conferences, and special activities.

# Traditional Classifications

The inns of old evolved from private homes. Today's hotel, even the mom-and-pop variety, is not represented as anyone's home. It is either a point of destination or an accommodation for those in transit. Yesterday's tavern offered the family meal to all who came. Dining today is a created experience in design, decor, and menu. The old inn was almost indistinguishable from its neighbours. Today's edifice is a sharp contrast in style and packaging.

Although the basic concepts of food, shelter, and hospitality remain, their means of delivery have changed. These changes have been marked by shifting terminology: **hostel**, tavern, public house, inn, guest house, hotel, resort, motel, motor lodge, motor inn, bed and breakfast, airtel, boatel, hometel, skytel, and condotel.

Despite the speed of change, several traditional classifications have withstood the test of time. Some have more objective measures than others. None are self-excluding: Hotels can fall into every category or into only some. Moreover, there are degrees of belonging. One **property** may be well within a classification, whereas another may exhibit only some of the characteristics. Each category has an impact on the scope and function of the front office.

## Size

Many methods could be used to measure the **size** of a hotel, but the number of **available rooms** is the traditional standard. Other possible measures of size (number of floors, amount of land, number of employees, gross dollar sales, or net profits) are just not used. Of course, an obvious relationship exists between the number of rooms and these other values.

**Hotels**  Hotels are grouped by size for purposes of study, for financial reporting, and for membership dues. A quick and easy classification considers 100 rooms or fewer to be a small hotel, between 100 and 300 rooms to be one of average size, and more than 300 rooms to be a large property.

The recent boom in hotel construction offers an interesting footnote. New hotels are small; 80 rooms is the average size of recent hotel construction, hardly surprising when the Hotel Association of Canada reports the average size of its membership at approximately 56 rooms. Visualizing such small properties as *the* lodging industry is difficult when one thinks of Canada's largest hotel, the Delta Chelsea in downtown Toronto with 1590 rooms, or the New Otani in Tokyo with 2057 rooms. More typical are cities such as Winnipeg, Manitoba, with some 58 hotel properties and about 6375 hotel rooms, an average of 110 rooms per hotel. In contrast, hotels in the European Economic Area, where family ownership still prevails, average fewer than 50 rooms per property. Japanese hotels average about 70 rooms per property.

**Motels** Attempts to distinguish hotels, motels, and motor inns (motor hotels, motor lodges) by size were abandoned long ago. Many motor hotels have in excess of 300 rooms and many hotels have fewer than 25. Still, people usually assume that motels are smaller than hotels.

The Canadian Provincial Conference on Tourism takes another view. It has developed three working definitions: A hotel is a commercial establishment in which the units (rooms) are accessible from the interior; motels have units that are accessible from the exterior; and motor hotels (or motor inns) have units that are accessible from both the interior and the exterior.

**Mom-and-Pops** Certain economics of size account for the decline of the small hotel. These start with financing and construction and involve every aspect of the operation from marketing to purchasing. Size determines the quality of management the property can afford. A motel with fewer than 100 rooms cannot budget management talent at the same level as a competitor with 300 rooms or a chain controlling several 100-room properties in the same area.

How, then, does the **mom-and-pop** establishment (the small, family-owned and -operated motel) continue to survive? In the same way that small grocery stores and tailor shops do. It offers individual attention by the owners and their families. Guests receive the personal attention that is impossible with any other kind of organization. Labour costs are almost non-existent, because the proprietor and the family babysit the establishment 24 hours per day, 365 days per year.

## Class

Hotels are ranked or graded into distinct classes. There are two objective methods of making the divisions, but properties are also classified subjectively. One often says or hears that a particular hotel is a "first-class" (or "fourth-class") property. Nothing measurable is used to arrive at the conclusion—it's just sensed. Fortunately, more objective measures are available, but even these are far from perfect. One approach uses the average daily room rate; the other uses a worldwide rating system.

**Average Daily Rate (ADR)** In large measure, the price that the guest pays for the room is the best criterion of class. Delivering elegance and service costs money. Large rooms, costly construction, and expensive furnishings mean larger finance costs, depreciation, taxes, power usage, and so on. All of these are recovered by higher room rates. If towels are elegantly large and thick, the higher costs of purchase and laundering (by weight) are recovered by higher room rates. Similarly, a high level of maintenance, 24-hour **room service**, sauna baths, and other extra services represent both a better class of hotel and higher room rates.

**Average daily rate** has generally been increasing in Canada with the exception of 2003, when it experienced a slight dip. However, this increase does not necessarily measure greater service or elegance (that is, class) across the industry, or even at an individual property. A higher ADR is needed to recover increased operating costs (labour, energy, interest, etc.). Furthermore, properties in small towns have a different measure than their big-city cousins. A $70 rate in Vancouver conjures up a totally different class of hotel than does the same $70 rate in a small rural town. However, at a given time and with a judicious concern for the size, type, and location of the hotel, the ADR seems to be a fair measure of class, so much so that published rates allow us to classify the nation's hotels (see Exhibit 1-4).

**Exhibit 1-4** ▶
Average daily rate can be used to categorize hotels, since room rate is one measure of class. The trade press often reports on these seven classifications.

## Classification of Hotels by Average Daily Room Rate

**Deluxe Hotels** (typical room rate: $600 plus/night)
Fairmont Hotels
Four Seasons Hotels
Ritz-Carlton Hotels

**Upper Upscale Hotels** (typical room rate: $400/night)
Le Meridien Hotels
Sofitel Hotels
W Hotels

**Upscale Hotels** (typical room rate: $300/night)
Hyatt Hotels
Marriott Hotels
Omni Hotels

**Midprice Hotels with Food** (typical room rate: $100/night)
Four Points (Sheraton)
Garden Inns (Hilton)
Best Western

**Midprice Hotels without Food** (typical room rate: $80/night)
Amerisuites
Hampton Inns
La Quinta

**Economy Hotels** (typical room rate: $60/night)
Baymont Inns and Suites
Red Roof Inns
Super 8

**Budget Inns** (typical room rate: $50/night)
EconoLodge
Microtel
Motel 6

**Full Service to Limited Service** Hotel/motel facilities are as diverse as the travelling public. Handling this enormous range of guests has created a heterogeneous industry, from the plush, full-service high-rise to the squat, limited-service motel. On the one hand is a group of operator–investors who maintain that guests want nothing more than a room with a good mattress and a clean bath. Guests get along nicely without swimming pools, lobbies, or closets, according to this view. This hotelier offers **limited service** at a limited charge. One hundred and eighty degrees away is the **full-service** deluxe hotel. Not only does this hotel include superior facilities, it also offers a full complement of services. Full service adds a menu of dining options and a range of extras, including lounges, in-room newspapers, and specialties such as swimming pools, exercise facilities, spas and a wide range of telecommunications. Between the two extremes lies the bulk of the industry, adding services where competition requires and costs allow, paring them as the market shifts and acceptable self-service equipment appears. In this chapter, we introduce these newer innovations to hotel keeping. Among them is the all-suite hotel. Commercial and leisure guests alike have been attracted to all-suite accommodations such as Marriott's Residence Inns or Hilton's Embassy Suites. By locating on less costly real estate and reducing the amount of public space, all-suites offer more guest room space at lower prices than at the luxury hotels. All-suites are closer to the limited-service hotel than to the full-service hotel.

**Number of Employees** Almost by definition, *full service* and *limited service* refer to the size of the hotel's staff: the number of employees. Thus,

$$\text{number of employees per guest room} = \frac{\text{number of employees on staff}}{\text{number of rooms available for sale}}$$

becomes another measure of class. As with room rates, the industry provides a wide range of offerings.

Budget properties, which have no restaurants, no bars, no room service, and no convention space, score as low as 0.25 employees per guest room. An 80-room hotel might have as few as 20 persons on staff. There's a limit to how small the staff can be. Regardless of the number of rooms, the desk must be staffed every hour of the day and night. Workers need days off. Housekeeping staff, maybe laundry workers, a night watch, a manager, and someone for repairs and maintenance must be among the count. The size of the hotel matters only after that basic staffing guide is met. A hotel of 60 rooms may have almost as many workers as one twice its size. Housekeeping would be the big difference. If a housekeeper can clean 15 rooms per shift, 3 or 4 additional employees are needed to do the extra 60 rooms if occupancy is around, say, 80 percent. Other staff members at the desk, the manager, the housekeeper, maintenance and grounds, the accountant, and so on, might number almost the same for each property.

The in-between class of hotel uses an in-between number of employees. That ratio ranges from 0.5 employees per room to as much as a 1:1 ratio. Depending on the services offered, a 300-room hotel could have as few as 150 employees and as many as 250 or so. The number is most likely to be about 200 to 225 if food service is provided and a bar needs staffing.

Full-service hotels staff a full complement of departments, including bell service, restaurants, turndown bed service, and telecommunications persons, among others. Hotels with theatre shows, hectares of grounds to be maintained, casinos, and 24-hour services require extra personnel and have still higher ratios, perhaps 1.5 employees per guest room. A 1000-room hotel/casino operating fully over 24 hours could easily have 1250 to 1500 employees.

Asian properties offer the best in service. Labour is less costly, so the number of employees per room is the world's highest. At the Bangkok Shangri-La, for example, 1073 staff members handle 697 rooms, a ratio of 1.5:1. Hong Kong's Peninsula Hotel ranks better still with a staff of 655 for its 300 rooms, better than 2:1.

**Rating Systems** Formal and informal, government-run and privately developed rating systems are another means of identifying the class of hotel. Using formal rating systems, the approach has been standardized, certainly more so within each country than across boundaries. Most members of the World Tourism Organization have adopted the WTO's five recommended classifications. Top is **deluxe** (or luxury) class, then **first class** (which is not top-of-the-line despite its name), followed by **tourist class**, sometimes called **economy** or second **class**. Third and fourth classes, which usually have no private baths, centralized heat, or even carpeting, are not for international tourists.

Each country implements its own categories. Local inspectors tend to be quite subjective in their ratings. If there is a pool on the premises, it will meet standards whether or not it is clean. An elevator adds to the ratings, whether or not it works. Government rating systems also fall prey to bribery, politics, and bickering within the trade association.

**Worldwide** Worldwide there are almost 100 rating systems. They range from the self-evaluation plan of Switzerland to the mandatory grading plan of South Africa, where tax incentives encourage properties to upgrade.

Europe's four- and five-star hotels always have restaurants and bars; those with three stars may or may not. Two-star properties almost never do.

**The North American Experience** In a uniquely North American way, government is not involved in the ratings; they are done by private enterprise. Mobil and the American Automobile Association (AAA) are the major competitors in the United States. In Canada, the Canadian Automobile Association (CAA), Mobil, and Canada Select are the major national organizations offering lodging ratings. Individual hotel chains have informal self-rating systems that emerge as a by-product of their efforts at market segmentation.

Membership in Preferred Hotels, a loosely knit affiliation of **independent** hotels, requires ratings of superior or above from one of the recognized services. Therefore, simply belonging to Preferred gives the property a superior-plus rating.

Canada Select was developed after extensive consumer research into what was expected and considered important at various star levels and categories of accommodations. Presently, nine provinces and one territory are delivering the Canada Select program: Newfoundland and Labrador, New Brunswick, Prince Edward Island, Nova Scotia, Ontario, Alberta, Saskatchewan, British Columbia, Manitoba, and the Yukon. It is operated by industry organizations in each of the provinces.

Canada Select is the most popular Canadian rating system, with more than 4000 rated properties, and has accommodations rated within six main categories: Hotel/Motel, Inn, Resort, Bed and Breakfast/Tourist Homes, Cottage, and Hunting and Fishing. To further confuse the issue, there are additional categories on the Canada Select Nova Scotia website such as Bed & Breakfast Inn, Condo Cottage, Farm Vacation, Guest Home, and Inn.

Canada Select and Mobil's ratings are done with stars; CAA/AAA uses diamonds. All organizations are stingy with their five-level ratings, awarding only two or three dozen although each looks at thousands of properties annually. In most cases, Mobil gives lower overall scores. All companies have field inspectors, who make on-site visits, often at the request of the particular establishment. Evaluations are based on written standards (see Exhibit 1-5); consumer voting is not their technique. Mobil refuses to disclose why stars are added or removed. Still, it is reported that a top rating by the Mobil guide can boost business by 20 percent! Similarly, as much as 40 percent of small hotel volume may be attributed to the CAA/AAA guide. We may eventually see a new environmental rating. Research indicates a willingness on the part of guests to pay more for environmentally friendly lodgings (EFLs). EFL could be another criterion for, or a completely separate rating from, the usual standards.

# Type

Size, class, type, and plan (discussed next) are the four traditional classifications describing the lodging industry. **Type** is subdivided into three parts: commercial hotels, resort hotels, and residential hotels. As with the distinction between hotel and motel, all definitions within the lodging industry have begun to blur. Traditional designations do not always provide the best descriptions for a changing industry. They make no provision for such new concepts as **conference centres** or condominium hotels. A host of

**Exhibit 1-5 ▶**
The Canada Select Star
Rating Program is used
by field inspectors to
rate properties.

**Explanation of the Canada Select Accommodation Rating Program**

Establishments voluntarily participate in Canada Select Accommodations and are rated within six categories:

- Hotel/Motel
- Country Inn
- Resort
- Bed & Breakfast
- Cottage
- Hunting and Fishing Lodge

The following are the star rating descriptions:

★ Modest accommodations meeting the Canada Select standards of cleanliness, comfort, and safety.

★ ⫯ A half-star is awarded to properties whose overall quality of facilities significantly exceeds the one-star rating.

★ ★ Modest accommodations with additional facilities and some amenities.

★ ★ ⫯ A half-star is awarded to properties whose overall quality of facilities significantly exceeds the two-star rating.

★ ★ ★ Above average accommodations with a greater range of facilities, guest amenities, and services available.

★ ★ ★ ⫯ A half-star is awarded to properties whose overall quality of facilities significantly exceeds the three-star rating.

★ ★ ★ ★ Exceptional accommodations with an extensive range of facilities, guest amenities, and services.

★ ★ ★ ★ ⫯ A half-star is awarded to properties whose overall quality of facilities significantly exceeds the four-star rating.

★ ★ ★ ★ ★ Luxurious properties; among the very best in the country in terms of their outstanding facilities, guest services, and quality provided.

other new concepts has appeared in recent times, and they are classified in the emerging patterns outlined in this chapter.

**Commercial Hotels** The **commercial hotel**, the largest category of North American hotels, is also called the **transient hotel**. It is a hotel for short-stay guests, guests who are transient, temporary, or coming for many reasons but chiefly for business. The corporate business traveller forms the core of the commercial hotel's customer base. By consensus, the commercial guest is viewed as the backbone of the lodging industry. The business traveller is equally critical to the large urban property and to the small roadside motel. Increasing leisure travel is quickly promoting the importance of the tourist within the mix.

A true commercial hotel is located close to its market—the business community—which means in an urban area. As the population centre has left the downtown area, so has the commercial hotel. Arterial highways, research parks, business parks, airports, and even suburban shopping centres have become favourite locations. This helps explain the poor weekend occupancy (business people are not working) of the urban hotel (see Exhibit 1-3 on page 8). Attempts to offset this weekend decline with tourists, conventions, and special promotions have been only moderately successful.

Transient hotels are usually full-service hotels. Until recently, business people have been expense-account travellers who wanted (and could afford) four- and five-star accommodations. Lately, the travel offices of many businesses have begun to monitor travel costs more closely. Travel costs do affect a business's **bottom line!**

**Residential Hotels** In contrast to the transient commercial guest, the residential guest takes up permanent quarters. This creates a different legal relationship between the guest and the landlord and may be formalized with a lease. In some locales, the room occupancy tax is not payable for a residential guest in a transient hotel.

Some **residential hotels** accommodate **transient guests,** and many transient hotels have **permanent guests,** with and without leases. Sutton Place Hotels in Toronto and Vancouver are a good example of this combination: their apartments house permanent, often famous guests.

*Apartment hotels* are another type of residential hotel. They offer very few services, so kitchens are provided in the apartments. Front desks are limited or non-existent in residential and apartment hotels.

**Extended-Stay Hotels** Extended-stay facilities offer more than a mere hotel room but are not the same genre as residential hotels, which denote permanency. Extended stay merely means long term. Guests include persons moving locations or having extended business assignments.

Extended-stay hotels provide kitchens, grocery outlets, office space—even administrative support and office equipment, fireplaces, exercise rooms, laundry facilities, and more—but all with room attendant service.

**Resort Hotels** Transient hotels cater to commercial guests, residential hotels to permanent guests, and **resort hotels** to social guests—at least traditionally they do.

Economics has forced resorts to lengthen their operating period from the traditional summer or winter season to year-round operations. Resorts have marketed to the group and convention delegate at the expense of their social guests. As this began happening, the commercial hotel shifted its design and markets toward the resort concept, dulling once again the distinctions between types. What emerged is a mixed-use resort. Sometimes these resorts are found in residential areas as part of a master-planned community.

Many believe that the modified resort is the hotel of the future. It is in keeping with the nation's move toward increased recreation and is compatible with the casual air that characterizes the vacationer. Unlike the formality of the vacationer of an earlier time, today's guest is a participant. Skiing, golfing, boating, and a host of other activities are at the core of the successful resort.

**The Megaresort** The megaresort, one of the lodging industry's newest segments, contains such a large variety of entertainment and recreational facilities that it is a self-contained unit. Guests need not leave the property during their entire stay. Size distinguishes the megaresort from similar self-contained properties, such as Club Meds. Canada does not have any true megaresorts, although examples exist, such as Whistler, which could be considered a destination offering many large properties and complete services in the town hub with the ability to compete with megaresort destinations.

Although the megaresort is a feature of Las Vegas, it is not specific to that location. Hilton's Hawaiian Village on Oahu's west coast (more than 2500 rooms), which contains rooms, condos, retail and office space, and a marina, also represents this genre.

Weather plays a key role in every type of resort. Geographic location is to the resort hotel what commercial location is to the transient hotel and population location is to the residential hotel.

## Types of Food and Accommodation Plans

The rates that hotels charge for their rooms are based, in part, on the plan under which they operate. By quoting the **plan**, the hotel identifies which meals, if any, are part of the basic charge. Rates will be higher if meals are included with the room charge, less if they are excluded. With very few exceptions, every hotel in Canada operates on the European or Continental plan. Classification by plan offers much more certainty than the other three classifications: size, class, or type. Either the meal is included or it's not.

**European Plan** When rates are quoted as **European plan** (EP), only the room accommodations are included. Evidence of the widespread use of the European plan is its lack of designation. Guests are not told, "This is the European plan." Rate **quotes** always assume EP unless otherwise stated.

**Continental Plan (Continental Breakfast)** More than any other meal, travellers eat breakfast in the hotel. A coffee urn with sweet rolls and juice left in the lobby when the dining room closes is often called a **continental breakfast**. Juice is included in Canada, but it is not usually served elsewhere.

**American Plan** Rates quoted under the **American plan** (AP) include the room and all three meals: breakfast, luncheon, and dinner. The AP, which is occasionally called bed and board, had its origin in colonial America, when all guests ate at a common table with the host's family. Conference centres and even some resorts still use AP but give it a more modern term, "all-inclusive plan."

**Adaptations of the American Plan** Many guests see the American plan in a negative way. They believe it is too restrictive because they must be at the hotel for meals at a given hour, and because it is too costly. Everyone pays the same price regardless of what is eaten. Cruise ships provide American-plan dining, but they don't use that terminology. Neither do all-inclusive resorts. Although the all-inclusive is not as popular in Canada as it is in the Caribbean, it is still marketed as an *all-inclusive* rate. Of course, drinks, activities, and even tips are then included as well as American plan meals.

A *dine-around* plan is another variation. Hotels offering the American plan (regardless of what it is called) allow guests to dine at other hotels in the vicinity.

**Modified American Plan** The **modified American plan** (MAP) is an astute compromise by which the hotel retains some of the AP advantages, and the guest feels less restricted. Guests get breakfast and dinner as part of the room rate quote, but not luncheon. This opens up the middle of the day for a flexible schedule of activities.

**Bed and Breakfast (B&B)** Bed and breakfasts in Canada take their cue from the British B&B, the Italian *pensiones,* and the German *zimmer frei* (room available)— lodging and breakfast offered by families in their own homes. The Japanese version of the Canadian B&B is *minshuku.*

B&B is a modern version of the 1930s rooming house, once called the tourist home. Like the rest of the industry, change is part of the B&B's vocabulary and no one definition fits all of the parts. There are many subcategories because the business is very individualized and localized. The B&B changes identity as it moves across the country. The B&B Inn, for example, is a product of California. It is a large version (more than half of the B&Bs in Canada are eight rooms or fewer) and is usually the owner's primary occupation. Some observers see another subcategory, the Country B&B, as an upscale boarding house because it serves all meals, not just breakfast. Country B&Bs have their origin in New England. In between the coasts is a variety of facilities serving their local markets (see Exhibit 1-6).

**Exhibit 1-6** ▶
Bed and breakfast oper-
ations in Canada listed
in the Canada Select
program are rated under
two classifications: Bed
and Breakfast and Bed
and Breakfast Inns.

In one way, B&Bs are no different from other Canadian hotels. They fight for business and rely on themselves for **referrals**. Since the Canadian government has never entered the tourist-rating business, several private rating and referral systems have emerged. Like the B&Bs themselves, these rating/referral systems come and go quickly. The Canada Select system has a classification for Bed and Breakfast and rates them with the same five-star system used for hotels.

**Boutique Hotels** Boutique hotels are a unique species that have their origin in very small inns (20 to 40 rooms, perhaps) but with all the amenities of a fine hotel without the size and bustle: sort of a grown-up B&B. Although they have become much larger now, they are still very fashionable, meaning that they are found in good urban locations, the "in places" of Montreal, Toronto, and Vancouver, all of which necessitates higher room rates.

The very nature of the boutique hotel—that it is something different—precludes a single definition. The term has been attributed to Steve Rubell, one of the founders of New York City's Studio 54, but the concept predated him. Asked for a description of his hotel, The Morgans, Rubell said that other hotels were large department stores, but Morgans is a small boutique. Boutiques suggest something different, very eclectic, always with flair, funky and artsy.

Ian Schrager, Rubell's partner, began developing the boutique in New York City. The concept spread rapidly, with Starwood Hotels introducing the W (for warm, welcoming, and witty) Hotels and Marriott redeveloping its Renaissance Chain with a facelift into the unexpected. The brand hotel chains have entered the fray because boutique hotels have had higher RevPar and occupancy figures (lower break-evens) than their more traditional cousins. The question remains whether a branded chain can deliver the unexpected and the quirky, which are the hallmarks of a boutique. Can a hotel be both mainstream and boutique?

Boutique hotels are being developed in major centres across Canada, with Montreal leading the way. The recent opening of the 135-room Le Place d'Armes Hotel & Suites in Montreal, which was purchased for $1 million by the Antonopoulos brothers who then spent $6 million in renovations, is an excellent example. Rates at this boutique hotel run from $194 to $1200 per night. Recently opened are new boutique hotels in Toronto (Pantages and Hotel Le Germain) and in Vancouver (Opus Hotel). Most of these have fewer than 200 rooms; it is their size that allows them to cater to the whims of pampered guests. Boutiques will feature some of the following: eye-catching hardwood floors, European-style kitchens, air purifiers, Jacuzzi-style tubs, luxurious duvets, rainforest shower heads, 100-percent-cotton bathrobes, 400-thread-count Egyptian cotton linens, fitness centres, and oversized plush pillows, to mention only a few. Many of these hotels cater to the business person who wants to be pampered, as well as to couples looking for romantic getaways.

# Evolution of Present-Day Lodging

The introductory material presented so far in this chapter provides a strong foundation from which the hotel industry can be viewed. It is to the credit of this industry that the traditional structures discussed are insufficient for today's tasks. Present-day lodging has evolved and restructured itself—and continues to do so almost daily, it seems—to meet the demands of rapid and continuous change. Throughout the centuries, innkeepers have reacted to the demands of the traveller. Seldom—until now—have they created the product or generated that demand. To meet its altered role, the industry has undergone major shifts and reconstructed itself into new patterns. In the remainder of this chapter, we look at four of these new patterns: product, market, ownership, and management.

# New Product Patterns

At first inspection, the ups and downs of the business cycle seem to have a negative impact on the hotel business. That's certainly true for many hotels caught in the downward draft. But it is less true for the overall industry. Forced from complacency by falling occupancies, astute innkeepers invent new products to rekindle the demands of a fickle public. Business is sustained by a variety of new subparts. No longer does one size fit all. At first, this process was called *brand stretching*; later, **segmentation**.[1] To counter falling occupancies, upscale hotels moved vertically downward (stretched their brands) into midscale operations. Marriott introduced Fairfield Inns, for example. Midscale chains moved both ways. Choice Hotels stepped up with its Clarion brand and stepped down with its Sleep Inns (see Exhibit 1.7).

Choice Hotels Canada Inc. is the country's largest lodging franchisor with more than 275 hotels open and under development, totalling 23 000 rooms. Worldwide, there are almost 5000 Choice Hotels open and under development in 46 countries, totalling almost 400 000 rooms. With eight distinct brands to choose from, Choice Hotels Canada has a perfect match for every franchisee. It became Canada's largest hotel chain in July 1993, when a 50/50 joint venture was forged between Journey's End Corporation (which became UniHost Corporation, then Westmont Hospitality Group Inc. and is now InnVest Management Holdings Limited) and Choice Hotels International, Inc.

Other chains segmented horizontally. Holiday Inn Hotels launched a new brand, Crowne Plaza, moving from traditional highway locations to compete in urban markets against the likes of Sheraton and Hyatt. Commercial chains even entered the resort business. Some of these changes brought new products to market; others merely put new faces onto older properties whose logos were no longer an asset.

| | Brand Names | | | |
|---|---|---|---|---|
| **Company Name** | **Low End** | **Midscale** | **Upscale** | **Suites** |
| Choice Hotels International | Comfort Inn<br>Econo Lodge<br>Rodeway Inn<br>Sleep Inn | Quality | Clarion | Comfort Suites<br>MainStay Suites<br>Sleep Inn Suites |
| Marriott International | Fairfield Inn | Courtyard<br><br>Residence Inn | Marriott Hotels<br>Ramada<br>    International<br>Renaissance<br>Ritz-Carlton | ExecuStay<br>Marriott Suites<br>Renaissance Suites<br>SpringHill Suites<br>TownePlace Suites |
| InterContinental[a] | Holiday Inn<br>Express | Holiday Inn<br>Posthouse | Crowne Plaza<br>Inter-Continental | Staybridge Suites |

[a]Formerly Six Continents
*Note:* Read horizontally, not vertically, because brand comparison is valid only for other brands within the same chain. It is not intended for comparisons between companies. Choice's midscale brand, for example, is not equated to Marriott's midscale brand. (The list is incomplete.)

The momentum accelerated, and the entire industry began offering new variations as a means of servicing specific guest needs and meeting marketplace demands. Segmentation is only the latest adaptation from an industry that responds to new conditions with dynamic innovations. (see Exhibit 1-8).

## Segmentation, Brand, and Image

Segmenting the industry has caused a good deal of confusion for both industry executives and hotel customers. The issue has been muddled by the creation of many new lodging designs and many new name brands. Unfortunately, putting a collection of similar hotels—or even worse, dissimilar hotels—under one name does not automatically create a brand. Customer recognition is what defines the brand. Hotel companies pour advertising dollars into creating that brand recognition. Brands are identified by their names and logos. Most hotel chains have several brands, some of which have been created and many of which have been acquired. There's no advantage to multiple brands unless the company can sell the customer on the differences and values among the brands.

Clarion Hotels have done probably the best job of segmentation, with eight main brands and several sub brands. They are Comfort Inns, Hotels and Suites; Quality Inns, Hotels, Suites and Resorts; Sleep Inns; Clarion Hotels, Suites, Resorts and Clarion Collection (boutique); Econo Lodge; and Rodeway Inns.

**Brand Equity** Brand equity is the value inherent in the shopper's recognition of the hotel brand. There is equity (value) in the brand only if that recognition carries a positive image. Basic to developing brand equity from mere brand recognition are four criteria: instant identification (Marriott), broad distribution (Holiday Inn Hotels), consistent quality (Hampton Inns), and level of service (Four Seasons).

**Exhibit 1-8** ▶
A segmenting industry increases the number of divisions and subdivisions by which it is identified. A single property may well fall into several categories.

## A Segmented Industry

**Segmented by Activity**
Casino hotel
Convention hotel
Dude ranch

**Segmented by Financing**
Public corporation
Private individual
Real estate investment trust (REIT)

**Segmented by Location**
Airport
Highway
Seaside

**Segmented by Management**
Chain
Management company
Self-managed

**Segmented by Markets**
Business
Groups
Leisure

**Segmented by Miscellaneous**
Collar
Hostel
Mixed use

**Segmented by Ownership**
Chain
Condominium
Mom-and-pop

**Segmented by Plan**
American plan
Continental plan
European plan

**Segmented by Price (ADR)**
Deluxe (above $100)
Midrange ($50–$90)
Budget ($35–$50)

**Segmented by Rating**
Five-star
Four-star
Three-star

**Segmented by Service**
Full service
Moderate service
Self-service

**Segmented by Structure**
High-rise
Low-rise
Outside corridor

**Segmented by Type**
Commercial
Residential
Resort

**Segmented by Use**
Bed and breakfast
Extended-stay
Health spa

Price (rate) is the offset to brand equity. With so many choices, guest loyalty often depends on nothing more than the rate quoted. Hotel rooms have become a commodity, much like wheat or oil. Brand managers fight an uphill battle as websites such as Priceline.com focus the buyer's attention on price rather than brand.

**Economy (Budget, or Limited-Service) Hotels** The original budget hotels were motor courts (1930s), very limited roadside facilities with no services (see Exhibit 1-9). Then came Kemmons Wilson's Holiday Inn Hotels. He founded this chain as clean, no-frill accommodations. Existing motor-court operators saw the inns differently, as **amenity creep.**

**Amenities and Amenity Creep** The history of lodging's budget segment is the story of amenity creep. An **amenity** is a special extra that a hotel provides in an effort to distinguish itself from competitors. After a time, guests expect the amenity. No longer do they view the extra product or service as anything special. Other hotel chains are then forced to provide as standard service what the industry previously viewed as something special. So the old amenity creeps into standard service, and a new round of amenities is forced upon the industry.

Little by little, small rooms grew larger. Direct-dial telephones were installed where there had been none. Free television replaced coin-operated sets; then remote controls were added. Expensive but infrequently used swimming pools were everywhere. Air conditioning, in-room coffee makers, and two wash basins in the room became standard. Guest room supplies such as three varieties of soap, combs, and lotions joined the rush of extras. Estimates place the cost of these toiletries at more than $10 per room per night.

Each upgrade pushed room rates higher. Hotel companies that started in the economy segment (Holiday Inn, Ramada) found themselves in the midrange.

**How Budgets Compete** As room rates inch upward, new chains fill the void at the lower end. New budget entries forego some amenities, but many amenities (telephone, remote television, acceptance of credit cards—even breakfasts and frequent-stay programs) are now seen as basic services. Today's budgets are competing with fewer bathroom amenities, better values in construction, and attention to operations and management.

Newer and newer rounds of economy chains employ newer and newer techniques. Rooms smaller than the standard are being offered now. Non-basic amenities such as pools, lobbies, meeting space, and restaurants have been eliminated once again. (Providing free continental breakfasts is actually less costly than operating a restaurant that loses money. Some budgets employ fewer than 20 employees per 100 rooms, almost 60 percent less than the traditional figures suggested earlier. Eliminating the dining room is just one technique for reducing labour. Planned savings like these require new, well-designed facilities. And these were built—and succeeded—during and despite the economic dips that began the decades of both the 1990s and the 2000s. Because it takes about 250 properties to ensure market identification, some emerging chains acquired old mom-and-pop operations at fire-sale prices in order to quickly establish themselves as viable budget operators. Days Inns was chief among them.

**Hard Budgets** The economy group has been lodging's fastest growing segment during the past two decades. It outperformed the other segments during both the down cycles and the upswings. Generalizations about budget hotels are hard to sustain because, like the whole of the lodging industry, they lack a single identity. They themselves are divided.

The entire low-end segment is called economy, budget, limited service, or simply low end. Adding confusion is a jumble of names and affiliations. There are upscale budgets—what an oxymoronic term—(La Quinta, for example), intermediate budgets (Red Roof Inns, for example), and low-end budgets (Super 8 Motels, for example). Hard budget, including truck-stop accommodations, is a fourth category of economy hotels. Hard budgets are located at airports and at the hundreds of truck stops that dot the interstate highways. Airports in Los Angeles and Honolulu offer rooms of 7m² (25 to 30 percent of a normal-sized room) for rest, showers, and stopovers between flights. Interestingly, France has a large number of hard budgets, reflecting perhaps its high payroll taxes and the need to minimize labour use.

**All-Suite Hotels** Each segment of the industry offers something unique. Boutique hotels, discussed earlier, emphasize soft attributes (fashion and spas) over hard values (room size and meeting space). Budget hotels offer rooms at half price. Two rooms for the price of one is the all-suite appeal.

Suite hotels were the brainchild of Robert Wooley, who created the first chain, Granada Royale Hometel. The idea was innovative—some say the best in a generation—but it borrowed from the traditional: the apartment hotel and the residential hotel.

The all-suite concept flourished after Holiday Inn acquired the Hometel brand. Holiday became the nation's largest all-suite chain, with two brands, Embassy Suites and Residence Inn. Embassy Suites, which was and is top of the line, was spun off from Holiday Inn to Promus (1990) when the Holiday Inn Corporation was broken apart. (Hilton bought Promus in 1999, acquiring Embassy Suites as part of the deal.) Residence Inn was sold in 1987 to Marriott when Holiday Inn was in need of cash. Holiday Inn (now part of InterContinental Hotels Group, which changed its name from Six Continents PLC) recently re-entered the all-suite market with its Staybridge brand.

Separate living–sleeping accommodations are attractive to personnel conducting interviews, and to others who require private space outside the intimacy of a bedroom. That's why the market shifted away from just extended-stay use. The living space contains a sofa bed and sometimes a second bath. That opened still another market: travelling families seeking economical accommodations.

Despite all-suites' tilt toward transient accommodations, two subdivisions—extended stay and corporate housing—continue to market the segment's original appeal.

**Extended Stay** Extended stay (5 nights or more—18 nights is the average stay) was the original concept of the all-suite hotel, and corporate users were the target market. The annual expenditure of extended-stay guests is four to five times that of transient guests, who stay but a night or two. Better to sell 4 weeks to one guest than 28 room nights to, say, 20 guests. Consequently, extended-stay hotels have higher occupancies than the norm and lower ADRs. Higher occupancy requires a good revenue management system, but problems are minimized by reduced room turnover and by the ability to accept transient guests.

**Corporate Housing** The original all-suite concept is re-emerging under a new name: corporate housing. This marriage of traditional hotels, apartment hotels, and all-suite hotels appeals to businesses that send many travellers to one city. The company takes a long-term lease on an apartment, but one that provides the services of a hotel. All departments of the corporation (sales, marketing, human resources, engineering) stay at the same corporate unit. Until recently, such accommodations were part of hotels or apartment buildings.

**Casino Hotels** The casino hotel has shaken up the established industry as nothing before in this generation. As legalized gaming (gambling) spreads, this unique destination resort shows signs of becoming the most important player in the lodging industry. That comes as no surprise when profits are counted. The operating profile of hotel casinos differs from that of the traditional hotel. Gaming revenues, called *win*, not room sales, become the major income producer. Therefore, having rooms **occupied** (potential casino players) is more important than the price for which those rooms sell. To generate casino volume, room rates are lower at casino hotels; single and double occupancy are the same rate to attract more players; and food and beverage are often viewed as loss leaders, a means of attracting traffic into the casino.

Casinos are relatively new to Canada but now exist in every province except for Prince Edward Island, Newfoundland and Labrador, and New Brunswick. Private individuals or corporations own the casinos in Alberta, British Columbia, and the Yukon. The host First Nations owns casinos in Saskatchewan, Manitoba, and Ontario. All casinos in Canada fall under provincial/territorial jurisdiction. Net profit for Canadian gaming is more than $7 billion per year based on more than $13.4 billion in revenue, with more than $4.7 billion of that revenue coming from casinos. Profits from Canadian gaming are broken up, with $2.2 billion going to charities, horse racing tracks, and First Nations, and $5 billion going to provincial governments. Gaming in Canada directly employs more than 50 000 people (more than 100 000 if you include horse racing). More than 75 percent of Canadians participate in some form of gaming. There are now seven casino hotels in Canada, with two more recently announced.

**Other Hotel Segments** The dynamic nature of the hotel business—out with the old and in with the new—has kept it viable and changing. New segments and new adaptations of older ideas are taking shape continually.

Some hotels have joined up with Routes to Learning Canada, a program designed to fill vacant dormitory beds during the summer. In this program, retired persons stay in hotels near a campus, where they choose from a variety of courses offered by distinguished professors.

Because of the manner in which they ring a city, suburban hotels have been dubbed *collar hotels*. These hotels have followed industry from high-rent downtown districts to the open spaces of the suburbs. Beltway roads, which collar the city, have made the transition possible. Suburban hotels are narrowly segmented with few opportunities to add to the customer pool other than from the industries they followed to the suburbs.

**Conference Centres Conference centres** are specialized "hotels" that cater to meetings, training sessions, and conferences of all types. Unlike the typical convention hotels, conference centres usually take no transient guests. Food service is also restricted to the **in-house** groups. Catering to this special market, conference centres provide a complete line of audiovisual materials, special seminar rooms and theatres, closed-circuit television with interactive teleconferencing, and simultaneous translation capabilities.

The special design of the meeting facilities distinguishes conference centres from other meeting places (see Exhibit 1-10). Conference planners do not always understand that distinction. Conference centres are not necessarily separate facilities, but they do have permanent and dedicated meeting space. Hotel meeting space is temporary as the function room changes from meetings to banquets, from trade shows to dances.

Other operational differences distinguish the conference centre from the hotel. Double occupancy is higher. Even top-level senior managers are doubled up. Two to a room encourages greater familiarity, which is one goal of conference planners. Lower management and upper management get to know one another.

Rates at conference centres are bundled. Room, food, and beverage are quoted as one figure. Conference centres call this quote a *corporate meeting package* (CMP), but the reader will recognize it as a variation of the American plan. CMP is a modern version of the AP because the conference centre is a modern marriage of the convention hotel and the traditional resort. When physically combined, a five-day workweek in the conference facility can be followed by a two-day weekend in the resort complex. Like convention hotels, conference centres are plagued by low weekend occupancy. Some have been forced to look at social guests to fill the hole.

**Spas** Spas are mineral springs or curative waters. Spas were known and used as far back as the Romans, who "took the waters" in the city of Spa, Belgium. Obviously, that is the source of the present-day term.

Today's spas are far different from those of the Romans or even such famous spas as Harrison Hot Springs and Radium Hot Springs (Canada's largest hot springs pool) in British Columbia and the famous Banff Springs in Banff, Alberta, which was introduced by Canada's First Nations to the railway pioneers. These spas and others were sought initially for their restorative properties and their promise as fountains of youth. It wasn't long before the spas became playgrounds for the rich and socially well placed.

The growth of the industry can be explained simply: Spas are profitable. Travellers expect them and, unlike swimming pools and kitchenettes, use them, even paying handsomely for the right. The business breaks down into two categories: the spa-destination resort—a resort with all amenities, including a spa; and the day spa, which may not even be in a hotel. Hoteliers originally outsourced their spa operations because they lacked expertise. Direct control means more profits, so spa departments with full-time employees have begun appearing.

Leading Spas of Canada, an association of various spa types, has just over 100 members across Canada (its website is listed at the end of this chapter).

**Unique Hotels** No hotel is more unique than Quebec City's Ice Hotel. It is the only ice hotel in North America and is based on the famous ice hotel in Sweden. The Quebec ice hotel is located 30 minutes west of Quebec City and is made from 15 000 tonnes of snow and 500 tonnes of ice. The hotel has 21 rooms plus 13 theme suites and can accommodate 84 guests per night. The ice hotel is rebuilt each year (since it melts each summer) and is open from January through April. In 2006, an ice bar also opened in Toronto to a great deal of fanfare.

# New Market Patterns

An explosion of choice has taken place around the globe in all goods and services that customers buy. Consumers are offered a rich selection of products, from bottled water to investment options. Such is also the case for lodging, which has joined the movement by introducing the new array of products that were just discussed. Now the problem is to entice the guest in.

## Marketing to the Individual Guest

Hotels zero in on particular market segments (niches) as their chief sources of business. Similarly, guests go to a particular hotel because they find there the kind of accommodations and services that they seek. So, the guest's very presence at a hotel tells us much about both the hotel and the guest.

**The Guest Profile** Guests stay at hotels under different circumstances. Consequently, what appeals to one guest may be a matter of indifference to another. Indeed, the same guest displays different responses during separate stays. The guest has a different profile as a business person than as a tourist. The single traveller has different expectations when returning as part of a business group or as part of a family unit. Looking at the guest under various circumstances enables the hotelier to build and manage for a variety of market segments.

Guest profiles have been developed by trade associations, governmental agencies, rating firms, purveyors, external consultants, magazines, and the hotel companies themselves.[2] The typical study focuses on demographic profiles. Age, income and job, gender, residence, education, and the number of travellers in a **party** are all determinable with a good degree of accuracy. Knowing the guests is the starting point for servicing them.

Some patterns take their lead from profiles less measurable than demographics. Developers differentiate between what have been called upstairs/downstairs buyers.

*Upstairs buyers* are more oriented toward the room. These guests want large sleeping and bathing facilities and a comfortable workspace. For this, they will sacrifice theme restaurants, bars, banquet facilities, and exercise rooms. Not so the *downstairs guests,* who want public space above all else.

*Extended-stay guests,* those who remain five or more days, attempt to recreate a little of their home in the guest room. They bring personal items such as pillows, photos, stuffed animals, and personal toiletries. The kitchenette is used, but mostly for breakfast or for snacks, less often for dinner preparation. The extended-stay guest wants working space and good lighting. So does the business traveller.

**Business/Leisure Travellers** Business people need to be at a given place at a given time. Therefore, price is less important—not unimportant, but less important—to the business guest than to the leisure traveller. Businessmen and -women are not apt to cancel a trip because of high rates, and they are not apt to make a trip because of low rates. Theirs is an *inelastic* market—there is very little change in demand from a change in price. The response from leisure guests is more dramatic: High rates repel them and low rates attract them. By responding to price changes, leisure guests represent a more *elastic* market.

All guests demonstrate some degree of elasticity. Even leisure guests may be inelastic; they just have to be there (a wedding, a funeral, etc.). Business guests may be elastic, rescheduling or postponing their meetings. Companies with travel desks, which schedule and buy travel (air, hotels, and car rentals) for their personnel, are more price sensitive. With someone other than the traveller doing the planning, businesses have shifted toward the elastic side. This shift helps explain the buyer's focus on the value of all-suite hotels.

Business travellers, male and female alike, use the room as an office. It is no surprise, then, that surveys indicate a comfortable desk and desk chair are high priorities. Telephones, extra lines for email and fax, and business centres with secretarial support are top "necessities" for business travellers. Women executives (upstairs buyers) rank in-room coffee makers almost as important as workspace; men (downstairs buyers) rank coffee makers at the bottom of the list.

Some leisure guests are looking for a change of experience rather than the leisure of lie-in-the-sun beach and ocean. This niche searches for a change of pace, not for idle leisure. Hiking, mountain climbing, planting trees, rafting, and archaeological digs are the sort of leisure activities that many resorts are offering and many vacationers are buying. Guests are willing to pay handsomely for these out-of-the-ordinary experiences.

The economy market is just the opposite. Price-sensitive guests form the core of the budget customers. Who are they? Government employees on a fixed per diem (per day) allowance make up one segment. Retirees, whose time is more flexible than their budgets, will go to the less convenient and less costly locations that economy properties require. Family vacationers and small-business persons sensitive to travel costs help round out this segment. International guests, who have different expectations than domestic travellers, are also part of the budget market, especially when the Canadian dollar is strong.

**The International Guest** Globalization requires special attention to the profile of the international guest. Foreign visitors are big business. Canada is the world's tenth most popular tourist destination, attracting almost 39 million international visitors per year. Since they spend more time and more money reaching their destinations, international guests stay longer than do domestic guests. Typically, theirs is a six-day visit, more than half again the usual domestic hotel stay. International visitors to Canada help the nation's balance of trade, representing some $57.5 billion in export equivalence. See Exhibits 1-11 and 1-12 for a breakdown of where international travellers to Canada come from.

## Travellers to Canada by Country of Origin, Top 15 Countries of Origin, 2005

| Country of origin[1] | Trips | Nights | Spending in Canada |
| --- | --- | --- | --- |
| | Thousands | | C$ millions |
| United States | 14 390 | 57 331 | 7 463 |
| United Kingdom | 888 | 11 882 | 1 246 |
| Japan | 398 | 4 750 | 557 |
| France | 351 | 5 836 | 463 |
| Germany | 311 | 4 900 | 410 |
| Mexico | 179 | 3 149 | 240 |
| Australia | 179 | 2 447 | 287 |
| South Korea | 173 | 4 466 | 247 |
| Netherlands | 118 | 1 580 | 131 |
| China | 113 | 3 723 | 219 |
| Hong Kong | 109 | 2 161 | 151 |
| Taiwan | 98 | 1 536 | 110 |
| Switzerland | 97 | 1 684 | 163 |
| India | 94 | 1 771 | 82 |
| Italy | 91 | 1 061 | 95 |

[1] May include more than one country.

**The New Amenities**   Traditional amenities (swimming pools, for example) are now viewed as basic services. Bathroom amenities (numerous deodorant soaps, toothbrushes, cotton balls) and historical amenities (shoehorns, sewing kits) have been de-emphasized as cost-cutting measures. Amenities remain important marketing devices, however, so new ones continuously take hold. Sometimes, they're practical amenities such as ironing boards, hair dryers, safes that hold laptops, and coffee makers. Often, they are just opulent: Jacuzzi tubs, air purifiers, towel warmers, sound generators, and more. To the business traveller, electronics is the best amenity.

High-tech, in-room amenities range from the frivolous to the essential: from bedside gadgets that operate the drapes to dual telephone lines, in-room faxes, and electronic check-in and check-out. Joining the list are electronic keys, in-room private voice mail messaging, and data ports. Telephone access without fees is a welcomed amenity. Providing these self-service amenities has allowed hotels to close expensive business centres or outsource the service at unattended but dedicated centres accessed by credit cards.

The Fairmont Vancouver Airport hotel features rooms with smart room technology. From your bedside on a touch-tone screen you can open/close the drapes, control the light and heating, ventilating, and air conditioning (HVAC), and control the room's audiovisual components. This same hotel has a hypoallergenic floor featuring foam or cluster fibre pillows and duvets that feel like feather. Rooms are cleaned with special

**Exhibit 1-12** ▶
This exhibit shows the
top 15 states in the U.S.
where travellers to
Canada originate. Are
there any surprises?

Travellers to Canada by United States State of Origin, Top 15 States of Origin, 2005

| State of origin | Trips | Nights | Spending in Canada |
|---|---|---|---|
| | Thousands | | C$ millions |
| New York | 1 771 | 5 833 | 680 |
| Michigan | 1 689 | 4 794 | 589 |
| Washington | 1 464 | 4 914 | 496 |
| California | 877 | 4 348 | 611 |
| Ohio | 698 | 2 377 | 285 |
| Pennsylvania | 642 | 2 751 | 361 |
| Massachusetts | 554 | 2 078 | 265 |
| Minnesota | 545 | 2 389 | 257 |
| Illinois | 477 | 2 038 | 308 |
| Florida | 466 | 2 815 | 338 |
| Texas | 419 | 2 018 | 325 |
| New Jersey | 417 | 1 629 | 238 |
| Wisconsin | 328 | 1 549 | 200 |
| Maine | 284 | 1 074 | 123 |
| Oregon | 265 | 1 203 | 147 |

non-allergenic cleaners, HEPA filters are installed on HVAC units, and water is filtered. The rooms' HVAC systems and lighting interface with the property's property management system (PMS) and motion sensors control lighting and HVAC, so when a guest leaves a room the lighting is shut off, as is the heating or air conditioning. All rooms in this hotel have a system called Vision Wall, which is a soundproof window system that keeps out the sound of the jet planes coming and going. The Fairmont Vancouver Airport is one of only three hotels in the world with Vision Wall soundproof windows.

**Frequent-Guest Reward Programs** Almost half of Marriott's room nights are from guests who belong to its frequent-guest program (FGP), Marriott Honoured Guest Awards. Marriott's is one of many FGPs offered at all price ranges. Hyatt's Gold Passport and Hilton's HHonors Club are two other examples of high-end programs. La Quinta's Returns is an example at the low end. In between are Priority Club by InterContinental Hotels and Best Western's Gold Crown Club.[3] Fairmont's President's Club, and Delta's Delta Privilege complete the offerings of Canada's largest chains.

No one is really certain whether FGPs or the airlines' frequent-flier programs (FFPs) actually increase business. It's difficult to determine when all competitors bestow similar rewards. Guests win as the chains gather more brands under one umbrella (see Exhibit 1-13).

These costly programs, estimated at more than $10 per room per night, have a positive side as well. Vast amounts of information help hotels profile their guests, who, by identifying themselves, signal their travel and personal habits. Hotel companies do a better marketing job with these demographic and preferential profiles. Some chains

## Selected Hotel Chains and Their Brands

**ACCOR** (approximately 3300 hotels with 370 000 rooms)

| | |
|---|---|
| ETAP Hotels | Motel 6 |
| Coralia Hotels | Novotel |
| Hotel Formule 1 | Red Roof |
| Ibis | Hotel Sofitel |
| Mercure | |

**CENDANT**[a] (approximately 6600 hotels with 550 000 rooms)

| | |
|---|---|
| AmeriHost | Knights Inn |
| Cuendet | Ramada |
| Days Inn | Super 8 |
| Fairfield | Travelodge |
| Holiday Cottages | Villager |
| Howard Johnson | Wingate |

**HILTON** (approximately 1750 hotels with 300 000 guest rooms)

| | |
|---|---|
| Conrad | Hampton |
| Doubletree | Harrison |
| Embassy | Hilton |
| Garden Inns | Homewood |

**STARWOOD** (approximately 750 hotels with 230 000 rooms)

| | |
|---|---|
| Four Points by Sheraton | St. Regis |
| Luxury Collection | W |
| Sheraton | Westin |

[a]Cendant also participates in global reservation systems: Galileo; Travel and Cheap Tickets; WizCom.

boast of membership rosters with 2 million names. Gifts and prizes are the inducements that entice guests to give up this personal information.

Gifts range from the simple to the expensive. Many are services that are available even to non-members under certain circumstances. Among them are room **upgrade,** daily newspaper, **late check-out, express check-in** and **check-out,** toll-free reservation number, and **guaranteed rates.** Other gifts are specials: room discounts; discounts with travel partners such as airlines, auto rental companies, or local tourist companies; health club membership; and free accommodations in exotic destinations. Tie-ins with credit card companies often mean double or triple points earned.

Despite costs and other issues, no one is daring enough to close a program. The hotel chain that first cancels its FGP will have some brave, and some say foolish, executives.

**A New Look at an Old Amenity** Food service is the oldest amenity of innkeeping. Yet hotel dining rooms are not favoured by today's travelling public, and they certainly are not profitable for the host hotel. Nevertheless, industry watchers were amazed when first the motels and economy hotels and then the all-suites eliminated restaurants. Many felt it to be a poor business decision. After all, travellers had to eat. The decision proved to be just the opposite, because alternatives were offered.

All-suite hotels provided free breakfasts—the Continental plan discussed earlier—the one meal that almost all travellers take in the hotel. Indeed, several surveys indicate that breakfast is one amenity for which guests are willing to pay extra. Those hotels without food service, chiefly economy properties, solved the problem by locating near free-standing restaurants.

Hotels have entered into partnerships, some with formal and some with informal agreements, with either national restaurant chains or well-reputed local operators. Often the result is a cluster. Three, four, or five brand-name hotels are built around the brand-name restaurant. Working with these neighbouring restaurants to accommodate their guests, even with room service in some cases, hotels are able to close non-profitable food outlets and improve their earnings picture.

The next move, one that is going on right now, was to invite these independent restaurants into the hotel building. Larger hotels have done that. Hamburger, chicken, and pizza franchises have opened in the lobbies—usually with street access also—of some very major hotels. Not only do they offer the type of food service that today's traveller prefers, but they pay rent as well!

**Non-guest Buyers** The price paid for many hotel rooms is negotiated by persons (usually legal persons, companies, and corporations) who are not guests and have no intention of becoming guests. Similarly, many rooms are sold to persons who never occupy them! These "non-guest" buyers act as intermediaries for the actual occupants. In later chapters that deal with reservations and room rates, we will sharpen these distinctions. Non-guest buyers are part of the modern marketing structure that has developed as a means of selling hotel rooms. Of course, each layer adds costs that must be recovered in the room rate. Non-guest buyers add an additional layer of organization between the hotel and the guest/occupant. As a result, hotels are not selling hotel rooms as much as they are trying to buy guests from these new marketing channels.

Because of their negotiating strength, non-guest buyers pay less for their rooms than do regular guests. Groups such as the Canadian Automobile Association (CAA) and the Canadian Association of Retired Persons (CARP) haggle with hotel chains over price. They obtain special rates for their members, although the hotel doesn't know who those members are until they arrive and claim the room. So widespread is the practice that almost every hotel entertains the request for a discount, whether negotiated or not, to stay competitive.

Another side of the reservation picture paints the third party as a buyer, not merely a rate negotiator. Business travel arrangements are often made by company travel desks, which may or may not be part of the traveller's business. Either way, paring travel costs is the mission of these tough negotiators. The range of third-party buyers is broadened further by the list detailed in the next section of this chapter. Group tours, incentive firms, and wholesalers make huge space commitments, but someone else actually uses the room.

## Marketing to the Group

Seeking out and servicing group business is one of the major distinctions between modern hotel keeping and the historic wayside inn. One group sale secures dozens, hundreds, or even thousands of room nights. With group business, the hotel is a destination site, rather than a transient accommodation. As with individual travellers, groups come both as tourists (leisure guests) and as business people (commercial guests).

**Tourist/Leisure Groups** Rising disposable income and broader travel horizons have made travel appealing to every level of society. As the relative cost of travel and accommodations decline, the market potential grows ever larger. The travel and hotel industries have finally embarked on the same kind of mass production that has brought increased efficiency to the manufacturing industries.

**The Tour Package** A new entrepreneur, the wholesaler—another party, another non-guest buyer—has emerged in the past 25 years to handle the mass movement of leisure guests. Entrepreneurs are risk-takers, and wholesalers are certainly that! **Wholesalers buy blocks** of rooms (commitments to take so many rooms for so many nights) from the hotel, blocks of seats from the airlines, and blocks of seats from the bus company. Then the wholesalers try to sell their **packages**, which now include transportation, ground handling, and baggage along with whatever else they are able to get without cost from the hotel (see Exhibit 1-14).

Quantity buying gives the wholesaler a good airline price. Special room and meal rates are negotiated with the hotel under the same umbrella—quantity discounts. With the promise of year-round, back-to-back charters, the hotel sales manager and accountant sharpen their pencils. One sale books hundreds of rooms. One correspondence confirms all of the reservations. One billing closes the books. There is no commission to

## Vacations—Round the Nation

### With the Vallen Chain

**⊟V**

*A Vallen Corporation Property*

| $497.20 | $667.50 | $733.33 |
|---|---|---|
| **In Las Vegas** | **In Orlando** | **In Maui** |
| Round Trip Air | Round Trip Air | Round Trip Air from LA |
| 4 Days/3 Nights | 4 Days/3 Nights | 5 Nights/4 Days |
| HOTEL PARADISE | HOTEL CARTOON | THE VALLEN MAUI |
| Taxes Included<br>Airport Transfers<br>Free Gaming Lesson | Room Upgrade If Available<br>$40 Daily Car Rental<br>Nonstop Flights from Major Cities | 6th Night Free<br>Includes Full Breakfast<br>Guaranteed Ocean View or Suite |

| $515.00 | $417.76 |
|---|---|
| **In New York City** | **In Boston** |
| 4 Days/3 Nights<br>2 Broadway Shows | 4 Days/3 Nights<br>Bottle Champagne Nightly |
| THE BIGGEST APPLE | FREEDOM TRAIL HOTEL |
| Apple Before Bed<br>One Breakfast-in-Bed<br>City Bus Tour | Guided Walking Tour of Historic Boston<br>$25/Day Food or Beverage Credit<br>Surprise Amenity |

**CALL: 1-888-555-5555 OR YOUR TRAVEL PROFESSIONAL**

Rates are quoted per person, double occupancy and are available until September 30. Unless otherwise stated, taxes and service charges are not included. Las Vegas offering is good Mondays to Thursdays only. All vacations earn Club Vallen points. Air trips, where included, require specific flights on carriers of the company's choosing. Other restrictions may apply.
The company strives for accuracy but will not be held responsible for errors or omissions in this advertisement.

**Exhibit 1-14** ▶
Sample of print advertising used by this hypothetical tour operator, *Vacations–Round the Nation*, to sell packaged vacations. Buying in quantity, which puts the wholesaler at risk, enables it to negotiate reduced prices from hotels and airlines and to resell at prices less than the sum of the individual parts.

credit card companies, and there is only minimum loss from bad debts. It is a bargain buy for the traveller, a profitable venture for the wholesaler, and a basic occupancy for the hotel, which also receives free advertising.

The travel industry, hotels included, gain as well because mass marketing has introduced many new customers to travel. Inexperienced guests find comfort in the safety and security of the group; experienced travellers find irrefutable savings in group travel. The downside is a loss of guest identity. Even the hotel staff senses a reduced responsibility when guests buy and pay through a third party.

Almost any destination hotel can host a tourist group if it can attract the group to the site. It must meet the price of a very competitive market to appeal to the wholesaler. And it must be large enough to accommodate the group and still handle its other guests. Hotels in out-of-the-way places cater to bus groups. They're a broader market because the number of guests is smaller and almost any hotel can handle them. With bus tours, hotels provide a mix of destination and transient service because after touring the area, the bus moves on, usually after one night.

**The Inclusive Tour (IT) Package** First, an explanatory note. This IT package is marketed to individual guests. Therefore, it could have been discussed under the topic "Marketing to the Individual Guest." It has been repositioned here as part of "Marketing to the Group" because it is best understood as a modification of the wholesaler's IT package, the tour package just discussed. Unlike the wholesaler's IT package, which requires numerous buyers to make it profitable, the hotel's IT package is directed toward an individual couple or a small group of friends.

The popularity of the wholesaler's IT package did not escape the notice of hoteliers. "Why give all of the profits to the wholesaler?" hotel managers asked. Because wholesale tour packages are very risky, involving air and land transportation costs outside the hotel's control, hotel ITs eliminate the transportation, and with it the risk. What is left is exactly what the hotel normally packages for the wholesaler room, meals, and drinks. Hotel packages add "free" use of the tennis court (or putting green, swimming pool, playground, shuffleboard, table tennis, etc.) and free admission to the theatre (or formal garden, exhibit, animal habitat, spa, exhibition matches, etc.). The products that the hotel includes look even better if small fees are normally paid for such services or admissions. Casino hotels often include one free play on the tables.

One hotel may offer several packages. Each package (a weekend package, a winter package, a golf package, and so on) is aimed toward a different market niche and includes different items at various prices. Hotel ITs must be marketed carefully because the hotel competes with itself (see Exhibit 1-15). IT packages are discounted rooms with extra services at lower prices than the room alone sells for. Later chapters dealing with yield management and room rates raise again this issue of self-competition.

**Business/Commercial Guests** Our fondness for forming into groups has produced an astonishing number of organizations. People come together under many umbrellas: business, union, fraternal, social, historical, veteran, health and medical, educational, religious, scientific, political, service, athletic, and so on without end. For short, the industry uses the acronym SMURF: societies, medical, university, religious, and fraternal. Each classification translates into numerous organizations, societies, clubs, and associations. Each of them meets, holds shows, and stages conventions. Functioning at local, provincial, regional, national, and international levels, these groups offer business to a variety of destination facilities.

**Conventions** Conventioneers assemble to promote their common purposes. These aims are as diverse as the list of associations that hold conventions. Some are professional, some merely entertaining. The members also interact individually, discussing common goals and problems. Professional conventions may serve as formal or informal job-placement forums.

Both urban and resort properties vie for convention business as the growth of mixed-use facilities spreads. To be competitive, the convention hotel must provide a range of self-contained facilities. Meeting space with appropriate furnishings and equipment and food facilities large enough to accommodate the groups at banquets are the minimum facilities needed. Conventioneers are a captive audience for the program and the planned activities. The more complete the property, the more appealing the site.

Sports activities, a change of scenery, and isolation from the hubbub of busy cities are touted by a resort's sales department. Urban properties respond with theatres, museums, and historical locations. Urban areas may have the advantage of publicly financed convention halls.

Hotels sometimes combine facilities with those of nearby competitors when the convention size is too large for one property. Although not the rule, conventions of 50 000 to 100 000 delegates have been recorded, usually when combined with trade shows.

**Trade Shows** Trade shows are exhibits of product lines shown by purveyors to potential buyers. Conventions and trade shows are often held together. Shows require a great deal of space, particularly if the displays are large pieces of machinery or equipment (see Exhibit 1-16). Space requirements and the difficulty of handling such products limit shows to a small number of hotels. The city convention bureau has a role here. It builds halls to accommodate the exhibits, leaving housing and guest services to the local hotels.

▲
**Exhibit 1-15**
Inclusive tour packages (rooms and some food, drinks, and entertainment) that hotels offer are similar to the wholesaler's package, Exhibit 1–14, except for transportation. Hotel packages compete with individual room sales, so they are offered and withdrawn by the hotel as occupancy dictates under a yield management system.

Exhibits of small goods (for example, a perfume show or a jewellery show) can be housed almost anywhere. They do not need public convention halls of 90 000 m² and more. Hotels with limited exhibit space can still accommodate trade shows by carefully choosing what market segments to pursue. Although less common, assigning several sleeping floors to such a trade show and converting guest rooms into individual exhibit spaces is still done by hotels with no dedicated meeting areas. Then the exhibitor occupies the exhibit room as a registered guest.

**The Single Entity** The single entity group is neither a tour package nor a convention/trade show. As its name implies, *single entity* has an adhesive that binds its members together. Attendees already belong to the group (a company, an orchestra, a college or university hockey team) before they come to the hotel. The unit (the company, the

**Exhibit 1-16** ▶

Public convention centres solicit and house trade shows whose delegates might number in the tens of thousands. What is good for the local hotel business has a major economic impact on the whole community. That value approximates $800 daily for each delegate during the three- or four-day convention.

orchestra, the college or university hockey team) makes the reservation, and the unit pays the bill. The single entity stays together during the engagement: They hold meetings; they perform; they play hockey.

The **tour group** offers a contrast. Tour group members have no previous relationships; they come together only for the trip. Each member pays the wholesaler a share of the cost; by contrast, with an entity, the single entity pays costs, not the individual members/players. The tour group dissolves after the trip; not so, the single entity. The hotel negotiates with the (team) manager of the single entity, who is also a team member, whereas the tour group negotiator is a business person seeking profit. Both commit to a block (group) of rooms, and both pay for that block.

Although the visiting athletic team is the best example of a single entity, hotels cater to a wide range of other groups. There are company sales and technical meetings, new product line showings, travelling concert groups, annual high school graduation trips, and others. Hotel/casinos have their own form of the single entity, the gambling junket. High rollers are brought to the hotel for several days of entertainment and play.

**Incentive Tours** **Incentive tours** are special kinds of single entities. Many businesses run incentive programs to encourage sales and production workers to improve output. A cash bonus, a prize, or an incentive trip—for example, a free vacation for two to a destination resort—is the reward for those who meet the announced goals.

Hotels like to **book** incentive tours because all of the participants are winners and only the best accommodations are chosen. Unfortunately, the deals for these facilities are frequently negotiated through intermediaries—incentive (tour) companies, which have emerged as still another non-guest buyer in the sale and distribution of hotel rooms. Incentive companies negotiate for hotel rooms and deliver them to clients, the companies holding the incentive programs. Often, the incentive companies are also the consultants handling the clients' incentive programs.

Tours, be they single entity, incentive, or as yet unnamed, are the group markets of tomorrow. One can foresee a growth of vertical integration with one large holding company owning the means of transportation, reservation system, tour wholesaler, incentive company, and hotel/resort. (At one time, Canadian railroads owned numerous hotels. These destination hotels hosted the guests that the transportation companies were trying to promote as passengers.) Canadian National (CNR) and Canadian Pacific (CPR) railways have owned destination hotels for some time. The same group that owns Sandals Resorts also owns Air Jamaica. The incentive is simply profits. One hotel room sold as part of an integrated sale that includes travel agent, airline, hotel, and entertainment fees is worth many times more than a single room sale made by a stand-alone hotel.

# New Ownership Patterns

The changes in guests and markets reviewed in this chapter have taken place at the same time that the industry has undergone major shifts in ownership structures and methods of raising money. New management patterns, discussed in the final section of the chapter, have appeared as well, adding to the dynamics of the industry.

## The State of the Industry

Historically, the inn was a family affair with the host–guest relationship paramount. That circumstance began to change in the early 1950s, when ownership and management became separate activities. As the separation widened, the famous hotel chains concentrated on managing both their own hotels and those belonging to others. Those others, who actually owned the buildings and lands on which the hotels stood, were concerned more with the hotels as properties, pieces of real estate. Income taxes, depreciation, rent, and financing are more important to owners than are day-to-day operational problems. That difference brought huge changes to the lodging industry.

**Churning and Turmoil** The hotel real estate business has been in turmoil for about 30 years, beginning in the early 1970s when real estate speculators set their sights on the hotel industry. The experience was worldwide, and was caused by an unhappy combination of low customer demand and high interest rates. Hotel owners were unable to pay off their huge debts, which included interest rates as high as 22 percent in Canada, because revenues were falling. Good room sales were needed to pay off the loans from expensive real estate transactions. However, as occupancy fell, so did rates. Hotel buyers were unable to meet the interest and loan repayments demanded by the banks. Estimates are that two-thirds of all hotel properties were in some level of financial distress.

As one real estate deal after another collapsed, so did the banking industry, which provided the loans. (All real estate, not just the hotel industry, suffered during this period of overbuilding and overspeculation.) With no payment flow, the banks were as badly off as the real estate investors. Banks began selling off the sick hotels, which were security for the loans. It was a fire sale—hotels were sold at substantial discounts from the original loan values. Although it hurt a great many hotel owners, it helped speed the recovery!

The turnaround gained momentum from the early 1990s onward and lasted for 10 years. As operating costs declined, the industry's break-even occupancy fell to less than 60 percent. Profits soared. By 2000, new construction began hinting of another cycle of overbuilding and a new downward spin. But before the characteristic cycle began anew, the terrorist attack of September 11, 2001, occurred and everyone, especially those in the travel and tourism business, experienced sudden churning and unforeseen turmoil. New issues surfaced as the lodging industry struggled to offset a dip for which it was completely unprepared. Deep discounting on websites wreaked havoc on RevPar (occupancy × rate) even as group business declined and attrition rates soared. In Canada, the effect of September 11 was furthered by severe acute respiratory syndrome (SARS) in Toro nto, the threat of mad cow disease in Alberta, avian (bird) flu in British Columbia, and the rising value of the Canadian dollar. Recently, as we approach the later part of the decade, the industry has improved in Canada to pre-2001 levels.

**A Consolidating Industry** Consolidation—bigger hotel companies and fewer of them—has been an ongoing strategy of the lodging industry (see Exhibit 1-17). Whether the cycle was up or down, the big guys got bigger. Acquisitions of competitors have enabled the surviving hotel chains to broaden their brands, add more rooms, and expand their market lines.

Acquiring other hotel chains is a function of stock market evaluations, but consolidation is more than a stock market game. Consolidation promises economies of scale and larger marketing and distribution networks for the chains. Growth comes faster and flashier from acquisitions than from internal growth. Buying instead of building produces immediate increases in revenues. It also makes good business sense. Acquiring hotels from an existing company costs less than building new ones. During the past several years, more than 100 acquisitions with multiple brands have consolidated into just a few large holding companies. The ownership saga of the Promus brand serves as a blueprint for the whole industry. Holiday Inn acquired Harrah's, a gaming company, in 1980. It then created a gaming division within Holiday Inn named Promus. Included

**Exhibit 1-17 ▶**
Consolidation has created large hotel chains, as shown in the listings of the top five Canadian hotel companies by number of rooms and by number of properties.

## Top Five Canadian Hotel Companies by Number of Rooms, 2005

| Company | # of Rooms | Company Type |
| --- | --- | --- |
| Choice Hotels Canada | 23 286 | Franchising |
| Westmont Hospitality | 19 969 | Management, Owning |
| InterContinental Hotels Group | 17 017 | Franchising |
| Best Western International | 15 864 | Non-profit association |
| Starwood Hotels & Resorts Worldwide | 13 430 | Franchising, Management, Owning |

## Top Five Canadian Hotel Companies by Number of Properties, 2005

| Company | # of Properties | Company Type |
| --- | --- | --- |
| Choice Hotels Canada | 269 | Franchising |
| Best Western International | 170 | Non-profit association |
| Westmont Hospitality Group | 159 | Management, Owning |
| Travelodge Canada Corp | 120 | Franchising, Management |
| InterContinental Hotels Group | 104 | Franchising |

in Promus's gaming unit were divisions of the original Holiday Inn (Homewood Suites, Embassy Suites, and Hampton Inns). Promus began an expansion of its own, but not before it spun away both its gaming division, now a freestanding company named Harrah's, and the original Holiday Inn chain.

Promus's Holiday Inn division was sold in 1990 to Bass, Great Britain's largest brewer. Bass also acquired Inter-Continental Hotels and renamed its hotel division Bass Hotels and Resorts. It renamed the hotels again to Holiday Hospitality, then Six Continents Hotels after adding Bristol Hotels and Staybridge Suites to its package, and then again to InterContinental Hotels Group.

Several major moves hurtled Promus into a good-sized chain. It merged with Doubletree in 1997. Doubletree had already merged with Guest Quarters (1993) and acquired Red Lion Inns (1996). Promus also formed a joint venture to develop Candle wood Hotels and a partnership with a REIT named Patriot America Hospitality, which owned Wyndham Hotels.

Having gulped down all the lesser fry, Promus had become a big fish by 1999. But not as big as Hilton, which continued the feeding frenzy that year by swallowing Promus and all of its parts. Hilton anticipated almost $100 million in savings, partly from folding these properties into its reservation system and frequent-guest program. Hilton paid less for the whole of Promus than Promus's single acquisition of Doubletree. Like the mom-and-pop minnows before them, consolidation appears to be hastening the end of even mid-size hotel companies.

Hotel companies, even consolidated ones, look tiny compared to international giants such as, say, Coca-Cola. Still, large-scale operations make it easier to compete nationally and internationally.

**The Global Village** The appearance of the global village (shorthand for "shrinking political differences and interlocking economic activity worldwide") has encouraged business interests to cross national borders and major oceans. Innkeeping has partici-pated along with almost every other type of business. Consolidation is caused, in part, by the realities of the global marketplace.

The direction of business flow often depends on the value of international curren-cies. Foreign investors who want to buy Canadian hotels need to have Canadian dol-lars. Before they can buy the hotels, they must buy the dollars. When the dollar is weak, fewer units of the strong foreign currency are needed. This makes the purchase price an attractive bargain to international buyers with strong currencies.

There is more to global participation than currencies. Companies go international to acquire a foothold on another continent, to acquire assets (management talent or reservation systems) they do not yet have, and to open new markets for their brands. Political stability is still another factor. Foreign investors may face serious financial loss from political uncertainty and upheaval in their own lands. Better to invest in Canada even if the purchase price is high or the chance of loss is significant. At least there is no political risk—the Canadian government is not likely to confiscate or nationalize the hotel. Furthermore, international investors differentiate, even more than do Canadian developers, between the hotel as an operating company and the hotel as a piece of real estate. Buying the hotel to get the real estate is a long-run view, and inter-national companies have a longer business horizon than do domestic companies.

**Global Village Examples** Hotel companies compete in a vast arena that stretches in every direction across the globe. European hotel companies are in North America, North American companies are in Asia, and Asian companies are in Europe. There are many examples of this global outreach. An example of the global outreach references the previous discussion of Harrah's, Bass, and InterContinental Hotels and Resorts (ICH). ICH has been in business for almost 75 years. It was originally owned by the now-defunct Pan American Airlines (Pan Am). In need of cash, Pan Am sold the chain to Grand Metropolitan of Great Britain, a competitor of Bass. In 1988, Grand Metropolitan sold the chain to Japan's retail and leisure conglomerate, the Seibu Saison Group, with the Scandinavian airline, SAS, taking 40 percent of the deal. Almost as an aside, ICH also entered into a joint venture with Hong Kong–based Dynasty Group. Once again, the chain was sold, this time back to Britain, to Bass PLC, which beat out Marriott and four other interested bidders. Undoubtedly, the strength of the British pound and the weakness of the Japanese yen contributed to the timing; the deal happened in 1998. Under Bass, ICH was teamed with Holiday Inn. Originally named Holiday Hospitality, the chain was renamed Bass PLC. Another change took place in 2001. Bass PLC sold its name and trademark, but not its hotels, to Interbrew. The Bass name went with the sale, so the hotel chain had to be renamed once again: Six Continents Hotels. Recently the hotel division was spun off and now operates as InterContinental Hotels Group. Renaming the corporation doesn't affect brand identity: The individual hotels retain the Holiday Inn or the ICH name.

ICH's parents have been the Americans, the Chinese, the English, the Japanese, and the Scandinavians! Globalization has been at work, but it isn't limited to the hotel segment of travel. Airlines and travel agencies have intraglobal connections. The marketplace requires it. More than 100 000 North American groups meet overseas annually. Still unclear is what impact there will be on globalization from Europe's new currency, the euro, or from the destruction of the World Trade Center in New York City.

Name changes such as ICH's have kept pace with globalization. Best Western became Best Western International; Quality Inns became Choice Hotels International. Hotels operate easily across national borders even without a global name. Paris-based Accor has spread into 30 countries, including a strong presence in North America with its Motel 6 and Red Roof brands.

## Ownership and Financing Alternatives

Early inns were family homesteads. The buildings were under the direct control of the innkeepers, so the hotel was owned and managed by the same party. This arrangement became more difficult as the size of the hotel grew. Large hotels required large sums of money, sums beyond the means of most families. Gradually, the financing of the hotel building separated from the operation of the hotel. This movement accelerated as the modern corporation matured. More recently, financing hotels has become a very creative undertaking.

**Individual Ownership**    There are still plenty of individually owned hotels. Best Western International is an affiliation of individual hotel owners. The small, local hotel may get equity (ownership) money from prominent professionals and business people who want to invest both for profit and for community pride. Investment groups, entrepreneurs, hotel companies, and franchise companies are examples of the more likely investors. In all cases, investors seek borrowed money to complete the deal. As projects grow larger, more equity money is needed. The public corporation becomes the likely source of invested capital and the means by which borrowed capital is obtained. Large amounts of borrowed money rely on bigger, money-centre banks or on insurance companies or pension funds. Some pension funds invest directly; others do so through mutual funds. As reviewed earlier, foreign investors are always a possibility. The 1980s to 1990s downturn in hotel prices saw companies that normally only franchise begin to buy and own—Choice Hotels, for example. Within a few brief years, a new financing vehicle emerged to take hold of the real estate market: the real estate investment trust.

**Real Estate Investment Trusts** Real estate investment trusts (REITs) raise the funds with which to acquire hotel (or apartment, office building, health care, etc.) real estate as much from the stock market as from borrowed money. REITs were introduced in Canada in 1993.

Canadian REITs are structured as trusts primarily to achieve tax efficiency. Unlike most Canadian corporations, REITs are generally not required to pay Canadian income tax if they distribute all of their net income for tax purposes (including the taxable portion of net realized capital gains) to unitholders at least annually. As trusts, they are also not subject to large corporation tax or capital tax—an advantage REITs enjoy over Canadian real estate corporations.

A well-known Canadian REIT is the Canadian Hotel Investment Properties Real Estate Investment Trust (CHIP REIT). CHIP Hospitality is one of Canada's and the United States' leading hotel and resort management companies. In Canada, it employs approximately 5000 hotel employees who service more than 7030 rooms in 30 properties across 9 provinces. It has franchise agreements with Crowne Plaza, Radisson, Coast, Best Western, Delta, Ramada, Quality, and Holiday Inn. CHIP Hospitality is the exclusive management company of its parent company, CHIP REIT, and also manages properties for third-party owners and investors, some of which may include financing or investment. CHIP REIT is a publicly traded company on the Toronto Stock Exchange.

REITs fuelled most of the hotel takeovers and expansions during the torrid 1990s. A large Canadian and U.S. REIT with its head office in Calgary, Alberta, is Royal Host, which currently owns 37 hotels, manages 123 properties, franchises 115 locations, and has involvement in 32 hotels across Canada. Royal Host also has Vacation Clubs offering timeshare opportunities, and was started by the Royer family in 1974 with one hotel in Red Deer, Alberta.

Another large publicly traded Canadian REIT is Legacy. Canadian Pacific Hotels was sold into this REIT (Fairmont maintains the management contracts on these hotels). Canadian Pacific Hotels and Resorts purchased the U.S.-based Fairmont brand and properties in 2000 and adopted the brand name. The REIT also purchased the Delta hotel chain and some Princess Resorts. This gave it a worldwide presence with a quality brand name (Fairmont) and provided expansion with the acquisition of Delta and Princess. At present they operate 24 luxury and first class resorts with more than 10 000 guest rooms in Canada and the United States.

REITs cannot operate hotels; instead, REITs rent property to the hotel managing company. After that, the REIT does not control the hotel's operation. So, the REIT forms its own hotel management company, which is a traditional corporation (referred to as a C-Corporation), which does pay income tax. The two work hand in glove, because the REIT owns the building and the management company owns and directs the operations.

**Condominiums and Timeshares** Both **condominiums** (condos) and **timeshares** (interval ownerships; vacation ownerships) have their origins in destination resorts. The industry's catchphrase is "Build Where Vacationers Go." Condos, which predate timeshare intervals by some 20 years, are a North American invention. Timeshares originated in Europe, but North America is a far larger market for them now.

**Condominium Ownership** Today's condominium owner buys for rental income, perhaps for hopes of real estate appreciation, and most likely for personal and family use. Guests own condominiums as they own any home. Common space and common grounds are also owned, but as part of the group association. Each unit is complete with all amenities, kitchen and general family space included. Owners furnish their units and maintain them according to personal preferences.

Since the owners are not always on-property, units are placed in a common rental pool. This requires on-site management to rent and service the units. Profits, if any, are paid to the owners on a pro rata basis. The complex might be part of a large resort facility operated by a well-known hotel chain or management company. Or, the condo owners might employ their own staff to operate and manage the units.

**Timeshare** Unlike condominium deals, the first timeshares were not real estate purchases. One did not *buy* the unit, so there was no property deed. One bought only the *right to use* the unit for so many days each year over a fixed period: hence the term *interval ownership*. "Buy a lifetime of vacations at today's prices" is a popular slogan these days. An earlier favourite was, "Don't rent for a night; purchase a week forever"— and some contracts were for forever: up to 40 years. At the end of the contract, the developer—not the guest who had paid for many years—owned the property. In contrast, condo owners took title from the start.

There are many timeshare and condominium developments throughout Canada. One of the largest players in this market is Intrawest, with sites across Canada from Whistler/Blackcomb, British Columbia, to Collingwood, Ontario, to Mont Tremblant, Quebec.

**Joint Ventures** In several ways, the joint venture is similar to a partnership arranged between two or more individuals. However, with the joint venture, the individuals are one of several entities: corporations, partnerships, individuals, and even governments. For example, Four Seasons Hotels and Resorts recently entered into a joint venture with Intrawest Corporation in Whistler, British Columbia. The $152 million, 242-suite Four Seasons Resort Whistler was sold within five hours of being offered for sale. The prices of the suites ranged from $350 000 to $2.3 million. This is the first time that buyers have been offered an opportunity to acquire whole ownership real estate in a Four Seasons hotel.

Marriott and Cendant formed a joint venture in 2002 to further develop and expand the Ramada and Days Inn brands in North America. Marriott contributed Ramada; Cendant contributed Days Inn.

Rising costs (land and construction) and huge enterprises (megaresorts and developments) make joint ventures, which are usually financial marriages, logical unions. On the other hand, strategic partnerships tap the capabilities of different organizations. The explosion in gambling serves as a good example. Gaming management is a skill that new types of developers (First Nations tribes, municipalities, and business development agencies) lack. Still, they want the benefits of casino ownership. Strategic partnerships bring the skills of gaming management companies to organizations that provide the sites, the licences, and the political muscle. The $2.5 billion development of Rama's Casino and Hotel was possible because of a joint venture that involved several casino companies and political entities. This casino is managed by Penn National Gaming, Incorporated.

# New Management Patterns

Our historical review has made clear that the era of the small innkeeper and the individual entrepreneur is waning. Erecting large, expensive buildings and competing in international markets require the management talent and the capital funding that only large public companies—the hotel chains—can provide.

## Chains

The very act of travelling evokes the unknown, the strange, and the unfamiliar. Within such an environment, travellers must select a rather personal service—a bed for the night. Examining or evaluating the experience beforehand is not possible. So, the hotel's reputation or its membership in a chain or affiliated group becomes the primary reason for the guest's selection. Overseas, the environment is stranger still. Brand recognition is even more critical to the selection. That is why North American hotels developed abroad when North America dominated the world's business scene. With international trade now more evenly balanced, foreign chains are appearing in North America for the same reasons.

Chains are defined as any group of two or more properties operated under a common name. Chain-controlled hotels now dominate the Canadian hotel industry. In Canada, some 41.1 percent of hotel properties with 30 rooms and more are branded, and 66.2 percent of hotels with 100 rooms or more are branded, representing 70 percent of the total rooms in Canada.

Modern business practices give chains an enormous operating advantage. Among their basic strengths are (1) expertise in site selection, (2) access to capital, (3) economies of scale (purchasing, advertising, reservations, etc.), (4) appeal to the best management talent, and (5) brand recognition.

As this chapter has stressed, hotel chains are no longer hotel builders. Just as often, the builders are not the owners, and the owners are not hoteliers. Therefore, the builder/developers and owners turn to the hotel chain for management skills. Institutional lenders trust these very same skills for the repayment of their loans. Obviously, then, successful enterprises involve mutually supportive skills from several participants.

**Parties to the Deal** There are five different parties involved in the development and operation of a hotel. The confusion is compounded when one of the participants wears two or three hats. The *developer* (party number 1) sees the opportunity and puts the plan together. That developer could be one of the hotel chains—Marriott, for example. The hotel might be part of a larger development—one element in a shopping mall, business park, or resort complex.

Financing is arranged from a bank, insurance company, pension plan, or other source. The *financier* is party number 2. As with all of the participants, financing could come in total or in part from one or more of the other parties. The developer or the hotel management company might participate in the lending, but more likely in the equity.

The equity—that is, the *ownership*—is party number 3. This party could be any of the others: a public corporation, a joint venture between one or more of the parties, or a separate entity making a passive investment.

If none of the participants is familiar to the consuming public as a hotel company, there will be no brand recognition. Then it is desirable that the group that manages the operation—the *management company* (party number 4)—has a recognizable logo. If the management company does not have a strong marketing presence, a franchise is licensed from a company (party number 5) that does.

Hotel chains are likely to be a combination of all five parties. They help with development and financing, hold a piece of the ownership equity, and supply management talent. Chains provide the critical name recognition and the essential reservation system. Whereas the chain might be part of all five parties in a big development, small-town projects use several different parties. The local business community may be the developer/owner but look elsewhere for the financing, the management, and the franchise.

**Membership Organizations** The growth of chains and franchises, with their interlocking reservation systems and easy identifications, put independent operators at a competitive disadvantage. For a long time, independent hotels struggled to maintain their freedom. Of late, the question has shifted from "if and when" to affiliate to "how to choose the right organization."

Reservation referrals are co-operative organizations initially designed to provide only one common service: marketing. Centralized reservations, standardized quality, joint advertising, and a recognizable brand with a logo are the limited objectives of most referral groups. This enables the individual property to compete but still maintain its independence. Best Western International is by far the best known membership/referral group. Each of its 4200 properties in some 80 countries is individually owned. Members have voting status for the board of directors that operates the association. By maintaining standards, quality accommodations, and fair pricing, Best Western provides the travelling public with consistency among the properties, whose uniqueness reflects the individual ownership that is still maintained.

Preferred Hotels and Resorts Worldwide is a different type of membership group. Its rates are at the other end of the price scale from Best Western. Although both are international in scope, Preferred's membership is about 120 hotels. Recently, it created a new holding company, IndeCorp Corporation, with several wholly owned brands. Preferred is now one of those brands. Under IndeCorp's umbrella are other independent brands such as Golden Tulip, Summit Hotels and Resorts, and Sterling Hotels and Resorts. By developing brands, IndeCorp emphasizes its consortium strategy with now nearly 1000 hotels.

Consolidation of the consortia follows the general consolidation movement of the whole industry. Leading Hotels of the World, which had been the largest consortium of the luxury independents, less than 420 members, also began consolidating with the addition of the Leading Small Hotels group of 70 hotels. It is likely that competition may force the consortia to move beyond mere branding to begin managing, even owning, hotels. They say that their structures already emulate Accor, InterContinental, and Marriott.

## Management Companies and Management Contracts

**Management Contracts** A management contract is an agreement between a hotel owner and a management company. The contract is a complex legal instrument by which the management company operates the hotel within the conditions set down by the contract. For this, the owner pays the management company a fee of 2 to 4 percent of revenues. Fees are paid whether or not there are earnings. Profits, if any, belong to the owner, but so do the losses. Since management fees are paid whether or not the property is profitable, management companies enjoy rapid expansion with little invested capital and almost no risk. Besides, most contracts provide increased fees for the management company if and when the hotel becomes profitable.

**Management Companies** The separation of hotel management from hotel ownership coincided with the industry's search for public monies with which to build ever-larger and more costly hotels. Professional management is critical to success when hotel owners are not operators themselves. It is enough that owners know to seek quality management.

A pure management company is almost unknown now. Some companies have equity (ownership) stakes in the properties they manage. They wouldn't get the contract otherwise. A bigger change has come from consolidation. Chains, which have their own management talent, have taken over many hotels that would otherwise be operating under management contracts. The number of independent properties that require management talent is declining even as the number of management companies is growing.

**Leases** Management contracts and lease contracts are almost opposite views of the industry's health. One or the other becomes popular depending on the position of the economic cycle. Leases are popular when times are good.

Hotels once owned the real estate and managed the operation. Owning real estate takes large sums of invested equity and significant risks from borrowing. As hoteliers became more sophisticated about finance (1960s), sale-and-leaseback became popular. The hotel company would sell the building to outside investors. The new investors would then lease (rent) the operation of the hotel back to the very hotel company that had sold the real estate. Since the operation was profitable, both parties won. The operating companies had profits after they paid the lease rent, and the owning company had a fixed flow of rental income with which it could secure the borrowing. The lease's long and successful history gives precedent to current REIT arrangements.

Management contracts gain popularity when the industry goes into a slump. The operating company cannot visualize any operating profits, so it steps back from lease arrangements. The owning company still has a hotel that needs management skills. It hires the management company, paying the company a management fee as prescribed by the management contract. Incentives are paid to the management company if it produces profits through increased sales or reduced costs.

The dynamics of hotel keeping allow for a variety of possibilities. Some hotel companies own and operate hotels. Sometimes, it is as a joint venture. Some hotel companies manage for a fee but contribute some of the equity (ownership). Some hotel companies just manage. Franchising is another option: Cendant just franchises.

# Franchises

Franchising is not a new idea, nor is it unique to the hotel industry. Tires, speedy printing, diet clinics, and more are all franchised these days. With a **franchise**, the buyer (called the **franchisee**) acquires rights from the seller (called the **franchisor**). Those rights give the franchisee exclusive use (a franchise) of the name, the product, and the system of the franchisor within a given geographic area. Buying a franchise enables the small-business person to operate as an independent but still have the benefits of membership in the chain. The franchise concept serves large absentee owners and small owner/operators equally well.

The franchisee pays a variety of fees to adopt the name and trademark of the franchisor (see Exhibit 1-18). In addition to an initial signing fee, the franchisee pays so much per room per night throughout the life of the contract. But that's not all. The franchisee also pays a rental fee for the company sign, a fee to access the reservation system, and a per-reservation fee for each room booked. In addition, the franchisee buys amenities from the parent company in order to get the franchise logo. Extra fees are charged for required training and for participating in the frequent-guest program. Competition has encouraged some management companies to pay all or part of the owner's franchising costs in order to win the management contract.

With those fees comes a variety of services. How many and which services depend on which franchise is purchased. The central reservations system, discussed in Chapter 4, is the major reason by far that franchisees sign up. Estimates place the number of reservations coming through the system at as high as 30 percent of the chain's total reservations and upward of half of all reservations for individual properties.

**The Franchise and the Flag** Hotel franchising probably began during the late nineteenth century. Cesar Ritz—*ritzy* now means the finest in luxurious accommodations—gave his name to a small number of hotels whose management he supervised. Kemmons Wilson made the next advance in hotel franchising with the development of the Holiday Inn chain.

Franchising is all about the brand recognition discussed earlier in the chapter. The franchisor is able to deliver immediate brand identity by selling its "flag" to the franchisee. Franchisee and parent company are so alike that guests do not distinguish between them. The physical hotels look identical. It's the ownership and management structures that differ. The chain (the franchisor) does not own the franchise property, the operator (the franchisee) does. The franchisor does not manage the property, the franchisee does. If the franchisee elects not to manage, it could hire the franchisor as its management company under a separate management contract. Or instead, it could hire an entirely different management company. So now another party, the franchisor (the franchise company), has been added to the interaction of the developer, the owner, the lender, and the management company.

**Exhibit 1-18** ▶
Hotel franchisors (franchise sellers) charge franchisees (franchise buyers) a variety of fees that might total as much as 8 to 10 percent of gross sales!

| Representative Franchise Fees[a] | | |
| --- | --- | --- |
| **Fee** | **Representative Terms** | **Alternative Terms** |
| Application[b] | The greater of $45 000 *or* $400 times the number of rooms | A lesser fixed amount plus a per-room fee over, say, the first 75 rooms |
| Royalty | 4–6 percent of room revenue | 3 percent of gross revenue; *or* a minimum per night, say, $5 |
| Advertising/ Marketing | 1.5–3.5 percent of room revenue | 2 percent of gross revenue; *or* a minimum per night, say, $1 per room |
| Training | 0.5 percent of gross revenue plus cost of attending school | None; franchisee bears all schooling costs for employees sent away |
| Reservation | 3 percent of room revenue plus $2–$5/reservation | $8–$10/reservation; *or* a minimum per night, say, $8 per room |

[a]Other possibilities include email costs, global reservation costs, termination costs, accounting charges, and participation in frequent-guest promotions.
[b]All or some (90–95 percent) of the application fee is returned if the application is not approved.

# Summary

The lodging industry continues to play an important role in the development of commerce and culture even as it undergoes rapid changes. Despite the introduction of many new lodging types, the industry retains its traditional measures of success: occupancy (percentage), average daily rate (ADR), and revenue per available room (RevPar).

To maximize the values of these measures, management must overcome several limitations that are inherent in the hotel business. These include a highly perishable product, an unmovable location, a fixed supply of inventory, a high break-even point, and seasonal operating periods. In addition, hotel keeping is a cyclical industry, with long up and down waves that sometimes last a decade: tough hurdles all. The average life of a hotel in North America is only 38 years.

Understanding the industry's traditional identifications (size, class, type, and plan) helps in identifying the new permutations (all-suite, B&B, boutique) that keep the industry economically sound and exciting as a career. Competition sharpens the new direction, and rating systems keep the individual hotel attuned. As the changes continue, new classifications and new categories are needed.

The twenty-first century opened with the hotel business at the peak of its cycle, in part because of the industry's willingness to try new things. New products were tested using new marketing approaches; new ownership patterns were introduced, calling for new management structures. Strategic changes such as these require rapid and decisive moves to meet the intense competition head on. Many new flags (brands) are flying even as consolidation shrinks the number of, and grows the size of, surviving hotel companies.

Shifts in the lodging industry take place within the global village, where ideas and innovations move swiftly between continents. Their speed and direction depend, in large measure, on the relative strengths of currencies. Hoteliers worldwide know that name recognition attracts the transient traveller. High fees notwithstanding, franchising is one concept that has jumped the oceans to further consolidate lodging and make it a true global industry.

For now, the inelastic business market continues to underpin the basic business of hotel keeping. Many predict that the rapidly growing elastic market of tourism and leisure will soon replace the business traveller as lodging's major guest profile.

The twenty-first century will build on the dynamic changes in products, markets, financing, and operations that continue to reshape this ancient industry.

# Questions and Problems

1. Explain where the hotel industry in Canada is in its economic cycle. Be specific. Is it at the bottom of the trough? The highest point of its rise? Somewhere in between? If so, in what direction is it moving? Submit evidence to support your position.

2. Identify the advantages and disadvantages to the career of a student who takes a job after graduation with a Hilton Inns franchise, and passes up an offer from Hilton Hotels, the parent company.

3. Someone once said, "If you try to be all things to every guest, you'll likely end up as every guest's second choice." Is that an accurate statement? Why or why not? Answer with special attention to the segmentation of the industry's product line.

4. Give three to five examples of each type of expense that is used to determine the cost portion of a hotel's break-even point: fixed expenses; semi-fixed expenses; variable expenses.

## CASE STUDY

### Consultant in Chilliwack

Shyam won a lottery three years ago, and his dream has always been to own a hotel. After investigating different markets, he settled on purchasing a 220-room, 20-year-old hotel in Chilliwack, British Columbia. This hotel was built as part of the Holiday Inn chain, but due to changing market conditions and possible poor management, it fell on hard times and was sold several years earlier to a private owner who operated it as an independent, with less than satisfactory results.

As the closing date for the purchase of the hotel rapidly approached, Shyam pondered several matters. He has hired you as a consultant to help him with the following important questions. What possible solutions would you offer to Shyam?

1. Shyam is not an experienced hotelier and is pondering whether to manage the hotel himself or hire an experienced general manager who would report directly to him. What other management options does Shyam have, and which one would you recommend to him and why?

2. Shyam is not sure how to flag (brand) his hotel. It was not successful as either a Holiday Inn or an independent. What are the options available to Shyam, and which would you recommend as the one most likely to succeed in terms of increasing occupancy? What are the advantages and disadvantages of flagging the property?

3. If Shyam chooses to remain an independent while having the additional features of an affiliation and computerized reservation referral service, what flag would you recommend?

## Notes

1. The lodging industry uses the term *segmentation* to mean product differentiation; that is, multiple products. Segmentation has a different, almost opposite meaning in marketing terms; that is, focusing on one product that is developed for one segment.

2. One chain recently identified its typical business guest as a male, age 25 to 44, holding a white-collar job that pays $54 400 annually. This traveller, who arrives alone by air, holds a reservation and pays an average of $67.20 per night.

3. These are registered trademarks.

# Weblinks

## Canadian REITs

Canadian Hotel Income Properties (CHIP) REIT
**www.chipreit.com**

Royal Host REIT
**www.royalhost.com**

## Canadian Hotel Companies

Four Seasons Hotels and Resorts
**www.fourseasons.com**

Fairmont Hotels & Resorts
**www.fairmonthotels.com**

Atlific Hotels & Resorts
**www.atlific.com**

Raffles Hotels and Resorts
**www.raffles.com**

## Canadian Gaming Association

**www.canadiangaming.ca**

## Leading Spas of Canada

**www.leadingspasofcanada.com.**

## Boutique Hotels

Hotel Godin
**www.hotelgodin.com**

Opus Hotel
**www.opushotel.com**

Pantages Hotel
**www.pantageshotel.com**

Quebec City's Ice Hotel
**www.icehotel-canada.com**

## Chapter 2

# The Structure of the Hotel Industry

## Learning Objectives

After reading this chapter, you will be able to do the following:

1. **Understand the management structure of a modern hotel, including an understanding of an organization chart.**

2. **Identify the role of the front office in this structure, including the design of the front office and the work hours and duties of its employees.**

3. **Understand hotel building structure from old to new.**

Hotel organizations are structured—put together—in many different ways. That's because the organizational structure is a method of arranging the workforce to carry out the goals and functions of a particular company. And what a variety of goals, functions, and companies there is! Certainly, Chapter 1 made clear the immense range of operations, segments, markets, and locations that falls under the single umbrella of the lodging industry.

Each organization takes final form from the patterns that make up the hotel industry. That's why the 1000-room, chain-operated convention hotel is no more like the mom-and-pop highway motel than a seasonal ski resort is like a casino hotel. And all of these differ again from the conference centre, the economy property, or the commercial hotel whose towers house residential guests.

Just as each hotel type calls for a different organizational structure, each calls for a different building structure, too. The ski lodge will probably have individual cottages or condos hidden in the woods. The resort may be a series of low-rise outbuildings surrounding the swimming pool. How different these structures are from the urban commercial giant, squeezed by high land costs, that adopts a high-rise configuration for its building design.

Differences notwithstanding, both the organizational structure and the building structure adhere to similar blueprints. Although differences distinguish the properties' lines, the basics are the same: the staff structured to serve the guest, and the guest room—the hotel's major product line—structured to accommodate the guest.

## The Organizational Structure

Hotels employ a vast number of persons with a variety of skills. Hotels have plumbers and accountants, bartenders and cooks, grounds managers and water purification experts, telecommunication specialists and computer trouble-shooters. The larger the hotel, the more specialized the tasks. Indeed, large hotels have bigger resident populations and provide more services than do many small towns.

Each hotel organizes this diversified workforce in different ways. Human and physical resources are combined to achieve company goals in the most efficient manner. Although each organization takes a unique form, the patterns that emerge are based on the industry's best practices.

Hotel organizations follow the pattern of other business or social institutions. They break up the workforce into separate departments, with each department entrusted with a share of the duties and sevices. Modern management techniques try to minimize the difference among the various departments becuase any one of them can destroy the best efforts of all the others. Coordinating the whole, unifying the different specialties, and directing their joint efforts are the job of the general manager.

## The General Manager

Management titles vary from hotel to hotel, just as their organizations do. The large hotel chains use titles at the corporate level that are similar to other Canadian businesses: chief executive officer (CEO), chief financial officer (CFO), and chief operating officer (COO).

**General manager (GM)** is the favoured title at the unit level—that is, for the individual hotel. This person is responsible for everything that happens in the hotel, for all of the departments (see Exhibit 2-1), and for the general profitability of the hotel!

If the general manager is a senior member of the corporation that owns the hotel, his or her title might be president (of the corporation) and general manager (of the hotel). Or the title might be vice-president and general manager. The GM who sits on the corporate board of directors could be director and general manager, or even managing director, but neither one is used very often. Managing director has a European flavour (directeur is French for manager), so managing director may be used as much for ambience as for organizational clarity. If the manager and his or her family own the hotel, owner-manager is standard terminology. Standing alone, the title of general manager implies no ownership affiliation. Then the GM is the employee most responsible to ownership, corporate or otherwise, and the one accountable for the full scope of the operation. Holiday Inn was indeed creative and captured the essence of the old hotel by calling its general managers "innkeepers."

When several properties of the same chain are located in one city and one person supervises all of them, the GM term might be assigned to that person rather than to the executives of the individual hotels. Chains use other titles as appropriate: *area vice-president for operations, regional director of marketing,* and *food and beverage manager, eastern division.*

Whatever the specific title, the top executive of the hotel reports to ownership directly or through other divisional executives. Ownership vests its authority in that top executive and holds that person responsible for all that happens.

Large hotel organizations support the GM with specialized departments, and sometimes with an assistant, the *executive assistant manager.* Like the general manager, the executive assistant has complete jurisdiction over the entire house. That distinguishes the executive assistant position from that of the *assistant manager,* which is a rooms department position only.

Hotels never close, and that places great demands on the energy and time of all hotel executives, but especially on the GM. Night, weekend, and holiday periods are covered in some hotels by rotating the entire management staff into a position called *executive on*

**Exhibit 2-1 ▶**
The organizational structure of hotels is changing almost as rapidly as their architectural designs. Flatter organizations (fewer supervisory levels) notwithstanding, new positions are being added. Among them are managers (or directors) of quality assurance, information technology, and revenue management. The chart is not complete except for the operations manager's line, which is the thrust of the chapter and the text.

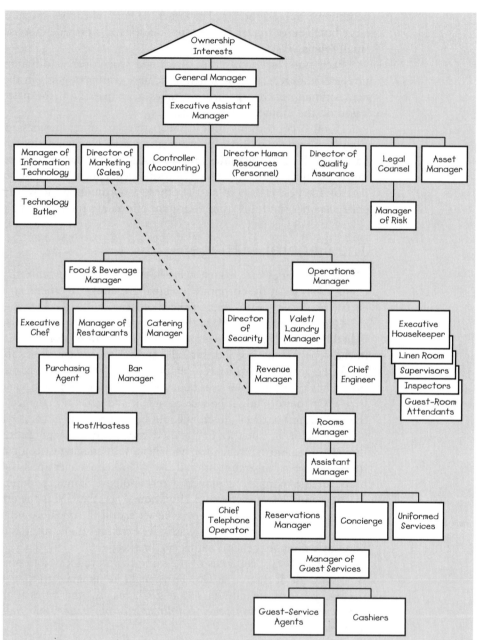

*duty* or *duty manager.* Every department head takes a turn. Thus, the reservoir of management talent is deepened and the experience of the individual manager is broadened.

**From Host to Executive** The many changes that were recounted in the previous chapter have affected the position and person of the general manager. During the period of one-person ownership, the general manager personified the specific property. The GM of this era was either the actual owner or a representative who stood in the owner's place. He (in those days, the positions were invariably held by men) was known as "Mine Host." His name was part of the advertising, his personality part of the aura, his presence part of the hotel's very identity. Hotels were smaller and the manager often visited with arriving and departing guests. The property reflected the qualities, personality, leadership, and the essence of this very special person.

In contrast, today, ". . . the amount of time spent with customers versus budgets is totally reversed. In fact, one room clerk working at a hotel for more than six months . . . [said] she had never seen the general manager [at] the front desk!"[1] GMs of an earlier period put their marks on properties because they were in one location for a long time. Not so today; the company's need for the special talents of a particular manager often means frequent transfers. Guests have also changed: Mass marketing and one-time arrivals make Mine Host less relevant. Executive talents now focus on a growing list of non-guest issues. Hence, many observers worry that "the business of hotels is no longer the hotel business."

**Support Departments** Hotel managers contend with an ever-growing list of issues that require special knowledge and expertise (see Exhibit 2-1). Large hotels support the GM with experts in specialized fields of law, employment, environment, taxes, marketing, technology, and more. If the GM carries a corporate title, so may these staff members. A president and general manager may have, for example, a vice-president of marketing rather than a director of marketing. Remember that even if there is no separate management company, the operating hotel is also a corporation, often a subsidiary corporation of the chain that carries the name.

Staff positions support the **operating departments** as well as the general manager. The rooms manager, for example, looks to human resources for help in filling job vacancies; to sales for help in filling rooms; and to accounting for help in credit card control and settlement. Staff members even make guest contact on occasion. Accounting, for example, may contact guests about unpaid accounts.

**Food and Beverage** Unlike the advisory nature of the support staff, the *food and beverage manager* has direct operating responsibility. F&B is one of the hotel's two major line departments (see Exhibit 2-1). The rooms department, which is the thrust of this text, is the other.

Food and beverage is subdivided into several operating units. Food preparation is headed by a *chef or executive chef,* and food service by a *manager of restaurants,* which large properties may title **maitre d' hotel**. Parties and banquets are handled by a *catering manager* (or banquet manager), although this position is sometimes assigned to the marketing department. All beverage outlets, including banquet bars, report to a *bar manager.*

The importance of the food and beverage department has been eroding during the past half century. F&B, which accounted for nearly half of the lodging industry's revenue in the 1960s, about equal with rooms, now contributes only 20 percent of total sales. This industry-wide statistic reflects the large number of lodging units that no longer have food service. But food revenues have declined even in full-service hotels. Declines in dollar volume and in the number of food outlets have reshuffled organizational charts. Many middle management positions (bar manager and restaurant manager, for example) and their assistants have been eliminated. In fact, middle management posts have been deleted in almost every department of the hotel. Fewer managers available means that either decisions are pushed to the operating employee (Chapter 7 examines this issue) or responsibilities are broadened for the managers who remain.

## The Hotel Manager

The **hotel manager,** also called the *house manager* or *operations manager,* is the front-of-the-house counterpart to the food and beverage manager. All operating departments, except those dealing with food and beverage, report to this position. Exhibit 2-1 outlines the divisions of the **front of the house** at a large hotel. Every department that services guests falls within the hotel manager's purview. Finding employees capable of dealing with such face-to-face contacts is a major challenge of the job. Coordinating—presenting the services of several different departments as those of one company—is another

In keeping with the industry's move toward flatter organizations (fewer management levels between top management and the employee on the spot), small hotels operate without a hotel manager. Small hotels have fewer operating departments—no F&B, perhaps—and fewer staff positions clamouring for the GM's time. Without intervening management levels, the heads of rooms, housekeeping, and security have the GM as their immediate supervisor.

For our larger-hotel illustration, these important departments remain with the hotel or house manager. He or she supervises a broad sweep of support positions, not merely rooms. Included are the departments of engineering (maintenance), laundry, valet, security, revenue control, housekeeping, credit, business centre, shop rentals, concierge, pool, spa, and more. (Exhibit 2-1 is not complete.)

Later sections of this chapter deal with security and the rooms department in detail. Also, in Chapter 3 we will examine another important responsibility of the house manager: housekeeping.

**Uniformed Services** The ranks of the service department—or uniformed services or bell department—are on the wane. At one time, this department included baggage porters, transportation clerks, and elevator operators for both guest and service cars. Now it comprises chiefly bellpersons and door attendants, and even these are decreasing in number.

There are several reasons for this decline. Changing travel habits and licensing requirements have eliminated the service department's role in travel arrangements. Second, guests travel lighter today than they did a generation ago. Suitcases are built lighter (and many have wheels), and shorter stays mean less clothing. Self-service is expected in many facets of Canadian life, so many guests carry their own luggage—all of which means fewer tips and less job appeal. As a result, fewer workers seek such employment.

The decline in the number of uniformed employees has another explanation: management cost-cutting. Today, everyone must be paid a minimum wage, whereas tips alone constituted the salary in an earlier era. Reducing the staff cuts labour costs and with them fringe benefits, which add as much as one-third more to direct labour costs. So, the hotel that services the entrance door around the clock is rare, and the motor hotel without any uniformed services is the norm.

If bell services are available, they will be the guest's first contact on arrival: if not a door attendant, perhaps a bellperson. Contact may be as early as the airport van driver, who is also a member of the service crew. In urban properties with separate parking, someone needs to be at the door to handle garaging and other auto services. Few urban hotels own their own parking spaces. They lease the space or have an outside contractor take a parking **concession**. (This outsourcing is still another explanation for today's smaller uniformed staff.)

Handling baggage for arriving and departing guests, including groups, is the major function of the service department. Laundry and valet service, ice, and transportation were once part of the department's duties, but they are less so today. Once roomed, few guests use bell service. Loudspeakers, telephones, and computer systems have even replaced the paging and message-service roles of the department.

With guest arrivals and departures as their main function, bellpersons can be scheduled at a ratio of 1 bellhop per 65 anticipated hourly arrivals/departures. If they exist at all in small hotels, the bell staff may handle room service, lobby cleaning, and pool maintenance along with their other duties.

The title of the modern service department head is *manager of services,* or *superintendent of services,* not nearly as romantic as the more traditional terms, **bell captain,** or its shortened version, *captain.* Recently, responsibility for the now-abbreviated service department has begun shifting to the *concierge,* a service-giver of a totally different type. If not organizational responsibility, which is still very tentative, certainly the services rendered are reminiscent of many previously provided by the uniformed services.

**Concierge** A relatively new front-office position has taken hold in Canada, but it has long been popular overseas, especially in France. The International Union of Concierges was founded in Paris, France, in 1952 and in Canada in 1976 as Les Clefs d'or Canada, with its head office in Montreal. It now has more than 100 members across Canada and 19 member countries. Some community colleges, such as Fanshawe in London, Ontario, now offer concierge programs. Members wear the Golden Keys (Les Clefs d'Or) that are their symbol of professionalism. The International Concierge Institute (ICI), Campus of the Americas, opened its doors in Montreal in 1995, and in 1999 the head office of the ICI moved to Montreal from Paris.

In Great Britain, where the front office is called the front hall, the **concierge** is the head hall porter. Like a French idiom, translating the nuances of the job into English leaves something to be desired. Many guests are still uncertain what the position entails, let alone how to pronounce it (*kon syerzh*).

The word comes from the Latin *con servus,* meaning "with service." Other translations offered are "fellow slave" or, more to the point, "building guard." According to the French, the *Comte de Cierges* (Count of Cierge) was in charge of the prisons, making him the keeper of the keys under the French monarchs. Thus, the European concierge appeared as a door attendant (building guard) and from that to the keeper of the keys, porter, and provider of various services.

These duties are still part of the European concierge's job, particularly in small hotels. Controlling the keys enables the concierge to watch the comings and goings of guests and thus to furnish a bit of extra protection and information. This is not the Canadian interpretation of the job, except when a hotel offers a concierge floor, or luxury floor. Even then, the added security is a secondary objective.

The keeper of the door, the lobby concierge (see Exhibit 2-2), provides all types of miscellaneous information and a variety of personal, but minor, services. Information and service shape the basic description of the concierge's job. Travel information, messages, tickets and reservations to a broad range of events, babysitters, language translation, and secretarial sources all fall within the purview of the concierge. Guests may ask the concierge to arrange for pet care, to provide extra chairs, to arrange flower delivery, to find lost items, to get medical care in an emergency, to recommend hair stylists, anything (see Exhibit 2-3).

As hotels retrench some services and automate others, the post of concierge becomes increasingly important. Guests can no longer turn to transportation desks, floor clerks, and elevator operators for questions and services. Those jobs no longer exist. Many of the gratuities that previously went to the uniformed staff have been

**Exhibit 2-2** ▶

To assure accessibility, the concierge is usually located in the lobby. Some hotels limit concierge service to special floors with extra services but at a higher room rate. The pleasant working conditions and the aura of confident service are highlighted in this lobby photograph.

**Exhibit 2-3** ▶

The duties of the concierge, a guest-service position in large, upscale hotels, range from A to Z.

| | | |
|---|---|---|
| A... | as in | Art supplies and restoration |
| B... | as in | Babysitting services for vacating parents |
| C... | as in | Churches for all denominations |
| D... | as in | Dinner reservations at sold-out restaurants |
| E... | as in | Errand and courier services for speedy delivery |
| F... | as in | Flowers for that special occasion |
| G... | as in | Galleries for antiques and arts |
| H... | as in | Helicopter services |
| I... | as in | Interpreters for an international symposium |
| J... | as in | Jewellers from whom one can buy with confidence |
| K... | as in | Kennels for a cherished pet |
| L... | as in | Libraries for source materials |
| M... | as in | Maps to navigate the city or the subway |
| N... | as in | Newspapers from distant cities and foreign countries |
| O... | as in | Orchestra tickets at the last minute |
| P... | as in | Photographers for that special occasion |
| Q... | as in | Queries that no one else can answer |
| R... | as in | Restaurants of every specialty |
| S... | as in | Scuba diving sites and services |
| T... | as in | Transportation: air; auto; bus; limo; taxi; train |
| U... | as in | Umbrellas on a rainy day |
| V... | as in | Virtual reality equipment |
| W... | as in | Wedding chapels |
| X... | as in | Xeroxing a last-minute report |
| Y... | as in | Yoga demonstrations and instructions |
| Z... | as in | Zoo directions for an outing with the children |

redirected to the concierge desk. For services rendered, a concierge may be tipped by the guest and commissioned by the service company (theatre, rentals, etc.).

A play on words has created the job of *compcierge,* in which *comp* stands for computer. A compcierge comes in two forms. The first is a *technology butler:* a technician or information technology (IT) expert who provides technology assistance to guests and conventioneers. The second form of compcierge is a computerized console that provides information about the local scene. Guests turn to the computer for directional information, theatres, restaurants, and similar listings. A computerized compcierge can stand alone or support a concierge's desk by freeing the live concierge for more complicated services.

**The Concierge Floor** The concierge floor is one amenity not discussed in Chapter 1. It is an extra service facility available at an extra charge. The concierge service is limited to guests on that special sleeping floor. Continental breakfast and evening cocktails are usually provided. As a premium floor, there are other extras. A terrycloth robe is furnished for the bath, shoes are shined, rooms are larger, arrival and departure procedures are expedited, and security is enhanced.

Access to the floor is limited and requires a special key for the elevator. The concierge is usually seated by the elevator, adding security as the floor clerk's position did before the Second World War.

All of the upscale chains have concierge floors. Hilton calls its Towers after the famed Waldorf-Astoria Towers, which is part of the Hilton chain. Hyatt uses Regency Club, Radisson uses Plaza Club, Delta uses Delta Privilege, and Fairmont uses Fairmont Gold. Add these names to the frequent-guest programs and the confusion of name segmentation increases dramatically.

InterContinental Hotels Group, the world's largest hotel group by number of rooms, has implemented the industry's most comprehensive virtual concierge service, eHost, for its Holiday Inn Hotels and Resorts brand. The move, which is the first by a major hotel chain, is part of the Holiday Inn brand's commitment to developing consumer-enabling technology for the ever-growing community of guests who seek products and services online.

Accessed via hotels' free high-speed Internet access systems, eHost gives Holiday Inn guests 24-hour access to the information normally provided by a traditional concierge, including area dining options, attractions, movies, shopping, transportation, and events in the immediate vicinity of the Holiday Inn where they are staying. eHost also provides weather and airline information, hotel-specific information, and Holiday Inn brand history, as well as email access to the hotel's general manager or staff to provide immediate feedback via an online survey tool. Guests can even play games and send e-postcards home to friends and family through eHost.

"With the growth of the tech-savvy, socialized Generation X customer base, our guests continue to expect the same superior service from Holiday Inn, but the way they want to interact with us is evolving," said Mark Snyder, senior vice-president of Brand Management for Holiday Inn Hotels and Resorts in the Americas. "eHost affords our guests more convenience, choice and control than ever before, allowing them to access the hotel's local community they are visiting in a way that is unique to them and customizes results for their individual needs."

**Telephone** The number of telephones in a large hotel often exceeds the number found in many of Canada's small cities. Nevertheless, computerization has reduced the size of this department just as automation has reduced the size of the uniformed services. Outgoing local and long-distance calls are handled by automatic, direct-dial equipment. Similarly, calls between guest rooms or from guest rooms to hotel departments (room service, for example) no longer require a telephone operator to complete the call. Electronic billing automatically records the telephone company's charges on the guest's electronic bill, eliminating the old position of charge operator.

In no other department of the hotel has the introduction of costly and complex equipment been so rapid and so complete, and worked so well. Supervising the few employees left in the department is the head telephone operator, called the *chief operator* or *telephone supervisor*. Depending on size, there might be an assistant or shift supervisor.

Operators may still answer incoming calls and direct them to their proper destinations. The caller's sole contact with the property is the disembodied voice of the telephone operator; therefore, incoming calls must be handled professionally and pleasantly. Some hotels still have incoming messages taken by the operator. More and more, the operator doesn't answer incoming calls and doesn't take messages. An electronic menu from which the caller chooses a service handles incoming calls. If the service chosen is a guest room call, the operator intercedes. Hotels do not give out the room numbers or telephone numbers of registered guests. Messages are different. The telephone mailbox allows a caller direct access to the guest's in-room telephone, where the message can be left with privacy and without the mistakes of transcription for which the hotel is always blamed.

Even morning wake-up calls have been automated. And furnishing an alarm clock in each guest room has reduced even this number. Some guests still prefer the assurance of human intervention, so the telephone operator provides this with a morning wake-up call, probably an automated one. However, some hotel chains such as Delta still do personal wake-up calls in the belief that a warm, friendly voice in the morning is better than a rude awakening to an alarm clock or automated device.

**Other Departments**    A previous paragraph noted the hotel manager's responsibility for all of the operating departments except food and beverage. This usually includes the hotel's numerous tenants. Among them are stores and shops (florists, beauticians, menswear, etc.), businesses that rent office space, and airline or privately owned tour desks. The business centre may be the hotel's, or it may be leased to yet another tenant. Negotiating the lease and rental contracts by which these relationships are established falls to the office of the hotel manager.

Thousands of persons pass through the hotel in a week. Medical emergencies must be anticipated and preparations put in place. That's another job for the hotel manager, although the assignment may be delegated, perhaps to the concierge. Many large cities have some form of *HotelDocs,* a private medical service. The physicians come without charge to the hotel; ill travellers pay for the care as they would at home. In Canada, it is more common to call emergency services or send or take the guest to the closest hospital emergency room.

Some hotels have the position of facilities manager. The post might be part of the engineering department, or even of housekeeping. Or it might be another responsibility reporting to the hotel manager. The care and maintenance of the physical plant includes new construction, repairs and maintenance, window washing, carpet maintenance, technology, and employee health and safety.

# The Rooms Manager

Full-service operations require some of the hotel manager's responsibilities to be moved down the organizational line. Rooms, which might include housekeeping, are then assigned to the next management level, the *rooms manager*. Reservations, telephone, concierge, and uniformed services are among the departments reporting to the rooms manager, as is the front desk. If the management load is still too heavy, the rooms manager may delegate oversight of the front desk to another line officer, the *front-office manager*. This manager assumes control over the front desk proper, including guest-service agents (front-office clerks), credit, cashiers, mail, messages, and information. The position of front-office manager is discussed later.

Few hotels need so many executives for the front of the house, and today we are finding a flattening of organization charts in Canadian hotels, with staff members required to handle more and more responsibility.

**Security**   The scope and purpose of hotel security has changed. From the single house detective or watchman walking a nightly fire patrol—adequate for the 1950s and 1960s—hotel security has matured to match present-day demands. Vigilance in the United States increased after the Persian Gulf War (1991) and moved to the forefront of all governmental and business activities after the destruction of the Twin Towers, which included Marriott's hotel at the World Trade Center (2001). Parts of the industry responded to these events with knee-jerk decisions. Some refused to accept or hold guest baggage at the bell desk. Package delivery, as well as some loading dock deliveries, were subjected to inspection and X-rays. Automobile trunks were examined before cars were parked in garages. Baggage had to be removed directly from guest rooms; corridor pickup was no longer allowed, even for large tour groups.

More reasonable, permanent changes were being initiated long before the 1990s. The lodging industry was forced to re-examine its overall security because of several widely publicized events. At the top of that list was the 1971 in-room rape of a well-known Hollywood actress. The lodging industry first responded with basic security measures and then moved toward professionalizing its security forces. Better, not merely more, security measures were implemented. First came the widespread installation of electronic locks (see Chapter 14), observation ports (peepholes in corridor doors), and better fire protection, including public address outlets in guest rooms. Perimeter lighting was improved. Smoke alarms and sprinkler systems were mandated. Properties that failed to comply suffered downgrades by rating agencies such as CAA and lost their franchise affiliations.[2]

A second phase of equipment upgrades is currently under way. It reflects improvements in security equipment of all types. CCTV (closed-circuit television) with improved video cameras enables one security person to monitor a vast array of corridors, parking areas, and public space. Special in-room alarms for the hearing and visually handicapped are being installed. Upgraded telephone and radio communications add to efficiency. Remote card readers control access to hotel facilities such as pools and garage gates. Perhaps biometric room systems, which are now in the pipeline, will serve as the room keys of the future. In the meantime, simple decisions such as sharing perimeter patrols with nearby competitors produce results.

An open, candid approach to the problem has been another shift in policy. Before now, lodging executives rarely spoke of security. Plain-clothes personnel were favoured over uniforms. Today, hotels go for visibility: uniforms or distinctive blazers in the lobbies, by the elevators (no floor access without a room key), and on patrol.

Good security has strong market appeal—guests want to feel safe—but that's not its major charge. Security has always had two basic responsibilities. It is charged with the protection of persons (guests and staff) and of property, including the hotel's property. Property losses come from several directions. Petty theft of towels and other furnishings, even televisions and clocks that are not secured to the tabletop, can be attributed to both employees and guests. Employees are believed to be the single greatest source of hotel larceny, but guests often take home more than memories.

Risk preparedness and crisis management have shifted the focus and structure of hotel security. Large chains have added a manager (even a vice-president) of loss prevention. Petty thieves, pickpockets, and prostitutes still demand attention, but many new flash points have been added to the basic assignment of loss prevention. Security now umbrellas and trains for a whole range of emergencies, including hazardous materials; bomb threats; fire; gas leaks; terrorism; riots and crowd control; elevator failures; CPR and medical emergencies, including food poisoning; and guest lawsuits. Security has focused more attention than ever before on risk management, on worker's compensation injuries, and on compliance with the Ontarians with Disabilities Act (ODA), which may soon follow in other provinces and territories (see Chapter 7). In certain locales, Hong Kong for one, hotel security even prepares for cyclones, tornados, and floods. Loss of electric power is a closer-to-home contingency.

Hotel security has moved up the organizational ladder in importance, even as other departments (bells and telephone) have been downsized. However, it functions as it always has. It acts first as a deterrent, then as a restraint, and only rarely as a police force. Hotel security must remain an iron hand in a velvet glove.

# Structure of the Front Office

## What Is the Front Office?

Physically, the **front office** is an easily identifiable area of the lobby. Functionally, it is much less so despite constant reference to it as the "hub" and the "heart" of the hotel. The overuse of such terms should not detract from the real importance of the front office. It is in fact the nerve centre of guest activity. Through it flow communications with every other department; from it emanate instructions for the service of the guest; to it come charges for final billing and settlement.

Organizational interdependence is not the only reason for the pre-eminent position of the front office. It is equally a matter of economics. Room sales produce more than half of the total revenue of the average hotel. For budget hotels, they produce all of the revenue. And for others, much of the revenue that comes from food and beverage originates in meetings and convention groups, whose search for site selection begins with rooms. More revenue (about 66 percent) is derived from room sales than from the total of food, beverage, and telephone.[3] Furthermore, rooms are more profitable than these departments. Every dollar of room sales produces approximately 73 cents in departmental profit. Food and beverage combined average out to less than 21 cents of departmental profit per dollar sale.

Hotel guests relate with the front office, and this adds to its importance. Guests who rarely see their housekeepers, who never see the cook, who deal with sales only on occasion, know the hotel by its desk. They are received at the desk and they depart from the desk. It is toward the desk that guests direct complaints and from the desk that they expect remedies. Guest identification, as much as profit or interdepartmental dependence, accounts for management's overriding concern with the front office.

Better to define the front office as a bundle of duties and guest services rather than as a fixed area located behind the lobby desk. Some divisions of the front office—reservations, for example—can be located elsewhere without affecting their membership in the front-office structure. Computerization's instant communication has reduced the need for all front-office segments to be within physical hailing distance of one another.

Someone once said that the front office was so named because it was close to the front door. Simple enough, but many hotels have substituted the term **guest-service area** in an effort to better define the role of the front office. By extension, the front-office manager becomes the guest-service manager; the front-desk clerk, a guest-service **agent**. Whatever their titles, the front-office managers and the guest-service agents operate the desk for the guest's convenience.

**Managing Rooms** How the front desk is managed and staffed depends on the hotel's pattern, its market segment, and its size. The organizational structure of a full-service hotel, for example, requires a very complete staff. Although few hotels have as complete an organizational structure as the full-service house, it serves as a model.

Full-service operations have three management positions on the hotel side (as differentiated from food and beverage or the support departments). The first of these positions, hotel manager (house manager, or operations manager), has already been discussed. Second is the *rooms division manager,* and then the *front-office manager.* The front-office manager reports upward to the rooms division manager, who reports upward to the hotel manager, and then to the general manager (see Exhibit 2-1 on page 50).

When the organization is structured this way, job responsibilities grow narrower down the organization's line. At the top, the hotel manager (the hotel manager is not the general manager) has responsibility for all operational functions except food and beverage. Included are departments that have not been discussed, such as maintenance and engineering, or laundry and valet. The hotel manager assigns responsibility for just the room functions to the rooms manager. That includes reservations, bell services, telephone, and the front office. The front-office manager takes control of the front office—clerks, mail and messages, guest information, credit, and so on. Some properties add yet another management level, the front desk. The front-desk manager is a supervisor usually responsible for a single shift.

Few hotels need three or four management positions, so the responsibilities of the positions remain but are handled by fewer persons. This chapter follows reality by including some of the rooms manager's duties under the headings of the hotel manager and the front-office manager. Remember: Many hotels just have one management level, or even none at all, between the employee on the desk and the general manager.

Whatever the manager's title, front-desk procedures require attention to detail. One study of the front-office manager indicated that performance and production are as important to success as is skill in dealing with people (see Exhibit 2-4). The fact is that performance and dealing with people are the same at the front desk, since handling details is the best means of attending to customer and employee needs.

**Manager of Guest Services** The organizational structure of a full-service hotel calls for one final level of management, the *front-office manager* or *manager of guest services. Assistant managers* might support this position during each shift, or a senior room

**Exhibit 2-4** ▶
The front-office manager or guest-services manager has a broad range of responsibilities beyond guest services, including departmental management issues: staff, profits, and legal and technical knowledge.

## PATH*FINDER*

| | |
|---|---|
| **Position:** | **Front Office Manager** |
| **Department:** | **Front Office** |
| **Hotel:** | **The Fairmont Royal York** |
| **Location:** | **Toronto, ON** |

The Front Office Manager reports to the Director of Rooms and is responsible for the day-to-day running of the Front Office. This leader will have a team of 14+ Supervisors and over 40 Front Line Agents reporting to them. The goal is to achieve levels of excellence in service in this 1365 Room property, to ensure a motivated energized work environment and fiscal responsibility for achievement of targeted or exceptional levels of profit.

**RESPONSIBILITIES:**

- Ensure the smooth and efficient operation of the Front Office and all related services to achieve maximum sales and guest satisfaction while adhering to established Company policies and procedures.
- Supporting Company and Hotel policies and procedures including the promoting and participation in SHARE, EOS, Health and Safety and GSI (JD Power).
- The ability to work effectively and provide leadership in a large management team with shared responsibilities.
- Co-ordinates all Front Desk, and related operations. Liaisons with key departments, including Guest Services, Reservations, Housekeeping, and Royal Service departments while on duty to ensure the highest levels of guest satisfaction.
- Ensures Service Standards are met and exceeded (i.e., Rooming the Guest; Anticipation of Guest Needs; Upselling and Cross Selling).
- Is thoroughly knowledgeable of all policies, procedures and systems including: relating to the Front Desk, Guest Services and emergency systems.
- Taking charge of groups and conventions from a Front Office perspective— attending Pre-Convention Meetings and ensuring all details are looked after.
- Participating and assisting with the Room Inventory, Yield and Revenue Management through maximizing revenues and Guest Services on Sell-Out nights and attending weekly Revenue Management meetings.
- Participating in interviewing, recruiting and selection of new team members.
- Harvests a cooperative team spirit amongst staff by listening, giving positive feedback, monitoring and following up. Reward performance!
- Monitors and controls staff performance and reviews communication strengths and weaknesses.

**Exhibit 2-4** ▶
(*Continued*)

- Assists in creating and maintaining manuals, which make available updated material relevant to safety procedures, hours of operation, promotions, guest service requirements etc.
- Conducts monthly staff meetings for Front Desk complete with minutes and in accordance with Fairmont Royal York standards.
- Liaise with VIP parties and special attention guests, ensuring their accommodation is in order, inspecting where necessary, greet, escort and contact when possible upon arrival.
- Schedule the staff within budgeted guidelines and provide best coverage for service demands.
- Thorough knowledge of Emergency Procedures and general Emergency Preparedness procedures.
- Design, implement, and follow up on staff incentive programs for guest service, quality and maximum revenue levels.
- Develop and implement new Front Office Initiatives, Systems and Standards.
- In periods of low occupancy, control distribution of rooms to maximize Housekeeping efficiency.
- Other duties as assigned by the Director of Rooms.

**POSITION REQUIREMENTS:**

- Minimum 2 years as Front Office Manager at a small to mid size hotel
- Excellent knowledge of Front Office procedures
- Highly organized, career and results oriented with the ability to be flexible with hours, days off, assignments and additional duties.
- Must be able to work well under pressure in a fast-paced and constantly changing environment
- Must be a strong team player with proven leadership, development and delegating skills
- Highest Guest Service skills, talent and knowledge with the vision and ability to lead employees to excellence. Professional manner, outgoing personality, and ability to work on own initiative
- Must possess excellent interpersonal and motivational skills
- Excellent written and verbal communication skills
- Diploma or Degree in Hotel Management an asset
- Second or third language an asset

clerk might do the job. With so complete a structure, job responsibilities grow narrower down the organizational ladder. Front-office managers control the immediate front-office staff, but the importance of the job makes it a pivotal assignment (see Exhibit 2-4).

**Guest-Service Agents** Different titles have attempted to describe the importance of the next organizational level. *Room clerk* and *front-office clerk*, which were Canadian favourites, have been replaced largely by GSA (*guest-service agent*). *Receptionist* is the favoured term outside North America.

Titles aside, guest-service agents have a host of duties concentrated in four functions: room sales, guest relations, records, and coordination (see Exhibit 2-5). Agents bring together the commitments made by reservations, the availability delivered by housekeeping, the minor repairs that so annoy guests, and the billing and collection required by accounting. Room clerks adjust minor problems and buffer management from the first blasts of major complaints. They are expected to achieve the company's average daily rate (ADR) goals by selling up (see Chapter 8). Thus, the guest-service agent is part salesperson, part psychologist, part accountant, and part manager.

**Exhibit 2-5 ▶**
The position description of a reception agent or guest-service agent is broad ranging, requiring persons with excellent people skills, great organizational skills, and exemplary communication skills, including those of a salesperson.

THE *Fairmont*
**ROYAL YORK**

## *CAREER OPPORTUNITY*

**Position:   Reception Agent**
**Department:   Front Office**

**RESPONSIBILITIES:**

- Provide effective, fast service in a friendly manner
- Check in and out hotel guests, making guest reservations, attending to internal guests
- Ensure the highest level of guest satisfaction
- Assist with Mail Desk and Guest Service duties as assigned
- Monitor for special rates and billing arrangements
- Pass on any guest comments to Assistant Reception Manager
- Other responsibilities connected with Front Office may be required
- Will rotate in various departments in Rooms Division either Royal Service, Fairmont Gold, Reservations, Guest Service, and Housekeeping

**QUALIFICATIONS:**

- A typing speed of 35 wpm
- Must have effective communication skills
- Must have a good command of the English language
- Hotel/Hospitality degree or diploma an asset

A new front-office position, which emphasizes the guest-service aspect of the desk, is appearing on the scene. The job has not yet been named, and it may disappear before it ever gets a title. With the introduction of computer-terminal registration, guests are able to bypass the front office and self-register using equipment similar to a bank ATM. To encourage reluctant guests, hotels have moved agents to the lobby side of the desk. Slowly walking guests through a learning process a time or two speeds up the work of the desk in the long run.

**Other Front-Office Functions** There was once a front-office position called mail, key, and information clerk. Modern circumstances have eliminated the position and even some of its functions. What remains has been taken over by guest-service agents or is now done electronically. Today, for example, most guest mail comes by fax; guests don't stay long enough to get letters through the traditional post. Heavy, metal hotel keys (and the front-desk traffic once generated by guests dropping them off and retrieving them later) have been replaced by electronic locks using disposable keys. Similarly, information and personal messages are handled today by electronic mail; in-room, closed-circuit television; and automated kiosks.

**Room Reservations** Reservations are requests for rooms from prospective guests who intend to arrive sometime in the future. These are received, processed, and **confirmed** by the reservations department, which is supervised by the reservations manager, who reports to the rooms manager (see Exhibit 2-1 on page 50). Reservations arrive by letter, fax, and email, or even directly across the desk occasionally. Most often, they are made over the telephone. Inquiries may come to the hotel's reservation office directly, but more likely they come through the chain's or franchise's central reservation office, the 800 or 888 number. In Chapter 4, we explain the procedure in detail.

The reservations department keeps records of who is arriving, at what time, and for how long they are staying. The information, including the type of facilities wanted, must be communicated to the front-desk clerk in anticipation of the guest's arrival. Tracking the number of rooms sold and the number still available for sale is the biggest responsibility of the reservations department. Groups and individual guests must be balanced to achieve a **full house** (100 percent occupancy) without overselling, which means not committing more rooms than are available. Reservations are maintained on a day-to-day basis for a year and in less detail for as many as three to five years ahead. Computerization has made the job easier and the decisions more accurate, as explained in Chapter 4.

**Cashiers** Cashiers are actually members of the accounting staff. Their location in the front desk and their relationship to many of the front-office positions place them in direct contact with the guest-services manager, who exercises control on a day-to-day basis.

Reorganization of the industry's front offices has blended the duties of the cashier into those of the guest-service agent. Both jobs are being rolled into one position except in large hotels. For money matters, the reporting line still flows through the general cashier.

Posting charges (recording them on guest bills), presenting final statements, resolving protests by departing guests, and handling cash and credit card transactions are the major duties of hotel cashiers. Other services once included cheque cashing and **cash advances**. Changes in the way that hotels do business have eliminated these banking services. Even guest service to **safe deposit boxes** has diminished as in-room safes have been installed (see Chapter 14).

As the guest-service agent is usually the guest's first contact with the front office, so the cashier is usually the guest's last. At one time, the cashier's window was a major source of guest irritation. Long lines and lengthy delays were the causes. Not so anymore. Computerization allows guests to use one of several forms of express check-out (see Chapter 13). As guests became accustomed to and began to prefer checking out themselves, and as hotels reined in the various financial services that the cashier had previously rendered, it became possible to eliminate separate cashier positions. Many hotels have started to do so.

## Design of the Lobby

Like so many other aspects of the front office, its design and location are also undergoing change. The bank teller look of the old-fashioned office has given way to an open style that is less formal and more inviting (see Exhibit 2-6). New, computerized systems have reduced the amount of paper and much of the clutter that typified the old front desk.

**The Lobby** Front-desk computers have also reduced the amount of floor space previously needed for the front office. This has encouraged new designs and configurations, which are coming at the same time that the lobby itself is enjoying a renaissance. For decades, the lobby was once the gathering place for business and social activities.[4] Hotel lobbies are providing that service again after a half-century of designs that limited use and discouraged lingering.

A well-designed lobby appears as if it were a town centre. Modern lobbies are great for networking. Small furniture groupings assure privacy for cellphone use and intimacy for cocktail gatherings. Big tables, large sofas, and heavy, overstuffed chairs have been replaced with smaller, more comfortable and eye-appealing settings (see Exhibit 2-7).

New or old, the lobby must provide easy access to the front office. Although the front office's architectural footprint has shrunk, new designs and images have made the desk more user-friendly than ever before.

**The Desk** The standard front-desk counter is about 114 cm high and approximately 76 cm across. The working space on the employee's side of the desk is lower by 15.2 cm or so. Reducing the height of the workspace allows the room clerk to carry out clerical duties comfortably. It also drops the equipment below the guest's eye level, permitting the employee and the guest to have better face-to-face interaction (see Exhibit 2-6).

Registration pods, which are non-standard front desks, are gaining popularity with new properties. Conversion costs are high, so pods, where both the guest and agent are seated in the lobby (see Exhibit 2-8), are limited to new construction. The setting is far less adversarial than the traditional across-the-desk barrier. Agents easily walk into the lobby to greet guests, to handle luggage, or to clarify directions. Registration pods have improved access for the handicapped, strengthening the industry's response to the Canadians with Disabilities Act. With careful training, the new design develops desk personnel into strong salespersons and greeters. In so doing, it changes the ambience of the desk and the sense of the lobby.

**Exhibit 2-6**
The modern front desk of a small hotel is open to the lobby to encourage a sense of welcome and to enhance security. The work level is below the desk level to reduce fatigue and encourage eye contact with the customer.
▼

**▲**
**Exhibit 2-7**
The once sterile and uninviting lobby has been revitalized as a dining spot and social centre. Hyatt Hotels pioneered the movement with its atrium concept.

Some front desks are nudged into lobby corners; others become the lobby's focal point. Whichever it is, the security of both employees and guests must be balanced with the desk's design and location. Employees, especially cashiers, must be secured (see Exhibit 2-9) and the desk positioned to monitor elevator traffic. Security is enhanced when front-office personnel have an unobstructed view of the lobby. Atrium hotels have all guest rooms opening into an atrium, an advantage in security design because all entry doors are in full view. Hyatt introduced the atrium in the late 1960s, and this revolutionized lobby design, helping to restore the lobby as a social and business gathering place. They now range from a few floors to more than 20 storeys high and add a spectacular scene to the lobby (see Exhibit 2-7).

Internal communication is another consideration in the design. Despite the many new marvels in telecommunications, face-to-face interaction at the desk remains an important means of handling the day's business. Most designs center the guest-service agent at the hub of activity (see Exhibits 2-9 and 2-10). From this advantageous position, agents coordinate the flow of business from reservations to departures. Groups are an exception. Hotels with large tour groups (sometimes called "tour houses") often build satellite lobbies where busloads of arrivals can be accommodated without interfering with the normal front-office traffic.

Aesthetic as well as practical workspace is the aim of modern desk design. Using lighting, form, and materials, architects must convey the image of the hotel: comfortable, open, organized, and professional.

## Working Hours

Hotels never close. The legal definition of a hotel requires that they do not. Therefore, work schedules must provide around-the-clock staffing, at least at the front desk. Other departments (personnel or accounting) work a more normal workweek. Work schedules must also provide for the peaks and valleys that bring daily, sometimes hourly, fluctuations to the volume at the desk.

**The Shift (or Watch)** Most desk employees work an eight-hour shift, five days per week, with two successive days off, which creates three equal shifts per day. Sickness, vacation time, and days off are covered by others, some of whom work part time. Although there are variations, especially in resort areas, the model in Exhibit 2-11 follows the pattern of other industries.

Most employees prefer the day shift because it follows the usual workday. Bellpersons opt for the **swing** shift, when arrivals and tips are the heaviest. Even senior front-office clerks choose the swing shift if tips are customary, as they especially are at resorts.

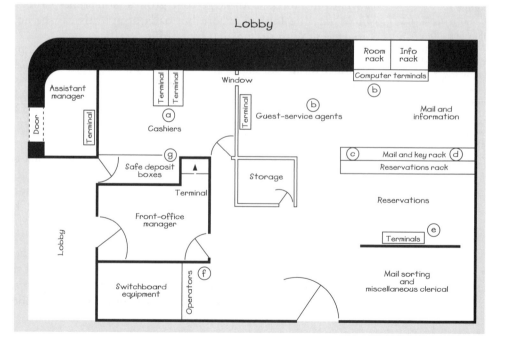

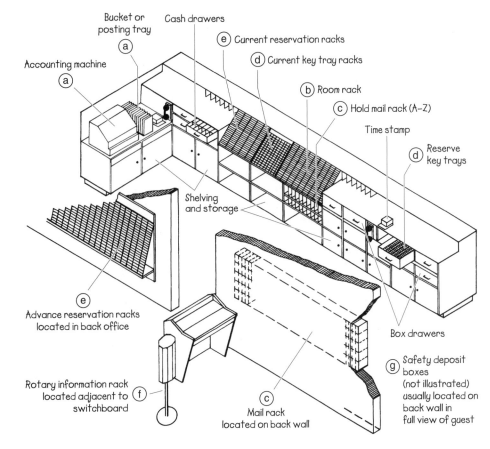

**Exhibit 2-10 ▶**
Design schematic of the front office, but not to scale. Letter references key the positions and equipment to a front-office design after the advent of property management systems (computerization), as illustrated in Exhibit 2-9.

| | |
|---|---|
| Day shift | 7:30 A.M.–3:30 P.M. |
| Swing shift | 3:30 P.M.–11:30 P.M. |
| Graveyard shift | 11:30 P.M.–7:30 A.M. |

▲
**Exhibit 2-11**
Typical working hours at a front office. Overlapping jobs often scheduled in 15- to 30-minute intervals to ensure consistency during shift changes.

The **graveyard** shift has the least guest activity, but it is during this shift that the **night audit** is completed. The night audit is more specialized than the other front-office duties. Thus, **night auditors** cannot take advantage of the general policy that allows senior employees to select their shifts. Few workers prefer graveyard, which is one explanation for the shortage of night auditors.

A special effort is needed to maintain morale during the graveyard **watch**. Graveyard work should be covered by formal policies. Employees must know that they are not locked into a career of night work. They are rotated when openings appear in the more desirable shifts. In the meantime, salary supplements are paid for night work, and careful attention may be paid to night meals in those hotels where the kitchen staff tends to short-change the night crew's menu.

Rotating personnel and shifts whenever possible, and where union contracts allow, enables employees to get to know one another. It also reduces the chance of collusion among employees who always work together. Sometimes day and swing shifts are switched en masse. This is done at the start of each month as employees' days off allow. It is unwise to make the switch on two successive workdays. The swing shift would close at 11:30 P.M., and the same employees would report for the day shift at 7:30 A.M. the following morning. Not only is this a burdensome procedure in a large city, where employees need commuting time, but it may also be illegal under provincial and territorial labour laws. Shift rotations should always follow the clock: day, evening, graveyard, off; day, evening, and so on.

Most front office positions follow the same work pattern. Cashiers, clerks, and even supervisors change shifts in concert. A 15-minute overlap offers a continuity that is lost with an abrupt change of shifts. If there are several persons in each job, individuals could leave in 15-minute intervals. If not, complementary jobs could be changed every quarter-hour. Cashiers might change at 3 P.M. and billing clerks at 3:15 P.M., for example.

**Forecast** Building a weekly or biweekly work schedule is part science and part art; both improve through experience. A **forecast** of room occupancy, which the reservation department completes (see Chapter 6), is the starting point. Human resource needs can be projected once the number of rooms occupied has been estimated. New computer programs match demand to the proper number of staff and even to the days-off/days-on preferences of the individuals.

With forecasting and advance scheduling, employees are given their days off during the slowest part of the week. Several may be off one day, and none may be off on a busy day. Part-time personnel can cover peak periods, or hours of the workday may be staggered. Each technique is designed to minimize payroll costs and maximize desk coverage when required.

The amount of help needed varies during the day, even within the same shift. Cashiers are busy in the morning handling check-outs and are less busy in the afternoon when the guest-service agents are busy with arrivals. Cashiers at a commercial hotel are slower on Mondays, when agents are busier, and busier on Thursdays, when agents are slower. An employee can be hired as a cashier for some days and as a clerk for others. Computer terminals are interchangeable, so agents can respond to traffic patterns, acting as either receptionist or cashier. Two job descriptions are then reduced to one.

# The Building Structure

As we noted in the introduction of this chapter, there is a good deal of similarity between the hotel's organizational structure and the structure of the building that is the hotel. Moreover, both structures are very similar property to property. Every hotel offers guest rooms, the basic product that the industry sells, and every hotel has staff members to deliver that basic product. Yet the differences that exist among the hotels—differences in the physical building and differences in the organizational staffing—are what distinguish the many properties. It is these differences that account for the industry's segmentation into numerous parts.

## The Old versus the New

Differentiating between hotels that were built before the mid-nineteenth century and those built since the Second World War is not difficult to do. Today's hotels take far more land—have a *large footprint,* in real estate terminology—because they are more open and because the individual rooms are so much larger. Exhibits 2-12 and 2-13 make the contrast clear. Some very famous hotels in the old design still exist. Best known among them are many of Fairmont's older CP Hotels such as Toronto's Royal York and Hotel Vancouver.

**Exhibit 2-12** ▶
Typical of the decades 1925–45, this upscale hotel offered accommodations in rooms smaller then today's budget inns. Light courts, designed to maximize land use, created odd-shaped rooms: 44, 61, and 65. (The building, the Hotel Benjamin Franklin, is a hotel no longer.)

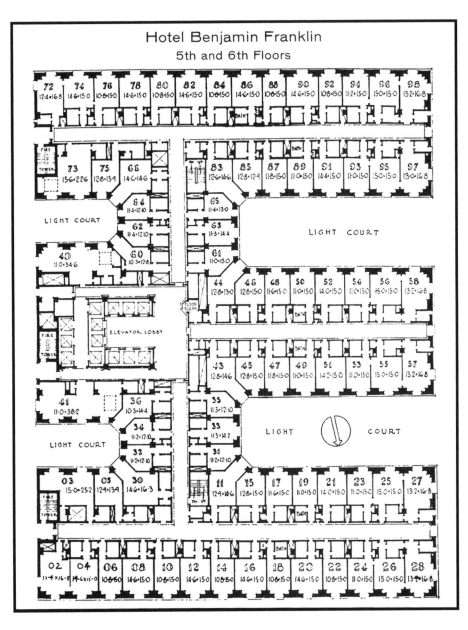

Exhibit 2-13 represents the open design of the world's new hotels. Except for suites, room shapes and sizes are identical in this new group. To emphasize that point, contrast again the shapes and sizes of rooms in Exhibit 2-12 with those in Exhibit 2-13. Furthermore, the shape of today's room is standardized across the industry. Of course, room sizes are different. Size means floor area, and floor area is part of construction costs and hence of room rate. Older hotels required a wider range of room rates to differentiate the variety of offerings. Current designs have reduced the number of room rates from a dozen or more in the 1950s to between three and five classes just over a half-century later. This eases the front desk's job of quoting rates and assigning rooms.

**The Old: Inside Rooms** Inside rooms have followed the semi-private (shared) bathroom (1930–50) and the public (served the entire floor) bathroom (nineteenth

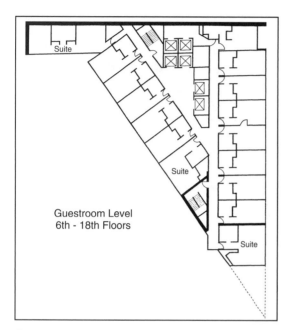

▲
**Exhibit 2-13**
The twenty-first-century hotel has a sweep of open design even in an urban setting. Unlike the prototype of an earlier century (see Exhibit 2-12), guest rooms are standardized in shape and size.

century) into oblivion. Rooms 58 to 97 in Exhibit 2-12 form a U shape of inside rooms around the light court. As illustrated, inside wings of the building enclose rooms. Contrast this inside view to the **outside rooms**, numbered 02 to 28 and 72 to 98, or to the entire design of Exhibit 2-13.

The view from the inside room is down, and the roof on the lower floor is often dirty and unsightly. Inside rooms are affected by the changing position of the sun, which casts shadows into these rooms even early in the day. The light courts produce some unusually shaped rooms—rooms 60 to 66, for example. Of course, smaller rooms and inside rooms are more economical in construction and land costs.

**The New: Suites and All-Suites** The traditional **suite** is a **parlour** (living room) with one or more bedrooms, illustrated in the modern hotel by Exhibit 2-14 and in the more traditional hotel by Exhibit 2-12, rooms 72 and 74. The traditional definition, a full wall—that is, separate rooms—is being challenged by new designs that use a low divider wall or even furniture to separate large accommodations (56 to 65 square metres) into "two rooms." Holiday Inn's Staybridge Suites accomplishes

**Exhibit 2-14** ▶
Folding doors separate the parlour and bedroom of this one-bedroom suite, which can be enlarged by unlocking the connecting door to the adjacent, second bedroom. Note the back-to-back plumbing and air conditioning (A/C) shafts.

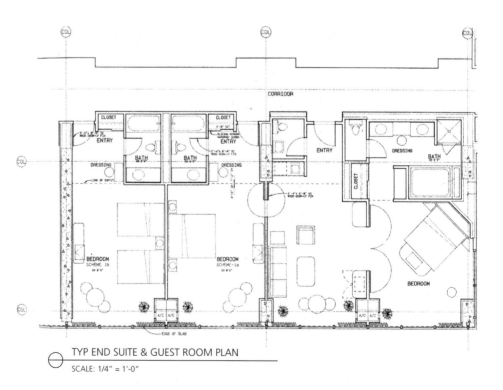

TYP END SUITE & GUEST ROOM PLAN
SCALE: 1/4" = 1'-0"

the division by designing the living part of the room at right angles to the sleeping portion.

Larger suites add second or third bedrooms and additional living space. More luxurious accommodations include kitchens and formal dining rooms, saunas or swimming pools, and even libraries. Almost every large suite contains a wet bar. Balconies and patios (**lanai** suites) are also common amenities. In the proper climate, suites have fireplaces. For a truly opulent experience, some hotels, especially casino hotels, offer a two-floor suite.[5]

Specialty suites are named, although they may also be numbered as standard suites are. The *bridal suite*, the *presidential suite*, and the **penthouse** *suite* are common terminology. Historical figures or local references that emphasize the theme of the hotel—for example, the Queen Elizabeth Suite—are other bases for choosing names.

Suites in all-suite hotels are a different product altogether. They are designed for a different market and a different use (Exhibit 2-15). The intent is for the all-suite to compete against the standard hotel room, not against the hotel suite. To compensate for the extra square metres offered by the all-suite unit, public space is reduced. Forty percent of the typical hotel building is allocated to public areas. The all-suite hotel cuts that figure by at least half.

All-suite and standard hotels alike employ a building technique that was invented by Ellsworth Statler in 1923. **Back-to-back** utility shafts reduce the amount of runs for piping, electrical, heating, and communication lines. There is economy in both the initial construction and continuing maintenance. It is not always possible, but kitchenettes, baths, and wet bars should be so constructed. Exhibits 2-12 and 2-14 show the baths back to back.

**Exhibit 2-15** ▶
The large size of all-suite facilities is appealing to the modern traveller and to the longer-term guest, to whom the concept was originally marketed. Either a fold-out chair or a sofa bed in the parlour provides extra sleeping accommodations. Candlewood is one of the newest entries in what is presently the fastest-growing segment of lodging.

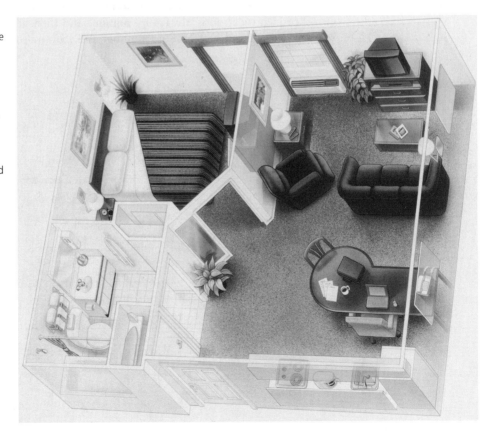

**Corner Rooms**  Corner rooms are the most desirable rooms on the floor. They offer a double **exposure** and therefore command a premium price. To enhance the price differential, corner rooms get preferential treatment from the architect. They are usually larger rooms, and they are frequently incorporated into the suite. Corner rooms were an integral part of the older hotel because its design created them (see Exhibit 2-12). Modern hotels have fewer building corners and thus fewer corner rooms; round hotel buildings have none at all.

**Motor Inns**  The highway hotel, child of the motel and grandchild to the tourist court, has its own, unique design. However, it isn't one that is widely applauded. In general, these have been inexpensive properties to build. Since the price of land is usually less than the cost of erecting a high-rise building, motor inns are almost always low-rise: one, two, or, rarely, three floors high. Consequently, they have the outline of a rectangle or a single strip of housing (see Exhibit 2-16). Providing easy access to outside parking, which is the aim of the highway property, necessarily limits design possibilities. Building an L or U shape helps with exterior appeal. Efforts are now being directed toward a more attractive exterior design, but the emphasis is on colour and facing materials and on the entryway of the **porte cochère** rather than on changes in the basic rectangular configuration.

## Numbering for Identification

Everyone uses the guest-room number for identification. Certainly, guests depend on the number to locate themselves. Desk personnel address guests by name, but within the front office identification is always by number and then, if at all, by guest name. Hotel rooms are identified first by floor number and then by room number.

**Exhibit 2-16 ▶**
The typical design of the small, often two-storey motor inn of 50 to 75 rooms is represented in this prototype. Ownership may still be mom-and-pop, but most motels are flagged with a franchise identity.

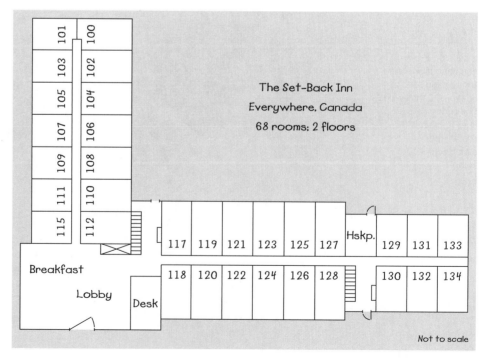

**Floor Numbering**   Floors are numbered upward sequentially, but most Western hotels omit floor 13. Toronto's Cambridge Suites Hotel is an exception: It has both a thirteenth floor and a room 13. Numbering systems reflect the culture of the hotel's location. In Asia, one never finds four as a room number, and sometimes not even numbers that add to four. Seven is a lucky number in Canada, as it is, along with six, in the Far East.

North Americans number the first sleeping floor as floor one regardless of the number of levels between it and the ground. Mezzanine, upper-ground floor, and shopping level are interspersed without any standard order. The sequence adds an array of non-numeric elevator buttons that confuse anyone who isn't a lifetime employee of the hotel. *M* is for mezzanine; *MM* is for the second mezzanine floor. Try to decipher *LM*, *SB*, and *S2* (lower mezzanine, sub-basement, and sub-basement 2).

The rest of the world begins numbering with the ground floor as floor one. Even without the intermediary floors, what would be the tenth floor in Canada would be the eleventh floor elsewhere.

A different numbering system needs to be used if the hotel comprises several low-rise buildings. Identically numbering each low-rise unit of, say, three or four storeys is one technique. Then each building is given a different name, and the keys for each are colour-coded. Others prefer to number the floors sequentially, moving in order from one building to the next. Guests become confused because only one unit has its ground floor numbered as floor one. Ground floors of the other units will have numbers in the teens or even twenties.

Hotels that have two or three towers have the same options. Either the towers are differentiated by name (the river tower) or direction (the east tower) with room numbers identical in each, or the floors are numbered sequentially with the bottom floor of the second tower using the next floor number in sequence.

**Room Numbering**   Assigning numbers to rooms is far more arbitrary than going up floor levels. Each hotel has a unique design, and that design determines where to begin numbering and what sequence to use. Sequential numbering is not possible in an old floor plan like the one shown in Exhibit 2-12—too many corridors run at right angles to one another. Even a plan as simple as Exhibit 2-16 offers choices.

Rooms are frequently numbered odd and even along opposite sides of the corridor. The numbering might begin at the elevator bay and progress upward as the sequence marches down the corridor: 101, 103, and 105 along one side; 102, 104, and 106 along the other. Of course, there is no rule that requires this. An atrium hotel may have rooms on only one side of the corridor and the numbering is sequential. All-suite hotel rooms are numbered in the usual manner because every room in the hotel is a suite.

Different floor designs present different numbering problems and require good signage. If the elevator empties into the centre of the sleeping floor, the logic of any system begins to break down. The numbering system becomes very confusing when a new wing is added to the original structure. Rarely is the entire floor, old rooms and new, renumbered in sequence. The new wing may be numbered sequentially from the old, without concern about the interface with the old numbers. Sometimes the old numbers are duplicated in the new wing by adding an identifying suffix or prefix, such as *N* for north wing.

Care in using certain numbers such as four and nine applies equally to room numbering as to floor numbering, as mentioned earlier. In Asia, correct positioning is also important. Many hoteliers there employ a fung shui (or feng shui) master who helps position the location of everything from doors and windows to desks and files and helps decide the most auspicious date to open a new hotel, a new dining room, and so on.

Adjoining or Connecting Rooms   Rooms that abut along the corridor are said to be **adjoining rooms**. Using the numerical sequence discussed above, 101, 103, and 105 would be adjoining rooms, as would 102, 104, and 106. If there is direct room-to-room access (a door between the rooms) without using the corridor (Exhibit 2-12, rooms 53, 55, and 57), the rooms are said to be connecting. Obviously, every **connecting room** adjoins, but not every adjoining room connects.

## Room Shape and Size

The guest room is the hotel's product. Therefore, its shape and size are critical to customer satisfaction. Size, especially, separates the industry into the several classes. Small rooms are associated with hard budget properties, huge rooms with deluxe accommodations. As the rate discussion in Chapter 9 points out, setting the different rate classes within the hotel also depends in part on the differences in the physical rooms.

**Room Shape**   There has been little overall change in the shape of guest rooms. As concave, square, and round structures are built, corresponding changes occur in the interior shapes and dimensions. Research may eventually show advantages in guest satisfaction or in reduced wear from certain shapes. Until then, the parallelogram remains the classic favourite, with the depth of the room approximately twice the width. The first increases in room size are made by adding to the depth. Width is improved next by increasing from 3.66 or 3.96 m to 4.88 m, which is a luxury-class room.

The presence of full or false balconies and French or sliding doors gives a sense of spaciousness to any room. Balconies are often part of a facade that adds interest to the outside of a building.

**Room Size**   Room shape is primarily an architectural decision; room size is derived from financial and marketing factors. Although the trend has been toward larger and larger rooms, the economy segment has capitalized on smaller accommodations and smaller rates.

In the final analysis, the market determines the rate structure and consequently the average room size and its furnishings. That market varies from hotel to hotel, so that the twin double beds of the family-oriented hotel might be inappropriate to a property servicing the business traveller.

A comparison of international accommodations illustrates the danger of trying to identify hotels as one industry. Japan's smallest budget rooms, called *capsule rooms,* are nothing more than sleeping accommodations. Guests change in a common locker area and crawl into a capsule approximately 1.5 m high, 1.5 m wide, and less than 2.1 m long. That is less than 4 m$^2$. Most hard budgets are larger. The Ibis chain, a European entry into the budget market, builds rooms of approximately 12 m$^2$. Econo Lodges and Super 8s have rooms of almost 19 m$^2$.

The surprise comes when comparisons are made between today's budget accommodations and the rooms of Hotel Benjamin Franklin (Exhibit 2-12), which was a first-class facility in its era. The 13.5- to 15.75-m$^2$ room of the prosperous 1920s was smaller than many of today's economy facilities, such as Choice Hotels International's Sleep Inn, at 18.9 m$^2$.

The Far East contributes to the other end of the scale as well. It has many of the world's opulent hotels, with large rooms and many extras. Hong Kong's Shangri-La Hotel offers a 45-m$^2$ facility (bath included). That size is immediately recognized as super luxury. (Guests do not get a feeling of luxury until the room size exceeds 36 m$^2$.)

The Four Seasons in New York City (370 rooms) compares favourably with luxury properties worldwide. Its rooms are about 55.75 m$^2$, including a 10.8-m$^2$ bath. The standard Canadian room measures approximately 23.3 to 32.5 m$^2$.

It's not enough to multiply the size of the room by the number of rooms to get the hotel's total square metres. Provisions must be made for service areas, public space, lobbies, offices, corridors, and so on. That requires almost a doubling of the total square metres needed for just the guest rooms. Even then, allowances must be made for the size, type, and class of hotel. A full-service convention property might require a total of 81 to 108 m$^2$ per guest room, although the room itself is only 32 to 36 m$^2$. An economy property with no public space might get by with as little as 54 m$^2$ per guest room, of which the room itself is 23 to 25 m$^2$. All of this bears on the amount of land needed to erect the property.

All-suite hotels provide a contrast in size, both to one another and in comparison with standard non-suite properties. All-suite properties are segmented into economy, midmarket, and upscale: Room size is the major difference. Guest Quarters pioneered the extended-stay hotel with a 68.5-m$^2$ unit. All-suite hotels include bedroom, parlour, bath, and kitchenette, making a unit rather than a room the standard of measure. The budget room of AmeriSuites is about 34 m$^2$; Park Suites measure some 43 m$^2$. Fireplaces carry Homewood Suites to 49.5 m$^2$. Extended-stay suites that range from 36 to 58.5 m$^2$ equate to the size of a standard apartment in many large Canadian cities!

**How the Room Is Used** Hotel chains use models to test guest acceptance and preview costs before proceeding with a new concept or with a major renovation of an existing property. The disproportionately high cost of building just one model room is offset by identification of design and furnishing flaws before the major project gets under way. For one thing, more thought is focused on how the room will be used.

Different kinds of guests use rooms in different ways. Within the same dimensions, a destination hotel furnishes proportionately more storage space than a transient property. A transient property allocates more space to sleeping and less to the living area than a destination facility. Such would be the case with hotels in major cities, where the average use of the room is eight hours. Very cold or very hot climates increase usage of the room.

Designers have become quite successful in making small rooms look larger. For example, nightstands can be eliminated by mounting bedside lamps on the wall. Mirrors do a good job of creating a perception of space. Wall-to-wall draperies and fewer patterned materials throughout the room add to the feeling of roominess. Designers also use mirrors and balconies to expand the sense of space. Nevertheless, it takes about 1.86 additional square metres before the occupant notices the larger size. That's the point where a rate increase could be justified if spaciousness is the only basis for the increase.

Clearly, there is no standard room. The hotel industry is moving in several directions at once. Miniprices use module units and measure 3.7 m from centre to centre. Luxury operations opt for 4.6-m centres and lengths of 9 to 10.7 m. (The standard carpet sizes of 3.7 and 10.7 m dictate the dimensions unless the plan calls for a custom job.) Costs of energy, borrowed money, and labour limit expansion even as competition pushes for more space. Comparisons, therefore, begin with the marketplace.

# Bed and Bath

The increasing size of the bed—Canadians are getting bigger—accounts in part for the increased size of the guest room. The new role of the bathroom—as a weapon in the competition wars—also contributes to the creep in total square metres.

**The Bed** Bed types, bed coverings, and bed sizes vary across the world and across time. Quilted bedding appeared in Japan about 1500. It is most certain that the nomads of the Middle East were using some form of stuffing in animal skins (early futons) to ease their sleep even earlier than the sixteenth century. The modern Canadian hotel room has gone through periods, which favoured first the double bed and then twin beds. Neither of these is popular today. Queen and king beds have taken over. If today's hotel wants a room with two beds, it opts for queen–doubles rather than traditional twin beds. Of course, larger beds mean larger rooms. Larger rooms mean higher construction costs and, hence, higher room rates.

Beds are being lowered as well as lengthened. The usual height of the mattress and box spring is 55.9 to 61 cm, in contrast to the average chair of some 43.2 cm. Lowering the bed to 43.2 cm makes the room appear larger because all of the pieces are on the same horizontal plane. It also makes the bed easier to sit on, and lower hotel beds are used for that purpose. Adequate seating is needed to reduce the heavy wear on mattresses when beds are used as chairs. It is a real conflict. Lowered beds make the room appear larger, but the mattresses don't last as long. Mattress life can be extended substantially if the mattress is rotated and turned on a regular schedule of four times per year. Good housekeeping departments do this as part of their quarterly deep cleaning. The position of the mattress is tracked by a system of arrows attached to the side of the mattress.

If every hotel room were a replica of every other room, room assignments would be greatly eased. Everyone would get the same room configuration, and the major decision for the desk would be which floor and what location within the floor. Although modern hotels are headed that way, as the earlier discussion on floor plans indicated, the front office still needs some shorthand symbols for designating different bedding and accommodations. These symbols, which were critical when hotels used **room racks** (see Exhibit 13-7 on page 404), have been carried over into computer equipment.

Bed Sizes and Bed Symbols    The terminology used to describe the capacity of the room is often confused with the terminology used to describe the beds in the room. For example, a single room is one that sleeps one person, but that person could be in one of several different beds. **Single** and **double** refer with equal ambiguity to (1) the room rate, (2) the number of guests housed in the room, (3) the number of persons the room is capable of accommodating, or (4) the size and type of the beds. It is possible to have a single occupant in a double bed being charged a single rate although the room is designated as a double, meaning that it could accommodate two persons.

A single occupant in a queen double sometimes needs assurance that no additional charge is being made for the unused bed. The single-room configuration—that is, one single bed for one person—is unknown today. Thus, to the innkeeper, "single" means single occupancy or single rate.

SINGLE BED    A single bed, symbol S, sleeps one person. A true single is 91.4 by 190.5 cm, but is very rarely used; it is simply too small. Instead, the rare single room (room for one person) is furnished with a single twin or, most likely, one double bed. When the room is furnished with one twin, the symbol S is used; when furnished with a double bed, the symbol is D. Single beds must measure at least 99 by 182.9 cm to win a CAA rating.

TWIN BEDS    A **twin** room, symbol *T*, contains two beds, each accommodating one person. (Two persons could also be roomed in a double, a queen, or a king bed.) **Twins** measure 99 by 191 cm each and use linen 183 by 275 cm. The 190.5-cm mattress has been replaced in all bed sizes with a longer length, called a **California length**. The 99 cm width remains with the twin, but the length has been stretched to between 200 and 215 cm. Additional centimetres are added to the linen length as well.

Because of their flexibility, twins once accounted for 60 to 70 percent of total available rooms. The trend shifted as twins were replaced by double–doubles, and then queens, and then by queen–doubles. Single business travellers actually prefer a two-bedded room: one for sleeping and one for spreading papers.

Because the double–double and queen–double sleep four persons, they are also called **quads** or **family rooms**. Motel owners will offer couples queen–doubles at reduced rates with the stipulation that only one bed be used. A survey done some time ago by Sheraton's franchise division showed that the second bed of a double–double or queen–double was used about 15 percent of the time.

DOUBLE BED   *D* is the symbol for double bed. The width ranges from 137 to 145 cm, and that's an important 8 cm. Like the twin bed, the length of the double has been stretching from 190.5 cm to the California 203-cm or longer. Linen sizes would be 228 to 236 cm wide and 287 cm long with a California mattress. Half a double bed is about 71 cm or so, narrower even than the single. That alone explains the double's loss of popularity among guests who are getting ever larger and heavier.

QUEEN AND KING BEDS   **Queen** and **king** beds (symbols *Q* and *K*) are extra wide (152 and 183 cm, respectively) and extra long. They made popular the California length, which has also been called a *European king*. Although designed for two, three or four persons might squeeze in when the room is taken as a family room.

Both beds require larger rooms (the critical distance between the foot of the bed and the furniture—a 91.4-cm minimum—remains) and larger sheets, 274 by 311 cm. Since laundry costs are calculated by weight, larger sheets mean larger laundry bills. A larger room with extra laundry costs can only mean a higher room rate even without consideration for the extra, upfront costs of the larger bed, mattress, and linen.

HOLLYWOOD BED   Two beds joined by a common headboard are called a **Hollywood bed**. Hollywoods use the symbol of the twins, *T*, since that's what they are. They are difficult beds to make, because the room attendant cannot get between them. To overcome this, the beds are placed on rollers and swung apart, resulting in rapid carpet wear. Because the total dimension of these beds is 198 by 190.5 cm (two twins), they can be converted into a king by replacing the two mattresses with one king mattress laid across both springs.

STUDIO BED (ROOM)   A **studio** bed is a sofa by day and a bed by night. During the day, the bed is slip-covered and the pillows are stored in the backrest. There is neither headboard nor footboard once the sofa is pulled away from the backrest to create the bed. Today's guest room serves a dual bedroom–living room function, so studio rooms should be popular with business guests. They once were. Studios are not popular anymore because the beds are not comfortable and the all-suite hotel serves the same dual purpose.

The **studio** room, once called an **executive room**, has been used to redo small, single rooms in older hotels. *UP*, undersized parlour, is one of the symbols once used for studios. In Europe, a parlour that has no sleeping facilities is called a salon.

DAYBED   **Daybeds** were once common additions to the family living room. They've made a comeback both in the home and in larger hotel rooms. Daybeds are like studio beds except that they are additions to the hotel room rather than basic furnishings, as they were in the heyday of the studio room. Both daybeds and studio beds are better as beds than as sofas. At 1 metre, they're too wide for sitting. Removing the pillows converts a daybed into a sleeping bed, but without the struggle often associated with converting a sofa bed.

SOFA BED    A **sofa bed** or bed chesterfield is similar in function to a studio bed. It is a sofa first of all, which makes sitting more comfortable. It is usually 43 cm off the floor, whereas the studio bed may be as high as 56 cm. Unlike the studio bed, which rolls away from its frame, the sofa bed opens in accordion fashion from the seat. Since it unfolds, the sofa bed is less convenient and requires more space than the studio.

Parlours are generally equipped with sofa beds as part of a suite (see Exhibit 2-14 on page 77), but a studio bed is usually a room unto itself. Sofa beds can be single, double, or even queen size, although the single is more like a three-quarter bed (122 by 190.5 cms).

Sofa beds are often called **hide-a-beds** and thus carry an *H* designation. Large rooms that contain both standard beds and hide-a-beds are called **junior suites**. Rooms in all-suite hotels offer a sofa bed in the parlour portion of the unit (see Exhibit 2-15).

ROLLAWAY BED (COT)    A **cot** or **rollaway** is a portable utility bed that is added to the usual room furnishings on a temporary basis. A rollaway sleeps one person, and a comfortable one measures 86.4 by 190.5 cm and uses twin sheets. Cots usually come smaller—76 by 183 cm, with linen 160 by 251.5 cm.

Setting up cots is costly in housekeeping time, primarily because the cots are rarely located conveniently. Cot storage never seems to be high in the designer's priority.

CRIB    Cribs for babies are rolled into the room on an as-needed basis similar to the call for rollaway beds. Deaths from unsafe cribs have made them a sensitive safety issue. Not that infants have died in hotels, but the issue was raised by a Consumer Product Safety Commission study that reported that most hotel cribs were unsafe. Infants could (*could,* not *did*) catch their heads between the slats, between the mattress and the bed frame, or in cut-outs in the headboards and footboards. A bigger danger is posed by the use of regular-sized sheets on a crib mattress. A call for better general maintenance (loose parts, protruding screws, broken slats) applies to rollaway beds as well as to cribs.

WATERBED    In two decades, waterbeds jumped from a novelty to a hot item and then fell back again. The bed is rarely found in hotel rooms, although it offers an alternative to innerspring and foam mattresses. Waterbeds have a long history, dating back to pre-Christian, nomadic tribes, which filled goatskins with water. Their use was rediscovered by a Californian who first tried starch and gelatin as fillers.

**The Bath**    *Bath* is the industry's jargon for bathroom; it is not the guest's bathing accommodation, not the bathtub. Into the *bath*[room] goes the toilet (or water closet), the sink (or lavatory), and the tub (or bathtub) and shower. The hotel bath underwent many changes throughout the twentieth century, but its position as a sound barrier between the room and the corridor remains. That location, abutting the corridor (see Exhibits 2-14 and 2-15) saves construction costs and leaves the desirable outside wall for windows or balconies. In more recent years, modular construction of the bath has gained some popularity. The bath is prefabricated away from the construction site and installed as one unit. Modular construction reduces the number of building trades required on the construction site and, some say, improves the quality of the work.

The bath accounts for about 20 percent of the room size. Thus, the baths in hard budget inns measure about 3.2 m² and in midrange properties measure about 6.3 m². The luxurious Four Seasons, mentioned earlier, has a bath of 10.8 m². What a contrast this is to the hotel of a century ago, when public baths served whole floors or entire wings. (Very early hotels had all of their baths in the basements because the mechanics of pumping water to higher floors was not yet in place.)

Stall showers, which occupy little space, gained favour as old hotels converted from rooms without baths. They fit easily into old, large closets or corners of renovated rooms. Tub and shower combinations were installed next when lifestyles changed again. Having both meets the cultural needs of all guests. The Japanese, for example, definitely favour tubs, just as they choose twin beds over all other choices. The bidet, which is installed in many other countries, has not found acceptance in the Canadian home and thus not in the Canadian hotel.

Upscale properties have cut back on low-cost amenities such as soap and shampoo. Strangely, they have gone all out in building larger bathrooms with expensive appointments: in-floor scales, in-bath telephones, electric shoeshine equipment, adjustable no-fog mirrors, and plush bathrobes. The Palmer House Hilton in Chicago, Illinois, which was renovated several years ago, has 300 guest rooms with his-and-her bathrooms. The same Four Seasons mentioned above features bathtubs that fill in one minute!

Not only is the bath larger, but the ancillary space has grown as well. Dressing areas and second lavatories outside the bath proper have also increased the overall dimensions. Replacing closets with open hanger space has helped compensate. Consolidating furniture also saves space. One vertical piece incorporates several horizontal space users. Into armoires, for example, have gone television sets, bars and refrigerators, writing desks with telephones, and several drawers for clothing. Reflected in the new design is the two-night stay and garment-bag luggage of today's traveller.

## Summary

Hotel architects have given the industry two important structures. One, the building, is designed to attract travellers and to provide comfort. The other, the organization, is designed to service guests and to earn their loyalty. Both forms are in change: adding wings and upgraded baths on the one hand and improving personnel and services on the other.

Good building designs recognize the diverse needs of consumers. Not all hotels offer the same accommodations. That variety provides a broad range of facilities, each designed to attract portions of the travelling public. Hard-budget hotels, for example, have rooms of 13.94 m²; rooms in upscale hotels exceed 55.76 m².

Good organizational designs are equally dynamic: changing as customer demand, technology, and service require. Today's guests are less inclined to pay for or wait for individualized care, opting instead for a measure of self-service. Less service has slashed the ranks of the uniformed services even as automation has reduced the size of the telephone department, and electronics, such as self-check-in and self-check-out, have altered the duties of the front office.

Hotel security is one department that is growing both in size and in responsibility. Recent world events have focused everyone's attention on security. Although hotels are not insurers of guest safety, they must exercise reasonable care to protect guests and their property. The hotel industry has responded with better trained personnel and larger security departments. Prevention and deterrence reduce the number of security incidents and, equally important, document those that are unavoidable.

Some organizational changes have shifted assignments as much as they have altered responsibilities or department size. In this respect, reservations is probably the most dynamic of all front-office departments.

## Questions and Problems

1. With special attention to front-office activities, prepare a list of duties carried out by one (or more) of the fictional staff in the book *Hotel* by Arthur Hailey (Garden City, NY: Doubleday & Company, Inc., 1965; also available through Bantam Books).

2. Using information provided in this chapter or acquired elsewhere, sketch to approximate scale a typical room with furnishings that Choice Hotels might be building in Europe. (That requires dimensions to be in metres and square metres.) Above the drawing list the several assumptions (as 1, 2, 3, and so on) that your drawing relies on. Cite references external to the text, if used.

3. Using information provided in this book or acquired elsewhere, *estimate* the total square metres of Vancouver's Pan Pacific Hotel. Show the several mathematical steps and label all of your figures.

4. Either as part of your travels this term or as part of a field trip, contrast the size, shape, bedding, price, and characteristics of two or more hotel rooms. Discuss.

5. Interview a hotel manager or a front-office employee. From the information obtained, construct the organizational chart of the front office, and prepare a description of any one front-office job, using Exhibits 2-4 and 2-5 as a guide.

6. Using the typical occupancy pattern of an urban hotel (see Exhibit 1-3 on page 8, plot the biweekly work schedule for the desk of a 300-room hotel that has separate room clerk and cashier positions. The switchboard is not at the desk. Strive for efficient coverage with minimum payroll costs. All full-time employees receive two successive days off and work an eight-hour day, five days per week.

## 🔑 CASE STUDY

### Challenging the Organizational Structure

As the director of operations for a small chain of eight hotels in eastern Canada, you have been challenged by Jeremy Jackson, one of your hotel general managers, to allow him to change the way in which his hotel has been managed.

It is a 150-room full-service hotel located in Halifax, Nova Scotia, and like most hotels of its size in Canada, it has a traditional management organization chart with a general manager at the top followed by an assistant general manager (food and beverage manager) and then the usual department heads in charge of housekeeping, kitchen, dining room, bar, maintenance and engineering, security, marketing, and conferences. The food and beverage department heads report directly to the AGM, while the other department heads report to the GM. The GM, of course, has overall responsibility for the successful operation of the hotel.

With this organization chart in place, Jackson has found a lot of duplication and overlap. Often food and beverage department heads would go to the GM for answers to problems, and the chain of command did not seem clear enough. Also, department heads, while competent, seemed to lack the initiative to make hard management decisions and depended on the GM or AGM to make decisions for them. Employees also often went to the GM or AGM instead of to their department heads for solutions to problems. Department head salaries were on par with competitor hotels, but not high enough to attract the brightest and the best. Company policy has been not to share financial information below the AGM level, as corporate office wanted to keep the financial status of each property a confidential matter.

Jackson's proposal is to eliminate the AGM position and distribute that salary to each of the department heads while giving them complete autonomy to run their own departments with the GM acting as a coach and facilitator. Paying better salaries at the department head level would also allow the GM to attract better qualified department heads.

As the district manager responsible for this property, you must respond to Jackson.

1. What are the pros and cons of Jackson's suggestion, if you decide to act on it?

2. Should the company change its philosophy of not sharing confidential financial information with its department heads? Why or why not?

3. What would you do with the displaced AGM and possible displaced department heads, should you allow Jeremy to enact this plan?

4. What effect would this change have on the motivation of the management team and employees? Most importantly, would this change make the hotel more profitable?

## Notes

1. Jeff Weinstein, "Old-Fashioned Hotelkeeping." *Hotels,* February 2001, p. 5.

2. Sheraton reportedly defranchised 215 properties in the early 1990s.

3. The sequence is different in casino hotels, where casino revenue accounts for 60 percent of the gross and rooms account for only 15 percent. Food is 12 percent, beverage is 9 percent, and other is 4 percent.

4. American President Ulysses Grant (1869–77) frequently walked from the White House to the Willard, now an InterContinental Hotel, to have a cigar and a drink. Petitioners waiting to argue their constituents' positions hovered in the lobby—thus, the term *lobbyists.*

5. The two-floor Governor's Suite of the Fontainebleau Hilton (Miami Beach) is 1800 m$^2$ (the size of a dozen average homes) and has five bathrooms.

## Weblinks

Society of Golden Keys, Canadian branch
**www.lesclefsdorcanada.org**

PKF Consulting, advisers to Canada's hospitality and tourism industry
**www.pkfcanada.com**

Pan Pacific Hotel in Vancouver
**www.vancouver.panpacific.com**

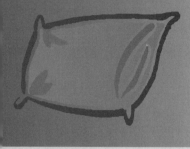

# Chapter 3 | Housekeeping

## Learning Objectives

After reading this chapter, you will be able to do the following:

1. **Recognize the importance, responsibilities, and roles of the housekeeping department and understand how the housekeeping department interfaces with the front desk.**

2. **Examine and understand today's trends in housekeeping operations.**

3. **Develop an understanding of guest and employee security as it applies to the housekeeping department.**

4. **Understand how supplies, equipment, and amenities are managed in the housekeeping department.**

5. **Develop an understanding of on-premise and off-premise laundry systems and management.**

6. **Understand how to control linens, uniforms, and storage.**

Over the past 40 years, some things have changed in the world of housekeeping, but a lot has remained the same.

Room design and materials have been upgraded; new things have been added, such as faxes, high-speed computer connections, interactive TVs, mini-bars, computerized locks, direct-dial portable phones, guest workstations, and other innovations leading to today's "smart room." Changes and innovations have been made to better meet the guests' needs, but little has happened to modernize the role of the housekeeping department.

While all of this has improved and changed from the guest perspective, the work of the room attendant has changed little over the last 40 years. Despite predictions of rooms that would almost clean themselves and robotic vacuums that would vacuum a room automatically, none of this has actually happened. It still takes a room attendant 30 minutes to clean a room, the same amount of time it took in the 1960s. Of course, modern materials and finishes may be easier to clean, but they still need cleaning; vacuums may have improved, but the carpets still need to be vacuumed; washrooms still need to be cleaned and beds do not make themselves. Despite all of the advances in technology, the job of the room attendant has changed little in the last 40 years.

# Responsibilities and Roles of the Housekeeping Department

The single most important item a hotel has for sale is a good night's sleep in a clean room. Room sales generate about 70 percent or more of the total revenue generated by lodging establishments, and they generate a much higher profit margin than does food and beverage (see Exhibit 3-1).

The housekeeping department is responsible for maintaining the cleanliness of guest rooms and common areas of the hotel. In survey after survey, cleanliness of the hotel is the number one reason guests choose to stay at and return to an individual hotel. In one 1990s survey conducted by research company Market Facts ("Bringing in the Business and Keeping It"), 63 percent of frequent travellers rated cleanliness and appearance as the most important reason they would return to a hotel. A more recent poll by Orkin Commercial Services[1] discovered that guests rated bathroom cleanliness as their top concern and that more than 90 percent of those polled said the one condition that would keep them from returning to a hotel or motel was a visibly unclean bathtub.

The housekeeping department has two prime functions: providing clean interiors in order to increase sales, and protecting the owner's investment in the property's interiors. The executive housekeeper is responsible for ensuring that these goals are met on time, on budget, and at the highest possible levels of quality.

## Housekeeping and the Front Office

The constant communication and co-operation that goes on between the front desk and housekeeping is the key to the operation of any hotel. Any breakdown in this communication link will quickly lead to unsatisfied guests.

At most hotels, front-desk clerks are not allowed to check guests into rooms that have not been cleaned, inspected, and released by the housekeeping department as being vacant and ready for sale. Typically, guest rooms are recycled for sale according to the process outlined in Exhibit 3-2.

The occupancy report is prepared by the front office (usually the night auditor) during the midnight shift and can be printed in the housekeeping department or provided by the front desk. It is the first form the executive housekeeper looks at in the morning. From this report, the executive housekeeper makes up the work assignment sheet for the room attendants. This report lists all rooms in the hotel

**Exhibit 3-1 ▶**
The Hotel Market,
Source of Total Revenue.

| Upper | %Room | %Food and Beverage | %Telephone | %Other |
|---|---|---|---|---|
| Luxury Hotels | 66.9 | 26.3 | 2.7 | 4.1 |
| Upscale Hotels | 67.3 | 26.9 | 2.5 | 3.3 |
| **Middle** | | | | |
| Mid-priced Hotels | 77.5 | 17.5 | 2.4 | 2.6 |
| **Lower** | | | | |
| Economy | 80.6 | 13.5 | 2.4 | 3.5 |
| Budget | 94.5 | 0.0 | 2.8 | 2.7 |

along with their status (see Exhibit 3-3). Exhibit 3-3 is from the Delta Halifax, and the abbreviations used may be unique to the Landmark property management system used by Delta Hotels. Other hotel chains and property management systems may have similar but different abbreviations. All systems communicate whether a

**Exhibit 3-2** ▶
Occupancy Report
(Housekeeping Report).
*Reproduced with permission from* The Rooms
Chronicle *(Volume 2,
No 5, Sept/Oct 1994),
NMRG Publishing , PO
Box 2036, Niagara
University, NY 14109.*

**Daily Communication**

**6 A.M.**
Front office to housekeeping:
- Rooming lists and times for arriving guests
- Special requests (adjoining rooms, rollaway beds, VIP rooms, etc.)
- Late check-outs
- Early check-ins

**8 A.M.**
Front office to housekeeping:
- Check-outs already departed
- Update of special requests and VIPs
- Assignment of showrooms for the day

**10 A.M.**
Housekeeping to front office:
- Results of vacant room check (for revenue check)
- Rooms that will not be cleaned today
- Rooms on maintenance (out of order) and the reasons

**Throughout the Day**
Front office to housekeeping:
- Late departures
- Extended stays
- Room changes
- Check-outs that have departed
Housekeeping to front office:
- Continual reporting of vacant and ready rooms
- Readiness of special requests
- Status update of room discrepancies

**Check-out Time**
Housekeeping to front office:
- Status of expected check-outs

**During Check-in**
Front office to housekeeping:
- Update on special requests
- Rooms needed as soon as possible

**End of Day**
Housekeeping to front office:
- Complete update of hotel status

▶ **Exhibit 3-3**
Partial Occupancy Report (Housekeeping Morning Report).

**DELTA**
HOTELS

**Delta Halifax** Page 1
**Report #300051** November 4, 20xx
**Housekeeping Report – 01 – Delta Halifax** 11:52:44

**Section 2**

| | | | | | Include: Clean, Ready, Maintenance & Discrepancy | | | | | | | |
|---|---|---|---|---|---|---|---|---|---|---|---|---|
| Room | Type | Name | Crd | St | Dp | Ar | Adl | Ch1 | Ch2 | Ch3 | Depart | Special |
| 101 | QS | Smith | 1 | OD | Y | | 1 | | | | Nov 6 | Delta P |
| 103 | DN | Khan | 1 | VD | | | | | | | | I'm On |
| 105 | DN | Khan | 1 | VD | | | | | | | | Early C |
| 107 | DN | Domi | 1 | OD | | | 1 | | | | Nov 8 | First S |
| 109 | DN | Watt | 1 | OR | | | 1 | | | | Nov 8 | Turnd |
| 111 | DN | Romi | 1 | VD | | | | | | | | Long St |
| 113 | PS | Katz | 1 | OR | | | 1 | | | | Nov 6 | Refrig |
| 195 | DN | McKay | 1 | VD | | | | | | | | VIP |
| 197 | DN | McKay | 1 | VD | | | | | | | | Late C |
| 199 | DN | Stutz | 1 | OD | | | 1 | | | | Nov 6 | Confide |

Message: Housekeeping Morning Report

Note: Abbreviations: Crd (Credit), St (Stay Over), Dp (Departure), Ar (Arrival), Adl (Adult), Ch1-3 (Child 1-3); Special column: Delta Privilege, I'm On My Way (Delta Privilege guest phones and room is guaranteed ready within one hour), Early Check-in, First Stay, Turndown Service, Long-term Stay, Refrigerator, VIP, Late Check-in, Confidential; Room Types: QS (Queen smoking), DN (Double non-smoking), PS (Parlour Suite) room is occupied and clean, occupied and dirty, checked-out and dirty, vacant and clean, and vacant and ready for sale (meaning that the room has been inspected and released for sale).

The front-desk or revenue manager will use the occupancy report to verify that revenues were charged for each room that is occupied. Generally, housekeeping will check all rooms that showed as vacant on the previous night's occupancy report and alert the front desk about any rooms that are occupied as discrepancies. The front desk would then endeavour to determine who is in that room and why they are not registered. The discrepancy can be caused by anything from the front-desk clerk giving a guest the wrong room key to unlawful use of the room.

**Technology and Communication with the Front Office** Today's system is much better than when the housekeeping department used to do a morning status report by knocking on the door of each room in the hotel around 8 A.M. and marking down the room status (occupied, check-out, vacant, etc.). This system resulted in many complaints from guests who were sound asleep at 8 A.M. This old system was also used to identify check-out rooms, so that room attendants could start cleaning. Today, this information (guests checking out) is relayed to housekeeping electronically and then to the room attendants either manually, by phone, by walkie-talkie, or by printer terminals on each floor.

# Hiring of Staff for Housekeeping

Shortages of employees who are willing to work in housekeeping are now becoming commonplace. Today's youth are not as interested in performing manual labour as were previous generations. According to Canadian Tourism Human Resource Council (CTHRC) studies, by the year 2011 there will be widespread shortages of hospitality employees and immigration will need to be increased to fulfill these worker requirements. We are already seeing the leading edge of this phenomenon in the fast-food industry, where in some areas of Canada, restaurants have had to close the midnight shift due to shortages of staff. This is also happening in housekeeping departments. Many hotels, hospitals, and long-term-care centres are now looking at contracting out the housekeeping function. This could result in a lower quality of service and cleanliness, which would lead to unsatisfied guests, lower occupancy rates, and losses in revenue—a downward spiral that eventually leads to bankruptcy and/or closure of the hotel. In discussions with the executive housekeeper at the Delta Halifax, it was pointed out that the hotel now uses an outside placement agency to source housekeeping employees. Predictions are that these staffing shortages will cause a major problem for future executive housekeepers. Wages for trained room attendants vary from $10.63 per hour in Halifax to $14.32 in Toronto and $15.02 in Vancouver. Outside of the major urban areas, wage rates may be considerably less. An executive housekeeper's salary will vary between $45 000 and $85 000 depending on the size, location, and quality of the hotel, and on whether the hotel is a member of a chain or is an independent.

Being an executive housekeeper is not an easy task, as you can see from the job description in Exhibit 3-4.

The position of room attendant is also quite a demanding job, as can be seen from the job description in Exhibit 3-5.

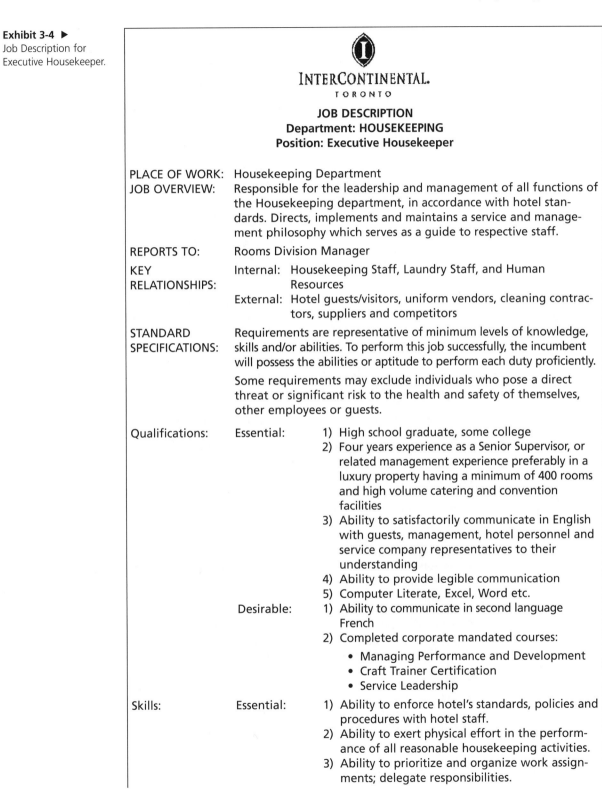

INTERCONTINENTAL.
T O R O N T O

**JOB DESCRIPTION**
**Department: HOUSEKEEPING**
**Position: Executive Housekeeper**

| | |
|---|---|
| PLACE OF WORK: | Housekeeping Department |
| JOB OVERVIEW: | Responsible for the leadership and management of all functions of the Housekeeping department, in accordance with hotel standards. Directs, implements and maintains a service and management philosophy which serves as a guide to respective staff. |
| REPORTS TO: | Rooms Division Manager |
| KEY RELATIONSHIPS: | Internal: Housekeeping Staff, Laundry Staff, and Human Resources |
| | External: Hotel guests/visitors, uniform vendors, cleaning contractors, suppliers and competitors |
| STANDARD SPECIFICATIONS: | Requirements are representative of minimum levels of knowledge, skills and/or abilities. To perform this job successfully, the incumbent will possess the abilities or aptitude to perform each duty proficiently. |
| | Some requirements may exclude individuals who pose a direct threat or significant risk to the health and safety of themselves, other employees or guests. |

Qualifications:  Essential:

1) High school graduate, some college
2) Four years experience as a Senior Supervisor, or related management experience preferably in a luxury property having a minimum of 400 rooms and high volume catering and convention facilities
3) Ability to satisfactorily communicate in English with guests, management, hotel personnel and service company representatives to their understanding
4) Ability to provide legible communication
5) Computer Literate, Excel, Word etc.

Desirable:

1) Ability to communicate in second language French
2) Completed corporate mandated courses:
   - Managing Performance and Development
   - Craft Trainer Certification
   - Service Leadership

Skills:  Essential:

1) Ability to enforce hotel's standards, policies and procedures with hotel staff.
2) Ability to exert physical effort in the performance of all reasonable housekeeping activities.
3) Ability to prioritize and organize work assignments; delegate responsibilities.

4) Ability to direct performance of departmental staff and follow up with corrections where needed.
5) Ability to promote positive work relationships with all departments.
6) Ability to ascertain department training needs and provide such training.
7) Ability to be a clear thinker who analyzes and resolves problems exercising good judgment.
8) Ability to focus attention to details.
9) Ability to input and access information on a computer.
10) Ability to remain calm and courteous with employees and/or situations.
11) Ability to perform job functions to standards under pressure of tense/confrontational situations.
12) Ability to ensure security and confidentiality of employee and hotel information.
13) Ability to work without direct supervision.
14) Ability to work as business dictates.
15) Ability to motivate staff and maintain a cohesive team.

Desirable:     1) Previous guest relations training.

**ESSENTIAL JOB FUNCTIONS:**

1) Assists in directing the work assignments of supervisory and non-supervisory personnel.
2) Monitors Housekeeping Personnel to ensure that guests receive prompt and courteous service.
3) Monitors Housekeeping personnel to ensure that rooms especially those of SCC members, known repeat guests, and other VIP's receive proper attention.
4) Informs other departments of housekeeping matters that concern them, particularly the Laundry Department, the Engineering Department, the Front Office and the Food and Beverage Department.
5) Establishes and maintains effective human relations.
6) Performs personnel related functions such as making recommendations for hiring, evaluating, suspending and termination of personnel.
7) Consults with the Rooms Division Manager on personnel matters.
8) Identifies training needs and makes recommendations for training programs.
9) Schedules and conducts routine inspections of all Housekeeping areas.
10) Inspects guest and public areas on a regular basis to ensure that the furnishings, facilities and equipment are clean and in good repair.
11) Makes recommendations to the Rooms Division Manager regarding the upkeep of furnishings, facilities, and equipment.
12) Maintains appropriate standards for dress, hygiene, uniforms, appearance, posture and conduct of housekeeping personnel.
13) Participates in regular departmental meetings.

**Exhibit 3-4** ▶
*(Continued)*

14) Ensures that housekeeping personnel are familiar with in house facilities for the purpose of assisting guests.
15) Monitors and removes substandard hotel linens from circulating inventory.
16) Maintains open channels of communication with the Assistant Executive Housekeeper on all matters affecting the housekeeping department.
17) Reports all shortages, damages, maintenance requests, problems to manager/proper department.
18) Maintains close liaison with laundry to ensure the service provided meets the hotel's standards.
19) Monitors and maintains the clean and orderly condition of department areas; ensure security of all hotel property.
20) Handles complaints, ensuring guest satisfaction.
21) Promotes positive relations with guests and employees.
22) Maintains complete knowledge at all times of: a) All hotel features/services, and hours of operation. b) Daily house count and expected arrivals/departures. c) Scheduled in-house group activities, locations and times. d) All hotel and departmental policies and procedures.
23) Helps monitor and control housekeeping tasks such as key control, chairs the environmental Committee and knows security and emergency procedures that help maintain the health and security of personnel and guests.
24) Handles other duties and projects as assigned.
25) Is prepared to implement assigned tasks during emergencies such as fires, power outages and bomb threats.
26) Fosters and promote a cooperative working climate, maximizing productivity and employee morale.

**Exhibit 3-5** ▶
Job Description for Room Attendant.

**Ⓘ**

**INTERCONTINENTAL.**
T O R O N T O

**JOB DESCRIPTION**
**Department: HOUSEKEEPING**
**Position: Room Attendant**

| | |
|---|---|
| PLACE OF WORK: | Guest Rooms, Guest and Service Corridors, Housekeeping Department |
| JOB OVERVIEW: | Clean guest rooms as assigned, ensuring the hotel's established standards of cleanliness. Responsible for reporting any maintenance deficiencies and handling guest requests or complaints. Ensures the confidentiality and security of all guest rooms. |
| REPORTS TO: | Executive Housekeeper, Assistant Housekeeper |
| KEY RELATIONSHIPS: | Internal: Executive Housekeeper, Assistant Housekeeper, Floor Attendants, Linen/Laundry Staff, and Engineering |
| | External: Hotel guests/visitors |

**Exhibit 3-5** ▶
*(Continued)*

| STANDARD SPECIFICATIONS: | Requirements are representative of minimum levels of knowledge, skills and/or abilities. To perform this job successfully, the incumbent will possess the abilities or aptitudes to perform each duty proficiently. |
| --- | --- |
| | Some requirements may exclude individuals who pose a direct threat or significant risk to the health and safety of themselves, other employees or guests. |

| Qualifications: | Essential: | 1. Ability to satisfactorily communicate in English with guests, co-workers and management to their understanding. |
| --- | --- | --- |
| | Desirable: | 1. 1 year's prior experience in cleaning hotel guest rooms. |
| | | 2. Guest relations training. |
| | | 3. Knowledge of proper chemical handling. |
| | | 4. High school graduate or equivalent vocational training. |
| Skills: | Essential: | 1. Ability to perform assigned duties with attention to detail, speed, accuracy, follow-through, courtesy, cooperativeness and work with a minimum of supervision. |
| | | 2. Ability to exert physical effort in being able to clean a certain number of rooms per shift in accordance with hotel productivity. |

ESSENTIAL JOB FUNCTIONS:

1. Use correct cleaning chemicals for designated surfaces, according to WHMIS and MSDS regulations and hotel requirements.
2. Clean guest rooms by category priority.
3. Transport cart with cleaning supplies, amenities and linens to assigned guest room and position securely.
4. Service assigned guest rooms.
5. Empty trash containers.
6. Remove all dirty terry linens and replace with clean par to designated layout.
7. Remove soil, dirt, soap build-up and hair from bathroom mirrors, vanity, sink, toilet, shower walls, bathtub, and floor.
8. Replace facial, toilet tissue and bathroom amenities in correct amount and location.
9. Replace fax paper correct size, amount and location. Inform Assistant Housekeeper if time on fax is not correct. Check fax machines to ensure they are plugged in.
10. Empty ashtray in toilet.
11. Inspect condition of bathrobes and replace soiled/damaged ones.
12. Remove dirty bed linen and make up bed with clean linen.
13. Replace laundry bags and slips.
14. Clean closets and door tracks on check-out rooms, removing dust and debris. Ensure correct amount and placement of hangers, pillows and luggage rack.

**Exhibit 3-5** ▶
*(Continued)*

15. Dust and polish all furniture.

16. Realign furniture to floor plan.

17. Open all drawers/doors in check-out rooms and remove items left by guest. Dust inside.

18. Check under bed(s), chairs and sofa for debris and remove if present.

19. Inspect condition of all furniture for tears, rips or stains; report any damages through Espresso Rapid Response System.

20. Remove all dust, debris and foreign particles from upholstered furniture including crevices and under cushions.

21. Dust pictures, frames and mirrors.

22. Remove dust and debris on television, VCR, clock radio, remote control cable box, fax machine and coffee maker.

23. Set correct time on clock. Inform Assistant Housekeeper to set time on VCR's.

24. Clean all lamps and light switches; check for proper working order.

25. Remove dust, spots and smears from windows, ledges and frames.

26. Remove dust, grease and smears from telephones and reposition properly.

27. Empty liquid from ice bucket and wipe all surfaces dry.

28. Remove dust, smudges and spills from mini bar; ensure it is plugged in and securely locked.

29. Remove dust on drapes weekly and realign to correct position daily.

30. Inspect condition of amenities in desk, drawers and guest service directory; replace designated amounts at proper locations within the room.

31. Remove cobwebs from guest room ceiling.

32. Inspect condition of planters and plants; remove debris.

33. Remove dust, dirt, marks and fingerprints from entrance door(s).

34. Ensure presence of fire safety, rate cards and DND sign. Inspect condition and replace as needed.

35. Remove dust, dirt and smudges from A/C unit, vents, grids and thermostat. Turn off thermostat in empty rooms.

36. Remove dust, stains and marks from all baseboards, ledges and corners.

37. Vacuum carpet in guest room.

38. Spray room with deodorizer.

39. Update status of rooms cleaned on assignment sheet.

40. Empty vacuum bag and wipe vacuum clean.

41. Ensure security of any assigned guest room keys or any other hotel key assigned.

42. Handle guest complaints by following the six step procedure and ensuring guest satisfaction.

43. Report any damage or maintenance problems through Espresso Rapid Response System.

44. Turn over any lost and found items from guest rooms to the Supervisor.

45. Thoroughly clean bath room area - tub, toilet, sink, vanity, mirrors, floor, cabinet and baseboards.

46. Spray periodically for mildew.

47. Always have entrance door closed with "Housekeeping in Room" sign on door knob.

# Staffing Schedules

Generally, housekeeping has the largest number of employees in the hotel. Schedules are drawn up weekly and the executive housekeeper must be able to build a schedule that satisfies all of the special requests from employees for days off as well as provide sufficient staffing to clean the rooms. Housekeeping schedules are done based on the occupancy forecast (see Exhibit 6-5 on page 180), which is prepared by the front office. This forecast is used by the housekeeper to decide how many staff members to schedule as room attendants, laundry staff, housepersons, inspectors, etc., and is also used to produce a schedule such as the one shown in Exhibit 3-6. The 10-day forecast needs to be updated on a daily basis; depending on whether occupancy goes up or down, the executive housekeeper would schedule more or less staff. For employees, this can mean that a scheduled day off becomes a workday or vice versa. Because of fluctuating occupancies, many hotels will have a mix of about 60 percent full-time employees and 40 percent part-time employees. In many cases, the part-time employees will experience the fluctuating work schedules as occupancy goes up and down. Part-time employees may also work most weekends, and for this reason they have to be intensely trained and supervised to ensure that the standards of cleanliness are just as high on the weekends as they are during the week. By comparing Exhibits 3-6 and 3-7, you can see how room attendants are assigned a particular floor and rooms to work on each day of the week. This allows the room attendant to relate better to a guest or family who may be staying on their floor and section for an extended period of time. It also creates a familiar environment for the room attendant, as the same vacuum, cart, and equipment would be used each day. In Exhibit 3-7, you can see how room attendants in training are given more rooms to clean each day until they reach the hotel standard of 16 rooms per day. At the Delta Halifax, the week's schedule starts on Friday and is posted on the Tuesday prior. At Christmas, staff schedules are posted for two weeks at a time.

## Work Assignment for Room Attendants

Different amounts of time can be allotted for a room attendant to clean a room, varying with room size, service level, construction materials, amenities, etc. (see Exhibit 3.8) The industry standard for most hotels is a room attendant being allotted 30 minutes to clean each room. Therefore, a room attendant would be expected to clean 16 rooms per day in an eight-hour shift. Exhibit 3-7 shows a work assignment sheet for the Delta Halifax, a 288-room hotel at which room attendants are expected to clean 16 rooms per day.

From the occupancy report, the executive housekeeper assigns the rooms to be cleaned by the room attendants. In Exhibit 3-7, you can see how workloads are assigned by floor. Most floors have 34 rooms. In this case, two room attendants are assigned to each floor, with one attendant cleaning the even-numbered rooms and another attendant cleaning the odd-numbered rooms. With each room attendant assigned 16 rooms to clean, the floor is covered except for two rooms. If all 34 rooms were occupied, then a room attendant from another floor who does not have a full complement of 16 rooms to clean would be assigned rooms under the "Send To" column. The "# Extra" column would be used if a room attendant were assigned more than 16 rooms to clean and, in that case, probably be paid overtime.

**▶ Exhibit 3-6**
Housekeeping Partial Official Schedule.

DELTA HOTELS

## Official Schedule

**Start and end times may change based on Guest's needs. We will evaluate daily.**

| | Friday | Saturday | Sunday | Monday | Tuesday | Wednesday | Thursday |
|---|---|---|---|---|---|---|---|
| October | 28 | 29 | 30 | 31 | 1 | 2 | 3 |
| House Count | 270 | 256 | 183 | 64 | 72 | 116 | 131 |
| Forecast | 280 | 260 | 200 | 80 | 100 | 150 | 210 |
| OT Needed | ? | Yes | ? | No | No | No | ? |
| Arrivals | 121 | 21 | 40 | 25 | 43 | 40 | 133 |
| Departures | 116 | 61 | 108 | 51 | 24 | 50 | 51 |
| Marion 5 odd | 7:46-4:16 | Training in Office 14 rooms 8:46-5:16 | XR | XR | 7:46-4:16 | 7:46-4:16 | Training in Office 14 rooms 7:46-4:16 |
| Michelle 4 even | 7:46-4:16 | XR | XR | Training Jani 8 rooms 7:46-4:16 | Training Jani 10 rooms 7:46-4:16 | Training Jani 12 rooms 7:46-4:16 | Training Jani 14 rooms 7:46-4:16 |
| Jani | X | X | X | Training with Michelle 8 rooms 7:46-4:16 | Training with Michelle 10 rooms 7:46-4:16 | Training with Michelle 12 rooms 7:46-4:16 | Training with Michelle 14 rooms 7:46-4:16 |
| Korri 2 Even Public Areas | Mod 12:30-9pm | Mod 12:30-9pm | Mod 12:30-9pm | XR | XR | Mod 5:00-9pm | Mod 5:00-9pm |
| Jessica Night R/A | 4 rooms 4-9:30pm | 6 rooms 3:30-9:30pm | 12-8:30pm | 4 rooms 4-9:30pm | 2 rooms 5-9:30pm | XR | XR |

Note: Abbreviations: XR (requested day off), XAD (anniversary day off), XWD (wellness day off), XRD (remembrance day off), OC (on call), MOD (modified duties), N/A (not available), School (in school); House Person: PA (public area), LR (linen room) and FL (floor house person).

DELTA
HOTELS

▶ **Exhibit 3-7**
Room Assignment Sheet.

Date:

| Section | R/A Name | Room Numbers | # of Rooms | Send To??? | Total | # Extra |
|---|---|---|---|---|---|---|
| 7 O | | 701,03,05,07,09,11,13,15,21,23,25,27,29,31,33,35 | | | | |
| 7 E | | 702,04,06,08,10,12,14,16,18,20,22,24,26,28,30,32,34,36 | | | | |
| 6 O | | 601,03,05,07,09,11,13,15,21,23,25,27,29,31,33,35 | | | | |
| 6 E | | 602,04,06,08,10,12,14,16,18,20,22,24,26,28,30,32,34,36 | | | | |
| 5 O | | 501,05,07,09,11,13,15,21,23,25,27,29,31,33,35 | | | | |
| 5 E | | 502,04,06,08,10,12,14,16,18,20,22,24,26,28,30,32,34,36 | | | | |
| 4 O | | 401,03,05,07,09,11,13,15,21,23,25,27,29,31,33,35 | | | | |
| 4 E | | 402,04,06,08,10,12,14,16,18,20,22,24,26,28,30,32,34,36 | | | | |
| 3 O | | 301,03,05,07,09,11,13,15,21,23,25,27,29,31,33,35 | | | | |
| 3 E | | 302,04,06,08,10,12,14,16,18,20,22,24,26,28,30,32,34,36 | | | | |
| 2 O | | 201,03,05,07,09,11,13,15,21,23,25,27,29,31,33,35 | | | | |
| 2 E | | 202,04,06,08,10,12,14,16,20,22,24,26,28,30,32,34,36 | | | | |
| 1 E/O | | 101,103,105,107,109,111,113,199,197,195,102,104,106, 108,110,112 | | | | |
| WA | | 155,156,157,158,159,160,161,162,163,164,165,166,167, 168,169,170,171,172,173,174 | | | | |
| W1 | | 175,176,177,178,179,180,181,182,183,184,185,186,187, 188,189,190,191,192,193,194 | | | | |
| EA | | 115,116,117,118,119,120,121,122,123,124,125,126,127,128, 129,130,131,132,133,134 | | | | |
| E1 | | 135,136,137,138,139,140,141,142,143,144,145,146,147,148, 149,150,151,152,153,154 | | | | |

Note: Numbers in the Section column represent floor numbers, either O (odd) or E (even). Wings of hotel designated as WA (West A), W1 (West 1), EA (East A), E1 (East 1).

**Exhibit 3-8** ▶
Time Spent on Room Cleaning.

| Hotel Type | Number of Rooms Cleaned per Day | Number of Minutes per Room |
|---|---|---|
| Five star with custom furnishings | 9 | 50 |
| Extended stay | 9 | 50 |
| Upscale all-suite | 11–14 | 32–40 |
| Five-star landmark | 13–14 | 32–35 |
| Four-star with standard furnishings | 17 | 27 |
| No-frills economy | 20 | 23 |

Deciding on the number of room attendants to schedule is simply a matter of dividing the number of rooms forecasted to be occupied by the number of rooms a room attendant is expected to clean in an eight-hour shift (e.g., 160 rooms occupied/16 rooms per shift = 10 room attendants to be scheduled). However, depending on the type of hotel, more or less time may be given to clean a room as suggested in Exhibit 3-8.

# Measuring Performance

Performance of room attendants is measured in several ways. As was mentioned earlier, there is an expectation that a room attendant will clean a certain number of rooms per eight-hour shift. These rooms must also be cleaned to the high expectations of the guest. In Exhibits 3-9 and 3-10 you can see how each of these items is measured.

## Room Inspection

Maintaining standards and a consistently superior level of cleanliness is accomplished in most hotels by a room inspections system similar to that shown in Exhibit 3-10. Many hotels will inspect every vacant room before it is released for sale by the front desk. Other hotels will perform spot checks or inspect a few vacant rooms in each room attendant's section per day. The Delta Halifax uses a system called CORE (Consistency, Ownership, Responsibility, and Excellence). New room attendants have every room inspected each day. Once room attendants have passed the three-month probationary period and are cleaning 16 rooms per day on their own, they are considered to have reached Green level and have all of their rooms inspected daily with 6 or more deficiencies out of 150 on the inspection form. The next level is Gold with four to six deficiencies per day and four room inspections. The top level is Platinum with three or fewer deficiencies per day and one room inspected. On a monthly basis, if a room attendant has three deficiencies or fewer on each inspection and have one room inspected per day, he or she receives a $50 bonus for the first month, a $75 bonus for the second month, and a $100 bonus the third month. The Delta Halifax's inspection form is one of the most complete in the industry, having about 150 items on it worth a total of 298 points.

Hotel chains may also have travelling inspectors that inspect the whole property as well as the guest rooms, and many hotels also use a system of mystery shoppers who report on everything they experience while staying at a property. Most hotels are also

**Exhibit 3-9** ▶
Sample Productivity
Standard Worksheet.

**Step 1**  Determine how long it should take to clean one guestroom according to the department's standards.
Approximately 27 minutes*

**Step 2**  Determine the total shift time in minutes.
8 hours x 60 minutes = 480 minutes

**Step 3**  Determine the time available for guestroom cleaning.

| Total shift time | 480 minutes |
|---|---|
| Less: | |
| Beginning of shift duties | 20 minutes |
| Morning break | 15 minutes |
| Afternoon break | 15 minutes |
| End of shift duties | 20 minutes |
| Time available for guestroom cleaning | 410 minutes |

**Step 4**  Determine the productivity standard by dividing the result of Step 3 by the result of Step 1.

$$\frac{410 \text{ minutes}}{27 \text{ minutes}} = 15.2 \text{ guest rooms per 8-hour shift.}$$

*Since performance standards vary from property to property, this figure is used for illustrative purposes only. It is not a suggested time figure for cleaning guestrooms. These times will also vary based on whether an employee is paid for breaks as in the above example. The performance standard should be based on fulfilling excellent inspection standards from one of your better room attendants. New employees may be given some time to reach these performance standards levels.

inspected by rating groups such as CAA (Canadian Automobile Association) and Canada Select.

# Supplies, Amenities, and Equipment Management

Some hotel chains such as Delta (which caters especially to the business person) have found that switching to an upscale brand-name amenities package has greatly enhanced the satisfaction of their guests (Exhibit 3-11). Delta Hotels has moved from a more generic Delta brand product to June Jacobs Spa Collection for their bathroom package. It now finds that guests take the amenities with them when checking out, which can be expensive but is a wonderful form of advertising and shows how satisfied guests are with the package.

## On-Premises and Off-Premises Laundry

Generally, it is accepted that a hotel can save about 40 percent of linen costs by installing its own on-premises laundry systems, rather than renting linens. A hotel also has the option of purchasing its own linens and paying an outside laundry company to launder them. When considering installing an on-premises laundry, a hotelier has to consider the space required as well as equipment, staffing, drainage, air handling systems, utility costs, and various other concerns. For many of these reasons, installing an on-premises laundry in an existing hotel may be very expensive and difficult. With new

**Exhibit 3-10** ▶
Partial Room Inspection
Form.

## DELTA
### HOTELS

| Room Inspection—Vacant/Occupied Ready | | Room Points |
|---|---|:---:|
| **Name:** | **Date:** | |
| **Bathroom Counter** | • Soap holder is clean next to sink | 1 |
| | • Sink is clean, free of hair | 2 |
| | • Chrome faucet/taps are clean & shiny | 1 |
| | • 2 clean rock glasses inverted on 2 clean coasters | 2 |
| | • Coaster "D" is facing the guest the correct way | 1 |
| | • Hairdryer cord is untangled & tidy | 1 |
| | • Hairdryer is clean & plugged in | 2 |
| | • Hairdryer is in good working order | 1 |
| | • Mirror is smudge free & clean | 1 |
| | • Pipes are clean under counter | 1 |
| | • Guest personal items are placed on a clean washcloth/towel | 1 |
| | • Bathroom door & knobs are clean | 1 |
| | • Bathroom door mirror is clean/door on a 45° angle | 2 |
| | • Bathroom garbage can is clean/proper place | 2 |
| | • Bathroom counter surface is clean, dust free edges (ashtray if applicable) | 3 |
| | • Mattress not sagging/pushed into proper place | 1 |
| | • Bedspread & bed skirt clean and hanging straight (duvet zipper down), proper size, not torn & matching | 4 |
| | • Pillows: Double-2, Queen-3, King-4, all even & matching | 3 |
| | • Headboard dust free | 1 |
| | • Breakfast menu clean & on bed, wrinkle free and menu side up/proper place | 4 |
| | • Underneath the bed is clean & dust free | 2 |
| | • Beds should be triple sheeted if applicable | 1 |
| | • Double beds should have the same kind of blankets | 1 |
| | • Bed is made according to the sheet change program, folds are straight & ends are tucked in | 1 |
| | • Extra pillow is left on bed—blanket folded neatly | 2 |
| | • Turndown card is removed if applicable | 1 |
| | • Hide a bed—made if applicable, "Make up Sign" should be present | 2 |
| | • Crib and or cot is made if applicable | 1 |
| **Comments/Maintenance Requests** | | |

Note: Partial inspection form shows only bathroom counter and bed items. Full inspection form is available on the instructors's website and also includes bedside table, work desk, television, ambience, amenity tray, toilet and bathtub, towels, closet, coffee setup, and bar tray setup. The total room inspection has 160 items and is scored out of 298 points.

**𝒹 DELTA**
HOTELS

**Bathroom Amenities Cost**

| | |
|---|---|
| Shampoo | $0.25 |
| Conditioner | 0.25 |
| Body lotion | 0.25 |
| Bath gel | 0.25 |
| Mouth rinse | 0.26 |
| Cream soap | 0.17 |
| Glycerine soap | 0.19 |
| Bath soap | 0.19 |
| Shoe mitt | 0.28 |
| Shoe disc | 0.30 |

**Other Items**

| | |
|---|---|
| Pen | 0.21 |
| Corkscrew | 0.67 |
| Laundry bags | 0.12 |

**What Guests Receive by Room Type**

*Delta Room*
Shampoo, conditioner, lotion, cream soap, bath soap, shoe mitt: $1.39

*Deluxe/Premier*
Shampoo, conditioner, lotion, mouth rinse, glycerine soap, bath soap, shoe disc: $1.69

*Suite*
Shampoo, conditioner, lotion, bath gel, mouth rinse, glycerine soap, bath soap, shoe disc: $1.94

construction, it is generally accepted that a hotel needs to have as few as 60 rooms to make installing an on-premises laundry a good investment. Another consideration is whether to add food and beverage linens (tablecloths and napkins) to the laundry system. Uniforms can also be added to the on-premises laundry, although experience shows that difficult stains, particularly on kitchen and maintenance uniforms, need special attention that may be better provided by an outside professional linen service.

## Controlling Linens, Uniforms, and Storage

Controlling costs is an important function of the housekeeping department. We have already looked at how housekeeping departments control labour costs, which is normally the largest portion of their budget. Now we look at controlling costs related to linens, uniforms, and storage.

**Linens** Hotels generally have 3 to 5 par of linen in stock, depending on whether they are using an on-premises or off-premises laundry. The amount of linen required to outfit all of the hotel's rooms once is considered 1 par. The theory behind stocking more

**Exhibit 3-12** ▶
Sample Linen Par
Calculation for 300 Beds.

## Par Stock for Queen-Size Sheets

This is a sample calculation to establish a par stock level for queen-size sheets for a hotel that uses an on-premises laundry operation and supplies two sheets for each of the property's 300 beds. This reflects an ideal situation, but many owners and managers are hesitant to tie up scarce financial resources in inventories. Therefore, the hotel may restrict linen stock to 3 or 4 par.

300 queen-size beds X 2 sheets per bed = 600 sheets (1 par)

| | | |
|---|---|---|
| 1 par in guest rooms | 1 x 600 = | 600 |
| 1 par in floor linen closets | 1 x 600 = | 600 |
| 1 par soiled in laundry | 1 x 600 = | 600 |
| 1 par replacement stock | 1 x 600 = | 600 |
| 1 par for emergencies | 1 x 600 = | 600 |
| Total number | | 3000 |

3000 sheets divided by 600 sheets per par = 5 par

than 1 par may be obvious; with an on-premises laundry, generally 3 par are required: 1 par is being used in the rooms, 1 par is dirty in the laundry, and 1 par is clean and on the room attendant carts and in storage. This assumes that the on-premises laundry is able to launder all dirty linens within a 24-hour period. If a hotel is using an off-premises laundry, another 2 par may be required to cover the extra day or two it takes for transportation to and from the laundry plant (see Exhibit 3-12).

Inventory shrinkage in addition to normal wear and tear is a costly item. Guests often take some linen from the room home with them, and linen has also been known to disappear from room attendants' carts and from storage. Normally, hotels need to replace 1 par of sheets per year, but with terries (towels and face cloths made from terrycloth) hotels face a larger loss in par; hotels may lose up to 5 par per year in face cloths. An average 300-room hotel will have a linen replacement budget of about $68 000 per year, or $226.66 per room. Most hotels do not bill guests for missing towels in rooms, as collection of the invoice is very difficult and hotels risk insulting a guest, losing that customer forever, and creating bad word of mouth.

As shown in Exhibit 3-13, Delta Hotels has a rather unique sign that is prominently displayed in guest rooms to help reduce linen laundry costs while at the same time address guest concerns about the environment.

▲
**Exhibit 3-13**
Sample Linens Card.

**Uniforms**  Many hotel departments have uniformed employees. In some cases, each department will inventory its own uniforms, while in other hotels it is the responsibility of the housekeeping department to fulfill this duty.

If the hotel has an on-premises laundry, uniforms may be laundered, pressed, and issued in the housekeeping department. If an off-premises laundry service is used, uniforms may be cleaned by the contract company or simply sent out for dry cleaning with the guest laundry. Usually, if a cost is involved in cleaning the uniforms, the hotel will absorb this cost, as it is in the hotel's best interest to have all employees looking clean, crisp, and comfortable. In smaller rural hotels, employees may be expected to launder their own uniforms, but this is probably not the norm. Generally, to ensure that employees return uniforms upon termination of employment and therefore to save costs, hotels will ask employees to pay a deposit on uniforms given to them when they are hired. This deposit is generally refunded when the employee returns the uniforms at the end of their employment period. In some cases, hotels will withhold an employee's final pay until all uniforms are returned (this may be illegal in some jurisdictions).

In most cases, employees are issued two uniforms so they have a clean one to wear while the other uniform is being laundered. Uniforms may be cleaned daily (kitchen, food service, and maintenance staff) or one or two times per week (front office and bellpersons). Many employees, such as management staff, are expected to wear business suits, and the cost of dry cleaning these would be paid by the hotel.

**Storage**  A lot of storage space is required for linens, uniforms, chemicals, and equipment used by or kept in the housekeeping department. These areas must be maintained neatly and safely while controls are in place to prevent employees and guests from stealing items. Most of the items used in hotels and stored in housekeeping are equally usable in someone's home. As an example, an employee mysteriously did not show up for work one day. When the hotel checked the employee's apartment with his landlord to verify that he was okay, it found that the apartment not only was furnished with hotel furniture, but also contained bathroom towels neatly embroidered with the hotel's logo. In fact, the apartment looked very similar to one of the hotel's guest rooms.

Therefore, housekeeping must be quite vigilant in safely securing many of the assets of the hotel that are in storage and on room attendants' carts.

# Guest and Employee Security in Housekeeping

How should hoteliers best convey a sense of safety in a high-alert world? Should they focus on improved technology in locking and surveillance systems? Should they focus on action plans to handle any crisis that may arise? The answer is probably both.

Should the tourism industry market Canada abroad as a neutral peacebroker on the world stage and therefore a safe destination to visit? Most hoteliers feel that this would be foolhardy, as it would take only one terrorist attack to dispel this myth. Most industry watchers believe that a terrorist attack could happen in Canada. One of the best solutions to ensure guest safety seems to be a well-trained and vigilant group of employees.

Recent technology improvements include digital surveillance and recording systems that allow hotels to store an entire week of surveillance on digital video recorders rather than on the older VCR technology. With digital, gone are the fuzzy images of a perpetrator we have become used to seeing on the late-night news when a bank or convenience store is robbed.

Locking technology has also improved, with systems that can now lock a room during scheduled non-occupied periods to keep out employees except when scheduled to clean the room. This reduces employee theft (if that is a problem) by giving a room attendant access to a particular room during a certain time period in the day. There also is a move to replace key locks with electronic locks on housekeeping storage rooms, electrical supply rooms, and conference rooms. Imagine a conference of 100 people leaving their laptops and cellphones in a meeting room to go for lunch. Modern technology could have that room locked automatically by motion detectors and turn on surveillance cameras while the guests are out. Surveillance cameras now also have smoked glass covers so it is impossible to tell in which direction the camera is pointed.

Crises action plans should be coordinated with local public agencies such as the fire marshal and police force. Vancouver's Pan Pacific Hotel, which is part of a 2-million-square-foot harbourside complex that houses a busy cruise ship dock, an office tower, and a convention centre, has trained more than 70 employees in emergency first aid through a local hospital as part of its crises management plans. Staff training and practice seem to be the best ways to have knowledgeable employees who are ready to jump into action whenever a crisis occurs.

In the housekeeping department, having a well-trained and vigilant staff can be vital to a hotel's security. Having a staff that notices suspicious guest or employee behaviour and reports this to management or security can go a long way toward maintaining guest and employee safety. Room attendants should be trained to report any suspicious items, such as drug paraphernalia or weapons, found in a guest room.

Security issues differ between a large urban hotel in Vancouver and a small hotel in rural Canada. The types of plans and interventions required will differ from property to property and location to location.

## Emerging Diseases

The industry suffered quite a scare when SARS hit Toronto in the summer of 2003. Front-desk clerks asked whether SARS could be caught from sharing a pen with a registering guest. Some room attendants asked for masks that could be worn while at work. And what about the handling of sheets and towels? There were many questions for which hoteliers had to find answers with which to satisfy the concerns of their employees and guests.

Many hotels now use a yellow hazard "sharps container" to dispose of needles as well as any other sharp objects found in rooms. The Delta Halifax uses an off-premises laundry and has been supplied with red laundry bags for linens that may be contaminated with blood or vomit. This contract laundry company also provides hospital linens and is specially equipped to clean and sanitize contaminated towels and linens.

In recent years, the world has gone from HIV (AIDS), legionnaires' disease, and ebola to SARS in Toronto, E. coli in Walkerton, bird flu in British Columbia, and mad cow disease in Alberta. We now live in fear of an emerging threat from avian flu, which may be spread to humans by birds. With jet travel shrinking the world and guests coming to Canada from all parts of the globe, the next pandemic may be just around the corner. Hoteliers remain on the alert, as does the rest of the travel community, but how can the industry do advance planning for something that even the medical and scientific community cannot predict? Will room attendants of the future wear space-like suits to protect them from disease? We hope not, but must remain vigilant for any surprises that the future may have in store.

# Summary

Many experienced hoteliers believe that the executive housekeeper or housekeeper has the best management skills of any of the department heads in the hotel. Why? Housekeepers are responsible for the main product that every hotel sells: a clean room. This product produces 75 percent or more of the profits of any hotel. Without a high level of occupancy, the hotel will soon fall into bankruptcy, as it cannot survive on the meagre profits produced by food, beverage, and other areas of the hotel. Housekeeping, along with engineering and maintenance, is also responsible for the condition and repair of the hotel's main property assets and indeed is responsible for protecting the owner's investment. Many times, a simple wrong choice by the housekeeper in choosing cleaners can destroy the finish on taps or some other amenity throughout the hotel. The housekeeper manages the largest staff in the hotel, usually manages the highest employee turnover (up to 200 percent annually) of any department, and hires individuals to do very demanding physical jobs at an average wage that is not heavily subsidized by gratuities from guests. Having said all of this, housekeeping departments churn out millions of clean rooms every year for the use and enjoyment of Canadians everywhere.

As many a smart hotelier knows, the success or failure of the hotel industry falls squarely on the broad shoulders of the men and women who work tirelessly in housekeeping every day.

# Questions and Problems

1. Develop an organization chart for a mid-sized hotel property with an on-premises laundry operation.

2. Why do you think many hotels are now hiring outside contractors to clean their rooms and/or public areas? In your opinion, what are the advantages and disadvantages of doing this?

3. If you were the executive housekeeper of a soon-to-open mid-sized hotel in Vancouver, what sources might you use to recruit housekeeping staff? Remember that advertising in newspapers is usually too expensive for your budget.

4. As a newly appointed executive housekeeper, do you think it is important to have all check-out and stay-over rooms inspected daily once they have been cleaned to ensure the high standards of cleanliness your hotel and guests demand?

5. You have been asked by your general manager to research and find a unique line of quality bathroom amenity products for the guest rooms. What sources would you use to accomplish this task?

6. Turnover in your housekeeping department has been close to 200 percent annually for far too long. What steps would you take to reduce this turnover and keep quality staff?

# CASE STUDY

## Team Scheduling

You are the executive housekeeper for a 320-room four-star hotel with an on-premises laundry. Based on a room attendant cleaning 16 rooms per day (30 minutes per room), you have to prepare a weekly schedule for 28 room attendants, 7 house persons, 7 supervisors, and 7 laundry persons (a total of 49 employees). To make this exercise less complex, we will assume that cleaning of public areas has been contracted out. You have found that it takes you half a day to prepare a schedule that meets the needs of your employees and hotel guests. You have read about the team concept of staffing and wonder if adopting this concept may solve your problems.

Each rooms division team will consist of a senior room attendant (supervisor), one house person, and five room attendants. Therefore, each team is capable of cleaning 80 (5 x 16) rooms per day. To clean all 320 rooms, four teams are required. They have been assigned names: Red Team, Blue Team, Green Team, and Orange Team.

The laundry team will have a laundry room supervisor (washer), one house person (helper/sorter), and five laundry attendants (two ironers and three folder/stackers).

You will also need two swing teams to cover for days off in both laundry and rooms. Each swing team will consist of a swing supervisor, one house person, and five room attendants. Each swing team will relieve two of the rooms teams on their two days off and relieve the laundry team on one of their days off.

Assuming full occupancy and a five-day, 40-hour workweek for all employees, make up a team staffing schedule for one week for your 320-room hotel, using the team staffing chart below. All teams will have two consecutive days off and will work their share of weekends.

Using the team staffing chart below, create six more weekly staffing charts by moving the days off for each team ahead by one day. When you are finished, you should have a seven-week rotating team schedule.

## Team Staffing Chart (Week 1)

| Team | Sat | Sun | Mon | Tues | Wed | Thurs | Fri |
|---|---|---|---|---|---|---|---|
| Red | | | | | | | |
| Blue | | | | | | | |
| Green | | | | | | | |
| Orange | | | | | | | |
| Laundry | | | | | | | |
| Swing 1 | | | | | | | |
| Swing 2 | | | | | | | |

1. Discuss in detail the pros and cons of team staffing in a larger hotel from the point of view of the guest, the executive housekeeper, and employees.

2. Would team staffing work for any other departments in the hotel?

3. Do you see any problems with a team schedule if your hotel was unionized? If so, how would you convince the union that team staffing is a good idea?

4. This schedule assumes 100 percent occupancy every night of the week. How would you adjust this schedule for fluctuating occupancy?

5. Study your seven schedules. Did anyone get more than two consecutive days off?

# Note

1. Orkin Commercial Services, 2006 Hospitality Poll, www.orkincommercial.com/apps/pressmanager/ ARFiles/HospitalityPollResultsOnline.pdf.

## Weblinks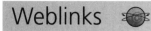

June Jacobs Spa Collection
**www.junejacobs.com/**

The Rooms Chronicle
**www.roomschronicle.com/**

Canada Career Consortium (Executive Housekeeper)
**www.careerccc.org**

Delta Hotels
**www.deltahotels.com/**

Cambridge Towel
**www.camtx.com**

Delta Hotels Spa Collection
**www.deltahotels.com/about/press_view.html?id=141**

# Part II
# The Reservations Process

From the largest chains to the smallest independent operations, significant investment is being made year after year in better, faster, and more enhanced reservations technologies. Whether the investment is tens of thousands of dollars for an independent property or tens of millions of dollars for a chain-wide system, the goal remains the same: to increase the accuracy, accessibility, profitability, and breadth of reservations venues for the property.

For the chain (or consortium of chains), the simple toll-free telephone reservations centres developed 40 years ago remain the foundation of the reservations process. However, through last-room availability technology, central reservations agents are now more informed and up to the minute in terms of space availability, rate structures, and even the ability to visualize (through CD-ROM or the Internet) each of the chain's properties. Through seamless connectivity technology, travel agents, wholesalers, airlines, and Internet providers offer additional options for making and taking a reservation. In almost all cases, the reservations are made in real time, directly to the chain's individual property being reserved. This saves the central reservations system (CRS) the task of forwarding reservations to the individual property and saves the property the task of updating its system with each CRS reservation received.

For the customer, these new technological enhancements lend ease, variety, and accessibility to the reservations process. In addition, the increasing sophistication of yield management technology is making the cost of a hotel room a real bargain for guests who are able to travel during the off-season or on the spur of the moment, or for those who are able to plan trip dates far in advance.

## Chapter 4

# Global Reservations Technologies

## Learning Objectives

After reading this chapter, you will be able to do the following:

1. **Describe the evolution of central reservations systems (CRSs) for hotels from the airline systems.**

2. **Elaborate on seamless connectivity between CRSs and global distribution systems (GDSs) using switch technology.**

3. **Elaborate on the history and current status of booking reservations at hotels.**

4. **Discuss the yield management revolution and automated yield management systems.**

Hotel reservations technology has certainly come a long way since Kemmons Wilson introduced Holiday Inn's (and the industry's) first **central reservations system**, Holidex, in 1965.[1] Rapid advancements in technology have changed—to the very core—the manner in which reservations are booked. Where just a few short years ago a hotel's posted available rooms were manually adjusted and sold on a daily (even hourly) basis, today's rooms are sold electronically through a myriad of channels with little or no human interaction (see Exhibit 4-1). That represents a substantial change in methodology over a few short years. What does the future hold for hotel reservations? Imagine the following rather futuristic scenario:

> Heading to the airport for a hastily scheduled business meeting, a technologically savvy corporate businessman accesses the Internet on his handheld personal digital assistant (PDA). Through the PDA, he checks availability at his favourite Vancouver hotel, discovers that room availability is tight, but manages to reserve a queen room for $269 that night. His credit card guarantee is transmitted automatically, and the confirmation number is conveniently stored in the PDA for later retrieval. A room reservation in hand, our corporate executive visibly relaxes as his taxi enters the airport's unloading zone.
>
> Several hours later, this futuristic scenario continues as our business traveller arrives at the Fairmont Vancouver Airport. The moment he steps foot in the hotel's lobby, his digital cellphone alerts him that a message is waiting. The text message on his telephone asks if he would like to proceed with electronic check-in. No wonder he loves this hotel. Of course, he readily agrees by simply typing "yes" into his cellphone and entering a preprogrammed personal identification number (PIN). Then, in one last attempt to upsell to the guest, the hotel's property management system prompts him

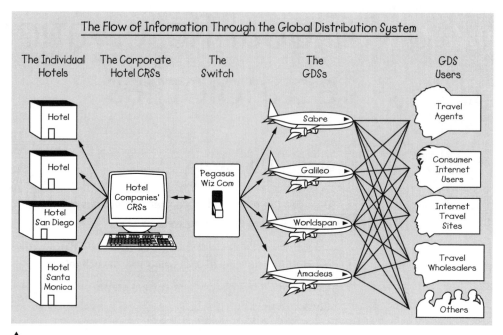

**▲**
**Exhibit 4-1**
The global distribution system is enormous in scope. Each of the four airline GDS systems processes roughly 100 billion transactions per year and about 300 million requests for information per day! Galileo alone, for example, is connected to 45 000 hotel properties, 43 000 travel agencies, 500 airlines, 40 car-rental companies, 360 tour operators, and all of the world's major cruise lines.

The flow of information works like this: The supply side of the flow begins with the hotel, where information (rate and availability) flows to the switches. The switches provide that information to all four airline GDSs. Travel agents, consumer Internet users, Internet travel sites, travel wholesalers, and a myriad of other end users (still to be invented) access the information through the GDSs. The demand side of the flow works in the opposite direction, with the resulting room reservation finally coming to rest in the hotel's reservations system.

*with several additional room-rate options. He decides to treat himself to a Fairmont Gold King at $359 and indicates as much on the cellphone.*

*As he walks across the lobby (secretly boasting because he's avoiding the growing check-in queue), a text message provides him with the room number and even directions to the room (not that he needs directions—after all, this is his favourite hotel). As he exits the elevator, the hotel's short-range radio-wave technology senses him and prompts his telephone by again requesting his PIN. As he approaches the guest room (within, say, 5 or 7 metres), the door automatically unlocks itself.*

What a truly seamless series of transactions our corporate guest experienced. Each transaction was fully electronic—both paperless and faceless (no printed receipts or mailed confirmations, and no one-to-one or guest-to-employee interactions). Quite futuristic, you must agree! But wait . . . that technology is already in place at many hotels across Canada today. Everything mentioned in the above scenario is available technology accessed regularly by today's corporate guests (see Exhibit 4-2). The future is here!

# Global Distribution

A complete understanding of today's complicated reservations technologies requires a look back to the beginning. Even before the advent of Holidex, the airline industry was

developing its own reservations systems. These airline systems proved to be an efficient and low-cost means for taking reservations. Based on these early airline successes, the lodging industry soon followed suit.

It is interesting to note that the lodging industry has historically followed airlines reservations technology ever since. The airlines have generally been the developers and investors in new systems, while the lodging industry has demonstrated itself to be somewhat more conservative. By choosing to wait on the sidelines in the early stages of development, hotel chains have ultimately saved money by taking advantage of existing technologies and systems.

## The Airline Systems

In the early 1960s, airlines began developing electronic reservations systems to ease the process for booking airline seats by in-house airline reservations clerks. Within a decade, the first airline reservations systems were being placed in travel agency offices. This was the first link in today's global distribution system networks.

It makes sense to let someone else book the reservation. The airlines knew this in the 1970s. Why have the travel agent call the airline to book a reservation when we have the technology to place the reservations system terminal in the travel agent's office? In addition, since the travel agent is a one-stop source for hotel as well as rental car reservations, the new airline systems soon transformed into global networks.

It wasn't long before every possible airline had a hand in some reservations network. But these networks were expensive (American Airlines alone had invested well over $1 billion by 1985), and most airlines were financially or strategically forced to join together in developing central reservations system (CRS) networks (see Exhibit 4-3). An excellent example of such a network is Worldspan, which joined the systems originally owned by Delta, Northwest, and TWA Airlines.

Air Canada developed its own reservations system known as Reservac and then purchased a 2 percent interest in Apollo, with United Airlines and U.S. Air. Apollo was sold to Galileo International for $1 billion in 1997. Air Canada and Tango now use Apollo, operated by Galileo Canada. Worldspan was purchased on June 30, 2003, by Travel Transaction Processing Corporation and Teachers' Merchant Bank.

Some of the most expensive components of airline CRSs were the individual terminals placed in travel agency offices. As such, larger agencies with access to more potential bookings received more terminals from the airlines than did smaller agencies. A travel agency with a large assortment of different airline terminals had more options than did a smaller agency. This difference in size and accessibility to airlines became even more pronounced as the airlines began offering hotel rooms and rental car bookings directly through their systems. Larger agencies were now able to sell a complete trip, while smaller agencies still needed to make reservations by telephone.

Smaller travel agents weren't the only ones left out of the picture. Many major lodging chains were not connected to airline reservations systems either. Although they were able to join, some lodging chains thought the costs were prohibitive. A single hotel property in the chain had to pay three separate commissions for a single reservation: The hotel paid the travel agent a 10 percent (or higher) commission, the airline took a fee for access to the airline reservations system, and the hotel chain took its normal fee for booking through the chain's central reservation office (CRO). Chains that chose not to join the airline reservations system were still available to the travel agent by telephone, but in many cases telephone reservations were not made.

To address this problem, many hotel chains began providing more efficient telephone reservations services to travel agents. In an attempt to encourage telephone bookings, hotel chains established private toll-free numbers exclusively for travel agents. Experienced reservationists who could answer questions and book reservations quickly staffed these private phone lines. As efficient as this may sound, to many agents the telephone approach was not as appealing as the direct-access airline computer terminal.

Also apparent during these years was the fact that the hotel information listed on the airline reservations system was old news. Just as the hotel chain's CRO was not full duplex (online, real time) at this stage, neither was the airline system. Hotels still needed to close availability when only a few rooms remained, they were still not able to alter rates at a moment's notice, and they were still only able to offer a few basic rate categories. In fact, many airline reservations systems only allowed a set number of changes to hotel information per day, and they required several hours' lead time. As a result, the risk of overbooking through the airline reservations system was high.

With the old-fashioned, one-way downloading of rates and availability, hotel chains and airline systems were constantly updating information. Not only was that

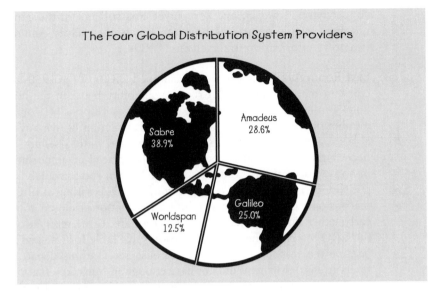

▲
**Exhibit 4-3**
It is difficult to keep up with the changing ownerships and affiliations of the four GDS providers. Sabre, the largest of the four, was the only GDS wholly owned by one airline (American Airlines). However, American Airlines spun off Sabre in 1996 and now owns a piece of Worldspan (along with Delta and Northwest Airlines). Amadeus (originally a partnership with Air France, Iberia, Lufthansa, and Continental Airlines) grew to its number two standing by purchasing System One (owned mostly by Continental Airlines) in 1998. Galileo was purchased by Cendant Corporation in 2001 for a whopping $2.9 billion!

Here is another interesting tidbit. While Sabre owns Travelocity.com, Amadeus owns OneTravel.com, and Galileo owns Trip.com; Worldspan does not own an Internet consumer travel site. Because of its strategy—staying out of the e-commerce competition game—Worldspan has become the largest processor of Internet bookings!

labour intensive and prone to errors, but it also created time lags between the creation of new data and its appearance on the CRS.

## Seamless Connectivity

By the late 1980s, the number of transactions between the airline **global distribution systems (GDSs)** and the hotel **central reservations offices (CROs)**[2] began outpacing the unsophisticated half-duplex communication interfaces that were in place at the time. Half-duplex systems (also known as *type B* systems) were basically one-way communication. A message would be sent in one direction; the response would be sent some time later. These type B systems required the travel agent to complete room requests (or requests for airline seats or rental cars) and forward them to the CRS. Minutes or even hours later, they received confirmation. This delay was costly, frustrating, and prone to numerous errors and overbooking mistakes.

The introduction of full-duplex (also known as *type A*) communication in 1989 was a first step in solving this problem. Type A communication provided immediate confirmation of reservations requests (usually within about seven seconds) and up-to-date rates and availabilities between the GDS and the CRO. Full-duplex communication between the GDS and CRS was an important landmark on the road to seamless connectivity. However, one key player was still not in the game—the hotel. The big question at this point was how the hotels themselves communicated their rooms' inventory information to the chains' CROs.

**Last-Room Availability** The old-fashioned CROs of the 1960s through 1980s required constant manual updating of room availability between the hotel and the CRO. The hotel's in-house reservations department was responsible for manually tracking the number of rooms sold by the CRO and calculating how many rooms remained available for a given date. The CRO would continue blindly selling rooms until it was notified by the hotel to close room sales. This placed an important responsibility on the in-house reservationist to notify the CRO when room availability was tightening. This notification became an exercise in timing and forecasting; as often as not, mistakes were made. Sometimes the hotel's in-house reservationist closed rooms with the CRO too early; other times, rooms were closed too late. If the reservationist closed rooms with the CRO too early, there were still rooms available for sale and those remaining rooms became the responsibility of the in-house reservations department. Many times, the reservations department did not have enough in-house reservations activity and the date would come and go with several rooms remaining unsold. On the other hand, if the in-house reservationist closed the rooms too late, the hotel was overbooked.

Commonly referred to as **last-room availability** or full-duplex systems, today's CRSs offer online, two-way communication with all **affiliated hotels** in the chain. No longer a hit-and-miss game of guessing when the last room will be sold, modern CRSs can literally sell the very last room at any hotel. This is because the CRS now has online real information about the actual status of rooms at every hotel within the system. This is a significantly more efficient system because it allows the CRS more opportunities to sell every room without either underselling or overselling the hotel.

In addition, last-room availability technology is a necessary first step in providing an automated yield management system to the chain. Without **online**, full-duplex communication, a hotel's room rates are difficult to update. In fact, some older systems required the hotel to publish rates 18 months in advance without allowing changes throughout the entire year. The hotel literally had to forecast its levels of business and live with those forecasts no matter what might occur. As a result, the only way a hotel could alter its rates upward or downward during busy or slow periods was to close room availability with the CRO. Once closed, all rooms had to be sold through the in-house reservations system, and rates could be changed as warranted. Today's online, last-room availability systems allow the property to update rates with the CRS as often as necessary.

**Electronic Switch Technology** The road to seamless connectivity was now almost complete. At roughly the same time that last-room availability technology was being introduced between individual hotels and their respective CROs, another brick was being laid between airline GDSs and travel agents. To understand why this brick needed laying, look back to the recent discussion on the1970s with the travel agents and their various reservation systems.

It took a new innovation, switch technology, to get all of the companies speaking the same language. Today, several major electronic switches are available. One system, THISCO, was developed by 11 major lodging chains (Best Western, Choice, Days Inns, Hilton, Holiday, Hyatt, La Quinta, Marriott, Ramada, Sheraton, and Forte) in conjunction with Rupert Murdoch's electronic publishing division. THISCO, which stands for The Hotel Industry Switching Company, was introduced in the early 1990s and is now owned and operated by Pegasus Solutions. Pegasus Solutions represents 48 000 hotel properties worldwide and 50 of the largest hotel companies, including Canadian Pacific Ltd's Fairmont, Delta, and Princess brands. Pegasus Solutions also owns and operates Travelweb.com, an Internet site for booking travel arrangements.

Switch technology functions like a clearinghouse. All reservations transactions are processed through the switch. The travel agent now needs to access just one terminal to communicate reservations requests and confirmations to literally any of thousands of airlines, hotels, car rentals, and other related products.

All of the benefits to the travel agent and hotel that accrue through last-room availability systems are becoming available through airline reservations systems. Now, the travel agent is literally looking at the same hotel reservations data as the in-house reservationist; if special rates or packages are available, the travel agent can quote them as readily as the hotel's in-house reservationist. This adds a new level of credibility to travel agents, who have often complained that their outdated data made them look unprofessional to the customer.

Another major advantage of the switch is that it enables the travel agent to learn just one set of procedures and to input just one set of codes. Switch technology functions as a translator as well as a real-time communicator. It translates codes into one hotel CRS or another. Now, when the agent is interested in booking a room with, say, two queens, the agent does not need to remember the exact input code. One chain might identify two queens with a QQ code; another chain might use 2Q or DQ for double queen. The electronic switch allows the user one system of codes and translates that information across each chain's CRS.

The introduction of the switch has allowed seamless connectivity across the spectrum of reservations systems. Now travel agents, airline reservationists, hotel central reservations agents, and in-house hotel reservations clerks access the same information at the same speed. All reservations are made in real time and update the rooms inventory the moment the reservation is confirmed.

**Online Reservations Bookings**   One of the fastest-growing means for personal access to the information superhighway is online subscription service. Online companies such as Rogers (Itravel2000.com), Bell Sympatico (Sympatico/MSN Travel), and AOL Canada (Sabre network) provide a direct link between the user and the server. Timely news and sports information, consumer and cinematic reviews, product ordering, and games are just a few of the common applications available to the online subscriber. Hotel reservations are another common application. Reservations can now be made by consumers through any hotel or airline website or through various travel websites, such as Travelocity.ca (owned by Sabre). Travelocity is the world's largest online travel agency and third-largest e-commerce site. Expedia.ca, owned by Microsoft, is a big competitor. Orbitz.com, formed in June 2001 by five of the U.S.'s largest airlines (American, Continental, Delta, Northwest, and United), is the new kid on the block. It has contracts with 35 other airlines to show their fares and expects to take 30 percent of the travel market from Expedia and Travelocity.

One of the more popular reasons for joining an online subscription service is to access major reservations systems. Prodigy, for example, allows the subscriber a direct link to the Sabre network. Sabre, American Airlines' central reservations system, is able to provide useful information on most major airlines, hotels, and car rental companies.

In October 2001, Sabre (Semi-automated Business Research Environment), the largest of the four remaining GDSs, was spun off by American Airlines and is now publicly owned. In 2001, the total global market handled by the four GDSs was $52 billion. Sabre has earned the leadership position in every travel market distribution channel, including travel agents (38 percent share in 2001), online consumers (44 percent share), and online corporate (71 percent share). Sabre controlled 48 percent of the North American market in 2001. In Canada, WestJet uses Sabre as well as its own in-house reservations system.

Galileo International—which owns Galileo Canada, now used by Air Canada—was bought by Cendant Corporation, the world's largest franchisor of hotels, in October 2001. Cendant also operates Lodging.com, another travel booking website. Galileo Canada's Apollo system is connected to a network of more than 100 000 terminals around the world. In Canada, Galileo is connected to 3000 travel agents with more than 10 000 terminals.

Once online with Sabre, for example, the user can check air, rooms, and car availability; rates and discount plans; flight schedules; and additional pertinent data. After the guest has played with the options and made a decision, entering the reservation request is simply a matter of following the computer-generated prompts.

Although the actual volume of online reservations is still quite small, it plays a greater role with each passing year. The Hotel Association of Canada suggests that, in Canada, about 20 percent of all hotel reservations are made through travel agents, with about 3 percent made by consumers directly over the Internet. With respect to Canada's $7.4 billion in rooms revenue, online reservations in 2001 probably accounted for less than $0.2 billion. But that is $0.2 billion more than just a few years before, when online reservations were non-existent.

Not only is the growth rate for online reservations astronomical, but there are some interesting trends with regard to who is using these services. Some of the best customers in the lodging industry are using online reservations technology. The profile of an average online user, who takes 25 trips per year, is an upper-income male with a high level of education. A recent survey by GetThere showed that 89 percent of companies were paying 42 percent less in travel agency fees for trips booked online.

## Application Service Providers

The historical evolution of CRSs from stand-alone call centres in the mid-1960s to today's seamlessly connected, last-room-availability GDSs has only been possible at a substantial price. Because of the heavy investment required, not all hotel chains are in the same place today in terms of their respective levels of sophistication.

Last-room-availability software requires an ability to integrate all of the chain's hundreds (if not thousands) of individual hotel property management systems. In terms of property management systems, some chains are still dealing with the mistakes they made decades ago. Mistakes such as allowing each hotel—franchised or corporate-owned—to select its own property management system hardware and software are still proving costly to lodging chains in a number of ways. That's because different hardware and software applications across each property in the chain require either new investment to bring like products to all properties or a myriad of programming changes to get all systems speaking roughly the same language. It is this challenge facing hotel chains that has lent itself to the successful introduction of application service providers (ASPs). ASPs are software companies (Pegasus's RezView and Swan's Unirez are two such examples) that offer a

**Exhibit 4-4 ▶**
Features Provided
Through an Application
Service Provider—The
Pegasus Solutions'
"RezView" Model.
Pegasus Solutions is
the lodging industry's
oldest (and most popular)
provider of ASP central
reservations software. Its
ASP application, known
as RezView, is used by
more than 10 000 hotels,
representing 71 brands
and 2 million rooms
worldwide.

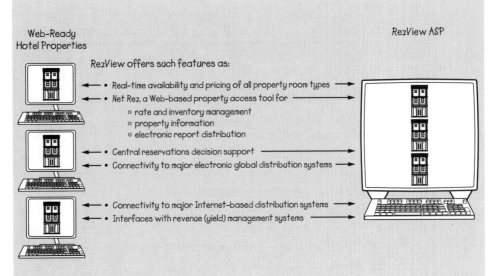

suite of software applications via Internet-based access. No longer is it necessary for a hotel chain to purchase and maintain specific property management system hardware and software for each affiliated hotel. Rather, through an Internet website, each hotel runs off the same suite of software by simply using any Internet-ready computer—even a laptop!

Generally, ASPs offer four primary functions in their arsenal of applications: a CRS, GDS connectivity, connections to "alternate" distribution systems, and Internet reservations. Hotels simply subscribe to the system, and all property-specific data are stored off-property in ASP-maintained warehouses (see Exhibit 4-4).

As you might imagine, numerous benefits are associated with ASP applications. Hotel chains do not have to make large capital investments in hardware and software. Nor do they have to employ a fleet of specialized software engineers to maintain the system and program new applications. Because every hotel uses the same software, multiple versions of poorly integrated applications are avoided. Best of all, new software enhancements are implemented immediately at the ASP site and available to all users instantaneously!

**Single-Image Inventory**   The biggest benefit associated with ASP applications is single-image inventory. Similar in concept to last room availability, single-image inventory allows all users to feed from the same database. One inventory—price and availability—is viewed by the GDS, central reservations call centres, and Internet-based distribution systems. The result is a lower error rate in reservations bookings and a resulting improvement in overall customer service (see Exhibit 4-5).

Although last-room-availability and single-image inventory (also known as *true integration*) appear quite similar, they are fundamentally different. The difference revolves around the fact that last room availability uses property management system inventory for its information. Historically, CRSs have interfaced with property management systems to determine availability and pricing. With single-image inventory, all

Electronic Commerce Households Shopping on the Internet from Any Location, by Type of Product and Service (Internet Shopper)

| | 2001 | 2002 | 2003 |
|---|---|---|---|
| | | % | |
| Books, magazines, and newspapers | 24.8 | 23.2 | 24.7 |
| Travel arrangements | 19.9 | 20.5 | 22.9 |
| Computer software | 14.7 | 13.7 | 14.5 |
| Automotive products | 18.5 | 18.3 | 16.9 |
| Music compact discs (CDs), tapes, and audio files (MP3) | 13.8 | 11.5 | 11.6 |
| Clothing, jewellery, and accessories | 27.2 | 25.7 | 28.6 |
| Computer hardware | 12.4 | 11.5 | 10.3 |
| Consumer electronics | 19.9 | 19.6 | 24.9 |
| Other entertainment (for example, tickets) | 9.5 | 9.0 | 9.2 |
| Housewares (furniture and appliances) | 23.5 | 25.3 | 27.7 |
| Videos and digital video discs (DVDs) | 7.5 | 7.6 | 9.2 |
| Hobbies | 3.7 | 3.7 | 4.6 |
| Food, condiments, and beverages | 3.3 | 3.8 | 3.0 |
| Toys and games | 9.1 | 7.8 | 7.9 |
| Real estate | 4.8 | 3.9 | 3.9 |
| Health, beauty, and vitamins | 7.0 | 5.9 | 7.6 |
| Flowers and gifts | 5.6 | 4.5 | 4.3 |
| Sports equipment | 9.7 | 8.9 | 9.5 |
| Other products and services (not elsewhere classified) | 16.2 | 19.9 | 18.1 |

▲
**Exhibit 4-5**

In the late 1990s, for the first time in the history of the Internet, online travel purchases outpaced online personal computer purchases. And travel bookings never looked back, continuing to grow at a rate faster than any other. That's because online travel bookings make sense—according to Internet experts, the travel industry is a natural for online bookings. Through the Internet, clients can readily compare prices, amenities, and other features before making their purchase decision.

But hotel bookings lag behind airline bookings in terms of online purchases. This is due, in part, to the fact that hotel bookings are more complicated for the average consumer—air is the simplest online purchase, followed by rental cars, with hotels coming in third for "ease of use." As such, just one out of every three or so Internet air bookings is accompanied by a related hotel booking.

reservations applications as well as property management system applications look at the same database and draw from the same well of information.

As such, the rooms inventory can become available for others to access. One result of having an accessible inventory is an overall savings on reservations commissions. Imagine negotiating a special corporate rate with Pepsi, for example. Rather than having Pepsi book its special rates through a travel agent (and paying commissions to the travel agent and fees to the GDS and other distribution system providers), the hotel could provide Pepsi with a unique access code. All reservations booked against the inventory using this special code would be virtually commission-free!

# Taking the Reservation

With the growing importance of the global distribution system, the telephone is losing ground in the reservations process. Conversely, websites and online bookings are growing in importance. Who knows what the future holds for the various players in the ever-changing reservations landscape.

**The Travel Agent** One certain shakeup involves the world's travel agencies. Hotels are quietly developing systems that circumvent the 500 000 travel agencies worldwide. You see, hotels pay numerous commissions on each room reservation booked. For example, let's say that a person visits a travel agent to book a ski trip. The travel agent (the first commission the hotel pays) books the lodging reservation through one of the switch companies (the second commission), which in turn is routed through an airline's global distribution network (the third commission) to the hotel chain's CRO (the fourth commission) and ultimately to the ski resort hotel itself. In an effort to save on all of these commissions, hotels are developing direct booking vehicles (such as web pages) that book reservations directly into the hotel's in-house reservations department commission-free (see Exhibits 4-6 (a) and (b) and Exhibit 4-7).

**Exhibit 4-6 (a)** ▶
Making reservations online is easy. In this case, go to Fairmonthotels.com and then click on the Fairmont logo. On the pull-down menu entitled "Select a Property," choose the Fairmont Chateau Whistler under "Canada" and then input your dates, room type, and number of occupants. The system searches and presents you with a list of available room types and rates. The web page provides information on the hotel amenities and facilities as well.

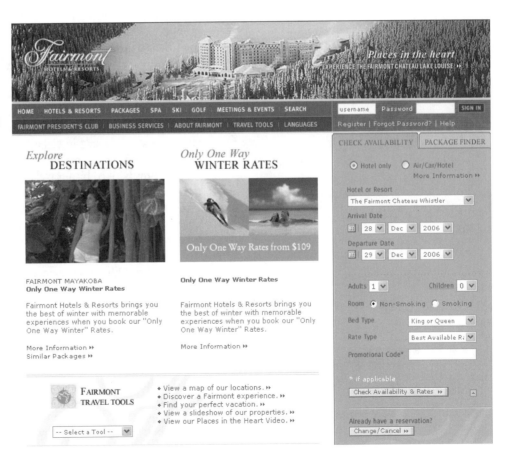

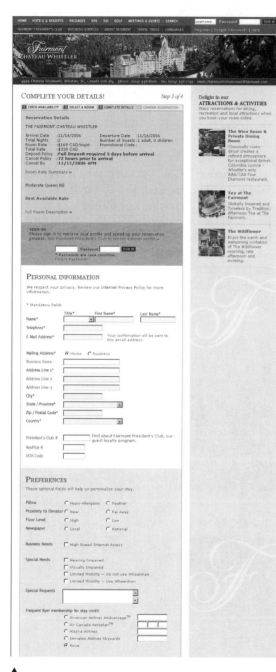

**▲**
**Exhibit 4-6 (b)**
After choosing from the "Select a Property" option in Exhibit 4-6 (a), you will arrive at the "Complete Details" screen, as pictured here. All reservation details are recapped. If you wanted to book the rooms, you would enter your personal information as requested before confirming the reservation.

In the mid-1990s, the airlines began to circumvent travel agencies. Several airlines announced commission caps ranging from $25 to $50 on retail air travel bookings. Some dropped online air reservations commissions to as little as $10. Indeed, in 2002, many airlines refused to pay commissions or only paid commissions on certain routes. This forced travel agents to begin charging fees to their clients, the consumer. Now travellers can avoid this service charge by booking directly with the supplier over the Internet from the comfort of their homes. This is causing a tremendous financial squeeze on travel agencies.

**The Hotel–Travel Agent Relationship** While some experts are predicting a similar reduction or ultimate elimination of travel agent commissions in the hotel industry, that seems doubtful. After all, there are literally tens of thousands of hotels compared with maybe a dozen airlines. Choose a community to visit for a few nights, and you'll be faced with selecting from numerous competing hotel properties (and other complementary options such as camping, bed and breakfasts, hostels, etc.). Even hotels working within the same chain or brand are, in essence, in competition with each other for limited travel dollars. Hotels therefore cannot afford to limit their chances of selling rooms by limiting the global distribution options they have in place. This discussion is expanded later in the section entitled "Automated Revenue Management Systems."

Travel agents are one of the major sources of hotel reservations. Travel agent bookings represent about 20 percent of all hotel rooms booked in Canada. Hotels pay a 10 percent commission—more in the off-season to generate volume—for all rooms booked by a travel agency. Fees are not governmentally regulated. Amounts paid vary from property to property and even within the same property over time. **Overrides,** additional points of 10 to 15 percent, are paid to encourage high levels of business from one agency.

Guests pay no direct charge to the agency for its service, although some agencies have started to charge fees for all services (not just for commission-less airline ticket bookings). Two areas of contention emerge from this relationship. One is a marketing problem; the other is a bookkeeping problem.

There are several marketing problems. Hotels complain that travel agencies (TAs) send business chiefly during the hotel's busy periods. Additional reservations are not needed then, and certainly not if they require a commission. According to the agents, hotels befriend them only when there is no business

**Exhibit 4-7** ▶

Some Interesting Facts
Related to Internet Hotel
Bookings.

- More than two thirds of all internet hotel bookings are for rooms selling below $100 per night.
- While the ADR for hotel rooms has been growing at roughly 7 percent per year, online internet hotel room rates have been growing more slowly—only 5 percent per year.
- Hotel rooms booked over the Internet sell for an average 2 percent lower rate than hotel rooms booked through other GDS channels.
- For rooms selling for $301 and higher, the internet actually sells a higher ADR than for hotel rooms booked through other GDS channels.
- The average length of stay for internet hotel room bookings is 2.1 nights. Hotel rooms booked through other GDS channels have an average length of stay of 2.2 nights.

and ignore them and their customers—who incidentally are also hotel guests—as soon as volume recovers.

If the travel agent's repeat bookings are few and widely spaced, commission cheques are small. Hotels find the cost of processing such cheques to be greater than the amount of the commission itself. Hotels also have problems with some bookings when they originate with unknown agencies whose credit status is unproven. For these and for other accounting reasons that are reviewed in a later chapter, commission payments are not as prompt as TAs would like them to be. Prompt, accurate payment heads the agenda of every travel agency–hotel meeting.

The macro view is rosier. Lodging industry payments to the travel industry increase each year. Hotels pay billions of dollars annually to the tens of thousands of individual TAs. Unfortunately for the client, those payments dictate which hotel the agency selects. If the guest has no preference (and most do not), the hotel that pays commissions promptly will be the one the agency selects.

The system operates through a patchwork of informal relationships. Few formal agreements are in place. Many hoteliers believe that they are in direct competition with the travel agent, fighting for the same business and paying a commission to boot. The appearance of powerful mega-agencies and consortiums of agencies are supporting that kind of thinking. Large-volume dealers stand toe to toe with national hotel chains. By securing the travel contracts of small and large corporations, these mega-agencies squeeze discounted rates from the national hotel chains anxious to get or retain a piece of the business.

**In-House Reservations Centre** No matter what their affiliation or level of automation, all hotels have some system for accepting direct or in-house reservations. In certain properties, the number of in-house reservations is quite minimal. In other operations, however, the bulk of hotel rooms are sold through the in-house reservations centre. This is especially true with non-affiliated, independent hotels where there is no CRS or where the CRS represents a small percentage of all reservations.

Direct or in-house reservations are also taken in quantity by hotels with large group sales business. Such business is generated by the hotel's own sales department, and those bookings bypass the CRS. For this reason, in-house reservationists have been incorporated into the sales departments of several hotel chains.

Experienced shoppers often call the hotel directly. The reservationist is more informed about the property. He or she has one hotel, whereas the CRS agent has hundreds or even thousands. If the hotel is full, reservations might be refused by the CRO but still be accepted on site.

A reservations manager, or supervisor, heads the division, which might number as many as a dozen persons. Large operations permit a degree of specialization, but the size scales downward until the room clerk alone carries out the function. Reports and room status computations may be the responsibility of one group of employees, and others may tend solely to tour groups. More often, several of these jobs are combined into one or two positions.

**Central Reservations System** The central reservations system (CRS) has historically been referred to as the central reservations office (CRO). Although there is a distinction between these two terms, today's jargon has made them almost fully interchangeable. Most managers refer to their central reservations centre as the CRS.

In reality, the CRS is the entire system, including all of the link-ups, **software**, switches, and nuances that will be described in this chapter. The CRO is the hotel chain's portion of this overall system. The CRO is the actual office or site at which the chain's reservationists operate (see Exhibit 4-8).

**Exhibit 4-8**
Central reservations offices (CROs) like this one may employ hundreds of reservationists. The office shown here is the global CRO for Fairmont Hotels and Resorts located in New Brunswick. A typical CRO takes less than three minutes per call and may handle 20 million calls annually.
▼

Historically, most chains maintained one CRO. Guests accessed the office simply by dialling the toll-free number that the chain advertised. It was not uncommon for one CRO to receive several million phone calls per year. That is a lot of telephone activity!

Therefore, CROs needed to locate in an area with a great capacity for telephone volume. In the United States, this area was the Midwest. The Midwest, especially Omaha, Nebraska, developed into a major central reservations hub because of the excess equipment in the area. The Bell system had unused capacity as a result of the massive defence grid built to accommodate the armed forces. With a promise of exceptionally good service and the support of the telephone system, hotel companies began opening reservations centres in the late 1960s. This created a specialized labour pool, making the area even more attractive. Four Seasons Hotels has its international CRO in Toronto, while Fairmont Hotels and Resorts has its CRO in New Brunswick.

Even today, Midwestern cities such as Omaha and Kansas City house a large percentage of the United States' CROs. However, as call volumes rose in the 1980s, most chains found themselves establishing several CROs scattered nationwide and even globally (England and India have both become major worldwide call centre regions). Today, the numbers are staggering. Some of the larger lodging chains boast more than 2 million calls per month and book well in excess of 1 million reservations per month.

**Processing the Call** Reservations agents receive incoming calls and usually process them in two to three minutes. They are assisted with incoming telephone calls by sophisticated telephone switching equipment. During busy call periods, automated telephone systems answer the calls and may segregate the callers according to a variety of options. The caller is asked to listen to the options and then select among them by pressing a specific number on the telephone keypad. Large chains use the telephone system to segregate callers according to the hotel brand in which they are most interested. Another common way to separate callers is according to whether their reservations are for a domestic hotel property, an American hotel, a European hotel, an Asian property, a Latin American operation, and so on.

Once callers have been properly routed, they may be placed on hold for the next available reservationist. During the holding period, a recording provides information about the chain, special discount periods, new hotel construction, and the like. Automatic call distributor equipment eventually routes the telephone call to the next available reservationist.

Time is money, with labour and telephone lines the primary costs of CROs. Therefore, the reservations manager battles to reduce the time allotted to each call. A sign in one office reads: "Talk time yesterday, 1.8 [meaning minutes]. During the last hour, 2.2. This hour, 2.1." Actually, more sophisticated devices are available. Some computer management systems monitor each agent, providing data on the number of calls taken, the time used per call taken, and the amount of post-call time needed to complete the reservation. However, employee evaluations must not be judged on time alone. Systems should evaluate the percentage of the agent's calls that result in firm bookings and the relationship of the agent's average room rate to the average being sold by the entire centre (office).

Reservations centres charge a fee for each reservation booked. Since the centre is usually a separate subsidiary of the corporate parent, even company-owned properties pay a fee of several dollars per booking. Franchisors often get more than just the booking fee. A monthly fee on each room plus a percentage of gross room sales may also be charged. Franchisees complain about the fee schedule, but the reservations system is the major attraction of franchising.

**The Hotel Representative** Although less common than in years past, hotels might maintain sales offices in distant cities, sending reservations from these offices to the hotel. Casino hotels usually maintain such offices in nearby cities: New York for Atlantic City, Los Angeles for Las Vegas. Casinos in Canada, such as those in Windsor and Rama, use toll-free numbers that connect callers to the casino's reservations office for group bookings.

Hotels more often establish their presence in other locations through the use of a **representative (rep)**. This person, or company, functions much as the traditional product representative, as a spokesperson and salesperson for many non-competing brands. Utell International is one well-known rep.

When many non-competitors (same-quality hotels in separate cities) associate with one particular rep, another alternative emerges. The independents band together to market the membership under one umbrella. Preferred Hotels and Resorts and Leading Hotels of the World are good examples of this kind of group. In Canada, you find member groups such as Ontario's Finest Inns (Ontariosfinestinns.com) that host websites for their member properties and provide marketing expertise and group buying discounts. These are non-profit affiliations.

The rep and the hotel negotiate a fee schedule, although a fee plus commission is not unusual. There may also be an initial membership fee. For that charge, the rep provides many sales and marketing services, including trade-show representation. Most important, the rep provides the CRO that the independent hotel lacks. Some international reps even service chains because the international rep provides language operators overseas and settles with travel agents in the currency of the local area. These are capabilities that the chain reservations office may not have.

Technology, with its access to travel agencies, transportation facilities, and company travel departments, is the key to the reservations business. Reps maintain their own systems, which they interface electronically with one or more airline computer systems, something quite difficult for the independent hotel to do.

**Independent Reservations Services** Membership in a CRS is one of the major advantages that chain-affiliated properties have over independent operations. The CRS provides each affiliated property access to sophisticated airline distribution systems, hundreds of thousands of travel agents, a convenient toll-free telephone number for potential customers, automated rate and inventory data, and a wealth of other automated benefits. Yet CRSs are extremely expensive, and the cost of developing a CRS is prohibitive for most small chains and independent operations.

Smaller chains can provide better guest service at a lower cost by leasing the reservations service. Leasing from an independent reservations service is commonly referred to as *outsourcing*. It makes sense for independent properties and small and new lodging chains. For example, Fairmont, Delta, and Princess hotels in Canada use Pegasus Solutions. In 1997, Utell International merged with Anasazi Inc. to become REZsolutions, which was purchased by Pegasus Solutions in 2000.

For hotel rep companies—Utell International (Utell.com), for example—the move is a natural extension of their primary role and should represent economies for each of their clients. UtellVision is a computerized reservations system for Utell member hotels. The system displays two screens simultaneously. The top screen is a series of high-resolution pictures of the member hotel and maps of the surrounding areas; on the bottom is an online reservations availability screen.

Independent hotels and small chains that join a private reservations service expect to gain efficiency and economies of scale, and they generally do experience a number of cost-saving benefits. They save significant investment in hardware and software by joining rather than developing their own system. They save operating and training costs. Reservations processing is more efficient due to the massive computer capacity of the independent reservations service. And salesmanship is enhanced by joining a group of professionally trained agents. If the independent reservation service is also an ASP, even more benefits are available to the small chain: the property management system database is web-accessible, single-imaging allows all users access to the same information, and yield management decisions can be made on a chain-wide basis. Refer to the discussion of ASPs earlier in this chapter (see Exhibit 4-4).

## Other Trends in Electronic Reservations

In just one week, the average North American adult is exposed to more information than a person living 100 years ago might have been exposed to in a lifetime. That statistical analogy speaks volumes in terms of the speed and quantity of information available today. And the trend will certainly continue. From voice recognition to "mapping" software, the future is anyone's guess.

**Voice Recognition** Amazing progress has been achieved in the area of automated voice recognition. Currently there are systems in place that can recognize tens of thousands of words spoken by a host of various users. Dragon Systems' NaturallySpeaking and IBM's Via Voice are the two leading personal computer applications. Each can recognize tens of thousands of words (more than 50 000) with virtually 99 percent accuracy (after a few minutes of training and the use of an acoustic optimizer).

We are probably not far from a time when straightforward rooms reservations are routinely handled electronically by voice-recognition and voice-synthesis (talking) systems. Indeed, thousands of voice-recognition systems are now at work across myriad other industries. Bell Canada uses voice recognition to assist the processing of directory assistance calls. Physicians' offices use voice recognition for transcribing detailed medical records. Business corporations use voice recognition for dictating letters.

The voice-recognition reservations program would generate a series of questions for the guest to answer. With each response, the program would acknowledge the answer, allow the guest to make changes as necessary, and generate a new series of questions based on the previous response. In those situations where the computer could not recognize the guest's voice due to a strong accent or other impairment, a fail-safe system would be in place—the guest might press the zero button twice on the telephone keypad, for example, to alert an operator that personal assistance is needed.

The computer system could check availability, quote rates, suggest alternative dates, and thank the guest in a manner similar to the reservationist. Of course, such a system would be significantly less personal than dealing with an actual reservationist.

**Mapping Capabilities** As global distribution systems gain sophistication, options that were previously unavailable (or manually performed) are increasingly being automated. One example of an old manual format now available as an automated system enhancement is *mapping*.

Commonplace requests such as a hotel's physical address, its distance from a popular destination, or specific travel directions were once manual tasks. Central reservations agents, representing chains of hundreds or thousands of hotels, were required to look up such information in databases provided by member properties. This was a slow and generally inefficient method.

Today, modern mapping systems can provide comprehensive geographical, pictorial, and textual information about every member property. Best Western was the first company of its size to offer a mapping feature with its new central reservations system. Now central reservations agents have immediate access to geographically related questions about property locations, distances, travel times, and so on.

Indeed, guests can retrieve the same information themselves automatically by calling any of the chain's 3400 hotels worldwide. For example, a call to the hotel's toll-free number from any location allows customers to determine the Best Western hotel that is closest to their desired destination and to get specific directions to the property.

**Guest History Databases** Another benefit of the global distribution system is the ability for hotels to share **guest history** information. Database information is currently used only within chains. As switch technology improves, guest history data may actually be shared across chains.

Even within a chain, hotels rarely take advantage of their wealth of data. Most management systems allow a guest history function. Standard information required for the reservation becomes a marketing tool, if properly administered. After all, the hotel already knows the guest's name and address, the dates of the last visit, the rate paid, the room type, the number of guests, and the method of payment. Add a bit of marketing information, such as the type of discount package purchased, the special rate or used, and whether the reservation was over a weekend or was a weekend getaway package, and the manager has an enormous amount of marketing data.

From guest history databases to voice recognition, automation is changing the global distribution system and the way in which hoteliers manage the reservations process.

# Automated Revenue Management Systems

An increasingly competitive and complex lodging industry has also changed the way in which hoteliers sell reservations. Rather than the old goal of simply "placing heads in beds," today's hoteliers selectively need to place the right heads in the right beds at the right price. You see, despite the large number of rooms that are available on an annual basis, not every reservation request is accepted. The decision depends on space availability and rate ranges available for the specific dates. An occupancy forecast determines the space situation for the day or days in question. Even if only one day of the sequence is closed, the reservation may be refused and an alternative arrangement offered. This is unfortunate if the declined reservation represented a request for a number of days. It is especially unfortunate if the period in question has only one sold-out date. Then the hotel is essentially trading a profitable, long-term reservation against a potential overbooking situation for one sold-out date. In many cases, the reservationist will override the system and book this type of reservation. Obviously, such a decision would be considered on a case-by-case basis.

In other situations, the sales ability of the reservationist comes into play. The telephone provides a two-way conversation during which the reservationist can gauge the behaviour of the guest. Some guests can be convinced to reserve their chosen date at a slightly higher nightly rate. Other guests' minds can be changed toward a slower occupancy period with the offer of reduced rates.

In any case, guests who cannot be accommodated represent lost revenues. The reservationist attempts to salvage lost reservations in a number of ways—offering premium rates during almost sold-out periods, offering different dates when rates are not as high, or even offering another sister property of the same chain in a nearby community. When all else fails, the reservationist can only thank the caller and ask him or her to try again another time.

Requests for accommodations are sometimes denied even if the house is not full. Most of the hotel's advertised packages are refused if the forecast shows that the house is likely to fill at standard rack rates. The inverse of this is also true. Reservationists must be taught to sell discounted packages or other reduced rates (weekend, commercial, governmental) only on request or when encountering rate resistance.

With a full house, requests from travel agents, to whom the hotel pays a commission, may be regretted. A low priority is assigned to requests from agents who are slow in paying. All reservations are refused if the caller has a poor credit rating, regardless of the occupancy forecast. Busy hotels give preference to higher-paying multiple-occupancy requests over single occupancy.

Casino hotels give preferential treatment to those who are likely to gamble, even to the extent of granting them free accommodations in preference to paying guests who don't play. Non-casino hotels do the same, allotting their scarce space to reservations from certain areas or markets that the hotel is trying to develop. Seasonal resorts quote **in-season** and **off-season rates** and frequently require a minimum length of stay on holiday weekends.

## The Yield Management Revolution

Revenue management, the act of controlling rates and restricting occupancies in an effort to maximize gross rooms revenue, is most commonly referred to as **yield management**. In its simplest form, yield management has been around for decades. Any seasoned manager who increased room rates as occupancy for a given date rose, or who quoted higher rates for holidays and special event periods, or who saved the last few room nights for extended-stay reservations was using yield management. The practice of yield management is not new, but the incorporation of revenue managers into dedicated senior staff positions and the automation of yield management into complex property management systems is.

Organizations were downsized and labour costs reduced during the low cycle of the early 1990s. Despite the squeeze on profits, many hotels added revenue managers (or yield managers) to their organizations (see Exhibit 2-1 on page 50). The revenue offset easily justified the move. Some 15 to 25 percent of recent average daily rate (ADR) growth has been attributed to yield management, the specialty of these new managers. Thus, a 400-room property with an overall 10 percent increase in ADR from, say, $118 to $129.80 could attribute about $2 of the nearly $12 increase directly to the new yield team. Assuming 70 percent occupancy, that produces some $200 000 annually (400 rooms × 70 percent × 365 days × $2). That's a wonderful return on the costs of yield management hardware, software, and new hires!

**A Brief History of Yield Management** As with other businesses, price (hotel room rate) is a major factor in the decision to purchase one product (one hotel) over another. That is especially true in light of the sharper guest segmentation that the industry has experienced over the last decade. Yield management works best when there are distinct market segments to attract. It is the price sensitivity of these market segments that made yield management practices successful in the first place.

**The Airlines' Role** Lodging has adopted yield management concepts from the airlines. Airline rate discounting was widespread in the early 1980s, and that contributed to the array of prices that the airlines found difficult to track. They began to experiment with adjusted rates based on demand forecasts. Discounted tickets purchased far in advance were used to establish a minimum level of seat occupancy and to forecast overall demand. Low and seasonal periods were also discounted. As the plane filled and departure time neared, higher and higher fares were charged. Full price was eventually charged for the remaining seats—a price that would have been virtually impossible to charge when the plane was empty.

Airlines and hotels are much alike. Both have a relatively fixed supply of product (seats and rooms), and both have products that perish with the passage of time. In the 1980s, airlines had one extra edge—large computer capability that was in place and was functional. It takes the capacity of these large systems to simultaneously track occupancy (seat or room) and the variety of price options that both industries market.

Hoteliers have employed price-sensitive concepts for a long, long time. Refining the practices and developing them into a program with rules and triggers, with a knowledge base and a strategy, awaited the superior computer capability of the airlines. Today, most major lodging chains have developed automated yield management systems that rival the best of the airline systems.

**Market Demand**  Airlines and hotels did differ in one respect—their view of the guest. Hotels had previously operated on the belief that their customer was not a discretionary traveller. The guest who came, hoteliers felt, was someone who had to come. Guests did not come merely because the price was reduced enough to lure them into the purchase. Urban hotels, which cater to the least flexible guest, the commercial traveller, first evidenced the change. In desperate need of weekend business, these properties began to market weekend specials to discretionary buyers. The march to yield management had begun.

Yield management has an economic rationale. It assumes that all customers are price conscious—that they are aware of the existence of and the significance of price variations. Furthermore, it assumes that customers are price sensitive—that their buying habits respond to increases and decreases in price.

All things being equal, the guest is motivated by lower prices. Theoretically, when a similar room type is available for a significantly lower rate at an otherwise equal hotel, the guest will select the lower-priced accommodations. In addition, guests who might not have left home at the rack rate are inclined to visit hotels when rates are low. As a result, low-occupancy periods are generally accompanied by lower average room rates.

Each customer class has different degrees of price consciousness and price sensitivity. Earlier discussions on segmentation (see Chapter 1) indicated the wide range of guests to whom the industry appeals. In simple terms, these are the business (corporate) class, the leisure (transient) guest, and the group (tour) buyer.

**Corporate Guests**  The business or corporate customer is less sensitive to price—not unaware of price, just less sensitive to it. Business people must travel when the need arises; they will not go merely because the price is reduced.

Business arrangements may be made only a few days or hours before arrival (see Exhibit 4-9). Location is very important, both to save travel time and to present the proper image. Business travellers need to be near the business centre, which means high-priced real estate and high room rates. These travellers are away from home a good deal. They seek and probably merit a higher level of comfort than the occasional leisure traveller.

**Leisure Guests**  The leisure guest, as the name implies, is 180 degrees removed from the corporate traveller. With leisure guests, lead time is long. Reservation bookings are well planned, with adequate time to shop for the best room rates. This class of guest is flexible as to the time of the trip, the destination of the trip, and the stopping places. These guests may not even use a hotel. High prices might drive them into camping or park facilities. Poor price value might send them to the homes of friends or family.

**Exhibit 4-9** ▶

Booking pattern of corporate travellers during a 30-day period. Although some corporate guests book 30 (or more) days in advance, the majority reserves rooms within a few days of arrival. This 275-room hotel receives approximately 60 percent of its business from corporate guests.

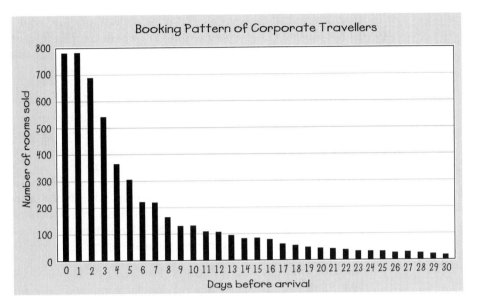

When prices of accommodations, fuel, toll roads, and gasoline are too high, this guest will just stay home.

**Group Guests** *Group business*, the last of the three general classifications, exhibits characteristics of both of the other two categories. That's because the group market forms from components of the business and leisure classifications. From the leisure category come social, fraternal, and hobby associations, sometimes called SMERFs (social, military, educational, religious, and fraternal). From the business segment come professional, union, and governmental groups.

Yield management has changed the interface between the sales department and the group buyer. Based on information from the yield management program, sales must decide to take the business, reject the business, or try to negotiate a different time at a different rate. Saturday arrival for a group might actually prove more profitable at $90 per night, for example, than a Monday arrival (which displaces full rack rate corporate guests) at $115 per night. A well-programmed yield management system should provide the answer. (A more detailed discussion of group business and related automation is available in Chapter 5.)

At issue is whether the discounted room rates requested by the group, plus the value of the group's meeting room and banquet business, is valued at more or less than the forecasted income from normal guests who will be turned away. Yield management systems can answer that question. The discretionary decisions still remain for the salespersons to evaluate. For example, is other new business likely to spin off from this meeting? Is this a single event, or is the hotel doing business with a meeting planner who controls 100 or more meetings per year?

Yield management means that function rooms are no longer booked on a first-come, first-served basis. Neither are guest rooms; there must be a price–occupancy mix.

**Tools for Measuring Results** The task facing the revenue (yield) manager is formidable. Each day represents a new challenge in terms of maximizing both average daily rate and occupancy, and the amount of information available to the revenue manager grows each year. It is no longer enough to understand your own hotel's rate and occupancy for a given period of time; today you must understand how your performance measures against your hotel's *competitive market set*—all competing hotels based on geography (they are proximate to your property) and/or quality or price (they offer a similar product or are similarly priced).

Gone are the days when revenue managers drove past their competitors' hotels and counted parked cars to gauge approximate occupancies. Gone are the days when the front-desk staff made a series of telephone calls to competing properties as an exercise in guessing how many rooms they still had available and for what rates. Instead, today's sophisticated hotels have access to an incredible assortment of reports and subscription services that provide a wealth of previously unavailable data. Thanks almost exclusively to the GDS, there is literally more information available to a well-connected revenue manager than anyone could ever use. You see, information is the by-product of inventorying and selling rooms, and some of the biggest providers of subscription information services are the very providers who sell millions of rooms each year—the GDS.

Let's look at some of the most popular reports.

**PHASER Complete Access Reports**    Provided by a company called Travel-CLICK, the *PHASER Report* is one of several popular formats available through this company. TravelCLICK is the pre-eminent provider of digital media and data solutions to the travel industry. By offering hotels and other travel suppliers detailed competitive reports, TravelCLICK helps hotels position themselves more aggressively within their marketplace.

TravelCLICK pulls its competitive information directly from the GDS (from Sabre and other GDSs), which is used by more than 480 000 (about 98 percent) of the world's travel agents. The report breaks the hotel rates into two categories, GDS and CRS, and the report looks for the lowest available rate in each of these areas. *PHASER Complete Access Reports* provide hotel managers with a custom-designed look at their own hotel as it compares with the competitive market set. Hotel managers can select the competing hotels they wish included in their market set and set the length of time they wish covered in each particular report.

Other features of this report include highlighted rates that have risen or dropped by a user defined amount (e.g., plus or minus $10), total hotel availability status by day in both the GDS and CRS, and details for every rate offered in the CRS by room type across each competitive hotel during the selected time period.

**Smith Travel Research's STAR Reports**    Founded in 1985 as an independent research firm, Smith Travel Research (STR) is one of the industry's leaders in providing accurate information and analyses to the lodging industry. With the most comprehensive database of hotel performance information ever compiled, STR has developed a variety of products and services to meet the needs of hotel revenue managers.

Although many reports used by revenue managers display future data (rates for a set of dates in the near future), *STAR Reports* are based entirely on historical data. This report answers the following questions: How well did I do in terms of average daily rate, occupancy, and RevPar against my competitors last week? Last month? Last year? Another key distinction is that *STAR Reports* do not share specific performance data for each competing property. Rather, all data are couched in aggregate, summary findings. In other words, a hotel can see how well it performed against the competitive market set of hotels, but cannot see how well each competing hotel performed individually (only as a set of hotels).

There are actually a series of *STAR Reports* providing a variety of ways of looking at historical data. The *STAR Trend Report,* for example, compares occupancy, ADR, and RevPar for a manager's property against the competitive market set for a series of months in the past. This report also provides an index (a measure of market penetration) that shows how well a manager's property performed against the competition (on a scale where 1.0 is performing exactly "on-market," a manager would hope to see numbers like 1.2 or 1.3, suggesting that his or her property performed 20 or 30 percent better than the market average).

The *STAR Competitive Set Positioning Report* shares similar data as listed above, but places the manager's property in rank order against competing hotels in the market set. The *DaySTAR Weekday/Weekend Report* compares competitive hotels by their success in filling rooms during the midweek and weekends. A number of other *STAR Reports* are available as well. In fact, revenue managers are excited about a new report still under development that compares how well their hotel performs against the competition in terms of transient versus group room bookings.

**Travel Information Management Services (TIMS)**  The *TIMS Report* also pulls its data directly from Sabre through an automated process. Rates are gathered through the CRS seamless connection, and the report displays discounts and lowest available rates for all hotels in the competitive market set.

**Hotelligence Report**  This is another popular report available through Travel-CLICK (see "PHASER Complete Access Reports" above). Not only does this report provide a wealth of information unavailable in other reports, but it is an extremely attractive report as well (see Exhibit 4-10). It compares a manager's rooms available with those available in the competitive market set. This establishes market share, and much of the report then compares actual history with theoretical market share. Data for the *Hotelligence Report* comes directly from Galileo, Sabre, and Worldspan—and the information from these three sources can be viewed both individually and in aggregate.

Specifically, the report compares room nights sold for the manager's hotel against room nights sold across the competitive set. Again, if the manager's hotel exceeds the theoretical market share, the report will show a market penetration of greater than 1.0. Similar statistics are available comparing overall revenue (yield) in the competitive set of hotels as well as average daily rate. Another thing this report does quite well is to show growth trends for current periods against similar periods the previous year.

**Expedia Competitive Price Grid Report**  For hotels that sell rooms through Expedia, this has become a valuable report. The primary reason a hotel wants to see the rates it is listing in Expedia, as well as the rates listed by its competitors, is to manage its own hotel-direct website. You see, the revenue manager must be certain that best available rates listed on Expedia are not substantially lower than best available rates listed on the hotel's own website. If rates on Expedia are significantly lower, the hotel is shooting itself in the foot by training its future guests to visit other websites (Expedia, for example) as opposed to visiting its own hotel-direct website. Remember, the hotel saves commission fees when it encourages guests to book rooms through the hotel's own website.

**Other Reports**  Listed here are several other popular reports used by today's revenue managers:

- Sabre.Net Reports
- Hotel Information Service (HIS) Reports
- CheckRate
- TrendFx

# THE HOTELLIGENCE REPORT

*Data Solutions for the Digital World*

| Subscriber | Vendor Code | GDS | Total Rooms | Data Exists | | | | | | | | | | | | | Fair Share |
|---|---|---|---|---|---|---|---|---|---|---|---|---|---|---|---|---|---|
| | | | | J-0 | F-0 | M-0 | A-0 | M-0 | J-0 | J-0 | A-0 | S-0 | O-0 | N-0 | D-0 | J-0 | |
| The Premiere Hotel | TC | Galileo | | Y | Y | Y | Y | Y | Y | Y | Y | Y | Y | Y | Y | Y | |
| First Avenue | TC | SABRE | 168 | Y | Y | Y | Y | Y | Y | Y | Y | Y | Y | Y | Y | Y | 11.4% |
| Chicago, IL 60601 | TC | Worldspan | | Y | Y | Y | Y | Y | Y | Y | Y | Y | Y | Y | Y | Y | |

**Competitive Set**

| Subscriber | Vendor Code | GDS | Total Rooms | Data Exists | | | | | | | | | | | | | Fair Share |
|---|---|---|---|---|---|---|---|---|---|---|---|---|---|---|---|---|---|
| Luxury Suites | AM | Galileo | | Y | Y | Y | Y | Y | Y | Y | Y | Y | Y | Y | Y | Y | |
| 392 Hampshire Blvd. | AM | SABRE | 121 | Y | Y | Y | Y | Y | Y | Y | Y | Y | Y | Y | Y | Y | 8.2% |
| Chicago, IL 60601 | AM | Worldspan | | Y | Y | Y | Y | Y | Y | Y | Y | Y | Y | Y | Y | Y | |
| Presidential Towers | PS | Galileo | | Y | Y | Y | Y | Y | Y | Y | Y | Y | Y | Y | Y | Y | |
| 6457 Washington Square | PS | SABRE | 154 | Y | Y | Y | Y | Y | Y | Y | Y | Y | Y | Y | Y | Y | 10.4% |
| Chicago, IL 60601 | PS | Worldspan | | Y | Y | Y | Y | Y | Y | Y | Y | Y | Y | Y | Y | Y | |
| Executive Suites | EX | Galileo | | Y | Y | Y | Y | Y | Y | Y | Y | Y | Y | Y | Y | Y | |
| 893 Circle Bend | EX | SABRE | 370 | Y | Y | Y | Y | Y | Y | Y | Y | Y | Y | Y | Y | Y | 25.0% |
| Chicago, IL 60601 | XE | Worldspan | | Y | Y | Y | Y | Y | Y | Y | Y | Y | Y | Y | Y | Y | |
| Capitol Towers | RR | Galileo | | Y | Y | Y | Y | Y | Y | Y | Y | Y | Y | Y | Y | Y | |
| 3000 Wilson Avenue | RR | SABRE | 140 | Y | Y | Y | Y | Y | Y | Y | Y | Y | Y | Y | Y | Y | 9.5% |
| Chicago, IL 60601 | RR | Worldspan | | Y | Y | Y | Y | Y | Y | Y | Y | Y | Y | Y | Y | Y | |
| The Tower | TT | Galileo | | Y | Y | Y | Y | Y | Y | Y | Y | Y | Y | Y | Y | Y | |
| 4101 Hurst Avenue | TT | SABRE | 237 | Y | Y | Y | Y | Y | Y | Y | Y | Y | Y | Y | Y | Y | 16.0% |
| Chicago, IL 60601 | TT | Worldspan | | Y | Y | Y | Y | Y | Y | Y | Y | Y | Y | Y | Y | Y | |
| Regal Plaza | RQ | Galileo | | Y | Y | Y | Y | Y | Y | Y | Y | Y | Y | Y | Y | Y | |
| 632 Forbes Avenue | RQ | SABRE | 288 | Y | Y | Y | Y | Y | Y | Y | Y | Y | Y | Y | Y | Y | 19.5% |
| Chicago, IL 60563 | RQ | Worldspan | | Y | Y | Y | Y | Y | Y | Y | Y | Y | Y | Y | Y | Y | |

▲

**Exhibit 4-10 (a)**

TravelCLICK's *Hotelligence Report* helps hotel executives make high-impact strategic and operational decisions as well as improve revenue management performance through the major GDSs. These reports are extremely useful for developing effective sales and marketing programs based on competitive information, evaluating the impact of promotional offers, and conducting performance benchmarking to fine-tune products and services.

The *Hotelligence Report* is 13 pages long—shown here are the first two pages. The first page (above) displays the subscriber hotel (the fictitious Premiere Hotel), lists competing hotels (Luxury Suites, etc.), and shows that information is available for each property across the dates shown (indicated by Y, as in Yes).

The second page (see Exhibit 4-10(b)) displays the Premiere Hotel's fair market share (11.4 percent) as compared with its competitive set. However, you'll notice that it sold far more rooms (market penetration) than suggested by its fair share—it sold 1.549 rooms for every 1 room it "should" have been able to sell against its competition. However, you will also note that the Premiere Hotel did less well when it comes to average room rate (bottom left corner of page 2).

Notes: Galileo figures include reservations made through Galileo and Apollo. Sabre figures include reservations made through Abacus and Axess. Total rooms are used from the TravelCLICK hotel database. All reservations displayed on the following pages are net of cancels in each GDS. Each reservation represents a stay that occurred during the month shown on the report (date of arrival). "Y" signifies that the hotel received at least one booking from the respective GDS during the month. Fair Share is calculated using the Total Rooms from the TravelCLICK hotel database.

**The Price–Occupancy Mix** Yield is calculated by multiplying occupancy (let's say 65 percent for a 250-room hotel) by average daily rate (let's say that the ADR is $75). In this example, yield is $12 187.50 per day. Yield can be increased by raising rates when occupancy (demand) is high. Rates are raised by refusing packages, requiring minimum lengths of stay, and charging groups the full rate without discounts. When occupancy (demand) is low, prices are dropped by promoting packages, seeking out price-sensitive

**Exhibit 4-10 (b)** ▶

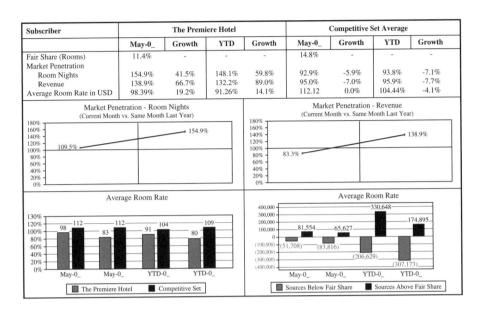

| Subscriber | The Premiere Hotel | | | | Competitive Set Average | | | |
|---|---|---|---|---|---|---|---|---|
| | May-0_ | Growth | YTD | Growth | May-0_ | Growth | YTD | Growth |
| Fair Share (Rooms) | 11.4% | - | - | - | 14.8% | - | - | - |
| Market Penetration | | | | | | | | |
| Room Nights | 154.9% | 41.5% | 148.1% | 59.8% | 92.9% | -5.9% | 93.8% | -7.1% |
| Revenue | 138.9% | 66.7% | 132.2% | 89.0% | 95.0% | -7.0% | 95.9% | -7.7% |
| Average Room Rate in USD | 98.39% | 19.2% | 91.26% | 14.1% | 112.12 | 0.0% | 104.44% | -4.1% |

groups, and creating special promotional rates. That's the dichotomy of the lodging industry: When times are good (high occupancy), they are very good (because with high occupancy comes high rate). Conversely, when times are bad (low demand), times are very bad (because all of the hotel's competitors are also lowering their prices).

Since yield is the product of the two elements, equilibrium is obtainable by increasing one factor when the other decreases. Exhibit 4-11 illustrates the mathematics. Yield in all three cases appears to be identical. With the same room revenue, a management choice between high ADR and high occupancy needs to be made.

All managers will not view the values in Exhibit 4-11 as being equal. Some would prefer the higher occupancy to the higher rate. Higher occupancy means more persons. More guests translate into more food and beverage revenue, more telephone use, more calls for laundry and dry cleaning. More guests mean more **greens fees**, more amusement park admissions, or more money spent in the casino. For these reasons, some hotels charge the same rate for occupancy by one or two persons.

A different group of operators would prefer to strengthen their ADR. These managers feel that ADR is a barometer of a property's service and quality levels. With the lower occupancy that accompanies higher ADR, hotels save on variable costs such as

| Hotel | Average Daily Rate | Percent Occupancy | Monthly Gross Yield | Potential Revenue | Yield Percent |
|---|---|---|---|---|---|
| A | $ 75 | 65.00 | $377 812.50 | $620 000 | 60.9 |
| B | 100 | 48.75 | 377 812.50 | 620 000 | 60.9 |
| C | 50 | 97.50 | 377 812.50 | 620 000 | 60.9 |

▲
**Exhibit 4-11**
Price–occupancy mix: Yield is the product of occupancy times room rate. Management decides whether a higher rate (ADR) or a higher occupancy is preferable. This exhibit assumes 250 rooms and a 31-day month. Potential revenue assumes 100 percent occupancy at an $80 ideal rate.

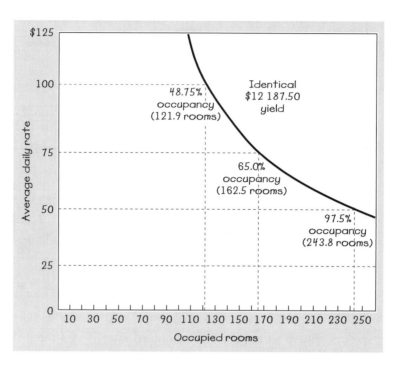

power, wear and tear on furniture and equipment, room amenities, laundry/linen costs, and staffing.

Clearly, price–occupancy mix is not a simple, single decision. Dropping rates to increase occupancy might not be the choice of every manager. Indeed, the manager might take that option at one hotel but not at another. Variations in the facilities of the hotel, in its client base, and in the perspective of its management will determine the policies to be applied.

**Revenue per Available Room** Yield is usually expressed in terms of gross revenue per day, per month, or per year (see Exhibit 4-11). However, there is a special advantage to quoting yield in terms of revenue per available room (**RevPar**). RevPar (see also Chapter 1) combines occupancy and average daily rate into a single number. Continuing the illustration: A 250-room hotel at 65 percent occupancy and $75 ADR produces revenue per available room (RevPar) of $48.75 (65 percent × $75).

Before the popularization of RevPar in the mid-1990s, hotel managers tended toward one of the two camps described above. They migrated either toward higher occupancies or toward higher ADRs. Managers who work toward maximizing RevPar, however, must seek a balance or equilibrium between occupancy and rate (see Exhibit 4-12).

The only difference between calculating yield and RevPar is that yield incorporates the number of hotel rooms into the calculation, whereas RevPar looks at revenue per available room. In fact, if you take RevPar for any given day and multiply it by the number of rooms available in the hotel, the product is that day's yield. To demonstrate, take the $48.75 RevPar calculated above in our ongoing example and multiply it by the 250 rooms available. The product is the same $12 187.50 yield calculated several paragraphs above in the discussion of price–occupancy mix.

The RevPar calculation is also beneficial to management as a quick-and-dirty glimpse into the hotel's success on any given day. If the hotel knows its fixed costs on a per-room, per-day basis (fixed costs include administrative salaries, mortgage debt, fixed franchise fees, and insurance, to name a few), it can quickly gauge how much, if any, of the RevPar can be contributed toward variable costs and profits. In our ongoing example, if RevPar is $48.75 and fixed costs are $23.25, then $25.50 per available room can be contributed toward variable costs and profit. Management can readily see how well the hotel performed on that given day.

## Automated Yield Management Systems

As far back as 1998, a study of hotel sales and marketing departments found that 80 percent of hotels were using yield management technology to assist their decision process when booking group business.[3] The figure begins to approach 100 percent when individual hotel room nights booked through chains or large independent properties are included. Clearly, yield management is an expense worth incurring.

Automated yield or revenue management systems are tools that aid management decision making. Indeed, in the absence of management, these systems can automatically change rates, restrict room availability, and monitor reservation activity. Here's a brief list of the functions generally attributable to yield management systems. The yield management system:

- establishes and monitors the hotel's rate structure.
- continually monitors reservations activity and sets inventory controls as needed (even in the absence of management approval).
- aids rate negotiations with travel wholesalers and group bookings.
- monitors and restricts the number of reservations that can be taken for any particular room night or room rate/room type.
- allows reservationists the tools necessary to be salespersons rather than mere order-takers.
- matches the right room product and rate with customers' needs and sensitivities.

Profits increase in all hotels that implement automated yield management systems. Certain properties, however, fare better than others. Generally, a property needs to have several characteristics in place to experience high returns on its investment in a yield management system. Some of these characteristics include a demand for rooms that can easily be segmented into distinct markets, a long lead time for some types of reservations, a variety of room types and associated rates, and high-occupancy/low-occupancy periods throughout the year.

**Artificial Intelligence Systems**   Yield management systems allow for instantaneous response to changing conditions. Seven days a week, 24 hours a day, the system compares actual performance with forecasted assumptions and adjusts rates accordingly. To make these changes, advanced computer systems use either standard logical functions or state-of-the-art artificial intelligence operations. Artificial intelligence (AI) or expert systems use stored data that have been developed over a period of time to form rules that govern yield management decisions.

Today's expert systems possess true artificial intelligence. They literally think through demand, formulate decisions, and provide the user with an opportunity to talk with the computer. Below is a list of the special features generally found in an expert yield management system. The expert system:

1. is able to deal not just with quantitative facts but with qualitative data as well.

2. includes an analysis of incomplete data when formulating a decision.

3. explains to the user how a given conclusion was reached.

4. allows a two-way communication interface with the user.

5. applies programmable rules and triggers to its set of facts.

6. can override basic rules and triggers when additional decision criteria warrant.

7. maintains a database of historical facts, including the following:

  • Demand for similar periods over a number of past years.

  • Room nights lost (regrets) through both in-house reservations and chain (1-800) sources over a number of past years.

  • Changes to demand (by various market segments) as forecasted reservations dates close in.

  • The ratio and demand for transient (leisure) room nights versus corporate room nights over a number of past years.

  • The demand for group room blocks (and the ratio of group room block "pick-ups") over a number of past years.

**Rules and Triggers**  The computer compares actual reservations activity with budgeted forecasts. When a particular date or period falls outside the rules for that time frame, the computer flags it. Once flagged, most systems will print a management report identifying periods that are exceptions to the forecast. In addition, expert systems will automatically change rates and other sales tools. The immediacy of the expert system is a major advantage. Hundreds and even thousands of dollars may be lost in the time it takes management to approve a given rate change. The expert system acts first and takes questions later.

To establish rules or triggers for the system to use, management must first segment the room count into market types. For example, a typical 250-room property might block 25 rooms for discounting to government guests or IT packages, 50 rooms for transient (leisure) guests, 100 rooms for business (corporate) customers, and the remaining 75 rooms for sale to tour groups and convention business.

Different guidelines are then placed on each of these market segments. To illustrate, assume that management expects 25 percent of the transient room block to fill by, say, 181 days out (days before arrival). It also expects that 91 days before arrival, transient rooms will be 60 percent sold, and by 61 days out, the entire block will be 90 percent reserved. These are the parameters that management has forecasted for transient rooms; its expectations for business rooms may be completely different. Once these triggers are identified, they are programmed into the yield management system. The computer then evaluates the effects of changing demand and acts accordingly. If, for example, 181 days out the transient room block was 35 percent reserved, the computer would flag the date as a potentially busy period and increase rates for all remaining rooms. How much the rates increase is also subject to advanced programming.

**Centralized Yield Management**  As the trend toward seamless connectivity, single-imaging, last room availability, and centralized property management systems (ASPs) becomes more prevalent, so too is the trend toward centrally driven corporate yield management systems. At the outset, centralized yield management looks much the same. As rooms are sold through in-house reservations (at the property) or the CRO, changes in inventory are automatically reflected in the centralized yield management system. As room types or dates begin to fill, the centralized system changes rates and inventory restrictions for the individual property. Similarly, if property-level management wants to tap into its own yield statistics and manually alter rates or restrictions, nothing prevents that.

What appears quite similar on the surface actually affords the chain and individual property unique advantages. Through centralized yield management, the entire global distribution system (GDS) becomes a yield management tool. In essence, the in-house **property management system** (**PMS**), the CRS, and the GDS are all reading from the same page. The chain can run a whole series of reports, which improves its understanding of certain market segments, lodging categories, dates, and trends. Price-sensitive group room blocks can be moved to sister properties across the chain rather than being lost because one hotel in one particular city was not able to meet its price on a given date.

**Yield Management Controls**   Aside from simply adjusting the room rate, hotels have several other tools with which they work. One common tool is **boxing** the date. Boxing dates (no through bookings are allowed) is another control device open to the reservations manager. Reservations on either side of the boxed day are not allowed to spill into that date. For example, if Wednesday, April 7, is anticipated as a heavy arrival date, the hotel might box it. Rooms sold for Monday or Tuesday must check out by Wednesday; rooms sold for Thursday or Friday cannot arrive a day earlier. Dates are blocked in anticipation of a mass of arrivals, usually a convention or group movement that could not be accommodated through the normal flow of departures. With such heavy arrivals, no one is permitted to check in before that day and stay through the boxed day, even though there is more than enough space on those previous days.

Another tool available to the reservations department is closing a specific date to arrival. Dates that are closed to arrival allow the guest to stay through by arriving on a previous date. Closed to arrival is used as a technique for improving occupancy on preceding nights before a major holiday or event.

A final example of reservations sales tools is the minimum length of stay. This technique is designed to improve occupancy on nights preceding and following a major event or holiday by requiring guests to book a minimum number of nights. For example, if New Year's Eve has a three-day minimum length of stay, the hotel will probably improve occupancies on December 30 and January 1.

**Nests and Hurdles**   Also known as *bid pricing, hurdle pricing,* or *inventory nesting,* this sophisticated yield management approach takes normal room allocations to a new level. By referring to Exhibit 4-13, let's assume that Hurdle Hotel is experiencing an unusually high demand for corporate rooms and has sold out of the $120 rate (Monday) while still offering discounted and rack rate rooms. It would make little sense to turn down a corporate reservation request at $120 while still accepting discounted rooms at $60, but that is exactly what might happen if room allocations are not continually monitored. That's where inventory nesting comes in. By incorporating a set of nesting rules, the property can ensure that high-rate rooms are never closed for sale when lower-rate rooms are still open.

### Data for the 250-Room Hurdle Hotel

|  | Discounted Rooms | Corporate Guests | Rack Rate |
|---|---|---|---|
| Normal rate structure | $60 | $120 | $150 |
| Normal room allocations | 75 | 100 | 75 |
| Current room demand |  |  |  |
| Monday (hurdle price is $150) | 60 | 100 | 57 |
| Tuesday (hurdle price is $120) | 53 | 82 | 48 |
| Wednesday (hurdle price is $60) | 34 | 51 | 22 |

The newest trend in nesting does away with the old concept of room allocations by market segment. Instead, a minimum rate, or *hurdle point,* is established for each day. Reservations with a value above the hurdle are accepted; reservations with a value below the hurdle are rejected. In Exhibit 4-13, if the hurdle point were set at or below $60, all room types would be available. If the hurdle were raised to $100, the discounted rooms would be closed while corporate and rack rates remained available.

Rather than selling rooms according to unreserved market segment allocations, the hurdle concept sells rooms based on total property demand. When demand is low, the hurdle price is low. When demand is high, the hurdle price is high. In essence, the hurdle price represents the theoretical price of the last room expected to sell that day. If the hotel expects to fill, the hurdle point might be set at full rack rate. A person making a reservation who is only willing to pay a lower rate is worth less to the hotel than the future value of the last room, and therefore such a reservation would be denied.

The real beauty of hurdle pricing is that hurdles can be added for subsequent days. For example, in Exhibit 4-13, let's say that the hotel is close to full on Monday (hurdle point $150), somewhat less full on Tuesday (hurdle point $120), and wide open on Wednesday (hurdle point $60). A guest wanting to stay Monday for one night only would need to pay $150 to get a reservation for the night. However, a guest checking in on Monday for three nights would get the benefit of adding the hurdles for those three nights. By adding $150 for the first night plus $120 for the second and $60 for the third night, this three-night reservation would pay a rate of $110 per night or possibly a different rate for each of three nights ($150, $120, and $60, respectively).

**Fenced Rates** A relatively new addition to the list of reservations sales tools has migrated to hotels from the airline industry. Fences or **fenced rates** are logical rules or restrictions that provide a series of options to the guest. Guests are not forced to select these options; their rate is determined by which (if any) options they choose.

As with yield management systems themselves, the airlines originated fenced rates. Examples of airline fenced rates might include the passenger who chose a lower but non-refundable fare, a customer who purchased a ticket at least 21 days in advance to receive a special rate, or someone who stayed over on a Saturday night to take full advantage of the best price.

Fenced rates are relatively new to the lodging industry. However, the few chains using them seem quite satisfied with their results. It will probably be standard practice in the future to offer discounts for advance purchases and non-refundable and unchangeable reservations.

# Summary

Sophisticated automation is changing the methods by which reservations are requested and accepted. Never before have hotels had reservations coming into their properties from so many varied directions. The introduction of last-room-availability technology has started a revolution in hotel reservations management.

Last room availability is real-time communication between central reservations offices (CROs) and property-level reservations systems. With last room availability, the entire global distribution system (GDS) can identify room types and rates at a member hotel and can literally sell to the very last available room. Electronic switch technology has afforded the industry increased access to member hotels. Travel agents, airlines, and subscription online services are all able to electronically access a property's reservations system.

With yield or revenue management (yield equals average room rate times the number of rooms sold), room prices change as a function of lead time and demand. Vacationing families, tour groups, and seniors often know as far as one year in advance their exact date and location of travel. These customers generally book early enough to take advantage of special discounts or packages; yield management works to their advantage. Conversely, corporate travellers frequently book accommodations at the last moment. In their case, yield management works against them by charging maximum rates to last-minute bookings when the hotel is nearing full occupancy.

# Questions and Problems

1. On busy nights, it is not uncommon for a front-office manager to remove several rooms from availability. Usually, the manager creates a fictitious reservation, thereby "selling" the rooms and removing them from availability. By holding on to a few rooms, the manager feels that he or she is in a better position to accommodate a special guest or request when the hotel is sold out. Even though the reason that management holds rooms may be very honourable, do you believe this practice undermines the very basis of last-room-availability technology? Explain your answer.

2. Central reservations systems are extremely expensive. Research and development, equipment, and staffing can easily run into hundreds of millions of dollars. How has this prohibitive cost structure changed the hotel industry? How will it change business in the future? And what options are available to the smaller and start-up chains in the industry?

3. Several studies indicate quite clearly that reservation calls made to a travel agent, to the reservations centre, or directly to the hotel may result in three different rate quotes for the same accommodations for the same period of time. Explain.

4. Discuss the merits of higher rates with lower occupancy versus lower rates with higher occupancy if you were the manager of (a) a budget economy property, (b) a commercial convention property, or (c) an upscale resort property.

5. Yield management programs often discount rates to the benefit of one segment of guests but charge full rack rate to others who book at the last moment. With attention to the rewards and penalties that such policies carry, discuss a proposed policy that (a) deeply discounts rates for non-cancellable reservations made 30 days in advance, and (b) discounts rates for standby guests who are willing to wait until 7 P.M. for vacancies.

6. Develop a list of fenced rate restriction possibilities. This list may include those currently used by airlines or possible restrictions you create.

## CASE STUDY

### Proposed Yield Management Software Purchase

Cynthia Mohammed has just taken over as general manager (GM) of a medium-sized, independent, 250-room hotel in Winnipeg, Manitoba. Her previous management experience was with Delta Hotels, a division of Fairmont Hotels and Resorts. Delta has practised yield management for many years, and Mohammed is certain that if she could convince the owner of her present hotel to purchase a yield management software addition to the present front-office software, she could increase occupancy and average rate, resulting in the hotel being more profitable.

The owner of the hotel, Mr. Slomka, is an old-time hotelier who still believes that computer systems create more problems than solutions. His idea of yield management is walking a single reservation in favour of a family who will pay a higher room rate and spend more money in his food and beverage outlets. Although this may be true, Mohammed knows from her experience at Delta that yield management is much more. She has a meeting scheduled with Mr. Slomka and the hotel's chief financial officer (CFO) and

hopes to convince them that the purchase of yield management software will enhance the operation and profitability of the hotel.

As the front-office manager of the hotel, Mohammed has asked you to attend the meeting. In preparation for this meeting, you are trying to anticipate some of the questions that may arise, as you know you will need solid answers if the hotel is to purchase this software.

1. Who else might be invited to attend this meeting? Think about people who would enhance your presentation.

2. Anticipate questions that Mr. Slomka and his CFO might have. Jot down these questions with your answers. For example: "I have heard that, with yield management, regular guests may be quoted different rates each time they book a reservation at our hotel."

3. Create a scenario that you will use as part of your presentation that explains how modern yield management works.

## Notes

1. Sheraton Hotels introduced its central reservations system shortly after the Holidex system, but Sheraton was the first major chain to offer a toll-free telephone line to its customers.

2. Hotel central reservations offices (CROs) are also commonly referred to as central reservations systems (CRSs). These two terms are interchangeable.

3. In a 1998 study, PKF Consulting found that 83.7 percent of sales and marketing departments use automated rooms inventory controls and 79.8 percent of sales and marketing departments use yield management technology.

## Weblinks

### Travel Websites
Travelocity
**www.travelocity.ca**
Expedia
**www.expedia.ca**
Orbitz
**www.orbitz.com**

### Corporate Websites
Pegasus Solutions
**www.pegs.com**
**www.utell.com**
Galileo Canada
**www.galileocanada.ca**

## Chapter 5

# Individual and Group Reservations

## Learning Objectives

After reading this chapter, you will be able to do the following:

1. **Identify the essential information required to make a reservation and the different types of reservations.**

2. **Discuss computerized reservations and the procedure for issuing confirmation letters.**

3. **Identify the importance of group rooms business and the different markets that produce this type of business.**

4. **Describe how to book group and convention reservations and understand the special requirements these markets have.**

# Components of the Reservation

Awash in technology, it is easy for a CRO to lose sight of its basic task: customer service. After running the potential guest through a gauntlet of automated telephone queries, telephone keypad number punching, recorded instructions, and on-hold background messages or music, the reservations agent can easily forget that there is a real human being on the other end of the telephone. To avoid this oversight, one chain actually pastes pictures of real customers on the office walls to remind central reservations agents that they are talking to real people!

Certainly, there is good reason for such automated telephone systems. Asking the guest to select instructions in English (press "1"), French (press "2"), or some other language (press "3") segregates callers to language-specific reservationists (see Exhibits 5-1 (a) and (b)). Further instructions may separate callers by domestic reservations (press "1") versus international reservations (press "2"). Even more sophisticated systems can electronically ask the caller to state his or her city of choice, dates of travel, and number of guests in the party (refer to the discussion of voice recognition in Chapter 4).

For all of the benefits such technology provides the call centre, one axiom is abundantly clear—the fastest reservation is not always the best reservation. Some years ago, in a study of a major lodging chain's reservation office, agents experimented with changing their initial telephone greeting from the rushed monotone so often associated with call centres to a warmer, friendlier greeting.[1] The results were

# TigerTalk for Innkeepers

### Correspond with Guests in their Own Language

1. Select language of guest: [French ▼]
2. Enter [TO:] guest's e-mail address and [FROM:] your TigerTalk code.
3. Click on "Check Box" of every theme (Guest ID, Room Availability, Innkeeper's Response),
   and item within a theme that you wish to include.
4. Type in data or select option for each item to be included.
5. Preview e-mail any time you wish by clicking on "Preview" button.
6. From preview page, send e-mail in selected language, or return to edit.

**TO:** (e-mail address)                    **FROM:** (Your TigerTalk Code)
[Gary.Vallen@NAU.edu]                       [TT001]

☑ **Guest ID**

Title: [Mr. ▼]    Last Name: [Reservation]    First Name: [Trial]

☑ **Room Availability**

Arrival Date:                          Number of Nights        Number of Rooms
[July ▼] [4 ▼] [2004 ▼]                [1]                     [1 ▼]

| Room | Adults | Children | Type | Beds | Smoking or Not |
|---|---|---|---|---|---|
| ...1... | [2 ▼] | [0 ▼] | [deluxe ▼] | [1 king ▼] | [No Smoking ▼] |
| ...2... | [0 ▼] | [0 ▼] | [standard ▼] | [single ▼] | [No Smoking ▼] |
| ...3... | [0 ▼] | [0 ▼] | [standard ▼] | [single ▼] | [No Smoking ▼] |

☑ **Innkeeper's Response**

☑ We can accommodate your room needs at the following rate
☐ We cannot meet your exact needs, but can offer the closest at the following rate
☑ Room 1: [100]  [Euro ▼]  Plus [10] % Tax and [10] % Service
☐ Room 2: [    ]
☐ Room 3:
☑ Breakfast  ☐ Lunch  ☐ Dinner included           Quote No. [123456]
☑ Please see description of our facilities at: [http://pretendhotel.com]

☑ Your reservation has been made.               Reservation No. [123456]
☑ Please confirm reservation with
    ☑ [100]  [Euro ▼]  ☐ Cheque/Money order by mail  ☐ Credit card info by fax
☑ Please see conditions for confirmation at: [http://pretendhotel.com]
☑ Your reservation has been confirmed
☑ Please advise of estimated arrival time

☐ Your reservation has been changed according to new room needs
☐ Sorry we cannot accommodate your room needs as requested
☐ Your reservation has been cancelled           Cancellation No. [    ]
☐ Please see conditions for cancellation at: [http://]

[ Preview ]    [ Clear All ]

A multilingual e-mail service for innkeepers worldwide by **Cyber Tigers Online**

▲
## Exhibit 5-1 (a)

Here is an interesting exhibit—multi-language reservations capabilities using Cyber Tigers' recent release of TigerTalk for Innkeepers. Since non-English-speaking Internet users are projected to overtake English speakers as the majority in the next several years, the market for effective email in multilingual and cross-cultural environments is growing rapidly. TigerTalk is a fast and free business-to-business (B2B) email service on the Web with near-flawless translations and little or no typing. TigerTalk is based on two main premises: Keyboard input and word processing in non-alphabetic languages such as Chinese can be cumbersome, and most routine reservations correspondence revolves around a limited list of basic elements. Using TigerTalk, guests can make reservations with very little keyboard typing. Rather, most input uses pre-programmed translations of key elements (e.g., check boxes).

The most popular languages currently used are English, Spanish, Japanese, and German (in that order). But TigerTalk is currently available in English, Spanish, Japanese, German, Chinese, French, Korean, Polish, and Russian (with more to follow). Exhibit 5-1 (a) shows a basic input screen (in English). You can then see the return email confirmation to the guest in both English and the requested language (French in this case; Exhibit 5-1 (b)). To try TigerTalk for yourself, visit www.cyber-tigers.com.

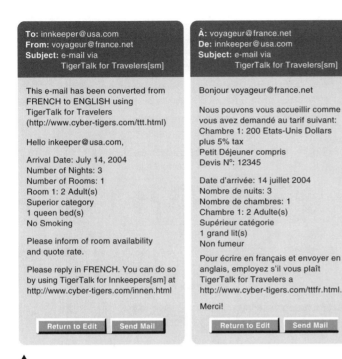

To: innkeeper@usa.com
From: voyageur@france.net
Subject: e-mail via
         TigerTalk for Travelers[sm]

This e-mail has been converted from
FRENCH to ENGLISH using
TigerTalk for Travelers
(http://www.cyber-tigers.com/ttt.html)

Hello innkeeper@usa.com,

Arrival Date: July 14, 2004
Number of Nights: 3
Number of Rooms: 1
Room 1: 2 Adult(s)
Superior category
1 queen bed(s)
No Smoking

Please inform of room availability
and quote rate.

Please reply in FRENCH. You can do so
by using TigerTalk for Innkeepers[sm] at
http://www.cyber-tigers.com/innen.html

Return to Edit    Send Mail

À: voyageur@france.net
De: innkeeper@usa.com
Subject: e-mail via
         TigerTalk for Travelers[sm]

Bonjour voyageur@france.net

Nous pouvons vous accueillir comme
vous avez demandé au tarif suivant:
Chambre 1: 200 Etats-Unis Dollars
plus 5% tax
Petit Déjeuner compris
Devis N°: 12345

Date d'arrivée: 14 juillet 2004
Nombre de nuits: 3
Nombre de chambres: 1
Chambre 1: 2 Adulte(s)
Supérieur catégorie
1 grand lit(s)
Non fumeur

Pour écrire en français et envoyer en
anglais, employez s'il vous plaît
TigerTalk for Travelers a
http://www.cyber-tigers.com/tttfr.html.

Merci!

Return to Edit    Send Mail

▲
**Exhibit 5-1 (b)**

astounding. Customers responded positively to the inviting greeting they received, and their perceptions of the CRO improved dramatically (ultimately, the reservations booking rate should improve as well). It took very little extra time for the reservationist to be nice and to "smile" through the telephone. The friendlier greetings added a mere 300 extra seconds (5 minutes) to each reservationist's day.

Today's hotel guests, whether corporate, leisure, or group, face more lodging choices than ever before. With so many options available, CROs (and in-house reservations centres) are realizing that a well-trained reservations agent makes a significant difference in guest satisfaction, booking rates, and return business. Technology can get the average reservation down to 180 seconds, but a speedy "businesslike" attitude does not necessarily translate into a successful reservation!

Seasoned reservations managers realize that effective communication skills are more important than basic computer skills. Training reservations agents to be salespersons is the key to success in this new millennium. Poorly trained reservations agents miss potential sales by failing to understand the guests' needs. Taking a step away from the rushed script allows the agent to develop a communicative information-gathering posture that may uncover personal information (needs) that can ultimately lead to a sale.

## Information Contained in the Reservation

The computer not only provides rapid input, but also prompts the reservationist to ask essential questions (see Exhibit 5-2). As one question is completed, the lighted computer cursor automatically moves to the beginning of the next question. In this way, essential information cannot be overlooked. In fact, if the reservationist attempts to enter an incomplete reservation into the system, the computer will beep and the cursor will blink at the beginning of the incomplete information field.

**Essential Reservation Data** The reservation process and especially the information obtained during the reservation are designed to improve the effectiveness of the front office. The facts communicated through the reservation form a valuable starting point from which the front-desk clerk can understand the guest's needs. Corporate guests may be placed away from the lobby in a quieter area of the hotel, while guests travelling with children may be roomed near the swimming pool. Late arrivals are noted on the reservation screen so the front desk is better informed should it need to make difficult overbooking and walked-guest decisions. Address information is collected so the hotel can contact the guest for marketing or billing purposes or in the event that the guest leaves behind a personal item (although for security and confidentiality reasons hotels do not automatically mail items to the guest, unless the guest calls and requests that they do so).

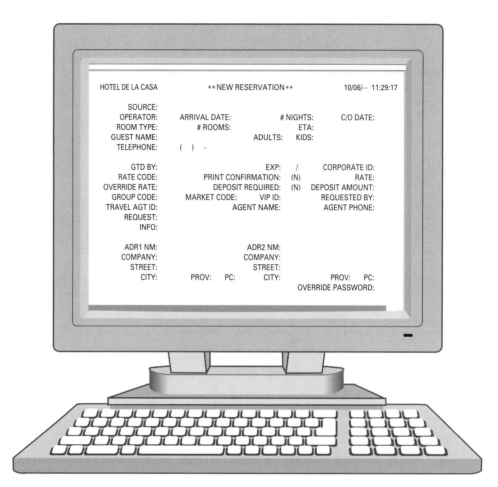

Arrival and Departure Dates In the reservations centres for national chains, the questions of arrival and **departure** come third, after "What city?" and "What hotel?" Telephone time is not used to gather the details that follow unless the clerk is certain that space is available at the time and place requested.

Number of Nights This bit of redundancy forestalls later problems if the guest's count of nights is not in agreement with the time between the arrival and departure dates. A common miscommunication occurs when the guest counts the departure day in the number of nights. It is important to remember that hotels sell room nights and not days, while guests generally think in terms of the number of days they will stay at the hotel. Many systems ask simply for the date of arrival (say, October 2) followed by a question related to number of nights (say, four nights). Then, the reservationist verifies information with the guest by replying, "So we have you checking out on October 6, is that correct?"

Number of Persons The number of persons in the party and its structure help clarify the kind of facilities needed. Two unrelated persons need two beds; a married couple could get by with one bed. Are there children? Is a crib required? A rollaway bed? Many hotels charge an extra fee for the second, third, and fourth persons in a room. This extra revenue contributes substantial profit to the bottom line and is easily justified when one considers the added utilities, linens, breakfast, and other items used by the extra person(s). See Chapter 9 for an additional discussion of double occupancy rates.

**Number of Rooms Required** Based on the size of the party and the types of rooms the hotel has available, additional rooms may be required. Most reservationists are authorized to handle requests for up to 10 rooms or so. As the number of required rooms increases above 10, the hotel's group sales department usually becomes involved.

**Type of Rooms Required** The question of room type is closely linked to the rate the guest is willing to pay. As the room type increases in luxury, the corresponding rate increases as well. Although the specific rate the guest wants to pay is the real question being asked, the reservationist certainly can't just offer a series of rates. That would be gauche. Instead, the reservationist offers a series of room types.

Generally, the reservationist attempts to sell from the top down. This is accomplished by offering the guest the most expensive room type first and then waiting for the guest to agree or decline before moving down to offer the next most expensive room type (see Chapter 8).

**Corporate Affiliation** Commercial hotels are very concerned with identifying all corporate guest reservations. The average corporate guest represents far more room nights than the average leisure guest does. In addition, corporate guests usually book their rooms with less lead time (and, as such, pay a higher average rate) than leisure guests do (see the yield management discussion in Chapter 4). As such, reservation data related to the guest's corporate affiliation are essential to the success of many commercial properties. In fact, asking the guest's corporate affiliation is often the first step in determining the rate to quote. Many corporate guests have negotiated a prearranged nightly room rate. Other corporate guests—usually less regular travellers to that particular hotel or region—are subject to the hotel's regular corporate rate.

**Price** The reservation (the sale) could be lost by the rate quotation. The agent may have no negotiating room if the yield management system has eliminated lower-priced options. Quoting the price is not enough. Descriptive matter intended to entice the buyer to the better rate must accompany distinctions between the prices.

**Name** The guest's name has become more important in recent years. In the past, the name was used for alphabetical filing of the reservation and was one of several means (confirmation number, date of arrival, etc.) by which the reservations agent or front-desk clerk could access the guest's reservation record.

Sophisticated reservations systems now use the customer's name as a means of gaining efficiency, saving time, and generating guest loyalty. Many systems integrate guest history into the reservations system. As the guest's name is entered into the reservation, a screen pops up for repeat customers showing the guest's address and phone number; rate, room type, and number of nights stayed during the previous visit(s); and other essential and non-essential information. With most information already in the system, the reservations clerk simply verifies that this is the same guest and asks whether the information is still accurate.

**Quality of the Reservation** The three quality types of reservations available—non-guaranteed, guaranteed, or advance deposit—are determined either by the guest or by the reservationist. The reservationist, for example, may be restricted from accepting non-guaranteed reservations as a function of policy or unusually high business levels for the hotel. Similarly, the guest may not have a credit card with which to guarantee the reservation or may have a card but not be inclined to use it. In either case, the reservation may fail to materialize because of disagreement at this stage in the process. See Chapter 6 for a complete discussion of the quality of the reservation.

**Non-essential Reservation Data** Depending on the reservations system in place and/or the amount of reservation activity occurring in the reservations centre at the time of the call, certain reservation information may not necessarily be required for each reservation. This less important information is categorized as non-essential or "nice-to-know" data. Examples of non-essential information include estimated time of arrival, special guest requests or needs, discounts or affiliations, and smoking or non-smoking room preference.

Although essential information must be complete for a reservation to be accepted into the computer system, non-essential information is not required. The computer will allow the input of a completed reservation into the system when non-essential data are missing. In fact, some computer screens display essential data in one colour while displaying non-essential data in a secondary colour. If time permits, the reservationist may request this additional data. Otherwise, it is often overlooked.

Overlooked, maybe. But just because the central reservations system doesn't mandate certain data as required fields before accepting the reservation does not necessarily mean the data are unimportant.

Some non-mandated information (smoking preference, for example) is still of critical importance to guest satisfaction!

**Estimated Time of Arrival** By knowing the guests' estimated time of arrival (ETA), the hotel can properly schedule front-desk clerks to assist with check-in, van drivers to retrieve guests from the airport, and bellpersons to room them. More important, hotels that are filling to capacity can be certain to save rooms for guests who are going to be especially late.

**Special Requests** Guest requests or needs run the gamut from simple, rather non-essential requests to extremely essential guest needs. That is why most reservationists provide guests with an opportunity to request any other items of importance before the close of the reservation process. If the request is essential (for example, a guest with a disability requesting a specially equipped room), the guest is usually certain to state the need. In other cases, the request (ocean view, near the Smiths' room, below the fifth floor) may be forgotten by the reservationist and the guest. It is the responsibility of the front-desk clerk to handle each request on a case-by-case basis at the time of check-in. Indeed, reservationists generally explain, "I'll note your request on the reservation, but I cannot promise you will get it."

**Discounts or Affiliations** Corporate, Canadian Automobile Association (CAA), Canadian Association of Retired Persons (CARP), or similar discounts or affiliations are usually handled during the room type and rate discussion earlier in the reservation. CARP members (membership restricted to those over 50 years of age) are offered minimum 5 percent discounts. In fact, many organizations (CARP, for example) require the guest to state his or her discount as a part of the reservation process. In such cases, the discount is void if the guest forgets to request it at the time of reservation.

**Smoking Preference** What was once merely a special request has become a standard reservation input field. Smoking preferences play an important role in guest-room satisfaction. Smokers and non-smokers alike are very committed to their particular preferences. As such, practically all domestic hotels offer smoking and non-smoking rooms for their guests' comfort. Some properties offer entire non-smoking floors, and one small chain even experimented with complete non-smoking properties.

With such a focus on smoking in today's society, it is surprising that guests' smoking preference is still classified as non-essential reservation data. Given the amount of guest satisfaction and comfort riding on the smoking preference, it is even more curious that hotel reservations departments do not guarantee the smoking status of the reserved room—yet that's the standard in the lodging industry. The guest's smoking preference is noted and the hotel tries to accommodate the request, but there are no guarantees that a smoking guest will get a smoking room, or vice versa!

**Address** The guest's address and/or phone number are requested by some hotels as a matter of record. Other hotels use the information to mail a confirmation card or confirmation letter when there is sufficient lead time. In the case of third-party reservations (as when a secretary or travel agent makes the reservation), the address and phone number of the person making the reservation are also requested.

## Confirming the Reservation

A letter of confirmation or a confirmation card is usually printed by the computerized property management system (or central reservations system) using the information collected during the reservation. There is a field on the reservation screen that asks "Print Confirmation? Yes or No." The system probably defaults to "No," requiring the reservations agent to enter "Yes" if a confirmation needs to be mailed. Some properties ask the guest, "Would you like us to mail you a confirmation?" Others do it as a routine activity when there is sufficient lead time. Most properties, however, do not mail a confirmation. Instead, the reservationist closes the conversation by furnishing the caller with a confirmation number generated by the computer.

## Reservation Information Flow

Once entered into the system, the reservation appears electronically in myriad formats and printouts until the date of arrival. On that date, the reservation changes from a future reservation to an arriving reservation. On the date of arrival, the overall responsibility for the arriving or incoming reservation changes from the reservations department to the front-office staff (see Chapter 8).

An arrival list (Exhibit 5-3) is printed by the automated reservations system each night for the following day's anticipated check-ins. The transfer of data is delayed until registration. The room clerk keys the material in, and the transfer is completed, but only after the guest arrives. Unlike the manual rack system, the computerized reservations system generally does not have a supporting correspondence file. Almost all supporting data are electronic in nature. Only under unusual circumstances will there be hard-copy support. Examples of these circumstances include reservation requests by mail or fax rather than telephone.

With computerized property management systems (or a central reservations system), all of the reservation information is stored in the computer's memory and can be recalled for viewing on the computer screen if the guest's name and the date of arrival are known. In a perfect world, the reservation or confirmation number would be known, and that also would bring the information forward.

Although the majority of reservations remain undisturbed until the date of arrival, a great number of reservations are changed. Common alterations to reservations include a changed date of arrival or length of stay, a changed guest name (as when an

**Exhibit 5-3** ▶

Computer display of expected arrivals (reservations) list. Identical hard copies are provided on the day of arrival to the desk, the uniformed services, and even to the dining room if it is an American plan hotel. Note the estimated times of arrival and reservations codes (see Exhibit 5-4 on page 150).

```
HOTEL DE LA CASA        **EXPECTED ARRIVALS**        10/06/--  11:32:10
                         FOR DATE 10/08/--

RES #  NAME                    CONV   #    TYPE  RATE  RES  EST     RESV
                               GRP    RMS  RMS   CAT   TYPE ARRIV   CODE
0261   ONITO, RANDAL                  2    K     2     4    11:00P  25
0005   OTTA, M/M ALFREDO              1    S     2     2    11:00P
0616   OUVIA & FAM, MRS JACK          1    D     3     2    8:00P
R111   RAMLETT, M/M JOHN              1    K     2     2            26 13
R260   ROADWATER, M/M REX             3    S     1     2            23
R312   RODEY, M/M FRED         ZTUK   1    K     3     2
R406   ROWN, M/M MIKE                 1    K     2     2    7:00P
R234   RUCHER, WM/SON                 1    H     3     1    10:00P  63
                                      W/KNIGHT
R400   RUDNICK, M/M DUANE             1    D     2     3    1:00A   44
R422   RUNKER,M/M WM           00E    1    D     1     1
R713   RURNSTEIN, M/M SCOTT           1    K     2     2
R646   RYANT, MS CISSY                1    K     1     2    5:00P
R456   RYER & FAM, M/M WAYNE          1    K     2     2
S121   SAMPBELL, M/M KRONE            1    K     1     2
S216   SAPP & PTY, M/M DONALDO        1    K     1     2    9:00P
S200   SAREY, TOMITHAN                1    S     4     2
S617   SARNIVELE, NICHOLAS    JOIN    1    S     4     1
S836   SARPENTER, MRS JULYE   WK      1    D     2     1
                                      W/BROWN
S855   SASTELLI, MONSIEUR     ZTUK    2    K     C     4            14
T202   TATO, D/M LOUIS                1    K     2     2
T008   TENTER & FAM, M/M DEAN         2    S     2     3    5:00P   25
T361   THANDLER, MR HAL               1    S     2     1    1:00A   44
                         PAGE 5 OF 6
```

existing corporate reservation is to be claimed by a different employee), a changed room type or discount request, and a cancellation.

No matter what the alteration may be, the reservationist cannot make a change without first accessing the pre-existing reservation. Only under unusual situations is the existing reservation difficult to locate. Difficulty in finding an existing reservation occurs when either the guest or the reservationist has made a clerical error. Common clerical errors include incorrect date of arrival or incorrect spelling of the guest's name.

In many cases, these errors are found and rectified. In other instances, the existing reservation cannot be located. If, for some reason, the reservation cannot be found, the reservationist may actually take a new reservation. This is risky, because chances are there will now be duplicate reservations in the system.

**Advance Deposits** Guaranteeing the reservation by means of an **advance deposit** has grown more popular and less popular at the same time. If the request is for cash (cheque), the procedure has become less popular. Handling cash or cheques requires a disproportionate amount of clerical time and postage relative to the economic gain.

The initial reservation procedure is similar whether or not a deposit cheque is requested. The reservation is confirmed, but only tentatively, since it contains notice that a reservation deposit is required. Two copies of the reservation confirmation may be mailed. The extra copy is to be returned with the cheque in the non-stamped, pre-addressed envelope that is enclosed. More often than not, the hotel mails nothing. Instead, the customer is instructed to mail the deposit and to write the confirmation number on the cheque to ensure proper credit. With enough lead time, a receipt is usually returned to the guest. Most hoteliers, however, feel that the cost, time invested, and delay make the procedure unwarranted. This is especially true considering the widespread availability of credit cards.

**Credit Card Guarantees** Even as requiring advance deposit cheques has decreased in practice, guaranteeing by credit card has gained in popularity. The reservations clerk takes the credit card number over the telephone and records it with the reservation. Nothing needs to be processed at this time. The charge will be forwarded only if the guest is a **no-show**, and then only if the hotel believes that collection is justified. In the usual sequence, the guest appears as expected and credit is established at registration.

Processing the credit card entails a fee that is not part of the cost of cash deposits. However, the fee isn't paid unless the charge is made. Cheque deposits have their own risk—they bounce.

Experienced travellers soon realize how much of a game the reservations process has become. Busy properties almost always insist on credit card guarantees rather than on a 4 P.M. or 6 P.M. hold. Credit card guarantees reduce the number of no-shows.

At the same time, guests know that many properties do not actually charge the card at the time of the reservation. With such properties, the guarantee is not processed until the expected night of arrival. A card that is charged at the time of the reservation requires another credit entry if the guest cancels in a proper and timely manner. So, to avoid making additional credit entries, many hotels wait to process the card until the night of arrival. The hotel's delay provides the traveller with a winning technique that costs the hotel unless the rooms manager is alert to what is happening.

Some unethical travellers play a credit card game: They provide the hotel with an inaccurate credit card number. In this way, if they fail to show, the hotel cannot charge them. On the other hand, if they do arrive and their false credit card number is challenged, they can blame it on poor communication or a clerical error. They invent the false credit card number by changing the sequence of one or two digits on their real credit card, which makes for a fairly believable excuse. For example, if their Visa card number is 4567 890 123 456, they could simply change the number to 4567 809 123 456. Now they have a believable excuse in the event that they do show up for their reservation—but a fictitious number in the event of a no-show.

Most hotel chains and individual properties are wise to this game and intercept "errors" at the time of the reservation. They accomplish this by having an automated reservations system that is interfaced directly to a credit card clearing centre. During the several minutes that the guest is on the telephone with the reservationist, the credit card number is input and approval verification is received. If the approval is denied, the reservationist gives the guest another opportunity to provide the correct credit card number.

**Cancellations** Cancellations require a change to the existing reservation. This is not necessarily a problem unless somehow it is improperly handled. Handling anything at the front desk in an improper manner generates problems as well as bad public relations. This is especially true with cancellations—imagine yourself in the shoes of a guest who previously cancelled the reservation. The hotel improperly recorded the cancellation and your credit card statement now reflects a $150 no-show charge for the unoccupied room night. That is exasperating!

Encouraging cancellation calls is in the best interest of the hotel. Such calls reduce the no-show rate. Fewer no-shows generate more room revenue from walk-in guests and reduce complaints from the anti-service syndrome of overbooking (Chapter 6).

The **cancellation number**, which is formulated like the confirmation number (discussed earlier), is the only major difference between a cancellation call and any other reservation change. Even then, its importance is limited to guaranteed reservations. The system must protect the guest who has guaranteed the room with a credit card (or other guarantee) from being billed if the reservation is cancelled in a timely manner. Non-guaranteed reservations are not generally provided with a cancellation number.

**Guest History Databases** One of the ancillary benefits associated with speed and accuracy has been increased data storage capabilities. Customer information, collected during the normal flow of the room reservation, can be stored in guest history databases, manipulated, and used for marketing and guest service/recognition purposes. It makes sense that the hotel's use of guest history data has risen with increased computer storage and processing capabilities.

The guest history revolution has been fought primarily at the individual property level. Until recently, centralizing guest history information at the corporate level has been too unwieldy to justify. Guest history use at the property level is more manageable.

Guest history improves the most basic component of guest service: recognition. Hotels have always known that guests appreciate personal recognition. Imagine the unwavering loyalty that can be gained, then, if the guests' basic needs and requests are recognized in advance. That is the promise of guest history.

In its most common form, guest history is applied at the property level during the reservations process. As stated earlier in this chapter (see the section entitled "Name"), the guest history function is used when the reservations agent pulls up a guest's previous-stay information and saves them both the burden of repeating address, credit card, and room type/rate preferences. However, guest history can accomplish far more than that. In upscale corporate and luxury properties, guest history databases often inform front-office personnel of the various likes and dislikes of the guest. Simple preferences such as ground-floor room, feather as opposed to foam pillows, extra pears in the fruit basket, and so on, go a long way toward generating loyalty and a sense of belonging.

It makes good business sense, too. Not only does the hotel gain the benefits of enhanced guest loyalty, satisfaction, and repeat visits, but guest history databases are valuable marketing resources as well. It takes little imagination to visualize the potential a mailed marketing campaign might have when focused on certain guest history parameters. For example, a hotel facing a slow autumn might mail a special promotion to those corporate guests who visited their property at least two times last year during September and October—now *that's* pinpointing the market.

**Centralized Guest History** Beginning around 1997, the industry saw increasing centralization of guest history information. What one property in Montreal, Quebec, knew about a particular frequent corporate traveller was now becoming available through the chain's central reservations system to, say, a sister property in Quebec City.

Corporate travellers have been demanding improved guest service (recognition) to compensate for rising room rates. Chains such as Marriott Hotels and Resorts, Ritz-Carlton, Preferred Hotels and Resorts (a referral group or consortium), and Carlton Hospitality Worldwide saw the need to centralize guest history databases and have taken the lead in this area of automation. These chains are banking on the premise that when frequent guests at one property are recognized like family in another of the chain's properties, the increased guest satisfaction will translate into increased brand loyalty.

Chain guest history databases have been developed from a variety of directions. Marriott's, for example, was designed around its existing Marriott Rewards frequent guest program. Since this program was already in place across its entire spectrum of properties, Marriott thought it made sense to use Marriott Rewards as the centralized starting point. As such, when Marriott rolled out its original guest history program it already had guest profiles from more than 9 million members. However, Marriott's guest history database system only stores basic guest information, such as bed type and smoking preference.

Some of the smaller chains have an operational advantage over Marriott because of their relative size. Ritz-Carlton, for example, took the complete encyclopedia of guest history information it had developed at individual properties and integrated it into a centralized database. Ritz-Carlton calls this database its Customer Loyalty Anticipation Satisfaction System (CLASS). Before the implementation of CLASS, regular Ritz-Carlton guests who were visiting a different Ritz-Carlton hotel for the first time would have been treated like first-timers. Now repeat customers at one property are repeat customers at all Ritz properties.

## Reservation Coding

The reservation's journey ends at the front desk (see Chapter 8). Sometimes the journey is long, as when the reservation was made a year in advance. In other cases, the reservation lead time is extremely short, as with reservations made minutes before arrival. In any case, the front desk is the final stopping point in the reservation's journey.

The first step in linking the reservation with the front desk is to change the status of the reservation from future reservation to arriving reservation. At the beginning of each day, some set of future reservations becomes that day's incoming reservations. In a computerized system, this change occurs automatically, either as the clock strikes midnight or as a step in the night audit process.

It is at this moment that guests' special requests and needs become the concern of the front desk. Armed with the knowledge of which rooms are clean and vacant, which rooms are due to check out, and which rooms are staying over, specific room assignments are developed in accordance with guest requests. Even in an automated property, the assigning of special rooms to match special requests is a manual operation. It is the clerk, operating with good judgment, who ultimately determines which requests can be met and which requests will be declined.

**Special Coding**  Whether operating under a manual or computerized system, certain reservations are different from the rest. They may be different in their method of payment, in the guests' specific requests, in the fact that they are **commissionable** to a travel agent, in their time of arrival, or in their affiliation. Whatever the case, the front-desk clerk needs to be alert and to treat these reservations differently.

The difference is generally highlighted somewhere on the reservation. In an automated system, a numerical coding scheme is commonly used. In this case, advance-deposit reservations will be indicated with one code number (see Exhibit 5-4, which uses code 40) and travel agent reservations with another code (Exhibit 5-4 uses code 55). The following is a brief discussion about some of these special codes. For a more complete understanding of their impact on the guest check-in process, refer to Chapter 8.

| Computer Code | Internal System Meaning | Actual Printout on Guest Confirmation |
|---|---|---|
| 11 | VIP | |
| 12 | Group buyer | |
| 13 | Honeymooners | |
| 14 | Comp | |
| 20 | Connecting rooms | *Connecting rooms, if possible* |
| 21 | Adjoining rooms | *Adjoining rooms, if possible* |
| 22 | Rooms on same floor | *Same floor, if possible* |
| 23 | Need individual names | *Please advise names of individuals in your party* |
| 24 | PS | *Petit suite* |
| 25 | RS | *One-bedroom suite* |
| 26 | LS | *Two-bedroom suite* |
| 30 | Send liquor | |
| 31 | Send champagne | |
| 32 | Send flowers | |
| 33 | Send gift | |
| 34 | Send fruit | |
| 40 | Require deposit | *Please send one night's deposit to guarantee your reservation* |
| 41 | Due bill | |
| 42 | No credit, require advance payment | |
| 43 | Walk-in | |
| 44 | Late arrival | *Anticipated late arrival of guest* |
| 50 | Special rate | *Special rate* |
| 51 | Airline rate | *Airline rate* |
| 52 | Press rate | *Press rate* |
| 53 | Convention rate | *Convention rate* |
| 54 | Non-convention rate | *Convention rate applies to convention dates only* |
| 55 | Travel agency | *Travel agency* |
| 60 | Cot | *Cot will be provided* |
| 61 | Crib | *Crib will be provided* |
| 62 | Bedboard | *Bedboard will be provided* |
| 63 | Wheelchair | *Wheelchair will be provided* |
| 70 | Casino guest | |
| 80 | See correspondence for very special instructions | |
| 99 | Print special message | *(Whatever that message is)* |

▲
**Exhibit 5-4**
Actual listing of reservations codes from a major hotel/casino operation. Code numbers correspond to an internal system description, policy, or abbreviation. Some codes (for example, code 54) print onto a special "comments" section of the confirmation form sent to the guest. Other codes (for example, code 11) are designed for in-house use only.

**Advance Deposits** Reservations with an advance deposit need to be specially noted. If the deposit arrived, the front-desk clerk needs to be certain to post the credit on behalf of the guest. If the deposit never arrived, the front-desk clerk will probably cancel the reservation if the hotel is nearing capacity.

**Late Arrivals** If front-desk personnel know that a given reservation is due to arrive late, they will be less likely to assume it is a no-show as the evening progresses. Also, most **late arrivals** require a guarantee of some sort to hold the room past the normal 6 P.M. (4 P.M. for resort properties) time frame for non-guaranteed reservations. (See Chapter 6 for a full discussion of the quality of the reservation regarding non-guaranteed and guaranteed reservations.)

**Credit Card Guarantee** Rooms guaranteed with a national credit card are theoretically held for the guest all night long. If the guest fails to arrive, the night auditor will charge the credit card for one night's room (see Chapter 6).

**Corporate Guarantee** The right to guarantee rooms with a corporation's good credit must be prearranged with the hotel. In case of a no-show, the room charge is billed to the corporation's **city ledger** account (see Chapter 6).

**Travel Agents** Special coding of travel agent (TA) reservations expedites the internal office procedure. After the guest departs, the hotel pays the travel agent's commission. (In those circumstances where the travel agent owes the hotel—an **account receivable**—the hotel bills the balance less the travel agent's commission.) When the reservation is placed, the agent identifies the agency, providing name, address, and **International Association of Travel Agents** (IATA) code number. Some hotels will not pay commissions, and the reservationist needs to explain that. If the customer wants the particular hotel, the agency will book the room and forgo its commission. Even if the hotel pays a commission, it may not do so on certain types of bookings. Deeply discounted rates (corporate or governmental, for example) are sometimes not commissionable.

Reservations are confirmed to the agency, not to the guest. In some cases, the hotel lacks the guest's address until registration time. To maintain accountability with the agency, the wise hotel manager sends a notice whenever one of the TA's clients fails to appear.

**VIPs** Very important persons (VIPs) are generally coded. These may be well-known dignitaries, celebrities, other hoteliers, or important members of an association that the hotel hopes to book later. VIP designations are made by a member of management or by the sales department. **Star reservation** is also used. A contact reservation is a VIP who should be met (contacted) and escorted to his or her room by the management.

**Riding Reservation** Reservations for which the date of arrival is vague may be allowed to "ride." The probable date is booked and then the reservation is carried until the guest shows or an allotted period of time passes, usually less than one week. Riding reservations are seldom used. They are generally found only at resorts or for VIP reservations.

**Convention Delegate** Group affiliation is a better term than convention delegate because the members of a group need not be part of a convention. Hotels cater to tours, company delegations, wedding parties, and other groups that need to be identified. Several codes are needed when different groups are booked at one time. For a more thorough discussion of group reservations, refer to the next section of the chapter.

# Convention and Tour Group Business

The term *group business* represents a variety of venues. Group business can range from major conventions and expositions (trade shows), to mid-sized corporate meetings and conferences, to smaller incentive travel packages, tour groups, and corporate retreats. From large to small, group business is a major player in today's lodging industry.

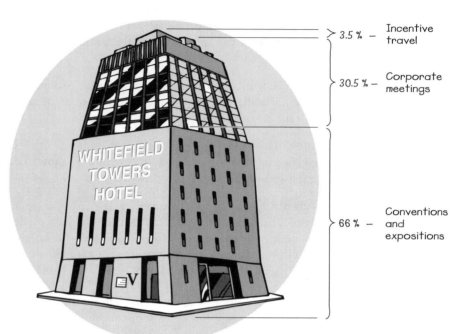

3.5 % — Incentive travel

30.5 % — Corporate meetings

66 % — Conventions and expositions

For some properties, group business is almost non-existent. Such hotels or motels may have limited or no meeting facilities, may be located in remote areas and face difficult group travel logistics, or may be so busy with leisure travel that there is no room for discounted group business. Conversely, major convention properties may derive upward of 90 percent of all hotel revenues from group activities. Although different types of properties have varying degrees of dependence on group business, the industry as a whole derives a significant portion of its revenues from this growing segment (see Exhibits 5-5 to 5-7).

Incentive travel, tour groups, conventions, and trade shows have become the mainstays of hotel sales in Canada and abroad. Such gatherings are clearly defined as group business. Business meetings and corporate retreats, though smaller in scale, are included in this broad definition.

Depending on the hotel, smaller gatherings lose the distinction of being classified and tracked as group business. A small wedding party requiring only five or seven rooms, for example, may be considered an individual rather than a group reservation. Several executives meeting in a conference room for a few days are often handled through the hotel's in-house reservations department as individual rooms. Indeed, even a convention/meeting planner visiting the property several weeks before the convention is probably handled as an individual (although complimentary) room. Technically, the meeting planner's accommodations should be tracked as part of the overall convention count.

Group reservations are handled differently from individual reservations. One difference is that the central reservations office (or reservations link-up) may not be entitled to handle the group. Many chains require that group accommodations deal directly with the specific hotel property. Even at the hotel property, larger operations remove group reservations from the responsibility of the in-house reservations department. Most large properties have a group sales department designed to handle (among other tasks) group rooms reservations. Finally, depending on business levels, policies, and property characteristics, large groups may be granted special rates and discounts.

**Exhibit 5-6** ▶
As you can see, almost 75 percent of a delegate's expenses are for accommodation, food, and beverage.

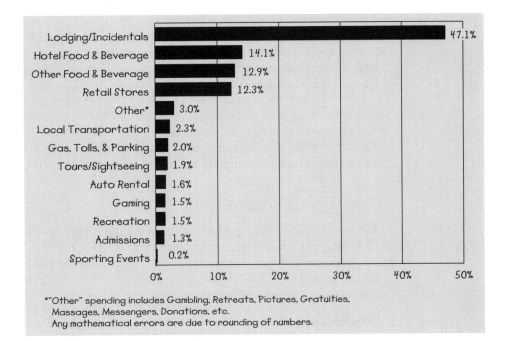

*"Other" spending includes Gambling, Retreats, Pictures, Gratuities, Massages, Messengers, Donations, etc.
Any mathematical errors are due to rounding of numbers.

**Exhibit 5-7** ▶
An out-of-town convention delegate spends more than four times as much as an in-town delegate, and the average stay of a convention delegate in Canada is 3.01 nights.

## Delegate Expenditures at Canadian Events

### All Events—Dollars Reported in Canadian Currency

|  | Total Expenditures | Daily Expenditures |
|---|---|---|
| Lodging and Incidentals | $388.38 | $129.03 |
| Hotel Food and Beverage | $115.88 | $138.50 |
| Other Food and Beverage | $106.04 | $35.23 |
| Tours/Sightseeing | $15.56 | $5.17 |
| Admission to Museums, Theatres, etc. | $10.92 | $3.63 |
| Recreation | $12.41 | $4.12 |
| Sporting Events | $1.22 | $0.41 |
| Retail Stores | $101.47 | $33.71 |
| Local Transportation (bus, taxi, limo) | $18.92 | $6.29 |
| Auto Rental (within event city) | $12.99 | $4.32 |
| Gasoline, Tolls, Parking (within event city) | $16.49 | $5.48 |
| Other* | $24.42 | $8.11 |
| **Total** | **$824.70** | **$274.00** |
| Out-of-town delegate expenditures | $888.14 | $295.06 |
| In-town delegate expenditures | $200.76 | $66.70 |

Average number of nights per delegate = 3.01

*"Other" spending includes Gambling, Retreats, Pictures, Gratuities, Massages, Messengers, Donations, etc.

These special deals are negotiated between the group's representative and the hotel's sales manager, with final approval granted by the general manager of the property.

Because of differing policies and definitions, group business is handled and characterized differently across various hotels and chains. Therefore, it is difficult to know exactly how great is the impact of group rooms activity on the lodging industry. A fairly large number of group activities are never counted. However, the convention industry (including conventions, expositions, corporate meetings, incentive travel, and trade shows) is conservatively estimated at $1.3 billion annually in Ontario alone. According to the Ministry of Tourism and Recreation, every year Ontario welcomes more than 1 million convention and meeting visitors from the United States and more than 400 000 international visitors.

## The Group Rooms Contribution

The contribution of group rooms revenues to total rooms revenues depends on the type of hotel. Some properties—conference centres, for example—are exclusively group-oriented (see Exhibits 5-8 (a) and (b)). Other operations choose to accommodate groups during slow periods and off-seasons. There are very few hotels that refuse to accommodate group business altogether.

**Why Groups?** There are three distinctions that separate group business from individual corporate and leisure travellers. These distinctions represent benefits (profits) associated with selling group rooms. Even though group rooms are usually sold at a discount from rack rate (as most things purchased in quantity are sold at a discount), it is still a very profitable venture for most hotels.

However, accepting a group booking for a given date is no simple matter. It must be evaluated in terms of the group's rooms revenues and related revenues (banquets, meeting room rentals, audiovisual equipment use, etc.), as opposed to displaced transient and corporate rooms business. Whether the group business justifies displacing normal hotel business (corporate and transient rooms) is a question for the hotel's yield management team (see Chapter 4).

There are three characteristics unique to group business that affect the hotel's interest in accepting group rooms:

1. Group business is a sizable market.

2. Groups provide certain economies of scale.

3. Group delegates spend more dollars.

**Exhibit 5-8 (a)** ▶
This exhibit illustrates the vast group capabilities of a major convention centre, such as the ones in Vancouver and Toronto. The Metro Toronto Convention Centre is Canada's largest convention centre. It measures 460 000 square feet and can handle groups from 40 to 40 000 in size.

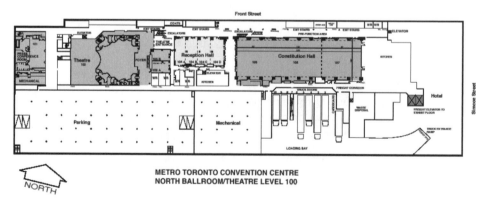

METRO TORONTO CONVENTION CENTRE
NORTH BALLROOM/THEATRE LEVEL 100

**Exhibit 5-8 (b)** ▶
This exhibit shows the capacities of only one part of the Metro Toronto Convention Centre's North Building.

# metro toronto convention centre

Schedule 'B'

## NORTH BUILDING - Dimensions and Capacities

**UPPER LEVEL — 300 - Exhibition Facilities**

| Room # | Overall Dimensions Feet | Usable Area Square Feet | Ceiling Height Feet | No. of 10x10 Booths | Theatre | Classroom | Banquet | Reception |
|---|---|---|---|---|---|---|---|---|
| A | 252 x 266 | 67,032 | 35/48 | 304 | 6,240 | 3,000 | 3,900 | 6,240 |
| B | 224 x 266 | 59,584 | 35/48 | 260 | 1,830 | 1,830 | 1,830 | 1,830 |
| C | 252 x 266 | 67,032 | 35/48 | 318 | 2,500 | 2,500 | 2,500 | 2,500 |
| Total | 726 x 266 | 193,648 | 35/48 | 1,000* | 11,000 | 8,100 | 10,400 | 10,570 |

**STREET LEVEL — 200 - Meeting Facilities**

| Room # | Overall Dimensions Feet | Usable Area Square Feet | Ceiling Height Feet | No. of 10x10 Booths | Theatre | Classroom | Banquet | Reception |
|---|---|---|---|---|---|---|---|---|
| 201A | 28 x 25 | 700 | 14 | | 75 | 40 | 70 | 70 |
| 201B | 28 x 30 | 840 | 14 | | 85 | 55 | 80 | 84 |
| 201C | 31 x 25 | 775 | 14 | | 80 | 45 | 70 | 71 |
| 201D | 31 x 30 | 930 | 14 | | 120 | 65 | 90 | 93 |
| 201E | 25 x 25 | 625 | 14 | | 70 | 35 | 60 | 63 |
| 201F | 25 x 30 | 750 | 14 | | 90 | 45 | 80 | 75 |
| Total | 84 x 55 | 4,520 | 14 | | 600 | 300 | 450 | 462 |
| 202A | 26 x 30 | 780 | 14 | | 85 | 45 | 70 | 78 |
| 202B | 34 x 30 | 1,020 | 14 | | 130 | 65 | 100 | 102 |
| 202C | 26 x 27 | 702 | 14 | | 80 | 45 | 70 | 70 |
| 202D | 34 x 27 | 918 | 14 | | 110 | 55 | 100 | 92 |
| Total | 60 x 57 | 3,420 | 14 | | 450 | 225 | 340 | 342 |
| 203A | 26 x 28 | 728 | 14 | | 85 | 55 | 70 | 73 |
| 203B | 37 x 28 | 1,036 | 14 | | 130 | 65 | 100 | 73 |
| 203C | 26 x 25 | 650 | 14 | | 70 | 35 | 60 | 65 |
| 203D | 37 x 25 | 925 | 14 | | 110 | 55 | 90 | 92 |
| Total | 63 x 53 | 3,339 | 14 | | 400 | 200 | 320 | 340 |
| 204 | 50 x 43 | 2,150 | 14 | | 170 | 95 | 190 | 215 |
| 205A | 35 x 27 | 945 | 14 | | 100 | 55 | 90 | 95 |
| 205B | 38 x 27 | 1,026 | 14 | | 130 | 65 | 110 | 102 |
| 205C | 35 x 29 | 1,015 | 14 | | 120 | 55 | 90 | 101 |
| 205D | 38 x 29 | 1,102 | 14 | | 140 | 65 | 110 | 110 |
| Total | 73 x 56 | 4,088 | 14 | | 500 | 250 | 400 | 414 |
| 206A | 36 x 27 | 972 | 14 | | 110 | 55 | 90 | 97 |
| 206B | 40 x 27 | 1,080 | 14 | | 130 | 65 | 100 | 108 |
| 206C | 36 x 32 | 1,152 | 14 | | 130 | 65 | 100 | 115 |
| 206D | 40 x 32 | 1,280 | 14 | | 140 | 65 | 120 | 128 |
| 206E | 36 x 27 | 972 | 14 | | 110 | 55 | 90 | 97 |
| 206F | 40 x 27 | 1,080 | 14 | | 130 | 65 | 100 | 108 |
| Total | 76 x 86 | 6,535 | 14 | | 780 | 400 | 600 | 646 |

**LOWER LEVEL — 100 - Meeting, Reception, Ballroom & Theatre Facilities**

| Room # | Overall Dimensions Feet | Usable Area Square Feet | Ceiling Height Feet | No. of 10x10 Booths | Theatre | Classroom | Banquet | Reception |
|---|---|---|---|---|---|---|---|---|
| 101 | 71 x 37 | 2,627 | 10/15 | | 270 | 150 | 180 | 262 |
| 102 | THEATRE | | | | 1,330 | | | |
| 103A | 41 x 28 | 1,148 | 12 | | 110 | 55 | 110 | 115 |
| 103B | 41 x 28 | 1,148 | 12 | | 90 | 45 | 110 | 115 |
| Total | 41 x 56 | 2,296 | 12 | | 200 | 100 | 220 | 230 |
| 104A | 62 x 30 | 1,860 | 12 | | 225 | 110 | 180 | 186 |
| 104B | 62 x 25 | 1,550 | 12 | | 200 | 100 | 120 | 155 |
| 104C | 62 x 31 | 1,735 | 12 | | 250 | 120 | 180 | 174 |
| 104D | 62 x 26 | 1,798 | 12 | | 190 | 95 | 120 | 180 |
| Total | 62 x 112 | 6,944 | 12 | 36 | 800 | 400 | 600 | 695 |
| 105 | 100 x 84 | 8,400 | 18/21 | | 1,000 | 500 | 700 | 840 |
| 106 | 100 x 112 | 11,200 | 18/21 | | 1,400 | 650 | 1,060 | 1,120 |
| 107 | 100 x 84 | 8,400 | 18/21 | | 1,000 | 500 | 700 | 840 |
| Total | 100 x 280 | 28,000 | 18/21 | 141 | 3,500 | 1,600 | 2,460 | 2,800 |

\* When using Exhibit Halls A, B & C together without operable walls
\*\* Capacities do not reflect sightlines or audio visual requirements

The first point, "group business is a sizable market," was addressed earlier in the chapter (see Exhibits 5-5 to 5-7). There is no question that group business is "sizable," and depending on the type of hotel and the market in which it operates, some properties get more than their share of group business.

The second point addresses the incredible economies of scale associated with group business. *Economies of scale* is a term that denotes the economic benefits of mass production. Most items produced in mass quantities benefit from reduced per-item production costs. The same is true for the hotel industry. Selling a bulk of group rooms provides the operator with specific economies of scale. The sales department benefits from the reduced work in booking one large group as opposed to booking numerous smaller visits. The reservations department benefits from having a block of rooms set aside for the group. Even the front office, housekeeping, and uniformed services benefit from group room bookings.

With group arrivals and departures, business levels are clearly understood. With a five-day convention, for example, the front office is especially busy on the first and last days: During the first day, the front office is busy with heavy check-ins; on the last day, it is busy with check-outs. The middle days, however, are relatively slow for the front office staff. During these slower middle days, the hotel saves labour costs by reducing its normal staffing levels. The same is true with the housekeeping and uniformed services departments. In many hotels, the housekeeping department spends less time cleaning stayover rooms than it does cleaning check-outs. Similarly, the bell staff is busiest when assisting guests with luggage at check-in and check-out. Uniformed-service positions are very slow during the middle days of a convention.

The third reason hotels like group business is that group delegates have a higher worth than do individual guests. No one understands this quite as well as casino hotels. Interacting with other conventioneers often puts group delegates in a festive mood. The trip is not just business—in many cases, there is fun and excitement in the excursion. And what better way to have fun than with an all-expenses-paid trip (see Exhibit 5-7)?

Many convention, exposition, and related group delegates are visiting the event at no personal cost. Their company or business has funded most of or the entire trip. Once at the hotel, delegates have a high likelihood of spending additional money. After all, their basic expenses (meals, lodging, transportation, and convention registration) have been paid. Therefore, they buy a round of golf they might not ordinarily purchase if they were paying for the trip on their own. They may have an extra cocktail or two and buy more expensive "premium" brands. They may select a souvenir from the gift shop or even a painting from the gallery. And, of course, they might gamble a few extra (or a lot of extra) dollars. Even when delegates attend a convention at their own expense, there are favourable tax deductions that often reduce the real cost of the trip.

**Casino Hotels** Casino hotels are interesting breeds in themselves. Casino hotels generally only accept groups that have a high likelihood of gambling. All things being equal, the casino manager may prefer a group of sanitation engineers, bottling managers, or morticians to a group of doctors, lawyers, or schoolteachers. In fact, the hotel may prefer a few empty hotel rooms to a hotel full of non-gamblers. Therefore, even when space is available, certain groups will be refused by casino hotels.

Assuming that sanitation engineers are considered to be good gamblers, the casino must decide how much they are worth. The question that must always be answered is: Will the group produce more casino revenues than the individual tourists the group is displacing? If the group has a strong reputation for casino play, it will be able to negotiate a better discount than a group with a lesser (or unknown) reputation.

Research shows that different delegates have different spending habits. Industries in which delegates have higher annual salaries (say, physicians) usually see more spending per person during annual conventions than industries with lower annual salaries (say, military officers). This is not necessarily the case with casino gaming. With casino gaming, lower-income delegates may spend more on the casino floor than wealthier delegates.

The reason for this dichotomy can be found in such socio-economic factors as education, aversion to risk, moral perceptions, and any number of other reasons for which a given delegate may or may not gamble. Therefore, a casino operator may prefer the military officers to the physicians, who have fewer propensities to gamble.

**Why Some Hotels Refuse Groups** Not too many years ago, select resort operations were less inclined to accept group business than they are today. They refused group bookings for a number of reasons. The primary reason was because the group alienated non-group guests staying at the property. That is still often the case. Staying in a hotel that is almost entirely occupied by a large group can be disconcerting to the individual, non-group guest. Walking the halls, playing tennis, eating a meal, and sitting in the lounge can be rather self-conscious activities when loud and boisterous group delegates surround the non-affiliated guest. Some exclusive resorts will not subject their individual guests to such an uncomfortable situation. In Canada, many resorts have found that snowmobile and ski markets do not mix well, as snowmobilers like to party at night while skiers get up early in the morning to be the first on the slopes.

Hotels may be less interested in group business for several other reasons as well. Group business requires a certain investment from the hotel—there is the need for public meeting space (see Exhibit 5-8 (a)), audiovisual equipment, tables and chairs, food service equipment, and so on. Also, there is the requirement of additional labour. Group hotels require a sales department staffed with one or more individuals, a convention and catering department, and food production areas. Finally, groups often negotiate discounted room rates. Hotels that find themselves in the enviable position of having strong year-round occupancy may be less interested in discounted groups.

## Categories of Group Business

The need to communicate an ever-increasing amount of information has given extra strength to the convention market. Even as the information superhighway is being paved, the conventions market is larger than ever. Meeting and speaking with other delegates face to face offers certain benefits that the impersonal computer, telephone, or Internet cannot provide.

As the convention market is growing, so is the group tour and travel market. The continued growth for this category of group business looks especially strong in light of the ever-increasing numbers of Canadians over the age of 55, retired, in good health, and with plenty of discretionary dollars. Lacking the expense account and tax advantages of the conventioneer, the group tourist seeks economy above all else. Group tour and travel rates are often substantially lower than rack rates.

Whereas convention business is sold as a group and guests are handled individually, tour business is sold as a group and guests are handled as a group. One sale, one reservation, one registration, one service, and one billing provide the savings on which the tour concept is built.

**Tour Groups** Tour groups are very convenient for the hotel, but that convenience comes at a price. Tour operators demand deep discounts. They get them because the entire burden is on the tour operator, with only minimal risk for the hotel.

The hotel deals with one party, the group tour company or wholesaler. The wholesaler leases the bus or plane, books the rooms, commits land transportation and entertainment, and then goes out to sell the package. Travel agents are the wholesaler's major sales outlets. Each agent receives a commission for the sale, and the wholesaler combines them into one group. In so doing, the workload of the front office is reduced considerably.

As much as 40 percent of the tour operator's original room estimate may be lost between the start of negotiations and the date of arrival, perhaps as long as one year later. Consequently, tour operators may be given the right to sell and report until as close as 7 to 14 days before arrival. **Sell and report**, also called status control, allows the wholesaler or tour operator to sell rooms and report back periodically. The right to this free sell is changed to sold-out status at the discretion of the hotel's forecast team.

Careful control is maintained over the right to sell and report because several agencies might be in that mode simultaneously. Specific dates are closed when the hotel is full and others may be closed to arrivals. Within the terms of the contract with the wholesaler, the hotel's forecast team can alter the closeout date for the tours, asking for the final rooming list one week, four weeks, or even five weeks before arrival. Nowhere in this process is the hotel's in-house reservations office involved. The wholesaler and that company's team of travel agents do all the selling. The sales office negotiates the deals, and the central reservations office is not generally involved.

**Convention Groups** Arrangements for a convention are made by a representative or committee of the organization and confirmed to the hotel with a contract of agreement. Large associations have permanent, paid executives in addition to the annually elected officers. These account executives are so numerous they have their own organization, the Canadian Society of Association Executives (CSAE).

If the organization is large enough to have a paid executive, he or she negotiates the arrangements with the hotel's sales staff. Details focus on many areas, including housing, meals, and meeting facilities. The organization (club, association, union) contracts with the hotel to buy meeting space (see Exhibit 5-8 (a)), banquet facilities, and rooms to house its own staff. It negotiates with the hotel for a block of guest rooms, but it does not pay for those rooms. Members deal individually with the hotel for accommodations.

The association sells function tickets to its membership for such events as banquets, cocktail parties, and luncheons. The money collected from these events is paid to the hotel at the negotiated price. If the association charges a higher ticket price, it will make a slight profit over the hotel's charge.

The organization is responsible for its own entertainment (although it may hire people through the hotel), speakers, films, and so on. For this, it charges the attendees a registration fee. Although some of the fee goes toward the costs of the program, the association usually profits here again.

Further gains may be made through the room rate arrangements. Sometimes organizations require the hotel to charge the attending members more than the negotiated room rate and to refund that excess to the group treasury. This raises many ethical concerns, particularly if the convention guest is unaware of the arrangement.

In no way does the association contract for rooms, except for those directly related to association headquarters, such as officers' and speakers' rooms. Room reservations are individually contracted between the hotel and each delegate. Billing is handled the same way, and collections become a personal matter between the conventioneer and the hotel.

**The Threat from Discount Travel Sites** The popularity of the Internet has made travel information more readily accessible than ever before. Broad availability of such information has affected the group travel side of the industry far more than anticipated. In the past, the group meeting planner negotiated with the hotel for the best possible convention rate, shared the headquarters hotel information—including rates—with association members and convention delegates months in advance, and assumed reservations against the group block would simply materialize. But the old way is certainly not the current way.

Discount travel sites (e.g., Priceline.com, Expedia.ca, Travelocity.ca, Orbitz.com, and LastMinuteDeals.com) have provided savvy delegates with several new options. Let's create a hypothetical situation; say that the fictitious Imperial Arms Hotel at a shore town in New Brunswick has the Canadian Billiards Club (CBC) convention visiting from August 3 to August 7. Delegates to the CBC convention likely made their room reservations many months ago at the group-negotiated rate of $139 per night.

However, in mid-July, delegates discovered that the same rooms could be purchased over discount Internet sites for just $79 per night. It is a small sacrifice to stay outside of the convention block—Internet-booked rooms outside the convention block will not be identified with the convention and therefore will not get turn-down service, a daily convention newsletter, or the nightly conference gift—so many delegates cancel their $139 convention room reservations and booked over the Internet at $79.

But the story does not end there. If rooms at the convention headquarters hotel are $79 on the Internet, there are almost certainly other rooms in town at substantial savings as well. It turns out that the fictitious William Lyon Mackenzie Hotel (just across the street) shows rooms for only $49 on the Internet. Other delegates decide to cancel rooms at the headquarters hotel in favour of an even better rate (although they'll have to walk across the street every day) at the William Lyon Mackenzie Hotel.

At this point, the meeting planner faces several serious issues. The availability of substantially lower rates makes for not only an embarrassing situation, but also a potentially costly one as well. The cost comes through group attrition (discussed in detail later in this chapter); if the convention does not generate a certain number of room nights, the difference is billable to the convention. The CBC group may potentially be liable for thousands of dollars in attrition costs because of the bargain-hunting antics of its delegates.

So what is to be done? Perhaps the meeting planner should simply talk to the hotel sales department, explain what has happened in the last few days before the convention begins, and ask for a new contract and a better rate. That action has been tried—it doesn't work. The hotel will stick to its guns and insist on maintaining the negotiated rate and the negotiated attritions clause.

Today's meeting planners therefore must negotiate several clauses into their contracts to combat this growing problem. One clause counts all members of the group against the guarantee. Even if members choose to stay at the hotel as unidentified delegates, if the group (CBC) can prove that the members were registered with the convention, the group will receive credit against the room-night guarantee. Another response to the problem of discounted rooms is a clause in the contract stating, "No lower rates shall be offered by the hotel, through any distribution vehicle, during the contracted meeting dates, unless offered to all attendees as well."

**Expositions and Trade Shows** Expositions and trade shows have many characteristics similar to conventions. In fact, trade shows are often held in conjunction with large conventions. The association (or trade-show entrepreneur) acquires space from the hotel or convention centre and leases that space to exhibitors (see Exhibit 5-8 (a)). Those managing the trade show invite guests, exhibitors, and shoppers.

The average guest stay is longer with a show because the displays, which are costly and elaborate, require setup and teardown time. Otherwise, reservation and front-office procedures are the same as for a convention or an individual guest. More city ledger charges (delayed billing) may occur because the exhibitors are usually large companies that request that type of settlement.

## Convention Reservations

Associations book conventions and expositions as many as 5 to 10 years in advance. For small to mid-sized conventions, two to three years is the norm.

Initially, the hotel commits a **blanket reservation** and a rate is negotiated. For large conventions requiring more than one hotel, a citywide convention and visitor's bureau (CVB) negotiates the blanket reservation on behalf of participating hotels (refer to the section entitled "Convention and Visitor Bureaus" below). The blanket reservation is little more than a commitment for a set number of rooms at a set rate for a set date. There is little additional detail until at least a year in advance.

**Adjusting the Room Block** As the date approaches, some six months to a year in advance, the hotel begins to examine the blanket reservation or room block. After discussions with the association, the hotel may adjust the number of rooms required if the association predicts its convention size will grow or shrink that year. Meetings with neighbouring hotels or the CVB may shed light on their management strategies with regard to the room block and the convention's ability to deliver the rooms committed. Finally, communication with other hotels where this group has previously been housed will give some sense of the group's attrition, casualty, or wash factor.

Convention hotels usually co-operate by furnishing each other with historical information about the group—numbers, no-shows, and the like. They do this because conventions usually move annually. A hotel in one section of the province or country is not competing with another if the organization has already decided to meet in another city. Similar information is available through local convention or tourist bureaus, which report to and have access to the files of the International Association of Convention and Visitor Bureaus (IACVB). The IACVB gathers data about the character and performance of each group handled by the member bureaus.

Reservation problems occur despite the best predictive efforts of the marketing and reservations departments. Association memberships change over time, and certain cities prove more or less appealing than previous sites. The **casualty factor** (cancellations plus no-shows) also varies from group to group, reducing the value of generalized percentage figures.

**Convention and Visitor Bureaus** Convention and visitor bureaus are publicly funded, quasi-governmental agencies found in all large and most mid-sized or small cities. CVBs (sometimes known as convention and visitor authorities) are a centralized entity designed to represent the city's hospitality industries. Usually, CVBs are funded by local lodging or room taxes (see Chapter 8); they may also receive some government funding and some membership dues. Because the vast amount of funding comes from lodging taxes, hotels are viewed as paying "customers" of the CVB and the CVB is, in essence, working for the betterment of the hospitality industry.

The CVB represents the city in numerous group rooms bids each year (see Exhibit 5-9). Many of these bids are made directly to the CSAE or a regional counterpart of the same. Hotel sales managers from some of the larger properties (or key properties bidding on a particular piece of business) often accompany CVB representatives on national sales trips.

Some group business may be booked directly with a hotel, particularly in smaller cities. In major cities across Canada, there is now a "live auction" several times per year. A major company such as General Electric, through a contract company operating a website similar to eBay, advertises its overnight room business requirements for the next year. Hotels are sent information prior to the live auction and advise whether they wish to bid on the business. If they decide to bid, they then enter the live auction at a pre-advised time and bid. Each hotel can watch as the private bids for the business become lower and lower; this is just the opposite of eBay, where bids go higher and higher. The bidding hotels are not aware of which competitors they are bidding against, and the end results are that General Electric gets great rates and the competing hotels further lower their average rate.

**Expanded Services** In recent years, CVBs have begun vertically integrating more and more group services. Such areas as transportation services (moving delegates to and from the airport and daily to and from the convention centre), on-site registration assistance (temporary staffing of booths), database marketing (identifying who attended

**Exhibit 5-9** ▶
The Metro Toronto Convention Centre has a list of upcoming events on its website, www.mtccc.com.

and from where they came), telemarketing (swaying potential delegates to attend the convention), promotion assistance (developing videos and print materials), and even special event or off-site banquet planning (managing extracurricular activities outside the convention centre) are now being offered by some CVBs.

Meeting planners are generally pleased with the trend toward expanded bureau services. After all, any value-added service included with the price of convention space will ultimately make for a better convention and might even save the association money. But at what cost? Just as meeting planners are happy about the trend toward vertical integration of CVBs, independent meeting suppliers are less pleased. They argue that CVBs are stepping outside their defined roles as convention and visitor bureaus. The job of the CVB, according to many meeting supply companies, is to bring business into the city. Once the CVB secures the business, independent meeting suppliers should be allowed to handle the details from there.

Certainly, the CVBs' expanded role encroaches upon the independent meeting suppliers' hard-earned turf. When the CVB offers transportation services, that affects the ground-handling companies. When the CVB offers on-site registration assistance, that affects the temporary employment agencies. Others who may be affected by these expanded services include independent research and marketing consultants, video production and media print services, caterers, and regional tour operators.

The CVBs understand the problem but often opt for the greater good to the greatest number of persons. You see, if a convention threatens to be lost to a competing city because that city is including additional services, like it or not, the CVB will have to match the bid. The alternative is to let the convention, and all of its associated community revenues (see Exhibit 5-6), slip away. With conventions of 10 000 delegates representing some $7 million to hotels, restaurants, transportation services, theatres, and shops in a community, CVBs cannot afford to lose business for the sake of a few independent meeting planners.

**The Housing Bureau** An important division or office within the CVB is the **housing bureau** (or housing authority). When the CVB is successful in bidding and committing citywide rooms to groups too large to be housed by one hotel, the housing bureau becomes involved.

Each hotel commits rooms toward the blanket reservation and a citywide commitment is made to the association. Rates remain the prerogative of the individual properties.

Reservation request cards (Exhibit 5-10) are returned to the CVB's housing bureau rather than to the individual hotel. The bureau relays to the hotel the guest's first, second, or third choice, depending on which hotel still has space. The hotel replies to the guest and sends copies of the confirmation to the housing bureau and to the association's headquarters.

Two properties may join forces if the convention is too large for one hotel but does not need a citywide commitment. It used to be that the property that booked the business became the headquarters site and booking office, with the second hotel (the overflow hotel) honouring the negotiated convention rate. This practice is now considered a violation of the Competition Act. Joint housing of delegates is permissible, but each property should negotiate its own rates.

**Overflow Hotels** Some hotels require an advance deposit from convention delegates. This is especially true of isolated resorts where there is little chance that walk-ins will fill no-show vacancies. It is also true of overflow hotels.

Conventions are often too large to be housed in just one hotel. Therefore, the association finds additional properties to supplement the rooms available at the headquarters hotel. These supplemental properties are commonly referred to as overflow hotels.

Overflow hotels often require an advance deposit sufficient to cover the cost of all nights booked. This is because overflow properties may lose occupancy to the headquarters hotel during the second or third day of the convention. Because of cancellations and

**Exhibit 5-10 ▶**
Group confirmation cards showing run-of-the-house (flat) rates (left) and spread rates (right). Spread rates offer a range of choices not provided by the flat rates. (The hotel's address is on the other side of the card.)

| Associated Tailors of Canada | Associated Tailors of Canada |
|---|---|
| May 4–8, — — | May 4–8, — — |
| **Herald Square Hotel** **Reservation Department** | **Herald Square Hotel** **Reservation Department** |
| Please make the following reservations quoted on European plan (no meals included). | Please make the following reservations quoted on European plan (no meals included). |
| Reservations must be received by **Herald Square** no later than April 15. | Reservations must be received by **Herald Square** no later than April 15. |
| ☐ Guest Rooms—Single            $82 | ☐ Guest Rooms—Single   $72  $78  $84  $90 |
| ☐ Guest Rooms—Double           $88 | ☐ Guest Rooms—Double   $78  $84  $90  $96 |
|  | (Please circle rate choice) |
| ☐ Suites: Petite            $110 | ☐ Suites: Petite            $110 |
|       Deluxe            $135 |       Deluxe            $135 |
| Will Arrive _____ Time _____ | Will Arrive _____ Time _____ |
| Will Depart _____ Time _____ | Will Depart _____ Time _____ |
| Name _____ | Name _____ |
| Address _____ | Address _____ |
| City _____ | City _____ |
| Province _____ Postal Code _____ | Province _____ Postal Code _____ |
| Credit Card No. _____ Exp. Date _____ | Credit Card No. _____ Exp. Date _____ |
| Reservations will not be held after 6 P.M. unless otherwise requested. | Reservations will not be held after 6 P.M. unless otherwise requested. |

no-shows, the headquarters hotel often has vacancies at the outset of the convention. Rooms available at the headquarters hotel are very appealing to delegates housed at overflow properties. After all, for roughly the same rate, they can stay in the main hotel with all of the exciting **hospitality suites** and activities it has to offer.

Therefore, overflow properties need to protect themselves against delegates who check out on the second day and move to the headquarters hotel. Overflow properties sometimes protect themselves by charging full advance deposits equal to the entire number of nights the delegate initially planned to stay. They may also change their cancellation policy to reflect 48 or 72 hours' advance notice.

## Negotiating Convention Rates

Convention rates are a unique breed because convention organizers bargain hard to obtain the best rates they can. Yet it is the individual convention delegate who actually reaps the benefit of the discounted rate when he or she pays the room bill. The association executive negotiates with the hotel(s) on behalf of the convention and its delegates. The sales manager, the director of sales, or even the general manager negotiates on behalf of the hotel.

For most conventioneers, the hotel room is the largest expense item (see Exhibit 5-6). Therefore, the convention attempts to negotiate a favourable rate so as to attract the most delegates possible. Conversely, the hotel needs to keep its profitability and yield management policies in mind as it sets rate parameters with the group.

Another factor that the hotel will probably consider is the attrition or wash factor for each particular group. Through contacts with other properties that have housed this group in the past, the sales manager gains an understanding of the attrition or pickup rate for this particular group. It makes no sense for the hotel to plan 800 rooms for five nights for the Associated Tailors of Canada conference (see Exhibit 5-10) if they'll be lucky to actually sell 650 rooms for an average of four nights. Associations have a tendency to exaggerate the number of rooms needed by delegates. Hotels must ascertain the attrition factor or pickup rate before committing to a specific room rate.

**Attrition** The group's attrition or wash factor and the group's pickup rate are actually reciprocals. They both provide the sales department with a measurement of the number of rooms actually reserved, in comparison to the number set aside in the reservation room block. They simply derive this measurement in slightly different ways.

The pickup rate looks at the actual number of rooms sold to convention delegates divided by the number of rooms originally blocked. For an example, let's look back to the Associated Tailors of Canada convention. Let's assume that the blanket reservation blocked 800 rooms for 5 nights—that's 4000 **room nights**. However, at the close of the convention, the hotel discovered that it sold only 650 rooms for an average of 4 nights—that's 2600 room nights. The pickup rate was 65 percent (2600 room nights sold divided by 4000 room nights blocked).

Conversely, the attrition factor looks at the number of rooms that were not sold or not picked up. The attrition factor measures the remaining unsold delegate rooms by the number of rooms originally blocked. Again, let's look to the Associated Tailors of Canada convention. If 2600 room nights were actually picked up against a block of 4000 room nights, 1400 room nights went unsold to convention delegates. These 1400 room nights may have ended up being sold to corporate or leisure guests, but only after the agreed-upon closeout date for accepting convention reservations. The attrition factor for this group was 35 percent (1400 room nights unsold divided by 4000 room nights blocked).

**Hotels Get Serious About Attrition** Hotel attrition policies are more prevalent (and taken more seriously) than ever before. Groups that fail to fill their contracted room block (usually a 90 percent pickup rate is considered acceptable) are charged attrition fees ranging from a few hundred dollars to hundreds of thousands of dollars! After all, when the hotel offers reduced group room rates, it is discounting them against the group's promise to fill them. If the room nights do not materialize, the hotel's bottom line suffers.

Automated attendee registration (systems like b-there.com, passkey.com, and 123sign-up.com) can alleviate costly attrition fees in several ways:

- *Email marketing.* You're attending the convention, but are your friends? Please send this email reminder to 10 of your closest associates.

- *Targeted marketing.* Which attendees who registered last year have failed to re-register this year?

- *Cancellation tracking.* Who cancelled in the past 10 days, and are any worrisome trends developing?

- *Hotel balancing.* The Omni is filled to 94 percent of its block (no attrition fees above 90 percent pickup), yet the Radisson sits at just 74 percent.

**Comp Rooms** Complimentary (**comp** or "free") rooms are one part of the total package. Complimentary rooms for use by the association are included at a rate of about 1 comp unit per 50 sold. The formula applies to both convention and tour groups.

Many hotels are beginning to take a hard look at how comps are earned and used. Attrition factors, no-shows, and cancellations are no longer counted in the computation. Credit is given only for the number of rooms actually sold; understays do not contribute to the count.

The use of comps is also being restricted. Comps are meant to be used by convention executives and staff during the dates of the convention and possibly several days immediately preceding or following the event. Comps are not designed for use months later as a personal vacation for the convention executive!

**Rate Quotes** Rates are quoted as flat or spread (see Exhibit 5-10). Under the **flat rate**, sometimes called **single rate** or **run-of-the-house rate**, all guests pay the same convention rate, which is usually less than the average rack rate. Except for suites, rooms are assigned on a best-available basis, called run-of-the-house. Some pay more for the room than its normal price, and others pay less. Run-of-the-house implies an equal distribution of room assignments. If half of the rooms have an **ocean view** and half do not, the convention group should get a 50–50 split with a run-of-the-house rate. One Hawaiian hotel advertises "run-of-the-ocean" rates. A fair distribution includes an equitable share of standard, medium, and deluxe accommodations.

A **spread rate,** sometimes called a sliding rate, uses the standard rack rate distribution already in place. The level is reduced several dollars below the rack rates. Assignments are made over the entire rate spread according to individual preference and a willingness to pay. The range of wealth and interest among the attendees makes spread rates more attractive to larger groups.

**Group Blocks** As individual requests arrive at a hotel, they are charged against the group block reservation. The hotel and the association re-examine the room commitment 45, 30, and 20 days before the convention begins.

Reservations received after the closeout date, 20 to 30 days before the convention starts, are accepted only if space remains—on an availability basis only. Reservations are confirmed individually, with an additional copy sometimes going to the association for count control.

Historically, handling group reservations, coordinating delegate rooms, and managing rooming lists has been a bit cumbersome. Housing bureaus collect convention delegate hotel preferences (see Exhibit 5-10) and prepare a list of delegates staying at each hotel. For smaller meetings, the company hosting the meeting probably develops the rooming list.

Once the names and addresses are prepared, the hotel may be responsible for sending a confirmation to each delegate. This is where the cumbersome nature of rooming lists is most apparent. The housing bureau (or meeting planner) rooming list is usually delivered to each hotel on paper, requiring the hotel to enter the data into its property management system by hand. That's where a lot of spelling and related errors occur.

New advancements on the market take advantage of the translation capabilities of switch technology (see Chapter 4) to download the information directly from the housing bureaus to each hotel, no matter which property management system they may be using. One of the leaders in this new technology is THISCO's UltraRes system.

**Unidentified Delegates** Some delegates slip through the carefully planned system and appear to the hotel as regular guests unaffiliated with the convention. This is usually accidental, but some guests deliberately trick the hotel to gain rate or room advantages. Many delegates make room reservations by telephone and fail to mention that they are with the convention. In addition, they do not mail back the reservation cards (see Exhibit 5-10).

One of two things may happen with these unidentified conventioneers: (1) the reservation might be denied (the convention block is open, but general reservations are closed), and the guest will go elsewhere; or (2) the reservation might be accepted as a non-convention guest (both the convention blanket and the non-convention categories are open). This second option leaves the hotel with duplicate space.

The situation takes a different twist when the conventioneer accepts space outside the blanket count because all of the convention spots have been filled. Once housed, this guest argues to get the special, reduced convention rate. If too many situations like that occur, the carefully balanced yield management system goes awry.

**Inclusive Tour Packages** The **inclusive tour** (IT) package is the hotel's move into the lucrative group market. The hotel combines housing, food, and entertainment—but no transportation—to offer an appealing two- or three-night stay at greatly reduced rates. The IT package affects group bookings, but it is not a type of group business.

IT packages can and do compete with convention reservations. For large conventions, the yield management committee closes the remaining rooms to all but high-priced rates. When relatively few rooms of the hotel are assigned to the convention, all rate classes remain available, including the package, priced at less and offering more than the convention rate. Keen convention shoppers book the IT package.

## Handling the Tour Group Reservation

The workload of the reservations department is affected relatively little by the demands of the tour group. Both the initial sale and the continuing contact rest with the hotel's marketing and sales department. That department may have a position called the tour and travel desk.

**Exhibit 5-11** ▶
Association executives
and professional meeting
planners evaluate numerous hotels before selecting the right property for
their group needs. Each
hotel is evaluated for
price, availability, size,
ability to meet the group's
unique needs, and so on.
Here is a sample page
(Accommodations) from a
site-inspection checklist.
This particular checklist
has 14 pages covering a
variety of categories and
observations.

SITE INSPECTION CHECKLIST

**ACCOMMODATIONS**

*Number of Rooms on Property:*

|  | Smoking | Non |  | Smoking | Non |
|---|---|---|---|---|---|
| Doubles | ____ | ____ | Queens | ____ | ____ |
| Kings | ____ | ____ | Parlors | ____ | ____ |
| Suite | ____ | ____ | Other | ____ | ____ |

*Total Number of Rooms Available for Group:*

|  | Smoking | Non |  | Smoking | Non |
|---|---|---|---|---|---|
| Doubles | ____ | ____ | Queens | ____ | ____ |
| Kings | ____ | ____ | Parlors | ____ | ____ |
| Suite | ____ | ____ | Other | ____ | ____ |

*ADA Rooms for the Physically Impaired:*

Doubles____ Queens____ Kings____ Parlors____ Suite____ Other____:

Complimentary room policy_____

Sprinklers and smoke alarms in rooms?          ≡ **Yes**      ≡ **No**

Emergency speakers in rooms?                   ≡ **Yes**      ≡ **No**

Room amenities (list) _____

Emergency lights?                              ≡ **Yes**      ≡ **No**

Hall lighting adequate and exits well marked?  ≡ **Yes**      ≡ **No**

Walls soundproof?                              ≡ **Yes**      ≡ **No**

Concierge/VIP Club level                       ≡ **Yes**      ≡ **No**

Concierge room amenities (list) _____

Guest phone charge policy/cost_____Long Distance_____

Data port on phone or in room?                 ≡ **Yes**      ≡ **No**

How many telephones in room? _____

Is there a desk with lighting?                 ≡ **Yes**      ≡ **No**

   Room Service? (open from_____ to_____)      ≡ **Yes**      ≡ **No**

Column headers (vertical): Accommodations · Dates of availability · Front desk · Public space · Meeting and banquet space · Food and beverage outlets · Services and parking · Other hotel information · Sports and recreational facilities · Facilities near property · Vendor recommendations · Meeting requirements and history · Site inspection evaluation · Negotiations

Yield management coordination is the major role for reservations during the time before the group arrives. Hotels doing a large tour and travel business maintain four-month horizons. Sell-and-report authorities are adjusted as forecasted demand equals, exceeds, or falls short of historical expectations.

Tour groups are almost always given shares-with rooms, since a premium is charged for single occupancy. The hotel gets a rooming list that shows each pairing. The entire block of rooms is **preassigned**. If the tour company brings in back-to-back groups, the very same rooms may be used again and again. Keeping the block together in the same floor or wing expedites baggage handling and reduces noise and congestion elsewhere.

Special group arrival sections, even special lobby entrances, reduce congestion as the group arrives or departs. Transportation is by bus, even if only to the airport. These transfer costs are part of the fee and are arranged by the tour company. Bell fees are also included, levied by the hotel over and above the room charge.

## Summary

Because reservations are in a sense contractual agreements, the hotel or corporate reservationist must be careful to document all pertinent information. Some reservation information, such as the date of arrival, number of persons and type of room, and guest's name and rate, is essential to the hotel. Other information, such as estimated time of arrival, special requests, and discounts, is less important to the reservation and may therefore only be collected in certain cases or by request of the guest.

Once the reservation has been agreed upon between the customer and the hotel or the central reservations office, its journey begins. In some cases the journey is short, as with those reservations made a few hours or days before arrival; other times, it is a long journey, as with reservations made many months—even years—in advance.

Although electronic reservations are gaining popularity for individual bookings, group reservations require person-to-person negotiations with the property sales department. Unlike the individual reservation, where most requests are straightforward, a personal touch is required for groups negotiating bulk rates, dates, meeting requirements, meal functions, and other hotel services.

## Questions and Problems

1. Many hotels are apprehensive about charging for corporate guaranteed reservations if a traveller fails to arrive. Even though a room was held and revenue was lost, the hotel is afraid to charge the no-show back to the corporation for fear of retaliation and loss of future business. Develop a series of strict—but fair—reservations policies that protect the hotel's interests while minimizing conflicts with the corporate account. In what instances would you charge the corporate no-show? When would you not charge?

2. The use of computerized reservations is far more efficient than the use of manual, handwritten reservations. Compare the manual reservations approach to the automated collection of guest reservation information. List as many benefits (efficiencies) created by automated reservations systems as you can.

3. As a follow-up to Problem 2, are there any disadvantages associated with automated reservations systems? Why are many reservations managers retraining agents to be more patient, friendly, and helpful? Does this retraining have anything to do with the computer age in which we live?

4. Guests generally prefer the choice associated with spread rates. Hotels find it easier to manage rooms inventory when they use flat rates. Which would you use as a hotel manager? Explain your response in detail.

5. As a prominent hotelier, you have been asked by the convention and visitor's bureau (CVB) to appear before the city commissioners during a CVB budget-review session. The commission is angry that the local CVB spends public funds to maintain a convention housing bureau and that those services are provided without a fee. Do the necessary research to provide hard facts to support your testimony in favour of the CVB.

6. The reservation of an unidentified convention delegate is treated as a corporate or leisure guest reservation. How might this lack of identifying the guest as a conventioneer affect the hotel? Could it benefit the guest? Could it hurt the guest?

## CASE STUDY

### Community Service versus Profitability

You have just taken over as general manager (GM) of a 300-room resort hotel within a two-hour drive of Vancouver. The hotel has extensive banquet and catering facilities that were underused during the tenure of the previous GM. When that manager arrived, he found that the function facilities were underused and decided to embark on attracting the business of various service and fraternal organizations in the city. He was quite successful at doing this, and now several service and fraternal clubs from the Kiwanis to the Shriners have their weekly dinner meetings at the hotel. The previous GM felt that exposing the hotel to these clubs, whose members also owned and operated local businesses, would expand its function business by attracting corporate and private functions from the membership of these clubs.

As the new GM, you know from your education and experience that the profitability of the hotel depends largely on the ability to sell more guest rooms and increase occupancy, as up to 75 percent of rooms revenue is profit. You feel that by offering a comprehensive conference package that would be marketed in Vancouver as an Executive Meeting Getaway, the hotel could attract overnight business. You believe that executives will have more productive meetings if they can get away from the distractions of the office and family that exist when companies hold day meetings at a downtown Vancouver hotel.

Your director of marketing has just come to you with a potential three-day, two-night booking by a corporation in Vancouver. The conference manager has rejected this booking, as several of the function rooms needed are already booked by the local service and fraternal organizations.

As GM, you need to answer the following questions:

1. Should you cancel the local service/fraternal organization bookings?

2. If you do cancel the local bookings, what are the ramifications?

3. What are the consequences if you choose not to cancel the local bookings?

4. How do you think the ownership group will ultimately judge your success or failure as the GM of this hotel, and does this affect your decision?

5. What might you suggest your director of marketing include in an Executive Getaway Package besides meeting space, accommodation, and food?

## Note

1. Information related to the study of central reservations offices can be found in the June 1997 issue of *Lodging Magazine*.

## Weblinks

### Convention and Visitor's Bureaus

Toronto Convention and Visitors Association
**www.tourismtoronto.com**

Tourisme Montréal
**www.tourisme-montreal.org**

Tourism Vancouver
**www.tourismvancouver.com**

Destination Halifax
**www.meethalifax.com**

Destination Winnipeg
**www.destinationwinnipeg.ca**

Canada Meetings, Conventions, & Incentive Travel
**www.canadameetings.com**

# Chapter 6 Forecasting Availability and Overbooking

## Learning Objectives

After reading this chapter, you will be able to do the following:

1. Identify the essential information required to make a simple unadjusted room count and a more complex adjusted room count.

2. Discuss the importance of forecasting and the uses of the rooms forecast by other departments.

3. Discuss the ramifications of a guest reservation as a legal contract.

4. Understand why hotels overbook and how to minimize the overbooking problem.

## Forecasting Available Rooms

The concept behind rooms inventory is simple enough. There is a one-to-one match between rooms in the hotel and rooms committed to either incoming reservations or stayover rooms. Each reservation reduces the available inventory until there are an equal number of reservations (and stayover rooms) matched with hotel rooms. At that point, the hotel is sold out.

As with most things in life, however, the simplicity of the system becomes increasingly complicated as the unique vagaries of customer contact affect the room count. Some guests stay an extra day or two despite their original intention to check out. Others depart a day or two earlier than anticipated due to circumstances beyond their control. Include in this growing list a few guests who cancel their reservations hours before arrival (or worse yet, guests who fail to even cancel their reservations and simply do not show up). Throw in another guest who arrives a day or two early and yet still expects to find room at your hotel (and it is in your best interest to accommodate early arrivals lest they cancel their future dates and stay elsewhere). Add to these circumstances the chance for human error—"Oh, I thought you said November 17, not September 17"—and the situation is further complicated.

# The Simple, Unadjusted Room Count

It makes sense to look first at a simple room-count forecast, before incorporating the numerous complications that can affect the count. A simple room count is also called an *unadjusted* room count, because various adjustments (such as overstays, understays, cancellations, etc.) have not yet been introduced. These adjustments will be discussed later in the chapter.

In this simple form, the unadjusted room count attempts to compare the rooms available in the hotel against anticipated stayovers and expected reservation arrivals. If any rooms remain uncommitted (i.e., there are more rooms available than are committed to stayovers and reservations), they are available for sale that day.

**Automated Inventory Tracking Systems**   At a moment's notice, the reservations department must be able to determine the number (and types) of rooms available for sale for a given date. With such pressing urgency, reservationists do not have the luxury of subtracting stayovers and expected reservations from rooms available to determine the room count. Therefore, they need to visualize the room count in some manner.

Automated property management systems offer various status reports under the reservations module. Although status reports (see Chapter 13) are determined in part by the particular property management system, most are quite similar. Some of the standard status reports found in the reservations module include:

- A 7-, 10-, or 14-day room availability report provides a window of time for which each room type is listed, and the number of remaining rooms available for sale are shown by date (see Exhibit 6-5).

- A current or one-day inventory report details all rooms in the hotel and their particular status. An example of such a report is shown in Exhibit 6-1.

- A reservations forecast report projects revenues and occupancies for each of several days into the future. Such a report usually displays the room and house count (number of guests in house) and projects the number of stayovers for each day. As the report reads further and further into the future (three to five days forward), the forecast becomes less and less accurate because it is based on each day's assumed check-outs and stayovers.

- A general manager's daily report looks at the current day. Group rooms picked up, guaranteed and non-guaranteed reservations, anticipated stayovers, out-of-order and out-of-inventory rooms, walk-ins, early check-outs, and more are all displayed in such a report.

- An arrivals list displays information about each reservation scheduled for that day's arrival. Each anticipated guest is listed alphabetically and can also be reviewed by affiliation: group reservations, travel agent bookings, late arrivals, and so on.

Other status reports may be generated, depending on the size of the hotel and the sophistication of the property management system.

**Simple Room Count**   Whether the reservations tracking system is manual or automated, exact room counts are performed several days prior to the actual date of arrival. By taking a more precise look at the next several days, the reservations department prepares itself for problems that may lie ahead. In fact, several room counts may be taken

| Business: MAY 25 | | | | 1-Day Room Inventory | | | | | MAY 25 17:15:49 |
| | | | | | | | | | Mon MAY 25-- |
| Room Type | Room Cnts | Rooms Offmkt | Rooms Sold | Rooms Avail | Rates 1per | | 2per | Close Level | Host Status | CTA MLOS |
|---|---|---|---|---|---|---|---|---|---|---|
| DDSU | 15 | 1 | 5 | 9 | 85.00 | | 85.00 | 4 | Open | |
| DDSN | 47 | 13 | 34 | 0 | 85.00 | | 85.00 | 4 | Closed | |
| KSU | 10 | 0 | 5 | 5 | 75.00 | | 75.00 | 2 | Open | |
| KSUN | 33 | 10 | 19 | 4 | 75.00 | | 75.00 | 3 | Open | |
| KHCN | 3 | 0 | 1 | 2 | 75.00 | | 75.00 | 1 | Open | |
| DDHN | 1 | 0 | 0 | 1 | 85.00 | | 85.00 | 1 | Open | |
| KEX | 1 | 0 | 0 | 1 | 85.00 | | 85.00 | 1 | Open | |
| KEXN | 5 | 2 | 1 | 2 | 85.00 | | 85.00 | 1 | Open | |
| D1HN | 2 | 0 | 1 | 1 | 75.00 | | 75.00 | 1 | Open | |
| Totals: | 117 | 26 | 66 | 25 | 56% Rack | | | | | |

Action:1 = Forward 1 Day   2 = Back 1 Day

▲
**Exhibit 6-1**
An example of a one-day rooms inventory screen. This is an actual Multi-Systems, Incorporated Property Manager screen (PM Version 8.11) from a 117-room all-suite hotel. Notice that 26 rooms are off-market (out of inventory due to an in-house renovation project), 66 rooms are sold (either to incoming reservations or to stayovers), and 25 rooms are available for sale. For information on CTA (closed to arrival) and MLOS (minimum length of stay), see Chapter 4. The various room types are listed in the first column from DDSU through D1HN. DD is two double beds, K is one king bed, S or SU indicates suite, EX stands for executive room, N means non-smoking (in the absence of N, the room is smoking), and H or HC means handicapped accessible.

throughout the day of arrival. Common times to readjust the day's room count are before arrivals begin (around 6 A.M.), just after the check-out hour (around 11 A.M. for many properties), and immediately before and after 6 P.M. for hotels that allow non-guaranteed (6 P.M.) reservations.

A simple room count taken during these times provides management with a true understanding of the rooms inventory status for the day. If the hotel has rooms available for sale (a plus count), it is important to know the number and types of these rooms. Armed with this information, the reservations department and the front desk can better sell the remaining rooms in the hotel. Maximum rates are charged against the last few rooms available (a yield management approach).

The hotel also needs to know when there are no rooms remaining (an even or zero count). It is especially important to be forewarned when the hotel finds itself in an overbooking situation (a minus count)—when there are more reservations and stayovers than there are rooms available. With advance knowledge, the hotel can arrange supplementary accommodations at other hotels, alert its front-office staff to handle the sensitive situation, and encourage the reservations department to accept cancellations if and when they occur.

Even in a computerized system, where the room count is available at a moment's notice, managers still need to understand the components that form the total rooms available count. Specifically, managers wish to know the number of rooms occupied last night, rooms due to check out, and reservations due to arrive.

**Committed Rooms** The process works on commitments. The hotel is committed to guests staying over from last night and to guests due to arrive today. If the total of these (stayovers plus reservations) is less than the total number of rooms in the hotel, there is a plus count. If the hotel has more commitments than rooms available for sale, there is a minus count (overbooked).

The concept of overbooking (having a minus count) is discussed in detail later in this chapter. However, it is important to understand that it is not necessarily a mistake to overbook the hotel. Overbooking is often a strategic decision made by the reservations manager in concert with the front-office manager, the sales manager, and the general manager. The idea behind overbooking hotel rooms is much the same as the reason that airlines overbook flights. The airlines (and hotels) know that some percentage of their customers will not arrive (no-shows) or will cancel. Therefore, the hotel reservations department plays a guessing game by projecting a series of adjustments onto the simple room count. The goal is to overbook the hotel just enough that the projected adjustments develop into a fully occupied hotel on the day of arrival. Too conservative a projection and the hotel has unsold rooms; too aggressive a projection and the hotel is forced to walk guests.

Refer to Exhibits 6-2 and 6-3. Exhibit 6-2 demonstrates a simple, unadjusted room count. The simple count looks at nothing more than rooms available, rooms committed to stayovers, and rooms committed to incoming reservations. These same figures are then reused in Exhibit 6-3. Exhibit 6-3, however, demonstrates an adjusted count. By including adjustments for overstays and understays, as well as for cancellations, no-shows, and early arrivals, the numbers are substantially different.

---

**Given**

A 1000-room hotel had a total of 950 rooms occupied last night. Of those 950 rooms, 300 are due to check out today. In addition, there are 325 reservations for today. There are 5 rooms out of order (OOO).

**Required**

Develop a simple, unadjusted room count using the given information above.

**Solution**

| | | |
|---|---|---|
| Rooms available in hotel | | 1000 |
| Occupied last night | 950 | |
| Due to check out today | 300 | |
| Equals number of stayovers | | 650 |
| + Today's reservations | | 325 |
| Total rooms committed for today | | 975 |
| Equals rooms available for sale | | 25    (with 5 OOO) |

Occupancy percentage is 975 ÷ 1000 or 97.5 percent.

---

▲
**Exhibit 6-2**

A simple, unadjusted room count. This is the first of two sample problems using the same basic information (also see Exhibit 6-3).

By subtracting committed rooms (650 stayovers and 325 incoming reservations) from rooms available (1000 rooms are available despite the fact that 5 rooms are out of order), the reservations manager knows that there are 25 rooms available for sale today (1000 minus 650 minus 325 equals 25).

Compare these results (25 rooms) with the findings in Exhibit 6-3. Although the same basic information was used for Exhibit 6-3, by incorporating a number of adjustments and projections, the end result is a substantially different room count.

**Given**

A 1000-room hotel had a total of 950 rooms occupied last night. Of those 950 rooms, 300 are due to check out today. In addition, there are 325 reservations for today. There are 5 rooms out of order (OOO). Note: This is the same information given in Exhibit 6-2.

**Historical Adjustments**

The hotel has developed the following historical adjustment statistics: understays, 6 percent; overstays, 2 percent; cancellations, 2 percent; no-shows, 5 percent; and early arrivals, 1 percent.

**Required**

Develop an adjusted room count using the given information and historical adjustments above.

**Solution**

| | | | |
|---|---|---|---|
| Rooms available in hotel | | | 1000 |
| Occupied last night | | 950 | |
| Due to check out today | 300 | | |
| Understays (6 percent) | + 18 | | |
| Overstays (2 percent) | − 6 | | |
| Equals adjusted number of rooms to check out today | 312 ⟶ | 312 | |
| Equals adjusted number of stayovers | | 638 ⟶ | − 638 |
| Today's reservations | 325 | | |
| Cancellations (2 percent) | − 7 | | |
| No-shows (5 percent) | − 16 | | |
| Early arrivals (1 percent) | + 3 | | |
| Equals today's adjusted reservations | 305 ⟶ | | − 305 |
| Adjusted total of rooms committed for sale | | | − 943 |
| Adjusted number of rooms available for sale | | | + 57 (with 5 OOO) |

Anticipated occupancy percentage is 943 ÷ 1000 or 94.3 percent.

▲
**Exhibit 6-3**
An adjusted room count. This is the second of two sample problems using the same basic information (see Exhibit 6-2).
   Using the same figures provided in Exhibit 6-2, this room count calculation incorporates a series of adjustments into the process. Stayover rooms, for example, are adjusted by understays (6 percent of rooms due to check out today) and overstays (2 percent of rooms due to check out today). Incoming reservations are adjusted by cancellations (2 percent of today's reservations), no-shows (5 percent of today's reservations), and early arrivals (1 percent of today's reservations).
   The net result (57 rooms available for sale) is far different from the 25 rooms found in Exhibit 6-2.

## Adjusted Room Count

Mathematics carries an aura of exactness that deceives any reservations department that relies on unadjusted figures. Most of the figures must be modified on the basis of experience. The reservations department collects data over the years, and this information allows for more precise projections. But even the adjustments change from day to day, depending on the day of the week and the week of the year. Percentages change with the weather, with the type of group registered in the house, and even with the news. Gathering the data is the first step; interpreting them is the second.

Each element in the projection can be refined over and over by using additional data or varying interpretations. Recomputing the count with these adjustments can make a substantial change in room availability (compare Exhibits 6-2 and 6-3).

**Computing Rooms Available** The actual number of rooms available in the hotel (1000 rooms for the continuing example shown in Exhibits 6-2 and 6-3) can change from day to day. For various reasons, rooms that were available for occupancy one day may be closed to occupancy on another day. If the removal is unexpected, removing the rooms from inventory can have an impact on the hotel's ability to accommodate guests with reservations.

When rooms are removed from availability, they are designated as being in one of two distinct categories: out of order or out of inventory. The difference between these classifications is of critical importance to management. The difference between out-of-order and out-of-inventory rooms affects more than the number of rooms available for sale. One of these two categories affects the occupancy calculation (the other does not); one may play a role in management bonuses (the other does not); and for publicly traded hotel companies, one can even influence stock market prices (the other does not). The difference between out-of-order and out-of-inventory (sometimes called offline) rooms is critical.

**Out-of-Order Rooms**  A room placed out of order is generally repairable within a relatively short time. A minor problem such as poor TV reception, a clogged toilet, a malfunctioning air conditioner, or a broken headboard will usually classify a room as **out of order** (OOO). Out-of-order rooms pose a special problem to management because in sold-out situations they must be repaired and returned to the market quickly. In periods of low occupancy, management may wait several days before returning such rooms to inventory.

Out-of-order rooms are, by nature, minimally inoperative—the problem that placed the room out of order is slight. As a result, in some situations out-of-order rooms are actually sold to the public. If the hotel is facing sold-out status and the few remaining rooms are out of order, management may choose to sell these rooms "as is" for a reasonable discount. A broken TV set may warrant a $10 discount; an inoperative air conditioner may warrant a $30 discount. No out-of-order room would ever be sold if it posed a hazard to the guest.

Because out-of-order rooms can be repaired and returned to the market, they are included in the total figure for rooms available for sale. In calculating room count statistics, out-of-order rooms are treated as if there is nothing wrong with them. Similarly, when calculating occupancy percentages, out-of-order rooms are left in the denominator as if there is nothing wrong with them. Some hotels, however, may show the number of out-of-order rooms separately on their daily report of revenues and occupancies.

In the continuing example, note that five rooms are out of order. Because out-of-order rooms are not removed from inventory, there are still 1000 rooms available for sale in the hotel. The occupancy of 97.5 percent (see Exhibit 6-2) has demonstrated no change in the 1000-room denominator.

**Out-of-Inventory Rooms** Out-of-inventory rooms cannot be sold "as is." Out-of-inventory rooms have significant problems that cannot be repaired quickly. Examples of major **out-of-inventory** (OOI) situations might include a flood that destroyed all carpet and floorboards in a room, a fire that has blackened the walls and left a strong odour, a major renovation that leaves half of the wallpaper removed as well as no carpet or furniture, and a murder investigation in which the police have ordered the room sealed until further notice.

By their very nature, out-of-inventory rooms are not marketable. The problem that placed them out of inventory is significant enough to remove the room from marketability until it has been repaired. In the continuing example, note that five rooms are out of order. To illustrate the points addressed above, let's see what happens if those five rooms were actually out of inventory. Remember, out-of-inventory rooms must be removed from the available rooms inventory. As a result, there will now be only 995 rooms available for sale in the hotel (1000 rooms less 5 out of inventory). The room availability total of +25 will also change. There will now be only +20 rooms available for sale [995 rooms less (650 stayovers plus 325 reservations)]. Out-of-inventory rooms have an impact on occupancy percentage as well. The rooms-sold numerator (975) remains the same, but the rooms-available-for-sale denominator would change to 995. The occupancy calculation (975 divided by 995) yields 98.0 percent. This is a different result from that in Exhibit 6-2, which showed 97.5 percent.

Exhibit 6-4 presents several additional examples of out-of-inventory and out-of-order computations.

**Computing Rooms Occupied Last Night** Rooms occupied last night is a precise number derived during the hotel's night audit function. This figure is simply the number of rooms physically occupied on any particular night. Relatively straightforward, yes, but certain adjustments or unique situations need to be considered in order that this be the most accurate figure possible.

**Exhibit 6-4** ▶
Out-of-order rooms do not affect inventory (rooms available for sale), while out-of-inventory rooms do. These two examples illustrate the difference this distinction can have on the resulting occupancy percentage. Each example is calculated in two ways: first the occupancy is calculated assuming that the rooms were OOO, and then the occupancy is recalculated assuming that the rooms were OOI.

1a. A 200-room hotel sold 125 rooms last night. If there were 10 rooms OOO, the occupancy would be as follows:
- Numerator (number of rooms sold): 125
- Denominator (number of rooms available for sale—remember, the denominator is not affected by OOO rooms): 200
- Equation: 125 ÷ 200
- Percent occupancy: 62.5

b. The same 200-room hotel sold 125 rooms last night. If instead the 10 rooms were OOI, the occupancy would be as follows:
- Numerator (number of rooms sold): 125
- Denominator (number of rooms available for same—remember, the denominator is reduced by the number of OOI rooms): 190
- Equation: 125 ÷ 190
- Percent occupancy: 65.8

2a. A 460-room hotel sold 375 rooms last night. If there were 22 rooms OOO, the occupancy would be as follows:
- Numerator: 375
- Denominator: 460
- Equation: 375 ÷ 460
- Percent occupancy: 81.5

b. The same 460-room hotel sold 375 rooms last night. If instead there were 22 OOI rooms, the occupancy would be as follows:
- Numerator: 375
- Denominator: 438
- Equation: 375 ÷ 438
- Percent occupancy: 85.6

Certain situations may require slight adjustments to the figure in the wee hours of the night audit. One example of such an adjustment is a very late arrival (usually after midnight). If the late guest is a walk-in customer (no pre-existing reservation), the auditor adds one more room to the already computed rooms-occupied-last-night figure. If the late guest has an existing reservation, the auditor similarly adjusts the rooms-occupied figure but also needs to credit the new guest's folio with the charge likely made hours earlier when it was assumed the guest would be a no-show (see the discussion on no-show guests later in this chapter).

Other considerations necessary for an accurate rooms-occupied count depend on unique hotel policies. For example, some hotels choose not to list comp (complimentary) rooms in their occupancy. As such, they are not counting comp rooms in the accounting processes for the preceding night. Therefore, the night auditor needs to remember to add all comp rooms to the rooms-occupied count. Similar errors crop up when the computer is programmed to count suites as two-room units even when the suite is not divided. The mistake comes in counting either two rooms as occupied or two rooms as checked out.

**Computing the Number of Stayovers** The number of rooms scheduled to check out today is not an absolute statistic. It is based primarily on the guests' initial plans at the time they made their reservations. Even when a well-trained front-desk clerk reconfirms the departure date during the check-in process, changes still occur. Corporate guests may complete their business a day or two earlier (or a day or two later) than expected. Leisure guests may decide to sightsee in town a bit longer (or shorter) than originally planned. Emergencies also occur, where guests may need to catch the next flight home, regardless of their original plans.

Each property collects historical data with which to project its understays and overstays. These data are usually expressed in terms of a percentage of the rooms due to check out that day. For example, in Exhibit 6-3, the understays percentage is 6 percent (0.06 times 300 rooms due out equals 18 understays), while the overstays percentage is 2 percent (0.02 times 300 rooms due out equals 6 overstays). Although these are both fictitious percentages, a real hotel would develop similar statistical projections over time.

**Understays** Some guests leave earlier than the hotel expected; they are known as **understays**. They are also sometimes referred to as *earlys*. When calculating the number of rooms due to check out, any understays will be added to the projected check-outs.

**Overstays** Some guests stay past their scheduled departure date; they are referred to as **overstays**. They are also sometimes known as **holdovers**. When calculating the number of rooms due to check out, any overstays will be subtracted from the projected check-outs.

| | | |
|---|---:|---:|
| Occupied last night | | 950 |
| Due to check out today | 300 | |
| Plus understays (6 percent) | + 18 | |
| Less overstays (2 percent) | − 6 | |
| Equals adjusted number due to check out today | 312 | −312 |
| Equals adjusted number of stayovers | | 638 |

By including understays and overstays in the continuing example, the number of rooms due to check out changes substantially. In the simple, unadjusted room count shown in Exhibit 6-2, the number due to check out today was 300. Once understays and overstays are included in the computation, however, that number changes to 312, as shown in the preceding table and in Exhibit 6-3. Similarly, the number of stayovers (650) demonstrated in the simple, unadjusted room count of Exhibit 6-2 changes with the inclusion of understays and overstays. In Exhibit 6-2, there are 650 projected stayovers. In the preceding table and in Exhibit 6-3, that number changes to 638 projected stayovers.

**Computing Today's Reservations** Just as some departing guests change their plans and overstay or understay their scheduled visit, some expected guests do not adhere to their original reservations. As a result, guests often cancel reservations, arrive a day or two earlier than expected, or never arrive at all. Each of these variables is assessed and adjusted according to historical data, to represent a closer approximation of reality.

**No-Shows** Some guests who hold reservations never arrive at the hotel. These guests are referred to as **no-shows**. No-shows may be caused by a multitude of factors. A change in business or personal plans, inclement weather or closed roads, cancelled or stranded flights, illness, or death may be some of the reasons a guest fails to arrive. Indeed, it is also possible that they simply forgot they had made a reservation.

No-shows present the hotel with a unique problem—namely, it is difficult to know when to classify the reservation as a no-show. For non-guaranteed reservations, the industry standard is 6 P.M. Non-guaranteed reservations that fail to arrive by 6 P.M. are considered no-shows, and those rooms are remarketed to walk-in guests.

Guaranteed and advance-deposit reservations are another story. The very nature of these higher-quality guaranteed or advance-deposit reservations suggests that the hotel will hold a room all night long. Therefore, it is literally impossible for a hotel front-desk clerk to determine when a specific guaranteed reservation changes from an expected arrival to a no-show. A front-desk clerk or night auditor can be fairly certain that a reservation that has not arrived by 11 P.M., midnight, or 1 A.M. is a no-show. An exception would be a reservation for newlyweds. However, there is always the chance that the guest has been detained and will still arrive in search of the reservation.

Most hotels will have a special code to identify newlyweds, as walking a newlywed couple is very distasteful for all involved. **Walking** a guest refers to the practice of sending guests with reservations to another hotel when your hotel is overbooked and unable to honour their reservation.

Asking for an estimated time of arrival on the reservation is one partial solution to this problem. By documenting the guest's expected arrival time, the desk clerk is better equipped to make difficult decisions about possible no-show guests. The earlier such decisions are made, the better the hotel's chances of selling the room to a walk-in.

**Cancellations** Although cancellations mean additional work for the reservations department and the front desk, they are still infinitely better than no-shows. Guests who cancel on the day of arrival are providing the hotel with an opportunity to resell the room. The earlier the cancellation is received, the better the chance of reselling that room.

Cancellation policies usually require notice at least 24 hours in advance of the reservation's arrival date. Cancellations made on the day of arrival are treated as no-shows and charged one room night. However, because cancellations (even last-minute cancellations) provide better information to the hotel than no-shows, many properties waive the one-night penalty to cancelling guests. Even if the hotel charges a late cancellation fee of, say, $25, that is better for the guest than being charged one full room night. That seems fair to all concerned, because a cancelled room has more opportunity to be resold than a no-show room. As a courtesy, many corporate hotels allow business guests to cancel without penalty until 6 P.M. on the day of arrival.

**Early Arrivals**   Cancellations and no-shows reduce the number of expected arrivals. Early arrivals increase the number of expected arrivals. **Early arrivals** are guests who arrive at the hotel one or more days prior to their scheduled reservation date.

There are a number of reasons why a guest might arrive at the hotel in advance of the expected reservation date. For example, the reservations department may have had a different date for the reservation than the guest understood, or possibly the guest's plans changed and he or she decided to arrive one or more days early. Whatever the reason, the front office will attempt to accommodate the guest.

Even in periods of 100 percent occupancy, the front office personnel strive to find accommodations for the early arrival. Not only is that good guest service, but also early arrivals often represent a number of room nights to the hotel—many early arrivals stay through the end of their originally scheduled departure. An early arrival that arrives two days early for a three-night reservation may very likely stay all five nights.

**Adjusting Today's Reservations**   The continuing example in Exhibit 6-2 on page 172 shows an unadjusted reservations count of 325 rooms. Assuming a cancellation rate of 2 percent, a no-show rate of 5 percent, and an early arrival rate of 1 percent, the numbers change significantly (see the following table and Exhibit 6-3):

| | |
|---|---|
| Today's reservations | 325 |
| Less cancellations (2 percent) | − 7 |
| Less no-shows (5 percent) | − 16 |
| Plus early arrivals (1 percent) | + 3 |
| Equals adjusted number of reservations | 305 |

A certain amount of mathematical rounding is necessary in these equations. A 2 percent cancellation rate with 325 reservations gives 6.5 cancellations. It is necessary to round 6.5 cancellations to 7. Similarly, no-shows round from 16.25 to 16 and early arrivals round from 3.25 to 3.

**The Adjusted Result**  With all of the adjustment components in place, a look at the adjusted room count (Exhibit 6-3) shows a substantial change from the simple, unadjusted room count (Exhibit 6-2). The number of stayover rooms has been adjusted from 650 to 638 because the number of rooms due to check out has been adjusted with understays and overstays. The number of expected reservations has been adjusted from 325 to 305 because of estimated cancellations, no-shows, and early arrivals.

The count of 57 rooms available for sale shown in Exhibit 6-3 is significantly higher than the count of 25 rooms available shown in Exhibit 6-2. With the same 5 rooms out of order, the hotel can now accept 57 rooms as walk-ins (assuming that it quickly repairs the 5 OOO rooms).

Exhibit 6-3 could just as easily have projected a change in the opposite direction. Second-guessing the actions of the guest is the reservations department's burden. A cautious projection with too few walk-ins accepted results in low occupancy and empty rooms despite guests who were turned away earlier in the day. An optimistic projection allows the desk to accept so many walk-ins that the reserved guest who arrives late in the day finds no room available.

This is the dilemma of overbooking: the need, on the one hand, to maximize occupancy and profits, and the pressure, on the other hand, to keep empty rooms for reservations that may never arrive. Hotels with heavy walk-ins, similar to the airline's standbys, are more flexible than isolated properties. Selective overbooking, 5 percent to 15 percent depending on historical experience, is the hotel's major protection against no-shows, double reservations, and "guaranteed reservations" that are never paid. Conservative overbooking begins with a collection of data, made easier by a well-programmed computer and a regular update of projections.

Data collection must be structured and accurate so the reservations office can rely on the figures. The computer can furnish the information if the database for accumulating the report was planned for in the programming. Data must be accumulated in a chronological fashion, day of the week matching day of the week. It is important for the second Tuesday in April, for instance, to match the second Tuesday in April of last year, irrespective of the calendar dates of those Tuesdays.

Dates do have importance, of course. The July 1 holiday is a more important date than the day on which it falls. Similarly, the days before and after such a holiday must be identified with other before-and-after days of previous years.

**Putting the Room Count to Use** Room forecasting starts with an annual projection and ends with an hourly report. In between are monthly, biweekly, weekly, three-day, and daily forecasts. Ten-day reports (see Exhibit 6-5) are sometimes used in place of biweekly projections, but most reservations managers prefer to see two weekends included in a report.

Every department of a hotel uses the room count projections as a critical tool for labour planning. Each department makes sales and labour forecasts from the anticipated room and guest count. Most departments depend on room occupancy for their own volume. This is certainly the situation with valet and laundry, room service, telephones, room attendants, food and beverage outlets, and uniformed services.

The reservations department should have its closest partnership with marketing and sales. Without that alliance, the property has little opportunity to maximize yield management policies. For example, how many discounted rooms has the sales department committed to wholesalers during a high-occupancy (thus, high-rate) period? The marketing department should be able to help reservations forecast no-shows, walk-ins, early arrivals, and so on, as they pertain to a particular group. Group figures differ from figures for independent guests and may vary from group to group.

**Periodic Recounts** The longer the period between the preparation of the forecast and its use, the less reliable it is. Without periodic updating, all departments, but especially the front desk, act on information that is no longer accurate. The three-day forecast

## Occupancy Forecast Report

Santa Rae Ranch
Ann Parker

Page Number:   1
22-DEC- 11:55 AM

**Occupancy Forecast Report**
For the Period from 03-JAN- to 12-JAN-
Percentages Include Out of Order and Off Market Rooms
Percentages Exclude Tentative Group Rooms

| | FRI JAN-03 | SAT JAN-04 | SUN JAN-05 | MON JAN-06 | TUE JAN-07 | WED JAN-08 | THUR JAN-09 | FRI JAN-10 | SAT JAN-11 | SUN JAN-12 |
|---|---|---|---|---|---|---|---|---|---|---|
| Total Rooms | 236 | 236 | 236 | 236 | 236 | 236 | 236 | 236 | 236 | 236 |
| - OOO | 3 | 2 | 3 | 3 | 2 | 0 | 3 | 1 | 0 | 0 |
| - OFF | 0 | 0 | 0 | 0 | 0 | 0 | 0 | 0 | 1 | 0 |
| Rooms Available | 233 | 234 | 233 | 233 | 234 | 234 | 233 | 235 | 235 | 236 |
| Rooms Occupied | 94 | 90 | 83 | 44 | 33 | 27 | 21 | 30 | 42 | 27 |
| - Non-Group Departures | 11 | 18 | 34 | 14 | 4 | 5 | 17 | 2 | 13 | 4 |
| - Group Departures | 12 | 3 | 14 | 1 | 2 | 2 | 0 | 1 | 5 | 4 |
| + Non-Group Arrivals | 18 | 13 | 9 | 4 | 0 | 1 | 15 | 14 | 3 | 0 |
| + Group Arrivals | 1 | 1 | 0 | 0 | 0 | 0 | 12 | 0 | 0 | 0 |
| Net In-House | 90 | 83 | 44 | 33 | 27 | 21 | 31 | 41 | 27 | 19 |
| + Estimated Pickup | 0 | 0 | 0 | 0 | 0 | 0 | 0 | 2 | 0 | 2 |
| + Excess Committed | 82 | 60 | 1 | 0 | 0 | 0 | 19 | 9 | 14 | 0 |
| + Tentative Grp Rooms | 5 | 0 | 0 | 0 | 0 | 0 | 2 | 0 | 0 | 0 |
| Net Rooms Reserved | 172 | 143 | 45 | 33 | 27 | 21 | 50 | 52 | 43 | 21 |
| Net Rooms Available | 61 | 91 | 188 | 200 | 207 | 213 | 183 | 183 | 192 | 215 |

◀ **Exhibit 6-5**
This computerized reservation forecast report displays a 10-day view of rooms activity. It details arrival and departure projections for individual as well as group rooms. Usually, such forecast reports also provide an estimate of each day's anticipated rooms revenues. (Note that unlike the treatment suggested by the authors, out-of-order rooms reduce rooms available. This technique boosts the percentage of occupancy, and so reflects better on the rooms manager.)

| | FRI JAN-03 | SAT JAN-04 | SUN JAN-05 | MON JAN-06 | TUE JAN-07 | WED JAN-08 | THUR JAN-09 | FRI JAN-10 | SAT JAN-11 | SUN JAN-12 |
|---|---|---|---|---|---|---|---|---|---|---|
| **Non-Group** | | | | | | | | | | |
| Projected Revenue | 7113.00 | 6527.50 | 3438.50 | 2757.50 | 2446.00 | 1810.00 | 1341.88 | 4265.37 | 3415.99 | 2913.49 |
| Avg. Rate | 103.09 | 101.99 | 88.17 | 95.09 | 97.84 | 86.19 | 70.63 | 137.59 | 162.67 | 171.38 |
| **Group (Reserved)** | | | | | | | | | | |
| Projected Revenue | 1064.00 | 965.00 | 221.00 | 175.00 | 47.50 | 0.00 | 1148.00 | 1100.50 | 590.00 | 190.00 |
| Avg. Rate | 50.67 | 50.79 | 44.20 | 43.75 | 23.75 | 0.00 | 95.67 | 100.05 | 98.33 | 95.00 |
| **Group (Excess Committed)** | | | | | | | | | | |
| Estimated Revenue | 5340.00 | 3925.00 | 20.00 | 0.00 | 0.00 | 0.00 | 1945.00 | 845.00 | 1280.00 | 0.00 |
| Avg. Rate | 61.38 | 65.42 | 20.00 | 0.00 | 0.00 | 0.00 | 92.62 | 93.89 | 91.43 | 0.00 |
| **Group (Tentative)** | | | | | | | | | | |
| Estimated Revenue | 375.00 | 0.00 | 0.00 | 0.00 | 0.00 | 0.00 | 150.00 | 0.00 | 0.00 | 0.00 |
| Avg. Rate | 75.00 | 0.00 | 0.00 | 0.00 | 0.00 | 0.00 | 75.00 | 0.00 | 0.00 | 0.00 |
| **Group (Totals)** | | | | | | | | | | |
| Projected Revenue | 6779.00 | 4890.00 | 241.00 | 175.00 | 47.50 | 0.00 | 3243.00 | 1945.50 | 1870.00 | 190.00 |
| Avg. Rate | 59.99 | 61.90 | 40.17 | 43.75 | 23.75 | 0.00 | 92.66 | 97.28 | 93.50 | 95.00 |
| **Totals** | | | | | | | | | | |
| Projected Revenue | 13892.00 | 11417.50 | 3679.50 | 2932.50 | 2493.50 | 1810.00 | 4584.88 | 6210.87 | 5285.99 | 3103.49 |
| Avg. Rate | 76.33 | 79.84 | 81.77 | 88.86 | 92.35 | 86.19 | 84.91 | 121.78 | 128.93 | 163.34 |
| % Occupancy Reserved | 38.63 | 35.47 | 18.88 | 14.16 | 11.54 | 8.97 | 13.30 | 17.45 | 11.49 | 8.05 |
| % Including Commits | 73.82 | 61.11 | 19.31 | 14.16 | 11.54 | 8.97 | 21.46 | 21.28 | 17.45 | 8.05 |

| TEN/ DEF | FRI JAN-03 | SAT JAN-04 | SUN JAN-05 | MON JAN-06 | TUE JAN-07 | WED JAN-08 | THUR JAN-09 | FRI JAN-10 | SAT JAN-11 | SUN JAN-12 |
|---|---|---|---|---|---|---|---|---|---|---|
| Canadian Building Consult | DEF | 30/0 | 20/0 | | | | | | | |
| Bavarian Bakeoff | *DEF | 0/1 | | | | | | | | |
| Bob's Bablo Island Tour | *DEF | 5/4 | 0/3 | | | | | | | |
| Brady Tours | DEF | | | | | | | 5/0 | | |
| Cardinal Group | DEF | 1/0 | 1/0 | 1/0 | | | | | | |
| Cups & China | DEF | 10/0 | | | | | | | | |
| Honda | DEF | | | | | | | 25/11 | 20/11 | 20/6 |
| MIPS | TEN | 6/5 | 5/5 | | | | | | | |
| Micro Data | DEF | | | | | | | 2/0 | | |
| Presentations Now | TEN | 5/0 | 5/0 | | | | | | | |
| Sky Line Displays | DEF | 5/0 | | | | | | | | |
| Cdn Clowns Inc. | DEF | 25/2 | 25/2 | | | | | | | |
| Cdn Water Polo Team | DEF | 12/1 | 12/1 | | | | | | | |

* This group's commitments must be cleaned up or all availability reports will be out of balance.

**Exhibit 6-5** *(Continued)*

permits a final push for sales and a tightening of labour schedules throughout the property to maximize occupancy and minimize costs.

By the time hourly projections are being made, responsibility has moved entirely to the front office. Overbooking problems, additional reservations, walk-ins, and stay-overs are being resolved by front-office executives.

Periodic or hourly forecasts improve the system in two ways. Obviously, the information is more current (see Exhibit 6-6). Less obvious is the increased accuracy in percentage variations as the day progresses. Were it known, for example, that 80 percent of all check-outs were usually gone by noon, a better guess of understays and overstays could be made at noon each day than at 7 A.M. Similar refinements are possible with cancellation percentages, no-show factors, and so on. In fact, it is possible to improve the accuracy of no-show forecasts by separating the total reservations into three categories—advance deposit, guaranteed, and non-guaranteed—before applying a different no-show percentage to each.

**Adjusting by Reservation Quality**   Returning to the continuing example illustrated in Exhibits 6-2 and 6-3, an improved adjusted room count is possible by separating non-guaranteed reservations from guaranteed and advance-deposit reservations. Instead of

| Royal Hotel Weekly Forecast for February 3 to February 9 | | | | | | | |
|---|---|---|---|---|---|---|---|
| | **3** | **4** | **5** | **6** | **7** | **8** | **9** |
| Rooms available for sale | 1206 | 1206 | 1206 | 1206 | 1206 | 1206 | 1206 |
| Rooms occupied last night | 1121 | 1190 | 1193 | 890 | 480 | 140 | 611 |
| Less anticipated departures | 444 | 396 | 530 | 440 | 350 | 55 | 20 |
| Stayovers | 677 | 794 | 663 | 450 | 130 | 85 | 591 |
| Reservations | 498 | 386 | 212 | 25 | 10 | 501 | 552 |
| Estimated out of order | 3 | 3 | | | | | |
| Rooms committed | 1178 | 1183 | 875 | 475 | 140 | 586 | 1143 |
| Estimated walk-ins | 12 | 10 | 15 | 5 | | 25 | 63 |
| Rooms occupied tonight | 1190 | 1193 | 890 | 480 | 140 | 611 | 1206 |
| *Group Arrivals* | | | | | | | |
| National Water Heater Co. | 80 | 140 | | | | | |
| Play Tours of America | | | 68 | | | | |
| Chevrolet Western Division | | | | | 5 | 183 | |
| Alberta Library Association | | | | | | 251 | 396 |
| Chiffo-Garn wedding party | | | | | | | 23 |

▲
**Exhibit 6-6**

This room-availability forecast demonstrates why statistics that depend on the cumulative results of previous days' forecasts grow less reliable the further the projected horizon. Each day's values build on estimates from previous days (see the arrows). If the actual number of rooms occupied in any preceding day is different than the mathematical base—and it always is—later forecasts become less and less accurate, since they begin with invalid figures.

For example, if the rooms occupied on February 3 are actually less than the 1190 projected (because of fewer walk-ins, more understay departures, etc.), then the rooms occupied on February 4 will also be lower than projected. After all, the count for February 4 is based on the number of rooms occupied the night before (1190). If the count for February 4 is lower than projected, then the count for February 5, 6, 7, and so on will also be lower than projected.

merely stating that 325 reservations are due in, it is more valuable to understand that, say, 100 reservations are non-guaranteed, 175 reservations are guaranteed, and 50 reservations are advance deposit.

If the hotel maintains statistical history by reservation quality or type, the accuracy of the entire projection is enhanced. In such hotels, the no-show percentage might be changed from the flat 5 percent for all reservation types to something more detailed. Assume that 20 percent of all non-guaranteed reservations are no-shows, 4 percent of all guaranteed reservations are no-shows, and 1 percent of all advance deposits are no-shows. The total number of no-shows would now change from 16 in Exhibit 6-3 to 28. This is calculated by taking 20 percent of 100 non-guaranteed reservations (20), plus 4 percent of 175 guaranteed reservations (7), plus 1 percent of 50 advance deposit reservations (0.5 rounds up to 1).

Similarly, cancellations are also a function of the quality of the reservation. Cancellations are more common with guaranteed and advance-deposit reservations, because such guests have an incentive to call and cancel (if the guest is not planning to arrive, he or she will save a no-show charge by calling and cancelling). Likewise, cancellations are less common with non-guaranteed reservations. The guest has nothing to lose with the non-guaranteed reservation, because the reservation is basically a courtesy hold until 6 P.M. In our continuing example (Exhibit 6-3), let's assume zero percent of all non-guaranteed reservations call to cancel, 4 percent of guaranteed reservations cancel, and 3 percent of advance-deposit reservations cancel. The total number of cancellations would now change from 7 to 9. This is calculated by taking zero percent of 100 non-guaranteed reservations (0), plus 4 percent of 175 guaranteed reservations (7), plus 3 percent of 50 advance-deposit reservations (1.5 rounds up to 2).

Accuracy can also be improved by attention to the character of the market. The type of group clues the reservations department to the no-show percentage. For example, teachers are very dependable. Tour groups are nearly always full because volume is as important to the tour operator as it is to the innkeeper. That generalization must then be balanced by knowledge about specific tour companies. Allocations versus use should be computed individually on wholesalers, incentive houses, associations, and other group movers. The washdown (number of rooms a group cancels between booking and arrival) history of groups may be enhanced by contacting the hotel that hosted them last year. Hotels will normally share this type of information.

Market research may prove that bookings from certain localities are more or less reliable depending on transportation, weather, distance, and the kind of guest the hotel is attracting. Commercial guests have a different degree of dependability than tourists, who differ again from conventioneers or referrals. A large permanent guest population needs to be recognized in any percentage computation involving stayovers and anticipated departures.

The overall goal of any room count projection is to forecast the number of rooms available for sale. This is especially critical during high-occupancy periods. When the hotel is nearly full, it is important to forecast the number of rooms that may become available for sale due to understays, no-shows, and cancellations. By understanding the interrelationship of these adjustments, the front office has a better chance of filling the hotel.

# Overbooking

Even when hotel management boasts of reaching 100 percent occupancy on a given night, there are usually a few unoccupied rooms left in the hotel. The hotel shows 100 percent occupancy because it has sold every available room, not necessarily because every available room is physically occupied. Rooms held for guaranteed reservations provide revenue in the form of no-show charges even when the guest fails to arrive at the property. Indeed, reaching the *perfect fill* or the *perfect sell-out* (where every available room is physically occupied) is actually a relatively uncommon occurrence even in well-managed properties.

## Reservations as Legal Contracts

Courts consider room reservations to be legal contracts. The request constitutes the offer, and the promise of accommodations represents the acceptance. Either the promise to pay or the actual transfer of a deposit is the third important element of a contract: consideration. Such promises may be verbal (as with a telephone confirmation) or written (as with a letter of confirmation). The parties are competent; the transaction is legal; and there is a mutuality of interest. All of the elements of a binding contract are in place.

If one party breaches the contract, the innocent party should be compensated for the injury. This has been the situation for many years. Recovery by either party has generally been limited to the natural or expected costs that the parties anticipated at the time of the agreement.

There have been few legal cases involving breach of reservation contract. That is because there is little to be gained by bringing suit. If the guest breaches the contract by failing to show up for the room, the hotel may have an opportunity to resell the accommodation. Even if the room cannot be resold, the monetary loss to the hotel is minimal. Similarly, if the hotel breaches the reservation contract by failing to provide a room, the guest is free to seek accommodations elsewhere. Even if a room cannot be found, the actual cost to the guest is still quite small (possibly limited to taxi fares and telephone calls expended in search of alternative accommodations). And courts are not willing to compensate the guest for inconvenience and depression.

**Others at Fault**   The fault for overbooking is not the hotel industry's alone. Canada does not have eviction laws that would allow hotels to evict a guest who has a reservation for one night and decides to stay for two or three nights. In fact, some guests will call to make a reservation for three nights and when they are told that only the first night is available they will book for one night, knowing that the hotel cannot evict them if they decide to stay for three nights. This is also complicated by the fact that hotels will do their best to accommodate regulars during overbooked periods and walk a non-regular guest who has a reservation.

Tour operators who bring planeloads of tourists to a town contribute to the overbooking problem. The group is usually divided among several hotels, with the guest's selection of a particular hotel determining the cost of the tour. The tour operator is playing the odds, estimating that a given number of guests on each plane will choose hotels in the same ratio that the tour operator has committed rooms. When too many people select one property and too few select another, the hotel is blamed for overbooking. Guests are unaware that the hotel and the tour operator had agreed on the number of rooms months before.

Convention executives must be hounded to keep their numbers current. No-shows are reduced if the number of rooms saved for the convention is adjusted to the group's history at other hotels. If possible, convention groups should pair their members at the meeting site as the individuals arrive. This reduces the number of single rooms created when previously paired delegates do not show. Failing this, the hotel can levy a compulsory room charge for no-shows.

Guests, too, are to blame! They are notorious no-shows. Guests will make reservations in more than one hotel and, if they do show, will change their length of stay without notifying the desk. The reservations department is always second-guessing guests' moves, and this means occasional errors no matter how carefully previous statistics and experiences are projected.

**Common Overbooking Policies** The burden of walking an arriving guest—sending that person away—falls to the room clerk (see Exhibit 6-7). Too often management leaves it at that, making no provision to train the clerk and no provision to house the guest. Where this is a frequent affair, the staff grows immune to the protests and even finds a bit of humour in walking one guest after another. In doing so, the staff reflects the apparent attitude of an unconcerned management. This is not the case in properties where quality assurance programs are in place (see Chapter 7). The situation is never treated lightly, even if a number of guests were walked that day.

Arranging substitute accommodations elsewhere is what the clerk should do. Providing the training to anticipate the incident is what management should do. Preparation includes preliminary calls to neighbouring properties as the situation becomes obvious. Many satellite properties depend on this type of overflow for business. Affiliated properties usually refer to each other before overflowing rooms business to neighbouring competitors—even to the extent that a full-service chain

**Exhibit 6-7** ▶
An overbooked hotel is no laughing matter!

property may walk guests to one of the same chain's budget operations and vice versa.

Managers need to be alert to unethical practices involving walked rooms. Some properties give a commission or kick back a payment to clerks of oversold properties when they refer walked guests their way. Even though the oversold hotel may specify to which properties guests can be walked, $10 or $20 from the unethical operation is incentive enough to disregard the rule. Indeed, such unethical clerks may begin referring walk-in customers to the other hotel even when rooms remain available at their own property.

Significant dollars are expended when walking a guest from those properties that have a quality assurance, guest-oriented policy in place. The hotel pays the round-trip cab ride to the substitute hotel. It underwrites the cost of one or more long-distance telephone calls (to the displaced guest's company and family). It also pays the room charge, regardless of the rate, at the alternative property. Some hotels give an outright gift (champagne, fruit basket, etc.) to apologize for the inconvenience. Others give a free room on the next visit as a means of bringing back a walked guest. If the guest has a reservation for more than one night, the hotel will try to get the guest back for the second and subsequent nights by offering a free room upgrade. Generally, in Canada, major hotel chains have a quality assurance plan similar to this one. Hotels do this to keep guest satisfaction at high levels, but also to avoid the chance of a guest entering into a lawsuit against the hotel. In Canada, lawsuits are rare because Canadian courts do not generally award guests punitive damages or damages for pain and suffering. Normally, a guest could only recover what he or she has lost; if the hotel has a quality assurance policy in effect, a walked guest is not financially out of pocket.

Assuming that the above-mentioned figures are cab, $30; telephone, $15; and room rate, $105, each incident costs $150. This computation ignores the value of lost sales in the other departments. Overbooking is not an everyday affair. If 3 guests per night are turned away 10 times per year, the hotel spends $4500 (3 × 10 × $150) in remedies. Walking guests does not make economic sense. The cost of failing to achieve 100 percent occupancy on the 10 nights is certainly less expensive than the overbooking outlay, especially when goodwill is added into the equation.

Ignored in the economic computation above is the cost of public relations. The iceberg effect of one extremely unhappy guest can add up to untold costs. Plagued by bad publicity from overbooking, the Bahamas Hotel Association (BHA) formalized an area-wide policy. The BHA recognized that being stranded on an isolated island without a room was not going to encourage tourism. The new policy carried the cab ride one step further, guaranteeing air taxi to another island if all accommodations in the host area were fully booked. A $20 cab ride is cheap compared with the cost of an air taxi!

Other localities have established programs to help themselves and the unaccommodated guest. Chambers of commerce or tourist authorities have set up hotlines. Equally important, the front desk can monitor what is happening throughout the city and adjust its own walk-ins based on citywide conditions. Generally, a hotel in a walk position will have a current list of hotels that are accepting walk-ins.

Clearly, steps can be taken to ease the impact of overbooking. An industry-wide policy of self-policing and public relations would minimize the incidence of overbooking and diminish the outcry from those cases that do occur. Success requires the support of each hotel and chain.

**Overbooking and the Anti-service Syndrome** While the majority of hotels are proactive in preparing their employees to handle oversold days, poorly managed properties simply place the "blame" on the guest. The common anti-service approach for such hotels is to act as if the reservation never existed. The clerk's pretence is what guests find most frustrating about the experience. To play out the charade, the clerk consults with co-workers, massages computer keys, and examines hidden room racks. Finally comes a proclamation. To the hotel, the guest is a non-person without a record and one for whom the hotel is not responsible.

To the dismay of the entire industry, certain properties give no attention to the matter of overbooking. They set a low priority on the loss of goodwill because they either have little repeat business or they have more business than they can handle. What is unimportant to these properties is of grave concern to the majority of hotel keepers. The majority act to minimize the frequency of overbooking. The minority exacerbate the problem to the detriment of all.

**No-Show Policies** As discussed earlier in the chapter, there is a high correlation between the incidence of no-shows and the **quality of the reservation**. The higher the quality of the reservation, the lower the likelihood of a no-show.

That's why hotels are less willing to accept non-guaranteed reservations. Non-guaranteed reservations frequently no-show, and when they do, the hotel receives no compensation short of selling the room to a walk-in guest after the 6 P.M. hold. Hotels have a different option where guaranteed and advance-deposit reservations are concerned.

Guaranteed and advance-deposit reservations are penalized for failing to cancel or use their reservation. Guests are usually charged the cost of one room night (one room night plus tax is the common amount requested for an advance deposit). For advance deposits, it is a simple matter for the hotel to claim the deposit. With guaranteed reservations, the process is less certain. Collecting against guaranteed reservations is often quite difficult because guests are unwilling to pay the charge against their credit card or corporate account. This disagreement often results in a fight between the guest and the hotel over the amount of one night's lodging. Even when the hotel wins, it loses because the guest may forever be lost as a valued customer.

**Cancellation Policies** Cancellation policies are another source of irritation to guests. Cancellation policies differ by chain, hotel, market, and destination. In Canada, for instance, Fairmont Hotels has a 24-hour cancellation policy, while Four Seasons requires that you cancel before 6 P.M. on the day of arrival. In addition, the cancellation policy often reflects the quantity of walk-ins experienced by the hotel. If the guest fails to cancel within the time frame established, a one-night charge may be assessed. In contrast, many resorts and isolated destination properties mandate more stringent cancellation policies. Some request that the guest notify the hotel 24 to 48 hours in advance. Others require as much as 7 to 14 days' notice. Indeed, more stringent cancellation policies may carry a weightier penalty: Some resort properties are known to charge the full prepaid stay.

The major credit card companies mandate cancellation times for properties that guarantee reservations against their cards. MasterCard and Visa require properties to accept cancellations until 6 P.M. on the day of arrival (resort operations are given the option of requiring cancellations up to three hours earlier). American Express and Diners Club understand that different markets may require different cancellation policies. Therefore, these two companies allow hotels to establish their own

## Credit Card Company

| | American Express | Diners Club | MasterCard | Visa |
|---|---|---|---|---|
| Name of guaranteed reservations program | Assured Reservations | Confirmed Reservations Plan | Guaranteed Reservation | Visa Reservation Service |
| No-show charge policy | Will support no-show charge if "assured reservation no-show" is written on signature line | Will support no-show charge if "confirmed reservation—no-show" is written on signature line | Will suport no-show charge if "guaranteed reservation/no-show" is written on signature line | Will support no-show charge if "no-show" is written on signature line |
| Cancellation policy | Property may determine its own cancellation times | Cancellations by 6 P.M. (4 P.M. for resorts) on day of arrival | Property may determine its own cancellation times | Cancellations by 6 P.M. if reservation made in past 72 hours; otherwise, property may set its own policy |
| Overbooking policy | Property must<br>• provide and pay for room in comparable hotel for one night<br>• pay for one three-minute call<br>• forward guest contacts to new hotel | Property must<br>• provide and pay for room in comparable or better hotel for one night<br>• pay for one three-minute call<br>• provide transportation to new hotel<br>• neither hotel can charge guest for room or guaranteed reservation | Property must<br>• provide and pay for room in another hotel for one night<br>• pay for one three-minute call<br>• provide transportation to new hotel | Property must<br>• provide and pay for room in comparable or better hotel for one night<br>• pay for one three-minute call<br>• forward guest contacts to new hotel<br>• provide transportation to new hotel |

▲
**Exhibit 6-8**
Third-party reservation guarantees are supported by all four major domestic credit card companies. If the room is guaranteed and the guest does not cancel within the established parameters, the hotel has the right to receive compensation for one night's stay. Of course, this means that the hotel must hold the room available for the guest until check-out time on the following day. As long as hotels abide by the policies established by each credit card company, they will be upheld by the credit card companies in all but the most unusual customer chargeback disputes.

cancellation times, provided that the hotels clearly explain the policies and procedures to all guests at the time of reservation. And verbal descriptions are not necessarily sufficient. Visa, for one, requires written notice of cancellation policies for reservations made at least 72 hours in advance. Exhibit 6-8 charts the policies of the several credit card companies. A hotel would process a guaranteed no-show by charging the amount to the guest's credit card. If a guest disputed this no-show charge with the credit card company, generally most credit cards will backcharge the amount to the hotel in the interest of keeping the credit card customer happy. The hotel then has to try to collect the no-show from the guest, which can be difficult at best. TD Travel actually guarantees the reservation to the TD Travel corporate card. The guest is then charged the no-show on his or her own personal card in this case.

## Minimizing the Overbooking Problem

There are really no perfect solutions to the problem of overbooking. As long as hotels overbook to compensate for no-shows and last-minute changes in occupancy, there will always be walked guests. The answer is found not in eliminating overbooking as a management tool but rather in minimizing the need to overbook on most occasions.

The issue boils down to this: A hotel overbooks because its guests change their minds. When guests change their minds, it often results in lower rooms occupancy than projected. Lower occupancy means less rooms revenue for the hotel. Therefore, in response to guest fickleness, the hotel has little choice but to second-guess the number of overstays, understays, cancellations, and no-shows for a given day. The operative word here is *guess*. And sometimes even the most scientific guesses go awry. That's when overbooking rears its head and guests lose confidence in the system.

Unfortunately, guests want the best of both worlds. They want the flexibility to understay or overstay as plans change, but they also want liberal cancellation and no-show policies for the times when they don't arrive. This leaves the hotel in a difficult position. If it charges a no-show guest for the **unoccupied** room night, the guest might never return to the hotel. If the hotel refuses a request for an overstay or tries to charge a fee to an early departing understay, it may also create ill will. The answer is probably to be found in more restrictive reservations policies and third-party involvement.

**Increasingly Restrictive Policies**  Certainly, the airlines are strict about their flight policies. Most tickets are non-refundable, non-transferable, and must be paid for at the time of reservation. Courtesy (non-guaranteed) holds on reservations usually expire within 24 hours. No-show guests (and cancellations) face "change" fees when they attempt to reuse their tickets. Indeed, unused tickets are only valid for a year.

The lodging industry is slowly beginning to adopt similar policies. Rather than simply using a credit card to guarantee a reservation, many hotels now charge the first night's stay on the guest credit card at the time of booking and will not refund the now-prepaid guest if he or she does not show. Merely adopting such reform, however, is not enough. The airlines went through a long period of guest education. And although the lodging industry will have a somewhat easier time educating its customers (because the airlines already broke much of the ground), competition among chains will surely affect the success of industry-wide reservations policies reform.

Slowly, such changes are taking place. One chain puts its toe in the water, and soon another follows suit. Yield management fences (non-refundable reservations, 21-day advance purchase, and stays over Saturday night) are some of the first toes in the water (see the yield management discussion in Chapter 4). Early departure charges are also being tested.

**Early Departure Fees**  Several major lodging chains, including both Hyatt and Hilton, have recently experimented with early departure charges. Although not terribly costly (most guests are required to pay between $25 and $50 as an understay penalty), such fees are designed to make guests think twice before departing early. Early departure fees are also expected to improve the accuracy of the reservation on the front end; once aware of an early departure penalty, guests will probably be more conservative in estimating the number of nights they plan to stay.

As with cancellation and no-show policies, early departure or understay fees must be clearly detailed at the time of reservation booking. Credit card companies expect properties to explain the policy in detail at the time of reservation, include a comment about the policy with mailed confirmations, and have guests sign a statement reiterating the standard during the check-in process. When these procedures are followed, credit card companies generally support the hotel with regard to guest disputes and **chargebacks** (see Exhibit 6-8).

**Third-Party Guarantees**  There is some logic in removing the hotel from direct involvement with the guest when fees or penalties are involved. It is easier for the hotel to charge a credit card company or travel agent the no-show charge than to assess it directly against the guest or the guest's corporate account. Although the guest still pays the charge in the end, the hotel is one step removed from the negative connotations associated with collecting such fees, and a third party is assigned that role.

**Trip Insurance**  The increasing popularity of trip or travel insurance is predicated on this same logic. By placing a third party into the equation, some of the negative feelings associated with paying a penalty are assigned elsewhere and the hotel looks a little less like the "bad guy."

Although few domestic hotels actually recommend travel insurance with their reservations, it is somewhat more popular in Europe. At the time of reservation, or mailed with the confirmation, is some explanation of the benefits associated with travel insurance. The benefits are simple enough: For a small fee, a third party will become responsible for cancellation, no-show, understay, or reservation change fees assessed for a given trip. The reasons the guest may change their plans are usually described with the insurance and may include illness, death, and a change in business plans, or even inclement weather.

The concept works something like this: With trip insurance, guests have no one to blame but themselves. You see, they should have purchased trip insurance (through a travel agent, tour operator, or trip insurance broker) if they thought their plans might change. Then, if they are charged a no-show, cancellation, change, or understay fee, the trip insurance will pay the cost. If they didn't buy travel insurance, how can they be mad at the hotel for charging them a fee clearly explained at the time of booking?

**Credit Card Guarantees**  Except for unusual circumstances, a credit card is charged if the reservation has been guaranteed. Unfortunately, charging the credit card does not always equate to receiving payment. In many instances, the guest will dispute the charge.

When such disputes arise, third-party involvement by the credit card company is necessitated. The credit card company usually requires the guest to issue a statement in writing. Such statements as "I never made that reservation" or "I cancelled that reservation well in advance" are difficult to prove.

That's why the costliest credit card chargeback category is no-shows. Hotels should arm themselves against such disputes by following standard procedures. Best Western, for example, always provides separate confirmation and cancellation numbers (unlike some chains, which simply add an "X" to the confirmation number to signify cancellation). In this way, Best Western can insist that the credit card company ask the guest to provide the cancellation number. No cancellation number ("I lost it," "I threw it away," "They never gave me a number"), no excuse. Similarly, Best Western doesn't accept the excuse "I never made the reservation." As a company, they find that excuse questionable—after all, how did the chain get the guest's name, address, phone number, and credit card number?

Once the statement is in hand, the third-party credit card company usually issues a temporary **credit** to the guest (and an offsetting **debit** to the hotel). This means that, temporarily, the guest does not have to pay the charge and the hotel does not receive the income.

At this stage, the statement is copied to the hotel and the property has an opportunity to respond. Many hotels stop at this point, believing that the case will never be settled in their favour. If the hotel chooses not to respond, the guest automatically wins the decision. Even when the hotel does respond, the case is still found in favour of the guest much of the time. Some critics of the system believe that credit card companies uphold the guests' claims because they want to keep them as customers. That is really not the case; if the hotel follows the credit card company's standard procedure, they should never lose a chargeback dispute (see Exhibit 6-8).

**Travel Agent Guarantees** A different type of third-party guarantee uses the travel agent. When a guest makes the reservation through a travel agent, the hotel removes itself from dealing directly with the customer. In the event of a no-show, the hotel receives payment directly from the travel agent. Whether the travel agent then charges the no-show customer is the travel agent's problem.

The only weakness with this system is that the hotel must have a credit relationship with the travel agent. In today's fast-paced travel environment, there is rarely enough lead time for the travel agent to send a cheque and for the hotel to clear the funds.

**Advance-Deposit Reservations** Probably the best of all methods for reducing the industry-wide problem of overbooking is to encourage advance deposits. Advance-deposit reservations (also known as paid-in-advance reservations) have historically maintained the lowest percentage of no-shows. Guests who pay a substantial amount in advance (usually the first night's room charge, although some resorts charge the entire payment up front) have a strong motive to arrive as scheduled.

However, advance-deposit reservations carry an extra clerical burden not found with other types of reservations. The reservations department, for example, has a tracking burden. If the guest responds by sending a deposit, the reservation must be changed from tentative to confirmed. If the guest doesn't respond, the reservations office must either send a reminder or cancel the reservation. Sending a reminder starts the tracking process all over again.

Handling the money, usually a cheque, involves bank deposits, sometimes bounced cheques, and accounting records. Refunds must be made in a timely manner when cancellations are requested. Processing and writing any cheque represents a measurable cost of operation.

For many hotels, these operational burdens are inconsequential compared to the benefits that accrue from advance-deposit reservations. However, even those hotels using advance-deposit systems would probably switch if and when new guarantee systems become available. And that is apt to happen as new electronic systems and new innovations in money substitutes appear.

## Summary

Accepting a reservation is really only half the battle. Tracking the reservation and forecasting house availability are also important components in a successful reservations department. Forecasting room availability is as much an art as it is a science. It is a simple matter to count committed rooms (those sold to stayovers and incoming reservations) as a means of forecasting the number of rooms available for walk-ins and short–lead time reservations. However, such a simple approach as counting committed rooms leaves untended a number of costly variables. Yet when the reservations manager begins to consider the potential for no-shows, cancellations, early arrivals, understays, and overstays, the art of forecasting becomes a bit like guesswork.

An error in predicting the number of cancellations and no-shows may prove disastrous to a nearly full hotel. Rooms may be overbooked, necessitating that guests be walked to a nearby property. When this is a rare occasion, the employees treat the situation with compassion and the walked guest is a satisfied one. However, when walked guests become a routine occurrence, the hotel is showing greed by purposely overbooking each day to compensate for the maximum potential no-shows and cancellations. In such cases, employees become jaded, guests receive little concern, and dissatisfaction inevitably results.

In reality, the lodging industry has done a superior job reducing overbooking complaints in recent years. Partially from fear of government regulation (as with airline overbooking policies) and partially from a desire to create lasting relationships and repeat business in a highly competitive industry, few hotel overbooking complaints have become public scandals in recent years.

## Questions and Problems

1. What is the difference between out-of-order and out-of-inventory rooms? Explain why one of these designations affects the occupancy count while the other has no bearing.

2. Prepare a simple unadjusted plus count from the following scenario: A 700-room hotel had 90 percent of its rooms occupied last night. Of those occupied rooms, 260 are due to check out today. In addition, there are 316 reservations scheduled for arrival today, and 10 rooms are currently out of order.

3. The rooms forecast committee is scheduled to meet later this afternoon. You have been asked to prepare remarks on group no-shows. Contrast the likelihood of no-shows for (a) business groups, (b) tour groups, and (c) convention groups. How would your remarks differ if the group reservation had been made by (a) the vice-president of engineering, (b) an incentive travel company, or (c) a professional convention management company?

4. The rooms forecast is a tool for managers throughout the hotel; it is not for the front office alone. List and discuss how several other departments (housekeeping, food and beverage, uniformed services, etc.) would use the rooms forecast.

5. A chain's corporate office launches a national campaign advertising its policy of honouring every reservation. Each property is notified that overbooking will not be tolerated. What policies can be implemented at the hotel level to meet corporate goals and still generate the maximum occupancies on which professional careers are built?

6. Two hours before the noon check-out hour, a walk-in party requests five rooms. The following scrambled data have just been completed as part of the desk's hourly update. Should the front-office supervisor accept the walk-ins?

| | |
|---|---|
| General no-show factor | 10 percent |
| Rooms in the hotel | 693 |

| | | | |
|---|---|---|---|
| Group reservations due (rooms) | 250 | No-show factor for groups | 2 percent |
| Number of rooms departed so far today | 203 | Understays minus overstays as a percentage of occupied rooms | 8 percent |
| Rooms occupied last night | 588 | Early arrivals expected | 2 |
| Total reservations expected today from all sources (including group rooms) | 360 | Non-saleable rooms and rooms that are out of inventory | 7 |
| | | Total forecasted departures for the day | 211 |

## CASE STUDY

# Overbooked in Calgary

On this particular morning, Amir had some apprehension as he dressed for work. He just received a call from the night auditor and it appears that, according to the preliminary room status report, the hotel is overbooked by 40 rooms this evening. It is a Tuesday in July at Amir's 300-room hotel in the heart of downtown Calgary, and the Calgary Stampede is just beginning.

During his career in the front office, Amir has handled some minor overbooking issues, and while working as a night auditor, he had to walk several guests to competing hotels. He has experienced first-hand irate guests who had guaranteed reservations in hand with no rooms available at the hotel. However, those were minor overbooking situations; today, Amir is faced with a major overbooking issue—and as he tightens his tie, his mind is anticipating the challenges ahead.

If you were Amir, how would you answer the following questions?

1. As you leave your house, your phone rings. The general manager of the hotel, who has been made aware of the impending disaster, wants to meet with you as soon as you arrive at work. She is going to ask how this overbooking situation occurred. What might be some of the possible reasons that caused this overbooking problem?

2. When you arrive at work, you start to go through the reservations to check for quality. The date on which the reservation was made is one of these quality checks. What other quality checks might you pursue? With each quality check, what information are you attempting to garner?

3. How would you handle VIP and repeat corporate reservations from local companies who patronize the hotel on a regular basis and always pay for guaranteed no-shows?

4. You know that the Calgary Stampede is under way and therefore other local hotels will quickly fill up if they're not already booked. These hotels are not prepared to take reservations from you without a guarantee. How do you handle this?

5. You know that you are going to have to walk guests with reservations. At what time during the day should you start doing this? What will you offer guests who are being walked as compensation?

## Weblinks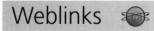

### Property Management Systems

Micros Fidelio Hospitality Solutions International PMS
**www.micros.com**

Maestro from Northwind PMS
**www.northwind.ca**

### Other

Meeting Professionals International
**www.mpiweb.org**

Hospitality Sales and Marketing Association International
**www.hsmai.ca**

# Part III
# Guest Service and Rate Structures

The subjects of service and prices have been referenced throughout Parts I and II. We know that guests choose their hotels on the basis of these two criteria, plus those of location and cleanliness. Guests give different weight to the several variables with each stay. Room rate seems to be of lesser consequence during economically "good times." Guests paid top dollar throughout the boom that closed the twentieth century. Then rates fell. Even as rates declined, guests assigned them greater weight in the buying decision.

Service is more constant. One portion of service, the number of employees per guest room, does fluctuate relative to the volume of business. But as the first chapter of this part explains, service is more than the number of housekeepers or food servers. Service is an attitude. The quality of that attitude and the evenness in which it is delivered must be immune to the ups and downs of the economic cycle. There is a correlation, however, between the number of employees and the attitude of their service. Overworked staff become surly if they feel exploited by large staff cuts.

Good service does not replace competitive pricing. Nor does competitive price offset unsatisfactory service. Part III brings the two together: opening the part with the role of service and closing it with the issue of price.

## Chapter 7

# Managing Guest Service

## Learning Objectives

After reading this chapter, you will be able to do the following:

1. Understand the concept of quality management and discuss its history and implementation in manufacturing.

2. Describe quality management and its application to the hospitality industry.

3. Implement guest service through an understanding of how to measure guest service, how to provide quality service guarantees, and how to handle complaints.

Guest service doesn't just happen; it must be managed—and it must be managed close to the action, not from afar. Accomplishing the shift from the traditional management-imposed culture to an employee-participative culture takes all of management's talent. It's slow, hard work. Many workers and even their immediate supervisors are not interested in taking on the job. They see guest service as management's job, not theirs. But today's innkeepers cannot be the guest's personal hosts as they were once seen to be (see Chapter 2). The task has sifted down through several organizational levels to the staffer on the floor. Getting those employees to recognize the importance of the task and the mutual interests that result from performing them is the role of managing for guest service. No easy task, that.

# Brief History of Quality Management

*Managing quality* originally meant reducing the number of manufacturing errors and improving the quality of mass-produced goods. Buyers still find inspectors' identifications in the manufactured products that they buy. This concept of quality management (QM) gradually shifted from manufactured goods to service delivery. As other measures of quality and new means of achieving it were introduced, quality management's definition changed. Thus, the broader concept of total quality management (TQM) came to the service industries. It reached the hotel business with a sharper focus on quality's delivery system: service personnel. With it has come the tentative beginnings of new terminology, customer relations management (CRM). For hotel managers with accounting, real estate, and marketing backgrounds, the shift was an abrupt one.

### Reasons for the Era of Human Resources

Realization that high touch is needed to balance high tech
Huge turnover among hotel staff (sometimes exceeding 100% annually)
Expectations and increased pressure from public, legislatures, and courts
Focus on hotel operations as well as on hotel investments
Cultural diversity in the general public and thus in the hotel workforce
Loss of supervisory management from organizational downsizing
Increased empowerment given to workers
Shortage of good job applicants at lodging's traditional salary levels

Quality management in innkeeping gets special attention when business slumps. That happened between the late 1980s and early 1990s, a low period following the previous decade of good times. The good cycle repeated itself, running again for some seven to eight years beginning around 1991. Volume fell again after the events of September 11, 2001. Through it all, attention to the service deliverer, the employee, gained ground. That's evidenced in the role of the hotels' human resources (HR) departments. In two decades, hoteliers have seen the introduction, maturation, and influence of HR departments where there had been none before (see Exhibit 7-1).

Sensitivity to customer needs is not special to innkeeping. Quality service must be a standard for all businesses. In one respect, then, lodging is, like all business, just one industry among many. In other aspects, chiefly face-to-face service, hotelkeeping is not like other service industries and is very different from manufacturing.

*We are in the people business. Not the hotel business, not the real estate business. Instead of machinery, we have people. Instead of automated conveyor belts, we have people. Instead of computers that hum and print stuff, we have people. We have not come to grips with this basic concept.*[1]

## Quality Management in Manufacturing

Worldwide markets, the advantage of globalization, come with worldwide competition. That competition grew intense as the world's economies blended into one. During this period, the quality of North American–made goods came into question. A reputation for quality, which North America had held since the end of the Second World War, passed into other hands. Industries formerly owned by North America, such as the automobile industry, were now being taken over by Japan and Germany. Nearly a quarter-century elapsed before the movement reversed again. A return to quality for all North American industries was signalled by Ford Motor Company's advertising slogan, "Quality Is Job One."[2]

The now-popular emphasis on quality had its North American origins in the manufacturing industries. The decline in the reputation of North American–made goods forced manufacturers to re-examine production techniques and the workers responsible for that production. North American manufacturing responded, but it did not originate the movement toward **quality management (QM)**.

The Japanese, for example, invented quality control circles, which are teams of employees focusing on special issues. Many hotels have used quality circles in their QM programs.

The Japanese also introduced the concept of zero defects. Zero defects are difficult enough to achieve in manufacturing, but impossible to achieve in service. Zero tolerance attempts to apply the same concept to the sociocultural environment. There, too, its application has failed. Taking up the challenge, some in the hotel industry have adopted "service quality that surprises," a level as near perfection as the human element allows.

## International Standards Organization (ISO 9000 2000)

*ISO* is the *International Organization for Standardization*. It is located in Switzerland and was established in 1947 to develop common international standards in many areas. Its members come from more than 120 national standards bodies.

ISO 9000 is sweeping the world. It is rapidly becoming the most important quality standard. Thousands of companies in more than 100 countries have already adopted it, and many more are in the process of doing so. Why? Because it controls quality. It saves money. Customers expect it. And competitors use it.

ISO 9000 applies to all types of organizations. It doesn't matter what size they are or what they do. It can help both product- and service-oriented organizations achieve standards of quality that are recognized and respected throughout the world.

ISO is available for all industries, including those in tourism; however, the tourism industry and the companies in it have chosen to create their own quality management and guest-service systems.

## Quality Management in Innkeeping

Locating this chapter on guest service in the middle of the book is not accidental. It is here as a fulcrum, balancing the how-to with the other elements of quality service, the guests and the staff. Every topic that precedes this chapter and every one that follows carries a message, understood if not always expressed, about the importance of guest service throughout the hotel, but especially at the front desk. Executive attention to rooms employees, and through these employees to the guests, is essential to the management of the front office. QM has spun off concepts, such as **quality assurance (QA)** and **total quality management (TQM)**. The terms seem to be interchangeable now. The essence of all three terms is that every person in the company has the opportunity, and needs the ability, to make a positive impact on the customer. Just consider the terminology. Retailers speak of *customers*, various professionals refer to *clients* or *patients*, economists cite *consumer* trends, and galleries talk of *patrons*. Only the hotel industry calls its business clients *guests*.

Hoteliers have brought many innovations to the business. Bathtubs were added to hotel accommodations before they appeared in the White House. At one time, fans, radios, TV sets, elevators, telephones, clocks, and swimming pools were unique products, installed in leading properties to attract guests. They are standard expectations today. To the credit of the hotel industry, QM is viewed similarly. Quality management was an innovation when it first came to the hotel industry. Today, it is thought to be so basic an accommodation that no hotel can operate without it. Thus, the standard of the whole industry moves upward just as it does when every hotel room has a personal computer and fax.

**Corporate Mission Statements** An organization's mission statement defines the unique purpose that sets one hotel or hotel company apart from others. It expresses the underlying philosophy that gives meaning and direction to hotel policies. Mission statements are not unlike a personal philosophy that gives each person direction in their life. Let's examine the following mission statement for Four Seasons Hotels and Resorts.

---

### OUR GOALS, OUR BELIEFS, OUR PRINCIPLES

#### Who We Are

We have chosen to specialise within the hospitality industry, by offering only experiences of exceptional quality. Our objective is to be recognised as the company that manages the finest hotels, resorts and resort clubs wherever we locate. We create properties of enduring value using superior design and finishes, and support them with a deeply instilled ethic of personal service. Doing so allows Four Seasons to satisfy the needs and tastes of our discriminating customers, and to maintain our position as the world's premier luxury hospitality company.

#### What We Believe

Our greatest asset, and the key to our success, are our people. We believe that each of us needs a sense of dignity, pride and satisfaction in what we do. Because satisfying our guests depends on the united efforts of many, we are most effective when we work together cooperatively, respecting each other's contribution and importance.

#### How We Behave

We demonstrate our beliefs most meaningfully in the way we treat each other and by the example we set for one another. In all our interactions with our guests, customers, business associates and colleagues, we seek to deal with others, as we would have them deal with us.

#### How We Succeed

We succeed when every decision is based on a clear understanding of and belief in what we do and when we couple this conviction with sound financial planning. We expect to achieve a fair and reasonable profit to ensure the prosperity of the company, and to offer long-term benefits to our hotel owners, our shareholders, our customers and our employees.

---

From the mission statement, a corporation then sets its goals. Goals are activities and standards a corporation must successfully perform or achieve to effectively carry out its mission. It may take several goals to achieve a mission, and goals need to be measurable so employees know whether the goal was attained or not. Goals must also be achievable or employees will soon become discouraged from trying to reach them. Corporations do long-term planning—usually a five-year plan—and then break this down into yearly goals, which may be further broken down into monthly goals.

A typical front-office goal may be to increase occupancy by two percentage points over last year. Other departments in the hotel, such as sales and marketing, would also be involved in reaching this goal. The employees and management would then establish strategies and tactics to reach this goal.

A typical plan to reach a goal may look like this:

Goal—to eliminate the need for guests to personally check out at the front desk.

Strategy—provide express check-out instructions to guests while they are checking in.

Tactic—install TV express check-out systems in guest rooms and print instruction cards for guests.

**Examples of Quality Management**   Hotels did not embrace QM terminology as early as manufacturing did. That fact doesn't distract from the lodging industry's long-held sensitivity to guest service. Guest service is an industry fundamental, although management's attention to it waxes and wanes over time. Industry-wide interest in guest service peaked anew when Ritz-Carlton Company, a hotel management company, won the 1992 Malcolm Baldrige National Quality Award. This award represents an example of quality management achievement for all of North America. As the first hotel company to win the award, Ritz-Carlton reawakened the entire industry to one of its basic tenets: Service the guests.

Winning an award in 1992 required the company to commit to excellence far earlier. Although Ritz-Carlton set the pace, many other hotel companies also initiated formal quality management programs. The American Hotel & Lodging Association (AH&LA) held the first Quality Assurance Conference in 1988, and in that same year the Educational Institute of the AH&LA published the first text on the subject, *Managing Quality Services*.[3] Both the text and the conference flowed from the 1981 annual meeting, when the AH&LA decided to create a Quest for Quality program. From that beginning, much of the industry came on stream. Many colleges, universities, and companies in Canada adopted these texts for instructing and implementing quality management. Recently, Ontario Tourism Education Corporation (OTEC) has developed two programs called Service Excellence and Managing Service Excellence. These are specific programs designed to meet the unique requirements of a service industry. Many provinces in Canada have training programs available in Superhost, a guest-service program developed for the Vancouver Expo in 1986. British Columbia has also developed Super Host Japan, a program that looks at meeting the unique guest-service needs of a specific market—Japan. Ontario developed an early guest-service program in the 1970s called We Treat You Royally. Holiday Inns created an advertising slogan of "No Surprises," widely used in the 1980s, meant to suggest that when staying at a Holiday Inn there were no unpleasant surprises.

Sheraton is now part of Starwood Hotels & Resorts. The culture of Starwood has been a mixed bag. In six short years, the company acquired a very diverse set of brands. There's the upscale St. Regis on one end and Sheraton's Four Point Hotels on the other. In between are the W Hotels, which are boutique-style properties and account for some 15 percent of total corporate revenues. In an effort "to integrate the company spiritually and to brand a [Starwood] culture,"[4] the corporation rolled out a system-wide initiative, Six Sigma. It is part of a total re-engineering designed to bring consistency to all corporate brands. In the full meaning of *total* quality management, the Six Sigma program incorporates every facet of operation from reservations to check-out, from service to cleanliness.

The Ritz-Carlton Hotel Company, like its Sheraton cousin, is no longer a freestanding chain. It's a division of Marriott, which also has a mix of brands (see Chapter 1, Exhibit 1-7). In contrast to Starwood, Marriott appears to be keeping its QM programs separated. Thus, Marriott's Renaissance brand has coined its own QM program, Savvy Service. Included are 20 principles that employees—Marriott prefers to call them *associates*—agree to work toward and enunciate during training sessions. Savvy Service aims to capture customer attention with the unexpected. Associates offer proactive service to win from guests, by means of personalized employee attention, the same level of delight that customers find in the unexpected design of a boutique hotel.

Broadening the basic quality management program to other employees and even to purveyors is part of the explanation for the emergence of the term *total* quality management. TQM views everyone as part of the program: guests, staff, and purveyors. Companies that employ the TQM philosophy treat their purveyors as part of the excellence team but demand of them the same performance levels that the hotel itself is striving to achieve.

Four Seasons Hotels have consistently led the industry with innovative guest service. "We have aspired to be the best hotel in each location where we operate," says Isadore Sharp, chairman and CEO. "Early in the company's history we decided to focus on redefining luxury as service and that became our strategic edge. And, in order to deliver on that promise, we needed to hire the 'best of the best' employees who are dedicated, committed and inspired to deliver great service. They are the standard bearers for the intuitive, highly personalized service we aspire to provide."

In 2006, for the ninth year in a row (one of only 19 companies to do so), Four Seasons Hotels and Resorts was named to *Fortune* magazine's list of 100 Best Companies to Work For. Four Seasons has made the list every year since its inception, in 2006 ranked twenty-eighth among leading employers in the United States, and, once again, was the only Canadian company to make the list.

At Fairmont Hotels & Resorts, formerly known as Canadian Pacific Hotels, employees are central to their operation's philosophy. A century of experience as hoteliers has created a tradition of hospitality that is evident in everything they do. They know that even the best locations and offerings would be meaningless without outstanding guest service. They believe that a well-trained, motivated workforce will naturally exceed guest expectations. Service Plus, their custom-designed service delivery program, gives their people the tools they need to succeed. They then carefully monitor progress through employee opinion surveys and guest feedback. Fairmont Hotels & Resorts has an outstanding reputation for environmental stewardship, community involvement, and innovative social programs. Their award-winning initiatives enhance employee satisfaction, win guest loyalty, and create a positive public profile for the brand as a whole.

**Ontario Tourism Excellence Program** The Ontario government has partnered with the National Quality Institute (NQI), industry stakeholders, and the Ontario Tourism Education Corporation (OTEC) to develop the Ontario Tourism Excellence Program. Building on the internationally recognized Canadian Framework for Excellence, this voluntary program provides a comprehensive set of criteria for management practices and principles that reinforce and sustain excellence. The criteria are based on years of accumulated knowledge and experience, and reflect the unique circumstances of tourism and hospitality organizations.

Empowering employees has another advantage: Fewer supervisors are needed if staff members have the authority to decide on their own. However, for this concept to work, better-trained employees are needed to carry out the empowerment—and, therefore, better salaries will need to be paid. There is no evidence yet that the hotel industry has accepted that rationale.

Whether a chain or an independent property, a conference centre or a franchise company, most of the industry has adopted some form or process that could be called quality assurance. Formal quality assurance programs are expensive, ongoing, and successful only when top management is committed for the long haul. That commitment often wavers over time because, like advertising, QM costs are easily measured but results are not.

# What Is Quality Management?

As we shall see shortly, there is no single, crystal-clear definition of quality management. At its core, QM seeks the co-operation of every staff member in achieving company goals, primarily those that stress guest service and guest relationships. In that, there is nothing new; management everywhere has this intent. Quality management brings a more formal tone, a more structured approach to the task. It recognizes, moreover, that guest service has many parts. Total quality management requires attention to all, not just some, of the parts. Among them is the physical product the hotel delivers.

## The Basic Product

Guests come to hotels to sleep. They willingly overlook missing amenities and poorly decorated lobbies if sleep, the hotel's basic product, is delivered. Above all else, hotel guests expect a good night's sleep. For quality management to achieve its goals throughout the hotel, guests must be satisfied with the delivery of the one product they have specifically purchased. QM begins with the guest room. Dissatisfaction with this basic product cannot be redressed by a smiling desk clerk wearing a happy-face button as part of a structured QM program.

**Bedding** The look of the bed and the look of the room become important once comfort levels are achieved. Each age has a different look. Shag carpets, the standard of an earlier era, have been replaced along with the florals and colours that identified them: mauve, pink, and burnt-orange. Sleigh beds and striped bedspreads are the "in" decor today, at least for Sheraton. So too are white bed linens, which convey a crisp, clean look and hold up better than colours in repeated washings.

Overall, the industry gets high marks for the quality of the mattresses and springs that complete the beds. A good hotel mattress lasts as long as 8 to 10 years; a top-of-the-line mattress, up to 15 years. A good-quality queen mattress costs about $300, or just $30 to $35 per year. It makes good economic sense to buy higher priced, longer lasting, matching mattress and spring sets. Housekeeping must devise a system for turning the mattresses at least four times annually (see Chapter 3), because equalizing wear ensures longer mattress life. Furnishing comfortable chairs also adds life to the bedding because guests sit on the chairs and not on the beds. Ergonomic chairs have been included in recent renovations at upscale properties. Fire-resistant bedding has reduced the number of in-room fires that result from smokers falling asleep in bed.

**Linen and Pillows** There is more to a bed than a mattress. Upgrading the sleeping experience requires close attention to the bed coverings (called the soft goods) and especially to the linen count. The standard is 180 count: 80 threads in one direction, 100 in the other. This is a durable product for the hotel and an acceptable one for the guest, who is probably using about the same count at home. Jumping to a 250 count, or even to 300, as some upscale chains have done for their top sheets, makes a noticeable difference. Sheets of that count are silky smooth and luxurious. Despite the moves of keen upscale competitors, the 180 count remains the choice of most hotels.

Crawling into a bed of 250- to 300-count bottom and top sheets, plus a third sheet of 180 count to cover the blanket, is a memorable experience. But there's more. No longer will one pillow do. Several pillows, each with distinctive characteristics, including hypoallergenic ones, are on the bed or available on call. Some hotels now offer "pillow menus" with feathers and down at the top of the list. Even wedge-shaped pregnancy pillows that lift and support the abdomen are offered.

Lighter down blankets or comforters, which have long been used in Europe, add another dimension to lodging's "new" beds. The comforters are enclosed in pillowcase-like covers, called duvets, another European adoption. Duvets are washable; traditional bedspreads are not. Savings from dry-cleaning costs can translate into more frequent laundering. Laundered bedcovers not only feel cleaner, they are.

**Cleanliness** No architectural design is more attractive than a sparkling bed. A recent survey among Canadian Automobile Association members who use the *Tour Book* ranked cleanliness as their top concern. Cleanliness was ahead of price, location, and amenities.

Bedding must be clean! Unfortunately, clean sheets don't always look clean. There has been a shift away from ironing sheets to using a sheet of 50 percent cotton and 50 percent synthetic fibre, no-iron sheets. No-iron sheets are fine as fitted bottom sheets because the wrinkles are stretched out, providing the appearance of a smooth, ironed sheet—except that fitted sheets are just not being used. They are difficult to fold and handle, require extra storage space, and tear at the corners, increasing replacement costs. Because of this, many hotels use regular, not fitted, no-iron sheets, which wrinkle and leave the impression of less-than-clean bed linen.

Cleanliness is not limited to bedding. Guests are very sensitive to the quality of housekeeping everywhere, especially in the bath. Tub/showers, toilets, sinks, and bathroom floors require special attention to remove hair and dirt. Cleaning into the corners and behind the toilets takes extra care. Chrome fixtures, particularly the sink and tub drains, must be cleaned and wiped daily.

Vacuuming, the final step in cleaning the guest room, may take place only between guests. Rooms for stayovers are not vacuumed unless the room attendant or housekeeper thinks there is need to do so. Elsewhere, the policy might be to vacuum every day, check-out or not.

Overall cleanliness, inside and outside the guest room, is taken for granted. Few guests ever compliment sanitation standards on guest-comment cards, but all will complain when it's missing.

**Noise and Temperature** Noise is another reason the industry fails to deliver its basic product: sleep. Even "road warriors" (business travellers who sleep away from home a great deal) complain about noisy rooms. Poor initial construction, which is not easily fixed after the fact, is high on a list of causes. Budget limitations force builders to ignore adequate sound barriers between rooms and in the utility and plumbing shafts. Back-to-back baths make for easy construction and maintenance, but play havoc in transmitting noises. In very bad cases, the plumbing is strapped inadequately, so noisy vibrations follow the opening of every faucet.

Poorly insulated rooms bring the neighbour's television set resonating into the sleeper's dreams. Everyday sounds from simple conversations to children playing come from rooms close by. Hallway noises, which include the whirr of ice machines, ice falling into buckets, ringing telephones, elevator doors, and late-to-bed revellers, add to the din. The worst noise offender is right in the room: the fan on the heating/air conditioning system. It is as much an annoyance as the room's temperature control.

Central heating and air conditioning systems are far superior to individual room units. Cost is, again, the determining factor. However, some window units are not even temperature sensitive. They run all the time unless they're turned off completely. It's up to the sleeper to decide which is worse. Occasionally, the units don't run at all. Maintenance of the systems is minimal and on demand rather than preventative. Guests may be housed in rooms with non-working units. Encountered occasionally are systems that deliver either heating or cooling, depending on the time of the year. No choice is available during swing months; guests get either heating or cooling, regardless of their own body temperatures.

Construction noise joins with street noise as still another QM challenge. TQM faces its toughest test when guests are roomed close to internal renovations or nearby external construction. Construction jobs always begin early in the morning. TQM requires the hotel to act. Reservations must alert the guest, and registration must remind the guest. Above all, the rate must reflect the unavoidable if the hotel is truly managing for quality. Airport hotels face another challenge, which has been addressed at the Fairmont Vancouver Airport Hotel by the use of sound proof "Window Walls."

The same kind of preventative action should be taken with all aspects of the hotel room. The Ritz-Carlton has done just that with its Care program. Care reduces the number of guest-room complaints through anticipative management. Preventing complaints relies heavily on the hotel housekeeping inspection that Chapter 3 discussed. So, the first hotel company to win the Baldrige Award for quality sees good sense in continuing TQM programs that attend to basic accommodations.

## Quality Management Defined

Defining quality management is as difficult a task as is delivering it. Some have tried explaining quality service by telling anecdotes, brief stories to illustrate the idea. Illustrations of this type are legend: A desk clerk makes certain that an important letter is typed for a guest after hours; a bellperson delivers a forgotten attaché case to the airport just in time; a housekeeper takes guest laundry home to meet a deadline; a door attendant lends black shoes to a guest for a formal affair.

Despite the difficulties, formal definitions are the vogue. Everyone gives it a shot—the authors try their hand at it a few pages on—even if the results are incomplete. Along with hundreds of other publications, *Managing Quality Services,* cited earlier, says that, "QA is a management system that ensures consistent delivery of products and services." Another puts it this way: "TQM is a way to continuously improve performance at every level of operation, in every functional area of an organization, using all available human and capital resources."[5] Both of these descriptions, which represent the general run of QA definitions, fail to emphasize the duality of the issue: TQM involves both the buyer–receiver of the service and the seller–giver of the service.

Part I explained how segmented the hotel industry is; its customer base is equally fragmented. Thus, the desire to deliver quality originates with innumerable sellers, even as the search to find quality has many, many buyers. Each side and each member of that side sees the issue from a different perspective. No wonder variations abound in the delivery and receipt of service, and consequently in its definition. Quality service, and the management of quality service, have no objective measures. Definitions are necessarily vague, evaluations are obviously imprecise, and delivery is clearly inexact. Still, everyone knows it when they see it.

**The Buyer's View** From the guest's viewpoint, quality is the degree to which the property delivers what the guest expects. If the guest is surprised by a better stay than anticipated, the hotel is perceived as high quality. If the visit fails to meet expectations, the property is downgraded.

Advertising, word-of-mouth comments, price, previous visits, and publicity create a level of expectation within the guest. Of course, almost every guest receives that barrage of communications differently with different perceptions. Moreover, those very expectations change over time and place, even within the same guest. Influencing the guest's expectations are components that may be outside the hotel's control: a late flight, a rude cab driver, and a bad storm.

Guests hold different expectations about different hotels, even different hotels within the same chain. Quality is measured against the expectation of that particular property at that particular time more than against different hotels in different categories.

Driving up to an economy property with a loaded family van and a pet, but without a reservation, carries one expectation. Flying around the world to an expensive resort—a trip that a couple has planned and saved for over many years—creates a much different level of anticipation. Coming to a busy convention property with a reservation made by the company's travel desk evokes still a third level of expectation. The hotel must meet each expectation with delivery at the highest level appropriate for the circumstances. Quality assurance attempts to do just that. It is a big, big order.

Consider two hypothetical properties. The first, an economy hotel offering minimal services, charges half its neighbour's rate. The neighbour, an expensive, upscale property and not a true competitor, has it all.

The economy hotel offers the following conveniences:

- No bell service, but parking is convenient and many luggage carts are in the lobby.
- No room service, but the hotel is located near a well-known restaurant chain and has an exceptional choice of vending options.
- No health club, but the swimming pool is clean, open at convenient hours, and has a good supply of towels.
- No concierge, but the room clerk is knowledgeable and affable.

The upscale neighbour offers the following conveniences:

- Bellpersons, whom guests are urged to call on. However, this hotel never schedules enough staff, resulting in long delays.
- Room service, but it is offered at limited times. This hotel suggests a pizza delivery company as an alternative.
- A well-reputed health club, but it is on lease, which means that this hotel charges for admission.
- A concierge, but the concierge has a recorded message that puts the guest on hold.

Extreme as the illustrations are, the point is obvious—quality is in the eye of the beholder. Managing for quality, therefore, must include standards set from the consumer's perspective. Doing so gives credence to the buyer's view of what quality service is all about. Management must first establish the systems and then the measurement standards for those systems—both to be based on the buyers' expectations. Management must also fix the procedure for achieving those standards. Successfully implemented, TQM matches the buyers' standards with the sellers' ability to deliver. When done right, the guest/buyer knows that the hotel delivers quality guest service.

**The Seller's View** Like every other policy and operating practice, TQM originates with management. Either management makes deliberate decisions to implement particular ideas or it passively accepts ongoing procedures. So it is with quality assurance. Management creates and carries out a program of enhanced guest service or there is none. Action doesn't always follow verbal support. A study of hotel general managers reported their belief in the concepts of TQM, but they downgraded its effectiveness in practice.[6]

Delivering quality requires management to focus on both employees and guests. The two are intertwined. Increasing guest services to satisfy the buyer's side of QM requires special attention to operational issues, the employees' side of QM. Staying close to the customer means stressing customer wants, ensuring consistency, remedying the mistakes that do occur, and concentrating on the whole with a passion that hints at obsession. However, all of these are also operational concerns. Nothing can be accomplished without attention to the employees entrusted with the delivery.

**Leadership** Adopting TQM as a company philosophy forces major changes in the definition of management. Traditionally, management is said to be a series of functions. Planning, organizing, staffing, directing, and reviewing are the classic list of management's responsibilities. TQM adds another element: leadership. Managing as a leader requires a change in both the style of management and the composition of the workforce being managed. When both components—management and workforce—focus on delivering quality above all else, the company is said to have a *service culture*.

With a leadership style, managers shift from their traditional position of review, which requires corrective action after mistakes are made, to a proactive style of supervision. Errors must be corrected, of course, but a proactive stance aims at error avoidance. Minimizing errors, whether on a production line or a registration line, is what TQM is all about.

Total quality management has come to mean almost any action designed to improve the operation. And that's just what it is: A series of small steps taken within an organizational culture that has the customer's experience as its central focus. Developing that culture requires a fundamental shift in management style. Management must lead by balancing its authority and discipline with delegation and flexibility.

Part of the sharing of responsibility and credit is the sharing of information that once was considered confidential. Staff members must be knowledgeable about the activities of their own departments and those departments whose functions overlap. Overlapping interests are reinforced through **quality circles (QOs)**. Quality circles, which are discussed again later in the chapter, are employee committees. Representatives within each department and sometimes from several departments meet and work on problems. QOs at the front desk, for example, may have representatives from housekeeping, sales, telecommunications, and accounting. Each representative would then sit on a QO within his or her own department. Soon a network exists across the entire property.

**Empowerment** Once so much of management's guarded interests are opened to the operating staff, the next step is almost anticlimactic. Some of management's power is given away, delegated down the line. Operative employees are authorized to make their own decisions as long as these fall within the scope of the individuals' job assignments. Entrusting the employee to act responsibly requires management to give that employee the authority to take action. Giving the workforce appropriate authority is empowerment.

Empowerment locates the problem solving and decision making at the source. Line employees can act effectively once they have both the information and the authority to use it. Moreover, empowering employees creates leaner and flatter organizations. The pancake-like structures make each department operate almost as a small company, with greater responsibility and accountability, under the umbrella of general management.

The first response to empowerment involves individual actions by single employees. The cashier settles a misquoted rate on the spot as the guest checks out. Apologies for an unmade room are expressed with a small bouquet ordered by the desk attendant. Individual acts by employees bring immediate responses from the guests who experience them. But empowerment is more than guest relations.

A second and broader delegation of empowerment is that given to quality circles. Originally, QOs were merely asked to identify problems and to recommend possible solutions. Where TQM has been implemented successfully, quality circles are actually executing their own ideas. They have been empowered to do so. QOs tackle two types of problems. One kind deals with guest relations, usually how-tos. The group considers how to speed check-ins and check-outs, how to reduce errors in reservations, how to expedite group baggage handling, and more.

The second type of issues faced by QOs also has an impact on quality service, but the relationship is less guest oriented. The attention is on in-house procedures (moving linen without tying up the **service elevators**), cost reductions (chargebacks by credit card companies), or operational irritations (maintenance's slow response to requests for guest room repairs). None of these has anything to do with immediate guest service, but all of them have everything to do with QM.

**The Employee** Convincing supervisors to adopt a leadership style of management is but half the battle. TQM requires employees to take on responsibilities, to accept the empowerment offered. Just as some managers and supervisors oppose the transfer of their power to employees, some employees decline to accept what's offered. Many prefer not to take on what they perceive to be a management job.

Similarly, the employer's willingness to share information about the business may not be matched by the employees' interest in receiving it—or receiving it, having the capacity to understand it, or the interest to use it. Even highly motivated employees may not comprehend what is offered or what is expected. Leadership requires followers; great leadership requires inspired and motivated followers. Quality management is burdened with the development of both leaders and followers, and that must be done within a workforce of great diversity in language, education, and cultural expectations.

DIVERSITY AND TURNOVER High job turnover is another reality of the hospitality workforce. Employees, and this term includes supervisors and managers as well, come and go at a costly pace. Many workers are in dead-end jobs. Boredom and monotonous repetition are blunted temporarily by moving to another property even though the new job has the same task routines. Turnover at the lowest levels of the organization, the spots where QM could shine, exceeds 200 percent annually in some jobs at some hotels. Every employee is replaced twice each year! Less dramatic but equally disturbing turnover occurs among managers and supervisors. Turnover feeds upon itself. Missing workers mean heavier loads for those remaining. Discontent grows so that establishing, maintaining, and improving TQM is put aside as resources are assigned to searching, finding, and replacing a turnstile staff.

It is far less costly to retain workers than to replace them. That's why retention plans, which have been in place in other industries for some time, are now finding their way into lodging. Stock options, year-end bonuses, and employee share ownership are relatively new concepts for this old industry. With them, workers are able to increase personal wealth by doing well the repetitive tasks that often make up hotel jobs. The low unemployment rate of the late twentieth century hastened the introduction of these industry-wide changes. Of course, several chains—Marriott, for one—adopted employee-participation plans years ago. Now, a shortage of applicants for low-wage positions has accelerated the introduction of financial incentives throughout the industry.

Rewards, financial and otherwise, must be part of any TQM retention plan. Incentives are especially important at the front desk, where TQM demands a great deal from moderately paid personnel. Every success should be celebrated, and every means to do so should be employed, from simple recognition such as a thank you from the manager to incentives that bind the company and reward the individual. Employee of the month is a widely used recognition. It is more effective if it carries a cash stipend and perhaps a special parking space along with a plaque on the wall and a photo in the newspaper. Some departments can accommodate flexible working hours, which may prove the best of all rewards for working parents. Although managers, especially supervisory managers not protected under wage-and-hour laws, are not above cash rewards, the hotel industry has another incentive to offer: time off. Long hours on the job cause hardships in the personal lives of many non-hourly (so-called exempt) workers. Incentives for them may simply be an extra day off.

Good staff at all organizational levels is the thread of the quality management weave. The commitment to finding and holding those persons is reflected in the salaries paid, the training offered, and the incentives rewarded. A company that concentrates on better human resources ensures a better delivery of quality service. The effort begins with selecting and retaining the right persons.

SELECTING AND RETAINING THE RIGHT EMPLOYEE Managing guest services by empowering employees and enlisting their help requires a broad effort. It reaches beyond the immediate delivery of services, stretching backwards to employment and forward to retention. Delivering quality service begins at the selection decision. How else can the right person be in the right place when the CRM situation requires? Hoteliers knows this, so the human resources office has been the launch site for most TQM programs.

Selecting the right employee—and TQM programs emphasize that it is *selection*, not *hiring*—is where good service begins. Imagine the impression when new hires meet the general manager who repeats that mantra: You've been "selected" because of your enthusiasm and your ability to smile when things go wrong. The industry has come to believe that it can teach technical skills, but it needs to select sensitive staff. Good service is actually intangible, not measurable, so the burden of delivery falls upon the employee who is on hand at that moment. Friendly, interactive applicants who have a sincere wish to help will solve problems of quality deficiency faster than do experienced technical workers who lack those qualities. Indeed, there are far more guest complaints about poor employee attitudes than about substandard facilities and broken TV sets.

Selecting the right person begins with searching for and finding the right pool of applicants. Human resource departments don't always clear that hurdle, because hotel job vacancies are frequent and difficult to fill. Too often, the first applicant to come is the one hired. Recruiting during good economic times takes imaginative work. Hotel companies begin with nominations from their own workforce, paying cash incentives when friends and relatives of current workers remain through a given time period. Websites are also widely used. Retention rates go up if new hires understand clearly what jobs they are about to take. Some properties ask the applicant to spend an hour observing the actual job. Others, like Doubletree Hotels and Resorts, go a step further. Applicants are interviewed by the very employees with whom they'll work, a practice called *peer group hiring*. That's part of a TQM program that puts employees in decision-making roles.

Once hired, retaining the right worker, like retaining the right guest, would seem to be of the highest priority. Strangely, despite the spread in costs, retention sometimes gets less attention than the original search. Yet retaining both the recruited guest and the recruited worker is at the very heart of TQM. Induction, helping the new hire ease into the company, is a common pitfall. After a company spends many recruiting dollars, a new employee may be alienated in the very next step: entering the work door.

TRAINING TQM views training as an investment, not as a cost. Continuous training can be likened to a program of continually upgrading the physical plant. Both the facilities and the employees are critical to guest satisfaction. Trained staff is able to do a better job for the house and the customer. This provides personal satisfaction for the employee and develops opportunities for both long-run promotions and short-run gratuities.

**The Authors' View** The entire TQM culture has been summarized in a brief phrase (an aphorism) that has become a favourite of the industry: "The answer is 'yes,' now ask me the question."[7] That clearly represents the type of employee (and management) attitude that TQM programs are supposed to instill. Applications of the adage apply equally well to employee–guest interactions, employee–management interfaces, and employee–employee contacts. Under an umbrella of so broad a coverage, this brief saying offers a simple definition of total quality management.

Closer inspection proves TQM culture to be very similar to the carefully cultivated culture of the concierge. With both, the attitude is expressed in Radisson's "Yes, I can!" slogan. Hotels that promote TQM understand that the concierge is not a department, not even staff. It is an attitude, the kind that one hopes all employees in a TQM program hold. Hence, the first part of the authors' definition: *Quality management is an attitude that has every employee acting like a concierge . . .*

Several times throughout this chapter the duality of quality assurance has been emphasized: The guest side (the display side) of the TQM equation is balanced by the employee side (the operational side). Thus, the second phrase of the authors' definition of TQM: *. . . and thinking like a manager.*

> *Quality management is an attitude that has every employee acting like a concierge and thinking like a manager.*

## Quality Management Denied

The hotel business is part of a vast hospitality industry that includes food, beverage, and entertainment facilities. Within that definition, hotel leaders see their industry as a service industry, their product as hospitality, and their customers as guests. Because this position has been verbalized so often, hotel patrons are confused by the anti-hospitality–anti-guest–anti-service syndrome that is part of some hotels.

**Exhibit 7-2** ▶
Who knows why?

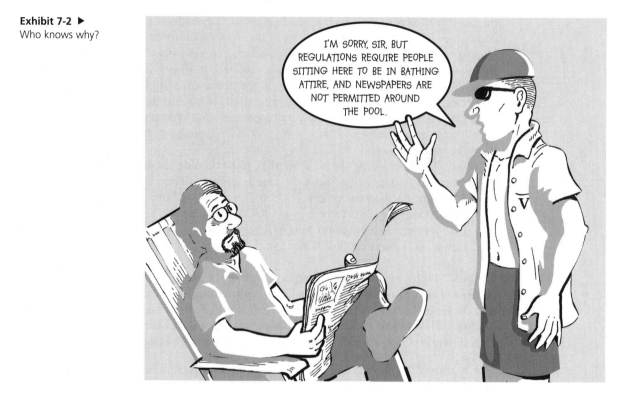

Guest expectations, one component of quality delivery systems, were reviewed earlier. Guests recognize that every property is not charged with the same level of product despite its grouping under the common umbrella of lodging. However, guests do not understand why minimal service means anti-service, and why a lack of personnel means a lack of courtesy. Management's failure to distinguish minimal service, justified by minimal rates, from anti-service, shown by employee negativism, has lead to the anti-service syndrome that some hotels demonstrate and many guests experience.

Total quality management is the industry's response to anti-service. TQM programs are designed to ferret out the problems, to train for the solutions, and to reward those who demonstrate the correct response. Sometimes, however, the very structure of the operation thwarts the best of intentions.

**Who Knows Why?**  Every organization develops standard operating procedures. They are to business routines as personal habits are to individual routines. Some of them are new and meaningful; some are bad and in need of change. Along with the new and the good, guests encounter the old and the useless. Like all bad habits, old and useless ways are hard to discard. Hotels that insist on keeping them irritate their guests unnecessarily and undermine the concepts of quality service (see Exhibit 7-2). To the observer, some practices seem to be almost intentional, as if inconveniencing the guest is easier than fixing the problem. For example, consider the following:

Who knows why?

- Sleepers are roused from their beds by:
  alarm clocks set by previous occupants.
  computerized calling systems asking for a breakfast order.

    maids knocking on the door: "Never mind, just housekeeping."
    running water in the neighbour's shower.

- Customers are assessed for:
leaving a day earlier than the four-day reservation.
incoming faxes, although incoming telephone calls are free.
late check-outs, even when occupancy is low.
gratuities, when they are part of the inclusive package.

- Guests find:
the pool closed when they are there and open when they're away.
dining dress codes more rigid than accepted social standards.
their requests cannot be met because of some "company policy."
hotel managers taking the best parking spots.

- Hotels:
sell double-occupancy rooms but offer only a single key.
require bell service for individual arrivals but not for groups.
have coffee stands that refuse service four minutes before opening time.
impose surcharges on telephone calls paid with credit cards.

- Policies dictate:
loud, public conversations when arrivals have no baggage.
different rate quotes from travel agents, reservationists, and websites.
no towels from the room, although there are none at the pool.
not providing clean linens for stayovers. Is it really ecological concerns?

# Implementing Guest Service

The modern hotel services mass markets. How different that is from the individualized attention that was the norm a century ago. Smiling, courteous, concerned employees working in a democratic culture have replaced the rigid, serve-food-from-the-left, clear-drinks-from-the-right, white-gloved autocracy of a past era.

Hotel companies have shifted from the formal to the informal; from pretence to expedited service; from rigid procedures to empowerment. Much of the change can be explained by the public's new attitude toward service. Aware of labour costs, functioning in a self-service environment themselves, sensitive to the employees' expectations of equality, today's guests no longer expect a servile attitude. And employees no longer deliver it. Guests do expect—and are entitled to receive during each encounter—a friendly face, an attentive ear, and a twinkling eye. After all, quality service, as previously defined, is an attitude that shines through.

## Measuring Guest Service

In Chapter 1, we discussed several measures for evaluating the industry's economic health. Occupancy percentages and average daily rates (ADRs) are the two basic measurements. Both figures rise or fall in response to the guest's experience with the service encounter. Happy guests mean good statistical results; unhappy guests mean poor ones. Other factors also affect occupancy and rate. The state of the economy, the condition of the building, and the level of advertising are just some of the issues that cloud the results. Waiting for low occupancy and poor ADRs to warn of guest-service problems may be a matter of waiting too long. Management must look elsewhere and everywhere.

| | | | |
|---|---|---|---|
| Number of rooms in the hotel | | | 300 |
| Percentage of occupancy | | | × .70 |
| Number of rooms occupied each night | | 210 | |
| Percentage of double occupancy | | | × .33 |
| Number of guest nights | | 280 | |
| **Moments of Truth** | | | |
| Arrival | 1 | | |
| Inquiry at the desk | 1 | | |
| Bellperson | 1 | | |
| Housekeeping | 1 | | |
| Telephone operator | 1 | | |
| Coffee shop host(ess) | 1 | | |
| Server/busperson | 2 | | |
| Cashier | 1 | | |
| Newstand | 1 | | |
| Total encounters per guest night | | × 10 | |
| Daily number of moments of truth | | | 2800 |

**Moments of Truth** Several years ago, a study was undertaken to measure the costs of poor service.[8] The amount of dollars and cents lost was calculated for each missed opportunity. Among the leading charges laid against the front office were overbooking, lost reservations, and discourtesy. Although one incident doesn't make a bankruptcy, poor service is insidious. Single episodes mushroom from minor, miscellaneous costs to staggering totals per week, per month, per year. Anti-service comes at a high cost.

Guests and staff interact more frequently in a hotel environment than in any other business setting. Hotel employees are asked to deliver an exceptional level of service over and over and over again each day. Exhibit 7-3 highlights the cumulative impact of having one's customers in residence.

With 70 percent occupancy and a double occupancy of 33 percent, employee–guest contacts number 2800 per day. The figure soars to more than 1 million per year for a hotel of only 300 rooms! The number multiplies even faster with full-service hotels, where more operating departments mean more employees. Not only are service expectations higher at the full-service property, so are the number of service contacts.

Opportunities for meeting guest expectations—or failing to meet guest expectations—have been called "**moments of truth**."[9] It is during these encounters, when the service provider and the service buyer meet eyeball to eyeball, that the guest's perception of quality is set. Some say the first 10 minutes are the most critical.

How does the staff respond? Does the final guest of the shift receive the same attention as the first arrival? For many, only a smile and an appropriate greeting are needed. More is expected by the next guest: the one with the problem, the one with the complaint, the one with the special need. If the employee is empowered to act, to respond with alacrity, to evidence concern, it is a shining moment of truth.

Total quality management requires similar moments of truth between supervisors and staffers. Employees will not shine outwardly unless there is an inner glow. Supervisors will not get positive moments of truth if they always second-guess subordinates who have been empowered. Supervisors will not get positive moments of truth if staffers are irritated, say, by late work-schedule postings that frustrate personal plans. Good results from service encounters begin with a good working environment. Shining moments of truth come best from a total quality program.

**Quality Control Through Inspection**  Review and evaluation are essential parts of the management function. That's no less true in managing guest services than, say, in managing cash. Cash management requires standards and procedures to account for the control of money. Service management, too, has standards and procedures for maintaining quality. Quality control (QC) enables hotel companies to maintain even standards throughout all properties of a far-flung chain. Guests rely on these standards, identifying them through corporate logos. To ensure the consistency promised by the logos, chains use inspectors to make on-site visits and evaluations.

Some chains have their own inspectors; others hire outside firms. Visits from the home company are both announced and unannounced. External inspectors usually come anonymously. Although there for a different purpose, inspectors from CAA, Mobil Travel Guide, Canada Select, and others are also on the road. In most cases, the inspectors provide a verbal report to the unit manager before filing a formal, written document with central headquarters. Generally, standards are enforced more stringently in company-owned or company-managed hotels than in franchised properties.

Each chain has its own policy for appraising quality. Hilton aims for three inspections per year. Choice Hotels International sets a two-visit minimum; Super 8 Motels, four visits per property per year. Most use a point system to measure compliance with the franchise agreement. Days Inn, for example, requires 425 points to maintain minimum company standards. Cendant, which inspects three to four times per year, makes its ratings public by assigning the property one to five sunbursts in its directory. Franchise contracts differ, so franchisees have 30 to 180 days to remedy serious defaults before the franchise is cancelled—and they do get cancelled! Radisson culls from the bottom up, using several criteria, including the comment cards that will be discussed soon. Differences among the chains account for the variations in procedure. For example, about 90 percent of Radisson's hotels are franchised, compared to, say, the 75 percent or so of Hilton's.

Quality control has many parts. One is an inspection of the physical facility. This involves a wide range of issues, from the maintenance of the grounds to the quality of the furniture and equipment to the cleanliness of the property. Are there holes in the carpets, burns in the bedspreads, paper in the stairwells? Check sheets used by the inspectors deal with a variety of details: working blow-dryers, cleanliness of air vents, number of hangers in the closet, and even the rotation of mattresses (see Exhibit 7-4).

Food is tasted and drinks are sampled in all of the food and beverage outlets, including room service. Large properties require several days for a full visit. Mystery shoppers, as inspectors are sometimes called, also check employee sales techniques. Does the room clerk sell up? Does the bellperson promote the facility? Does the telephone operator know the hours of the cabaret?

Security is another QC point. Both guest security (keys, locks, chains, and peepholes)[10] and internal security (staff pilferage from the hotel and theft from guests) come under scrutiny during the visit. Do bartenders ring up every sale? Does cash paid to room service waiters reach the bank deposit? Security shopping is designed to uncover dishonesty and criminal acts. That's far different from the intent of the typical inspection visit.

Mystery shoppers are not police. Neither are they consultants or critics. They are reporters of the scene. Evaluating service and employee attitude and testing the staff's

## Inspection Report

Auditor _____          Hotel _____

Identification no. _____     City _____

                                   Date(s) _____

| | Excellent | Good | Fair | Poor | Comments |
|---|:---:|:---:|:---:|:---:|---|
| **Registration** | | | | | |
| 1. Waiting time | | × | | | About 2 minutes |
| 2. Greeting | × | | | | Used my name in conversation |
| 3. Friendliness | | × | | | |
| 4. Efficiency | | | × | | PMS was slow |
| 5. Staff on hand | × | | | | Other clerks handled telephone |
| 6. Grooming | | × | | | Except for Grace's hair |
| 7. Accuracy | × | | | | |
| **Rooming** | | | | | |
| 1. Bellperson offered | | | | × | No, had to call housekeeping |
| 2. Elevator wait | × | | | | 3:00 P.M. |
| 3. Floor signage | × | | | | |
| 4. First impression | | | × | | Not too clean; stale odour |
| **Guest Room** | | | | | |
| 1. Hangers | × | | | | |
| 2. Paper products | | | × | | Facial tissue box nearly empty |
| 3. Sanitation | | | × | | Shower curtains need attention |
| 4. Desk | × | | | | |
| 5. Telephone and book | × | | | | Displayed card with fees listed |
| 6. Bed and linens | | × | | | |
| 7. Lighting | | | | × | Bulb burned out, standing lamp |
| **Services** | | | | | |
| 1. Call housekeeping | | × | | | Delay in acquiring extra pillow |
| 2. Send fax to self | × | | | | Prompt, no charge to receive |
| 3. Get maid to let in | | | | × | Took $3 tip and let me in |
| 4. Ask for second key | | × | | | Clerk remembered me, or said so |
| 5. Ask for toilet repair | | | × | | 38-minute delay |

▲
**Exhibit 7-4**
Secret shoppers making quality-control inspections uncover operating weaknesses to which management and staff must attend.

mettle during moments of truth are the purposes of quality inspections. Quality is maintained when management acts on the QC reports, using them to reinforce good habits. Training, not punishment, follows when reports are negative. When that really is the intent of the practice, the staff learns about the mystery shoppers in advance, and the inspectors' evaluation sheets are made available to all. How else will the standards that management hopes to establish be known?

## Quality Guarantees

Quality guarantees (QGs) are simply assurances that the hotel will deliver on its promise of quality service . . . or else. With QGs, the company puts its money where its advertising mouth is. Guaranteeing a satisfactory level of product and service takes gumption. It contradicts the not-my-fault phenomenon currently evident across Canada. Service guarantees take responsibility for everything that happens. QGs announce unequivocally to customers and employees alike that management is confident enough to stand behind its advertising. It is a courageous stand and a sign of management's confidence in the programs it has implemented. Sure, it backfires at times.

QGs are not like discounted rates, used and discarded as occupancy declines and recovers. Quality guarantees become part of the operating philosophy of the business: They are the very essence of the operation. Such a potent tool must be introduced carefully as the ultimate result of an ongoing and successful program of quality management. Guarantees fail miserably when they evolve from an advertising need rather than an operational TQM plan.

Several years ago, a well-known hotel chain jumped on the QG bandwagon with a promise of "complete satisfaction." No modifiers or limiting exceptions—just complete satisfaction guaranteed. An incident arose when a guest relying on that policy stopped at one of the properties. There was no hot water for a shower on the morning of departure. Citing the well-advertised guarantee, the guest asked for a free room or an **allowance** against the standard charge. The member property declined, explaining that the malfunctioning boiler was beyond its control. So much for a guarantee of complete satisfaction.

QGs need to be narrowly defined at first. Once a standard is established, the guarantee can be aimed at a target and delivered accordingly. Implementing guarantees in stages, by specific expectations within certain departments as capabilities come online, announces to guests and staff that service quality is in place. Marriott, for example, guarantees to deliver room service breakfast within 30 minutes. Failure to do so means a free breakfast. Wrapped up in this simple promise are an advertisement, a departmental promotion, an employee empowerment, an assurance of quality, and a willingness to be measured.

Other hotel companies offer different guarantees—Westin's no-overbooking policy, for example. Each Westin hotel keeps open enough empty rooms to ensure the property's compliance. Strict enforcement minimizes cash restitutions because guests are almost never walked. Obviously, there is still the cost of empty rooms that might have been rented. From a practical side, however, the guarantee is inexpensive to deliver. Hotels do not reach full occupancy very often. When they do, careful counting can almost always accommodate every reservation. Only on a few occasions will rooms be left vacant in order to meet the guarantee.

Meeting planners have begun asking for and receiving service guarantees. The groups they represent guarantee room, food, and beverage numbers, so they are asking the hotels to do the same. They ask for guarantees that there will be no noise from adjacent meeting rooms, and guarantees that coffee breaks will be served within five minutes after the session breaks. Just as the group's guarantees carry monetary penalties, so must the hotel's.

Quality guarantees are a two-edged sword. Failing to pay off after announcing a guarantee alienates guests far more than the incident itself. Guarantees must be unambiguous, limited in scope, and focused on specific objectives that are easily understood. With such guarantees, a failure to deliver is evident to all. There is no quibbling about payment, which—when made promptly—leads to guest loyalty and positive word-of-mouth advertising.

Nothing highlights operational weaknesses more than having to pay off guarantees that arise from legitimate complaints.

**Canadians with Disabilities**  The **Americans with Disabilities Act (ADA)** is a quality standard of a special nature. It was enacted into law in 1990 and became effective in 1992 in the United States. The ADA provides for changes in physical structures and hiring practices to accommodate people with disabilities, be they guests or employees. The ADA applies to all industries, including lodging, which is covered by Title III of the Act. This law guarantees certain levels of quality service to some 43 million Americans with disabilities. Unlike the guarantees of hotel companies, the law levies stringent penalties, under civil rights legislation, for failure to comply.

Canada has been slow to implement an act similar to the ADA and has chosen to see how the ADA plays its way through the courts and industry.

One exception to this trend has been the Ontario government, which has enacted legislation. On September 30, 2002, the Ontario government finally proclaimed in force most of the provisions of the new Ontarians with Disabilities Act 2001 (ODA). Many Ontarians with disabilities, 1.9 million strong, will watch closely to see whether the new disabilities legislation lives up to its promise.

The ODA is designed to ensure the following in Ontario: a barrier-free province for persons with disabilities; that no new barriers will be created against persons with disabilities; that the provincial government will enact mandatory regulations covering all sectors, including the private sector; and that specific accessibility results will be achieved in the public and private sectors. The law provides that people with disabilities will have greater access to goods, services, facilities, jobs, and significantly improved opportunities across Ontario, making a meaningful difference in their lives.

The Ontario government's ODA and the lodging industry's TQM converge on the same two subjects: Both treat guest and employee issues. One legislates changes and the other implements them as a matter of good business. Hotel companies hired employees with disabilities long before the laws were enacted, although less was done to accommodate guests with disabilities. Radisson was an early employer of people with disabilities, and so was Ritz-Carlton Company. Holiday Inn, especially its Worldwide Reservation Center, was still another.

**Accessibility Assessment**  An accessibility assessment may be used by meeting planners and should include the meeting space and the facility in general. Hotel rooms should also be assessed if the event includes an overnight stay.

Examples of physical features of an accessible facility include the following:

- Automatic doors and obstacle-free pathways for people using mobility aids.
- Tactile signage for persons who have visual impairments.
- Access to the outdoors to allow persons to walk their guide/service dogs.
- Meeting room layout that allows ample space for participants to move around freely without running into obstacles or requiring the removal of objects during the event.

- Meeting rooms that are large enough to accommodate assistive listening systems, translation booths, and seating for sign language interpreters.
- Doorways to meeting rooms that are approximately one metre in width to allow easy access.

  Accessible hotel rooms should include the following:

- Door handles, sinks, faucets, and other accessories that are easy to use for people with limited dexterity.
- Easy access and exit to the bedroom and washroom for persons using wheelchairs.
- Flashing alarm system to ensure safety, as well as access to a TTY to ensure telephone service for persons who have auditory impairments.

**Across Canada** Other jurisdictions do not seem to be as proactive in this area as Ontario. There are, however, federal, provincial, and territorial laws that have some impact on the hotel industry.

The Canadian Human Rights Act took effect in March 1978 and prohibits discrimination against people with physical disabilities. However, the legislation only applies to the federal government and organizations regulated by the federal government. Therefore, this act applies to about 10 percent of Canadians. However, the remaining 90 percent are covered under laws in the provincial or territorial jurisdiction in which they work.

The Employment Equity Act (EAA) came into effect in 1986. It applies to federal Crown corporations and federally regulated private sector organizations with at least 100 employees. This act is designed to address the imbalance in the employment of women, Aboriginal people, visible minorities, and people with disabilities. In addition, most Canadian provinces and territories have some form of pay equity legislation requiring "equal pay for the same or similar work" and "equal pay for work of equal or similar value." These types of legislation are too complex to be covered in detail in this text; however, they have had a large impact on human resource management policies in the industry and therefore are also part of most quality assurance programs.

All or parts of these legislations affect all departments of the hotel, including the rooms division. Each responds with a different solution. Housekeepers learn to leave guest's personal belongings exactly in place. Cashiers count cash aloud, announcing which denominations are being returned. Folios and registration cards are enlarged to further help people with vision problems. Similar alterations in procedures and space accommodate workers with disabilities. Equipment might be modified or even totally replaced. Enhanced lighting, power to recharge wheelchair batteries, or other alterations are sometimes warranted. Hiring practices and other personnel procedures are often more difficult to change than the equipment or work area. Included in these special human resources needs are revised approaches to hiring, testing, job structures, position descriptions, and more.

**Physical Accommodations** Physical accommodation of persons with disabilities may also be covered federally in the National Building Code, as well as locally in provincial and municipal building codes. Local departments of health that oversee construction of public washrooms in hotels and restaurants enforce some of these regulations. Various liquor control boards may oversee regulations provincially for establishments licensed to serve alcohol.

Most provincial governments have some form of Workplace Accessibility Tax Incentive (WATI). Under this program, incorporated businesses are able to deduct up to 100 percent of qualifying expenditures (to a maximum of $50 000) to accommodate new employees with disabilities. Unincorporated businesses are eligible for an equivalent refundable tax credit of 15 percent. Qualifying expenditures include disability-related modifications and equipment allowed as deductions under the federal Income Tax Act, such as interior or exterior ramps, electric door openers, modifications to bathrooms, and visual fire alarm indicators.

The Canada Transportation Act underlines the Government of Canada's commitment to equitable access to transportation services by all travellers. The National Transportation Policy contained in the Act states that accessible transportation is essential to serve the needs of persons with disabilities. Under the Act, the Canadian Transportation Agency has the power to remove "undue obstacles" from Canada's transportation network, which includes the following:

- Air carriers and airports.
- Passenger rail carriers and stations.
- Interprovincial ferry services and their terminals.

This means that unnecessary or unjustified barriers should not restrict travellers with disabilities. To achieve the goal of accessible transportation, the Canadian Transportation Agency interacts with both the industry and travellers with disabilities.

**Signage**  The ODA will bring renewed attention to signs. In Canada, signage requirements may be found in federal, provincial, and municipal building codes. Lack of signage and poor signage are irritants for all visitors, not only for those with disabilities. By requiring compliance for Braille and raised lettering as well as a host of other requirements, the law helped focus the entire issue of good signage. The Canadian Automobile Association has established its own signage requirements as part of its rating system, but this does not include accommodations for meeting or recreational facilities.

Signage for people with vision impairments must be provided inside and outside elevators, on guest room keys when requested, and on the outside of accessible rooms. Audible elevator signals (once for up; twice for down) supplement the traditional Braille or raised numbers. Some properties are testing audio signs that are broadcast from small transmitters to the guest's receiver. The audio signal tells guests where they are and how to proceed to a room or to the elevators.

Guests who are disabled in ways other than sight rely on signs for different reasons. The wheelchair symbol used by tour books indicates special parking and wheelchair accessibility to the lobby, the desk, at least one food and beverage outlet, and, of course, to and within the guest room.

Good signs and directions are not special to guests with disabilities. Managers must "walk" their properties, leave their offices, and note—not just see—what guests encounter as they enter and proceed through the property as strangers. Are there fire-exit signs? If the exits are alarmed, a sign should say so. Are non-smoking rooms and floors marked? Is the entire ambiance of the hotel destroyed by a bunch of supplemental handwritten signs? Can one actually find a guest room following the posted directions? Are some rooms named rather than numbered? Are all of the bulbs in electric signs functioning? Exterior signs on the building are often forgotten and lack maintenance and repair.

The alert manager should question the staff at the desk, in uniform, or on the guest floors about the location of certain sites. Employees who have no reason to be in particular areas of the hotel are often unable to direct guests to a banquet facility, the swimming pool, the spa, or the guest laundry.

# Complaints

Complaints are another tool for directing management's attention to troubled service areas. Unfortunately, too few guests actually complain. Most merely mumble quietly, never to return. That's why those complaints that are registered must be resolved quickly and corrected for the future. Measuring customer unhappiness is like trying to compute the costs behind the moments of truth. Neither offers any mathematical accuracy, but both make many believable points.

Putting dollar values to the cost of complaints requires some assumptions. These assumptions have never been proven, but they are quoted frequently nevertheless. It is said, for example, that 10 percent of guests would not return to the property of their most recent stay. Using the same values as in Exhibit 7-3, a hotel would lose 21 **guest nights** each day (300 rooms at 70 percent occupancy multiplied by the 10 percent loss). That totals a whopping 7665 guest nights per year for a 300-room hotel. Based on an assumed average daily rate of, say, $65, the failure to resolve complaints in this example would be nearly $500 000 per year (7665 guest nights at $65 per night). The figure stretches into the stratosphere of nearly $5 million when 3000-room hotels are involved.

Some argue, moreover, that labour-intensive industries such as lodging increase productivity only by improving service encounters. The failure to do so represents additional labour costs as well as costs from lost business. Here, too, there is not much empirical evidence to support the hypothesis.

Every complaint has an impact on the bottom line, but not every complaint takes dollars to resolve. One major investigation reported just the opposite: Only one-third of all written complaints involved a financial issue. Money is more often at stake with face-to-face encounters. Exhibit 7-5 offers another tidbit: Better to spend a bit to hold that guest than to invest five times the amount to solicit a new customer.

**Exhibit 7-5** ▶
Widely quoted, but rarely referenced, figures emphasize the importance of a proactive stance in handling complaints.

**Loss of Guests**
- Sixty-eight percent of non-returning guests quit because of indifferent service.
- Thirty-two percent is lost to death, relocation, competition, and poor products.

**Complaints**
- Less than 5 percent of dissatisfied guests speak out—so for every 1 that does there may be 20 who do not.
- More than half of the silent majority refuse to return—an iceberg floating beneath the surface.
- Non-complaining guests do complain to friends and acquaintances.
  - 10 to 11 others will hear of the mishap.
  - 13 percent of the group will gripe to 20 others.
- Two-thirds of the iceberg could be won over if they were identified—about half of these could become boosters.

**Costs**
- It costs more than $10 to write a complaint letter (including the cost of writing time, follow-up time, and postage).
- It costs five times more to get a new customer than to keep an existing one.

**Still Another Calculation**    Still another calculation is shown in Exhibit 7-5. Like the others, it begins with a bunch of widely quoted but vaguely grounded assumptions. Still, the conclusions are startling.

*Premise 1:* Sixty-eight percent of non-returning guests stay away because of indifferent service. (Deaths, relocations, competition, and poor products account for the other 32 percent.)

*Premise 2:* About 2.5 percent of dissatisfied guests actually voice their unhappiness. There is an iceberg effect here. Below the surface floats the vast bulk of complaints, never voiced and never resolved. Of this silent majority, it is said that well over half will not patronize the hotel again. Worse yet, they will tell 10 to 11 others not to do so; some tell as many as 20 others. This fact is so irrefutable in the view of many that a "rule" has been created, the 1–11–5 rule. One unhappy guest will tell 11 others, and each of the 11 will tell 5 more.

*Premise 3:* About two-thirds of the icebergs can be warmed and won over by resolving the complaint. About one-third of complainers can be converted from blasters to boosters if their complaints are handled quickly and properly. Implicit here is the guest's willingness to speak up. Guests will do so when they are very angry or when management creates an environment that encourages guests to register complaints.

**Preventing the Complaint**    Identifying the reluctant complainer is a challenge. It will not be met by asking departing guests the rote question, "How was everything?" Desk personnel and managers from all operational and organizational levels must ask direct and specific questions. That means talking to guests, whether in the lobby, by the pool, or elsewhere. The dialogue may start with pleasantries: an introduction, a comment on the weather, and an inquiry about the frequency of the guest's visits. But then the conversation must elicit the negatives, if there are any. "Did you use room service?" opens a chain of related questions. "How was the bed?" directs the conversation in a different direction. "Can you tell me about any especially pleasant (or unpleasant) experiences you have had here?"

Issues that flow from these solicitations are not complaints in the truest sense, but they give management direction for improving service and pre-empting complaints from someone else later on. More important, they bring out the guest's concerns and give the hotel the opportunity to redirect the dynamics and make friends. Many of the issues raised require no immediate actions, no costs, and no allowances. They form the base for operational changes and they build the relationships that promote returning guests, especially if the questioner follows the brief interview with a letter of thanks to the candid guest.

Management must be knowledgeable if it hopes to prevent complaints. Executives who don aprons and get to ground zero by working in different departments—say, once a month—do more than create public relations photo ops. They learn, for example, that the location of the dish machine is the cause for high breakage, that the housekeepers' vacuums really don't work, or that customer service warrants the front-desk purchase of umbrellas for guest use. Managers who telephone their own hotels test departmental procedures and the disposition of their staff.

**Early Warning**    Complaints can be forestalled if the staff is honest with the guest and tells it like it is. Alerting guests to bad situations allows them to decide whether to participate. So, the reservations department explains that the pool is closed for repairs during the dates under consideration. A request for connecting rooms is impossible to promise, so the request is noted but the reservationist makes no guarantee. And that is so stated, not just implied.

Similarly, sales executives must warn small groups about other large parties in the house during the anticipated booking period. Room service reports elevator problems and thus some delay before the order will be delivered. Room clerks offer special rates in a certain wing because ongoing renovations there are noisy at times and create extra dust.

Complaint management acknowledges how the "squeaky wheel" gets the best results. Attending promptly to the squeak may mean better service for all. Observant guests often side with the hotel when an obnoxious squeaker rolls up to the desk. They will cede their priority in line to get the pest out of the way. Similarly, handling families with tired or irritable children outside the sequence actually improves service for others.

Preventing the complaint by anticipating the problem and providing unsolicited, accurate information is far preferable to assuaging angry guests after the fact. Explaining the circumstances makes guests feel better about the situation and forestalls their complaints. "The maid will not get to the room before luncheon, so we can accommodate your early arrival but not before 1 o'clock."

If a policy of candour works wonders in reducing complaints, the opposite is also true. Misleading information, either directly or by implication and omission, enrages guests who feel that they have been cheated—as they have.

**Comment Cards** The effectiveness of guest comment cards is subject to debate. Detractors say that managers intentionally ask the wrong questions, tilting the questionnaires toward the hotel's strengths. Maybe so, but the battle to improve guest service needs every weapon that can be mustered. Comment cards are just another device for getting guest input. Like other information-gathering techniques, they have advantages and disadvantages. Innovative approaches to this old standby strengthen the instrument and improve its quality. The better the questionnaire, the more information is available for managing guest services.

Hoteliers complain that guests use questionnaires to gripe. Guests do not balance the good and the bad, hoteliers protest, but concentrate their comments on operating weaknesses. Actually, that's good. Uncovering and remedying shortcomings is what TQM programs are all about. As noted earlier, too few guests ever bring their concerns to the hotel's attention. Guest comment cards help overcome the iceberg effect, the reluctance of the complainer to complain. Management's grumbling about the disproportion of positive and negatives probably has its origin in its personal promotion and bonus decisions, which often include comment-card data.

Critics attack the validity of comment cards on the basis of very low response rates, typically 1 to 2 percent of the guest population. Long, detailed questionnaires account for some of the low numbers. Guests just won't take the time to answer. Small cards with a narrow focus, one that changes periodically, improve the overall response rate. It might be done in one of two ways. Short, themed questionnaires about a single concern—cleanliness or courtesy, for example—could be distributed throughout the entire hotel. Separate, specialized forms for use within each department is another means of shortening and focusing the inquiry. Although not an actual questionnaire, good success is obtained with a form that asks the guest to submit requests for in-room repairs (see Exhibit 7-6).

Simply asking guests to participate increases the number of returns. Some of the best results come during the check-out procedure, when response rates improve

**Room Maintenance**

Having everything work as it's supposed
to is important to your comfort and to our
level of service. Please help us maintain
the quality accommodations that make
your stay comfortable and enjoyable. We
are proud of the cleanliness and condition
of this room, but items are sometimes
overlooked by housekeeping or
maintenance. If anything needs attention,
please complete  the card and leave it at
the front desk or call extension 111.

ROOM NO. _____

PLEASE ATTEND TO:

_____

_____

_____

Thank you,
*Doug Douglas, Manager*

▣V
*A Vallen Corporation Property*

tenfold. Locating touch-screen terminals in the lobby near the cashier solicits direct responses from departing guests. Even here, though, the number of questions and the speed with which the guest can respond is critical to success. Marriott's Fairfield Inns calls its exit survey the Score Card System. Strategic placement of the equipment encourages adult use and dissuades random input from children, another criticism that is occasionally voiced.

Participation rates increase when guests have an incentive for completing the cards. The rate of return goes up with every dessert coupon the desk issues. (This tactic also gets guests into the coffee shop.) Similarly, room upgrades for the next visit combine incentives with room promotions. Immediate upgrades are given when the solicitation is made during registration.

Awarding elaborate prizes from a drawing of comment-card participants is another incentive for guests to complete them. It also flags the importance that the property attributes to quality assurance. Moreover, contest information enables the hotel to match guest names with comments. That isn't always possible otherwise, because some guests prefer anonymity.

Modern communications have taken questionnaires to another level. Hotel companies have followed other industries by providing and advertising toll-free telephone numbers for disaffected consumers. The additional costs of doing this are balanced by the additional demographic data obtained. Besides, immediate attention to consumer complaints builds enormous goodwill quickly. Provided, that is, that the call is answered by an actual person, who has the ability to resolve the issue and the personality to make friends with the caller. Like so much of the TQM concept, it is easier to create the system than it is to implement it effectively.

Every comment card or telephone call should receive an immediate and personal response from someone with authority to act. Guests then know that they are getting the highest level of attention. Telephone calls suggest a sense of urgency and often elicit further details of the incident. Carefully done, very carefully done, a letter supposedly originating with the employee involved may produce exceptional results. Far too often, the hotel's response is a bland, standardized letter or a generic apology that fails to address the issues raised by the guest.

**Quality Circles** Quality circles, or quality teams, are still another method of getting information. Circles are small groups of employees who meet regularly as quasi-permanent teams to identify issues in delivering quality service. The terminology differs, but guests are occasionally added to the teams, especially at resorts. If the circle catches problems before complaints are registered, TQM is working perfectly. Sometimes the remedies come after the fact, arising from management's referral of a series of complaints.

Quality circles in the service industry are very much like those in manufacturing. Small, continual improvements—creative changes—are the goals. Spectacular break-throughs or innovations are not customarily part of the circle's design. Consequently, the group's composition is taken from all levels and across departmental lines. Delays in room service at breakfast, for example, may prove to be housekeeping's fault—moving linen between floors ties up the elevators just when room service demand is highest!

Total quality management requires each employee to service other departments as if they were guests. A cross-departmental team, therefore, has members who are inter-nal customers of one another. Teams may function in several capacities, or different teams may be organized for specific, corrective action. In addition, there are focus groups (short-term, one-issue teams) and ongoing self-managing units.

Canadian culture emphasizes the individual and not the group. Circles have been very successful in some hotel environments and have flopped terribly in others. Like comment cards or lobby interviews or toll-free calls, the circle serves as another piece in the quality mosaic. It is both a source of information on which to act and a means of finding the solution with which to act.

**Handling the Complaint** Quality assurance aims for error-free service, but that is a goal more than a fact. Experience keeps a tight rein on reality, making complaint-free environments desirable but very unlikely. Only the number, timing, or place of the complaint is uncertain, not whether one will occur. As TQM programs reduce the number of complaints, the remaining complaints gain in importance. Besides, not all complaints are subject to quality management solutions. Systems, procedures, and training aside, the unexpected will always happen. Door attendants do lose car keys, for example.

**Preparing for Complaints** Preparing for complaints begins by acknowledging their likelihood. Training programs must first emphasize the probability of a complaint. Employees with a proper mindset, those not caught unaware, recognize the importance of attitude in receiving and resolving complaints. Proper preparation minimizes the impact and cost of the complaint. Preparing properly means making the best of the worst. Readying employees to receive and resolve complaints has become an integral part of QM programs.

Although the specifics differ, complaints follow a theme in each department. This gives quality circles an effective role in training. Within the circle, members share their individual experiences and solutions, and the group adopts the best ideas as depart-mental standards. Employee empowerment, the authority to accept responsibility and to remedy the situation, is implicit.

For front-desk employees, common themes spring from specific encounters. What is the proper response to a departing guest who protests a folio (guest bill) charge? What should be done with an irate arrival whose reservation has been sold to another? What accommodations can be made if the guest tenders a travel agent's coupon that is not acceptable to the hotel? Common situations all, playing themselves out time and again in a fixed pattern if not an exact duplication. None are rare, unexpected encounters. A series of options must be readied and employed as needed (see Exhibit 7-7).

Directing employees to kick the problem upward is an option required by certain circumstances. Even empowerment programs limit employee authority to certain deci-sion levels. Preparing employees for the complaint must include information about when and why and to whom to refer the matter. Rarely do the sessions train for the

## Hotel Anywhere, Canada
### Internal Memorandum

To:        Guest-Service Agents

From:      Holly Wood, Rooms Manager

Subject:   Empowerment Guidelines

Date:      January 1, 20--

Effective this date, all guest-service agents who have completed the four training hours have authority to make the following adjustments using their own discretion. Managers and supervisors are always available for consultation.

An apology is the first response! Apologies are free; we give away as many as necessary, but be sincere and listen carefully.

Where appropriate, verify information before acting.

| Issue | Intermediate Response | Maximum Response |
|---|---|---|
| Noisy room | Relocate, if stayover | Upgrade now or next visit, gift to the room |
| Incorrect rate | Correct the paperwork | Allowance for the difference, ticket to club or spa |
| Engineering problems: Heat and AC, TV, plumbing | Send engineer, change rooms | Upgrade, up to 25 percent off rate |
| Protest charges: | | |
| Telephone | Allowance for local | Allowance for long distance |
| In-room film | Allowance | One per day |
| Valet parking | Allowance | Full amount |

next (frequently necessary) step: What is to be done when the next level of authority is not available? Leave the fuming guest to wait . . . and wait . . . and wait?

Complaints may arise because the spread between guest expectations and service delivery widens dramatically after arrival. However, complaints are not always of the hotel's doing. Hotel staff may just be the most convenient recipient of the guest's bad day. Tired and grumpy travellers, those who have done battle with family members or business associates, who have fought against cancelled flights and lost luggage, may find the hotel employee—especially an inexperienced one who dithers and dathers—an ideal outlet for a week of frustrations. Preparing for the complaint means understanding this.

Preparing for the complaint means putting up with drunks and being tolerant of the show-off and the braggart performing for the group. Preparing for the complaint allows one to overlook exaggerations, sarcasm, and irony. Preparing for the complaint recognizes that senior persons sometimes berate younger staff in a replay of the parent–child relationship. Preparing for the complaint means understanding that some persons can never be satisfied whatever the staff may try.

**Responding to Complaints** No complaint is trivial in the eyes of the guest. What the hotel's representative perceives as trivial often originates from a series of small, unattended-to issues that smoulder until management's casual attitude fans the fire of dissatisfaction. Suddenly, the trivial explodes into a major conflagration.

BY LISTENING To bring about change, the complaint must be received and understood. Complaints are communicated only if the complainer speaks and the listener listens. It is not enough for the complaint-taker to hear passively; he or she must listen actively. Careful listening is fundamental to resolving every complaint. Full attention to the speaker moves the problem toward prompt resolution even before the explanation is complete. Experienced complaint-handlers never allow other employees, guests, or telephone calls to distract them from hearing out the complainant.

Complainers do not always begin with the real issue—which is true, of course, with many conversations. Questions are appropriate provided that they are not judgmental, but interrupting unnecessarily angers the speaker and pushes the conversation to another level of frustration before all of the facts are in hand.

Listening requires good eye contact and subtle supportive body movements. Appropriate nodding, tsh-tshing, mouth expressions, and hand movements encourage the speaker and convey attention, sympathy, and understanding. It is important to remain in contact with the speaker and empathetic toward his or her experience throughout the recitation.

Guests do not like being rushed along; they want the whole story to come out. The listener must be sensitive to his or her own body language, careful that negative signals are not halting the complainer or dropping a cold blanket over the encounter. Watching for the guest's non-verbal signals helps interpret the guest's readings of one's own signals.

IN A PROPER VENUE Complainers who grow hostile or overly upset, loud, or abusive must be removed from the lobby. Shifting to a new venue should be done as quickly as possible. Don't wait for the issue to intensify or the time committed to the situation to outgrow the lobby discussion. Perhaps the pretence can be that of comfort: "Let's sit down in the office; we'll be more comfortable there, and there will be no interruptions."

Walking to the new location offers a cooling-off period. It provides an opportunity to shift the topic and to speak in more conversational tones. Walking changes the aggressive or defensive postures that one or the other might have assumed in the lobby. The office location adds to the manager's authority and prestige.

The louder the guest growls, the softer should come the response, which usually brings an immediate reaction: Loud complainers quiet down to hear replies that are given in near whispers. A harsh answer to abuse or to offensive language only elevates the complaint to a battle of personalities. Above all, the hotel wants the guest to retain dignity. Divorcing the interaction from personalities helps do that. The facts are at issue, not the persons; certainly not the employee, who may be the original target of the guest's ire.

Ultimately, the manager may refuse to discuss the issues further unless the guest modulates language and tone. The hotelier tells the complainer that he or she is being addressed politely and that he or she expects the same courtesy from the complainer. In a worst-case scenario, say with a drunk or drug-crazed guest, the hotel may need to call the police.

BY MAKING A RECORD Asking permission to record the complaint by taking notes indicates how seriously management views the matter. It also allows the guest to restate the issue and have it recorded with accuracy, at least from the guest's point of view. The hotel's representative gets an additional opportunity to express concern and sympathy as the issues are restated aloud. It also slows the conversation, helping to cool emotions. Contributing to the written report makes the complaining guest sense that already something is being done. Thus, the stage is set for resolving the problem.

Front offices maintain permanent journals of the day's activities, including complaints. These logs improve communications with later shifts since the issues often carry over. The documentation helps the participants recall the incident later, provides a basis for training, and supports legal proceedings if the matter goes that far. Serious accidents are documented again by security and by the hospital or the police, depending on circumstances.

The record keeping goes further. Getting the guest's folio, registration card, or reservation data helps the manager understand what happened. Calling an employee into the office or on the telephone in the guest's presence broadens the investigation, clarifies the facts, and mollifies the complainer. Employees should get as much courtesy as the guest. Training or discipline, if appropriate, is done elsewhere in private. Both the staff member and the guest should be addressed with civility, certainly using surnames and appropriate titles: Mr., Mrs., Dr., and Ms.

WITH A SETTLEMENT Once registered, the complaint must be settled: resolved somehow and closed. The complainant expects some satisfaction or real restitution for the embarrassment. The hotel wants to keep the customer, strengthen the relationship, if possible, and send the guest forth as a booster who tells the world how fairly he or she was treated. Still, the hotel doesn't want to give away the house atoning for mistakes that caused no harm and little damage.

Apologies are free—we can give away as many as needed; and indeed, only an apology may be needed. Apologies are in order even if the complaint seems baseless or unreasonable. The effectiveness of the apology depends on the guest's reading of the manager. And that reading often reflects the importance of and the guest's involvement in the delivery of the service. A transient family views situations differently than a family celebrating an important anniversary. A business traveller's anger increases directly with the importance of the message that wasn't delivered.

Does the unhappy guest see the hotelier as truly contrite or merely mouthing niceties as a means of getting a quick solution? There are different ways of apologizing, but none are effective unless they ring true. The standard, "I am sorry, and I apologize on behalf of the hotel," goes a long way toward settling minor issues quickly and satisfactorily. "I am sorry" can take on different nuances with different levels of emphasis ("I *am* sorry"), additional words ("I am *so* sorry"), or deleted words ("I'm sorry").

Although it is not necessary to fix blame for the incident—and doing so may be counterproductive—the hotel's staff clearly may be at fault. When pertinent, admitting as much helps to set the tone, as long as the admission doesn't include minimizing the incident or offering lame excuses. Use a simple statement about "our" mistake.

Managers may want to go beyond the apology and send gifts to the room. The traditional fruit basket, a tray with wine and cheese, or even a box of amenities serves this function. Apologies appear on the card once again.

Complaints that are settled with apologies are the least expensive kind and often prove to be the most satisfying for both sides. Subsequent telephone calls or letters reinforce the apologies that were expressed during the face-to-face encounters.

After hearing out the guest, quieting down the situation, and offering appropriate sympathy, the hotel manager must provide restitution and lay the issue to rest. The quicker the problem can be resolved, the better. That is what happens with most complaints. But serious items are not settled that easily. Smashed fenders, dentures broken, and snagged designer dresses are not remedied on the spot. Insurance companies, or law firms in more serious instances (a fall in the tub), work their wares slowly. Nevertheless, sympathy, concern, and prompt, on-the-spot action reduce the longer-run consequences and costs.

More concrete solutions are needed when apologies are not enough. A list of options should be identified for the hotel's representative as part of the preparation process (see Exhibit 7-7). Heading the list are items that cost the hotel little or nothing, as would an upgrade. Even here, there are degrees: Should we upgrade to another level? To the concierge floor? To an expensive suite? The upgrade is offered for this visit or for another. If for another, the manager's card with a direct number—"call me personally and I'll arrange it"—reinforces the special nature of the solution. Some managers preface every offer by hinting that the arrangements are special. By implication, deviating from standard procedure recognizes the guest's importance and the hotel's desire to make things right.

Annoying but inconsequential incidents can be handled with small gifts. Tickets to an event that is being held by the hotel are welcome. Athletic contests (tennis tournaments), presentations (distinguished speakers), theatre-style entertainment, and the like are almost without cost if seats are plentiful.

Admission to the hotel's club or spa, tickets to local activities such as theme parks or boat rides, or transportation to the airport in the hotel's limousine are other options. Cash refunds are the last choice, but they may be the only appropriate response. Damage to property requires reimbursement, and extraordinary circumstances necessitate an allowance against folio charges.

Usually, the situation is less serious. The guest has twice before reported an inoperative television set. Or, the guest's request to change rooms has been ignored. Or, the long delay in getting a personal cheque cleared for cashing is irritating and embarrassing. Complaints of this type need fast and certain action. Once the solution is resolved, a wise manager explains what is to be done and how long it will take. It is better to overestimate the time—then a more rapid turnaround will impress the guest with the hotel's sincerity.

BY ASKING THE GUEST Guest demands soften if the episode is handled well and if the guest feels that the treatment is fair. To get that kind of response, the hotelier needs to get inside the guest's head, to view the situation from the other side. If the interview appears to be moving favourably, the guest can be brought into the decision loop. Carefully, the hotel's agent elicits the guest's expectations, which often are less than the hotel's, and draws the guest into formulating the remedy. The complainer becomes part of the solution, and the process gains momentum toward a quick and satisfactory conclusion.

All of which is easier said than done. Standing near an experienced complaint-handler—listening to what is said and how it is said—is the best learning experience the manager can have. It is especially helpful if the claim is denied.

Customers are always right! Except that sometimes they aren't. The first reference is to the attitude with which management hears the guest's complaint; the second reference is to the context of the complaint. Management can listen attentively, sympathize completely, and communicate in a caring manner, but still *say no* to outrageous requests based on non-events.

Refusing compensation—remember, apologies are always in order—may cost the customer's patronage. It is a fine judgment call, as repeat patronage may already be lost. In denying restitution, inexperienced managers resort to "company policy" as the reason. Company policy is a great turnoff! Better to explain the answer in terms of fairness, safety, service to other guests, economic reality, or past experience.

Unhappy guests may request the intervention of higher authority. If that is appropriate, the next manager must be formally introduced and the issue recapped aloud to expedite the meeting. Thereafter, the first interviewer remains silent unless questioned and allows the second conversation to progress without interruption.

Complaints that are resolved quickly and equitably make friends for the hotel. Resolved or not, management's attitude, as expressed in words and movements, goes far toward minimizing (or aggravating) the damages.

UNDER CONTRACTUAL AGREEMENTS There is very little wiggle room for negotiating complaint settlements if guests have a pre-existing "contract" with the hotel. Too often, the public relations/advertising people put the operational/management people in just such a non-negotiable, no-win situation. Advertisements that promise a 100 percent satisfaction guarantee (first offered in 1989 by Promus) allow for little discretion. The hotel has already agreed to settle for the guests' demands. If it doesn't, the company's credibility suffers immeasurably.

Recognizing the pitfalls of such open-ended pledges, hotel companies have shifted away from unequivocal guarantees to lesser promises of attention. Limited exceptions still guarantee 100 percent satisfaction: for example, breakfast in 30 minutes or it's free. Otherwise, the guarantee is 100 percent but only if the opportunity to remedy the shortfall fails. In other words, there's a promise to attend to the complaint. Failing that, some payment may follow.

Radisson says:

> *Our goal at Radisson is 100% guest satisfaction. If you aren't satisfied with something, please let us know and we'll make it right or you won't pay. Please dial 0 now and tell the hotel staff what service you require or what we can do to improve your visit. If the staff is unable to satisfy you, call our corporate customer service department at 1-800-333-3333 for assistance.*

The Sheraton Service Promise is:

> *If you're not entirely satisfied, we'll take care of it. And we'll make it up to you with an instant discount, points for our rewards program, even money back. And that's a promise.* [*]
>
> [*]*Service Promise applies to hotel services in the Continental U.S. and Canada and excludes group transactions. Level of compensation is at the discretion of hotel management.*

# Summary

TQM, total quality management, has many definitions and practices even within a single industry such as lodging. TQM's goals are simple to express but difficult to implement because guest service involves two parties. Managing for the first, the guest, is not new; it is part of the industry's heritage. Bringing the second party, the employee-server, into the management process is the inspiring idea.

Attitudinal changes take place over time. Once hoteliers attended to guest needs within the accommodations that the host provided. Today's hotels furnish what the market demands, not what management wants to offer. By so doing, each company reinforces the brand image that was discussed in Chapter 2. Above all else, guests want quality rest in a physically comfortable room with service delivery in a comfortable human relations environment. As the market dictates both, the guest's perception of quality and the reality of the quality offered move closer together.

Guest satisfaction stems from the hotel's delivery of its product by courteous and empowered staff members during the many moments of truth that occur on hotel floors each day. Recognizing the employees' critical role, management is changing its methods of supervision to enlist their co-operation and initiative. Winning that commitment is an ongoing process. Empowering staff members to make decisions within their own level of authority is one of the most dramatic redefinitions of the role of the worker.

TQM has introduced new terms and new expressions. If history is any guide, the language of TQM will soon fade away. Fads in management come and go like other fashions. Carlson's recent adoption of CRM (customer relations management) heralds new guest–employee terminology. Hotel managers must retain the vision behind the management of service even as such terms as *quality circles*, *quality guarantees*, or even *TQM* itself disappear.

# Questions and Problems

1. Using a computer, create a simple spreadsheet showing the form and functions that management can use to summarize and analyze complaints originating within departments of the rooms divisions.

2. Prepare and briefly discuss a list of three quality guarantees that are defined narrowly enough to be communicated easily and achieved successfully; for example, room service breakfast delivered within 30 minutes or it's free. Be certain to include the penalty to be paid by the hotel if the guarantee is not met.

3. Explain why Marriott's guarantee of breakfast is, in the words of the authors, "an advertisement, a departmental promotion, an employee empowerment, an assurance of quality, and a willingness to be measured."

4. Compute how many moments of truth occur in a full-service convention hotel of 630 rooms during a typical month. Comment.

5. From readings and personal experience, discuss six of the most difficult elements of resolving a complaint.

6. List five incentives a hotel might offer to encourage guests to complete a comment card. Make a special effort to have the incentive encourage cross-advertising, through which one department awards incentives for use in another department.

## CASE STUDY

### Snowmobilers versus Skiers

Sally Maitland is the general manager (GM) of a mid-sized resort just north of Montreal. The director of marketing has created packages that have been successful in attracting two distinct winter markets: snowmobilers and skiers. Unfortunately, these two markets do not seem to gel well. Skiers are early to rise and early to bed, spending most of the day on the slopes; snowmobilers are late to rise and very late to bed, and their noise has resulted in complaints from skiers who have been awakened at 2 A.M.

Maitland has called a meeting with the director of marketing and the front-office manager to discuss these problems and possible issues with other groups. Help Maitland with some solutions to and suggestions for her problems.

1. What can the hotel do to alleviate the conflict between snowmobilers and skiers?

2. Can you think of any other markets that may clash and result in complaints and loss of business for the hotel?

3. Most hotel marketing gurus suggest that a hotel should cater to no more than three major markets, believing that a hotel cannot be "all things to all people." Do you agree with this general theory? Does it apply to all hotels in all locations?

## Notes

1. Steven J. Belmonte, president and CEO, Ramada Franchise Systems, Inc. Talk delivered at Ramada's Annual Conference in Orlando, Florida, December 1999.

2. Trademark of the Ford Motor Company.

3. Stephen J. Shriver, *Managing Quality Services* (East Lansing, MI: Educational Institute of the AH&LA, 1988).

4. Christina Binkley, "Starwood Sets Effort to Enhance Quality and Improve Cash Flow," *Wall Street Journal*, February 5, 2001, p. PB-4.

5. Shriver, p. 3; Bruce Brocka and Suzanne Brocka, *Quality Management: Implementing the Best Ideas of the Masters* (Burr Ridge, IL: Richard D. Irwin, Inc., 1992).

6. Robert Woods, Denny Rutherford, Raymond Schmidsall, and Michael Sciarini, "Hotel General Managers," *Cornell Hotel and Restaurant Administration Quarterly*, December 1998, p. 41.

7. Rick Van Warner, in *Nation's Restaurant News*, October 26, 1991, attributes the aphorism to Keith Dunn, who cites Don I. Smith as the original source.

8. Stephen Hall, *Quest for Quality: Cost of Error Study* (n.p.: American Hotel & Lodging Association and Citicorp Diners Club, n.d.).

9. The term *moments of truth* has been attributed to Jan Carlzon, former chairman of SAS Airlines.

10. To be approved for inclusion in CAA's lodging guide, hotel rooms must have deadbolts, automatic locking doors, and peepholes, and provide facilities for people with disabilities.

## Weblinks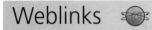

Human Resources and Social Development Canada
(persons with disabilities)
**www.hrsdc.gc.ca**

Access to Travel
**www.accesstotravel.gc.ca**

Guide to Planning Inclusive Meetings and Conferences
**www.tbs-sct.gc.ca/pubs_pol/hrpubs/TB_852/
gpimc-gprci1_e.asp**

Persons with Disabilities Online
**www.pwd-online.ca/**

Canadian Human Rights Act
**http://lois.justice.gc.ca/en/H-6/**

National Quality Institute
**www.nqi.ca**

# Chapter 8

# The Guest Arrival, Registration, and Rooming Process

## Learning Objectives

After reading this chapter, you will be able to do the following:

1. Understand the guest pre-arrival and arrival process and its "moments of truth."

2. Identify the steps in completing guest registration, including the room selection process and establishing guest credit.

3. Understand the rooming process, including the function of uniformed services and the bellstaff.

## The Arriving Guest

The guest arrival process blends a wide range of hotel functions into the guest's first five or ten minutes on property. These broad functions are fairly constant across the industry—the guest arrives, registers, and arranges payment for the room, and ultimately enters the room and cursorily examines it for overall acceptability. The manner in which each hotel accomplishes these broad objectives, however, is quite varied.

The arrival process varies by guest; by hotel brand, segment, and size; and even by employee. As standard or routine as the arrival, registration, and rooming process initially appears, no two experiences are exactly alike. Guests arrive armed with a wide range of expectations—while some are seasoned, others may be novice travellers or have little experience with this particular brand or property. Similarly, each hotel provides a different experience—even properties in the same chain differ due to location, service level, management, and other factors. Certainly, employee personalities and training influence the guest arrival experience as well.

While the broad objectives of the arrival process (arrival, registration, and rooming) remain consistent for all hotels, the actual delivery of these objectives and performance of the numerous tasks required to accomplish them varies. Add to this complexity the fact that today's lodging industry has developed a number of full-service and self-service options to meet the growing variety of guests needs, and the list of potential arrival experiences grows exponentially. To illustrate the point, let's imagine two guests staying at the same downtown Vancouver hotel. The first is a leisure guest visiting the hotel for several nights as part of an extended vacation. Knowing little about the property, this leisure guest arrives at the airport and is picked up by the hotel's shuttle, delivered to the front door, greeted by a doorperson, and escorted to the front desk. At the desk, many attributes of the hotel are explained to the leisure guest (location of the pool, hours of the dining room, the name of the duo playing in the lounge, etc.), and following registration, a bellperson shares even more information while rooming the guest. Now that's a full-service arrival complete with a number of distinct employee–guest interactions.

Change focus for a moment and follow the experience of our other hypothetical guest. This gentleman is a frequent traveller and regular corporate guest of the hotel. Upon arrival at the airport, he rents a car and drives to the property, opting to pull his own car into the parking garage rather than have it valet parked. He wheels his one piece of luggage onto the elevator, rides to the lobby, and passes directly in front of the desk on his way to a self-check-in kiosk. There, he accesses his existing reservation, scans his credit card and writes his own electronic room key, and is assigned a room number. Moments later, on his way to the room, he visibly relaxes as he considers how much he loves this hotel—even though he had not one employee–guest interaction throughout the entire arrival process.

In both scenarios, the ideal check-in goes unnoticed by the guest because all hotel and front-office functions flow smoothly. Aside from the actual reservation (which may or may not have been made by the guest), this is the guest's first opportunity to see the hotel in action. First impressions are critical, and that is why the arrival and check-in process is often referred to as a **moment of truth**. The front-office staff does not get a second chance to make a good first impression.

## A Moment of Truth

Different segments of the lodging industry offer differing levels of service. At no time is this difference in service as pronounced as it is during the arrival and check-in process. Limited-service properties offer no employee interaction between the porte cochère (the canopy in front of most hotel lobbies under which arriving guests temporarily park their vehicles) and the front desk. In a limited-service property, the guest may not see or speak with any employee other than the guest-service agent. In fact, for hotels that offer self-check-in terminals or kiosks, limited-service guests may not see any employee at all upon arrival to the hotel.

Full-service hotels, on the other hand, place several ranks of employees between the front door and the front desk (see Exhibit 8-1), and each of these encounters is a separate moment of truth, a separate opportunity for the hotel to excel (or in some situations, to fail the guest). The guest may encounter a valet parking attendant, a doorperson, and a bellperson before ever arriving at the front desk.

**The Valet Parking Attendant** The first employee that guests often encounter in a full-service hotel is the valet parking attendant. The parking attendant greets the guests as they pull their vehicles under the porte cochère, opens their car door(s), assists with placing luggage on the curb, and takes responsibility for parking and securing the vehicle. Similar services are provided to guests arriving by taxi, airport shuttle, and other means of transport.

**Exhibit 8-1** ▶
The guest arrival process is a complex choreography of departments and responsibilities. When their efforts come together seamlessly, the guest has a positive "moment of truth." Shown here is an arrival flow pattern for a full-service corporate hotel. Luxury resorts might add several functions to the flow pattern (golf, dinner reservations, or table assignments for an American plan resort). Limited-service properties might provide none of the services displayed here.

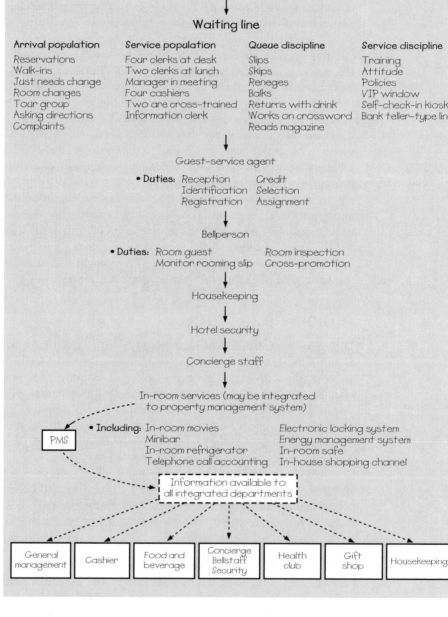

Guest arrives
↓
Valet parking attendant
↓
Doorperson
↓
Lobby rotations of bell staff
↓
**Waiting line**

| Arrival population | Service population | Queue discipline | Service discipline |
|---|---|---|---|
| Reservations | Four clerks at desk | Slips | Training |
| Walk-ins | Two clerks at lunch | Skips | Attitude |
| Just needs change | Manager in meeting | Reneges | Policies |
| Room changes | Four cashiers | Balks | VIP window |
| Tour group | Two are cross-trained | Returns with drink | Self-check-in kiosk |
| Asking directions | Information clerk | Works on crossword | Bank teller-type line |
| Complaints | | Reads magazine | |

Guest-service agent

- **Duties:**  Reception      Credit
              Identification  Selection
              Registration    Assignment
↓
Bellperson

- **Duties:**  Room guest           Room inspection
              Monitor rooming slip  Cross-promotion
↓
Housekeeping
↓
Hotel security
↓
Concierge staff
↓
In-room services (may be integrated to property management system)

PMS

- **Including:**  In-room movies       Electronic locking system
                Minibar              Energy management system
                In-room refrigerator In-room safe
                Telephone call accounting  In-house shopping channel

Information available to all integrated departments

| General management | Cashier | Food and beverage | Concierge Bellstaff Security | Health club | Gift shop | Housekeeping |

**Exhibit 8-2** ▶
Example of a hotel offering both doorperson and valet parking services (note the sign to the right of the doors). At the Wedgewood Hotel, doorpersons and parking attendants are one and the same. Although most small four-star hotels would probably not offer both services—the Wedgewood has just 51 luxury standard and executive rooms, 34 one-bedroom suites, and 4 penthouse suites—their average room rate ($220 to $498) is sufficient to warrant it.

Valet parking is an amenity or service provided by many fine hotels. However, not all full-service hotels offer valet parking. It is most commonly found in urban, city-centre hotels where space is at a premium and guest self-parking is inconvenient (see Exhibit 8-2).

This department is a revenue centre for some hotels. By charging the guest a fee for parking each day, the valet parking department generates income to help defray the costs of maintenance and insurance on the parking lot or parking structure. The parking fee (which runs as high as $50 or $60 per day in city-centre hotels) is added directly to the guest's folio or account. In addition, many guests tip the attendant each time their car is returned.

Hotels may lease or subcontract the operation of this department to a private parking company. With leased operations, a private company takes responsibility for parking the guest's car, insuring it against damage, and staffing the department. They also pay the hotel a monthly lease for the privilege of using their parking lots and garages. In such cases, the guest is unaware that valet parking is a contracted department.

**The Doorperson** Not all full-service hotels (or even resorts, for that matter) offer a doorperson. In an era of rising labour costs, that's one position easily eliminated. This is especially true when you realize that it is a non-revenue-producing department. As a result, only the finer hotels can afford to provide doorpersons. And as such, the doorperson makes a statement both about the opulence of the hotel and about its concern for providing the finest in guest service.

To many guests, no position represents the hotel quite like the doorperson. The uniformed services position of doorperson is part concierge, part bellperson, part tour guide, and part friend all rolled into one. The doorperson may offer the guest suggestions, point out interesting historic sites, explain difficult directions, and hail a taxi. For newly arriving guests, the doorperson assists with removing and securing luggage from the car until the bellperson retrieves it for delivery. In addition to all of these tasks, the doorperson also opens doors! (See Exhibit 8-2.)

In potentially dangerous urban downtown settings, the doorperson supplements the security department by serving as an early-warning defence against suspicious non-guest "visitors" and other possibly hazardous situations. Due in large part to the doorperson's physical location at the front of the hotel, these staff members prove excellent early-warning security enhancements. Likewise, the very nature of the job, observing and greeting all who pass by, recognizing and chatting with regulars, and providing verbal suggestions and directions to those who ask, lends itself well to observation and scrutiny of would-be thieves. Certainly, all employees should be trained to observe the warning signs of suspicious visitors, but the doorperson is especially critical in watching for the following telltale signs:

- A person occupying a vehicle under the porte cochère who refuses to move or has no discernable purpose for being there.
- A person who passes by regularly, aimlessly, or with no particular direction.
- A person who watches the hotel front doors or exits, or intently watches a particular employee station, or a person who intently watches another guest (especially a guest with a laptop computer or briefcase).
- A person carrying a suspicious package or who displays a bulge under his or her shirt or jacket.

## Guest Registration

After being greeted at the curb and the front door, the guest arrives at the front desk (see Exhibit 8-1). In a small property, the desk itself is small and probably staffed with just one or two agents (see Exhibit 8-3).

In large hotels, guest receptionists or guest-service agents have distinct responsibilities. During busy check-in periods, however, most other activities are placed on hold until the arriving guests—the highest priority—are handled. Arriving guests can easily tell which guest-service agents are handling check-ins. For one thing, their stations are usually marked with signs reading "reception," "registration," "check-in," or "arrivals." Additionally, there may be a line (queue) of guests standing in front of each guest-service agent. For further information on waiting lines, refer to the discussion on queuing theory later in this chapter.

Two types of guests present themselves at the front desk: those with reservations and those without. Those with reservations are generally handled without problem. The agent reconfirms the accommodations requested, the guest signs the registration card, a method of payment is secured, a room is selected, and some pleasantries are exchanged. In a computerized property, the entire reception process can be handled quickly—say, in several minutes.

Guests holding reservations may encounter two problems: no record of the reservation and no space available. The arrival and reception should go quickly, even if the reservation has been misplaced, provided that space is available. As unobtrusively as possible, the clerk elicits the reservation information again and makes the assignment. No reference to the missing paperwork is made. Far more composure is necessary if the clerk is to handle an overbooking situation successfully. With proper training, the emergency procedures described in Chapters 6 and 7 are implemented, and the moment of truth is achieved without incident.

**Exhibit 8-3** ▶
This exhibit shows the front desk of the Fairmont Hotel Macdonald in Edmonton, Alberta.

## Walk-In Guests

The registration process is more time consuming for walk-in guests than for guests who have an existing reservation. If space is available—and it usually is (even hotels boasting 100 percent occupancy on a given night often have one or two unoccupied rooms)—the guest-service agent must collect the same information from the walk-in guest that the reservations department collects during a routine phone call. The difference is that now the guest is standing in front of the desk. Patiently, the agent asks about the room configuration and number of beds preferred, guests in the party, number of nights required, and so on.

Careful handling of walk-in guests is critical to the hotel's healthy bottom line. Yet, before the agent can ask questions about the party's needs, the walk-in guest is often concerned with one thing—rate. Indeed, in transient properties, the guest may literally run in and ask the "rate" question ("How much is a room?") while the car is running, the kids are fidgeting, and the spouse is losing patience. Improperly trained guest-service agents do not seize the moment and simply spit out "$129 plus tax." The potential guest turns on his or her heels and heads back out the door.

Many experts believe that the hotel industry, as a whole, does a poor job focusing on the sales opportunities presented by walk-in traffic. After all, the guest is standing in front of the desk asking about rooms and rates. That places the hotel in a far more advantageous position then if the guest were on the telephone at the airport. Phoning guests have it easy; they can call one hotel after another until they find the rate they're seeking. It is far more difficult to get back into the automobile, pull out of the driveway, and head down the street to another property.

Besides, the guest is standing in the lobby and has already been affected by his or her first impression. If the lobby shows well, and the agent is personable, there is no reason why the potential walk-in guest should turn around and leave. A well-trained agent knows that rate alone tells the guest nothing. Rather, the agent needs to describe the accommodations, explain how the hotel meets the travellers' needs (swimming pool for kids, very quiet rooms for tired corporate guests, breakfast included for price-conscious customers, etc.), and provide a list of rate options. Then, ask for the sale.

**Registered, Not Assigned**   Very early arrivals, especially those that appear before the day's **check-out hour**, may be required to wait until a departure creates a **vacancy**. Even then, the room must still be cleaned. Baggage-check service is offered to all guests who must wait, and a complimentary beverage may be given to some if the hotel is responsible for the wait. In anticipation of an upcoming vacancy, the clerk may have the guest **register**. The account is marked **registered, not assigned (RNA)** and kept handy until the first appropriate departure takes place. The assignment is made but the guest is kept waiting until housekeeping reports the room ready for occupancy; guests are not sent to unmade rooms.

Guests who arrive after the room is vacated but before housekeeping has cleaned it—a status called **on change**—are assigned at once but not provided with a key until the room has been cleaned and inspected. This is not an RNA.

RNAs occur whenever the hotel is very full with simultaneous arrivals and departures of large conventions, or when tour groups overlap. Busy holidays cause RNAs at the type of resorts where arrivals come early and departures stay late.

Waiting for the room is a distressing experience, especially as the hours tick away. On some occasions it may be necessary to assign guests temporary rooms, changing them to a permanent assignment later. This type of costly duplication should be avoided except in special circumstances. Most front-office systems, including computerized ones, allow RNAs to create charges even though no room identification is possible.

In corporate hotels, RNAs are less frustrating. Corporate guests who arrive early in the morning are happy to register and leave their luggage secure. They then go about their business until the workday ends later that afternoon. Upon returning to the hotel, they find that their room number has been assigned and their luggage is waiting for them in the room.

**Early Check-In Policies**   Generally, hotels have rooms available from the night before. Even when last night's status was "sold out," there are usually rooms available. That's because a few of last night's rooms probably never arrived (for a discussion of no-shows, see Chapter 6). The hotel received its revenue by billing the no-show guest, but the room itself was never occupied. Therefore, a guest checking in at, say, 7 or 8 A.M. is likely to find a room available.

The real question is: Will the front-desk clerk allow the guest to check in? Check-in time for most hotels is between 1 and 4 P.M., allowing housekeeping ample time to clean check-out rooms. A guest checking in at noon or 11 A.M. is no big deal, but a guest who wants access to the room at 7 or 8 A.M. poses a problem for some hotels— their policies do not allow early check-in without imposing a fee. Similar to a late check-out fee (for guests who stay beyond 2 or 3 P.M.), the idea behind an early check-in fee is that the guest is using the room for a number of hours before the start of the official "day."

Imposing such a fee does more harm than good. The guest feels taken advantage of. Moreover, letting the guest into the room early will probably result in a few breakfast meals and some telephone revenue as well. Crowne Plaza Hotels and Resorts encourages early check-in for corporate members of its Priority Club Worldwide. It advertises corporate check-ins beginning at 7 A.M. (and late check-outs until 3 p.m.) without extra charge!

**Waiting Lines**   Early check-in and RNA policies do more than get the guest into the room early; they get the guest out of line, too. Few check-ins occur early in the day, and therefore the front desk should accommodate such guests whenever possible. Otherwise, those guests may return during the busiest check-in times. For corporate hotels, the busiest check-in times are usually from 5 to 8 P.M. The busiest check-out periods are 7 to 9 A.M.

There is probably nothing more frustrating after a long day of travel than to arrive at a congested front office. From early in the morning, the travelling guest has been waiting—waiting to park the car and get a parking stub; waiting to have the airplane ticket validated; waiting for the plane to begin boarding, take off, land, and deplane; and waiting to be shuttled to the hotel. Imagine the frustration when walking into the lobby of your home away from home to see yet another waiting line. Indeed, that is one of the appeals of the new self-check-in kiosks, discussed later in this chapter.

It is the job of hotel management to adequately staff busy check-in periods. This is hard to do, because guests can (and do) arrive at literally any hour. Add to this uncertainty the constrictions of a limited budget, union and non-union labour laws (meal breaks and the like), employees who are not yet fully trained, and sick call-ins, and the problem becomes amplified. It becomes even more exaggerated when you realize that the industry is larger and busier than ever before. How else can you check thousands of guests into a megaresort except one guest at a time?

**Long Lines Equal Poor Service**   Some theorists suggest that today's guests are more impatient with check-in lines than ever before. The blame, they say, is on the computer industry, which has created a "get it now" society. Through modern technology, we can communicate at lightning speed, send documents by modem, and reach cellular phone customers wherever they happen to be. Maybe that's why guests are so impatient.

Whatever the reason guests are so impatient, it is in the hotel's best interest to minimize the wait. That is because the check-in process—and its accompanying wait in line—is one of the most memorable moments of the guests' stay. A long wait can ruin the check-in and ultimately the entire stay. The check-in is probably the first, or one of the first, face-to-face encounters the guest has with hotel staff. The first encounter should be memorable, and a long wait in line certainly is memorable (just not the kind of memory we wish to create). In addition, arriving guests have little else to occupy their minds. They quickly become restless and critical of the front-office operation. Finally, guests have a certain expectation with regard to the check-in process. A limited wait is reasonable; a long wait becomes synonymous with a poorly run hotel. That is especially true when there are few guests in line. When the wait is due to some hidden element, guests become indignant.

To empathize with the waiting guest, management needs to understand and train for three important factors:

1. Empty minutes go faster when the guests' time is filled with something to do.

2. For waiting guests, not knowing how long they'll be waiting is worse than knowing an estimated length of wait, even if the wait is expected to be quite long.

3. Anything the guest(s) can do to make the check-in process more efficient is understood and appreciated. Guests want to help.

**Queuing Theory** In the early twentieth century, A.K. Erlang, a Danish mathematician, introduced a theory called *telephony*. Originally designed as a mathematical model for solving telephone traffic line usage, the theory found other applications during the Second World War. Each modification resulted in other names as the application changed slightly. Erlang's traffic theory has been renamed queuing theory, congestion theory, and for its application to lines, waiting line theory. The uses are manifold: toll booths, 911 calls, traffic lights, airports, parking lots, hospitals, data processing, and more.

Queuing theory is a mathematical tool that management uses to obtain an optimum rate of customer flow. It balances the costs of making customers wait against the costs of serving them more rapidly. Queuing theory attempts to quantify the dilemma regarding ideal levels of guest service.

Too little service and the guest waits in line, or waits on the reservation telephone line, longer than expected. Dissatisfied guests, formal complaints, a low percentage of repeat business, or lost revenue from guests who leave are the consequential losses from too little service.

Responding to too little service (a definition that varies with the class and pattern of the hotel), management adds more registration windows, more employees, more computer terminals, and self-check-in kiosks. The guest is served more rapidly but at a significant cost in labour, equipment, and lost lobby space. And herein lies the dilemma: What is the optimal point between these two extremes? Let the guest wait too long, or invest in systems and labour to eliminate the wait?

Queuing theory requires an understanding of probability statistics as well as of differential and integral calculus. Computer programs are available to do the computations. Four key elements must be quantified: arrival population, service population, queue discipline, and service discipline (see Exhibit 8-1). The quality of the assumptions and facts behind these four components dictates the level of success that the final solution takes.

ARRIVAL POPULATION  A number of factors affect the size of the population arriving at the desk. Certain hours of the day and certain days of the week are busier arrival times than others. The quantity of group business has an impact, as does the method of handling it. Are they registered at the desk or in a separate area? All guest transactions are not the same. Guests stand in line to check in, to ask questions, to complain, to get change, and to obtain and return keys (see Exhibit 8-1).

SERVICE POPULATION  The kind and number of available agents and their configuration behind the desk is the service population. Intrinsic to this component are several special issues. The ability of the clerk; the number of clerks, and whether that figure is fixed or variable; and the assignment of duties (does each position handle every request, or are there special windows for special needs?) are all elements of the service population.

QUEUE DISCIPLINE  Queue discipline refers to the behaviour exhibited by the guests who are waiting in line. This is the element that changed waiting line theory from a mathematical science to a behavioural one. Guests cry, "Unfair" or "Don't cut into line" when someone who arrived after them is served before them. Skips and slips (when one guest skips or "cuts" ahead of a waiting guest, resulting in the original guest slipping further back in line) are the most infuriating of all. Additionally, queue discipline addresses the guest's reaction to the line: Does a guest refuse to join the line because of the length (a "balk")? Does a guest switch lines as the respective lengths vary? If a guest leaves the line (a "renege") after waiting for some time, is that decision determined by the length of the line, or is it a random move? Do others allow the line-jumper back in? Little is really known about the behaviour of hotel guests standing in line to be registered.

SERVICE DISCIPLINE Service discipline is the last of the four key elements. It examines the server's attitude and approach as the queue discipline questions the guest's behaviour. Are guests handled on a first-come, first-served basis? How are interruptions fielded from a "one quick question" interloper? Is priority treatment provided for special VIPs and frequent-guest members?

**Creative Solutions to Long Lines** Responses to the problem of long waits have come from all industries. Banks have addressed the problem by implementing a single waiting line so that waiting customers don't have to be frustrated by picking the slowest clerk. Grocery chains have developed an approach that solves the problem and also serves as a marketing tool. They advertise: We'll open a new line whenever more than two customers are waiting. Fast-food chains, airlines, and many others send an employee to the rear of the line to take orders and ease the bottleneck at the cash register. Customers respond as much to the company's demonstrated concern as to the actual solution.

Some solutions can be, and have been, borrowed from other industries. The single waiting line is the most apparent. Snaking the line back on itself, as is done in theme parks, makes the line appear shorter, but it does take up costly lobby space. Telling the guest the estimated waiting time recognizes the human behaviour part of waiting, but it does nothing to speed up the process. Neither does another technique, which merely assuages the guest's irritation from waiting. Borrowing from pizza-delivery philosophy, guests who wait in line longer than five minutes get a monetary reward: cash, reduced room rate, or an upgrade.

Radio-assisted registration has been tried, but only the largest hotels are able to work this out. Customer-service staff works the rear of the registration line or catches new guests as they enter the lobby. The reservation information is radioed to back-office computers. Using a different computer provides temporary relief to the property management system (PMS) and to the front-office crew. The guest is directed to a special window to sign the registration form and pick up the room key.

Separating certain guests from the regular line saves time for both those separated and those remaining. A concierge or executive check-in that accommodates special categories such as guaranteed reservations, negotiated corporate accounts, and frequent-guest patrons are sample categories.

However, some of the best ideas are the most creative. The Mirage Hotel and Casino in Las Vegas boasts a 75 000-litre saltwater aquarium behind its front desk. It's hard to get bored when live sharks are swimming just a few metres in front of you. Other major hotels transform the wait into a party. They bring in jugglers, magicians, and comedians who perform for the waiting guests. And of course, the amusement parks have it down to a science. Which of the following ideas can the lodging industry adopt from theme parks?

- *Pre-shows:* an informative video describing various aspects of the resort and designed to run on a continuous loop.

- *Time signs:* describing the approximate wait in line from this point forward.

- *Live entertainers:* for example, the jugglers, magicians, and comedians described above.

- *Segmented queues:* allowing guests to see just a small section of the queue at a time to create the illusion of short lines.
- *Video screens:* entertaining video clips of various topics.
- *Interactive participation:* guests decipher codes, draw graffiti on walls, converse with robots, and so on.
- *Themed environments:* aquariums, jungles, pyramids, and the like to give guests plenty to look at while waiting in line.

**The Registration Card** Registration is not essential to the common-law creation of a legal guest–hotel relationship. In Canada, registration is a statutory requirement, and a "registered guest" has a higher level of entitlement in the eyes of the law than does a "visitor," someone who is coming to the hotel for dinner or to use other hotel services but is not registered. In contrast, other countries not only require registration cards but use them as police documents. In Canada, the police may ask to see a guest registration if doing an investigation, and the hotel has to produce a list of guests, indicating which guests are in wheelchairs, in the event of an emergency. Guests furnish foreign innkeepers with passports and a great deal of personal information that has value only to the authorities (see Exhibit 8-4). Indeed, hotel registration in Brazil requires the guest to fill in the names of both mother and father. Age, gender, date of birth, next destination, previous stop, and nationality are never found with registration information collected in Canada.

In manual (non-automated) properties, registration information is collected by handing the guest a blank **registration card** to complete. Today's PMSs have eliminated the need for manually collecting guest information. For the most part, information collected at registration is the same as information collected during the reservation. Automated properties preprint registration cards from the information collected at the

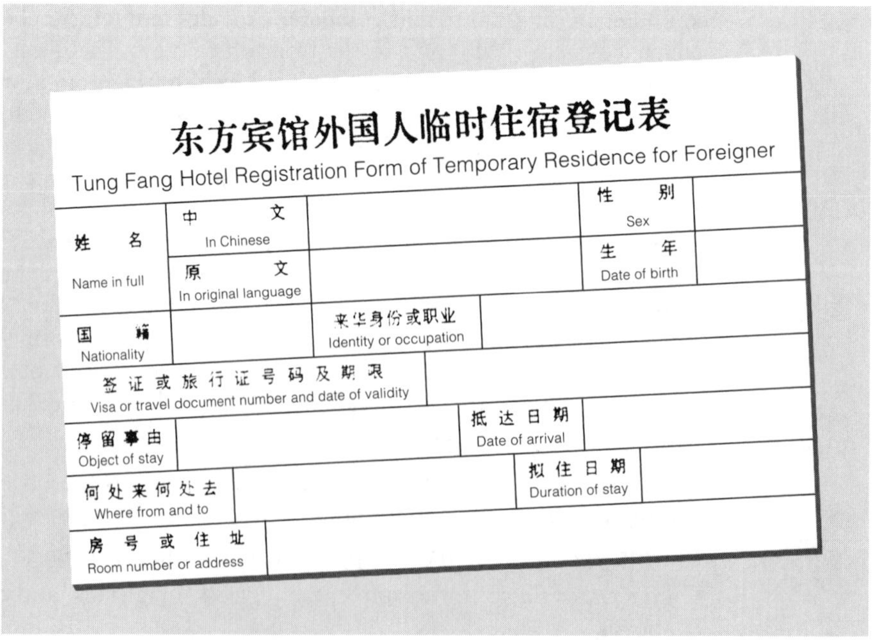

东方宾馆外国人临时住宿登记表
Tung Fang Hotel Registration Form of Temporary Residence for Foreigner

姓名 Name in full
中文 In Chinese
原文 In original language
性别 Sex
生年 Date of birth
国籍 Nationality
来华身份或职业 Identity or occupation
签证或旅行证号码及期限 Visa or travel document number and date of validity
停留事由 Object of stay
抵达日期 Date of arrival
何处来何处去 Where from and to
拟住日期 Duration of stay
房号或住址 Room number or address

**Exhibit 8-4 ▶** Domestic hotels would never think of asking age, sex, travel plans, or names of the guests' mother and father. Indeed, such questions would surely be construed as an illegal invasion of privacy in Canada. However, these are the types of questions asked of the guest on many foreign registration cards, including this one from the Tung Fang Hotel, Canton, People's Republic of China. In some foreign countries, the registration card can actually be used as a police document!

time of reservation (see Exhibit 8-5). Now, instead of burdening the guest with completion of an entire card, the front-desk clerk merely asks the guest to verify the accuracy of the information and sign at the bottom of the card.

**Number in the Party** The number of persons (the house count) has importance for statistics that are developed during the night audit. In addition, the number of persons in the room determines the rate charged, although many North American hotel chains now charge the same rate for single or double occupancy and do not charge for children 18 and under if sharing the same accommodation as their parents. When indicating the number of guests in the room, many hotels separate adults from children (see Exhibit 8-5). This is especially true in an American plan hotel that probably charges less for young children's meals than for adult meals.

**Name and Address** An accurate and complete name and address is needed for credit and billing and for the development of mailing lists for future sales promotions. A complete address includes such things as postal or zip codes, apartment numbers, and even province, territory, or state of residence since the names of many cities are common to several provinces, territories, or states. Commercial hotels often ask for the patron's business address and organizational title in addition to the residential address (see Exhibit 8-5).

Greater credit may be extended at some hotels to a guest whose address has been verified through an exchange of reservation correspondence than to a walk-in. Generally, all hotels today require that a valid credit card be provided upon arrival to establish credit. A guest paying cash without a credit card will have a "no-post status" on their account and will not be able to charge at any of the hotel's revenue centres. Whereas those intent on fraud will use false addresses, vacant lots, or temporary box numbers, unintentional **skippers** (people who forgot to check out or inadvertently left a portion of their folio unpaid) can be traced, billed, and subsequently collected from if an accurate name and address are on file.

**Room Number** Even as the hotel industry seeks higher levels of courtesy and guest service, the guest is known as much by room number as by name. Once the guest is

**Exhibit 8-5 ▶**
With a computer-prepared registration card, all a guest needs to do is verify the accuracy of the information, read the disclaimers, and sign. A detailed and accurate reservation saves the hotel duplicate work. Assuming that the name has been spelled properly, the address is correct, and so on, the information collected at the time of reservation is reused again and again (on the letter of confirmation, the folio, the rooming slip, the arrivals list, and so on).

| | | | RATES DO NOT INCLUDE TAXES |
|---|---|---|---|
| **2059** Room | **M/M Paul D. Ligament** Name | **6/14/** Depart | Res. # 122 ABC 9821 |
| **DLX K N/S** Type | **Western Athletes** Firm or Group | **6/11/** Arrive | Group # WA |
| **ABC** Clerk ID | **2A/1K** Party | | Deposit |

Address     Rate Plan
Street 1234 Achilles Tendon Way     (160)
City/Province Wounded Knee, BC 00000-0000
Company Horsn Around, Inc.
Date Departure 6/14/
Signature *Paul D. Ligament*

I agree that my liability for this bill is not waived and I agree to be held personally liable in the event that the indicated person, company, or association fails to pay for the full amount of the charges.

I would like to handle my account by:
☐ Cash/Cheque ☐ MasterCard ☐ Visa
☐ Diners Club ☒ American Express
☐ Discover Card

**HOT WIRE HOTEL**
**Shocking Behaviour Drive**
**Electric City, Manitoba**
**L4X 2M2**

**NOTICE TO GUESTS:**
This hotel keeps a fireproof safe and will not be responsible for money, jewellery, documents, or other articles of value unless placed therein. Please lock your car.

registered in the PMS and a room number has been assigned, all subsequent transactions are referenced and billed to the room number rather than to the guest's actual name. The room number is the major means of locating, identifying, tracking, and billing the guest. Even before the guest arrives, the reservation number (or with some systems, a preassigned folio number) is used to locate the guest and credit advance deposits (see Exhibit 8-5).

**Date of Departure** The guest's expected date of departure is of critical importance during the check-in process. By double-checking the guest's departure plans, the front office ensures the accuracy of future room availability figures.

Many front offices require the guest to sign a statement or initial the registration card next to their date of departure (see Exhibit 8-5). This is especially true for busy periods when a scheduled departure is necessary to provide the room to a newly arriving reservation (see Exhibit 8-8). Of course, plans change, and some percentage of guests will invariably depart earlier or later than they originally thought. In such cases, the front office strives to accommodate the guest. There is usually no extra charge for early departures and most unscheduled stayovers are accommodated (see the section entitled "Early Departure Fees" in Chapter 6).

**Discounts or Corporate Affiliations** Another issue resolved during the check-in process is the guest's corporate affiliation or qualified discounts. The corporate affiliation (if applicable) is often logged and tracked by the front desk on behalf of the sales and marketing department. This corporate information is critical to the sales department because many companies have accounts with individual and chain properties. By tracking corporate guest visitation, the sales department is able to continue offering discounts and special rates to companies who frequent the property. Many corporations have agreements with the chain (or with an individual hotel) to stay a certain number of room nights per year. Tracking use is critical to the success of such ongoing relationships.

Even when a corporate guest's company has not negotiated a special room rate, the hotel is usually willing to grant a standard corporate discount. Such discounts range from 10 percent to 20 percent or higher depending on the type of hotel, the date, and the season of visitation.

Even non-corporate guests may qualify for discounts. Leisure guests are often members of national or worldwide organizations such as Canadian Automobile Association (CAA) or Canadian Association of Retired Persons (CARP). CAA and CARP are two of the largest membership organizations in Canada. Most hotels grant CAA or CARP discounts to qualified guests. A complete discussion of rate discounts is found in Chapter 9.

**Clerk Identification** The front-desk clerk who checks the guest into the hotel is automatically identified in the PMS from the password the clerk used when logging onto the computer. Clerk identification is important in case a problem or other issue arises. By knowing who checked the guest in, management can return to that clerk and ask related questions. Possibly the guest was pleased with the process and complimented management on the clerk's performance. On the other hand, maybe the clerk provided an insufficient discount, was rude, or forgot to establish a method of payment.

**Folio Numbering** All hotels assign a unique folio number to the guest's account. In a computerized property, this account number is provided at the time of reservation. The number is assigned early in case the guest sends advance payment. The folio (or account) number references the guest's automated file just as readily as the room number or guest name.

Computerized numbering serves as a control device when one employee is clerk, cashier, and supervisor all in one. It is possible for such an employee to sell the room as clerk, pocket the money as cashier, and cover the discrepancy as night auditor. When the staff grows large enough to permit a separation of duties, numeric form control becomes less important.

Another major advantage to a computerized PMS is the ease of storing records. Although according to some management consultants the standard is seven years (three years for registration cards), many properties find themselves storing folios, registration cards, and accounting records for even longer periods. Canada Customs and Revenue Agency requires that hotels keep financial records for seven years in case of a future audit. In an electronic hotel, storage is easy when daily records are downloaded onto tape or disk. In a manual property, storage consumes considerably more space.

**Disclaimer of Innkeeper Liability** Almost every registration card carries a statement concerning the hotel's liability for the loss of guest valuables. Such a disclaimer is shown in Exhibit 8-5. The form and content of the statement are prescribed by provincial or territorial statute, and consequently, these vary. If the innkeeper meets the provisions of the statute, and public notice on the registration card is usually one such provision, liability for the loss of valuables is substantially reduced. Were it not for the dollar limits set by provincial or territorial legislatures, innkeepers would have unlimited liability under common law.

Common law is far more stringent than statutory law; it makes the hotel responsible in full for the value of guests' belongings. Most provinces and territories limit the innkeeper's liability to a fixed sum, usually $40 even when the guest uses the safe provided. Other statutes prevent recovery against the hotel if the guest fails to use the safe, provided that the hotel has complied with every provision of the law (see Exhibit 8-6). Provincial and territorial legislatures have extended this principle of limited liability to checkrooms and to goods that are too large for the ordinary safe—salesperson's samples, for example. In most jurisdictions, appropriate signage has to be posted in a prominent place to notify guests that they are leaving items at their own risk. None of these measures protect the hotel if negligence is found on behalf of the hotel or its employees.

Notices, which must be posted in the rooms, must include the maximum rate charged for the room (see bottom of Exhibit 8-6). Charges sometimes exceed that figure when a yield management system is in operation or when rates are changed frequently. The hotel may charge what it wishes, but there is a danger in not changing the permanent rate schedule that must be posted in each guest room.

**Catering to Pets** Over the past five years or so, the number of pet owners who travel with their pets has increased from 30 percent to 65 percent.[1] Pet owners are becoming a sizable market, one not overlooked by the lodging industry. Many pet owners think "its the cat's meow" when luxury properties cater to their pets. The Chicago Ritz-Carlton, for example, offers a gourmet room service menu for dogs and cats, a Pet Recognition Program that provides a treat to the guest's pet each time it visits, and even an on-site grooming and pet-walking service. The Four Seasons hotel group offers similar services at some of its properties, complete with a ceramic feeding bowl, dog biscuits, and a sleeping pillow. Holiday Inn, Ramada, Motel 6, and a growing list of other chains also accommodate guests' pets.

---

# ONTARIO  HOTEL  LAW

Section 4 of the Innkeepers' act being Chapter 217 of the Revised Statutes of Ontario, 1970, read as follows:

"4    (1)    No Innkeeper is liable to make good to any guest for any loss of or injury to goods brought to the Inn, not being a horse or other live animal, or any gear appertaining thereto, or carriage, to a greater amount than the sum of $40 except,

(a)    where the goods have been stolen, lost, or injured through the willful act, default, or neglect of the Innkeeper or the Innkeeper's employee:

(b)    where goods have been deposited expressly for safe custody with the Innkeeper.

(2)    In case of such deposit, it is lawful for the Innkeeper if the Innkeeper thinks fit, to require, as a condition of liability that the goods shall be deposited in a box or other receptacle fastened and sealed by the person depositing the goods. R.S.O. 1970, C. 223 S. 4."

The Criminal Code, Chapter 36, of the Revised Statutes of Canada, 1927, provides as follows:

"405    (2)    Everyone is guilty of an indictable offence and liable to one year's imprisonment, who in occurring any debt or liability, obtains credit under false pretences, or by means of fraud."

COMPLIMENTARY SAFETY DEPOSIT BOXES ARE AVAILABLE AT
THE FRONT DESK FOR THE STORAGE OF VALUABLES

RATE OF THIS ROOM

| ROOM NO. | 1 PERSON | 2 PERSON | 3 PERSON | 4 PERSON | CHECK-OUT TIME |
|----------|----------|----------|----------|----------|----------------|
| 2103 | $1450 | $1450 | $1450 | $1450 | 11:00 A.M. |

---

Registering pets has some serious potential costs, including the discomfort of other guests. Some hotels refuse all animals except Seeing Eye dogs. Others, as explained above, seek pet owners as a distinct portion of their market. Most pet owners appreciate the innkeeper's problems and make restitution for damages. Additional protection is provided when a contract (or a deposit) is signed by the owner agreeing to pay for any damages that occur.

**Points of Agreement**    Even as management strives to expedite the process, extra reading matter is being added to the registration card. The content of these extra messages differs among hotels and chains. Each has different problems and legal experiences. The presence of the messages meets legal requirements, but it is doubtful whether any guest actually reads messages during the hurried moments of registration. The message is repeated on the rooming slip, however, and that slip is left with the guest.

Despite the printed comments that guests are supposed to read, legitimate misunderstandings (about the rate, the date of departure, etc.) do occur. To minimize the likelihood of misunderstandings, hotels often train front-office personnel to elicit the guest's agreement on several of the more sensitive issues.

The room rate is one such issue. Although it is bad form to mention the guest's rate aloud, it is important to reach agreement on the nightly charge before rooming the guest. Rather than discussing the rate aloud, it has become standard practice to ask the guest to initial the rate. Usually, the clerk circles the rate (see Exhibit 8-5), passes the registration card to the guest, and asks for the guest's initials. If there are any disputes about discounts or special pricing arrangements, now is the time for the guest to mention them.

Another point of agreement sometimes stressed on the registration card is the smoking status of the guest's room. Smokers and non-smokers alike are adamant about their personal preferences. Non-smokers want a fresh room without the stale odour of smoke; smokers want a smoking room complete with ashtrays and matchbooks.

Hotels can spend considerable funds making non-smoking rooms truly smoke-free. Window and wall coverings, bedspreads, and carpet have never been exposed to smoke. Should a guest smoke (or allow a friend to smoke) in such a setting, it could cost the hotel hundreds of dollars to make the room smoke-free again. As such, non-smokers are sometimes asked to initial the non-smoking status (N/S in Exhibit 8-5) as a reminder to keep the room smoke-free.

Also frequently included on the registration card is a statement by which the guest agrees to stand personally liable for the bill if some third party (the company, the association, or the credit card company) fails to pay (see Exhibit 8-5).

**Going Green**   The environmental programs offered by the hotel are also sometimes mentioned on the registration card. Although more likely to be included on the rooming slip (so the guest has more time to read about them), hotels are beginning to promote the "greening" of their workplace more regularly.

Not only is the greening of our industry the politically correct thing to do these days, but it is also quite profitable. It is profitable in two ways: from a marketing standpoint as well as a cost-savings one. Environmental consciousness is great for public relations and generates positive feedback from hotel guests. Although guests may be slightly inconvenienced by the green programs in place, hotels that offer such initiatives say that guests rarely complain. In fact, they become involved. By hanging up wet towels to use again, initialling an agreement to have bed linens laundered every other day,[2] and walking into a warm room because the air conditioning adjusts to an energy-savings mode when **unoccupied**, the guest takes an active role in the hotel's green consciousness.

Although the more sophisticated energy, water, and waste management savings systems are usually engineered into the initial design of the facility, many conservation opportunities are available to hotels for little or no investment. For a discussion of automated energy management systems, see that section in Chapter 14; see also Exhibit 8-7.

Simple low-investment programs usually concentrate on saving money through energy and water conservation. Hotels are different from other businesses because lights stay on 24 hours a day. Merely turning off unnecessary lighting, changing 100-watt incandescent bulbs to 20-watt fluorescents, and putting exterior lighting on timers will save considerable money and help the environment. With the average hotel room spending between $5.50 and $6.00 per night on energy consumption, a simple conservation program can result in substantial savings. In fact, after some basic staff training, in-room brochures, and changing a few high-wattage light bulbs, most properties see a reduction

of 30 to 50 percent for in-room energy consumption. For a 250-room property (with 70 percent occupancy), that translates to energy savings of $110 184 to $183 641 annually!

Additionally, retrofitting guest-room showers, faucets, and toilets pays for itself quickly with the savings in water consumption. Even low- or no-investment policies such as serving water in the restaurant only upon request or laundering linens less often makes a big impact when multiplied over hundreds of guest rooms.

One of the leading companies in the world with a very extensive Green Program is Fairmont Hotels and Resorts. Check their website under the heading of "Environment" for an update on all of their activities.

# Completing the Registration

At registration time, many things are going on simultaneously: The reservation is being located; the guest is being welcomed; accommodation needs are being determined or re-evaluated; some small talk is taking place; the clerk is trying to sell up; the guest's identity, including the correct spelling of name and address, is being verified; certain public rooms or services in the hotel are being promoted; the anticipated departure date is being verified; both the guest and the clerk are completing their portions of the registration card; the credit card is being validated; the computerized room key is being made; and mail or messages are being handed over. Finally, a bellperson is called and the guest is roomed.

All of this normal activity notwithstanding, the clerk must remain alert to special cases. Room clerks issue the coupons that accompany each inclusive tour (IT) package, and there could be a dozen of them. Room clerks are the point position for advertising contracts (rooms traded for advertising), travel agency vouchers (the guest has paid the travel agency that booked the room), and special rates. Conventions, for example, sometimes have reduced rates before and after the convention dates (pre- and post- convention rates) and sometimes they don't. Often hotels will offer very low rates for a convention guest who checks in on Sunday, the least busy night of the week, or offer special rates for spouses to increase guest count. And, of course, if a mystery shopper is checking in, a few more curves will be thrown at the overworked front-desk clerk (see Chapter 7).

Throughout the procedure, which could take anywhere from 1 to 15 minutes, the clerk must remain calm, dignified, and friendly. Some feel that the clerk's attitude is the most important part of the entire registration, reception, and room selection process.

## The Room Selection Process

Early each morning, front-desk clerks look at the rooms they expect to have available for sale that day. Rooms that were not occupied the previous night are immediately available; rooms that are due to check out on that day will eventually be available (assuming that they actually check out; see Exhibit 8-8). By comparing the **housekeeper's report** against the PMS, the clerk identifies all available rooms. A determination is

**Exhibit 8-8** ▶
Check-out reminders like this one may be printed on cards or letterheads and placed under the guest's door or on the pillow the night before. Reminders are used only when the hotel expects an overbooking situation the following day.

# Just a Reminder

Ms. Angelica Chuckee          Room  3308

You indicated upon checking in that you would be departing today. Your room is reserved for an incoming guest and your check-out time is 12 noon.

Should you need to stay in Montreal an additional day, please contact our assistant manager, located in the main lobby or on Ext. 123. The assistant manager will make the necessary arrangements to reserve a room for you in a nearby hotel, as all our rooms have been reserved for today.

You can also make reservations for your next hotel stop before departure through our worldwide central reservation service.

**Thank You.**

made at this point as to how many additional walk-ins will be accepted. The decision will be revised many times throughout the day (see the discussion in Chapter 6).

**Blocking Rooms** Every room has distinct features, and a well-trained desk clerk understands these distinctions. Not all double–doubles are the same. Some are better than others because of location, view, newer furnishings or paint, or any number of other enhancements. The task of the front desk is to align reservations with available rooms.

**Blocking,** or preassigning rooms to guests, ensures a high level of certainty that special requests will be accommodated. When the room count identifies a high number of rooms available for sale, few rooms will be preblocked. For example, there is no purpose in blocking a standard queen reservation when there are numerous standard queen rooms available. Conversely, when the room count is tight (few rooms available to walk-ins) all incoming reservations will be blocked against the list of available rooms. In this way, the few unblocked rooms remaining are easily identified for walk-in customers. Theoretically, the best available rooms should be saved for guests with reservations, leaving the less desirable rooms to walk-in customers. Even when there are dozens of executive kings available, for example, some are less desirable—possibly they are noisier due to their location next to elevators or the housekeeping office; maybe the view is unattractive because they overlook dumpsters, parking lots, or the roof of another building; or maybe they still have the old furniture and have not yet been renovated. Whatever the reason, less desirable rooms should be offered to walk-in guests and the better accommodations saved for those who made advance reservations.

In the event that the house count is negative (the hotel is overbooked), a priority list is established. Management-made reservations, VIPs, and guaranteed reservations head the priority list. The rest of the reservations will probably be filled on a first-come, first-served basis. Regardless of projections, a careful rooms manager always blocks special cases early in the day. Included in this category are connecting rooms, early check-ins, **handicapped rooms**, management-made reservations, suites, and VIPs. If the house is very crowded, even special request assignments may need to wait for checkouts. The desk knows who the anticipated departures are, although it's never really certain. The desk does not know what time the departures are leaving relative to the arrival of the new guests. So special requests are assigned first to vacant rooms (if the rooms meet the requirements of the request), and then to other rooms as the guests depart.

The room numbers of the preassigned rooms are entered into the PMS. This prevents duplicate room assignments to other arrivals. It also provides immediate display for the clerk when the guest approaches and requests the reserved accommodations. Changes in the original assignments are made throughout the day as new information surfaces. If the arriving guest reports a change in the size of the party, or in the date of departure, or if the party appears before the preassigned room has been vacated, changes will need to be made.

**Assigning Rooms** Whenever possible—and it's possible more than it's practised—the agent should attempt to **sell up**—to sell the guest a higher-priced room than was originally reserved. Good selling is the key to rooms profits (see Exhibit 9-15 on pages 298–299).

The best way to sell up (or upsell) the product is to show it. At resorts, where longer stays are the norm, guests may prefer to see the room before signing in. That can be done—and has been done—with a screen monitor at the desk. With sophisticated reservations systems, the same image can be projected into the home to sell the reservation directly to the buyer via the Internet. The use of a front-desk photo album is another common (and inexpensive) way to demonstrate to the guest the various differences in room types.

Obviously, the better the clerk knows the product, the more rapidly and satisfactorily the assignment will be made. It has been jokingly said that the fewer the rooms available, the easier it is to make assignments. With few rooms, the guest must take what's offered or have nothing.

**Property Management System Algorithms** The computer uses an algorithmic function to search its memory for appropriate room assignments. Algorithms are a series of "if–then" statements by which the computer arrives at the proper response. The algorithm comes into use when the computer displays an arrival list, an over-the-credit-limit report, or similar statements. It does the same with room assignments, but the program is more sophisticated.

Suppose that a double–double is to be assigned to the arriving party. The system can be made to display the first choice (the computer's first choice) and the room is then assigned. Or, if the clerk wishes, the screen will display all double–doubles, including those ready, those on change, and those that are out of order (see Exhibit 8-9). Management can control the display—the first double–double displayed is the one that management wants sold first, and the final room on the list is to be sold last.

Without sophisticated computer algorithms, the computer would simply display available rooms in numerical order (see Exhibit 8-9). If this were the case, the first rooms displayed (rooms numbered in the 100s, 200s, etc.) would be sold far more often than rooms with higher numbers. With computer algorithms, management controls the order in which rooms are displayed (and ultimately sold) to accomplish any of several goals: to rotate room use equally, to concentrate occupancy in newly refurbished rooms at a higher rate, to restrict wings or floors to save energy, and others.

**Upgrading** Upgrading a room assignment—giving a better accommodation for the original rate—is one technique for resolving complaints. It has other applications as well. Upgrades might be given to frequent-guest program members, to VIPs, to business people from companies with negotiated corporate rates, and even to guests as a reward for patiently queuing.

Upgrades are also used if there are no rooms available at the rate reserved. In such cases, a well-trained and motivated front-desk clerk tries to upsell the guest. More frequently, the guest is given the better room at the lower rate, but the upgrade is explained. If the differential is significant, the guest is moved the following day when the lower rate opens. The costs of moving, to both the guest and the hotel, warrant leaving the upgraded assignment for a few nights if the rate spread is small.

**Did Not Stay** A party that registers and leaves is a **did not stay (DNS)**. Dissatisfaction with the hotel or an incident with a staff member may precipitate the hasty departure. The guests sometimes seek remedy first, or they may leave without saying why. The cause isn't always the hotel. Emergency messages may be retrieved upon arrival, or a telephone call might come in soon after the room assignment. As a courtesy and to ensure good guest relations, usually no charge is levied if the party leaves within a reasonable time after arrival, even if the room was occupied for a short period.

As a control device, DNS guests are referred to the rooms division's supervisory staff. Upon further investigation, supervisors may uncover poorly trained employees, a weakness in the reservations system, or some other root problem as a result of the DNS

## The Lodge at River's Edge

### Room Status Report

Date: 06/06/__  10:37

| Room Number | Discrpncy | Room Type | Clean Sectn | Hskpg Credits | # of Guest | Room Status | Description |
|---|---|---|---|---|---|---|---|
| 102 | | DDSN | R1 | 1 | 0 | VACANT, CLEAN | RIVER N/S CONNECT 103 |
| 103 | | DDSN | R1 | 1 | 2 | OCCUPIED, CLEAN | RIVER N/S CONNECT 102 |
| 105 | | KEX | R1 | 1.5 | 0 | VACANT, CLEAN | RIVER S |
| 106 | | KKEX | R1 | 1.5 | 2/2 | OCCUPIED, CLEAN | RIVER S |
| 107 | | KN | N1 | 1 | 2 | OCCUPIED, CLEAN | POOL N/S |
| 108 | | DDN | N1 | 1 | 0 | VACANT, DIRTY | POOL N/S |
| 109 | | KK | N1 | 1 | 2 | VACANT, CLEAN, BLOCKED | POOL S |
| 110 | | KEX | N1 | 1.5 | 0 | VACANT, CLEAN | POOL S |
| 111 | | PEXN | S1 | 2 | 0 | VACANT, DIRTY | MTN VIEW N/S CONNECT |
| 112 | | DDN | S1 | 1 | 0 | VACANT, CLEAN | MTN VIEW N/S CONNECT |
| 115 | | QSN | S1 | 1 | 0 | VACANT, CLEAN | MTN VIEW N/S |
| 116 | | DDSN | S1 | 1 | 2/3 | OCCUPIED, CLEAN | MTN VIEW N/S |
| 117 | | K | S1 | 1 | 3 | VACANT, CLEAN, BLOCKED | MTN VIEW S |
| 118 | | QS | S1 | 1 | 0 | VACANT, CLEAN | MTN VIEW S |
| 119 | | K | S1 | 1 | 2 | VACANT, CLEAN, BLOCKED | MTN VIEW S |
| 120 | | DD | S1 | 1 | 1 | VACANT, CLEAN, BLOCKED | MTN VIEW S |
| 121 | | PEXN | P1 | 2 | 1 | OCCUPIED, CLEAN | SPA N/S |
| 123 | | PEXN | P1 | 2 | 2 | OCCUPIED, DIRTY | SPA S CONNECT 125 |
| 125 | | PEX | P1 | 2 | 1 | VACANT, DIRTY, BLOCKED | SPA S CONNECT 123 |

MORE

| | | |
|---|---|---|
| Due check out: 30 | Occupied: 114 | Occupied/dirty: 52 | Occupied/clean: 62 |
| Blocked: 24 | Vacant: 146 | Vacant/dirty: 15 | Vacant/clean: 131 |
| Dirty: 67 | | |
| Clean: 193 | | |

▲
**Exhibit 8-9**
This room status report displays rooms in numerical sequence. Other options allow the clerk to call up rooms by status and room type (display only clean, executive parlour, non-smoking rooms—PEXN). With a computer algorithm, the system might call up rooms in reverse numerical order, or even randomly.

complaint. Although the vast majority of DNS situations (which don't occur all that often) are legitimate, some caution is urged.

The most common DNS ruse happens when a conventioneer finds an open room at the headquarters hotel down the street. That's why caution is always urged with overflow guests housed in another hotel. Some managers actually ask the complaining DNS guest (who probably said something like "this room does not meet my standards" or "I've received an emergency call and must leave immediately") to wait a moment. The manager then phones the headquarters hotel and asks if they are holding a reservation for the guest. If the response is "yes," the manager will explain to the DNS guest that the hotel must charge him or her for a one-night stay. When such guests realize that their trickery has been uncovered, they usually settle down and spend the night(s) in the hotel after all.

**Cash-Only Guests** Although all guests are asked to establish credit at check-in, few actually pay their bills in advance. Instead, most guests imprint a credit card or use their corporate account to establish credit against charges to be incurred during the visit. Only a small percentage of guests choose to pay cash (or a cash equivalent such as a traveller's or personal cheque) at check-in.

Under the law, hotel room charges may be demanded in advance. In addition, the law provides innkeepers with the right to hold luggage for non-payment. This prejudgment lien is under court challenge. Rather than testing the issue, hotel keepers rely on the credit card and on their right to collect in advance.

Paid-in-advance or cash-only guests are "flagged" with a "no-post status" to prevent charges being made from other departments. Once the room is **paid in advance**, other departments must also collect cash for services rendered. Communicating that to the other departments often results in costly errors, although with computerized point of sale (POS) systems integrated with the PMS system this is much more efficient, as the POS will not accept the charge to the room. You see, few hotel guests are cash-only customers. Even those who prefer to pay with cash at check-out are encouraged to leave their credit card on file during the visit. In this way, explains the front-desk clerk, they can charge various expenses incurred around the property back to their hotel room account—it's far more convenient. Later, they can replace the credit card charges with cash upon check-out, if that's their preference.

As such, few hotel guests are paid-in-advance customers (it is common in budget properties). Therefore, other hotel departments (restaurants, lounges, golf courses, health spas, clubhouses, gift shops, etc.) are relatively unaccustomed to dealing with cash-only guests. These other departments often forget to check their POS systems (which are usually interfaced with the PMS) to verify the guest's credit standing. In the end, they inadvertently deliver room service meals, extend access to tennis courts, and even allow merchandise charges to cash-only guests.

This places the burden of payment on the shoulders of the front desk. A guest who has "charged" a $50 room service meal must now pay for it. Some front-office managers will phone the guest's room and explain that a bellperson is coming to collect payment; others leave a less intrusive message to please settle the account with the front desk. If the incident was accidental, the money is forthcoming. However, those guests who were trying to defraud the hotel make themselves scarce at this point and never settle their account!

By the way, telephone charges are a common source of lost revenues from paid-in-advance guests. When checking in the paid-in-advance guest, with so much else on their minds, front-desk clerks sometimes forget to deactivate the in-room telephone from outgoing calls. Only during the night audit shift does the hotel then realize it has a cash-only guest owing $35 in long-distance charges. Certainly, the desk can't wake the guest at 2 A.M., so it leaves a note for the morning crew. When the morning desk staff follows up, they find that the guest has already departed.

**VIP Guests**   Reservations may carry the designation **VIP (very important person)**, **SPATT (special attention** required), Star Guest, or some other similar code. All of these designations mean that the guest is an important person and the clerk should provide service in keeping with the visitor's stature. The guest could be the executive officer of a large association that is considering the hotel as a convention site, a corporate officer of the hotel chain, or perhaps a travel writer.

Such a designation sometimes requires the assistant manager to accompany the arriving guest to the room. It sometimes means that the guest need not register. It may also mean that no information about the guest will be given out to callers unless they are first screened.

There is a difference between a VIP and a DG (distinguished guest), according to one professional publication. The VIP represents either good publicity for the hotel or direct business, whereas the DG is honoured because of position rather than economic value. Presidents, royalty, movie stars, and celebrities rate a DG designation. Meeting planners, company presidents, or committee chairpersons get the VIP treatment and then only during the tenure of their office. VIPs are treated to comp rooms, baskets of fruit, and bottles of wine or champagne.

**Self-Check-In Kiosks**   Even as hotels strive to provide higher levels of guest service, automated devices enable the guest to perform more and more front-office functions. The best example of customers serving themselves is self-check-in/self-check-out terminals or kiosks. Located in the lobbies of some of the finest hotels in the world, guest-operated terminals are no longer viewed as a reduction in service. Instead, self-check-in devices provide the guest with another long-awaited option. Rather than queuing at the front desk for an undetermined length of time, today's sophisticated traveller can opt for a self-check-in (see Exhibit 8-10). Not only does it save waiting in line, but the overall self-check-in process is faster too. According to Hilton Hotels Corporation, the average self-check-in takes between 30 and 45 seconds. That compares quite favourably with the average check-in time at the front desk of 210 seconds (3.5 minutes).

Integrated directly into the PMS, the self-check-in/self-check-out terminal offers choices much like a guest-service agent would. The guest can select room numbers and room types from an online inventory of clean and available rooms. In addition, many of these machines are portable, thereby allowing the hotel to strategically locate the terminal in busy areas (say, for a large group check-in). Some hotels even locate the system in their shuttle vans for registration en route from the airport. Other hotels staff front-desk receptionists at airport luggage claim areas. While guests are waiting for their luggage, they can register using a hand-held terminal, and the room key is waiting upon arrival.

**Prerequisites**   Most self-check-in terminals require the arriving guest to hold an advanced reservation and a valid credit card. Although that is the current standard, these prerequisites are changing. Some of the newest self-check-in devices now provide an option for walk-in customers. However, the self-check-in process becomes more detailed for the walk-in guest. All of the basic information obtained during the reservation process (name, address, length of stay, etc.) must be input by the guest into the

**Exhibit 8-10** ▶

AutoCheck is an excellent example of a self-check-in kiosk. At the touch of a screen, this full-colour system retrieves the guest reservation, verifies credit, authorizes in-house charges, checks the guest in the PMS, assigns a room, generates a keycard, prints the room number and directions, produces amenity coupons, and activates the phone, voice mail, movie, and energy management systems.

terminal. Some self-check-in terminals now accept cash. These are especially popular in limited-service motels that continue to sell rooms after-hours via automated terminals (see "Case Study" below).

**Features** Many self-check-in systems display an electronic map of the property. In this way, guests can knowledgeably select rooms most convenient to them. In addition, it is possible for the terminal to display messages, promote certain aspects of the hotel, and even upsell the guest to a higher-priced room!

Most self-check-in/self-check-out terminals feature a built-in printer that provides the guest with a receipt of the transaction. This receipt may actually be used as a guest identification card during the stay. Some of the newer self-check-in systems use touch-screen technology. Self-check-in terminals also provide the guest with a room key. Although some of the older systems required the guest to visit the key clerk at the front desk, most of the more recent terminals include an automated key function. At the end of the self-check-in process, the system dispenses a key or prompts the guest to remove a blank key card from the stack and swipe it through the electronic key-writing slot. As an added bonus, many systems allow guests to use their personal credit cards as the room key.

**Case Study** Numerous chains have introduced self-check-in systems over the last few years. Hyatt Hotels' Touch and Go system is available at almost all of its non-resort properties. Cendant has built its AutoCheck system into every one of its Wingate Inns. The list, including Promus, Hilton, Choice, and others, continues to grow.

Choice Hotels created a whole new chain based around the premise that some guests prefer efficiency to service. This chain, MainStay Suites (all-suite properties with rates ranging from $50 to $110), doesn't even have a front desk! Instead, guests proceed to a kiosk, where they choose the language (English, Spanish, or French) with which they prefer to check in. They then select a task from one of four icons: check-in, check-out, other hotel services, or community information.

During the check-in process, an automated voice takes the guest through each step. The voice asks the guest to swipe the same credit card used to make the reservation. The card number then accesses the reservation particulars from the central reservation system, Choice 2001. The voice then asks a series of questions related to departure date, room preference, and rate. Once the particulars are verified, the system asks the guest to create and confirm a PIN number. This number is used to access the MainStay Suites system during the remainder of the guest's stay.

At this point, the self-check-in kiosk dispenses a key (or keys), displays a bird's-eye view of the property, and prints an advance folio. The folio reiterates the room rate, check-in and check-out dates, and the room number. It also tells the guest how to find the room and where best to park. The folio is the only place where the guest is addressed by name or room number—for security reasons, the system never displays the guest's name or room number except on printed receipts. When everything is concluded, guests press the "finish" button and the system wishes them a nice visit.

Soon to come to hotels will be a cashless system similar to that used on cruise ships. Guests have their electronic room key validated with credit approval for their stay. When signing charges anywhere in the hotel, guests simply present their computerized room keys and the amount is automatically charged to their room. This automatic charge system can be valid in all hotels outlets, including gift shops, and could also be used to book off-site tours and shows through the concierge desk. As cruise line guests will tell you, this "cashless system" usually leads to the guest spending more money during their stay at the hotel than they would otherwise. Guests also enjoy the added convenience and service that this system provides.

## Establishing Guest Credit

Accurate identification at check-in is so important as to be mandated by many local statutes. By accurately knowing the guest, the hotel protects itself and provides a valuable service to local law enforcement agencies. Information about transient visitors can be of critical importance. In Vancouver, British Columbia, a guest was found murdered. The hotel had obtained no identification at check-in, and it took authorities many days to identify the victim.

Proper identification also serves to protect the hotel. When cash customers are allowed to check in without producing identification, the hotel opens itself to a number of potential problems. A classic case in Halifax, Nova Scotia, illustrates this point. A guest checked in to a one-storey motel, paid cash for the room, and signed the registration card with a phony name. In the dead of night, the guest proceeded to load his van with all of the room's furnishings. The next day, the guest was gone, the motel room was bare, and the motel had absolutely no recourse, having failed to obtain proper identification. (And the room was truly bare. The guest had taken everything—the TV set, bed, and dresser, as well as the toilet, tub, and carpet!)

Even if the guest has no intention of stealing, securing guest identification aids the hotel in a multitude of ways. Knowing the guest's name and address allows the hotel to return **lost and found** items, bill and collect late charges, and maintain a valuable database.

**Credit Cards**   Every registration card asks the guest to identify the method of payment (see Exhibit 8-5). If a personal or company cheque is the answer, credit approval must be obtained from the rooms division manager. More likely, a credit card is tendered. If there is a choice, the desk should always request the card for which the hotel has negotiated the best merchant fee (see Chapter 12).

With a PMS, the credit card data are entered into the electronic folio either through the computer keyboard or by means of a credit card reader. Using a credit card reader, the room clerk gets a simultaneous authorization of the card from the credit card company. The terminal reads the magnetic strip and communicates that number electronically to the credit card clearinghouse. Use of electronic credit card scanners integrated with PMSs saves about 40 valuable seconds during the check-in process. The number can be punched in manually if the strip signal is damaged or inoperative. Back comes an authorization number (or a denial), which appears on the screen of the credit card reader. The authorization number is the hotel's guarantee that the credit card is legitimate.

Part of the communication between the credit card company and the hotel involves the amount of charges that will be added to the guest's balance. Limits exist for both the hotel and the individual. These "floor limits" are explained in Chapter 12. That discussion also includes the next steps in the credit card story: processing the card at departure and collecting from the credit card company.

**Back-Office Records**   Front-office records post departmental charges incurred by the guest against the credit established at check-in. Back-office records track those charges through the bank or credit card company until payment has been received. Credit cards are just one of several records initiated by the front office but completed by the back office. Final settlement of travel agency bills clears through the back office, although the reservation and paperwork begin at the front office. Frequent-guest records and frequent-flyer partnership records are another front-office/back-office relationship. The disposition of these various records is explained in Chapter 12. It is not a matter that concerns the clerk at the point of registration.

Record keeping for frequent-guest or frequent-flyer programs is a new job for the front office. It has just recently been incorporated into the PMS at many properties. Guests using automatic-teller registration may still be required to go to the desk to get frequent-guest credits.

# The Rooming Process

While the guest registration process nears completion, a bellperson may arrive to escort the guest to the room. As the guest moves into the realm of the bell department, a number of critical functions are accomplished. The bellperson explains various locations and departments throughout the hotel, details a list of current hotel activities and promotions, and serves as final inspector before the guest prepares to occupy the room.

## Uniformed Services

The bell staff is part of a much larger department commonly referred to as uniformed services. Throughout the guest's visit, the uniformed services department attends to various needs and services. Valet parking, doorpersons, concierges, hotel security, and the bell staff all play a key role in enhancing the property's image. No other department has the degree of personal one-on-one time with the guest as does uniformed services.

Like all members of uniformed services, the bell staff serve as goodwill ambassadors who turn an ordinary visit into a warm and personable experience (see Exhibit 8-11). By developing close, professional relationships with the guest, a well-trained bellperson successfully promotes a number of hotel services. Suggestive selling and gentle persuasion are invaluable skills for a bellperson to possess.

**Guest Communication**  Bellpersons, like all members of the uniformed services staff, are encouraged to engage the guest in conversation. Whenever staff members see a guest, they should make the effort to smile and at least offer a simple greeting (see Exhibit 8-12). By taking such steps, the guest comes to know and trust one or more members of the uniformed staff.

It is interesting to watch which uniformed personnel are attracted to which guests. Sometimes it is a matter of personality type or due to a relationship formed during the **rooming** process. Whatever the reason, many guests develop a favourite among the bellpersons or other uniformed services staff. Management encourages such relationships, as long as they remain within the boundaries of professional behaviour.

By developing such personable relationships, the bellperson is well situated to know when the guest's visit has gone awry. The bellperson can then approach the guest and solicit the complaint. Careful training places the bellperson in the critical role as bridge between the dissatisfied guest and the responsible department. When management works to keep open these lines of communication, the bellperson performs a key function in the hotel's quality assurance program (see discussion in Chapter 7).

**"Wired" Bellpersons**  Generally, outfitting the bell department with inconspicuous earpieces, a voice-activated mouthpiece, and an attached belt pack costs less than $100 per employee. Having direct and instantaneous communication with bell staff (along with other front-of-the-house departments) is critical, especially in upscale properties. Today's guests have less patience waiting for an employee to answer a page, find a

**Exhibit 8-11 ▶**
The legendary elegance of the Fairmont Hotel, built atop San Francisco's Nob Hill in 1907, is embodied in the bell department. A large **bellstand** (centred in the lobby just behind the bellperson standing in the photo) staffs more than 20 bellpersons for this 600-room property.

**Exhibit 8-12** ▶

CAA inspectors rate hotels based on a number of criteria. Listed here are the bell service guidelines for four- and five-diamond properties.

Among the requirements for a Four- and Five-Diamond ranking by the Canadian Automobile Association are the following services expected of bellpersons:

**All Bellpersons Must**
- be neatly uniformed;
- wear tasteful nametags;
- be friendly, courteous, and helpful;
- be knowledgeable of hotel and area;
- make good eye contact with guests; and
- acknowledge the presence of guests (e.g., when passing in corridors).

**On Guest Reception**
- welcome guest to the hotel;
- address guest by name (should pick up on name from desk or luggage tags);
- explain food and beverage department, recreational and other facilities;
- hang garment bag in closet;
- take out and set up luggage rack; suitcase should be placed on luggage rack, not on bed or floor;
- explain operation of lights, TV, and thermostat;
- offer ice at a Four-Diamond, expected to be automatic at a Five-Diamond;
- point out emergency exits or diagram;
- offer to open or close drapes;
- explain any unusual features within the room;
- explain turn-down;
- check bathroom supplies; and
- offer additional services.

**On Check-Out**
- arrive promptly (wait should not exceed 10 minutes);
- check around room and in bathroom for belongings that might be left behind; and
- offer to arrange for car delivery.

house phone and call the desk, or answer a cellphone. Talkabout headsets not only are instantaneous, but also give the entire staff a look of crisp professionalism and service-readiness. Additionally, in this day of heightened security, they allow the bellperson to perform a critical role as the mobile eyes and ears of the hotel.

**Uniformed Services Training** Although a professional dialogue is encouraged, it is often difficult to monitor and maintain. All uniformed services staff (but especially the bellperson) have ample opportunity to speak with the guest on an intimate level. By design, bellpersons have a great deal of autonomy. During the rooming process, while driving the airport shuttle, and at other times, the bellperson can be with a guest—and out of management's sight—for 10 or 15 minutes at a time. Therefore, it is difficult for management to know what is actually being discussed with the guest during these one-on-one conversations.

There are numerous examples of bellpersons stepping over the line of acceptable behaviour. Distraught with the job, a bellperson might badmouth the hotel or senior management to the guest. Disappointed with the lack of gratuities that day, a bellperson might boldly ask for a more generous tip from the guest. There are even cases where bellpersons dealt drugs and prostitution to the guest! Minimizing such occurrences begins with proper hiring and continues with constant training.

**Mystery Shopper Services** Because it is so difficult to assess the bellperson's professionalism while he or she is rooming the guest, many managers stress its importance with secret shopper services. Such services work on the premise that employees act differently when they sense that management is watching. On the other hand, a secret shopper posing as a hotel guest is able to truly observe the employee's professionalism on the job.

Secret shoppers visit the property and stay one or more nights (see Chapter 7). During this time, they attempt to engage employees in a number of usual and sometimes unusual activities. Although employees are probably forewarned that secret audits may be conducted, they usually have no idea that they are being observed. As a result, secret shopper services are an excellent way to monitor the effectiveness of employee training—especially in the uniformed services department.

## The Bell Staff

Several innovations have affected the uniformed services department's functions and means of earning income. Self-service icemakers and vending machines on the floor, and in-room refrigerators and minibars, have reduced the kind and number of service calls that bellpersons make. Group arrivals and self-check-in kiosks, in which individuals room themselves, further reduce the service functions of this department.

**Rotation of Fronts** Tips comprise the bulk of the bell department's earnings. Total earnings usually exceed that of other front-office employees, including some management positions.

The bellperson who comes forward to take the rooming slip and room the guest is called a **front**. Fronts rotate in turn. The one who has just completed a front is called a **last**. Lasts are used for errands that are unlikely to produce gratuities. Cleaning the lobby is a responsibility of the last. Lasts are also assigned **dead room changes**, with no chance of a **gratuity**, such as lockouts and moves carried out in the guest's absence.

Between the front and the last, positions rotate in sequence, moving forward in the rank as each new front is called. A particular post in the lobby should represent each position in the sequence. One station might be by the front door to receive incoming luggage; another across the lobby; a third by the elevators. Staffing requirements for a full-service bell department run approximately 1 bellperson for every 40 to 50 estimated check-ins.

The procedure is much less formal today. Fronts wait by the bellstand, which is visible from the front desk. As the clerk completes the registration, the front is summoned to the desk by lights or signals or verbally by the clerk calling, "Front!" Aware of the routine, the front rarely needs prompting.

With a PMS, remote printers located at the bellstand print the rooming slips, so the bellpersons approach the guests aware of their names. By coding the printout, the desk communicates additional information (VIP, heavy luggage, etc.) to the bell department. The PMS also maintains a record of fronts.

A record of fronts assures each person a proper turn, although the sequence may be altered if a guest requests a specific person or if a last is still away on some long-term errand. The record, maintained at the bell captain's desk, tracks the crew, which is the most mobile department in the hotel. By noting the bellperson's presence on various floors at various times, the record offers protection from accusations in the event of theft or other trouble. It fixes responsibility about the rooming procedure or lost luggage. The comings and goings of the bell staff, the purposes of their errands, and the times elapsed must all be recorded.

**Responsibilities of the Bell Staff**  Depending on the level of service for the particular hotel, there may be no uniformed services department at all. In many small hotels, the bell staff is a catch-all department that performs a multitude of tasks. Small operations may ask the bellperson to drive the shuttle van, act as doorperson, make room service calls, deliver cocktails to guests relaxing in the lobby, and even aid the front-desk staff during meal-break periods.

Certain responsibilities are outside the scope of the bell department's duties. Bellpersons do not quote rates or suggest room assignments. They call the room clerk for a second assignment whenever the guest is dissatisfied with the room.

Bellpersons, or just the captains, share in other incomes. Auto rentals, tickets to local attractions, and bus tours are available at the captain's desk. Each of these companies pays a commission (usually 10 to 15 percent) that more often accrues to the uniformed services than to the hotel. This may also hold true when the hotel contracts an **outside laundry** or dry cleaner for guest service.

**Luggage**  The doorperson, or just as often the guest, carries in the baggage from the cab or car. It stays on the lobby floor until the guest is finished registering. The room clerk gives a rooming slip to the bellperson, who now takes over the guest's service. Jointly, the guest and the bellperson identify and retrieve the luggage and head toward the elevator. The guest, the bellperson, and the baggage might ride up together. Or the bellperson might leave the guest in order to transport the luggage on the service (rear) elevator, while the guest rides the guest (front) elevator. They meet at the elevator lobby on the guest's assigned floor.

**Final Inspection**  Rooming guests is the primary task of the bell department. Although many individuals room themselves, it is preferable to go in the company of a staff member. Guests who are in the company of a bellperson avoid the embarrassment of walking in on an occupied room. Service personnel always knock and wait before unlocking the door.

Once inside, the bellperson performs another inspection function. First, the bellperson hangs the guest's loose clothing and hefts the baggage onto the luggage rack or bed (see Exhibit 8-12). Temperature controls are checked, and the room is inspected for cleanliness, towels, soap, toilet tissue, facial tissue, and other needs. Lights, hangers, television sets, and furnishings are examined. Special features of the hotel are explained—the spa or the operating hours of room service, for example.

Self-service items are pointed out—the ice machine or the in-room refrigerator. Connecting doors are unlocked if the party is to share several connecting rooms. Unless there is a special request for service, the bellperson leaves the key and the rooming slip and accepts the proffered tip, if any. Before leaving, there may be a final sell for a particular dining room or lounge and a final "good day."

**Group Luggage Handling**  Tour groups are easy for the bell staff to handle and are generally quite profitable. Using the guest list furnished by the group, the desk **preregisters** the party. Roommates, whom the tour company has identified, are assigned, and keys are readied in small envelopes for quick distribution. Similar key envelopes are prepared for rapid distribution to airline crews when permanent reservations have been negotiated with the airline.

The PMS can print the key envelopes (coded by groups), the rooming lists (knowing who is with whom and where is very important to the tour guide or the company meeting planner), identification cards for in-house use, baggage tags, and every other form needed for a successful group meeting. All of these items are derived from the same basic information, which is fed into the computer only once.

Final instructions to the tour members are given on the bus. Communication is impossible once the captive audience is lost. Tour members are reminded that charges not included in the tour price will need to be settled individually with the hotel. A notice to that effect is also included in the key envelope (sometimes called the key packet). The envelopes are distributed in the lobby (or on the bus) by the desk, the tour coordinator, or sometimes the bell staff. Guests find their own rooms without help from the bell department while the baggage is being unloaded from the bus.

Group baggage can be a headache as well as a backache for the uniformed services if bags are improperly marked or hard to identify. Putting some procedures in place makes the task easier. The tour company should provide each traveller with brightly coloured tags to attach to the luggage before departure. The colour identifies the group, expediting baggage handling in and out of the airport and the hotel. The individual's number is written on each tag, and that number corresponds to that person's place on the master rooming sheet. Copies of the list should have been given to every hotel on the tour. The number, which is easier to read than a name, helps the bell staff match the bags with room numbers.

There is another variation: Each bag can be marked with the correct room number from a computer-printed list of adhesive-backed labels. The bellperson removes the room number from the printed list and slaps it on the bag for delivery.

All hotels that cater to tour and meetings business use similar techniques for delivering group baggage. Although it has the appearance of anti-service, delivering the group's luggage in bulk is really the only efficient manner for handling the task. By eliminating the one-on-one rooming of each guest, the bell department can move through luggage deliveries quickly. Aside from being escorted to their rooms, group guests don't miss much else. Information normally shared during the rooming process—hours of the restaurant, for example—is shared by a desk clerk or bell captain during a short presentation to the captive audience on the bus. This frees the bell department to get right to luggage deliveries. Within 30 to 45 minutes, most small and mid-sized groups will have received their luggage. Some creative hotels hold an arrival punch reception for the tour group, and while the guests are enjoying this, hotel management can officially welcome the group and sell the property and services. During the punch reception, ice and luggage can be delivered to each room.

Group luggage is the bellpersons' bread and butter. That's because the bell department is paid a small stipend for every group guest arriving and departing that day. Group contracts include a negotiable charge commonly referred to as "baggage in and baggage out." Group baggage handling rates run as little as $2 per person in and $2 per person out, to as much as $6 per person in each direction. Group baggage handling rates may be a factor of unionization (unionized bell departments may set a minimally acceptable rate), the time of year that the group arrives, the room rate paid, and so on. The entire fee (both in and out) is paid at the time of contract, and a hotel that handles a lot of group business can easily supplement paycheques by several hundred dollars per bellperson per week.

**Rooming Slips**   The **rooming slip** serves as a vehicle for communication between the front desk and both the bellperson and the guest. The bellperson uses the rooming slip to better understand the guest and the rooming situation. The slip provides the bellperson with information related to the guest's name, the guest's affiliation or corporate name (if appropriate), the room number assigned, the guest's home city (great for making small talk), and the number of nights reserved. As explained earlier, the rooming slip also serves as a support document to prove the bellperson's whereabouts during a specific period in question.

Although not intended for that purpose, the slips have been used by the Canada Customs and Revenue Agency. Estimating the average tip per front and counting the number of fronts according to the rooming slips provides a fair estimate of tip income. The estimate is then compared to that reported by the employee.

**Content** The guest uses the rooming slip for two purposes: as a receipt and as guest identification. As a receipt, the rooming slip provides the guest with an additional opportunity to verify the accuracy of information. For example, the rooming slip may show that the guest's name has been misspelled. The room rate, date of check-out, or some other information may also be inaccurate. Many rooming slips restate hotel disclaimers as a means of strengthening the hotel's legal relationship with the guest (see Exhibits 8-13 and 8-14).

**Informative**
Floor plan of the property
Aerial view of the property
Telephone directory of services
Kinds of lobby shops
Foreign language capabilities of the staff
Airline, taxi, and limousine telephone numbers
Local sites to see and things to do
Airport bus: times of operation and rates
Currency exchange capabilities
Map of the city with highway designations

**Marketing**
List of restaurants: prices, hours of operation, and menu specialties
A message of welcome or a note of appreciation
WATS number for other hotels in the chain
Recreational facilities: tennis, golf, pool, sauna

**Regulatory**
Check-out hour and check-in hour
Rate of gratuity applied to the room charge
Regulations for visitors
Limitations on pets
Dress code

Availability of the safe for valuables
Settlement of accounts
Expectations for guaranteed reservation holders
Deposit of room keys when leaving the property
Fees for local telephone calls

**Identification**
Clerk's identifying initials
Identification of the party: name, number of persons, rate, arrival and departure dates
Room number
Key code—where room access is controlled by a dial system key

**Instructional**
Express check-out procedure
Electrical capacity for appliances
What to do in case of fire
How to secure the room
Notification to the desk if errors exist on the rooming slip
How to operate the in-room films; their cost
How to operate the in-room refrigerator; cost
Rate of tax applied to the room charge

▲
**Exhibit 8-13**
The size and breadth of the property dictates the size and breadth of the rooming slip. Small hotels may provide little more than a simple receipt to the registered guest. Other hotels, anxious to market in-house services, local attractions, paid advertisers, and legal disclaimers, may provide a multi-page rooming booklet. This exhibit demonstrates the variety of content found on rooming slips in North America.

**Exhibit 8-14** ▶

Example of a rooming slip and computerized key packet presented to arriving guests at the Niagara Falls Hilton Hotel. The packet includes information on the various revenue centres, Niagara scenic tours, express check-out, key card instructions, check-out time, early departure fees, and guest-service hotline.

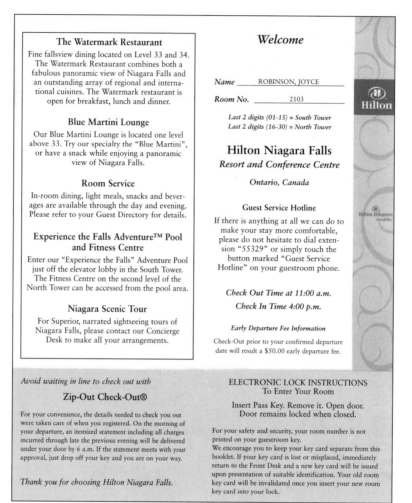

### The Watermark Restaurant

Fine fallsview dining located on Level 33 and 34. The Watermark Restaurant combines both a fabulous panoramic view of Niagara Falls and an outstanding array of regional and international cuisines. The Watermark restaurant is open for breakfast, lunch and dinner.

### Blue Martini Lounge

Our Blue Martini Lounge is located one level above 33. Try our specialty the "Blue Martini", or have a snack while enjoying a panoramic view of Niagara Falls.

### Room Service

In-room dining, light meals, snacks and beverages are available through the day and evening. Please refer to your Guest Directory for details.

### Experience the Falls Adventure™ Pool and Fitness Centre

Enter our "Experience the Falls" Adventure Pool just off the elevator lobby in the South Tower. The Fitness Centre on the second level of the North Tower can be accessed from the pool area.

### Niagara Scenic Tour

For Superior, narrated sightseeing tours of Niagara Falls, please contact our Concierge Desk to make all your arrangements.

---

*Welcome*

Name ___ROBINSON, JOYCE___

Room No. ___2103___

*Last 2 digits (01-15) = South Tower*
*Last 2 digits (16-30) = North Tower*

### Hilton Niagara Falls
*Resort and Conference Centre*

*Ontario, Canada*

#### Guest Service Hotline

If there is anything at all we can do to make your stay more comfortable, please do not hesitate to dial extension "55329" or simply touch the button marked "Guest Service Hotline" on your guestroom phone.

*Check Out Time at 11:00 a.m.*

*Check In Time 4:00 p.m.*

*Early Departure Fee Information*

Check-Out prior to your confirmed departure date will result a $50.00 early departure fee.

---

*Avoid waiting in line to check out with*

## Zip-Out Check-Out®

For your convenience, the details needed to check you out were taken care of when you registered. On the morning of your departure, an itemized statement including all charges incurred through late the previous evening will be delivered under your door by 6 a.m. If the statement meets with your approval, just drop off your key and you are on your way.

*Thank you for choosing Hilton Niagara Falls.*

---

ELECTRONIC LOCK INSTRUCTIONS
To Enter Your Room

Insert Pass Key. Remove it. Open door.
Door remains locked when closed.

For your safety and security, your room number is not printed on your guestroom key.
We encourage you to keep your key card separate from this booklet. If your key card is lost or misplaced, immediately return to the Front Desk and a new key card will be issued upon presentation of suitable identification. Your old room key card will be invalidated once you insert your new room key card into your lock.

---

Overseas hotels use the rooming slip as a sales tool for their own property and for local, non-competing businesses. Few Canadian hotels sell such advertising space. With their more extensive services and facilities, they need all of the space themselves.

The Canadian rooming slip is an interesting mix of selling, services, and legal safeguards. Depending on management's inclination, the rooming slip is either a simple slip of paper or a complete, elaborate sales tool in a variety of colours. Caesars Palace in Las Vegas has a rooming booklet of 20 pages! Exhibit 8-13 lists the range of information that a hotel might try to communicate to the guest, and Exhibit 8-14 shows an example.

Colour-coded rooming slips, like that of Hyatt's Passports, may also serve as a guest identification card. The colour tells the cashiers in the bars and dining rooms whether the guest is a paid-in-advance guest, a tour group member, a VIP, and so on.

Although the guest is just arriving, check-out information and a check-out form are frequently provided in order to plan for a quick departure. Quick check-out has been in place far longer than self-check-in/self-check-out terminals. Innovative departure systems that did not need computer hardware were inaugurated as early as 1975. However, they all require the guest to use a credit card or other form of advance credit.

## Summary

Arriving guests face a number of opportunities to meet members of the uniformed staff. Valet parking, the doorperson, guest-service agents, and the bell department all play critical roles in the arrival process. The first impressions made by these employees create a positive (or negative) lasting effect on the guest's perception of the hotel operation.

The check-in procedure represents an especially sensitive segment of the arrival process. The front-desk clerk communicates with the guest in an unscripted fashion where few rules dictate their interaction. A wise front-desk clerk evaluates the guest and attempts to understand unique requirements. Too rapid a check-in and the guest leaves with a sense of rudeness or having been rushed. Too slow a check-in and the guest perceives inefficiency in the hotel operation. Add to this sensitivity the need for the desk clerk to retrieve payment, extract additional information, get a signature on the registration card, ask credit questions, and attempt to upsell to a higher-priced room, and the check-in process can be a tense several minutes.

The bell department spends the last moments with the arriving guest. Rooming the guest is a complex process of small talk, suggestive selling, room inspection, and overall guest service. Oh, yes—bellpersons carry the luggage as well.

## Questions and Problems

1. Reorganize the following jumbled list of events, persons, and job activities into a logical flow from start to finish of the guest arrival process:
   - (a) Room selection
   - (b) Establishing guest credit
   - (c) Registered, not assigned
   - (d) Bellperson
   - (e) Valet parking attendant
   - (f) Rotation of fronts
   - (g) Room assignment
   - (h) Obtaining guest identification
   - (i) Rooming slip
   - (j) Upgrading and/or upselling
   - (k) Rooming the guest
   - (l) Preblocking rooms
   - (m) Doorperson
   - (n) Registration card
   - (o) Check-out reminder
   - (p) Room status report
   - (q) CAA/AAA discount
   - (r) Pet deposit

2. Foreign registration cards often require significantly more personal information than is required on domestic registration cards. Some management personnel feel that this extra data amounts to an invasion of the guest's privacy. Other managers, however, believe that this extra information aids the hotel in providing better security and service levels to the guest. With whom do you side? Why might a hotel legitimately need to know your future and past destinations, your mother's maiden name, and your date of birth?

3. Intentional bias can be programmed (through computer algorithms) into the room-selection sequence of a property management system. Rooms will then appear in a prescribed order rather than in sequence or at random. Certain rooms can be offered first, or not, depending on management's criteria. Give examples explaining why management might wish to decide which rooms appear in which sequence in order to direct the clerk's selection.

4. A local merchant, whose attempts to service the hotel's guest laundry and dry cleaning business have been frustrated, visits with the

new rooms manager. (The laundry of this 600-room, commercial hotel does not clean personal guest items.) The conversation makes the rooms manager realize that she has never seen commission figures on any of the reports. She learns that the bell captain, who doesn't seem to do any work—that is, he doesn't take fronts—gets the commissions. The rooms manager initiates a new policy. All commissions from car rentals, bus tours, ski tickets, laundry, balloon rides, and so on, will accrue to the hotel. An unresolved issue is whether the money will go into the employee's welfare fund. A very angry bell captain presents himself at the office of the vice-president of the rooms division. Explain with whom you agree (the rooms manager or the bell captain) and prepare an argument to support your opinion.

5. Some hotels upgrade corporate guests to nicer rooms when space is available. Usually, the guest need not even ask for this courtesy—it is offered as standard operating procedure. Managers of such properties believe that the corporate guest appreciates the courtesy and the nicer room. And since the room is not likely to sell anyway, why not make someone happy? The reverse side of this argument, however, suggests that the guest comes to expect this treatment and even feels slighted if only standard rooms are available. In addition, hotels that give upgrades away for free are doing themselves a disservice in terms of upselling corporate guests to a higher rate. After all, why should corporate guests ever select higher-priced rooms (or concierge-floor rooms) when they are given at no extra charge as a matter of standard practice? How would you respond to these arguments?

## CASE STUDY

### Facilitating Marketing to and Registration of Bus Groups

Joseph Shembri, the general manager of a small resort hotel outside Quebec City and just off the Trans-Canada Highway, noticed that many bus tour groups were driving past his hotel, although last year only three stayed there overnight. Shembri has a relative in the busing business and enquired why none of these buses were staying at his hotel. He was told to take a math compass and draw two circles around the location of his hotel on a map of North America—one at 500 kilometres and one at 850 kilometres. Shembri was told that overnight bus business would originate between those two circles. The circles identified the potential bus markets as being east and west of Quebec City within Canada and several northeastern states in the United States.

Shembri and his director of marketing sat down to devise how to market to these bus groups, now that they knew where they were located. Help Shembri with answers to some of the questions he has for this meeting.

1. How does the hotel find out what bus tour companies are in the geographical area identified?

2. What demographic age group takes bus tours?

3. What should be included in the hotel's package for the bus tour groups that would entice them to stay at the hotel rather than at a competitor? Competitors are offering a free room to either the bus driver or the tour escort, and not much else.

4. How will the hotel handle speedy registration of the groups?

## Notes

1. According to the American Hotel & Lodging Association (AH&LA), pets are welcome in more than 23 000 U.S. lodging establishments, up from 10 000 hotels in 1994. Additional information can be found in CAA/AAA's PetBooks series of guides listing pet-friendly accommodations across Canada and the United States.

2. One 291-room full-service property demonstrated savings of 27 240 litres of water and 182 litres of detergent per month just by laundering bed sheets every other day. And that was for an optional program in which not all guests chose to participate.

## Weblinks

American Hotel & Lodging Association
**www.ahma.com**

Canadian Automobile Association
**www.caa.ca**

Hotel Registration of Guests Act
**www.e-laws.gov.on.ca/DBLaws/Statutes/English/90h17_e.htm**

Innkeepers Act
**www.e-laws.gov.on.ca/DBLaws/Statutes/English/90i07_e.htm**

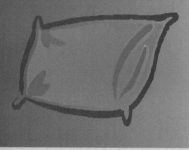

# Chapter 9

# The Role of the Room Rate

## Learning Objectives

After reading this chapter, you will be able to do the following:

1. Identify factors used in establishing the room rate.

2. Discuss the concepts of hotel room demand, rack rate discounts, and other rate variations.

3. Identify methods of determining the correct room rate using traditional rate calculations as well as understand the impact of upselling and discounting.

## Factors in Establishing the Room Rate

In recent years, average room rates have risen from two to six times the national rate of inflation. There are a number of reasons why rates are rising so quickly. Inflation is certainly part of the answer. But also to blame for recent rate increases are higher daily operating costs (including rising labour rates) and an increased consumer demand for hotel rooms. The result of these factors is an industry whose prices are sometimes surprisingly strong (see Exhibit 1-2 on page 6).

In 1991, the Hotel Association of Canada reports that the average daily rate (ADR) for Canada was $70 with revenue per available room (RevPar) of $41. In 2004, the ADR was $117.49 with a RevPar of $72.96. This represents an increase in ADR of 67.8 percent in 13 years for an average annual increase of 5.22 percent (almost double what average inflation rates were during the same period). Based on this rate of increase, in 20 years you could be paying $415 per night to stay at your local Holiday Inn.

### Hotel Room Demand

Probably the biggest culprit in the industry's flight to higher room rates is the nation's economy itself. The late 1990s represented the greatest non-wartime boom the world, especially North America, has ever experienced. A natural result of a booming economy is an increased demand for hotel rooms. To respond to this demand, the industry has been building hotels at a feverish rate. Today, there are more hotel rooms available in Canada than ever before, but room demand is higher than ever before, too.

**Exhibit 9-1** ▶
In 2004, a very high percentage of revenues in Canadian hotels resulted from the sale of rooms. This is probably not surprising, and as we will find out, this single revenue area (rooms) contributes up to 75 percent of revenue to profits.

## Distribution of Revenue by Type of Service for Hotels and Motor Hotels, by Province, 2004

| | Rooms | Meals | Alcohol | Merchandise | Service |
|---|---|---|---|---|---|
| **CANADA** | 60% | 20% | 10% | 1% | 9% |
| NF | 62% | 22% | 7% | 1% | 8% |
| PE | 73% | 17% | 5% | 0% | 5% |
| NS | 69% | 17% | 5% | 1% | 8% |
| NB | 68% | 23% | 4% | 0% | 5% |
| QC | 62% | 22% | 7% | 1% | 8% |
| ON | 63% | 20% | 5% | 0% | 12% |
| MN | 36% | 18% | 34% | 3% | 9% |
| SK | 52% | 19% | 20% | 2% | 7% |
| AB | 57% | 21% | 12% | 1% | 9% |
| BC | 61% | 19% | 11% | 1% | 8% |
| YI | 51% | 26% | 13% | 3% | 7% |
| NT | X | X | X | X | X |
| NN | X | X | X | X | X |

Note: X indicates confidential data. Canada totals include all provinces and territories.

The result is a form of inflation—inflation at a microeconomic level, affecting just the travel industry. Inflation occurs when too many dollars are chasing too few goods. The result of such a dilemma is a rise in consumer prices, and the entire travel industry (hotels, air travel, rental cars, and restaurant meals, to be specific) has experienced an inflation of prices over the past several years. The largest percentage of revenue in a hotel is realized from the rooms division (see Exhibit 9-1).

The amazing thing about the great economic boom of the late 1990s is that most other industries demonstrated extremely low inflation. The national Consumer Price Index (CPI) reflected low single-digit inflation (generally 2 to 3 percent) during most of the boom years. Most products, the travel industry excepted, cost little more today than they did, say, five years ago—but not so with hotel rooms. Hotel rooms represent a microcosm of the overall economy, and a unique microcosm at that. When the whole economy is booming, salespeople are travelling; companies, both large and small, are hosting more lavish corporate retreats; and conferences are boasting record attendance. The leisure travel market, flush with its own sense of wealth, is also travelling more.

The result is increased rooms demand. And of course, increased demand means higher average rates. That's the uniqueness of the situation—the rest of the economy is booming but inflation is staying in check, while the hotel industry is seeing rapid rate increases—increases that are averaging about twice the inflation rate of other industries. The thing about "averages," however, is that there are highs and lows. Some markets (mostly major urban areas) are seeing rate increases even higher than those described above. Other markets are stagnant in terms of room rate inflation. The effects of September 11, 2001, caused a 17 percent drop in hotel occupancy in downtown Toronto from the rate in 2000 (although occupancy was already down 10 percent before September 11, signalling the beginning of a recession) and a smaller drop in most other major Canadian cities. Most of the markets had bounced back by the fall of 2002, with the exception of downtown Toronto and Ottawa. Many American conferences were either cancelled or moved to New York City as a measure of support for the devastated city.

In early 2003, Toronto (along with other areas of the world) was hit with an outbreak of severe acute respiratory syndrome (SARS). This outbreak had a devastating effect on hotels, as occupancy dropped from 70 percent to 30 percent. This is a far greater drop in occupancy percentage than any other in recent history, including the drop experienced with the threat of terrorist attacks. Travel from the United States to Canada has dropped drastically since 2001; some speculate that this is because of Americans' fear of travel, some say it is a result of Canada not entering into the Iraq War with our American friends, and of course the continuing rise in the Canadian dollar has had an impact. Canada is no longer a cheaper vacation for American travellers. The proposed requirement for passports to cross the Canada–U.S. border may further reduce the number of Americans travelling to Canada. These same concerns are shared by our American neighbours, as Canadian business is very important to border states and vital to states such as Florida and California.

**Competition** Just as operating costs dictate the minimum rate a hotel can afford to charge, competition sets the maximum it can expect to get. External competition from neighbouring facilities prescribes the general price range. Internal physical differences within the rooms determine the rate increments.

Supply and demand, the degree of saturation, and the extent of rate cutting in the community fix the rate parameters. Customers comparison shop, and hotel management should do the same. Differences in both the physical facilities and the range of services offered justify higher rates than the competition. The physical accommodations are easier to compare; they are there for the looking. Swimming pool, tennis courts, meeting rooms, restaurants, and a lobby bar head a long list of differences that give one property a competitive advantage over its neighbour. Room size, furnishings (bed and bath types), location, and exposure differentiate the internal product.

The condition of the facilities can offset their competitive advantage. "Clean and neat" sends an important subliminal message. Hotels with burnt-out bulbs in their signs, wilted flowers in the planters, and dirty glass in the entrance doors lose out to hotels with lesser facilities that look fresh and new.

Differences in service are more difficult to discern, but they add to the room rate charge as substantially as do other components. Twenty-four-hour room service, pool guard on duty, and an extensive training program for employees head another, less visible list of competitive advantages. Like the capital outlays of the physical accommodations, these costs must be recaptured in the room rate as well.

**Room Rate Elasticity** Elasticity is the change in demand (rooms sold) resulting from a change in price (room rates). If demand increases with a drop in price (or decreases when price is raised), demand is elastic. If demand appears unaffected by drops or increases in price, demand is inelastic. Hotel room rate reductions in an elastic market generate new business (higher occupancy). Hotel room rate reductions in an inelastic market generate little or no new business.

The hotel industry has always believed that reductions in rate produce less new revenue than is lost from lowering the unit price, thereby suggesting that room demand is somewhat inelastic. The supposition was supported by actual experience. Room income (occupancy multiplied by ADR) actually rose during the low-occupancy periods of the past decade because increased room rates did not drive away significant

**Exhibit 9-2 ▶**

Curve A represents a normal elastic demand curve, characteristic of the leisure market. As room rates fall, room demand increases by the leisure market. When the rate is reduced from $140 to $40, occupancy jumps from 25 percent to 75 percent. The corporate travel market, on the other hand, is considered inelastic (curve B). Corporate travellers are little concerned with rate, so a reduction in room price will not create increased demand.

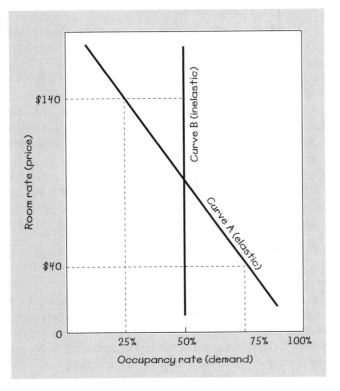

amounts of sales (occupancy). It did not, goes the reasoning, because room demand is inelastic (see Exhibit 9-2).

Elasticity of demand for hotel rooms is exceedingly complex. An inelastic property can actually increase rates during an economic slump with profitable results. Rate changes can be disastrous—or very beneficial—depending on the elasticity of demand for the property and market in question.

Different markets have different degrees of sensitivity. Tour properties are more elastic, and commercial demand is more inelastic. Hotels experience different degrees of elasticity throughout the year. That is what the demand pricing behind seasonal rates is all about. A given hotel may have numerous seasons throughout its annual cycle.

Elasticity of demand was the catalyst for major change throughout the travel industry from the 1970s to the 1990s. During this period, customer profiles began to form into distinct buyer segments. The airlines—after deregulation—were the first to capitalize on the emerging distinctions between corporate travel and the leisure market. The hotel industry wasn't far behind.

This parameter shift was the beginning of a conscious attempt to segregate buyers by their price sensitivity, the concept behind yield management. Both industries discovered that demand was elastic for the leisure market and inelastic for the business segment in terms of both time and price. Demand is a little of both for the group rooms market.

The art of managing these distinct markets cannot be taken lightly. Success from discounting to the leisure market (where lower rates result in incremental increases in occupancy) does not hold true with the corporate market (where lower rates are not offset with increased occupancy). Similarly, offering alternative dates to move the guest into discounted low periods of occupancy works well with the leisure market (whose vacation periods are relatively flexible) but poorly with corporate guests (whose travel dates are on a need-to-go basis). Discretionary leisure buyers may even change location to save the lodging budget, while corporate guests are last-minute shoppers with extremely little flexibility (see Exhibit 9-2).

Complicated as this may seem, group rooms business throws yet another dimension into the picture. Tour groups, which are usually price sensitive, take on many of the characteristics of the leisure segment—elastic in terms of rate, flexible with regard to date. Conventions, trade shows, conferences, and corporate retreats generally demonstrate the characteristics of the corporate market—inelastic with regard to rate, inflexible in terms of travel dates. But remember one thing: Even an inelastic market becomes elastic at some point. There may be little or no difference in corporate occupancy when the rate fluctuates between $80 and $160. But if the rate becomes too high, say $260, some sensitivity will ultimately result. A growing trend—corporate guests finding last-minute bargains via Internet leisure travel sites—is adding a new twist to the old formula.

**Rate Cutting** According to many industry experts, there is a distinct difference between rate cutting and discounting. **Rate cutting** occurs in an inelastic market. Unwarranted rate cuts generate new business for one property only by luring the customer away from another property. Discounting, on the other hand, attracts new customers to the industry, benefiting all properties. Discounting seeks out the stay-at-home customer, the visit-friends-or-family customer, and the let's-camp-out customer. Rate cutting aims at the guest already staying in a competitor's hotel across the road or down the boulevard.

Competitors, who are the source of the new business, counter with rate cuts, and the price war is on. A decline in price per room and in gross sales, rather than the hoped-for increase in occupancy, is the net result. Some resort localities outlaw price wars by making it a misdemeanour to post rates outside the establishment. Printed rate schedules are permitted; however, advertising on the marquee is not allowed. Conversely, other communities actually require room rates to be posted outside the property. In such cases, the lowest and highest posted room rates on the marquee establish the rate parameters that the customer can expect to pay. This reduces the unsavoury practice of "sizing up" the walk-in guest before quoting a room rate.

The long list of special rates (discussed later in the chapter) proves that not all rate variations are viewed as rate cutting. Perhaps they must merely stand the test of time. The **family plan**, in which all children roomed with their parents are accommodated without charge, caused dissension when it first appeared. It is today a legitimate business builder. So, too, is the free room given to convention groups for every 50 or 100 paid rooms. Like any good sales inducement, special rates should create new sales (elasticity), not make the product available at a lower price. For once sold at a lower rate, it is almost impossible to get the buyer to pay the original price.

Once established, rates are not easily adjusted. Increases must be undertaken slowly if they are not to affect patronage. It does not matter that the rate was too low to begin with. Rate reductions will bring no complaints if the initial rates were too high. Opening with rates that are too high may do devastating damage before the adjustment is made. Excessive rates create bad word-of-mouth advertising that takes time and costly sales promotions to counteract.

**Elasticity of Lodging Taxes** One rate component over which hotel managers have little or no control is local lodging taxes. In Canada, taxes are imposed at three levels: (1) property taxes go to the local municipality, (2) taxes on food, beverage, and rooms go to the province (PST), and (3) goods and services tax (GST) goes to the federal government.

**Exhibit 9-3** ▶
This exhibit demon-
strates the high taxes
paid by the hotel indus-
try (excluding property
taxes, which appear in
Exhibit 9-4).

## Room Taxes on Accommodation Industry in Canada, 2004

| Province | Supplementary Room Tax | PST and/or GST on Rooms | PST and/or GST on Other Goods |
|---|---|---|---|
| British Columbia | 2%[1] | 15% | 14% (Liquor 17%) |
| Alberta | 5% | 7% | 7% |
| Saskatchewan | | 13% | 13% |
| Manitoba | | 14% | 14% |
| Ontario | 3% Toronto[2] | 12% | 15% |
| Quebec | $2 per room[3] | 15%[4] | 15%[4] |
| New Brunswick | | 15%[5] | 15%[5] |
| Nova Scotia | 1.5% Halifax[7] | 15%[5] | 15%[5] |
| Prince Edward Island | | 17% | 17% |
| Newfoundland | 3% St. John's[6] | 15%[5] | 15%[5] |

[1]An additional 1% or 2% municipal and regional district tax on accommodation is collected in Chilliwack, North Vancouver, Oak Bay, Parksville, Prince Rupert, Qualicum Beach, Richmond, Rossland, Saanich, Smithers, Surrey, Vancouver, Victoria and Whistler. In Vancouver, 100% of funds go to Tourism Vancouver. Also 1.65% of the 8% sales tax on hotels province wide is dedicated to funding Tourism BC.

[2]There is a 3% Destination Marketing Fee on hotels in the Greater Toronto Area (GTA).

[3]There is a room tax of $2.00 per room. The PST and GST are then calculated on the room taxes (cascading tax). The money is returned to each tourism association minus 2% collection fee.

[4]Montréal, Laval, Québec City and area, Outaouais, Charlevoix, Saguenay-Lac-Saint-Jean, Chaudière-appalaches, Eastern Townships, and in July 2003, Gaspésie and Centre-du Québec.

[5]The PST and GST have been harmonized (HST).

[6]In St John's there is an additional 3% room tax. Two percent is used to fund the Avalon Visitors and Convention Bureau and 1% to bring down the debt on the Convention Centre.

[7]The City of Halifax has a 1.5% tax with 1% going to the Visitor and Convention Bureau and 0.5% placed in trust for special marketing promotions.

Provincial taxes (PST) and federal taxes (GST) are charged on rooms in most areas of Canada, as well as on a host of other items, including food and beverage purchases by the guest (see Exhibit 9-3). Operating with increasingly tight budgets, cities are lured into the easy money available from increasing property taxes on the hotel industry (see Exhibit 9-4). As you can see, many Canadian cities have the highest property tax rates in North America.

**Taxing Demand** According to the Hotel Association of Canada, in 2004 the hotel industry paid out the following amounts in taxes:

| | |
|---|---|
| Federal | $2.2 billion |
| Provincial | $1.8 billion |
| Municipal | $0.9 billion |
| Total | $4.9 billion |

Looking at 50 destinations around the globe, the World Tourism Organization (WTO) concluded, "taxes on tourism are proliferating . . . in some cases they can stifle tourism and cause a net loss in revenues for a destination." According to the WTO, roughly 73 percent of the destinations studied had raised tourism-related taxes over

**Exhibit 9-4** ▶
Canadian cities pay some
of the highest property
taxes in the world. In
fact, Toronto, Ontario,
has the highest property
tax on hotels of any city
in Canada.

| Property Taxes as a Percentage of Hotel Revenue | |
|---|---|
| **Toronto** | **12.5%** |
| **Montreal** | **8.5%** |
| **Halifax** | **7.9%** |
| **Vancouver** | **7.5%** |
| **Edmonton** | **7.5%** |
| New York | 6.9% |
| San Francisco | 6.5% |
| Dallas | 5.6% |
| **Calgary** | **4.5%** |
| **St. John's** | **4.2%** |
| Atlanta | 3.7% |
| Los Angeles | 2.49% |

the past several years. Indeed, governments are finding creative ways to levy new taxes against tourists—more than 40 different kinds of taxes were identified, including many new ones (like environmental taxes) that had never before existed.

The Hotel Association of Canada is consistently lobbying governments for reduced taxes, pointing out among other things that the hotel industry is one of the few industries in the country that consistently creates jobs and generates large amounts of foreign revenue.

## The Discounting Dilemma

In those markets where demand is strong, competing hotels continue to push rates to new ADR heights. Hotels find it easier to sell expensive rooms, and price-sensitive guests find few properties willing to bargain on rate. This is not the case in all markets. In markets where demand is soft, the industry tears down the very prices it worked so hard to build. And like anything else, it is easier and faster to destroy than to build. In markets where discounting is rampant, the only sure winner is the customer who buys a quality product for a fraction of the price. If and when occupancy demand finally catches up to rooms supply, the industry finds itself dug into a deep hole. After becoming accustomed to discounted rates, customers perceive full rates as a very poor value.

Hotel customers are becoming increasingly aware of the room rate discount game. Travel articles tout the same mantra to all customers: shop around for your best rate. Many customers have trained themselves to ask for the discount when booking lodging accommodations. This creates the image that standard prices are unfair and that the industry needs to discount because the quality of the product does not warrant full price.

**Discounting Profitability** Room discounting is designed to increase occupancy at the cost of a lowered room rate. If the resulting occupancy increase is sufficient, it covers the lost revenues from reduced rates. In such a situation, both parties are happy—the guest pays less for the room and the hotel makes a higher profit from having created more room demand.

However appealing these potential profits are, rate discounting has a negative side as well. In fact, the whole idea of discounting rates to increase demand

| Current Occupancy (%) | Percent of Rate Discount | | | |
|---|---|---|---|---|
| | **10%** | **15%** | **20%** | **25%** |
| 50 | 55.56 | 58.82 | 62.50 | 66.67 |
| 55 | 61.11 | 64.71 | 68.75 | 73.33 |
| 60 | 66.67 | 70.59 | 75.00 | 80.00 |
| 65 | 72.22 | 76.47 | 81.25 | 86.67 |
| 70 | 77.78 | 82.35 | 87.50 | 93.33 |
| 75 | 83.33 | 88.24 | 93.75 | 100.00 |

▲
**Exhibit 9-5**
Shown is a rate-discounting equivalency table. Figures in columns two through five (listed as 10 percent through 25 percent) reflect the new occupancy percentages required in order to produce the same gross revenues the hotel was generating before the rate discount. For example, a hotel that discounts rates by 20 percent must increase occupancy from its current 65 percent level to 81.25 percent, or room revenue will fall.

is somewhat suspect. Let's assume that a given hotel property was operating at an annualized occupancy of 60 percent with a $70 ADR. Because the property decides that it wants to increase occupancy, it establishes a rate discounting program. Exhibit 9-5 shows that for this example, a 10 percent rate discount (second column of Exhibit 9-5) requires occupancy to rise to 66.67 percent in order to gross the same revenues as previously earned. That's an 11 percent increase in occupancy required to offset a 10 percent discount in price—just to gross the same revenues!

An 11 percent increase in occupancy may not be easy in a community experiencing, say, only a 3 percent demand growth. To accomplish an 11 percent increase, some other lodging operation(s) will lose customers. Herein lies the biggest problem: As competing lodging properties catch wind of your discounting program, they too will begin to discount. Ultimately, a rate war will ensue, and the only winner will be the customer who pays the reduced rate.

**Examples of Discounted Rates** Discounted or special rates come in a variety of shapes and sizes. Some merely provide a slight discount from the rack rate, as when a hotel offers a 10 percent price reduction for CAA or CARP members. Other special rates, such as volume discounting programs and seasonal price reductions, are quite significant, reducing the posted rate up to 50 percent, 75 percent, or even more.

The reordering of rates is part of the shakeout of segmentation. Rates are a function of supply and demand, and in a perfect economy these two variables move toward equilibrium. However, for now, *special rates*—a term that is preferable to *discounted rates*—are in. The list of those entitled to special rates is limited only by the imagination of the marketing department.

One hotel chain has special rates for teachers and a different rate for students. Most have discounts for senior citizens; almost all allow children to stay in the room with their parents at no charge. Special introductory rates are a common tactic for launching a new hotel. The same tradition that gives police officers discounts in the coffee shop gives other uniformed groups such as the clergy and the military discounts off the room rack. And so the list grows.

Travel agents and travel writers usually get free accommodations while they are on familiarization trips. At other times, the special rate is a standard 50 percent discount, unless, of course, they come during the height of the busy season.

Hawaii's *kamaiina* rate (literally, "old-timer's rate") is an interesting case of special rates. A class-action suit was filed by a Californian on the grounds that the 25 percent discount granted to Hawaiian residents was discriminatory. The court denied the argument. The judge found that "offering a discount to certain clients, patrons, or other customers based on an attempt to attract their business is [not] unlawful." The decision is important because it shows the other side of the issue. Rates that are raised to discourage business from certain persons might well be judged as discriminatory. Rates that are lowered to attract certain persons are viewed quite differently, at least by one court.

All rate discounts should be aimed at the development of new markets and should be phased out as that market stabilizes. It does not work that way in practice. Over time, many special rates become part of the established rate structure. Described below are some of the more common examples of discounted rates found in most hotels.

**Seasonal Rates** Posted rack rates can be changed, or they can include seasonal variations. Season and off-season rates are quoted by most resort hotels, with incremental increases and decreases coming as the season approaches and wanes (see Exhibit 9-6). The poor weekend occupancy of urban hotels has forced them to offer a seasonal rate of sorts—a discounted weekend rate.

Hotel capacity in many resort communities is vast, able to handle great numbers of tourists during periods of peak demand. Because of this glut of hotel rooms available for high-season demand, low-season rates are often deeply discounted—so steeply, in fact,

**Exhibit 9-6 ▶**
The Bear Trail Ultra Luxury Couples Resort, located in Algonquin Park, Ontario, shows a rate sheet with different rates for different days of the week and different periods of the year.

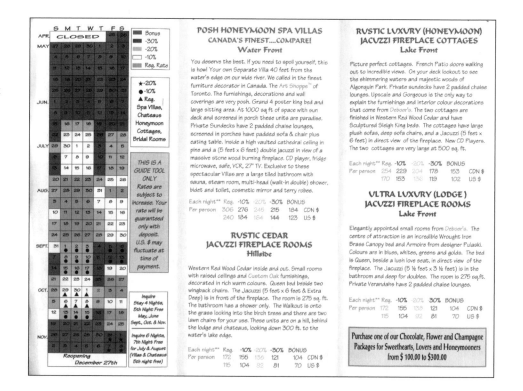

that many resort properties once closed their doors during low-occupancy seasons. This practice changed some 10 or 15 years ago. Today, very few resort properties actually close for the off-season. The expense of reopening the facility, training and hiring new staff each year, and operating a skeleton crew to maintain the closed facility combined to change the economics of closing the property. Instead, resorts remain open, steeply discounting rooms to value-conscious guests. In Canada, many resorts spent large amounts of money winterizing their properties. The growing popularity of winter sports such as cross-country skiing, snowmobiling, and ice fishing has contributed to this growth market.

**Weather-Related Discounts** When it comes to negotiating group rates, even nature gets involved. A growing trend designed to reduce the length of the low or shoulder season at certain resorts is a weather discount factor. Credits or discounts against the rate are offered to guests for each day it rains or stays unseasonably cool.

Obviously, this is risky business, and few resorts are yet offering such plans. However, select Hiltons and Marriotts are currently on the bandwagon, and others are sure to follow. Indeed, at least one Marriott resort offers a "temperature guarantee" package that they have insured through Lloyd's of London!

**Weekly Rates** Weekly rates, which are less than seven times the daily rate, are offered occasionally. Improved forecasting and increased revenues in all the other departments compensate for the reduction in room revenue.

Both the daily rate—assume $170—and the weekly rate—assume $1050—are recorded by the clerk on the registration card and, later, on the guest bill. The $170 rate is charged daily through the sixth day, when a $30 charge is posted. In this way, the daily charge is earned until the guest meets the weekly commitment. If one-seventh of the weekly charge were posted daily, the hotel would be at a disadvantage if the guest left before the week was up, as frequently happens. One variation on weekly rates leaves the daily rate intact but discounts services such as valet, laundry, and greens fees.

**Corporate Rates** North America's corporations do a great deal of business with the nations' hotels. Corporations and hotel chains are synergetic. Corporations have offices and plants worldwide. Employees at all levels (management, personnel, sales, engineering, accounting) travel in vast numbers. They visit the very countries and cities in which the hotel chains have opened their properties worldwide. The synergy works when the employees of a certain corporation stay in the hotels of a given chain. By guaranteeing a given number of room nights per year, the corporation negotiates a better rate, a corporate rate, from the hotel chain.

Reducing room rates is only part of the discount. Reducing the number of rooms needed to close the deal is a more subtle form of discounting. Not many years ago, corporate rates required 1000 room nights per year. Recent figures place the level as low as 50.

The figures were pushed lower by the appearance of third-party negotiators rather than by the astuteness of corporate travel desks. Corporations with numbers that were too small to negotiate on their own were included under the umbrella of room consolidators. Third-party volume buyers who were in no business other than negotiating discounts with hotels (and airlines) represented numerous companies and developed a tough rate-negotiating base. Hotels responded by dealing directly with the smaller corporate accounts, bypassing the travel agents and the consolidators.

Technology has altered the corporate discount picture as well. In the past, major corporations negotiated favourable rates by promising a large annual room volume with a given chain. However, no one really counted, and room volume (actual or anticipated) was never verified. With the increasing sophistication of central reservations systems (CRSs), most major hotel chains are now able to accurately track a corporation's total room volume chain-wide. Corporate room activities at franchised properties, parent properties, and through the CRS are combined into a quarterly volume report. Renaissance Hotels, for example, produces quarterly reports for more than 1800 of its major corporate accounts. These reports take the guesswork out of room rate negotiations and give both the hotel chain and the corporation an accurate picture of used volume.

Corporate rates are now one of the panels in the mural of discounting. However, their implementation has left still another irritant between travel agents and hoteliers. Slashing rates low enough to compete for corporate business leaves the hotel little margin for paying commissions. Travel agents get no commission when they book rooms for corporate clients who have negotiated special rates with the hotel. The travel agent who makes the reservation to accommodate the corporate client is in a dilemma. Either book the room and get no commission or tell the corporate clients to book their own rooms.

**Commercial Rates Commercial rates** are the small hotel's answer to corporate rates. Without the global chain's size to negotiate national corporate contracts, smaller hotels make arrangements with small commercial clients. Such understandings might account for 5 or 10 room nights per year for a manufacturer's representative or salesperson travelling on a personal expense account. Few hotels actually distinguish between corporate and commercial rates. The two terms are effectively synonymous.

**Government Per Diems** Federal, provincial or territorial, and local governments reimburse travelling employees up to a fixed dollar amount. This per diem (per day) cap is made up of two parts: room and meals. Reimbursement is made on the actual cost of the room (a receipt is required) but no more than the maximum. Anyone travelling on government business is reluctant to pay more than the per diem room allowance, since the agency will not reimburse the excess unless preapproved. Meal reimbursement is a given number of dollars per day and generally requires no receipts.

Key cities, those with higher costs of living, are given higher caps. The Treasury Board of Canada Secretariat publishes the per diem rates for meals and incidentals that apply to federal employees. The distinct market segment covers all federal civilian employees, military personnel, and recently, cost-reimbursed federal contractors.

In Canada, hotels may submit a tender for government business on Canada's official public-sector electronic tendering service called MERX (www.merx.com). MERX has levelled the playing field so that businesses of any size can have easy, affordable access to billions of dollars in contracting opportunities with the federal government and participating provincial and municipal governments.

Hotels approved for use by government employees must accept their special rate (normally the best discounted rate) reservations on a last-room availability basis and cannot reject these discounted rates. Some other special rates are on a space-available basis, but not government rates. *Space available* means that rooms are not confirmed until close to the date of arrival. All government employees carry a photo ID card and government contractors would have an introduction letter.

**Employee Courtesy Rates** Special rates are extended to employees of the chain when they travel to other properties. Indeed, for the large chains, this is actually a market segment. Substantial discounts from the hotel's minimum rate plus upgrade whenever possible result in a very attractive bargain. Special rates are always provided on a space-available basis. Employee-guests are accepted only if rooms are vacant when they present themselves (some chains allow reservations a few weeks before arrival if projected occupancy is below 75 percent or so.)

Offering a complimentary or discounted employee room is an inexpensive way for chains to supplement their employee benefits packages. Because such rooms are provided on a space-available basis, there is little associated cost (aside from house-keeping) to providing the employee with a free or deeply discounted rate. And many chains find some real benefits in increased morale and motivation as employees take advantage of the chain's discounted rooms.

Indeed, some chains actually listen to their employees. They request visiting employees to fill out evaluation forms complete with comments and suggestions for improvement. If carefully monitored and tracked, this type of "secret shopper" program can have enormous advantages to the chain.

**It Pays to Pay Rack Rate** Although not really a discount, some upscale chains are experimenting with added perks for guests who actually pay full rack rate. The perks include such valuable amenities as free use of a cellular telephone, limousine service to the airport and nearby shopping, free dry cleaning, and even free food items. Several Ritz-Carlton properties allow full–rack rate guests an extended checkout until 6 P.M. Four Seasons hotels give deluxe accommodations (a free upgrade) to rack rate guests.

**Senior Citizen Rates** According to the 2001 census, there are currently more than 9.2 million Canadians over the age of 50, representing 28.5 percent of the Canadian population. In addition to these age-related statistics, it is important to note that senior citizens (defined as 50-plus years of age by some organizations) represent the fastest-growing travel market. Canadian Association of Retired People (CARP) has more than 400 000 members in Canada.

Although seniors are by no means a homogeneous group, they have certain features and expectations in common. First, people over the age of 50 are the best money savers in the world. As such, when they travel (and they love to travel), they're careful with money. They try to find travel bargains, aided by the fact that they have such flexible travel schedules. When asked about their preferences, seniors listed discounted buffet breakfasts, complimentary newspapers, and free cable television as their top lodging amenities. They also seem to appreciate hotels where grandchildren stay for free, low-cholesterol and low-sodium menu items are offered, bathtub grab bars are provided, and large-digit alarm clocks and telephones are available. Chains such as Ramada Inns, Howard Johnson, and Hilton, to name a few, are among the leaders in marketing to senior travellers.

**Infinite Other Discounts** There are an unlimited number of additional rate discounting possibilities. Large groups, such as CAA and CARP, no longer have a monopoly on special rates. Any group that can produce even a few room nights per year is negotiating discounted rates.

One growing mid-sized market is bank clubs. Members of credit unions or banks and holders of numerous credit cards now find discounted rates part of their incentive package. Some of these groups charge for the service; others provide it free as a means of attracting and holding bank customers.

The Entertainment Card, Quest International, and other travel clubs carry more clout today than ever before. By providing members with deep discounts (usually about half of rack rate) for travelling during off-peak periods, such clubs provide a win–win–win product. The travel club wins because it charges members a fee to join,

▲
**Exhibit 9-7**
Since its introduction in 1998, Priceline.com has sold more than 7 million hotel rooms through its online auction service. In its own words, here is how the process works:

> *Every night, thousands of hotel rooms go unsold throughout the country. That's lost revenue for the hotels, and a great opportunity for priceline customers! Tell us where and when you want to go, select the hotel quality level (1–5 stars), tell us how much you want to pay, and guarantee your request with a major credit card. We'll take your offer to all the participating hotels in the city or area you select (with priceline, you'll always stay in a nationally recognized, name-brand or quality independent hotel). If your offer is accepted, we'll immediately book the room(s) you requested, at the price you want to pay!*

members win by gaining access to substantial travel discounts, and hotels win when rooms fill (albeit at discounted rates) during less busy periods.

Hotels must be extremely careful, however, to limit the use of such discounts to the slower periods of the year. It's a costly mistake to replace a full-paying rack rate or corporate guest with an Entertainment Card customer on a sold-out night. On the other hand, it makes good sense to attract such deeply discounted business on nights when the hotel is unlikely to fill. Yield management is the tool for making this decision.

Auctioning is a form of discounting that is gaining popularity even at the smallest market level—the individual traveller. Auctioning allows hotels, airlines, and rental car agencies to enter a product-available database marketed directly to the traveller through technology available to the average person (see Exhibit 9-7). The guest—say, Carl Jones—decides where he is travelling to, the dates and times he wishes to travel, and any specifications (must be a four-star property, a mid-sized car, etc.) related to the trip. He is then asked to quote his own rate!

If a hotel, airline, and/or rental car agency informs the database that this is a reasonable offer, Jones gets the deal as bid. He never knows until the offer is accepted which airline he will fly, which hotel will accommodate him, or which rental car he will drive. If the bid is too low, Jones places a time limit on his offer and waits to see whether the various travel components in question will respond favourably.

Companies such as Priceline.com, Bid4Travel, LuxuryLink.com, SkyAuction.com (to name a few) have taken inventory auctioning to new levels. By matching millions of potential buyers with millions of vacant rooms (and available rental cars, empty airline seats, etc.), travel auction companies have created a growing niche for themselves. To qualify for deep discounts, travel auction companies often require a degree of flexibility on the part of the customer (non-prime-time flight schedules and less-popular travel dates are the norm). As the popularity of travel auction websites continues to grow, and their contribution to total rooms and other services sold continues to rise, customers will find their purchasing clout rising as well. The result will be more peak-time and high-demand travel bookings.

**Complimentary Rooms** Hotel managers should be as reluctant to give away complimentary (**comp**) rooms as automobile sales managers are to give away free cars. However, both the perishability of the room and the low variable cost of housing an occupant change this reality. Comps are used for business promotion, as charitable giveaways, and as perks.

By custom, complimentary rates are extended to other hoteliers. The courtesy is reciprocated, resulting in an industry-wide fringe benefit for owners and senior managers. Such comps rarely include food or beverage (costs are too high), even in American plan hotels. As mentioned earlier, another portion of the travel industry—travel agents and travel writers—are comp'd during **FAM trips**. Deregulation permitted FAM trip comps by the airlines, which have now joined the hotel industry in developing site inspection tours for the travel industry.

Association executives, who are considering the property as a possible meeting place, also make site inspections. Site visits are comp'd even though some association executives have been known to abuse the industry standard by using site inspection opportunities to vacation with their families. Comp rates as part of the group's meeting were discussed previously, and these are considered to be acceptable standard practice.

Comps are given to famous persons whose presence has publicity value. Comps are used as promotional tools in connection with contests in which the winners receive so many days of free accommodations. In gambling casinos, comps extend to food, beverage, and even airfare from the player's home. In Canada, regulations are tighter, particularly with regards to alcohol, and some giveaways can be seen as an "inducement to gamble" and therefore are regulated or not allowed by law. After all, in a brief period of table play, a high roller can lose many times the cost of these promotions, which on close inspection prove to be surprisingly inexpensive.

**Posting the Comp** Internal control of comps is important! In most hotels, the night auditor is required to submit a report of comps granted each day and by whom. To that end, the actual room rate is recorded in the rate block on the registration card and marked "COMP." Daily, or at the end of the stay, the charge is removed from the folio with an allowance (see Chapter 10). Under this procedure, a daily room charge is made so the room and the guest are both counted in the room and house counts. The total allowances at the end of the accounting period provide statement evidence of the cost of comps.

Some casino hotels have the comp paid by a paper transfer to another department (sales, casino, entertainment). The departmental manager has accountability, and the amounts of the comps appear on that departmental budget.

Recording no value at all is another method for handling free accommodations. No dollar value is charged each day and, therefore, no allowances are required to remove the charges. Neither is a permanent dollar record of comps available. Comps are not usually recorded in room and house counts under this procedure.

The night auditor prepares rate-discrepancy reports for all types of discounts and comps. They are a quick product of a property management system (see Chapter 13). The PMS has all the rack rates in memory. Every room assigned at a special rate is identified and reported to management.

## Additional Rate Factors

Not all variations to the rack rate involve discounting. Some factors actually raise the room charge to a premium level above the posted rack rate or charge additional fees of some form or another. Special, high-demand, premium dates (New Year's Eve, for example) may find rooms selling for rates substantially higher than the hotel's normal rack pricing. Likewise, many hotels post additional charges for extra guests occupying the room. Another example of room prices rising above rack rates can be found in long-term group room negotiations. When the group is contracting for rooms to be delivered years into the future, inflationary issues need to be factored into the quoted rate. Other fees or additional charges increasingly evident in the past several years are the energy surcharge, "resort," and other non-room fees.

**Premium Periods** Some hotels find themselves in the enviable position of having too much business—too much demand during certain premium periods. These premium periods are generally characterized by a national or regional holiday, major sporting event, or other sizable attraction. For example, when Toronto, Vancouver, or Montreal hosts the Grand Prix, when a Canadian Football League (CFL) city hosts the Grey Cup, or when Toronto celebrates winning the Stanley Cup, hotel rates rise dramatically.

Premium rates are charged when normal demand significantly exceeds room supply. In such cases, hotels have been known to charge several times their standard rack rate. Such rate adjustments may be based on "gut feel" and knowledge of what other properties are charging, or yield management software may be used to assist with the decision-making process.

Indeed, rate alone is not the only adjustment the guest will be forced to accept. Other standard practices include closing specific dates to arrival and requiring minimum lengths of stay (see Chapter 4). By carefully following such practices, a manager can extend a sold-out day—say, Grey Cup Sunday—into a sold-out weekend or three-day event.

**Double Occupancy** Double occupancy refers to the use of the room by a second guest. Traditional rules increase the single-occupancy rate by a factor (normally not two) whenever the room is double occupied. However, the price spread between single and double occupancy has been narrowing. One rate is being used more frequently because the major costs of a hotel room are fixed (debt service, taxes, depreciation). Having a second or third occupant adds relatively few incremental costs (linen, soap, tissue). As such, one charge for both single and double occupancy is gaining favour.

Convention rates are almost always negotiated with double occupancy at no extra charge. The more persons in the hotel, the more the hotel benefits from sales in other departments: banquet, bar, casino. Suite charges have also followed that pattern. The room rate is the number of rooms that compose the suite, not the number of guests who occupy it. The room, not the guest, becomes the unit of pricing.

Several arguments support the movement toward a single room price. The fewer rate options, the less confusion there is, and the more rapidly the telephone reservationist can close the sale. Price is a critical issue in package plans or tour bookings, and rates can be shaved closely because the second occupant represents a small additional expense. A third occupant adds a still smaller incremental cost. The incremental cost is almost unnoticed if the extra person shares existing beds. That is what makes family-plan rates attractive. An extra charge is levied if a rollaway bed, which requires extra handling and linen, is required. Suite hotels are popular because the extra hide-a-bed is permanently available as a sofa bed in the room.

With rollaway beds, the used bed is returned to the housekeeping office, where linens are changed and the bed is stored for its next use. With sofa beds, however, the housekeeping department must remember to look at the sofa bed linens after each guest check-out. Guests often use sofa beds during their stay and then fold the sofa bed back up before check-out as a means of straightening the room and creating more floor space. Without careful follow-through by the housekeeping department, new guests can check into a room and find that the sofa bed has been previously used.

Unless the family-rate plan has been quoted, a charge is generally made for the third and subsequent occupants of a room. Even in hotels where single and double occupancy is charged at the same rate, a third or fourth guest probably pays an additional fee. Usually, that added charge is a flat fee—say, $20 per extra person.

Many hoteliers find a flat $20 fee illogical in light of the numerous room types available at the property. Where $20 may be fine for a $100 standard room, it does not seem high enough for a $150 deluxe room or a $200 executive parlour. Indeed, if the hotelier can make the argument that we charge for extra guests because they cost the hotel incremental expenses, that argument is doubly true in premium rooms.

In a standard room, extra guests (whether the second, third, or fourth occupant) cost the hotel in a variety of ways, including extra water and electricity, additional amenities, more towels and linens, and, of course, some wear and tear. These costs are not identical for a standard room and deluxe accommodation. Hotels outfit deluxe rooms with larger bathtubs, more expensive personal amenities, heavier-quality linens, and higher-quality furnishings. An additional person in a deluxe room has a higher incremental cost to the hotel than does an additional person in a standard room.

A flat $20 rate represents a declining percentage of the rate as the quality of the room increases. In a $100 standard room, $20 reflects a 20 percent surcharge. Yet in a $200 executive parlour, $20 reflects only a 10 percent surcharge. In fact, if the $100 standard guest is willing to pay $20 for an extra occupant, it makes sense that the $200 executive-parlour guest would be equally willing to pay something like $40 for an extra guest.

## Time Is Money

Although the actual date of arrival and departure is the primary consideration for establishing the guest charge, the number of hours of occupancy may someday play a role in rate determination. In simple terms, time is already a rate criterion in many hotels.

**Arrival Time** The day of arrival is listed on the reservation, the registration card, and the guest folio. The time of arrival is also indicated on the folio by means of an internal electronic clock operating in the property management system. Assuming that the clock is accurate, the actual minute of check-in is recorded on the electronic folio.

The actual time of arrival is more critical to the American plan hotel, where billing is based on meals taken, than to the European plan operation. American plan arrivals are flagged with a special meal code.

The hour of arrival at a European plan hotel is less critical. An occasional complaint about the promptness of message service or a rare police inquiry might involve the arrival hour. Very, very late arrivals, such as a guest who arrives at 5 A.M. are the exceptions. Somewhere in the early morning hours (5 to 7 A.M.) comes the break between charging for the night just passed and levying the first charge for the day just starting.

Check-in hours are difficult to control. Guest arrivals are dictated haphazardly by travel connections and varying distances. Still, many hotels have established check-in hours. The termination point of a night's lodging is more controllable, so every hotel posts an official check-out hour.

**Departure Time** Check-in and check-out hours are eased or enforced as occupancies fall or rise. Setting the specific check-out hour is left to each hotel. It might be established without any rationale, or it might be the same hour that nearby competitors are using. The proper hour is a balance between the guest's need to complete his or her business and the hotel's need to clean and prepare the room for the next patron.

Seasoned travellers are well aware that check-out extensions are granted by the room clerk if occupancy is light. Under current billing practices, the effort should be made cheerfully whenever the request can be accommodated. If anticipated arrivals require enforcement of the check-out hour, luggage should be stored in the checkroom for the guest's convenience.

Resorts are under more pressure than commercial hotels to expedite check-outs. Vacationing guests try to squeeze the most from their holiday time. American plan houses usually allow the guests to remain through the luncheon hour and a reasonable time thereafter if the meal is part of the rate. Some 90 percent of the resorts surveyed in an American Hotel & Lodging Association (AH&LA) study identified their check-out hour to be between noon and 2 P.M., in contrast to the 11 A.M. through 1 P.M. range used by transient hotels. These same properties assigned new arrivals on a "when-available" basis.

Special techniques in addition to that shown in Exhibit 9-8 have been tried to move the guest along. On the night before departure, the room clerk, the assistant manager, or the social host/hostess calls the room to chat and remind the guest of tomorrow's departure. Today, this task could be assigned to a computer. A more personal touch is a note of farewell left by the room attendant who turns down the bed on the night before departure. A less personal touch is outlined in Exhibit 9-9.

**The 24-Hour Stay** Recently, some hotels have been experimenting with true 24-hour stays. There is no official check-in time and no posted check-out hour. Rather, guests explain their travel plans at the time of reservation and identify their estimated times of arrival and departure. They are then welcome to stay at the hotel an entire 24-hour period for one set room rate.

**Exhibit 9-8** ▶
Permanent bureau tent
card left in each guest
room. Many hotels place
a similar statement on
the registration card.

## CHECK-OUT TIME: 1 P.M.

We would like to ask your cooperation in checking out by 1 P.M. so that we
may accommodate travellers who are beginning their stay. If you require
additional time, you may request a two-hour grace period (until 3 P.M.) from
the assistant manager or the front office manager. If you wish to check out
later, we regret that there must be a $12-per-hour charge, from 3 until 5 P.M.,
for this added service. An additional half-day rate will be charged to guests
who delay their departure until between 5 P.M. and 8 P.M. After 8 P.M., a full-
day rate will be charged. Of course, you are then welcome to remain until
the following afternoon at 1 P.M.

**As an incoming guest, your comfort and convenience depend on these
stipulations. We hope you will visit again soon.**

To qualify for these 24-hour programs, guests must make advance reservations and
identify their estimated hours of arrival and departure at the time they make the reservation. Additionally, guests must pay rack rate—discounted packages do not qualify
for the 24-hour programs. The logic behind such rate/time programs becomes more
evident when you realize that these programs are most likely found at airport properties. Guest arrivals (and departures) are predicated on flight schedules. As such, a hotel
that will accommodate guests' unique 24-hour stays may develop a favourable reputation and earn higher market share.

Therefore, it makes sense to view these 24-hour day programs as marketing tools.
They drive higher rates and hopefully attract unique customer segments who appreciate the unusual policy. Today, these programs are viewed as marketing "gimmicks,"
but so are any policies that differentiate a hotel from its competitor. Only time will tell
if these programs are ushering in a new era of room pricing.

**Incentive Rate Systems** Incentive rate systems have been suggested as a means of
expediting check-outs. First, the check-out period for a normal day's charge would
be established—say, between 11 A.M. and 1 P.M. Guests who leave before 11 A.M.
are charged less than the standard rate, and those who remain beyond 1 P.M. are
charged more. Flexible charges of this type require a new look at the unit of service, shifting from the more traditional measure of a night's lodging to smaller blocks
of time.

Unlike other service industries, hotels have given little consideration to time as a
factor in rate. Arrival and departure times establish broad parameters at best. We can
expect these to narrow as hotel keepers become more concerned with the role of time
in rate structuring. Taken to the other extreme, it is conceivable that the hour will eventually become the basic unit for constructing room rates. Under current practices, a
stay of several hours costs as much as a full day's stay (see Exhibit 9-10).

The total length of stay may also be an issue in the guest's level of satisfaction with
the hotel. Guests with few hours to visit scarcely get enough time to sleep and bathe.
It is the guest with sufficient leisure hours who truly enjoys the property by taking
advantage of relaxation and recreational activities (see Exhibit 9-10).

**Exhibit 9-9** ▶

An excerpt from "The Late Check-Out," in the March 1997 issue of *Lodging Hospitality*. Written by Megan Rowe, Senior Editor, and used with permission.

Recently, while staying at one of the San Antonio Marriotts, I had occasion to make this request. I would be in meetings all morning, and I wasn't scheduled to leave until 3 P.M. I figured I could have lunch, go back to my room and dig out my winter coat and boots, then check out.

The night before I was to leave, I made my request. The clerk asked me what time I wanted to check out. "Three o'clock," I answered.

"You can stay until three, but we'll charge you for a half-day," he said.

At first, I was stunned by the sheer greed this response implied. When I recovered, I asked whether this was an arbitrary decision on his part or a policy of the hotel.

"It's our policy," he said, defensively.

"Is it a new policy?" I responded, trying to keep a smile on my face, "because I've never heard of such a thing."

"No, it's not new, and I don't know what kind of hotels you've been staying in, but it's very common."

First deny my simple request, then try a subtle insult. Good thinking.

This kind of treatment would probably have bothered me in any hotel, but it seemed terribly out of place at a hotel with an otherwise extraordinarily friendly and accommodating staff.

The next day, I visited the front desk, posed the same request—hypothetically—to a different employee, and asked how he would handle it. He said he would ask how late, check to see if the room was booked, and possibly okay it based on whatever information he got from the reservations system. If he wasn't sure, he would check with someone in the back office, and they would most likely okay it. Standard operating procedure, in my experience.

| Guest | Rate Paid | February 14 Arrival | February 15 Departure | Total Hours |
|-------|-----------|---------------------|-----------------------|-------------|
| 1 | $225 | 1 A.M. (FEBRUARY 15) | 6 A.M. | 5 |
| 2 | 225 | 2 P.M. | 11 A.M. | 21 |
| 3 | 225 | 8 A.M. | 3 P.M. | 31 |

▲
**Exhibit 9-10**
Shown are three different hotel room use schedules. Even though each guest pays the same $225 rate, they experience three significantly different lengths of stay.

The first guest arrives very late (1 A.M.) and checks out early (6 A.M.) the next morning. The second guest exactly parallels the hotel's standard check-in and check-out times (2 P.M. and 11 A.M., respectively). The third guest extends arrival and departure times by taking advantage of light occupancy and normal front-office courtesies.

No wonder hotels are looking more closely at hours occupied as one variable in establishing rate. These three guests paid the same rate, yet one guest occupied the room 620 percent more hours than another!

A popular journalist once observed facetiously that the length of time one spends in a hotel room is inversely proportional to the quality of that hotel room. When you arrive at, say, 1 A.M. and need to get some rest for a 7 A.M. flight the next morning, the room will be lavish—there will be vases of roses, trays of food and drink, soft music, a Jacuzzi tub, and candlelight. Conversely, when you have no time commitments and all day to spend in the hotel, it is invariably a poor-quality establishment—there will be no restaurant or lobby, fuzzy TV reception, and a drained swimming pool!

**The American Plan Day** Meals are part of the American plan (AP) rate, as they are with the modified American plan (MAP). Accurate billing requires an accurate record of arrival and departure times. Arrivals are registered with a meal code reflecting the check-in time. For example, a guest arriving at 3 P.M. would be coded with arriving after lunch but before dinner.

A complete AP stay technically involves enough meals on the final day to make up for the meals missed on the arriving day. A guest arriving before dinner would be expected to depart the next day, or many days later, after lunch. Two meals, breakfast and lunch, on the departing day complete the full AP charge, since one meal (dinner) was taken on the arriving day. MAP counts meals in the same manner, except that lunch is ignored.

Guests who take more than the three meals per day pay for the extra at menu prices, or sometimes below menu prices. Sometimes, guests who miss a meal are not charged. That is why it is very important to have the total AP rate fairly distributed between the room portion and the meal portion. Meal rates are set and are standardized for everyone. Higher AP rates must reflect better rooms, since all guests are entitled to the same menu.

AP and MAP hotels have a special charge called tray service. It is levied on meals taken through room service. European plan room service typically contains hidden charges as a means of recovering the extra service. Menu charges are greater than the usual coffee shop prices when the food is delivered to the room. This device is not available to the American plan hotel because meals being delivered to the room are not priced separately. Instead, a flat charge of several dollars per person is levied as a tray service charge.

**Day Rate Rooms** Special rates exist for stays shorter than overnight. These are called **part-day rates**, **day rates**, or sometimes use rates. Day rate guests arrive and depart on the same day.

Day rates make possible an occupancy of greater than 100 percent. Furthermore, costs are low. Nevertheless, the industry has not fully exploited this possibility. Sales of day use rates could be marketed to suburban shoppers and to small, brief meetings. Unfortunately, better airline service has cost hotels day rate business, although capsule rooms at international airports have had some success. Airport properties have promoted their locations as central meeting places for company representatives coming from different sections of the country.

A new day rate market is becoming evident. Motels near campsites and along roadways are attracting campers as a wayside stop during the day. A hot shower, an afternoon by the pool, and a change of pace from the vehicle are great appeals when coupled with a low day rate.

Check-in time is often early morning. Corporate guests prefer to start their meetings early, and truck drivers like to get off the highway before the 8 A.M. rush hour. If clean rooms remain unsold from the previous night, there is little reason to refuse day rate guests early access to the room. Indeed, they may order room service coffee or breakfast as an added revenue bonus.

Since rooms sold for day use only are serviced and made available again for the usual overnight occupancy, the schedule of the housekeeping staff has a great deal to do with the check-out hour. If there are no night room cleaners, the day rate must end early enough to allow room servicing by the day crew. On the other hand, low occupancy would allow a day rate sale even late in the day. Nothing is lost if an additional empty room remains unmade overnight.

There are no rules as to what the hotel should charge for the day room. Some purists suggest that it must be half of the standard rack rate. Others appreciate the extra revenue and are willing to charge whatever seems appropriate. Corporate hotels must remember that their day rate rooms compete with their convention and meeting facilities. A small group of executives might prefer to meet in the day rate guest room with its attached bathroom and access to room service rather than in the larger, impersonal convention meeting room. This can prove detrimental to the hotel if the meeting room sells for two or three times the day rate room.

# Determining the Proper Room Rate

Because a sound room rate structure is fundamental to a sound hotel operation, every manager is sooner or later faced with the question of what is the proper room charge. It is a matter of exceeding complexity because room rates reflect markets and costs, investments and rates of return, supply and demand, accommodations and competition, and not least of all, the quality of management.

Divided into its two major components, room rates must be large enough to cover costs and a fair return on invested capital, and reasonable enough to attract and retain the clientele to whom the operation is being marketed. The former suggests a relatively objective, structured approach that can be analyzed after the fact. The latter is more subjective, involving factors such as the amount of local competition and the condition of the economy at large. There is little sense in charging a rate less than what is needed to meet the first objective; there is little chance of getting a rate more than the competitive ceiling established by the second limitation.

Yield management, the balancing of occupancy and rate, has emerged as the number one component of rate making. Yield management has attracted attention because it introduces two new concepts to room pricing: (1) the industry is selling rooms by an inventory control system for the first time, and (2) the pricing strategy considers for the first time the customer's ability and willingness to pay. This discretionary market, with sensitivity to price, is itself a new phenomenon (see Chapter 4).

In years past, the rate structure was built from the standpoint of internal cost considerations. Yield management has not eliminated that focus. Important as they are, customers are not the only components of price. Cost recovery and investment opportunity are reflected there as well. Depreciation and interest as well as taxes and land costs are outside the hotel–guest relationship but not external to the room charge.

The more traditional components of rate deal with recovering costs, both operating and capital. They deal with profits and break-even projections. Mixed into the equation are competition, price elasticity, and rate cutting. And in the end, the average daily rate earned by the hotel is partly determined by the ability of a reservationist or room clerk to sell up.

# Traditional Rate Calculations

Hotel room rates are derived from a mix of objective measures and subjective values. Expressing room rates numerically gives the appearance of validity, but when the origins of these numbers are best-guess estimates, the results must be viewed with some measure of doubt or uncertainty.

Facts and suppositions combine when hotel managers calculate the room rate. As useful and respected as the following mathematical formulas may be, they are still merely an indication of the final rate. Fine-tuning the formula, establishing corporate and double occupancy prices, and adjusting the rate according to the whims of the community and the marketplace are still the role of management.

**The Hubbart Room Rate Formula** The **Hubbart room rate formula**[1] offers a standardized approach to assigning room rates. The Hubbart formula sets rates from the needs of the enterprise, not from the needs of the guests. The average rate, says the formula, should pay all expenses and leave something for the investor. Valid enough—a business that cannot do this is short lived.

Exhibit 9-11 (a) illustrates the mechanics of the formula. Estimated expenses are itemized and totalled. These include operational expenses by departments ($1 102 800 in the illustration), realty costs ($273 000), and depreciation ($294 750). To these expenses is added a reasonable return on the present fair value of the property: land, building, and furnishings ($414 000). From the total expense package ($2 084 550) are subtracted income from all sources other than room sales ($139 200). This difference ($1 945 350) represents the annual amount to be realized from room sales.

Next—see Exhibit 9-11 (b)—an estimate of the number of rooms to be sold annually is computed. Dividing the number of estimated rooms (22 484) to be sold into the estimated dollars ($1 945 350) needed to cover costs and a fair return produces the average rate to be charged ($86.52). The computations are simple enough; the formula is straightforward enough. Deriving the many estimates is where the weakness lies.

**Shortcomings of the Formula** Like many such calculations, the Hubbart room rate formula is only as accurate as the assumptions on which it was projected. Several such assumptions come immediately to mind for the Hubbart formula: What percentage is "reasonable" as a fair return on investment? What occupancy rate appears most attainable? What are the cost projections for payroll, various operating departments, utilities, and administrative and general?

The formula leaves the rooms department with the final burden after profits and losses from other departments. However, inefficiencies in other departments should not be covered by a high, non-competitive room rate. Neither should unusual profits in other departments be a basis for charging room rates below what the market will bring.

There is some justification in having rooms subsidize low banquet prices if these low prices result in large convention bookings of guest rooms. (Incidentally, this is one reason why the food and banquet department should not be leased as a concession.) Similar justification could be found for using higher room rates to cover unusually high dining room repairs and maintenance, or advertising costs. The trade-off is wise if these expenditures produce enough other business to offset lost room revenue resulting from higher room rates.

Additional shortcomings become apparent as the formula is studied. Among them is the projected number of rooms sold. This estimate of rooms sold is itself a function

|  | | | | Example |
|---|---|---|---|---|
| **Operating Expenses** | | | | |
| Rooms department | | | | $467 400 |
| Telecommunications | | | | 60 900 |
| Administrative and general | | | | 91 200 |
| Payroll taxes and employee benefits | | | | 178 200 |
| Marketing | | | | 109 800 |
| Utility costs | | | | 138 900 |
| Property operation and maintenance | | | | 56 400 |
| Total operating expenses | | | | $1 102 800 |
| **Taxes and Insurance** | | | | |
| Real estate and personal property taxes | | | | 67 200 |
| Franchise taxes and fees | | | | 112 200 |
| Insurance on building and contents | | | | 37 200 |
| Leased equipment | | | | 56 400 |
| Total taxes and insurance | | | | $ 273 000 |
| **Depreciation (Standard Rates on Present** | *Value* | | *Rate* | |
| **Fair Value)** | | | | |
| Building | $_____ | at | % | 168 750 |
| Furniture, fixtures, and equipment | $_____ | at | % | 126 000 |
| Total depreciation | | | | $ 294 750 |
| **Reasonable Return on Present Fair** | *Value* | | *Rate* | |
| **Value of Property** | | | | |
| Land | $_____ | at | % | |
| Building | $_____ | at | % | |
| Furniture, fixtures, and equipment | $_____ | at | % | |
| Total fair return | | | | $ 414 000 |
| Total | | | | $2 084 550 |
| **Deduct—Credits from Sources Other Than Rooms** | | | | |
| Income from store rentals | | | | 14 850 |
| Profits from food and beverage operations (if loss, subtract from this group) | | | | 131 400 |
| Net income from other operated departments and miscellaneous income (loss) | | | | (7050) |
| Total credits from sources other than rooms | | | | $ 139 200 |
| Amount to be realized from guest-room sales to cover costs and a reasonable return of present fair value of property | | | | $1 945 350 |

▲
**Exhibit 9-11 (a)**
Although the Hubbart room rate formula was first introduced in 1952, it is still the most widely used means of computing zero-based room rates. By dividing annual fixed costs, variable expenses, and a reasonable return on the property by the estimated number of rooms projected to be sold for the year, the Hubbart formula provides a fairly reliable minimum average rate calculation.

| | Example |
|---|---|
| 1. Amount to be realized from guest-room sales to cover costs and a reasonable return on present fair value of property [from part (a)] | $1 945 350 |
| 2. Number of guest rooms available for rental | 88 |

| | | Example |
|---|---|---|
| 3. Number of available rooms on annual basis (item 2 multiplied by 365) | 100% | 32 120 |
| 4. Less: Allowance for average vacancies | 30% | 9 636 |
| 5. Number of rooms to be occupied at estimated average occupancy | 70% | 22 484 |
| 6. Average daily rate per occupied room required to cover costs and a reasonable return on present fair value (item 1 divided by item 5) | | $ 86.52 |

▲
**Exhibit 9-11 (b)**
Computing the denominator, the estimated number of rooms to be sold for the year, requires an occupancy projection. But it is difficult to project the occupancy before one knows the average rate to be charged—a real conundrum!

of the very rate being computed. How can a hotel estimate the number of rooms it will sell before first knowing the average rate for which it will sell each room—yet that is exactly what the Hubbart formula requires! Rate, in turn, is a function of double occupancy. Yet the increased income from double occupancy is not a component of the Hubbart formula. Neither component (the impact of rate on occupancy and the impact of double occupancy on rate) is projected.

The average rate computed ($86.52) is not the actual rate used by the hotel. Hotels use a number of rate classes, with various proportions of the total number of rooms assigned to each classification (see Exhibit 9-6). The actual average rate will be a weighted average of the rooms occupied. Reflected therein are the range of accommodations that the hotel is offering and the guest's purchase of them based on nearby competition.

**Square Foot Calculations** To compensate for the fact that the Hubbart room rate formula provides no rate detail by room classification, some managers use a square foot calculation. The basis for this is the fact that more expensive and higher-quality guest rooms are invariably larger than standard rooms at the same property. Therefore, rather than calculating the Hubbart room rate per room sold, this variation calculates the rate on a per-square-foot basis.

To illustrate, assume that the hotel presented in Exhibit 9-11 has a total of 27 250 square feet of space in its 88 guest rooms. With occupancy of 70 percent, there would be an average of 19 075 square feet sold per day. With an annual required return of $1 945 350, the daily required return is $5329.73 ($1 945 350 divided by 365 days). Therefore, each square foot of rented room space must generate $0.27941 per day ($5329.73 divided by 19 075 square feet sold per day), or almost 28 cents in daily revenue. As a result, a 300-square-foot room would sell for $83.82 (300 square feet times $0.28) and a 450-square-foot room would sell for $125.73. Assuming that the hotel sells all room types in equal ratios to the number of rooms available in each type, this square foot calculation works as well as any other means for determining individual room type rates.

**The Building Cost Room Rate Formula** Time and repetition have created an industry axiom saying that rate can be evaluated by a rule of thumb (the building cost rate formula): The average room rate should equal $1 per $1000 of construction cost. For a 200-room hotel costing $14 million (including land and land development, building, and public space but excluding furniture, fixtures, and equipment—FFE), the average rate should be $70 ($14 million ÷ 200 rooms ÷ $1000).

The building cost method is about as reliable as an old cookbook's direction: "Flavour to taste." Despite some very radical changes throughout the years, the rule is still being quoted on the theory that rising construction costs are being matched by rising room rates. Higher construction costs are a function of room size as well as building materials and labour. Current rooms are 100 percent to 200 percent larger than rooms were even 25 or 30 years ago.

Cost of construction (including the costs of land and land improvement) includes other factors: type of construction, location, high-rise versus low-rise buildings, and the cost of money. Luxury properties can cost five or six times as much per room as economy hotels. Land costs vary greatly across the nation. Comparing Vancouver and Winnipeg is a lesson in futility. Toronto and Vancouver may be stretching toward a $400-per-night room rate, but that is not the expectation of the hotel manager in Regina, Saskatchewan.

Economy chains have stopped advertising a minimum national rate. Each locale has its own cost basis for building, borrowing, taxing, and paying labour. Budgets aim only for a percentage rate below that of local competitors. Advertising a single rate as part of the national company logo is no longer feasible.

According to the Hotel Association of Canada, the average price per room for a hotel sold in Canada has increased from $29 700 in 1994 to $63 000 in 2004, an increase of 53.5 percent in just ten years. In 1994, 47 hotels (4056 rooms) changed hands compared to 47 (5633 rooms) in 2004. The peak of the market appears to have been in 2001 when 39 hotels sold in Canada (6426 rooms) for an average per room price of $111 300. Averages can however be misleading as the figures above do not denote location or quality of the hotels sold.

In terms of new supply of rooms across Canada, the total inventory of rooms was increased by 1.3 percent in 2004. Other years are as follows: 2003, 1.3 percent; 2002, 1.1 percent; 2001, 1.6 percent; and 2000, 2.2 percent.

Conditions seesaw, first supporting the rule and then undermining it. The general rise in land and construction costs has been offset by improvements in design and reductions in labour force. The rise in financing costs has been offset by the lower costs of older hotels still in use. Since building costs are tied to historical prices, older hotels have lower financing costs (and probably lower real estate taxes, too) to recover. That is true, at least, until they're sold.

The building cost formula, a standard whose first known reference was in 1947, is still as roughly accurate today as it probably was back then.[2]

**The Cost of Renovation** The costs of additions, property rehabs, or new amenities such as pools fall within the scope of the $1 per $1000 rule. First, the cost of the upgrade is determined on a per-room basis. The installation of an in-room air conditioner might be priced at $1500 per room. A general-use item such as a sauna would need a cost-per-room equivalent. The cost (assume $150 000) would be divided by the number of rooms (100) to arrive at the cost per unit.

Exhibit 9-12 illustrates an example of a major hotel renovation program. This exhibit assumes that a 200-room hotel spends $1 303 240 renovating its rooms, for an average cost of $6516.20 per room. The exhibit also assumes that the hotel has a 12 percent cost of funds (interest rate), although today financing may be available for a considerably lower interest rate. With a $6516.20 expense per room at 12 percent interest and 15 years of debt repayment, $956.74 is the annualized cost of principal and interest per room per year. Therefore, the rule of thumb established in the building cost rate formula suggests that the hotel needs to charge an additional $0.96 per occupied room night to compensate for the expense incurred due to renovation. With that kind of information, management can evaluate the likelihood of the additional investment being competitive in the eyes of the guest who is asked to pay the increased price.

**The Ideal Average Room Rate** The firm of Laventhol & Horwath designed the ideal average room rate as a means of testing the room rate structure. According to this approach, a hotel should sell an equal percentage of rooms in each rate class instead of filling from the bottom up. An occupancy of 70 percent should mean a 70 percent occupancy in each rate category. Such a spread produces an average rate identical to the average rate earned when the hotel is completely full—that is, an **ideal average room rate**.

Exhibit 9-13 illustrates the computation used to derive the ideal rate. This formula assumes that each room type (standard, executive, deluxe, and suite) fills to the same percentage of rooms sold as every other room type. At 70 percent hotel occupancy, 70 percent of the standard rooms will be sold, 70 percent of the executive rooms will be sold, 70 percent of the deluxe rooms will be sold, and 70 percent of the suites will be sold.

Once calculated, the manager is armed with a valuable figure, the ideal average room rate. As long as rates remain constant and the ratio of double occupancy does not change, the manager has a valid ideal rate. If the actual average rate on any given day or week is higher than the ideal average rate, the front-office staff has been doing a great job of upselling guests. Either that or the hotel has failed to provide a proper number of high-priced rooms. Such a hotel's market appears to be interested in rooms selling above the average, so room types and rates should be adjusted upward.

An average room rate lower than the ideal, and this is usually the case, indicates several problems. There may not be enough contrast between the low- and high-priced rooms. Guests will take the lower rate when they are buying nothing extra for the higher rate. If the better rooms do, in fact, have certain extras—better exposure and newer furnishings—the lack of contrast between the rate categories might simply be a matter of poor selling at the front desk (discussed later in the chapter).

Check-in at the front desk represents the last opportunity to upsell the guest to a more expensive room accommodation. Good sales abilities coupled with a differentiated product gives the hotel a strong chance to increase middle- and high-priced room sales. Such comments as "I see you have reserved our standard room; do you realize for just 12 more dollars I can place you in a newly refurbished deluxe room with a complimentary continental breakfast?" go a long way toward satisfying both the guest and the bottom line.

A faulty internal rate structure is another reason why the ideal room rate might not be achieved. The options—the range of rates being offered—might not appeal to the customer. Using the ideal room rate computation, the spread between rates could

### 1. Renovation Project Parameters

| | Guest rooms: Cost per Room | Hallways: Cost per Door | Meeting Space: Cost per Square Foot | Lobby: Cost per Square Foot | Food & Beverage Outlets: Cost per Seat | Total Project |
|---|---|---|---|---|---|---|
| Soft costs[a] | $       515 | $       194 | $       2 | $       3 | $       212 | N/A |
| Hard costs[b] | 3305 | 755 | 5 | 18 | 1342 | N/A |
| Subtotals | $ 764 000 | $ 189 800 | $ 105 000 | $ 73 500 | $ 170 940 | $1 303 240 |

### 2. Basic Hotel Information

- A 200-room full-service airport hotel
- 15 000 square feet of convention space
- 3500 square feet of lobby space
- One 110-seat restaurant and bar
- 12 percent cost of funds interest rate
- Total renovation cost $1 303 240 (as shown above)

### 3. Project Cost per Average Guest Room

- $1 303 240 project divided by 200 rooms equals $6516.20 per room.
- Assume that the $6516.20 project cost per average room is to be repaid over 15 years at a 12 percent cost of funds rate.
- The combined principal and interest charge is $956.74 per room per year.

### 4. Impact of the Building Cost Room Rate Formula

- The $956.74 annualized cost per average room divided by $1000 rule-of-thumb formula equals $0.96 increase per average room night sold.

[a]Soft costs include professional and contractor fees, sales tax, and shipping fees.
[b]Hard costs include construction costs, labour, materials, and all FF&E.

▲
**Exhibit 9-12**
Figures developed in this exhibit come from an actual renovation project of a 200-room full-service hotel. Applying the $1 per $1000 building cost room rate formula to this project results in roughly an added 96 cents in required per-room revenue. Note: Unit measurements are indicated in square feet.

be adjusted. According to the authors of the formula, increases should be concentrated in those rooms on those days for which the demand is highest. That begins with an analysis of rate categories.

**Rate Categories** The discrepancy between the rates the hotel furnishes and those the guests prefer can be pinpointed with a simple chart. Guest demands and the hotel offerings are plotted side by side.

Guest demands are determined by a survey of registration card rates over a period of time. The survey should not include days of 100 percent occupancy when the guest had no rate choice. Special rate situations would also be excluded. Using elementary arithmetic, the percentage of total registrations is determined for each rate class.

| Room Type | Number of Rooms by Type | Percent of Double Occupancy | Single Rate | Double Rate |
|---|---|---|---|---|
| Standard | 140 | 30 | $ 80 | $ 95 |
| Executive | 160 | 5 | 105 | 105 |
| Deluxe | 100 | 25 | 120 | 140 |
| Suite | 75 | 70 | 160 | 160 |
| Total rooms | 475 | | | |

**Calculation Steps**

1. Multiply all standard rooms (140) by their single rate ($80) to get a product of $11 200. Then take the double occupancy percentage for standard rooms (30 percent) times the total number of standard rooms (140) to get 42, the number of double-occupied standard rooms. Next, take the 42 double-occupied standard rooms times the differential between the single and double price ($95 double rate minus $80 single rate equals $15 differential) to get $630. Finally, add the room revenue for standard rooms calculated at the single rate ($11 200) to the additional room revenue received from standard rooms sold at the double rate ($630) to get the full-house room revenue for standard rooms, a total of $11 830.

2. Follow the same procedure for executive rooms: 160 rooms times $105 equals $16 800. The differential between single and double occupancy for executive rooms is zero, so there is no added revenue for double occupancy. The full-house room revenue for executive rooms is $16 800.

3. Follow the same procedure for deluxe rooms: 100 rooms times $120 single rate equals $12 000. In terms of double occupancy, there are 25 deluxe rooms (25 percent double occupancy times 100 rooms equals 25 rooms) sold at a $20 differential ($140 double rate minus $120 single rate equals $20 differential) for a total double occupancy impact of $500. The full-house room revenue for deluxe rooms is $12 500.

4. Follow the same procedure for suites: 75 rooms times $160 equals $12 000. The differential between single and double occupancy for suites is zero, so there is no added revenue for double occupancy. The full-house room revenue for suites is $12 000.

5. Add total revenues from standard rooms ($11 830), executive rooms ($16 800), deluxe rooms ($12 500), and suites ($12 000) for total revenues assuming 100 percent occupancy—ideal revenues. That total ($53 130) divided by rooms sold (475) is the ideal average room rate of $111.85.

*No matter what the occupancy percentage, the ideal average room rate remains the same.*

Try this problem again, assuming, say, 70 percent occupancy. The end result will still be an ideal average room rate of $111.85.

▲
**Exhibit 9-13**
Although Laventhol & Horwath, the firm that developed the ideal average room rate, is no longer in business, the formula lives on. Follow these steps to develop an ideal average room rate for any hotel.

Exhibit 9-14 illustrates the contrast between what the guest buys and what the hotel offers. It also points to the rates that need adjustment.

Exhibit 9-14 assigns 40 percent of the hypothetical hotel to the average room rate. Two additional categories of 20 percent and 10 percent, respectively, appear on both

**Exhibit 9-14** ▶
An analysis of registration cards, over a period of time, will reveal which room rates are purchased most regularly. This sample hotel has five rate classes, representing 10, 20, 40, 20, and 10 percent of all hotel rooms, respectively. However, an analysis of rates purchased suggests a disproportionate percentage of guests opt for class 3 (and fewer guests than expected choose classes 4 and 5).

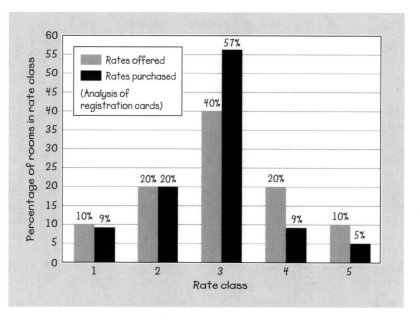

the lower and upper ends. It is the sad history of our industry that hotels fill from the bottom up. Lower-priced rooms are in greatest demand. This means that low occupancy is accompanied by a low average daily rate. It is felt, therefore, that there should be more categories at the lower end of the price scale. These lower categories would be bunched together, while the higher rates would be spread over fewer categories. That might be the reason that Hilton advises its franchises to concentrate on the minimum single rate as the key in competition.

**Upselling Premium Accommodations** The room rate policy faces a moment of truth when the front-office staff and the buying public come face to face. Fashioning a room rate policy is a futile exercise unless management simultaneously prepares its staff to carry out the plan. The selling skills of reservationists and clerks are critical to the ADR until the house nears capacity. Since nearly full occupancy is a rare occasion, earning a consistently higher ADR on the 60 percent to 70 percent day is achieved only when a program for selling up is in place.

The hardest sell comes from the guest-service agent. A guest who approaches the desk with a reservation in hand has already decided to buy. Already committed, the new arrival is susceptible to a carefully designed and rehearsed sales effort (see Exhibit 9-15). The hardest job is that of the reservationist, who doesn't even see the buyer. Too hard a sell, too firm a price, and the guest is lost early on. Teamed up, the reservationist and the room clerk deliver a one–two punch to the ADR, although they could be 1600 kilometres and 30 days apart.

A firm sale begins with product knowledge. That's why good sales executives travel to the central reservations office to brief the operators there. On property, both the reservationists and the room clerks need continual training about the facilities and accommodations of the hotel. This is rarely done. Few hotels ever assign 15 minutes per day for staff visits and inspections. Hotels spend millions of dollars upgrading rooms and modernizing facilities, but the room clerk never sees the changes. A simple and consistent training program assures management that reservationists and front-desk clerks know their product.

If the desk staff knows the product, a repertoire of reasons can be developed to upsell. A 10 percent upsell of $10 to $20 is not a large increment in terms of today's rate. Since every dollar of the increment goes to the bottom line, it represents a large annual figure, even if only a portion of the attempts are successful. The focus might be to move the commercial guest from standard service to a concierge floor. The weekend shopper of that commercial hotel needs a different approach. This discretionary buyer may turn away if the rates quoted at check-in fail to reflect the package plan booked at the time of reservation.

Each guest looks at the incremental dollars differently, and so does the employee. Management must be cognizant that the basic room rate and especially the incremental upsell seem excessive to employees working for an hourly wage. Part of the training must attend to the employee's frame of reference. Having some type of incentive plan for the employee does help change attitudes.

**Incentives to Upsell**   Motivated room clerks are better selling tools than cut rates and giveaways. They are less expensive, too, even with an incentive-pay plan. And it takes a good incentive plan coupled with proper training to make the system work.

Incentive systems stimulate interest and emphasize the goals of management. Rewards are especially important during heavy discounting periods, when guests know that low rates are available and sales resistance is high. Unlike some other places of the world, clerks in Canada do not share in any mandatory **service charge**, with the exception of some all inclusive package resort properties. Therefore, a special cash pool is needed for incentive distributions.

Incentive systems require an accurate and easily computed formula. Flat goals can be established, or the focus can be on improvement from last year, or last month, or last week for that matter. Most front-office incentives are keyed to average daily rate. Occupancy is a factor in total revenue, which suggests other bases for setting goals.

Most systems establish a pool that is shared by the team. Individual competition is restricted to the clerks, but selling up is a function of the reservations office, the telephone operators, the bellpersons, and others. That's why the pool, with its spin-off in morale and teamwork, is preferred.

The cash pool is generated from a percentage—say, 10 percent—of room sales that exceed projections. Management projects either the total room sales or the average daily rate. Management projections might be based on the ideal room rate (see Exhibit 9-13) or the budget forecast. If actual sales exceed target sales, the bonus becomes payable. The bonus period is important. It must be long enough to reflect the true efforts of the team but short enough to bring the rewards within grasp.

Higher ADRs are a win–win–win situation. The clerk wins by receiving increased payroll as an incentive for upselling. Management wins because upselling contributes proportionately higher profits to the profit and loss statement. And the guest wins by receiving exactly the room desired—this is where training is so important. The clerk isn't forcing anything on the guest that the guest doesn't want. Guests are more than ready to pay top dollar for the best accommodations. That's been demonstrated time and again over the past decade as room rates and room quality continue to rise.

## Mastering the Basics of Selling

### 1. Impressing the Guests

- Maintain an appealing physical appearance, including good posture. Don't lean or hang over the front desk. Bring to the job your own sense of spirit and style.

- Organize and keep the front-desk area uncluttered.

- Get to know your property's every service and accommodation type thoroughly. Make frequent forays around the property to learn firsthand about each kind and category of room so that you can better describe the facilities to potential guests.

- Memorize or keep close at hand an up-to-date list of the locations and hours of operation of all food and beverage facilities; entertainment lounges; recreational and sports rooms; and banquet, meeting, exhibit, and other public areas.

- Learn the names and office locations of the general manager and all department heads, including directors of marketing, sales, catering, convention services, and food and beverages.

- Be friendly to guests, greeting them warmly and, whenever possible, by name and title. For instance, when requesting a bellperson's service, ask him or her to take "Mr. Smith to room 340." (To ensure the guest's privacy, be discreet in mentioning the room number to the bellperson.) Call the bellperson by name as well.

- Give guests your undivided attention.

- Answer all questions completely, but concisely and accurately, based on your in-depth knowledge of hotel operations. Refrain from boasting about accommodations and services; instead, offer simple, to-the-point descriptions of features.

- Assume a polite, patient manner in explaining the various options available—for example, the size of rooms, kinds of reservations (confirmed or guaranteed), and the terms American, European, or modified American plan.

### 2. Winning the Guests

- Expand prospects' accommodations horizons with descriptions of the room and service possibilities awaiting them. Potential guests may think of a hotel as simply a building filled with bedrooms, but you know better. So inform them about rooms with views, rooms near the health spa, twin-bed rooms, suites, rooms furnished according to a certain historical period, or ultramodern accommodations with Jacuzzis. Lay everything out for prospects, dwelling on the positive, distinctive appeals of each choice. Throw in the tempting intangibles associated with each type of room; for instance, the prestige of having a room on the same floor as the hotel's exclusive club for special guests, or the pleasure of staying in a room equipped with a VCR or a fireplace.

- Attempt to sell a room to suit the client. Observe people and try to read their particular hankerings. If a guest is new to the hotel, a room with a nice view might be impressive. Business travellers might prefer a quiet room at the back. Guests with children, people staying for an extended visit, honeymooners, and celebrities are among those who might be interested in suites.

- Sell the room, not the rate. If a guest asks flat out for rates, avoid quoting a minimum or just one rate; instead, offer a range, portraying in detail the difference in accommodations that each rate affords.

- Should a prospect look unsure or reluctant to book a room, suggest that the guest accompany a hotel employee on a walkthrough. A tour of the premises gives guests a chance to settle any doubts they might have and demonstrates the hotel's policy of goodwill and flexibility.

- Keep abreast of special sales promotions, weekend packages, and other marketing strategies, and dangle these offerings to prospects. (To make sure you're informed, you might ask your sales department to hold regularly scheduled presentations to front office staff on their latest schemes.)

- Look for opportunities to extend the sale—there are many. If a guest mentions that he or she is hungry or arrives around mealtime, promote the hotel's dining facilities; if a guest arrives late, talk up the entertainment lounge or room service. As the person most in contact with guests throughout their stays, you are in the enviable position of being able to please both your guest and hotel management. You can delight guests merely by drawing their attention to the multitude of services your hotel offers, whether it's quick dry cleaning or a leisurely massage. And you can thrill the boss by advancing a sale and hotel revenues through your promotion of in-house features.

3. **Wooing the Guests**
   - When a guest arrives, upgrade the reservation to a more luxurious accommodation whenever availability allows, ask whether the guest would like to make a dinner reservation, and ask whether he or she would like a wake-up call.
   - Record and follow through on all wake-up call requests.
   - Deliver mail and messages promptly.
   - Avoid situations that keep guests waiting. For instance, if you're unable to locate a guest's reservation and a line is beginning to form on the other side of the counter, assume that the hotel has plenty of the desired accommodations available and go ahead and book the guest. Finish registering anyone else who is waiting, and then search for the missing reservation.
   - Should mishaps occur, whether a reservation mix-up or a housekeeping error, handle the matter with aplomb without laying the blame on any individual employee or department.
   - Dispatch each departing guest with a favourable impression of the hotel. In other words, treat the guests with care and courtesy during check-out. Regardless of whether guests enjoyed their stay, they will remember only the hassles experienced at check-out if you allow them to occur. Therefore, don't. That is, be sure there are useful, comprehensive procedures for dealing with guests who dispute postings and payments, and follow those procedures with assurance and professionalism.

▲
**Exhibit 9-15**
Master the basics of selling. Common sense advice from the Foundation of the Hospitality Sales and Marketing Association International's pamphlet entitled *The Front Office: Turning Service into Sales*.

# Summary

A proper room rate is as much a marketing tool as it is a financial instrument. That's because the room rate needs to be low enough to attract customers while high enough to earn a reasonable profit: Easier said than done. Even in this day of sophisticated computer technology, calculating the room rate still involves plenty of guesswork and gut instincts. There is an unquantifiable psychology involved in the room rate. A rate that is attractive to one person may appear too high or too low to another guest. For some, high rates suggest a pretentious operation; for others, a low rate suggests poor quality.

Searching and working toward the perfect rate is difficult, indeed. Even after the rate has been determined and established, it is immediately changed. Rates fluctuate by season, they change according to room type, they vary with special guest discounts, and they shift as a function of yield management.

Although there are some well-established methods for calculating the proper rate, these should never be used to the exclusion of common sense and market demand. The Hubbart room rate formula and the building cost rate formula are two of the most common means for determining the rate. In addition, the ideal average room rate formula adds a dimension of retrospection to understanding the appropriateness of a rate in terms of the local marketplace.

# Questions and Problems

1. Assume that the ideal average room rate for a given property is $87.25. Month after month, however, the hotel consistently outperforms its ideal average room rate by at least $5 to $10. You are the general manager of the property, and you know you can extract much information from these data. Based on the fact that the hotel's actual ADR is consistently higher than its ideal average room rate, what do you know about the front-office staff's ability to sell rooms? What do you know about the price sensitivity of your customers? And what do you know about rate tendencies in the surrounding marketplace? Armed with these data, what type of action might you now consider?

2. Upselling at the front desk is paramount to enhancing hotel profitability. Yet upselling also has the potential to cause the guest discomfort and to appear pushy or aggressive. There is a fine line between professionally upselling the room and appearing as if you are "hustling" the guest. How might you attempt to upsell each of the following types of guests? Acting as the guest-service agent, prepare a professional upselling dialogue for each of these situations (make up your own room types and rates as necessary):

   (a) Standing before you is an executive on your corporate-discount plan. He is stretching and yawning from a hard day of air travel and local meetings.

   (b) About to check in is a mother with her three young children. She is alone—her husband doesn't arrive until tomorrow. The kids are obviously excited about the prospects of swimming and running around the courtyard.

   (c) Two gentlemen from a recently arrived bus tour are standing in front of you. Even though the rest of the tour group is housed in standard queen doubles, these men are commenting that their room is much too small.

   (d) A female executive with an extended-stay reservation is currently checking in. She comments on the fact that she must stay in your hotel for at least 10 days. How can she possibly survive 10 days away from home?

3. A commercial hotel offers a deeply discounted rate on Friday, Saturday, and Sunday nights. Discuss what should be done or said in each of the following situations:

   (a) A guest arrives on Saturday but makes no mention of the special rate and seems unaware of the discount possibilities. The desk clerk charges full rack rate. On check-out Monday morning, the cashier notices the full rate charged for two nights, but the guest (after reviewing her folio) says nothing.

   (b) The situation is the same as that in part (a), but this time the guest does comment that she thought a discounted rate might apply.

   (c) A corporate guest stays Wednesday through Wednesday on company business. He receives a slightly discounted commercial rate for all seven nights, but his rate is still much higher than the special weekend rate available to anyone off the street. He knows about the special rate and asks that his three weekend nights be reduced accordingly.

   (d) Create a fourth scenario of your own.

4. Explain why hoteliers differentiate between discounting practices and rate cutting. Create a list of similarities and differences between discounting and rate cutting. Then conclude whether you believe they are substantially different activities or really two different statements for describing exactly the same practice.

5. The Hubbart room rate formula calls for an average room rate that will cover expenses and provide a fair return to investors. Compute

that rate from the abbreviated but complete set of data that follows: Investment (also fair market value)

| | |
|---|---|
| Land | $3 000 000 |
| Building | $25 000 000 |
| Furniture and equipment | $6 000 000 |
| Non-appropriated expenses, such as advertising, repairs, etc. | $1 200 000 |
| Income from all operating departments except rooms, net of losses | $3 200 000 |
| Rooms available for sale | 563 |
| Non-operating expenses, such as insurance, taxes, and depreciation | $510 000 |
| Desired return on investment | 16 percent |
| Interest on debt of $25 000 000 | 14 percent |
| Percentage of occupancy | 71 |

6. Using the data from Problem 5, compute what the typical room charge should be according to the building cost rate formula.

## CASE STUDY

### Opening Rack Rates in Fredericton

Abraham has been hired as general manager (GM) of a hotel being built in Fredericton, New Brunswick. The owner of the hotel and Abraham have spent some time trying to establish the opening rack rates for their new hotel, using several formulas such as the Hubbart formula, the building cost formula, and the ideal average rate formula. Each of these formulas has produced a different answer. Some of the results have been of concern, as they suggest that the opening rack rate should be much higher than those of competitors.

Can you help Abraham with the answers to some of the questions going through his mind?

1. In your opinion, what ultimately decides the rate you can charge for a room?

2. Will the application of yield management help this new hotel maximize its rates and maximize occupancy at the same time? Substantiate your answer.

3. Can a new hotel command a higher rate than its existing competitors? Why or why not?

4. The owner has suggested that the opening rates should be less than those of competitors. Why has the owner suggested this, and what are the ramifications of instituting such a rate policy?

## Notes

1. *The Hubbart Formula for Evaluating Rate Structures of Hotel Rooms* (1952) is available from the American Hotel & Lodging Association, 1201 New York Avenue, NW, Suite 600, Washington, D.C. 20005, and is used here with the association's permission.

2. An August 1995 letter to the editor of *Cornell Hotel and Restaurant Administration Quarterly* stated that the earliest reference the author, Bjorn Hanson, could find was a 1947 publication of *Horwath Accountant* (a newsletter of a now-defunct accounting firm). The author of this newsletter, Louis Toth, stated that for the $1 per $1000 rule of thumb to work, several things needed to be in place: (1) The rule referred only to the cost of the building, not the entire project; (2) the hotel needed to receive rent from concessionaries to cover debt service and taxes on the land itself; (3) the hotel needed a 70 percent occupancy; (4) the cost of furniture, fixtures, and equipment (FF&E) could be no more than 20 percent of the cost of the building; and (5) income before fixed charges must be at least 55 percent of room sales.

## Weblinks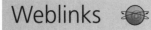

Hotel Association of Canada
**www.hotels.ca**

Hospitality Sales and Marketing Association
International
**www.hsmai.ca**

PKF Consulting, advisers to Canada's hospitality and
tourism industry
**www.pkfcanada.com**

Canadian Tourism Commission
**www.canadatourism.com/ctx/app/**

# Part IV

# The Hotel Revenue Cycle

The sequence of the text is designed around the flow of guests as they pass through the several stages that structure their relationship with the hotel. First come reservations, which are described in Part II. Modern telecommunications have changed the mechanics of reservation requests, and modern technologies have improved the hotel's techniques of forecasting and processing room availability. Once the reservation contract is agreed upon, the hotel confirms the understanding and begins tracking the expected arrivals through its reservation system.

In Part III, the guest arrives, sometimes carrying the reservation made in Part II and sometimes unexpectedly as a walk-in. The mechanics of that arrival, including room rate decisions, room assignments, and the rooming process, are examined thoroughly in this middle section of the book. Here, too, are discussed the special guest-service relationships that set the tone during the arrival time (Part III) and throughout the subsequent sale of services (Part IV).

Part IV brings us to the reason for the guest's visit: the sale of services, especially room sales, by the hotel. Selling services is only one part of this section. Recording the sales, collecting the amounts, and establishing the accounting procedures make up the content of Chapters 10, 11, and 12. In Part V, the cycle closes, and the guest checks out. There are still records to keep after the guest's departure—as there were throughout the guest's entire stay. Part IV attends to the records of the sale and Part V to the accuracy of those records.

Computerization has improved the techniques of recording and reviewing the records from guest sales and services. Fundamental to the process is an accounting base, whose essential rules have remained unchanged despite the speed and accuracy of computerization. In Part IV, we review the rules of basic accounting over and over again. This teaching technique—the recitation of rules—helps the student clear the hurdles of accounting's debits and credits. In this manner, Part IV establishes a firm base for understanding the ideas behind accounting even if the reader lacks formal courses in the subject. Too often the non-accountant rejects the accounting explanations as being too difficult. Not so; the repetition of the rules will indicate how narrow an understanding of accounting is needed to be wise about front-office folios.

In part, the business environment for hotels is a non-cash one, with credit, credit cards, debit cards, and smart cards the new media of exchange. We explain this in Chapter 12. Despite the popularity and convenience of the cards, cash retains its hold on many business activities. In Chapter 11, we review the money form of cash as well as its substitutes, old standbys such as traveller's cheques and personal cheques. Before we examine cash and credit cards, an overview of the entire billing process is provided in Chapter 10.

All of the preceding carries the guest (and the text) to the final stage of the sales/collection process, the audit. In Part V, we emphasize the changes in audit techniques that computerized property management systems have brought. For one, they have reduced the piles of paper and make possible the megaproperties (hotels of 2000 rooms and more) that have appeared in the past decade.

# Chapter 10 Billing the Guest Folio

## Learning Objectives

After reading this chapter, you will be able to do the following:

1. **Understand the simple accounting process encountered while posting charges and credits on a guest folio.**

2. **Understand accounts receivable as they apply to the front desk.**

3. **Describe the billing procedure as it applies to hotel guests.**

There's a tempo, a rhythm, to the flow of guests through the hotel. Reservations sound the first beat. The full swell of services begins after guests arrive and register. The melody doesn't end until they depart and settle the amounts owed. Between check-in and check-out, guests enjoy the facilities of the hotel. Selling those facilities is what the business of hotel keeping is all about. Hotel incomes are earned from the sale of such services. How those incomes are recorded is what this chapter is all about.

## Accounts Receivable

Except at the retail level, most commerce is carried on without immediate payment. Businesses buy and sell to one another without a direct exchange of money. Payment is delayed until a more convenient time in order to complete the sale as quickly as possible. Hotels also work that way. Guests are not disturbed during their sleep in order to collect the room rates! Instead, charges are made to the folio and collections are made later. Guests usually settle at checkout time. During the period between the sale (room, food, beverage, etc.) and the payment (at departure), the guest owes the hotel. A customer who owes a business for services that have not been paid is known as an **account receivable**.

### Types of Account Receivable

Hotels have two types of accounts receivable because there are two types of hotel guests. The most obvious guest (or account receivable) is one who is currently registered and occupying a room. Oddly enough, this most visible class of guest is not the largest dollar debt (accounts receivable) that the hotel is owed. More money is owed by the second type of accounts receivable: persons or companies that owe the hotel for services but are *not* registered and *not* occupying a guest room. Registered guests are called *transient guests*; non-registered accounts receivable are called *city guests*. Both owe the hotel for services rendered and sold. One group, the city receivables, are not even in the hotel and may never have been!

Guests can and do change categories; **transient accounts receivable** usually become **city accounts receivable**. When guests check out, leaving their transient classification, they usually settle their folios (that is, pay the bill) with a credit card. The amount owed is now a debt of the credit card company. The hotel will be paid by a city ledger receivable: Visa, MasterCard, Diners Club, or other credit card. Credit card companies obviously are not registered guests occupying a room. The credit card debt is owed by an account receivable that is not registered: a city account receivable.

**The Ledgers** There are numerous accounts receivable in both the transient and the city categories. Hotels as large as those in Chapter 1 (see Exhibit 1-1) might have several thousand guests registered, and approximately the same number of folios. Accountants call a group of folios a **ledger**. Since all of the parties are registered—that is, transient—guests, this particular group of records is called a **transient ledger**. The individual folios of transient guests are viewed as one record, a transient ledger.

City accounts receivable are combined similarly. The total records of city accounts—that is, debtors to the hotel who are not registered currently—are called a city ledger. The individual accounts of city guests are viewed as one record, a city ledger.

**The Transient Ledger** *Transient ledger* is shorthand for the transient **accounts receivable ledger**. Hotel professionals use other jargon to identify this particular ledger. Because the ledger—that is, the total record of debt to the hotel by registered guests—is available at the front office, it is frequently called the front-office ledger. Since it is made up of registered guests, it is also called the guest ledger. Room rates are the largest source of charges to guest folios, so **rooms ledger** is still another term used for the transient ledger.

The variety of terms used to identify the transient ledger spills over to the folios that make up this ledger. Thus, the single transient folio may be called folio, or guest folio, or front-office folio. Since the folio is a record of the guest's account with the hotel, the folio is also called an **account card** or **guest bill**.

**The City Ledger** There are numerous subcategories of the city ledger, as explained in Chapter 12, but there is but one general term, *city ledger*. That makes city ledger references easier to remember than the variety of labels (guest ledger, rooms ledger, front-office ledger) used for the transient ledger.

The guest ledger is located at the front desk, the city ledger in the accounting office. With computerization, ledgers have no real physical location. They can be accessed wherever a control terminal allows. Timing is the major difference between the two ledgers. Charges, which are the records of services rendered, are *posted* (recorded) immediately to the guest ledger since the guest might choose to leave at any time. City guests, who must establish credit in advance, are billed periodically. This permits some delay in posting city ledger charges. Like many other businesses do, hotels bill city accounts monthly. Often, a three-day cycle is used for the first billing. These variations in timing are accommodated by different ledger forms as well as by different posting and billing procedures.

**What Is and Isn't Accounted For** Each folio is an account receivable, a record of the guest's debt to the hotel. Since folios deal only with accounts receivable, persons who pay cash for services received, as they might in cocktail lounges and restaurants, are not part of the front-office billing procedure. It makes no difference whether the buyer is a guest or not; there is no account receivable, no debt owed, when settlement is made immediately with dollars.

Non-guests without front-office folios can still purchase food and beverage on credit. They do so with credit cards. A credit card charge creates an account receivable within the city ledger, not the front-office ledger. It is, of course, an account for the credit card company, which is a non-registered debtor. That's the definition of city ledger. As a result, the non-guest owes the credit card company and the credit card company owes the hotel as a city ledger account. The exception is when guests pay with a bank credit card (Visa or MasterCard); these are deposited in the bank as cash and do not become a receivable.

Hotel guests use dollars at times to pay for meals or other services. Since that is a cash payment, no account receivable record (no folio) is involved. Also like non-guests, registered guests may elect to use credit cards to pay for services. Then the credit card record becomes part of the city ledger.

To summarize, both registered and non-registered guests pay for services in one of two methods: they pay cash/debit card, or they charge services to personal credit cards. Guests have a third option of payment, one not available to non-guests: they charge services to their rooms—that is, to their front-office folios. By merely signing for the charge, the guest acknowledges the debt. The amount is then posted to the folio. Payment for the folio with all of its charges comes later, usually as the guest checks out. Much of this chapter concentrates on this third method of paying for services. Cash is treated in Chapter 11 and credit cards in Chapter 12.

## The Folio: The Individual Account Receivable

Folio, bill, **guest account**, account card, guest account card, and guest bill are used interchangeably to refer to the individual account receivable that is opened for each registered guest. Of course, one folio may serve a party of several persons, as it does with a family, for example.

**Location and Filing of the Folio** Modern hotels have adopted computerized folios without exception. Computerized folios (see Exhibit 10-1) are maintained in electronic memory and are visible only when printed or on the computer screen. Therefore, the desk needs input and output devices (keyboards, scanners, screens, and printers) to input and access the information.

Older, hand-prepared, pencil-and-paper folios (see Exhibit 10-2) had to be physically stored at the desk in a *cashier's well*, also called a *cashier's bucket* or *cashier's pit* (see Exhibit 10-3). Folios were separated there by heavy cardboard dividers. Guest folios were kept in room-number sequence because room numbers, even more than guest names, were and still are the major means of guest identification. Not all hotels have done away with cashier's buckets. The need still exists under some PMSs for filing paper records, but not folios, by room number.

Whether maintained electronically or by hand, the folio is the responsibility of the guest-service agent or the front-office cashier. Hand-prepared folios generated such large quantities of paper that billing clerks (or posting clerks) supported the cashier. As the chapter explains later, recording charges on the folio is now done electronically at computer terminals in the various departments providing the services (food, beverage,

☐V

*A Vallen Corporation Property*

**HI-JINKS HOTEL**

**1000 NOAH VAIL
ROTTEN PUMPKIN POND
SHERBROOKE, QC  L1X 2Z2
1-888-555-5555**

| RES#  43 RLG 1234 | ACCT#  5941 |
|---|---|

| IN      11-02- | OUT      11-04- |
|---|---|

NAME:    Iona Carr

| RATE   100 | ROOM   444 |
|---|---|

ADDRESS:  S.N. Eaky Rd.
         Calgary, BC  X4X 5Y4

| DATE | DESCRIPTION | REFERENCE | | CHARGES | CREDITS | BALANCE |
|---|---|---|---|---|---|---|
| | | | | | | 100.00 |
| 11/02/ | ROOM | 444 | 18-1 | 100.00 | | 105.50 |
| 11/02/ | ROOM TAX | 444 | 18-2 | 5.50 | | 119.48 |
| 11/03/ | COFFEE SHOP | 444 | 38-1 | 13.98 | | 130.58 |
| 11/03/ | TELEPHONE | 444 | 43-2 | 11.10 | | 136.58 |
| 11/03/ | FAX | 444 | 43-3 | 6.00 | | 159.18 |
| 11/03/ | LOUNGE | 444 | 26-2 | 22.60 | | -0- |
| 11/04/ | VISA#1111111 | 444 | 50-4 | | 159.18 | |

. . . . If you were a Vallen ☐V Associate Member,
you would have earned 320 Club Membership points.

TRANSFER TO CITY LEDGER
I AGREE THAT MY LIABILITY FOR THIS BILL IS NOT
WAIVED, AND AGREE TO BE PERSONALLY LIABLE IF
THE INDICATED PERSON, ASSOCIATION, OR COMPANY
FAILS TO PAY ANY PART OF THESE CHARGES.

_____
SIGNATURE

For Reservations: 1-888-555-5555   •   Fax: 1-888-555-5554   •   E-mail: vallen@hotel.com

spa, etc.). Thus, there are fewer desk employees and fewer paper errors. As front-desk jobs are combined (see Chapter 2), guest-service agents with broader responsibilities take on what was once the job of front-office cashiers and billing clerks.

**Number of Folios** The size of the hotel determines the number of folios in use, more or less. Essentially, there is one folio for each occupied room. There are exceptions, however. Several friends sharing one room might request several folios, and a single person occupying a four-room suite may need but one.

**Exhibit 10-2** ▶
The folio here illustrates a pencil-and-paper folio, normally prepared with a carbon copy that is given to the guest. Compare the format to Exhibit 10-1.

| ROOM NO. | 409 | | | | | E69080 | |
|---|---|---|---|---|---|---|---|

*m*  M/M Art E. Fishal
86 Bates Boulevard
Port Alberni, BC  V1T 8T4

| ARRIVED | RATE | PERSONS | COT | REG. CARD # | PREV. INV. # | CLERK |
|---|---|---|---|---|---|---|
| 12/23/ | 78 | 2 | N/A | 69080 | N/A | SB |

| DATE | 12/23/ | | 12/24/ | | | | | | | | | | |
|---|---|---|---|---|---|---|---|---|---|---|---|---|---|
| BROUGHT FORWARD | | | 99 | 24 | | | | | | | | | |
| ROOM | 78 | – | | | | | | | | | | | |
| TAX | 6 | 24 | | | | | | | | | | | |
| RESTAURANT | 15 | – | | | | | | | | | | | |
| " | | | | | | | | | | | | | |
| TELEPHONE-LOCAL | | | | | | | | | | | | | |
| -LONG DISTANCE | | | | | | | | | | | | | |
| TELEGRAMS | | | | | | | | | | | | | |
| LAUNDRY & VALET | | | | | | | | | | | | | |
| CASH ADVANCES | | | | | | | | | | | | | |
| " | | | | | | | | | | | | | |
| NEWSPAPERS | | | | | | | | | | | | | |
| TRANSFERS *from 407* #69081 | | | 84 | 24 | | | | | | | | | |
| TOTAL DEBIT | 99 | 24 | 183 | 48 | | | | | | | | | |
| CASH | | | | | | | | | | | | | |
| ALLOWANCES | | | | | | | | | | | | | |
| CITY LEDGER | | | | | | | | | | | | | |
| ADVANCE DEPOSITS | | | | | | | | | | | | | |
| CREDIT CARDS | | | 183 | 48 | | | | | | | | | |
| TRANSFERS | | | | | | | | | | | | | |
| BALANCE FORWARD | 99 | 24 | 0 | | | | | | | | | | |

ALL ACCOUNTS ARE DUE WHEN RENDERED

The number of occupied rooms does not determine the number of city ledger accounts. City ledger accounts are established for individuals and companies who want credit privileges with the hotel. In pre–credit card days, large hotels had thousands of city ledger accounts. Not so today, when almost everyone carries national credit cards. Now, the bulk of the city ledger can be accounted for in a half-dozen national credit card accounts. Electronically tying city ledger accounts to the computers of credit card companies and banks speeds processing and reduces administrative costs.

**Master Accounts** The master account is its own person, much like a business corporation has a legal identity separate from that of its individual owners. This accommodates tour companies, trade associations, convention organizations, and single-entity groups that incur charges that are not billable to any one person (see Chapter 1 for an explanation). Group services—an awards luncheon, for

▲
**Exhibit 10-3**
The **cashier's well**
(**bucket** or **pit**) separates
pencil-and-paper folios
by sequential room num-
bers. Computerized prop-
erties use the bucket to
separate and locate pre-
printed folios, correspondence, and vouchers.

example—are charged to this non-person folio, the **master account**. Master accounts allow group charges to be distinguished from personal charges. These accounts are not city accounts receivable, because they represent the organization currently registered. So long as the group is in the hotel, its master account is a standard guest folio, such as Exhibit 10-4.

As with all folios, master accounts are settled at check-out. Settlement involves a joint review of the many charges by representatives of the hotel and the organization. Then the folio is transferred to the city ledger for direct billing. Obviously, then, the city ledger has more than just credit cards. Individual accounts receivable with billing to be made to the person, company, or organization (rather than through credit cards) are also part of the city ledger.

Master accounts are complex. They may number 25 pages and more. It takes telephone calls, faxes, and emails to resolve what the hotel believes it is owed and what the association believes it owes. Conflicts arise over the number of persons at each function, over who signed for services, over the number of comp rooms, over sales taxes due, and so much more. The discussion of the city ledger in Chapter 12 explains the final billing and settlement.

**How Master Accounts Are Structured** Decisions about master account billing are made well in advance of the group's arrival. Service details, credit terms, and authorized signatures are part of the negotiations between the hotel and the organization. How charges are to be distributed between individual folios and the master account is the group's decision, not the hotel's. The hotel is responsible for billing as instructed.

SINGLE-ENTITY GROUPS  Employees gathering for company business or groups travelling together—say, to perform—are examples of single-entity groups (see Chapter 1). Charging all room rates to a single master account is one method of billing such closely related groups.

CONVENTION GROUPS  Unlike single-entity groups, convention delegates hail from many locations and companies. Delegates pay their own room and personal charges. No master account would serve for room rates, since delegates have no relationship other than their mutual attendance. However, the association staging the event has a master account for banquet costs, cocktail parties, and meeting expenses. Other general costs, such as telecommunications and room charges for employees or speakers, also go onto the master account. Such charges must be authorized by the signature of the person or persons identified during the early negotiations.

Many master accounts are created during a large convention. Participating companies in attendance at the convention may have exhibits, employee rooms, hospitality suites, and other services that require charges to that subgroup. As affiliated or allied members, they may see public relations benefits from sponsoring a meal. Each, then,

**Exhibit 10-4** ▶

Debits (charges) and credits (payments) can be visualized within a T: debits in the left column and credits in the right one. Mentally draw the line between the columns and then draw a horizontal arm across the two columns. Note the similarity of format and content to Exhibit 10-1. The final entry involves a direct, city ledger billing to the sponsoring organization.

Daytona Beach
**Hilton**
Resort

2637 S. Atlantic Avenue
Daytona Beach, Florida 32118
904-767-7350

DB
In      Out      Folio
10/25-10/28      12977
Rate 59.00 PAGE 1   A

Name:   VALLEN, JEROME   MR.

Address:   SECOND AVE.
DIGBY, NOVA SCOTIA
T4N 1X9

TRAVEL AGENCY

DEAC01      Room  621

| Date | Description | ID | Ref. No. | Charges | Credits | Balance |
|---|---|---|---|---|---|---|
| 10/25/ | ISLANDER      01 | XAQ | 419354 | 9.00 | | |
| 10/25/ | VID-COM | XAQ | E3 | 8.43 | | |
| 10/25/ | VID-COM | XAQ | E5 | 8.43 | | |
| 10/25/ | ROOM | XAP | 621 | 59.00 | | |
| 10/26/ | 201-595-7796 | XAQ | 18:18 | 3.36 | | |
| 10/26/ | VID-COM | XAQ | E5 | 8.43 | | |
| 10/26/ | ROOM | XAP | 621 | 59.00 | | |
| 10/27/ | ISLANDER      01 | XAQ | 419995 | 19.62 | | |
| 10/27/ | ROOM | XAP | 621 | 59.00 | | |
| 10/28/ | SUNROOM CAFE 01 | XAQ | 814544 | 7.31 | | |
| 10/28/ | DIRECT BILL | BEL | | | 241.58 | |
| 10/28/ | C/O TIME 08:16 | BEL | | .00 | | |
| 10/28/ | DIRECT BILL | BEL | | | 241.58– | |
| 10/28/ | ADJUST MOVIE | BEL | | | 8.43 | |
| 10/28/ | ADJUST PHONE | BEL | | | 3.36 | |
| 10/28/ | DIRECT BILL | BEL | | | 229.79 | .00 |

Checked In 07:16 pm TDO
CR:      OT:   AB:   R:N HH:

Checked Out 08:16 am BEL
AL:      A#

*Jerome Vallen*
Guest

Firm

Address

City                     State                     Zip

Rates do not include applicable sales, occupancy or other taxes:

Transfer to credit ledger
I agree that my liability for this bill is not waived and agree to be held personally liable in the event that the indicated person, company or association fails to pay for any part or the full amount of these charges.

Guest Signature

has its own master account. There is no accounting relationship to the association's master account. The hotel tracks and bills each separately.

TOUR GROUPS Master accounts for tour groups differ from master accounts for convention groups. Convention attendees pay their own bills. Tour group participants pay the tour company in advance, and the tour company negotiates with the hotel. So the tour company is responsible for payment of all charges included in the package. The tour company's master account includes the room charges for everyone in the group, plus whatever else was sold with the package: meals, drinks, shows, golf, and so on. Personal expenses—those not within the package—are charged to the guest's personal folio.

**Split Billing** The distribution of the charges between the master account and the guest's personal folio is called split billing or split folios. Both the master folio (often called the **A folio**) and the guest or **B folio** are standardized forms of the types illustrated throughout the chapter. A and B are used merely to distinguish the group entity from the individual person. The A folio is the major folio where the large charges of the association, tour company, or business are posted. Sometimes, the hotel itself is the A folio. Such is the case with casino comps and frequent-stay customers.

**Casino Comps** Casino hotels sometimes provide complimentary (free) accommodations to "high rollers" (big players). Split billing is used to account for the comps. To the A folio is posted all charges that the hotel/casino will comp. Depending on the size of the guest's credit line, the comp could be for room only, or for room, food, beverage, and telephone. Even airfare might be reimbursed. Items not covered are posted to the B folio, which the guest pays at departure.

**Preferred-Guest Programs** Preferred-guest (or frequent-traveller) programs employ the flexibility of split billing. Two different folios are opened when a guest checks in with frequent-traveller points. The full rate of the room is charged on the A folio. On departure, the guest pays the non-room charges, which have been posted to the B folio. The A folio is transferred to the city ledger, and either the parent company or the franchisor is billed. According to the frequent-traveller contract, one of these is now the account receivable obligated to pay the room charge.

The actual amount paid to the hotel under the preferred-guest program is always less than the rate quoted to the guest. Most programs pay full rack rate only if occupancy of the hotel is above a given figure—90 percent, perhaps. Below that figure—and occupancy is usually below that figure—the program reimburses the participating hotel for its operational expenses: linen, labour, and energy. So, the reimbursement may be set anywhere from $20 to $50. No provision is made for recovering fixed costs such as taxes, interest, or fair wear and tear.

## Understanding Charges and Credits

Familiarization with accounting and with its system of charges and credits gives front-office associates a big assist in handling folios. The knowledge is especially helpful in understanding how front-office records (the transient ledger) interface with back-office records (the city ledger). Since many guest-service agents lack accounting knowledge, front-office forms are designed without that requirement. Exhibit 10-11, for example, uses plus (+) and minus (−) to indicate increases (charges) or decreases (credits) to folios.

Exhibits 10-4, 10-5, and 10-10 mark the differences by using two columns. One is titled "Charges" and the other "Credits." Charges for services rendered increase the guest's debt to the hotel (Exhibit 10-4, line 1, the ISLANDER Restaurant). Credits reduce the guest's debt (Exhibit 10-4, line 11, DIRECT BILL). With enough credits, the folio is paid; the balance is zero (Exhibit 10-4, final line).

A third technique for distinguishing charges from credits is illustrated in Exhibits 10-8 and 10-12. Only one column is used, but credits are marked "CR." Figures that are not marked are understood to be charges. Most folio postings are charges.

**The Meaning of Debits and Credits** Accounting language speaks of debits and credits instead of charges and credits. Debits (or charges) increase the values of certain accounting records. In this chapter, the focus is on folios, which are accounts receivable. Other accounts—cash, for example—are also increased with debits. Cash and accounts receivable are among the many assets (things that hotels own) that follow the same accounting rules. Accounting records, assets among them, that are increased with debits are decreased by credits.

Increases in assets, including *accounts receivable* and *cash*, are made with debits.

Decreases in assets, including *accounts receivable* and *cash*, are made with credits.

Accounting students will recognize the folio as a T-account, where debits are on the left side and credits are on the right. Exhibit 10-4 is highlighted with horizontal and vertical lines to reinforce the visual similarities between an account receivable folio and an account receivable T-account.

**Assets** An asset is something a business owns. Hotels own many assets, including land, buildings, furniture, and kitchen equipment. Only two of the numerous assets owned are important to the front office and its folio responsibilities. Accounts receivable, which are debts that customers owe the hotel (the hotel owns the debt), is one of those assets. Cash is the other. Cash is money: money in the bank, money at the desk, money in the bar till. Cash has become less important to the records of the front office because both guests and hotel keepers prefer folios to be settled with credit cards.

**Sales or Incomes** Hotels are in the business of selling services. It's those sales that produce income and eventually profits for the business. The sale of rooms is the hotel's major product. Depending on the size, class, and type of property, income is also earned from the sale of other products and services. Guests pay for these services by charging them to the folio (establishing an asset called account receivable) or paying for them with cash. Sometimes they use credit cards. The delivered product or service is the same, they're just paid for differently. The record of service is different from the record of payment, although the two records take place simultaneously, as we shall see next in the discussion of equality.

Customers who buy services with cash in the lounge, the coffee shop, the newsstand, or other hotel departments increase the hotel's cash asset. There is no record on the guest's folio, but there is an increase (debit) to cash according to the accounting rule:

> Increases in assets, including accounts receivable and *cash*, are made with debits.
> Increases in incomes (sale of rooms, *food*, beverage, spa, etc.) are made with credits.
>
> Debit: Cash                                                      33.00
>    Credit: Proper Department (room, *food*, beverage, spa, etc.)        33.00
> *Explanation*: Sold coffee-shop meal for cash.

Debit/credit rules are different for sales (incomes) than for assets. Just as all assets follow one asset rule, so all incomes follow one income rule. It is an opposite rule.

> Increases in assets, including *accounts receivable* and cash, are made with *debits*.
> Increases in incomes (sales of *rooms*, food, beverage, etc.) are made with credits.
>
> Debit: Accounts Receivable/Guest's Folio                          100
>    Credit: Proper Department (*room*, food, beverage, spa, etc.)           100
> *Explanation*: Guest occupied room.

**Equality of Debits and Credits** Every accounting event has two parts. This dual accounting system always requires equal dollar amounts of debits and credits. For example, two things happen when a bar bill is paid with cash. One, the hotel has more cash in the till. Two, bar sales, or bar income, has also increased. Both increase by the same dollar amount. The $33 food example above illustrates that equality.

If the bar drinks are charged to the room, the accounting entry changes somewhat but the equality of debits and credits remains the same.

# Posting to Accounts Receivable

Hotels extend credit to guests. They do so because the guests' identities have been confirmed through reservations, registrations, and credit card verifications. Except in unusual cases (see Chapter 8), guests are permitted—indeed, expected—to charge goods and services to their front-office folios. Front-office folios are the records of accounts receivable.

Most guests take advantage of the system, but some elect to buy goods and services with cash. Paying for a bar drink or a buffet breakfast with cash does not affect the folio. Folios are accounts receivable. Guests who pay with cash owe nothing, so no accounts receivables, no folio records, result from cash purchases.

Certain items—for example, room charges or telephone calls made from the room—always sell on credit. There is no practical way for the hotel to collect cash for these sales. Telephone calls are recorded automatically on the folio by a tie-in with the telephone company. Room charges are recorded nightly by the night auditor. No one expects the room charge to be collected in cash in the middle of the night. So, both are folio charges. Both are sales made on credit.

Guests may also elect to use credit cards for drinks or meals. Credit card companies are accounts receivable too, but they are not registered; they are city ledger receivables. Front-office folios involve transient receivables only. Neither cash purchases nor credit card purchases appear on the front-office folios of registered guests.

Cash and credit cards especially do have a role at the front desk. They are used at check-out time to settle (pay for) the folio balance. We discuss this at the end of the chapter.

## Overview of the Billing Procedure

Electronic folios gained popularity in the mid-1980s. Pencil-and-paper folios (see Exhibit 10-2) were the norm during the previous half-century.

**Preparation of the Folio** Computers format the folios (see Exhibits 10-4, 10-5, etc.) as guests arrive and register. The data come from the registration card (see Chapter 8, Exhibit 8-5) entered by the guest-service agent as the arrival procedure unfolds. The PMS can even incorporate reservation information onto the folio. In fact, some hotels prefer to use the reservation information to print the registration card or the folio the night before. One or both are then ready when the guest arrives.

Many bits of information appear on the folio. In Exhibit 10-4, the folio indicates the time of the guest's arrival at the bottom, and eventually the time of departure is printed. Usually, that information appears at the top of the folio, as it does in Exhibit 10-5, where the arrival time is 12:29. Also shown there is the group's identity, American (top left), and its code number, 6566 (top right).

**Exhibit 10-5** ▶

A computer-prepared folio showing group affiliation, American; group identification, 6566; the clerk's identification, 54; the account number, 20539; and the guest agreement on the ultimate liability of the bill.

## (IP) Radisson Hotel Ottawa Centre

100 Kent Street, Ottawa, Ontario, Canada  K1P 5R7  Telephone (613) 238-1122

**LA RONDE** FINE CUISINE          **CAFE TOULOUSE**          *Lautrec's*

| ROOM / CHAMBRE<br>2228 | NAME / NOM<br>STEIN, FRANK N. | RATE / TAUX<br>75.00 | DEPARTURE / DEPART<br>14/10/ | TIME / HEURE | ACCT#<br>20539 |
|---|---|---|---|---|---|
| ROOM / CHAMBRE<br>1K1A | FIRM OR GROUP / COMPAGNIE OU GROUP<br>AMERICAN | PLAN | ARRIVAL / ARRIVEE<br>09/10/ | 12:29 | |
| 54 | P.O. BOX 1211          DB<br>LANSING MI 90125-0012 | | | | GROUP<br>6566 |
| CLERK<br>COMMIS | ADDRESS / ADRESSE | | METHOD OF PAYMENT<br>MODE DE PAIEMENT | | |

| DATE | REFERENCE/RÉFÉRENCE | CHARGES | CREDITS / CRÉDITS | BALANCE DUE / SOLDE DÛ |
|---|---|---|---|---|
| 09/10 | ROOM          2228, 1 | 75.00 | | |
| 09/10 | ROOM TAX      2228, 1 | 3.75 | | |
| 10/10 | TOUL POS      000000 | 17.12 | | |
| 10/10 | LNG DIST      315-386- | .57 | | |
| 10/10 | ROOM          2228, 1 | 75.00 | | |
| 10/10 | ROOM TAX      2228, 1 | 3.75 | | |
| 11/10 | ROOM          2228, 1 | 75.00 | | |
| 11/10 | ROOM TAX      2228, 1 | 3.75 | | |
| 12/10 | LNG DIST      315-386- | 1.14 | | |
| 12/10 | LNG DIST      315-386- | 1.14 | | |
| 12/10 | ROOM          2228, 1 | 75.00 | | |
| 12/10 | ROOM TAX      2228, 1 | 3.75 | | |
| 13/10 | TOUL POS      000000 | 9.86 | | |
| 13/10 | TOUL POS      000000 | 16.58 | | |
| 13/10 | ROOM          2228, 1 | 75.00 | | |
| 13/10 | ROOM TAX      2228, 1 | 3.75 | | |
| | | | | 440.16 |

FIRM / COMPAGNIE _____ ADDRESS / ADRESSE _____

CITY _____ PROV. _____ POSTAL _____
VILLE                                POSTALE
ATTENTION _____

GUEST SIGNATURE    X _____
SIGNATURE DU CLIENT

I AGREE THAT MY LIABILITY FOR THIS BILL IS NOT WAIVED AND AGREE TO BE HELD PERSONALLY LIABLE IN THE EVENT THAT THE INDICATED PERSON, COMPANY OR ASSOCIATION FAILS TO PAY FOR ANY PART OR THE FULL AMOUNT OF THESE CHARGES.

IL EST CONVENU QUE MA RESPONSABILITÉ DE CETTE FACTURE N'EST PAS ABROGÉE ET JE CONSENTS A L'ASSUMER DANS L'ÉVENTUALITE OU LA PERSONNE INDIQUÉE, SOCIÉTÉ OU ASSOCIATION REFUSE DE PAYER LE MONTANT EN TOTALITÉ OU EN PARTIE.

There is common information in every folio exhibit of the chapter. Exhibit 10-5 can serve as the source. Illustrated are the room assigned (2228), the rate charged ($75), and dates of arrival and anticipated departure (9/10 and 14/10). Included, of course, is the guest's name, Frank N. Stein, and address. The number of persons is usually shown, but not in Exhibit 10-5 (see Exhibit 10-8).

Folios are numbered sequentially as a means of identification and accounting control. The folio account number of Exhibit 10-5 is 20539. Folio numbers are especially important for internal control when the hotel uses pencil-and-paper folios, and almost always appear in the upper right corner (see Exhibit 10-2).

Nearly every folio now carries at the bottom of the page a statement about liability for the bill (see Exhibit 10-1 and others). With so many persons (employers, associations, credit card companies) other than the guests accepting the charges, hotel lawyers want to make certain that eventually someone pays. The odd part about the statement is how rarely the guest is asked to sign it.

**Presenting the Bill** Common law protects the innkeeper from fraud by requiring guests to prove willingness and an ability to pay. Credit is, therefore, a privilege that management may revoke at any time. Nervous credit managers do just that whenever their suspicions are raised. The folio is printed and presented to the guest with a request for immediate payment. Even the traditional delay until the guest checks out is revoked. Motor hotels may go one step further by collecting in advance either in cash (rare) or by obtaining credit card identification/authorization.

Since most guests are not credit risks, bills are normally presented and paid at check-out time. It works that way for the vast majority of guests who stay for several nights. A folio is printed on demand as the guest departs. If there are any adjustments, an amended copy is printed for the guest to take away. Many hotels deliver the customer's initial copy under the guest room door sometime during the previous night. If a hard copy is not needed, the folio can be viewed on a front-office monitor or more leisurely on the television in the guest room.

Long-term guests are billed weekly, and they are expected to pay promptly. Regardless of the length of the stay, folios are also rendered whenever they reach a predetermined dollar amount. The class of hotel, which reflects room rates and menu prices, determines the dollar figure that management sets as the ceiling. No charges are allowed beyond that value.

**Communications** Guests can buy and charge services as soon as the folio is opened, even before going to the room. That was always possible, but the computer opens the folio immediately. Pencil-and-paper systems required front-desk agents to recopy the registration information onto the folio. Recopying caused long delays because it was not an agent's first priority at a busy desk.

Guests buy services from dining rooms, cocktail lounges, newsstands, room service—from all of the many departments of a full-service hotel. Getting the charge information from the point of sale to the folio at the front desk is critical to the accuracy and the completeness of the billing process. The computer, the hotel's PMS, has done away with handwritten vouchers and control. Communication is electronic. The distant department is tied electronically to the front desk by means of the PMS. Cashiers in the dining rooms, lounges, and room service enter the cheque into an electronic cash register, called a **point-of-sale (POS) terminal** (see Exhibit 10-6). Instantaneously, the information enters computer memory. The guest's folio is always current and late charges are minimized. Moreover, the PMS gives the departmental cashiers additional capability to verify guests' identities and their right to charge.

Property management systems with point-of-sale terminals are expensive installations. Management might make an economic decision to leave certain minor departments, which generate a small amount of revenue, without POS capability. Therefore, some hotels have a mixture of electronic and pencil-and-paper systems.

**Exhibit 10-6 ▶**
Point-of-sale terminals
(POS) are located at various revenue centres
(restaurants, lounges, gift
shops). Each POS terminal interfaces with the
hotel's property management system (PMS), electronically posting
transactions to guest folios; this is the location
for the screen shown in
Exhibit 13-2.

## Posting Charges to Accounts Receivable

Charges (increases to accounts receivable folios) and credits (decreases to accounts receivable folios) are posted (entered on the folios) to keep guest accounts current. Our discussion centres first on posting the charges and then on the meaning of each charge.

**Understanding the Line of Posting** Each charge line on the folio represents two things. One is the change in the value of the account receivable. The amount the account receivable owes the hotel gets larger with each charge posting.

The purchase of goods and services are charges, and they increase the amount owed by the guest. Exhibit 10-7 illustrates several of these departmental charges. Among them are room sales (line 1, Exhibit 10-7), restaurant sales (line 5, Woodlands), and telephone calls (lines 4 and 6). Each line in Exhibit 10-7 increases the debt owed by the guest/account receivable to the hotel. Note that lines 2, 3, 8, and 9 are not sales (income). They are taxes. That discussion is several pages ahead.

REMINDER: If the guest paid with cash or a credit card in the Woodlands restaurant, there would be no folio record! Folios are accounts receivable, guests who still owe. Obviously, nothing is owed when payment is made with cash or credit card.

The second, but less evident, event that each line represents is the departmental record. Charges made by the guest are sales to the departments. Each line of posting is a charge by the guest and a simultaneous record of hotel income by department. As guest account balances increase, so do the income flows from the particular departments.

Each folio illustrated in this chapter carries the same format. There is a single line record for each activity. The printed information in the centre of the folio identifies the source of the income. The fact that a line of posting exists means that the account receivable is also affected.

**Exhibit 10-7** ▶
The format of all electronic folios is much the same, although some have two columns (debit and credit) and some have only one, leaving the reader to distinguish between charges and credits. Note the sales tax postings on lines 2, 3, 8, and 9. Stouffer is no longer a hotel chain.

STOUFFER WESTCHESTER HOTEL
80 WEST RED OAK LANE
WHITE PLAINS, NEW YORK 10604
(914) 694-5400

TOWNS, SEYMOUR

123 NORTH STREET
CHARLOTTETOWN, PEI
Y24 1X2

| | ARRIVAL | 3/11/ |
| | DEPARTURE | 3/13/ |
| | NO. IN PARTY | 2 |
| | RATE | 89.00 |

ACCT. NO.    801936        ROOM NO.    346

| # | DATE | DESCRIPTION | AMOUNT |
|---|------|-------------|--------|
| 1 | 3/11/ | ROOM/346/2/2/4 | 89.00 |
| 2 | 3/11/ | SALES TAX/346/2/2/4 | 6.19 |
| 3 | 3/11/ | COUNTY OCCUPANCY TAX/346/2/2/4 OCCUPANCY TAX | 2.67 |
| 4 | 3/12 | LOCAL/LOCAL TOLL/346/3120XX4006/1/4 09:56/6987991 | .75 |
| 5 | 3/12/ | WOODLANDS/346/736334/1/4/113355 | 24.03 |
| 6 | 3/12/ | LOCAL/LOCAL TOLL/346/312CXXX011/1/4 11:41/6987991 | .75 |
| 7 | 3/12/ | ROOM/346/2/2/4 | 89.00 |
| 8 | 3/12/ | SALES TAX/346/2/2/4 | 6.19 |
| 9 | 3/12/ | COUNTY OCCUPANCY TAX/346/2/2/4 OCCUPANCY TAX | 2.67 |
| | | * BALANCE DUE * | 221.25 |

ACCOUNTS PAST 30 DAYS SUBJECT TO SERVICE CHARGE OF 1 1/2% PER MONTH (ANNUAL RATE OF 18%)

*PRINTED ON RECYCLED PAPER* ♻

COMPANY                    STREET                    ZIP

CITY / STATE

I agree that my liability for this bill is not waived and agree to be held personally liable in the event that the indicated person, company or associations fails to pay for any part of these charges.

SIGNATURE _____

Increase in assets, including *accounts receivable* and cash, are made with debits.

Increase in incomes (sales of *rooms, food, telephone*) are made with credits.

Increase in liabilities (debts owed to banks and *governments*) are made with credits.

Line 1    Debit accounts receivable, credit room sales for $89.00
Line 2    Debit accounts receivable, credit sales taxes payable for $6.19.
Line 3    Debit accounts receivable, credit occupancy taxes payable for $2.67.
Line 4    Debit accounts receivable, credit telephone sales for $0.75.
Line 5    Debit accounts receivable, credit restaurant sales for $24.03.
Line 6    Debit accounts receivable, credit telephone sales for $0.75.
Line 7    Debit accounts receivable, credit room sales for $89.00
Line 8    Debit accounts receivable, credit sales taxes payable for $6.19.
Line 9    Debit accounts receivable, credit occupancy taxes payable for $2.67.

**Reference Numbers** Exhibits 10-4, 10-5, 10-7, and 10-8 display reference numbers on each line of posting. These numbers identify departments in the hotel's chart of accounts. A chart of accounts is a coded numbering system by which the hotel classifies its records. Each department within the hotel is identified by code, but it isn't a secret code. Having codes makes record keeping easier. There is no uniform coding system among hotels, but there is consistency within the individual property and sometimes within the chain.

Consider the reference numbering of Exhibit 10-8. In the second column under "Description," the number 2315 appears on lines 2 to 11. That's the room number, the number of the account receivable being charged. In the third column is a second series of numbers, which represent the departments generating the postings. Lines 2, 3, and 4 contain the numbers 518, 519, and 520, respectively. The rooms department is identified by the number 5. Hence, 518 is room sales, 519 is room tax, and 520 is room tax for a second governmental agency.

**Exhibit 10-8** ▶

Line 1 of the folio illustrates an advance deposit made by a credit card, an unusual posting. Note references to the chart of accounts in the centre under "Description." Each debit posting is to the room number, 2315. Equal and opposite credits are charged to their respective departments: 518, 519, and 520 are accounting codes for rooms; 5996 is beverage; and 1382 is food. The balance due will most likely be charged to the same credit card.

## HAWAII PRINCE HOTEL

W A I K I K I

⊙ *PRINCE HOTELS*

*Hawaii Prince Hotel, 100 Holomoana Street, Honolulu, Hawaii 96815*
*Telephone: (808) 956-1111  Facsimile: (808) 946-0811*

A-STANDARD

DECAT, M/M BILL
234 PENNSYLVANIA AVENUE
REGINA, SK
M4I 1X4

| ARRIVAL DATE | 6/21 |
|---|---|
| DEPARTURE | 6/22 |
| NO. IN PARTY | 2 |
| RATE | 125.00 |

ACCOUNT NO. 67877   ROOM NO. 2315

| NUMBER | DATE | DESCRIPTION | | | AMOUNT |
|---|---|---|---|---|---|
| 1 | 5/31 | ADV DEP VISA MASTER | 4000 0000 0000 0000 | | $130.21CR |
| | | 1NT RM/ST TAX | 67877 | | |
| 2 | 6/21 | ROOM | 2315 | 518 | $125.00 |
| 3 | 6/21 | EXCISE TAX | 2315 | 519 | $5.21 |
| 4 | 6/21 | ROOM TAX | 2315 | 520 | $6.25 |
| 5 | 6/21 | LOCAL PHONE | 2315 | 621XXX9005 | $.75 |
| | | 13:57     9564902 | | 67877 | |
| 6 | 6/21 | PROMENADE DECK | 2315 | 5996 | $23.00 |
| 7 | 6/21 | PROMENADE DECK | 2315 | 5996 | $3.00 |
| 8 | 6/21 | PROMENADE DECK | 2315 | 5996 | $.96 |
| 9 | 6/22 | PRINCE COURT | 2315 | 1382 | $18.00 |
| 10 | 6/22 | PRINCE COURT | 2315 | 1382 | $2.00 |
| 11 | 6/22 | PRINCE COURT | 2315 | 1382 | $.75 |
| | | * Balance Due * | | | $54.71 |

SIGNATURE

I AGREE THAT MY LIABILITY FOR THIS BILL IS NOT WAIVED AND AGREE TO BE HELD PERSONALLY LIABLE IN THE EVENT THAT THE INDICATED PERSON, COMPANY OR ASSOCIATION FAILS TO PAY FOR ANY PART OR THE FULL AMOUNT OF THESE CHARGES.

**Getting the Posting onto the Folio** Charges are posted throughout the day as the guest uses the hotel's services. Often, the same charges appear again and again as they do for food (see Exhibit 10-8, lines 9 to 11), beverages (lines 6 to 8), or telephone. Depending on the type and class of hotel, additional charges may be generated in the laundry/valet department or in any of a variety of other minor departments. Among the others are garage or parking fees; saunas and health clubs; in-room safes, bars, and films (see Exhibit 10-4, lines 2 and 3); and sports and recreational charges such as green fees, ski-lift tickets, skeet shooting, horseback riding, and more.

In every instance, the charge must be communicated to the desk from the distant department providing the service. Either the desk accesses the information from the computer or receives it in paper-and-pencil form. In the first case, the department uses a POS terminal and the communication is electronic. If there is no POS terminal, the voucher is delivered by hand, telephone, or remote printer, and the guest-service agent enters the charge into the PMS through the front-office terminal.

**The Rooms Department** Posting rooms-department charges is different than posting charges from other departments. Room charges are posted only once each day. Food, beverage, and telephone might have several daily postings. Furthermore, room charges are posted by the night auditor during the early hours of the morning. Other charges are posted as they occur throughout the day. The final difference is the location of the charge. Room sales originate at the desk, so there is no need to communicate electronically or with vouchers.

With a pencil-and-paper system, the night auditor removes each folio from the well, writes the room charge and tax on each, and totals the account (see Exhibit 10-2). This is a very time-consuming and error-prone procedure.

Property management systems keep the room rates in memory, compute the taxes automatically, post and total electronically, and print on demand. With a PMS, the night auditor initiates a program that posts the room rates and taxes to all folios, as illustrated in Exhibit 10-8, lines 2 to 4, and in other illustrations throughout the chapter.

Four exceptions, all infrequent ones, require room rates to be posted during the day rather than by the night auditor. Exception one is the day rate: Guests arrive and depart on the same day—leaving before the night audit even takes place. Late check-outs are another example. The auditor posts the previous night's room charge in the normal manner, but the premium for staying beyond the check-out hour is added by the cashier as the guest departs. It's something the auditor has no way of knowing. Situation three is a recent innovation. Guests who check out earlier than the guarantee on their reservations are compelled to pay a penalty, which is posted by the guest-service agent on duty. Again, the auditor has no way of knowing about the early departure.

Paid-in-advance guests—say, those without luggage—are the final exception. Often, but not always, room charges are posted at the same time that the guests make payment—that's even before they go to the room. With this procedure, guests get receipts at check-in and do not return to the desk at check-out, having already settled their accounts. At the time of the audit, the night auditor finds that the folios have already been posted.

Although posted at a different time and in a different manner, room sales have the same impact as sales in other departments. All increase the amount owed by the guest, the account receivable. Most folio postings do that: increase the amount owed by the guest. The critical posting is the guest's settlement of the account. That's when the debt is paid and the account receivable is reduced to zero. *It is* always *reduced to zero.* Before examining account receivable settlements, let's review sales taxes as another of the charges (increases) to accounts receivable.

**Sales Taxes** Taxes levied by municipal, county or region, provincial or territorial, and federal governments on room sales are universal to hotel keeping. Governments find taxing visitors easier than taxing residents. Making the hotel collect the tax just adds insult to injury. With rare exceptions, every room charge is followed by a tax posting. The amount owed by the account receivable increases with each room sale, which belongs to the hotel, and with the room tax, which the hotel collects for the government.

Taxes payable is a debt that the hotel owes to the government. Until the quarterly payment is made, it is due and payable. In other words, the hotel is an account receivable of the government just as the guest is the hotel's account receivable. Logically enough, one becomes an *account payable* when situated on the other side of the owe–owed relationship. Collecting taxes from guests as an arm of the government makes the hotel liable to (owing) the state and/or local agencies. The amount due is labelled as *taxes payable*. Exhibits 10-4, 10-5, 10-7, and 10-8 show those tax entries.

Periodically, perhaps quarterly, the hotel pays the governmental agencies the taxes due.

## Posting Settlements to Accounts Receivable

As the guest folio (an account receivable) is increased by charges, so it is decreased by credits (payments). Simply put, paying the bill by one of three means reduces the guest's obligation to the hotel.

Although charges occur and are posted numerous times throughout each day, settlement of the account usually waits until check-out time. Of course, guests can and do make payments during the stay. With reservations, payments are often made in advance, prepaid. Irrespective of when and how the payment is made, the transient folio (the guest bill, the front-office account) *must* always have a zero balance at check-out! That is, total debits posted throughout the stay and total credits, whenever posted, must equal at departure. Departed guests can have no transient folio balance if they are no longer registered. The first few pages of the chapter made clear that only registered guests can have accounts in the transient ledger.

**Three Methods of Settling Accounts** Hotels have many services to sell, and they result in an array of charge postings. Payments, often called credits, are easier to track because there are only three means of settling the account debt: *There are only three methods of settling a folio.* These can be applied separately or in combinations.

1. Cash is one method, but it is used infrequently. Cash means any kind of money: bills and coin; foreign currency; domestic and international traveller's cheques; personal cheques; bank cheques; cashier's cheques; even casino chips. Payment with cash is discussed thoroughly in its own chapter, Chapter 11.

2. Allowances, reductions to the amount owed, are a second method of settlement. One study suggested that billing errors that require allowance adjustments may occur as often as one in four postings!

3. Transferring the folio balance to someone else is the third method of settlement. Credit card transfers are the best examples. Guests move their folio balances to other accounts receivable. That is usually a credit card company, but not always. That "person" eventually makes settlement with the hotel.

**Allowances** Just as retail stores allow the return of unsatisfactory goods, hotels give credit for poor service, misunderstandings, and mathematical errors. The retailer's exchange of merchandise is the hotel's allowance. Legitimate adjustments to guest complaints are considered so important that lease provisions usually give the hotel authority to grant allowances for unsatisfactory service by concessionaires renting space in the hotel.

Even computerized properties use paper-and-pencil allowance vouchers, also called **rebate** slips. A written record requiring an authorized signature highlights the issue both for the guest and for the company anxious to minimize errors in guest service (see Exhibit 10-9). Improving weaknesses in the operation starts with knowing what the failures are.

An allowance report is prepared daily as part of the night audit. As hotels empower employees (Chapter 7) to make decisions such as granting allowances, reports to management increase in importance as a control technique. Employee empowerment aside, good fiscal management requires a supervisor's signature when the value of the allowance exceeds a given amount. That limit would vary with the class of the property.

Allowances are given to adjust the bill after the fact. Problems brought to management's attention early enough will be corrected. Allowances are warranted only if it is too late to rectify the complaint. A range of circumstances requires allowances: a higher room rate is posted than appears on the guest's rooming slip; a guest room never receives service from housekeeping; the hotel fails to deliver promised services or a basic commodity such as hot water; or a complimentary (comp) guest.

Comp Allowances The authority to compliment rooms or other services—the "power of the pen"—should be restricted and carefully monitored. Because comps are subject to abuse, management should require a daily comp report (see Chapter 13). Misuse starts when comp guests are not registered. Then there is nothing to report: no room count, no house count, and no room income. Proper handling of room comps starts with a daily posting of the full room rate. To allay the guest's concern, the rate is flagged on the rooming slip, "100 COMP" for example. An allowance valued at the sum total of daily folio postings is granted at the time of departure.

**Exhibit 10-9** ▶
Prenumbered allowance vouchers provide pencil-and-paper records of guest complaints and company errors.

**REBATE CREDIT**
Allowance Voucher

Date _July 6_ _____ 12501

Name _Jones L. K._          Room _1617_

| Explanation | | | |
|---|---|---|---|
| _Laundry lost tie_ | | 23 | 50 |
| | | | |

GUEST SIGNATURE _L.K. Jones_          Cashier _ABC_

Kayco NCR Form 126          O.K. By _____          Manager

The allowance illustration presented under the topic of sales or incomes is repeated here with the tax added on. If the guest stayed four nights, the first entry would be made four times, once each night, but on the folio and in folio format (see Exhibit 10-7, for example). Here, the folio entry appears in accounting form.

> Increases in assets, including *accounts receivable* and cash, are made with debits.
>
> Increases in incomes (sales of *rooms*, food, beverage, etc.) are made with credits.
>
> Increases in liabilities (debts owed to banks and *governments*) are made with credits.
>
> Debit: Accounts Receivable/Guest's Folio 107
>     Credit: Proper Department (*room*, food, beverage, spa, etc.) 100
>     Credit: Sales Taxes Payable 7
> *Explanation:* Comp guest occupied room.

Reversing the room sale (or any other sale) with one allowance results in no charges to the guest and no room (or other) income earned by the hotel. However, a clear record of what occurred is now on the books. Some jurisdictions require room taxes to be paid on comp rooms.

**Allowances for Poor Service** Accidents happen: A shirt is scorched in the laundry; a skirt is torn on a rough cocktail table. And service delivery fails: a food server spills coffee on a guest; a child's crib is never delivered. Service mishaps are bound to occur when servicing hundreds of visitors each day.

If the problem is caught immediately, management remedies the mistake: delivers the crib. If not caught immediately, or if the problem has no remedy (the shirt is burned), there is little to do but reimburse with an allowance. Every allowance, whether for comps or adjustments, results in reductions of both the account receivable (the guest's folio) and the departmental income. If the original charge was made to a credit card (as it might be in the lounge where the skirt was torn), the adjustment would be made to the credit card, not to the folio.

All allowance entries follow the same format as the room comp allowance above. The specific departmental allowance is substituted for the room allowance of the illustration.

**Allowances to Correct Errors** Handling small late charges is one of several clerical errors requiring correcting allowances. A late charge is posted to the folio of a guest who has already checked out. If the charge is large enough to pursue by mail, a transfer—soon to be explained—is used. If the late charge is too small to warrant the costs of collection, including guest annoyance, it is wiped off. Accounts receivable is credited and the hotel absorbs the error.

Some errors are just carelessness in posting. Exhibit 10-10 shows the allowance for 99 cents that was inadvertently posted as part of the room charge by the night auditor. Exhibit 10-4 (third line from the bottom) adjusts for a dual posting of an in-room film (lines 2 and 3).

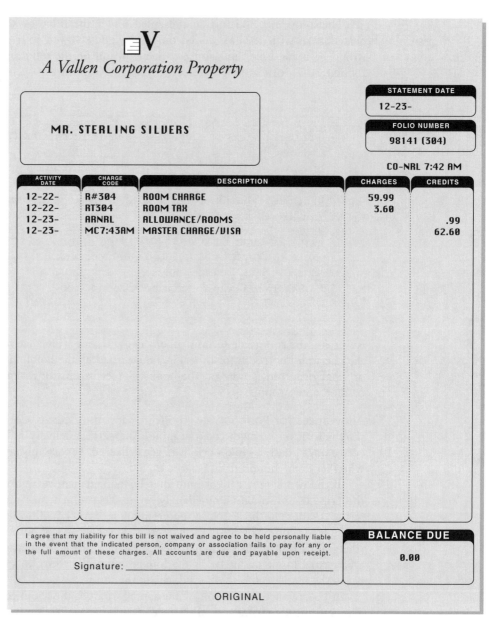

Many errors originate in misunderstandings or lack of attention. For example, a couple arrives for several days but one spouse leaves early. Although the desk is aware of the situation, the double occupancy rate continues for the entire stay. An allowance is needed to reduce the debit balance by the difference between the single and the double rates multiplied by the number of nights overcharged.

In theory, it should not happen, but sometimes a guest folio is carried one night beyond the actual departure day. An allowance corrects the error. This happens most frequently with one-night, paid-in-advance guests who do not bother to check out.

Every protested charge is not the hotel's error. This is why having old vouchers accessible to the cashier is helpful. (New PMS programs display vouchers from previous days, reducing the time needed to search manually.) When shown a signed voucher, guests often recall charges they had vehemently protested only moments earlier. Large bar charges fall into this category when viewed with a sober eye on the following day. This also happens when two persons share a room and one makes charges but the other pays. When the first guest has already checked out, it is especially necessary to prove to the remaining guest that the charge was made.

Although computers reduce the number of errors, they do not compensate for guest forgetfulness or for honest misunderstandings or mistakes.

**Extended-Stay Allowances** Some resorts allow a reduction in the daily rate if the guest remains for an extended length of time. To make certain of the guest's commitment to remain, the full daily charge and not the pro rata charge of the special rate is posted. Either an allowance is given on the final day to adjust the weekly rate or the charge for the final day is reduced to meet the special weekly total.

**Recording the Allowance** Allowances, as well as the other two methods of settling an account (cash and transfers), are usually resolved at the time of departure. Once the issue has been settled, a voucher is completed and an authorized signature is obtained (see Exhibit 10-9). As Chapter 7 explains, empowered employees are authorized to sign off within a given dollar range.

The allowance is used with either or both of the other payments to settle the bill. Exhibit 10-10 illustrates settlement with an allowance and a credit card transfer.

**Transfers** Like allowances and cash payments, transfers are usually, but not always, recorded as the guest checks out. A transfer simply moves the balance of one record (a front-office folio) to another record (most often a city ledger account). The balance of the front-office folio gets smaller, usually falling to zero. The balance of the other record gets larger by the same amount.

All or part of a folio balance can be transferred. Transfers can be made between accounts in the same ledger (registered guest to registered guest in the transient ledger) or between accounts in two ledgers (registered guest in the transient ledger to city account in the city ledger). The first transfer type, registered guest to registered guest, is easier to track because both folios are available to the front-office staff. Transfers between transient folios and city accounts, usually credit card companies, may appear incomplete to the front-office staff because the city ledger is not at the front desk. It is maintained by the accounting office.

**Transfer of Transient Ledger to Transient Ledger** Exhibit 10-11 illustrates transfers recorded on PMS folios. Note that both parties have folios, and both stay for two nights. Both folios have room and tax charges of $230.80 ($190 plus $22.80). On June 14, Guest Berger, Room 301, settles his account with a credit transfer to Guest Meade, Room 723 (line 009). Meade's account increases and Berger's decreases by the same value, $230.80. With the credit transfer, Berger's account is zeroed out as required of all check-outs. Guest Meade, Room 723, pays the total amount.

**Transfer of Transient Ledger to City Ledger: Credit Card** Credit cards are the most common method of settling transient folios. The guest "pays" the transient folio by

**Exhibit 10-11 ▶**
Line 9 of both folios illustrates a transfer from Room 301 (left page) to Room 723. That transfer zeros the account of 301, and the guest checks out. Room 723 also checks out after making a different type of transfer, one from the guest ledger to the city ledger using an American Express credit card. Sales taxes (GST) are summarized on each folio. Note the plus (debit) and minus (credit) signs used instead of two columns.

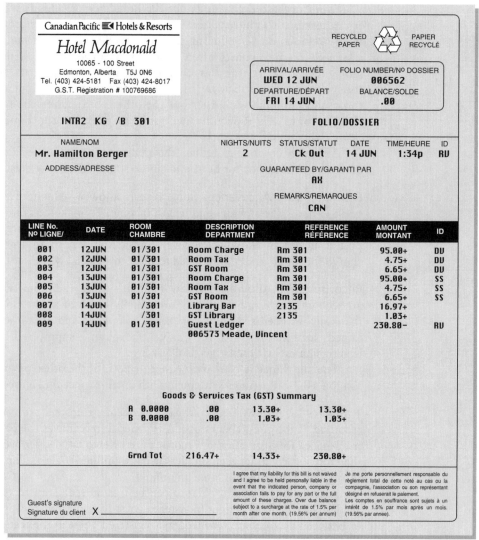

transferring the balance to a credit card account in the city ledger. The front-office cashier sees the transient folio brought to zero and leaves collection from the credit card company to the accounting office, which is covered in Chapter 12.

Three exhibits illustrate the mechanics. Exhibit 10-10 shows a credit card used in conjunction with an allowance. The two credits totalling $63.59 balance the debit total of $63.59. Note the zero balance on the bottom right. Now the hotel must collect from Visa, the city ledger account. **Bank cards** such as Visa and MasterCard are usually handled in the same manner as cash, although a special payment key may be used. The credit card vouchers are deposited in the bank the next day, or immediately if electronic settlement (similar to a debit card transaction) is used, and are credited to the hotel's bank account. Non-bank cards such as American Express may still have to be invoiced on a daily basis.

**Exhibit 10-11 ▶**
*(Continued)*

Canadian Pacific **ЖⰈ** Hotels & Resorts

## Hotel Macdonald

10065 - 100 Street
Edmonton, Alberta    T5J 0N6
Tel. (403) 424-5181   Fax (403) 424-8017
G.S.T. Registration # 100769686

RECYCLED PAPER    PAPIER RECYCLÉ

| ARRIVAL/ARRIVÉE | FOLIO NUMBER/No DOSSIER |
|---|---|
| **WED 12 JUN** | **006573** |
| DEPARTURE/DÉPART | BALANCE/SOLDE |
| **FRI 14 JUN** | **.00** |

INTR2  KG  /B  723                          **FOLIO/DOSSIER**

| NAME/NOM | NIGHTS/NUITS | STATUS/STATUT | DATE | TIME/HEURE | ID |
|---|---|---|---|---|---|
| **Mr. Vincent Meade** | 2 | **Ck Out** | 14 JUN | 1:34p | RV |

ADDRESS/ADRESSE

GUARANTEED BY/GARANTI PAR
**AX**

REMARKS/REMARQUES
**USA**

| LINE No. No LIGNE/ | DATE | ROOM CHAMBRE | DESCRIPTION DEPARTMENT | REFERENCE RÉFÉRENCE | AMOUNT MONTANT | ID |
|---|---|---|---|---|---|---|
| 001 | 12JUN | 01/723 | Room Charge | Rm 723 | 95.00+ | DV |
| 002 | 12JUN | 01/723 | Room Tax | Rm 723 | 4.75+ | DV |
| 003 | 12JUN | 01/723 | GST Room | Rm 723 | 6.65+ | DV |
| 004 | 13JUN | 01/723 | Long Distance | 0 - 54-6 8 | 4.68+ | |
| 005 | 13JUN | 01/723 | Long Distance | 0 - 51-1 6 | 5.57+ | |
| 006 | 13JUN | 01/723 | Room Charge | Rm 723 | 95.00+ | SS |
| 007 | 13JUN | 01/723 | Room Tax | Rm 723 | 4.75+ | SS |
| 008 | 13JUN | 01/723 | GST Room | Rm 723 | 6.65+ | SS |
| 009 | 14JUN | 01/301 | Guest Ledger 006562 Berger, Hamilton | | 230.80+ | RV |
| 010 | 14JUN | 01/723 | American Express Thank you | | 453.85− | RV |

### Goods & Services Tax (GST) Summary

| | | | | |
|---|---|---|---|---|
| A | 0.0000 | .00 | 13.30+ | 13.30+ |
| B | 7.0000 | 9.58+ | .67+ | 10.25+ |

| Grnd Tot | 209.08+ | 13.97+ | 223.05+ |
|---|---|---|---|

Guest's signature
Signature du client  X _____

I agree that my liability for this bill is not waived and I agree to be held personally liable in the event that the indicated person, company or association fails to pay for any part or the full amount of these charges. Over due balance subject to a surcharge at the rate of 1.5% per month after one month. (19.56% per annum)

Je me porte personnellement responsable du règlement total de cette noté au cas où la compagnie, l'association ou son représentant désigné en refuserait le paiement. Les comptes en souffrance sont sujets à un intérêt de 1.5% par mois après un mois. (19.56% par année).

**Transfer of Transient Ledger to City Ledger: Direct** Master accounts are the best examples of direct city ledger transfers. The firm, association, or group is billed at the conclusion of the event. Doing so saves the hotel the service costs of using a credit card company. When the group leaves, the master account—the A folio in the transient ledger—will be credited (see Exhibit 10-4) and the association's account in the city ledger will be debited. In Exhibit 10-4, the $229.79 balance is credited (with a transfer credit) in the transient ledger and subsequently debited (with a transfer debit) to the association in the city ledger. Billing and collection then take place through the mail.

Coupons Direct city ledger transfers sometimes involve coupons. A guest who is booked by a travel agent or airline may pay the transient folio with a coupon. This is a receipt by which a third party, the travel agent, acknowledges that it has already been paid by the guest. By accepting the coupon, the hotel agrees to bill the travel agency or other third party directly. This is accomplished by transferring the transient guest's folio to the third party's account in the city ledger and billing by mail (see Chapter 12).

**Transfer of City Ledger to Guest Ledger: Advance Deposits** Transfers of advance deposits flow in a direction opposite to the other two interledger transfers. Credit card and direct city ledger transfers shift the account receivable *from* the transient ledger (the front-office folio) *to* the city ledger. The accounting office then makes billing. Advance deposits move the other way. The balance starts in the city ledger and moves *from* the city ledger *to* the folio in the guest ledger. Since the deposit precedes the guest's visit, the transfer appears on the folio's first line (see Exhibits 10-8 and 10-12, lines 1). But how does the deposit get into the city ledger to begin with?

Guaranteed reservations require a deposit, either a credit card deposit (see Exhibit 10-8) or a cash deposit (see Exhibit 10-12). The hotel receives the asset, either the account receivable with the credit card company or the cash by means of a cheque. Note that advance deposits in cash are rare, usually limited to resorts. Most advance deposits are made with credit cards, but these too are rarely processed as advance deposits. Rather, they are handled as guaranteed reservations and processed after the fact, but only if the guest does not arrive (see Chapter 6).

The hotel's obligation to provide service equal to the deposit cannot be recorded on the front-office folio. There is no front-office folio, because the guest hasn't arrived. Only registered guests have transient folios, so the hotel opens a city ledger record called Advance Deposits. Advance deposits from all guests are accumulated in this one record.

With advance deposits, the hotel has collected payments even though the guests owe nothing. This makes the hotel liable (owing) for services sometime in the future. Just as the hotel has liability for room taxes collected but not yet paid to government, so it has liability to provide paid-in-advance guests with future services.

The record of the hotel's city ledger liability, advance deposits, remains in the city ledger until the guest arrives days or weeks later. Upon arrival, the balance is transferred from the city ledger to the guest's newly opened folio in the transient ledger. As with other transfers between ledgers, guest-service agents at the front office may see only the transient-ledger half of the entry.

The hotel still owes the guest; the transfer has not changed that. Purchases during the guest's stay (rooms, food, and so on) are applied against the original deposit. Either the hotel still owes the guest at the end of the stay, or the guest has charged more than the original deposit. With the former, a refund is necessary, and that is explained in Chapter 11. More likely, the guest checks out owing an additional amount because deposits are usually one night's room rate only. Then the cycle begins again with payment at check-out.

Payment on check-out can be made in one of three ways: allowances, cash (see Exhibit 10-12), or transfers (credit card or direct). Most likely, settlement will be by credit card. This moves the balance *to* the city ledger *from* the transient ledger, whereas the deposit shift had been *from* the city ledger *to* the transient ledger (see Exhibit 10-12).

**Exhibit 10-12** ▶

This folio opens with a credit balance, a cash deposit transferred from the city ledger. Another cash payment zeros the account as the guest checks out. Cash payments like these are one of three methods for settling folios. Exhibit 10-10 illustrates the other two methods, allowances and credit cards.

30 PITT STREET
SYDNEY NSW 2000 AUSTRALIA
TELEPHONE: (02) 259 7000
FACSIMILE: (02) 252 1999
TELEX: AA127792
A.R.B.N. 003 864 908

SYDNEY
**RENAISSANCE**
HOTEL

| GUEST | | |
|---|---|---|
| VALLEN, M/M J | ROOM | 2003 |
| EASTER PACKAGE | RATE | 170.00 |
| 2ND AVE BEACHSIDE APPTS | No. PERSONS | 2 |
| BURLEIGH HEADS  QLD  4220 | FOLIO No. | 152490 |
| | PAGE | 01 |
| | ARRIVAL | 04/12/ |
| CH-A  BUNNY | DEPARTURE | 04/16/ |
| | DEPOSIT | $680.00 |

| DATE | REFERENCE No. | | DESCRIPTION | CHARGES / CREDITS |
|---|---|---|---|---|
| 19 | | | | |
| | | 00754 | DEPOSIT | 680.00CR |
| APR12 | 401 | 01859 | 99LOCAL CALL | .70 |
| APR12 | 011 | 02003 | 00ROOM CHG | 170.00 |
| APR13 | 131 | 04071 | 61BRASSERIE | 22.00 |
| APR13 | 401 | 02145 | 99LOCAL CALL | .70 |
| APR13 | 011 | 02003 | 00ROOM CHG | 170.00 |
| APR14 | 181 | 02003 | 43MINI BAR | 2.50 |
| APR14 | 011 | 02003 | 00ROOM CHG | 170.00 |
| APR15 | 401 | 01736 | 99LOCAL CALL | .70 |
| APR15 | 011 | 02003 | 00ROOM CHG | 170.00 |
| APR16 | 001 | 00001 | 23PAID CASH | 26.60CR |
| | | | TOTAL-DUE | .00 |

TRAVEL AGENCY
LOVE   TRAVEL
JENN
SH8  HIGH  ROAD
SOUTHPORT   QLD   4215
CHARGE TO

I AGREE THAT MY LIABILITY FOR THIS BILL IS NOT WAIVED AND AGREE TO BE HELD PERSONALLY LIABLE IN THE EVENT THAT THE INDICATED PERSON, COMPANY OR ASSOCIATION FAILS TO PAY FOR ANY PART OR THE FULL AMOUNT OF THESE CHARGES.

SIGNATURE

SYDNEY RENAISSANCE HOTEL - INSPIRED BY THE PAST, DESIGNED FOR THE FUTURE. SM
FOR RESERVATIONS: AUSTRALIA (008) 222 431, IN SYDNEY (02) 251 8888  ●  BANGKOK 02 236 0361
HONG KONG (852) 311 3666  ●  JAPAN (0120) 222 332, IN TOKYO (03) 3239 8303  ●  KUALA LUMPUR
(03) 241 4081 AND (03) 248 9008  ●  SEOUL (02) 555 0501

AUSTRALIA ● CANADA ● CARRIBEAN ● CENTRAL AMERICA ● CHINA ● EUROPE ● HONG KONG ● INDIA
INDONESIA ● JAPAN ● KOREA ● MALAYSIA ● MEXICO ● MIDDLE EAST ● PAKISTAN ● SRI LANKA
THAILAND ● UK ● USA                    FORM No. FO 001 12/92

# Summary

Hotels sell their services to strangers and to registered guests. Whereas strangers must pay immediately for services such as food and beverage, guests may delay payment until check-out. In the interim, guests owe the hotel; they are accounts receivable. A record of that debt, called a folio, is maintained in the front office. All of the folios together are called a ledger. Hence, the billing records of registered guests are in a front-office or transient ledger. Non-registered parties—credit card companies, for example—may also owe the hotel. Their records are maintained in a different ledger, the city ledger, by the accounting office.

Usually, guests settle their individual folios as they check out. That's the time they pay for all of the services (room, room taxes, food, beverage, spas, golf, etc.) that have been charged to them. Payment is by cash (rare), by allowances (for service adjustments), and by credit cards (the usual method). Credit card settlements transfer the balance of the front-office folios to the records of the credit card companies in the city ledger. The accounting office bills and collects from credit card companies.

Master accounts, which track the charges of groups, are also maintained on folios. These, too, are transferred to the city ledger when the association or company checks out. (Every folio must have a zero balance after check-out!) Master accounts are billed directly to the group's headquarters. That's different from billing credit card companies for third-party folios. Both types of billing originate in the city ledger, having been transferred there from the front-office ledger. That discussion resumes in Chapter 12.

Hotels have not only accounts receivable, but also accounts payable. Receivables are something the hotel owns. Payables are something the hotel owes. Hotels owe governments for room taxes collected but not yet paid. Hotels owe employees for tips collected but not yet paid. Hotels owe guests with advance deposits (not common) for services not yet delivered.

# Questions and Problems

1. Differentiate the following:
   (a) Debit from credit
   (b) Master account from split account
   (c) A folio from B folio
   (d) Transient guest from city guest
   (e) Charge from payment

2. Use a word processor to replicate the folio that would be produced when the Arthur Jones family checks out. Mr. and Mrs. Jones and their infant son, George, reside at 14 Big Mountain Drive, Quebec City, Quebec L1R 2X4. Their reservation for three nights at $125 per night plus 5 percent tax was guaranteed May 17 with a $200 cash (cheque) deposit for one night. They indicated that they will arrive late. They check in at 10 P.M. on June 3 and take one room (1233).
   (a) Breakfast charge on June 4 is $12.90.
   (b) Mrs. Jones hosts a small luncheon meeting for her company, and a $310 charge for the meeting room and meal is posted to the folio.
   (c) The family decides to leave earlier than planned and notifies the front desk of a 7 P.M. check-out.
   (d) A long-distance call of $8 is made.
   (e) The family checks out. They raise the issue of no clean linen—the laundry had a wild-cat strike—and argue for an allowance. One is given—$25. The rooms manager then charges 30 percent of the normal room charge for the late departure.
   (f) Payment is made with an American Express card, no. 33333333333.

3. Create a pencil-and-paper folio; use Exhibit 10-2 as a guide. Post the events of Problem 2, as they would appear on a hand-prepared folio.

4. Under which of the following circumstances would management grant an allowance? What would be the value of that allowance? What else might be done if an allowance were not granted?

(a) Guest sets the room alarm clock, but it fails to go off, which causes the guest to miss a meeting that involves thousands of dollars of commission.

(b) Same circumstance as (a), but the guest called the telephone operator for a morning call, which wasn't made.

(c) Guest checks out and discovers the nightly room charge to be $15 more than the rate quoted two weeks earlier by the reservations centre.

(d) Same circumstance as (c), but the discrepancy is discovered soon after the guest is roomed.

5. How would the following transfers be handled? (Answer either by discussion, by offering the accounting entries, or both.)

(a) A departing guest discovers that a $60 beverage charge that belongs to another guest, who is still registered, was incorrectly posted yesterday to the departing guest's account.

(b) Same circumstance as (a), but the $60 beverage posting was made today.

(c) Same circumstance as (a), but the other guest has departed.

(d) Two days into a guest's four-day stay, the reservations department realizes that the guest's advance deposit was never transferred to the front-office account.

(e) Same circumstance as (d), but the discovery is made by the guest, who writes to complain about the omission one week after check-out.

6. Check your understanding of accounting by proving the debits and credits for each of the following situations, which were not discussed in the text.

(a) The hotel pays the quarterly sales taxes of $8925 due to the local government, the City of Halifax, Nova Scotia.

(b) The hotel receives a cheque from Diners Club for payment of credit card balances due of $1000.

(c) Same as (b), but Diners Club withholds 4 percent as a fee.

(d) The hotel receives a cheque from its parent company for $1500, representing the total payment due for several frequent-stay guests who used their points at your hotel. The amount of room charges generated by those guests was $5500.

## 🗝 CASE STUDY

### The Sleeper Problem: A Simple Front Desk Error Results in Divorce

Veronica, a guest-service agent (GSA), was confident in her ability to handle almost any guest situation. However, the demanding customer at the front desk had a unique problem. Mrs. Smith was clutching in her hand an invoice from the hotel for one night's accommodation and taxes, and she was sure that no one in her household had stayed there. In fact, her husband had been away on a business trip on the date stated on the invoice. Although Veronica knew that under the Freedom of Information Act she was not allowed to discuss this guest registration invoice with Mrs. Smith, it possibly revealed a deeper problem with the hotel's front desk.

Mrs. Smith was introduced to the general manager (GM), who moved the discussion to her office to remove the debate from a public area to a more private one. Unable to reveal the details of the registration to Mrs. Smith, the GM promised to look into the complaint and call her to discuss it. The GM, who had worked as a GSA and front-office manager earlier in her career, was sure she knew what had happened—this invoice was probably the result of either a skip or a sleeper.

The GM asked Veronica to print out a copy of the guest folio and attach to it the registration card. The registration was indeed for a Mr. Smith who had given the address that the invoice was sent to. It showed that that Mr. Smith had checked in to the hotel, paying cash for one night of accommodation (October 16, departing October 17).

The folio showed a zero balance on the morning of October 17 and subsequently had a second day of room and taxes posted for the night of October 17.

Veronica was asked by the GM to explain how this error had happened.

1. What two key areas of daily checks required by the front desk had it failed to do or done poorly?

2. What could be done in the future to ensure that an error like this does not happen again?

3. In your opinion, what may be the ramifications for the hotel when Mrs. Smith confronts Mr. Smith with this invoice?

## Weblinks

American Express Canada
**www.americanexpress.ca**

MasterCard in Canada
**www.mastercard.com/canada/**

Visa Canada
**www.visa.ca/en**

Diners Club International
**www.dinersclubnorthamerica.com**

# Chapter 11 Cash Transactions

## Learning Outcomes

After reading this chapter, you will be able to do the following:

1. **Understand the proper handling of cash transactions, including cash receipts, paid-outs, and house receipts and expenses.**

2. **Understand the cashier's report and the income audit.**

3. **Create systems for detecting counterfeit currency and safe-guarding cheque cashing.**

## Handling Cash Transactions

Due to the ease, security, and prevalence of credit cards and debit cards, departing guests rarely pay hotel room folios with cash. Conservative estimates place cash payments during check-out at something less than 5 percent of the time. Cash payments are probably more common in budget or economy properties; they are even less common in corporate hotels (where employer-provided credit cards are frequently used) and resort properties (where the folio from a one-week stay might easily reach $3000 or more).

In today's electronic age, cash is simply less convenient than credit cards, debit cards, or other forms of electronic payment. After all, compared with credit (or debit) cards, cash is bulkier, less secure, provides a less detailed transaction trail, and requires an exchange to local currencies when visiting foreign countries. For corporate guests, an added step is required when using cash—the corporate guest must either obtain a cash advance before beginning the business trip or be out-of-pocket the amount of cash expended until the company reimburses his or her travel costs. No wonder so few guests pay cash at the front desk.

In spite of the small amount of cash that changes hands over the front desk, its relative importance to the operation of the hotel is substantial. Full-service properties monitor daily cash balances in cashiers' drawers to ensure that there is enough cash on hand to manage the numerous non-payment cash transactions that regularly occur. Guests expect to cash traveller's cheques, even personal cheques at times. They may need to change large bills. We should expect that foreign currency conversions at Canadian hotels will increase substantially with the introduction of the euro, the single European currency. Front desks also handle cash advances to guests and provide upfront money for many hotel uses. So, cash is not going to disappear.

Even as cash grows less popular as a means of folio settlement, its security becomes more of a concern. Cash is very negotiable, easily pocketed, and a continuing target of the bad guys. Counterfeiters, bad cheque artists, photocopiers, and short change manipulators work their wares at hotel desks. They would rather try the hotel desk than busier retail outlets. Guest-service agents handle less money than most other retailers, and are, therefore, less skilled at identifying bogus paper. When speaking of money, eternal vigilance is trite but true.

## Cash Paid-Outs

Cash at the front desk flows both ways, in the form of *cash receipts* and *cash paid-outs*. In every other operational department of the hotel, cash flows in to the various departmental cashiers (cash receipts). Only at the front desk does cash flow in both directions.

Cashiers in the front office, as in all hotel departments, may receive cash as payment to settle a guest account. However, as already noted, cash is less frequently used at the front desk to settle the guest folio than it is in various other departments, where the purchase is substantially less (e.g., breakfast in the dining room, a few beverages in the lounge, or a newspaper in the gift shop).

Another difference between the front office and other hotel departments is worth noting: While cashiers in other departments receive cash to settle purchases of various departmental products (e.g., breakfast, beverages, newspaper), cash transactions at the front office settle accounts receivables. Front-office cashiers have no product to sell. Conversely, outlet cashiers have no record of accounts receivable and are not able to accept payments from departing guests. Each cashier type accepts cash from guests but for different reasons.

Here is a simple formula for understanding the relationship of cash to accounts receivables:

Increases in assets, including accounts receivable and *cash,* are made with debits.

Decreases in assets, including *accounts receivable* and cash, are made with credits.

**Cash paid-outs** are the exclusive right of the front-office cashier. Except for tips paid to employees (wait staff, for example), no paid-outs are ever made by cashiers in other operating departments. Paid-outs to guests are, in fact, small loans made by the front office to or on behalf of the guest. Paid-outs are debits to the guest folio and increase the amount that the guest owes the hotel (accounts receivable). Similarly, the paid-out requires a cash outlay and therefore reduces the amount of cash in the front-office cashier's drawer. Again,

Increases in assets, including *accounts receivable* and cash, are made with debits.

Decreases in assets, including accounts receivable and *cash,* are made with credits.

Tips to employees are the most common paid-out, but there are others as well.

**Tips to Employees**  Tips are the most common cash advances. They are paid to an employee upon request of the guest. A signed cheque from the dining room or bar is the usual method of request. The guest, when signing for the service, adds the amount of gratuity to the cheque. When the signed voucher reaches the clerk, the departmental charges are separated from the tip. The tip is posted under the cash advance category, not the food or beverage category. After all, the tip is not departmental income, so it must not appear under a departmental heading.

Acting on the guest's signature, the front-office cashier pays the tip to the server, who signs for the money on a cash advance voucher. The cash advance voucher is then posted to the guest's folio along with the departmental charge (food, beverage, or whatever). At the end of the shift, this paid-out appears on the cashier's balance report as a reduction to the cashier's drawer.

Since the procedure is not an unusual one, a traffic problem could develop at the front desk if employees from all over the hotel came to collect their tips. To forestall this, tips are paid by the cashiers in the various dining rooms and bars. In a way, the problem handles itself. Most tips are added to national credit cards. Charges to national credit cards do not usually come to the front office. Only charges to the guest's folio, whether there are tips or not, flow through the front office. Even a credit card charge (restaurant, bar) made by a registered guest will not pass through the guest's folio, but rather will be deposited as income directly by the department involved.

Front-office cashiers still process tips to front-of-the-house employees: bell, house-keeping, and delivery persons. Most hotels pay their employees' tips on receipt or at the end of the shift. This is wonderful for the employee, but it can often result in the hotel subsidizing its employee gratuities in three common ways: **float** (that is, the time value of money), merchant discount fees on credit cards, and potential non-collectible accounts. Granted, it may be a minimal sum of money when considered on a per-employee basis, but over time (and in large properties with hundreds or thousands of employees) it can quickly add up to a significant amount.

**Float** Because of the time value of money, it is expensive to prepay an employee's tip before the guest's bill is paid. Yet this is exactly what happens with many paid-out tips. To illustrate the point, let's follow the payment cycle for a newly arriving guest, Diane Green.

Upon arrival, Green asks the front desk to issue a $10 tip to the bellperson as a paid-out against her folio. Because this is the first day of a lengthy visit, let's assume that Green's folio will not be settled for nine days. In this example, the hotel has ostensibly paid the bellperson with money it will not receive for nine days.

To add insult to injury, Green's bill will probably be settled by a national credit card. Certain credit card companies take weeks before they pay the hotel. It is conceivable, therefore, that the hotel has paid the bellperson a tip with money it will not receive for some 20 or 30 days! That is a costly employee benefit.

Yet almost all hotels conduct this practice. There really is no other way to handle employee tips without creating additional burdens. Hotels could refuse to allow guests to charge tips against their folio. Although this would save hotels the cost of the merchant discount fee, the practice would create far more ill will than it would save in expenses. Similarly, hotels could wait to pay employee tips until the guests' bills actually cleared. This would save hotels those expenses related to both float and non-collectible accounts. It would, however, create an accounting and tracking nightmare that would be hard to justify. Hotels look upon tip expenses as another cost of doing business, a large one at that.

**Cash Loans** Paid-outs to hotel guests are generally quite rare, occurring under unusual circumstances and only to those guests well known by the hotel's management. Advancing money to the guest as a paid-out (debit) against the folio runs the same costs and risks discussed above (float, credit card merchant discount fees, and potential losses from uncollectible accounts). However, just as few hotels charge processing fees to employees who receive tips against credit cards, equally few hotels charge fees to guests desperate for a cash loan.

▲
**Exhibit 11-1**

Advanced ATM machines offer many more features than the standard ATM cash machines, including cheque cashing for personal, corporate, and payroll cheques with no risk to the hotel or merchant. Risks are minimized by the Mr. Payroll ATM, which uses a security system based on facial recognition. With biometrics technology, the ATM "never forgets a face."

**Automatic Teller Machines (ATMs)** By far the most common method used by today's guests for generating cash is the automatic teller machine (ATM). There are presently 15 950 ATM machines across Canada at a cost of almost $100 000 each. The use of ATMs (see Exhibit 11-1) is not limited to Canada: ATMs are rapidly becoming the accepted norm for quick currency worldwide. The two most popular overseas networks, Cirrus (linked to MasterCard) and Plus (linked to Visa), can be accessed by more than 90 percent of the ATM bank cards in circulation in Canada. Another attractive benefit to using worldwide ATMs is that the ATMs' foreign exchange rate is often lower than the rate charged by local banks.

Corporate and leisure travellers have benefited in recent years from the growing number of available ATMs. This is especially true in foreign countries, where travellers gain the convenience of local currency at the touch of a button without the concern of exchanging just the right amount of money. Also, using international ATMs allows the traveller to float the currency exchange for some 20- or 30-plus days.

Additionally, ATM machines in hotel lobbies likely increase revenues. Cash retention is generally quite high with ATM users. In other words, some of the money dispensed to the guest through the ATM probably stays in the hotel. Research shows that 30 to 33 percent of cash is retained from ATMs located in large retail stores; 35 to 40 percent is retained from ATMs located in small retail stores; and 70 to 80 percent is retained from ATMs located in nightclubs. No research is yet available for hotel lobbies.

**ATMs Dispense More than Cash** The newest ATMs are fast becoming important new marketing tools for hotels and local merchants. ATMs promote products through coupons and/or on-screen graphics. Many ATMs allow a hotel to custom-design one or more coupons for the back of the guest receipt. A coupon might be worth a free drink in the bar or a free appetizer in the restaurant. In addition to this approach, ATMs can flash messages and promotional screens to the guest while waiting for the transaction to process.

Because today's hottest ATMs are wired directly to the Web, literally anything goes. Guests can pay utility bills, apply for a new car loan, or trade stocks. Indeed, the ATM can print cashier's cheques, make a pitch suggesting that the customer try the hotel's new credit card, even show the guest tomorrow's weather forecast.

**Paid-Outs to Concessionaires** Full-service hotels often arrange for local merchants to provide guest services that the hotel is unable to offer. These merchants may actually have an outlet inside the hotel (for example, a beauty salon, florist, or gift shop), or they may contract services off-premises (for example, a travel agent, valet cleaning, or a printing shop). These private vendors are commonly referred to as concessionaires; their shops are known as **concessions**.

The concessionaire–guest relationship often mandates that the hotel act as an intermediary. In circumstances where the hotel relays the goods on behalf of the guest (laundry is usually delivered to the guest's room by the bell staff, for example) or where the concessionaire looks to the hotel for collection (say, when a guest charges her hair-styling to the room folio), the hotel is acting as an intermediary. As such, the hotel is sometimes entitled to a fee or commission for its part in the process. It is not uncommon for hotels to earn 10 to 20 percent of the laundry and dry cleaning revenue (the other 80 to 90 percent accrues to the vendor) as their share of providing laundry bags, bell staff pickups and deliveries, storage, and collections.

The hotel also finds itself stuck in the middle when dealing with problems or complaints. When a piece of clothing has been lost or destroyed, the guest is not interested in learning that the laundry service is a private concession. Quality guest service dictates that the hotel solve the problem on behalf of the guest!

### Accounting for Paid-Outs to Concessionaires

The hotel also acts as intermediary in terms of disbursing revenues to the concessionaire. Payment is made to the merchant when the service is completed and charged to the guest's folio as a paid-out. Specifically, the clerk debits accounts receivable (a paid-out on the guest's folio) and credits cash. The clerk then removes the cash from the drawer in the amount of the paid-out (remember, the paid-out charged to the guest may be different from the amount of cash handed over to the concessionaire, because the hotel may keep a portion of the proceeds as its share of the transaction). The concessionaire then signs the paid-out voucher and the money is handed over.

At the end of the shift, the cashier's balance report reflects the reduction of cash in the money drawer. In essence, the hotel has loaned the money on behalf of the guest and awaits repayment when the guest checks out. Of course, all of the costs associated with float, credit card discount fees, and uncollectible accounts are issues for negotiation between the hotel and the concessionaire.

Paying the concessionaire in cash each time the service is used is expensive and time consuming, for the merchant as well as for the hotel, since the concessionaire must wait for the cash and sign the paperwork. In many cases, a different plan is arranged. The hotel bills the guest just as if the concessionaire were a department of the hotel, collects on check-out, and reimburses the merchant periodically. In such cases, the guest's folio looks a bit different. Rather than reflecting a paid-out posting, the charge instead is posted to an actual department (say, laundry or valet). The net effect—the guest owes the hotel—remains unchanged.

### Refunds at Check-out

On occasion, the hotel owes the guest a refund at the conclusion of the stay. This happens for one of several reasons. Either there was a substantial deposit with the reservation, or a large payment on account was made on (or after) arrival. If the guest shortens the stay, or the hotel adjusts the rate downward, there could be a credit balance at the time of departure. Paid-in-advance guests who leave additional deposits to cover other charges to their rooms (such as for telephone calls) may also show a credit balance.

At check-out, the hotel pays the guest. Zeroing the credit balance of the account requires a debit or charge entry. A paid-out voucher is prepared for the guest's signature in the amount the hotel owes. At the end of the shift, the computerized cashier's balance report subtracts the amount of the paid-out from the total cash remaining in the money drawer.

Cash is never refunded if the original payment was not made in cash! If the guest's personal credit card were the source, for example, the hotel would issue a rebate against the credit card. Similarly, large cash deposits made by the guest may not be refundable on check-out. Before receiving the large cash deposit, the clerk should explain hotel policy regarding paid-outs. Some hotels restrict the size of the paid-out to, say, $100. Anything above that amount requires a cheque to be processed by the hotel accounting department and mailed to the guest's home. This prevents guests from depositing illegitimate traveller's cheques, personal cheques (discussed later in this chapter), or counterfeit money and then attempting to collect legitimate cash against that amount the following day.

## Cash Receipts

We have already emphasized that cash paid-outs are limited to front-office cashiers. Cash paid-outs are advances to accounts receivable. Eventually, those advances are repaid by the guest, the account receivable, at the front desk. That normally takes place when the balance of the folio is settled, typically at check-out. Guests settle their folios, as Chapter 10 stressed, in one of three methods: with cash, with credit card, or with an allowance. Cash paid by the guest and received by the hotel is the thrust of this chapter.

Increases in assets, including accounts receivable and *cash,* are made with debits.

Decreases in assets, including *accounts receivable* and cash, are made with credits.

**Cash Receipts at Check-out** Only a small percentage of check-outs elect to settle with cash. Most guests pay by credit card or request direct billing through the city ledger. Very few use cash, traveller's cheques, or personal cheques.

Posting cash paid to the folio has the opposite effect of posting a cash paid-out to the folio. Whereas the paid-out increases the amount owed by the guest (debit to accounts receivable), cash receipts decrease the amount owed by the guest (credit to accounts receivable). In all cases, the amount collected from the guest is the exact amount required to reduce the folio balance to zero.

It is a quick procedure: The computerized property management system maintains a cumulative balance, which indicates the amount due. Some hotels display the folio on the computer screen for the guest to scan, others deliver pre-printed hard copies to all departing guests, and still others encourage self-check-out via the television screen (see Chapter 14).

Whatever the method, all cashiers are trained to inquire about very recent charges that may still be unrecorded. Catching unposted telephone or breakfast charges minimizes the number of late charges, with their high rate of non-collection and guest displeasure.

**Cash Receipts on Account** Payments may be requested at any time, not just at departure. Long-term guests are billed weekly, as a means of improving the hotel's cash flow and keeping the guest as current as possible. Guests who exceed certain credit limits or guests who generate too many charges (especially items normally paid for in cash) are billed at the hotel's discretion. Sometimes, guests themselves decide to make payments against their accounts.

At check-out, departing guests are given a copy of the zero-balance folio as a receipt for their cash payment. Similarly, guests who make cash payments on account are given a copy of the folio to serve as a receipt of the payment. The only difference is the timing: The folio given in the middle of the stay is probably not a zero-balance folio. In fact, paid-in-advance customers usually maintain a credit balance on their folios throughout some of the visit.

The desk is frequently faced with a guest—especially one who hasn't travelled extensively—who tries to pay on the day before departure. Because of possible late charges, the desk tries to discourage guests from making payment too early. In fact, day-early payments require special attention by the cashier, who must be certain to collect enough to cover the upcoming room night and room tax that will not be posted until the auditor arrives. So, the employee convinces the guest to wait until the next day rather than paying in full on the previous day in anticipation of an early departure. Naturally, many guests find it incomprehensible that they are dissuaded from concluding their business until the next morning. This is much less a problem in modern hotels, which provide the guest with a number of rapid automatic or self-check-out options.

**Cash Receipts at Check-in** All guests are asked to establish credit at check-in. Most simply proffer their credit card and the desk clerk verifies it for a predetermined floor limit. Direct-bill guests are not asked about credit at check-in because their company has a previously established account on file with the hotel's accounting department. Only cash guests, then, are actually asked to pay their room charges up front. Cash guests include those paying with currency, traveller's cheques, and personal cheques (if allowed).

Unless an additional deposit is made, no other room charges are allowed against a paid-in-advance guest, who often departs the hotel without stopping at the desk. An additional room charge is made and collected on each succeeding day the customer remains. Unless this is received, someone on the desk automatically checks out advance payments by the check-out hour of the following day. Some limited-service properties may actually lock out guests who remain beyond the check-out hour. Less extreme measures, including telephone messages, are usually used to communicate with the paid-in-advance guest.

Automatic check-out of a paid-in-advance guest requires coordination and communication. The front desk must be careful not to prematurely show as vacant any room that was paid in advance. Prior to automatically checking out the guest, a bellperson or housekeeper is asked to inspect the room. Only after he or she communicates that the room is truly empty should the front desk complete the check-out.

**Reservation Deposit Receipts** Just as cash is seldom used to pay the folio at the front desk, so is cash rarely used when requesting an advance deposit. Most guests simply guarantee the reservation with a credit card. Still, some hotels (particularly resorts where reservation lead time may be several months) request advance deposits to hold the reservation. In such cases, the easiest means of collecting the deposit is simply to charge the guest's credit card upon taking the reservation.

Some properties, however, do not choose to collect deposits against guest credit cards. Who can blame them? When there is sufficient lead time, a mailed-in deposit (cheque or money order) has no merchant discount fee associated with it. For the hotel that collects an entire season's worth of advance deposits, this small distinction may represent thousands of dollars in savings.

Different hotels handle these deposits in different ways, usually as a function of the size and sophistication of their accounting systems. The easiest but least businesslike method assigns the cheque to the front-office cash drawer. There it stays, unrecorded, until the guest arrives weeks or months later. The cheque is then applied to a newly opened folio as if the money were just received on that day. This procedure simplifies the bookkeeping, especially if there is a cancellation, but it has little additional merit even for a small hotel. Lack of a proper record and the failure to clear the cheque through the bank indicate poor management of both procedure and funds.

Sometimes the actual folio that is to be assigned to the guest on arrival is opened when the deposit cheque is received. This procedure is extremely cumbersome for manual or semi-automated properties that use prenumbered folios. However, in computerized properties, this procedure works quite satisfactorily. That is because one major difference between manual and computerized properties is the timing as to when they assign the guest folio. In a manual property (unless a reservation deposit is received), the folio is not assigned until check-in, which may be months later. In a computerized property, a folio identification number is assigned immediately, at the moment of reservation.

**Establishing a City Ledger Account**　The most common method for handling reservation deposits uses the city ledger (see Chapter 12 for a complete discussion of the city ledger). An account is established in the city ledger for advance-deposit receipts. Guest deposits are credited to that account and later transferred to the folio on guest arrival.

With a city ledger advance-deposit account, the front-office cashier sees only one side of the transfer, the credit made to the account of the arriving guest. The debit portion to the city ledger advance-deposit account is made by the accounting office, not by the front-office cashier.

As an additional control, the reservations office keeps both the front-office cashier and the city ledger accountant current with the names and amounts of advance deposits. Each day's anticipated list is compared to the actual arrivals, and oversights are corrected. Deposits applied that day by the front-office cashier become the basis of the city ledger debit entry made by the accountant. Some unclaimed deposits will be returned because of timely cancellations. Others will be **forfeited** to pay for the rooms that were saved for the no-shows.

## House Receipts and Expenses

Although the front-office cashier is primarily responsible for handling rooms-related revenues and disbursements, other responsibilities are assigned as a function of convenience. Because of the fact that the front desk is centrally located and accessible to all departments of the hotel, the cashier in the small hotel takes on a set of hotel-related cash responsibilities, both house receipts and house expenses.

**Assorted City and Guest Ledger Receipts**　Some hotels, especially small properties that lack a full accounting staff, elect to funnel all cash and cheque receipts through the front office. This adds another person and record to the process, which strengthens the internal control. It also adds another set of responsibilities to the front-office cashier.

Examples of assorted city and general ledger receipts that are not affiliated with the rooms division include receipts for meetings or banquet functions, reimbursements or rebates for overpayment to vendors, refunds or credits from taxes, and lease revenues from merchants or concessionaires. In small hotels, the front-office cashier might serve as dining room or lounge cashier. Magazines, newspapers, and candy may be sold across the desk. Coin collections from vending machines or sales of miscellaneous items such as kitchen fat (to tallow-rendering plants) or container deposits may all flow through the front desk. Meal tickets in American-plan resorts are also commonly sold at the front desk to non-guests.

Depending on the accounting system in place, the cashier records a credit to some type of general account and a debit to cash on the front-office documentation. The specific detailing of the general account (each affected account must be updated) is later handled by the accounting department on an item-by-item basis.

**Assorted House Paid-outs**　Just as some of the cash receipts collected by the front-office cashier are not actually transient guest receipts (rather, they are city or general ledger receipts), some of the paid-outs made by the front-office cashier are not actually

**Exhibit 11-2 ▶**
Petty cash vouchers are often simple, handwritten forms. When available, a store receipt documenting the exact amount of the purchase should also be attached.

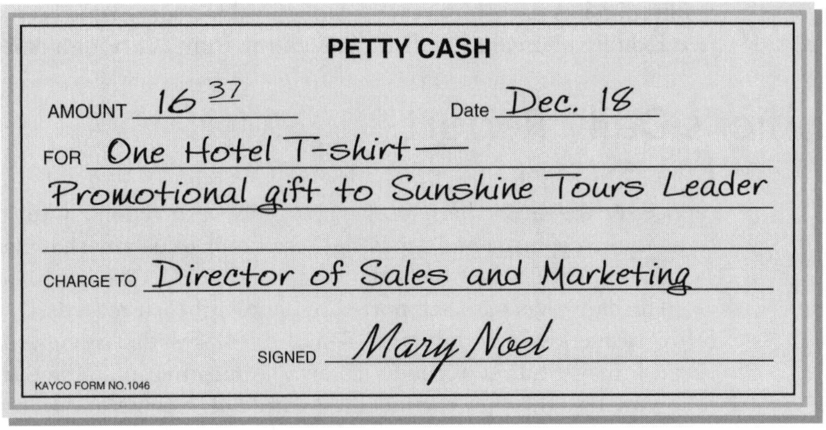

PETTY CASH

AMOUNT 16.37 Date Dec. 18

FOR One Hotel T-shirt— Promotional gift to Sunshine Tours Leader

CHARGE TO Director of Sales and Marketing

SIGNED Mary Noel

KAYCO FORM NO.1046

guest paid-outs (rather, they are house paid-outs). The front-office cashier acts, on one hand, as a depository for the accounting department and, on the other hand, as the accounting department's disbursing agent.

Unlike guest paid-outs, which have an impact on the cashier's drawer, house paid-outs do not. As such, house paid-outs are not posted to the property management system—guest paid-outs most certainly are. The reason that house paid-outs do not affect the cashier's drawer is because the cashier treats house paid-outs (petty **cash disbursements**) just like cash.

The person receiving the money (say, the bellperson who just purchased $30 worth of flour for the kitchen) signs a **petty cash** voucher (see Exhibit 11-2). The voucher is kept in the cashier's drawer and treated as if it were cash. It is cash, because the accounting department's general cashier will buy the petty cash voucher at some later point. The purchase of this voucher by the general cashier reimburses the front-office cashier and leaves the cash drawer intact—as if the petty cash disbursement had never been processed in the first place.

**The Imprest Petty Cash Fund** If the front-office cashiers are reimbursed daily, the accounting department's general cashier administers the petty cash fund. If the front-office cashiers are only reimbursed when petty cash vouchers reach a sizable sum or at the end of the month, it is known as an **imprest petty cash** fund. An imprest fund authorizes the front-office cashier to hold petty cash vouchers in the drawer day after day.

The cashier holds the house petty cash vouchers until some predetermined point is reached. This point is usually a function of both time and amount. A cashier is assigned a limited bank from which to conduct all of the day's transactions. If the cashier's ability to make change and serve the guest is compromised by a large petty cash holding, it is time to sell the vouchers to the general cashier. Some hotels have a specific policy that when the total petty cash vouchers in a given cashier's drawer reach, say, $25, the amount must be turned over to the general cashier. Petty cash vouchers are also cleared from front-office cashiers at the end of each accounting cycle, usually the last day of the month.

A wide range of small expenditures is processed through the petty cash fund. Salary advances to good employees or termination pay to employees the hotel wants immediately off the premises might be paid by the fund. Some freight bills need immediate cash payment under International Chamber of Commerce (ICC) regulations.

Stamp purchases, cash purchases from local farmers or purveyors, and other payments (see Exhibit 11-2) are handled through the front office of a small hotel.

# The Cashier's Daily Report

Every cashier in the hotel—whether at the front office, the dining room, the bar, room service, or the snack bar—prepares a daily cash report. With the report, the cashier turns in the departmental monies. These funds (plus any that clear through the general cashier) constitute the hotel's daily deposit made to the bank.

The daily deposit is supported by a flow of cash records. The records of the front-office cashiers (see Exhibits 11-3 and 11-4) are first reviewed by the night auditor because they contain accounts receivable information. They are processed again the following day through the income audit. The income audit combines the front-office cash records with the records of the other departmental cashiers. This creates a support document (see Exhibit 11-5) for the bank deposit.

## Preparing the Cashier's Report

The front office **cashier's report** is much more complicated than standard cashier reports found in other departments. This is because of the two-way flow of front-office cashier's responsibilities. Whereas departmental cashiers only receive payment from guests, front-office cashiers both receive funds and pay them out.

| CASHIER: ARDELLE | | | REPORT DATE: 03/09/-- | | | | 15:27:30 |
|---|---|---|---|---|---|---|---|
| | | | **CASHIER'S BALANCE REPORT** | | | | |
| CODE | ROOM | LAST NAME | FIRST NAME | ACCOUNT | RATE | TIME | AMOUNT |
| → 0001 | 217 | JOHNSON | LINDA | CASH | RACK | 06:57:23 | 48.52 |
| 0026 | 1171 | VANLAND | TOM | VISA | GRP | 07:11:10 | 179.37 |
| 0024 | 678 | HARRISON | GEORGE | DSCV | TOUR | 07:12:12 | 87.50 |
| 0025 | 456 | LENNON | JOHN | MC | TOUR | 07:16:44 | 87.50 |
| → 0011 | 319 | WILSON | BILL | CHCK | DISC | 07:17:17 | 82.50 |
| 0011 | 337 | ADAMS | JOHN | CHCK | RACK | 07:21:50 | 67.21 |
| 0031 | 902 | GREENBACKS | LOTTA | POUT | RACK | 07:24:01 | −17.50 |
| 0026 | 842 | STUART | LYLE | VISA | GRP | 08:10:15 | 161.40 |
| 0024 | 212 | JONES | ROBERT | DSCV | DISC | 08:34:20 | 242.59 |
| 0011 | 711 | GREGORY | GARY | CHCK | TOUR | 09:10:10 | 111.77 |
| 0011 | 315 | GONNE | CONNIE | CHCK | RACK | 09:44:30 | 96.20 |
| 0031 | 107 | MOORE | MANNY | POUT | TOUR | 10:10:15 | −20.00 |
| 0025 | 371 | ORTIZ | RAUL | MC | RACK | 10:40:29 | 68.57 |
| 0011 | 211 | JACKSON | ANDY | CHCK | DISC | 11:04:41 | 46.31 |
| 0011 | 551 | WASHINGTON | BOB | CHCK | TOUR | 11:57:01 | 1278.71 |

▲
**Exhibit 11-3**
In the Account column of this cashier's balance report are shown cash, cheques, city ledger (credit cards), and paid-outs. Follow the arrows marking Ardelle's cash guests, Johnson and Wilson, Exhibits 11-4 and 11-5.

| CASHIER:   ARDELLE | | REPORT DATE: 03/09/-- | | | | 15:28:41 | |
|---|---|---|---|---|---|---|---|

**CASHIER'S BALANCE REPORT BY CODE**

| CODE | ROOM | LAST NAME | FIRST NAME | ACCOUNT | RATE | TIME | AMOUNT |
|---|---|---|---|---|---|---|---|
| → 0001 | 217 | JOHNSON | LINDA | CASH | RACK | 06:57:23 | 48.52 |
| TOTAL | CASH | | 0001 | | | | 48.52 |
| | | | | | | | |
| → 0011 | 319 | WILSON | BILL | CHCK | DISC | 07:17:17 | 82.50 |
| 0011 | 337 | ADAMS | JOHN | CHCK | RACK | 07:21:50 | 67.21 |
| 0011 | 711 | GREGORY | GARY | CHCK | TOUR | 09:10:10 | 111.77 |
| 0011 | 315 | GONNE | CONNIE | CHCK | RACK | 09:44:30 | 96.20 |
| 0011 | 211 | JACKSON | ANDY | CHCK | DISC | 11:04:41 | 46.31 |
| 0011 | 551 | WASHINGTON | BOB | CHCK | TOUR | 11:57:01 | 1278.71 |
| TOTAL | CHECKS | | 0011 | | | | 1682.70 |
| | | | | | | | |
| TOTAL | AMERICAN EXPRESS | | 0021 | | | | 0.00 |
| | | | | | | | |
| TOTAL CARTE BLANCHE | | | 0022 | | | | 0.00 |
| | | | | | | | |
| TOTAL DINERS CLUB | | | 0023 | | | | 0.00 |
| | | | | | | | |
| 0024 | 678 | HARRISON | GEORGE | DSCV | TOUR | 07:12:12 | 87.50 |
| 0024 | 212 | JONES | ROBERT | DSCV | DISC | 08:34:20 | 242.59 |
| TOTAL | DISCOVER | | 0024 | | | | 330.09 |
| | | | | | | | |
| 0025 | 456 | LENNON | JOHN | MC | TOUR | 07:16:44 | 87.50 |
| 0025 | 371 | ORTIZ | RAUL | MC | RACK | 10:40:29 | 68.57 |
| TOTAL | MASTERCARD | | | 0025 | | | 156.07 |
| | | | | | | | |
| 0026 | 1171 | VANLAND | TOM | VISA | GRP | 07:11:10 | 179.37 |
| 0026 | 842 | STUART | LYLE | VISA | GRP | 08:10:15 | 161.40 |
| TOTAL | VISA | | 0026 | | | | 340.77 |
| | | | | | | | |
| 0031 | 902 | GREENBACKS | LOTTA | POUT | RACK | 07:24:01 | −17.50 |
| 0031 | 107 | MOORE | MANNY | POUT | TOUR | 10:10:15 | −20.00 |
| TOTAL | PAID-OUTS | | 0031 | | | | −37.50 |

▲
**Exhibit 11-4**
A cashier's balance report by code (the hotel's chart of accounts). This portion of the report shows payment methods against which the cashier reconciles cash, cheques, and charges. This report shows payment by room number. Other reports would also be printed showing activity by departmental sales (say, telephone, restaurant, or lounge). This exhibit is the second in a continuing series of interrelated Exhibits 11-3 through 11-7 that follow the arrows of cashier Ardelle.

**The Cashier's Bank** Each cashier receives and signs for a permanent supply of cash, called the **bank**. The amount varies depending on the position and shift that the cashier has. A busy commercial hotel needs front-office banks of as much as $10 000, but the night cashier at the same hotel might get along with $250. It is partly a question of safety and partly a question of good financial management. Excessive funds should not be tied up unnecessarily; temporary increases can be made for busy periods.

CLERK: THOMAS

REPORT DATE: 3/10/--

09:39:17

## CASH RECEIPTS SUMMARY REPORT

| DEPARTMENT | CASHIER | CASH SALES | COLLECTION TRANSIENT RECEIVABLES | COLLECTION CITY LEDGER RECEIVABLES | TOTAL CASH RECEIPTS | PAID-OUTS TRANSIENT | PAID-OUTS CITY LEDGER | NET CASH RECEIPTS | ADD:OVERAGES LESS:SHORTAGES | TURN IN FOR DEPOSIT |
|---|---|---|---|---|---|---|---|---|---|---|
| FRONT OFFICE | ARDELLE | | 452.51 | 1278.71 | 1731.22 | −37.50 | 0.00 | 1693.72 | −.76 | 1692.96 |
| FRONT OFFICE | BABETTE | | 1171.14 | 622.50 | 1793.64 | −49.00 | −25.00 | 1719.64 | 1.20 | 1720.84 |
| FRONT OFFICE | CHARLES | | 850.19 | 1460.51 | 2310.70 | −11.50 | −5.00 | 2294.20 | 0.00 | 2294.20 |
| FRONT OFFICE | DIANE | | 67.10 | 0.00 | 67.10 | 0.00 | 0.00 | 67.10 | 0.00 | 67.10 |
| FRONT OFFICE | EDWARD | | 572.46 | 604.27 | 1176.73 | −12.90 | 0.00 | 1163.83 | −2.41 | 1161.42 |
| FRONT OFFICE | FRANCES | | 934.72 | 210.58 | 1145.30 | −18.65 | −14.00 | 1112.65 | .87 | 1113.52 |
| GIFT SHOP | GARY | 687.14 | 0.00 | 0.00 | 687.14 | 0.00 | 0.00 | 687.14 | 0.00 | 687.14 |
| GIFT SHOP | HARRY | 901.73 | 0.00 | 0.00 | 901.73 | 0.00 | 0.00 | 901.73 | −1.47 | 900.26 |
| LOUNGE | ILONA | 1262.85 | 0.00 | 0.00 | 1262.85 | 0.00 | 0.00 | 1262.85 | 1.01 | 1263.86 |
| LOUNGE | JEROME | 2411.59 | 0.00 | 0.00 | 2411.59 | 0.00 | 0.00 | 2411.59 | 0.00 | 2411.59 |
| RESTAURANT | KATE | 816.44 | 0.00 | 0.00 | 816.44 | 0.00 | 0.00 | 816.44 | −.25 | 816.19 |
| RESTAURANT | LOUISE | 1017.55 | 0.00 | 0.00 | 1017.55 | 0.00 | 0.00 | 1017.55 | −.61 | 1016.94 |
| SNACK BAR | MARC | 469.68 | 0.00 | 0.00 | 469.68 | 0.00 | 0.00 | 469.68 | 2.71 | 472.39 |
| SNACK BAR | NANETTE | 371.02 | 0.00 | 0.00 | 371.02 | 0.00 | 0.00 | 371.02 | 0.00 | 371.02 |
| DAILY TOTALS | | 7938.00 | 4048.12 | 4176.57 | 16 162.69 | −129.55 | −44.00 | 15 989.14 | .29 | 15 989.43 |

▲
**Exhibit 11-5**
This cash receipts summary recaps records of all departmental cashiers and serves as the source document for the income auditors' daily bank deposit. Information shown for Ardelle corresponds with Exhibit 11-4, from which Washington, a city ledger collection, appears in column 5. The total of the other cash collections, Johnson through Jackson, appears in column 4 as transient collections. Paid-outs (column 7) originate in the bottom three lines of Exhibit 11-4. Follow the balanced cashier report of Ardelle across a continuing series of interrelated Exhibits 11-3 through 11-7.

A careful review of all **house banks** may release sizable sums for more profitable use. One major accounting firm reported that the total of house banks and cash on hand is about 2 percent of total sales (about $600 per room). An excessive percentage suggests that cashiers are borrowing from their banks or that daily deposits and reimbursements are not being made, which means that extra funds are required to operate the banks. There are other reasons, of course—infrequent reimbursement of the petty cash fund, for example, which makes the fund unnecessarily large.

Cashiers lock their banks in the safe or hotel vault after each shift. The cashier's bank may not be used for personal loans. To ensure that all funds are properly held in the cashiers' bank, the accounting office sporadically schedules surprise counts. When the cashier comes on duty, he or she will find the safety deposit box inaccessible—access to the safety deposit box requires two keys: one is the cashier's key and the other is the accounting office's master key. To open the box, the cashier needs to summon an auditor, who takes a few minutes with the cashier to count and verify the contents.

Unfortunately, common banks for several employees to share are not unusual. These are seen in every department from the bar to the front office. With shared banks, control is difficult to maintain, and responsibility almost impossible to fix. Custom and convenience seem to be the major reasons for continuing this poor practice, although it obviously requires less hotel funds than required to stock shared banks.

A bond should cover everyone handling money. Bonds are written to cover either individual positions or as blanket coverage, whichever best meets the hotel's needs.

The bank must contain enough small bills to carry out the cashiering function. There is no value in a bank comprising $100 bills. Two examples follow: with a $500 bank for the text discussion and a $1000 bank for the separate discussion of the exhibits.

**Net Receipts** Net receipts represent the difference between what the cashier took in (receipts) and what was paid out. Since only front-office cashiers are permitted to make advances, net receipts in the bar and coffee shop are the same as total receipts except when tip advances are made. Net receipts at the front office are computed by subtracting total advances (paid-outs), city and transient, from total receipts, city and transient. House paid-outs and miscellaneous receipts are not included because they're counted as cash (as discussed earlier in the chapter).

For discussion, assume the totals of the front-office cashier's balance report to be:

| | |
|---|---|
| **Receipts** | |
| Transient receivables | $2376.14 |
| City receivables | $ 422.97 |
| Total receipts | $2799.11 |
| **Paid-outs** | |
| Transient ledger paid-outs | $ 107.52 |
| City ledger paid-outs | 27.50 |
| Total paid-outs | $ 135.02 |
| **Net Receipts** | |
| Total receipts | $2799.11 |
| Less paid-outs | 135.02 |
| Equals net receipts | $2664.09 |

Exhibit 11-6 ▶

Preparation of Ardelle's front-office cashier report requires an understanding of the computations. Refer back to Exhibits 11-3, 11-4, and 11-5 to understand the numbers shown under "cash receipts," "paid-outs," "cheques," and so on. Remember, this exhibit is based on the figures shown in the continuing series of Exhibits 11-3 to 11-7, and is *not based on the text discussion,* which provides a look at a *different* example.

**Given**

1. A starting bank of $1000

2. The cashier's balance report shows:

   | | |
   |---|---:|
   | Cash receipts (both transient and city ledger) | $1731.22 |
   | Paid-outs (both transient and city ledger | 37.50 |

3. Count in the cash drawer at the close of the watch

   | | |
   |---|---:|
   | Cheques | $1682.70 |
   | Currency | 821.00 |
   | Coin | 177.26 |
   | House vouchers | 12.00 |
   | | $2692.96 |

**Computation**

1. Net receipts (gross receipts minus advances)
   NR = $1731.22 – $37.50 = $1693.72

2. Overage and shortage (what should be in the drawer minus what is in the drawer)
   O&S = ($1000 + 1693.72) – 2692.96 = $0.76 short

3. Turn-in (cheques, vouchers, other non-negotiable items, and all cash except the bank)
   TI = $1682.70 + 12.00 = $1694.70

4. Due bank (amount needed to reconstitute the bank)
   DB = $1000 – (821.00 + 177.26) = $1.74.

5. Verification (the excess of the turn-in over the amount due)
   DB = $1694.70 – ($1693.72 – 0.76) = $1.74.

The front-office cashier accesses this information through the cashier's balance report. See Exhibits 11-3 and 11-4 for examples of a cashier's balance report. Note, however, that this current example (total receipts of $2799.11 and total paid-outs of $135.02) does not correlate to the figures shown in Exhibits 11-3 through 11-7. For an example of a net receipts calculation using the figures found in Exhibits 11-3 and 11-4, see Exhibit 11-6.

Some balance reports provide only summary data such as those described in this section—total transient ledger receipts, total city ledger (and general ledger) receipts, total transient ledger paid-outs, and total city ledger paid-outs. Other balance reports are very complete, telling the cashier exactly how much net receipts to have in the drawer.

Whether the system provides detail for net receipts or not, this figure is a simple number to compute. In this example, net receipts are total receipts ($2799.11) less total paid-outs ($135.02), which equals $2664.09 in net receipts.

**Over or Short**   No cashier is perfect. The day's close occasionally finds the cash drawer over or short. Sometimes the error is mathematical, and either the cashier finds it without help or it is uncovered later by the auditor.

Cash errors in giving change are usually beyond remedy unless they are in the house's favour. Guests may not acknowledge overpayments, but they will complain soon enough if they have been short-changed. Restitution after the fact is possible if the cash count at the end of the shift proves this to be so.

**Over or short** is the difference between what the cashier should have in the cash drawer and what is actually there. It is the comparison of a mathematically generated net total against a physical count of the money in the drawer. The cashier *should* have the sum of the bank plus the net receipts. The money on hand in the drawer is what the cashier *does* have. Over or short is the difference between the *should have* and the *does have* amounts.

In our continuing example, the front-office cashier should have $3164.09 on hand at the close of the shift. This is calculated by taking net receipts of $2664.09 (see discussion on page 346) plus starting bank ($500), which equals $3164.09.

| Should Have on Hand | |
| --- | --- |
| Net receipts | $2664.09 |
| Starting bank | 500.00 |
| Total of should have | $3164.09 |

Once the cashier knows how much should be in the drawer, it is a simple matter of comparing that total with the actual cash on hand. The cashier's drawer probably contains personal and traveller's cheques, currency, coin, and petty cash vouchers. Credit cards are not included in this discussion of the cashier's drawer because they are often electronically deposited to the hotel's bank or handled by the accounting department as a city ledger accounts receivable. A full discussion of credit card processes is included in Chapter 12.

| Does Have on Hand | |
| --- | --- |
| Cheques (personal and traveller's) | $2704.60 |
| Currency | 356.00 |
| Coin | 62.13 |
| House petty cash vouchers | 42.50 |
| Total cash on hand | $3165.23 |

The cashier apparently has more in the drawer than there should be. In such a case, the cashier has an overage. If the amount of cash on hand was actually less than what there should be, the cashier would be short. The amount of the overage or shortage is simple enough to compute—just subtract the amount there should be ($3164.09) from the amount of cash on hand ($3165.23). The net total ($1.14) is the amount of overage. A positive net number is always an overage; a negative net number is always a shortage.

**The Turn-In** When the cashier has calculated net receipts, determined the amount there should be, and counted the actual cash in the drawer, it is a simple matter to compute the **turn-in**. However, in many hotels, the cashier is not responsible for counting the drawer.

**The Front Office Turn-In** The turn-in of the front-office cashier is more complicated than the turn-in of the departmental cashiers. The front-office bank is used to cash cheques, make change, and advance cash, as well as to accept receipts. Assume, for example, that nothing took place during the watch except cheque cashing. At the close of the day, the bank would contain nothing but non-negotiable cheques. It would be impossible to make change the next day with a drawer full of personal cheques. Therefore, the cashier must drop or turn in all non-negotiable items, including cheques, traveller's cheques, foreign funds, large bills, casino chips, cash in poor condition, vouchers for house expenses, and even refund slips for inoperative vending machines.

The objective of the cashier's turn-in is to rebuild the starting bank in the proper amount and variety of denominations to be effective during the next day's shift, and "drop" the rest of the contents of the cash drawer. Sometimes, there are enough small bills and coins in the cashier's drawer to rebuild tomorrow's bank quite easily. At other times, there are too many large-denomination bills or non-negotiable cheques and paper to effectively rebuild tomorrow's bank. In such cases, the cashier must turn in all of the large bills and non-negotiable paper, leaving tomorrow's bank short. That's okay, because the income audit staff will leave currency and coin in requested denominations for the start of tomorrow's shift. By adding these new funds to the short bank, tomorrow's drawer will be both accurate and effective.

Our continuing example helps illustrate the concept of turn-in or drop. Remember that the cashier has a total of $3165.23 on hand, comprising cheques ($2704.60), currency ($356.00), coin ($62.13), and house petty cash vouchers ($42.50). The cashier must turn in all of the non-negotiable paper, including cheques ($2704.60) and house petty cash vouchers ($42.50), which equals a $2747.10 total turn-in.

**Due Bank** At this point, it is quite obvious that the cashier does not have enough negotiable money to rebuild tomorrow's $500 starting bank. In fact, tomorrow's bank will be short by $81.87. This shortage is commonly referred to as the **due bank**. It is also known as the **due back, difference returnable, U-owe-me,** or the **exchange.**

The due bank is calculated by subtracting the amount of money retained by the cashier, $418.13 ($356 in currency plus $62.13 in coin) from the amount needed to open the next day's bank, $500.

| Due Bank Computation | |
| --- | --- |
| Original bank | $500.00 |
| Cash on hand | 418.13 |
| Due bank | $ 81.87 |

Since the cashier always retains the exact bank, it is apparent that the turn-in includes the overage or allows for the shortage. The hotel, not the cashier, funds the overages and shortages. A due bank formula, which produces the same due bank figure as the simple subtraction computation, mathematically illustrates the hotel's responsibility for the over or short.

| Due Bank Formula |
| --- |
| Due bank = turn-in – (net receipts ± over or short) |
| Due bank = $2747.10 – ($2664.09 + $1.14) |
| Due bank = $2747.10 – ($2665.23) |
| Due bank = $81.87 |

To keep their banks functional, cashiers specify the coin and currency denominations of the due bank. There is little utility in a due bank of several large bills. For the very same

## DEPARTMENT CASHIER'S REPORT

DAY *TUE*    DATE *3-9*

CASHIER *Ardelle*

DEPT *F.O.*

SHIFT *8:00*    A.M. ☑ / P.M. ☐    TO *4:00*    A.M. ☐ / P.M. ☑

| | | AMOUNT | ✓ |
|---|---|---|---|
| CURRENCY | $1.00 | | |
| " | $5.00 | | |
| " | $10.00 | | |
| " | $20.00 | | |
| " | $50.00 | | |
| " | $100.00 | | |
| COIN | 1¢ | | |
| " | 5¢ | | |
| SILVER | 10¢ | | |
| " | 25¢ | | |
| " | 50¢ | | |
| " | $1.00 | | |
| BAR STUBS: | | | |
| PAID-OUTS: | | | |
| | | | |
| VOUCHERS AND CHEQUES: | | | |
| Bank of Montreal-Wilson | | 82 50 | |
| Bank of Nova Scotia-Adams | | 67 21 | |
| CIBC-Gregory | | 111 77 | |
| TD Bank-Lesage | | 96 20 | |
| Laurentian Bank-Jackson | | 46 31 | |
| CIBC-Trudeau | | 1278 71 | |
| Postage Stamp Voucher | | 12 — | |
| | | | |
| TRAVELLER'S CHEQUES | | | |
| | | | |
| LESS SHORT | | 76 | |
| TOTAL AMOUNT ENCLOSED | | 1694 70 | |
| NET RECEIPTS WITH O & S | | 1692 96 | |
| DIFFERENCE | | 1 74 | |

▲

**Exhibit 11-7**

Cashier's envelope for preparing the "turn-in" (or "drop") at the close of the shift. Refer back to Exhibits 11-3 to 11-6 to understand the source of cheques enclosed, the postage stamp voucher, the "due bank" difference of $1.74, and so on. Note that the net receipts figure includes the $0.76 shortage (O & S stands for "over" and "short").

reason, the turn-in may be increased with large bills to be exchanged for more negotiable currency. More often, the change is obtained from the general cashier before the shift closes, or from another cashier who has coins and small bills to exchange.

Exhibits 11-6 and 11-7 offer a second example complete with cashier's turn-in envelope, but with different values from the text discussion.

## The Income Audit

Income auditors and general cashiers are members of the hotel's accounting department. They usually perform the income audit each morning to process the cashier drops made on the preceding day. One purpose of the income audit is to verify that each department's (and, indeed, each shift's) cashiers have accurately dropped (turned in) the amount indicated on the deposit envelopes (see Exhibit 11-7). Although this function is performed in a vault or safe room, there are several general cashiers present and the audit may even be videotaped as an additional safeguard.

The income audit includes both front-office cashiers (who probably calculate the exact amount of their turn-in and know shift by shift whether they are over or short) and departmental cashiers (who may or may not precalculate their turn-in before preparing the deposit envelope).

**Paying off the Due Bank** Many cashiers turn in more money than necessary. The excess amount of their drop is the due bank. As discussed above, due banks are caused by a variety of factors: there may have been a large house paid-out that used most of the drawer's cash, there may have been too many large-denomination bills and too few small ones to effectively rebuild tomorrow's starting bank, or there may have been too many cheques cashed to leave sufficient money for tomorrow. Whatever the reason, the income audit staff pays each cashier's due bank from the growing pile of turned-in cash before preparing the hotel's daily deposit.

Most operations use a signature and witness system to facilitate returning the due banks to each cashier. One main cashier (often a front-office cashier) is given a series of due bank envelopes with the name of each cashier to whom the envelope is owed. The departmental cashier then signs for the sealed envelope in the presence of the main cashier and adds the contents of the envelope to the department's starting shift bank. Of course, the envelopes were prepared during the cashier audit and were therefore witnessed by several general cashiers as to the correct amount sealed inside. Although simple, these signature and witness systems are generally quite effective.

**Paying off the House Vouchers** In hotels that use an imprest petty cash fund, front-office cashiers are asked to hold their house vouchers until they build to some predetermined amount (say, $25). Front-office cashiers write house vouchers for a pop machine refund ($0.75), a video game refund ($0.50), and a tank of gas for the shuttle van ($19.50). These are kept in the cash drawer until they exceed the predetermined amount ($25). Even at the close of the shift, as the cashier is building tomorrow's starting bank, the vouchers are still kept by the cashier. Tomorrow, however, if the cashier writes a few more house vouchers (say, a container of sour cream was purchased from the grocery store for $4.59), the entire sum of all vouchers will be turned in.

In this example, the sum to be turned in is $25.34. The cashier turns in all of the house vouchers, not merely the one or two vouchers that put the total over the predetermined amount. The income audit staff counts the house vouchers as cash and credits the drop envelope with the total amount of the house vouchers. In some cases, a due bank may be caused by an extremely large house voucher (say, a large cash-on-delivery shipment arrived).

**Tour Package Coupons** Hotels that operate in busy tour and travel markets often incorporate the redemption of package coupons and certificates into their cash drawer procedures. Such coupons or certificates are found primarily in departmental cashier turn-ins, but front-office cashiers may also have an opportunity to redeem them under some circumstances.

Generally, package tours provide the guest with substantially more than just a hotel room. Breakfast each morning of the visit, two free rounds of golf, a discount in the gift shop, several free drinks, and a dinner show are all examples of products that might be included in a packaged tour. To identify themselves as members of the tour, guests are presented with a coupon booklet that contains redeemable certificates.

As an example, when a couple arrives at the dining room for breakfast, the servers and cashier may not be aware that they are tour customers. In fact, they are treated like any other customer until the end of the meal. Then, instead of paying for the breakfast in cash, credit card, or room charge, the tour couple need only redeem their complimentary breakfast coupons.

It's at this point that many accounting systems break down. Departmental cashiers forget to collect tour coupons with the same determination they show when collecting cash. After all, the cashier thinks, the meal is complimentary; if the tour guest accidentally forgets the coupon booklet in the room, what's the harm? This overlooks the fact that someone is paying for the guest's complimentary meal (golf, drinks, or whatever). In fact, the redeemed coupon serves as documentation to the travel wholesaler for payment. Redeemed coupons are proof that goods (breakfast, in this case) were exchanged and become the basis for the account receivable. That's why redeemed coupons often become part of the departmental cashier's daily turn-in.

**Foreign Currency** Foreign currency is not regularly accepted in Canada, with the exception of the U.S. dollar. However, international tourism is growing at an amazing rate, with more increases to come in the years ahead. More foreign currencies are being tendered across hotel desks, and more language capability is being encouraged among front-office staffs.

Cities with large numbers of foreign tourists, such as Toronto, Montreal, and Vancouver, have developed adequate exchange facilities to accommodate international tourists. These privately owned, franchised currency-exchange companies, such as Money Mart, have been supported by local tourist bureaus, Chambers of Commerce, and the Canadian Tourism Commission, which see the importance of the international tourist to the balance of trade. Exchange agencies allow the hotels to service the currency needs of the international guest with a reasonable ceiling on costs. Servicing the guest is all that Canadian hotels appear to do. It is a limited service at that—limited to a very few hotels that deal only in a few popular currencies because they have identified a well-defined international market segment for themselves. Overseas, foreign exchange is a profit centre for the hotel. There is a profit to be made because both domestic and foreign hotels exchange currency at something less than the official rate. That's a double insult because even the official rate, which is determined by open market bidding, provides a spread between buy price and sell price.

Since it is not desirable to inventory money from around the world, hotels do not provide for the reconversion of local currency into foreign funds as the visitor prepares to go home. Therefore, the hotel's concern is only with the bid rate. Money brokers quote both a buy (bid) rate and a sell (ask) rate. The desk buys foreign currency from the guest at a rate that is lower than the broker's bid rate, reselling later to the broker at the bid rate. The hotel might buy American dollars, for example, at 8 cents less than it sells them for, although the official spread might be only 4 cents. The extra spread between buy and sell may be further enriched by a supplemental exchange fee. This fee, which currency dealers call *agio,* provides the hotel with additional funds to pay for bank charges or to offset unexpected variations in foreign currency value. The latter makes it especially important to process foreign currency quickly and to include it in the turn-in every day.

If the hotel is dealing in foreign currencies, the accounting office must furnish the cashier with a table of values for each currency traded. (Several airlines quote currency rates, including rates on foreign traveller's cheques, as part of their reservation system service.) If currency values fluctuate over a wide range, a daily or even hourly quote is necessary to prevent substantial losses. More likely, the hotel will just refuse that particular currency.

**Foreign Cheques** Rare indeed is the hotel that will accept a foreign cheque. However, if payment were made by foreign cheque, the hotel would make an additional charge, passing on to the guest the bank's fee for foreign exchange. The amount of the fee is a function of both the size of the cheque and the variation in the rate of exchange.

Foreign traveller's cheques (especially U.S. traveller's cheques) are more readily accepted than personal cheques. Although cashiers are cautioned to use the same level of scrutiny with foreign traveller's cheques as they use with Canadian traveller's cheques (accepting traveller's cheques is discussed in depth toward the end of this chapter), there is an additional catch. Foreign traveller's cheques look identical to Canadian traveller's cheques, with one simple difference: Instead of stating, "Pay to the order of (name) in Canadian dollars," the foreign traveller's cheque states "Pay . . . in U.S. dollars," or whatever currency is applicable. Many a time has a clerk accidentally cashed a foreign traveller's cheque thinking it was payable in Canadian funds. This can represent a considerable loss to the hotel or to the guest, depending on the foreign currency and its rate of exchange against the Canadian dollar.

# Cash and Cash Equivalents

Even as the ratio of guest folios paid with cash and cash equivalents (traveller's cheques, personal cheques, and corporate cheques) is decreasing, the incidence of counterfeiting and forgery is at an all-time high. Due to advances in technology and print quality, computers are responsible, in part, for the rise of cash-related crimes proliferating nationwide. The busy hotel, with its hundreds or thousands of new guests each day, creates the perfect haven for such crimes. That's why it is of paramount importance that managers be trained in the secure handling of cash and cheques.

Hotels are likely targets for professional counterfeiters for several reasons. First, agents are often rushed with numerous small transactions, allowing the professional counterfeiter easy access and egress. Second, hotel cashiers are inundated with so many guests that they would probably have a difficult time remembering (much less describing or identifying) the professional counterfeiter.

Finally, as discussed earlier, hotels handle relatively little cash as a percentage of all sales volume. Although that may sound contradictory, counterfeiters often seek establishments that deal in little cash. That's because cashiers who handle a lot of cash become very adept at spotting a phoney. Conversely, hotel cashiers (who handle relatively little cash) are poorly prepared to spot fake currency.

## Counterfeit Currency

Counterfeit bills in Canada are still a problem, with almost $10 million in worthless bills being passed in 2005 (see Exhibit 11-8).

**Detecting Counterfeit Currency** Security features on bank notes are quick and easy to use, as well as being reliable (see Exhibit 11-9). To verify that a bill is genuine, simply touch it, tilt it, and look at and through it. Always check more than one security feature when deciding whether a bank note is real or not. Always compare a suspect counterfeit note to a genuine note. Remember that applying water, rubbing, or folding the note is not a reliable test.

**Exhibit 11-8**
Counterfeit Canadian bank notes passed, by denomination, in 2004 and 2005. © *HER MAJESTY THE QUEEN IN RIGHT OF CANADA as represented by the Royal Mounted Police (RCMP). Reprinted with the permission of the RCMP.*
▼

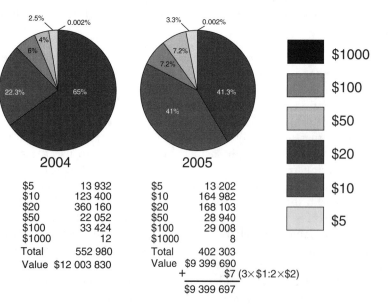

| 2004 | |
|---|---|
| $5 | 13 932 |
| $10 | 123 400 |
| $20 | 360 160 |
| $50 | 22 052 |
| $100 | 33 424 |
| $1000 | 12 |
| Total | 552 980 |
| Value | $12 003 830 |

| 2005 | |
|---|---|
| $5 | 13 202 |
| $10 | 164 982 |
| $20 | 168 103 |
| $50 | 28 940 |
| $100 | 29 008 |
| $1000 | 8 |
| Total | 402 303 |
| Value | $9 399 690 |
| + | $7 (3×$1:2×$2) |
| | $9 399 697 |

| | |
|---|---|
| ■ | $1000 |
| ■ | $100 |
| ■ | $50 |
| ■ | $20 |
| ■ | $10 |
| ■ | $5 |

**Other Cashier Applications** Hotel cashiers may also be interested in a number of relatively inexpensive counterfeit detection devices that have hit the market in recent years. One of the most common is an ultraviolet light. This light highlights the planchettes. (see Exhibit 11-10).

Whatever their approach, hotels are urged to use caution when accepting currency. Counterfeit currency can cost a hotel a considerable amount of money in a relatively short amount of time because counterfeiters usually pass a number of bills in quick succession. Counterfeit bills are like ants, you never find just one! And when the hotel finally realizes what has happened and

**Exhibit 11-9** ▶
Detecting counterfeit
Canadian currency. ©
*HER MAJESTY THE
QUEEN IN RIGHT OF
CANADA as represented
by the Royal Mounted
Police (RCMP). Reprinted
with the permission of
the RCMP.*

| | |
|---|---|
| **Touch the bill** | Does the paper feel like your other currency? |
| | Raised ink, intaglio: run your finger over the large numeral and the other areas that have a lot of ink to feel the difference in texture. |
| **Tilt the bill** | If checking new series $5 and $10 notes: Look for iridescent maple leaves. Tilt the note; the three maple leaves will change from a faint image to a shiny gold. The outline of the leaves is clearly defined, and there are no detectable raised edges. |
| | If checking new series $5 and $10 notes: Check for the hidden number. Hold and tilt the note at eye level. The number 5 or 10 will become visible. |
| | If checking bird series $20, $50, and $100 notes: Check the colour change patch (optical security device, or OSD) found in the upper-left corner of a genuine note. Ensure that the patch changes colour—from gold to green and back again—when tilted back and forth. There is a far less noticeable colour shift (and sometimes none) on a counterfeit bill. |
| | If checking new series $20, $50, and $100 notes: A mirrored stripe on these bills contains holographic images of the denomination of the bill and maple leaves that will appear to move and change colour as the bill is tilted. There is a colour split on the maple leaves, and the mirrored stripe itself is curved. The security thread on the back of the note shifts from gold to green. |
| **Look at the bill** | Does the colour of the note look similar to other notes you've seen? |
| | If checking birds series $20, $50, and $100 notes: Planchettes (green dots) can be removed if scratched. |
| | All Canadian paper currency makes use of fine-line patterns. Observe the sharp, well-defined lines that make up the facial features of the portraits, the circles within the eyes, and the background patterns of the note. |
| | All Canadian notes also make use of micro-printing, tiny words that never appear blurry. On the $5 note, for example, the text FIVE 5 CINQ is printed in clear, small characters. Text to the right of the West Block of Parliament gradually becomes smaller but remains clear and sharp. |
| | Serial numbers never repeat. |
| | Those equipped with ultraviolet lights will be able be able to see glowing threads or fibres on newer bills and the glowing planchettes (confetti-like dots) on the older $20, $50, and $100 bills. On new bills, the denomination of the bill and the words BANQUE DU CANADA BANK OF CANADA glow over the portrait. |
| **Look through the bill** | If checking new series $20, $50, and $100 notes: A watermark portrait, see-through number (marks that come together like a jigsaw puzzle to form a number when looking through the bill), and top-to-bottom woven security thread will only become fully visible when held up to a light or window. |

▲
**Exhibit 11-10**

Detection devices such as MoneyChecker supplement front-office training designed to recognize counterfeit currencies and related products. Detection devices are generally inexpensive and require minimal training. The least expensive (and least sophisticated) detection comes with special pens designed to change colour when they contact the starch in paper counterfeits—real currency is made from cotton fibres. However, inexpensive detection pens are easily thwarted by coating the fake bills in plastic (usually with a sprayed-on Scotchgard-type product).

A slightly higher investment by the front office affords substantially improved detection in the form of ultraviolet (UV) lamps. UV lamps (like those found in the MoneyChecker) readily illuminate the colour-coded security threads found in all $5, $10, $20, $50, and $100 Canadian currency bills. A built-in template on all MoneyCheckers shows the location and colour of each denomination's security thread. Additionally, the UV lamp can help authenticate credit cards, driver licences, and travellers' checks, many of which now boast logos or overprinted areas visible only under the specific wavelengths of UV light.

calls the police or the RCMP, they are in for another shock—the counterfeit bills will be confiscated without restitution.

**Fraudulent Credit Cards**   At the end of fiscal year 2005, approximately 56.4 million credit cards were in circulation across the country, with a sales volume exceeding $190.6 billion (MasterCard and Visa.) See Exhibit 11-11 for a breakdown of credit card losses.

Payment card counterfeiters are now using the latest computer devices (embossers, encoders, and decoders often supported by computers) to read, modify, and implant magnetic stripe information on counterfeit payment cards.

As well, phoney identification has been used to obtain government assistance, personal loans, unemployment insurance benefits, and for other schemes that victimize governments, individuals, and corporate bodies.

**Exhibit 11-11** ▶
Summary of credit card losses in Canada, 2005. © HER MAJESTY THE QUEEN IN RIGHT OF CANADA as represented by the Royal Mounted Police (RCMP). Reprinted with the permission of the RCMP.

| Payment Card Partner Losses by Type, 2005 | | | |
|---|---|---|---|
| **Category** | **$ Loss** | **No. of accounts** | **$ Avg. loss per account** |
| Lost | $14 771 080 | 25 363 | $586.75 |
| Stolen | $26 112 623 | 40 827 | $638.86 |
| Non receipt | $7 856 411 | 3 803 | $2 041.71 |
| Fraudulent applications | $8 909 580 | 4 872 | $1 733.24 |
| Counterfeit | $126 824 292 | 114 795 | $1 050.02 |
| Fraudulent use of account | $88 364 181 | 147 911 | $595.86 |
| Miscellaneous, not defined | $7 305 414 | 5 069 | $1 496.07 |
| TOTAL | $280 143 582 | 342 640 | $798.00 |

**Categories of Credit Card Fraud** The criminal use of credit cards can be divided into the following categories:

- *Counterfeit credit card use.* This represents the largest category of credit card fraud involving Canadian-issued cards, with 37 percent of all dollar losses. Organized criminals have acquired the technology that allows them to "skim" the data contained on magnetic stripes, manufacture phoney cards, and overcome such protective features as holograms.
- *Cards lost by or stolen from the cardholder.* Lost and stolen cards represent 23 percent of all credit card fraud losses. Typically, the cards are stolen from the workplace, vehicles, health clubs, golf clubs, etc.
- *Fraud committed without the actual use of a card (no-card fraud).* No-card fraud accounts for 10 percent of all losses. Deceptive telemarketers and now fraudulent Internet websites obtain specific card details from their victims, while promoting the sale of exaggerated or non-existent goods and services. This in turn results in fraudulent charges against victims' accounts.
- *Fraud committed on cards not received by the legitimate cardholder (non-receipt fraud).* Non-receipt fraud, where cards are intercepted prior to delivery to the cardholder, account for 7 percent of all losses. Losses attributable to mail theft have declined as a result of "card activation" programs, where cardholders must call their financial institution to confirm their identity before the card is activated. In 1992, this category accounted for 16 percent of all losses.
- *Cards fraudulently obtained by criminals who have made false applications.* Fraudulent applications involve the criminal impersonation of creditworthy persons in order to acquire credit cards. Although false application losses represent only 4 percent of all losses, the numbers are increasing.

## Cheque-Cashing Safeguards

Even in the smallest hotel, management cannot make every credit decision every hour of the day. Instead, it creates the policies and procedures that will minimize losses and retain customer goodwill. A credit manual or credit handbook is the usual manner of communicating management's position. Each company reflects its own approach in policies, but procedures for handling personal cheques (and traveller's cheques) are much alike from hotel to hotel and from handbook to handbook.

Many hotels today will not accept personal cheques from guests. Some major chains such as Fairmont Hotels extend cheque-cashing privileges to guests who belong to their frequent-guest program, the Fairmont Presidents Club. Many other hotels have similar services. Some credit cards, such as American Express, provide their cardholders with cheque-cashing privileges and guarantee the cheque to the hotel if a problem arises. Today, even in smaller centres, there are cheque-cashing establishments such as Money Mart to which a hotel can send a guest who wishes to cash a cheque. These places provide the service to the guest without the liability to the hotel.

Hotels train their front-office personnel to be pleasant, courteous, and accommodating. Cheque scam artists are usually loud, rude, and threatening. By pushing in during rush hours, harassing the clerks who have been taught to "take it," and pressuring for service, passers of bad cheques walk away with millions. Losses can be reduced when certain procedures are put in place.

**Procedures for Minimizing Fraud** Hotel operations are 100 times more likely to lose money to forged and fraudulent cheques than they are to armed robbery! Using proper cheque-cashing procedures is critical to avoiding significant losses from this form of theft.

As with counterfeiting, computer technology has made cheque-cashing forgery a simple crime for anyone to perpetrate. Basic desktop publishing and scanning equipment is all one needs to ably copy and alter personal cheques. And since cheques are paid by computer automation as well, the altered cheque will clear provided that the account has sufficient funds.

Unfortunately, hotels that accept forged or worthless cheques have little recourse. Banks are not responsible for losses incurred from bad cheques passed against them. The hotel ends up holding the bag—prevention is the only cure.

The Canadian Payments Association (CPA) has published new specifications for Canadian cheques in preparation for the transition to image-based clearing. Under the new specifications (to take effect on June 30, 2007), all cheques used by customers of financial institutions operating in Canada will require some changes. The new specifications, as outlined in CPA Standard 006, Part A, are necessary to ensure that high-quality cheque images can be captured, both for clearing purposes and for delivery to clients, and to enhance processing efficiency.

In the Canadian clearing system today, paper-based payment items, primarily cheques, are exchanged between financial institutions daily at six regional exchange points across the country. In each of these locations, cheques are exchanged between up to 12 direct clearers (major financial institutions that also may act as clearing agents on behalf of other financial institutions, known as indirect clearers).

The process begins when a customer deposits a cheque at his or her branch. Near the end of the day, that branch's cheques are bundled, totalled, and sent by air or ground courier to the regional processing centre for that financial institution in one of six cities across the country. A similar process is in place for cheques deposited at automated teller machines (ATMs).

At the regional processing centre, the amount of each cheque is encoded on it in magnetic ink to facilitate automated processing. Then cheques are passed through high-speed readers and sorted based on the financial institution holding the accounts on which they have been written. Once the total number and value of the cheques have been confirmed, they are bundled once again and then transported to another processing centre that serves the financial institution of the person who wrote the cheque.

There the items are unbundled and processed again through a high-speed reader to verify the number and value of cheques received. Next, the cheques are put through the machine again to sort them based on the branch that holds the account on which the cheque was written. Depending on the financial institution's internal processes, the cheques may then be shipped to the various branches. If a cheque cannot be honoured (for example, due to insufficient funds or a stop payment order), it retraces the entire journey back to the branch where it was initially deposited.

This entire process may involve processing a paper cheque through the reading and sorting machines up to eight times and transporting it up to four times.

Once image-based clearing begins, Canadians will continue to write cheques as they do now, and will continue to deposit them at their financial institutions as usual (e.g., at the branch or through an ATM). Financial institutions will, for the most part, follow their current practices for delivering deposited cheques to their processing centre.

From that point on, the clearing process will change. At the data centre, the amount of a cheque and its electronic code line data, as well as a digital image of the front and back of the cheque, will be captured. Then, instead of shipping the actual physical cheque, the data centre will transmit the data captured from the cheque and the image file to the institution that holds the account on which the cheque was written (referred to as "the drawee institution") or its clearing agent. As "time in transit" for the electronic files will be significantly reduced, the drawee institution will have access to the cheque image and data much faster to make a decision on whether to honour the cheque based on this electronic information.

After the image has been captured at the processing centre and sent to the drawee institution, the original paper cheque will no longer serve much purpose. Shortly after the usability of the image has been confirmed, the financial institution in possession of the paper cheque will see to its destruction. Since physical cheques will no longer be available for enclosure in customer statements, financial institutions will introduce new image-based services to provide equivalent information to clients about the cheques they have written. Although the services will vary somewhat between financial institutions, it is anticipated that most will offer a form of "image statement" on which copies of the cheques written by that customer will be reproduced as well as online access to images as part of the electronic banking services. Images may also be offered on CD-ROM for business customers with high volumes of cheques.

**Endorsements**   Procedural protection requires proper and immediate endorsement after the cheque is received. This is particularly true with open endorsements containing only the payee's name. The cashier should use a rubber stamp that reads as follows:

For Deposit Only

The ABC Hotel

The stamp should contain space for identification, credit card number, room number, and the initials of the person approving the cheque. This stamp should also be used for traveller's cheques, although approval of management is usually not required for traveller's cheques.

**Debit Cards**   Canadians are the highest users of debit cards in the world. In 2003, Canadians made 81.7 debit card transactions per person, and in 2004, Canadians made 1.1 billion ATM transactions. Debit cards provide the hotel with immediate payment through the guest's bank account. Rather than writing a personal cheque, the debit card electronically debits the guest's bank account and credits the hotel's account. Payment is immediate, and the risk associated with accepting personal cheques is removed. For additional discussion of debit cards, refer to Chapter 12.

It is safe to use a debit card, as the banking industry has sophisticated security systems and teams of security experts to protect customers and the debit card system. As the biggest users of debit cards in the world, Canadians enjoy the convenience and 24-hour access to banking services that their debit cards provide. Chips are being introduced to debit cards in Canada in 2007, and this new mini-computer technology will greatly enhance security.

Banks have a zero tolerance for fraud and work to protect you. Security measures are constantly being enhanced, technology is being upgraded, and the banking industry assists police in investigations to help catch criminals and put them behind bars.

When using your debit card, you are protected by the Canadian Code of Practice for Consumer Debit Card Services, which guarantees that if you are a victim of debit card fraud, you will get your money back from your financial institution.

**Traveller's Cheques**   American Express pioneered the traveller's cheque, and it has retained its pre-eminent position ever since. Visa and MasterCard entered the field in the late 1970s and early 1980s as extensions of their credit card business. Several banks and travel agencies round out the slate of participants. It is a competitive business. However, because of primarily the proliferation of ATM machines (discussed earlier in the chapter), the traveller's cheque industry has stagnated in recent years. With easy access to electronic cash, travellers feel even more secure carrying their plastic ATM cards as opposed to dozens of bulky traveller's cheques. As such, the traveller's cheque industry stalled in the late 1990s at about $50 billion per year. It will probably decline in volume over the coming decades, even as the industry has found renewed popularity through the use of gift cheques (traveller's cheques given instead of cash for weddings, birthdays, etc.).

Generally, traveller's cheques are purchased by the consumer prior to a trip. They are used as if they were cash, with the issuing company guaranteeing their replacement against loss or theft. The charge is usually 1 percent, but the cheques are often issued without charge. Even without charge, there is plenty of competition for the business. Large sums of interest-free money are available for investing. The time lag (the float) between the purchase of the traveller's cheque and the use of the cheque might be months. Some 15 to 20 percent of traveller's cheque sales are never claimed. No wonder American Express advertising encourages buyers to hold their cheques for some distant emergency.

Buyers sign the cheques at the time of purchase and countersign when they cash the instruments. Signature comparison is the main line of defence against fraud. Cheques must be countersigned under the scrutiny of the cashier or re-signed if they were initially endorsed away from the cashier's view. Some traveller's cheques provide for dual countersignatures (usually to accommodate a husband-and-wife team), yet only one signature is required to cash the cheque.

Traveller's cheques are very acceptable, and some hotels will cash them even for non-registered guests. Other hotels are extra cautious and require additional identification or compare signatures to registration cards. Comparing signatures is all that's required. In fact, many issuing companies do not even want the cashier to ask for additional identification. That is because extra identification takes the cashier's focus away from the signature line. And the identification may also be invalid—in more than half of the instances of stolen traveller's cheques, the identification has also been stolen!

Prompt refund of lost or stolen cheques is their major appeal. Hotel desks, with their 24-hour service, represent a logical extension of the issuing company's office system. It is both a service to the guest and a marketing device for the chain.

**Traveller's Cheques Deterrents** The best defence is to watch carefully as the guest signs the traveller's cheque. Cautious cashiers should never remove their eyes from the cheque being signed. Indeed, some cashiers never even remove their hand from the cheque, always holding on to one corner while the guest is signing. It is a simple matter for someone to produce a stolen traveller's cheque, pretend to sign it while the cashier's attention is focused elsewhere, and then quickly substitute a previously signed traveller's cheque with a well-forged signature.

Like their commercial counterparts, traveller's cheques employ a magnetic code on the lower left portion of the paper.

Although forgers can easily alter the clearinghouse transit codes, they cannot easily copy the high-quality, high-speed laser images that major companies print in their traveller's cheques. These images can be seen when holding the traveller's cheque to the light (don't confuse these highly detailed laser imprints with simple watermarks found in paper). MasterCard and Thomas Cook, for example, show a Greek goddess on the right side of the cheque.

American Express uses a somewhat different safety approach. Red dots are visible in the cheque if held up to the light, but a wet finger is the acid test. It will smear the cheque when applied to the denomination on the back left side but will not smear the back right side.

The components of this chapter—cash, cash paid-outs, and cash equivalents—represent a small percentage of the transactions that occur at the front desk. Most transactions are handled by credit card or credit transfer to a city ledger account. In Chapter 12, the focus changes to the issues of credit. Because credit cards and credit equivalents represent the lion's share of front-office transactions, poor or lazy procedures can harm front-office profitability. In Chapter 12, we explain credit-handling procedures and caution managers to treat credit transactions with the same care as cash transactions.

## Summary

Even as the quantity of cash circulating in hotels declines, the need for careful cash-handling practices increases. This is especially true for front-desk cashiers because they not only receive cash but also pay it out.

Front-office cashiers receive cash from a number of potential sources. Guests may pay cash on their room folio at check-in, at check-out, or in the middle of their stay. Cash is also received at the desk on behalf of other departments (as when a customer pays for a banquet) and for auxiliary revenue centres such as vending machines or video games.

Cash is paid out by the front-office cashier for a number of reasons as well. On check-out, the guest who overpaid the folio may receive a refund. Employees may receive charged tips in cash, concessionaires may receive charged purchases in cash, and guests themselves may receive cash advances against the folio. Add to this list of paid-outs the use of an imprest petty cash account and the front-office cashier's job becomes a complicated and sensitive task.

To make the job even more difficult, cashiers must remain alert to potential cheque-cashing, credit card, or cash transaction frauds. Hotel front desks are favourite targets for counterfeit currency, forged cheques, or stolen credit cards. Front-office managers need to train cashiers carefully to identify situations in which fraudulent practices may occur.

## Questions and Problems

1. An international guest tenders $171 in Canadian funds and #2000 from his native country to settle an outstanding account of $206.20. The exchange rate the hotel is paying is $3.50 Canadian for each #. What must the cashier do now to settle the account? Assume that the guest has more Canadian dollars; assume that he or she doesn't. The hotel cashier has no foreign funds in the drawer.

2. Explain how international tourism helps balance the trade deficit of Canada. How does international tourism worsen the deficit?

3. Sketch and complete a cashier's envelope for October 11 showing the details of the turn-in and the amount of due back. (The accounting office handles city ledger collections. No provisions are made for cash over or short; the cashier covers both.)

**Given for Problem**

| | |
|---|---|
| House bank | $1800.00 |
| Advances to guests | $181.15 |
| House vouchers | $16.20 |
| Vending machine refunds | $0.50 |
| Received from guests | $7109.40 |
| Cash in the drawer exclusive of other cash listed below | $1721.00 |
| Traveller's cheques | $2675.00 |
| Personal cheques: | |
|   Todd Bertussi | $75.25 |
|   Don Cherry | $310.00 |
|   Doug Gilmore | $44.98 |
|   Mats Sundin | $211.90 |

| Markus Naslund | $55.00 |
| Others | $1876.85 |
| Bills of $100 denomination | 10 |
| Torn and dirty currency | $60.00 |
| Coins | $682.14 |

4. Imagine that your hotel operates in a community in which the incidence of counterfeiting is quite high. Develop a procedure for all front-desk cashiers that addresses accepting Canadian currency. Remember to be sensitive to the amount of time it takes to examine a bill properly and the fact that the cashier may be busy with other guests in line. Also, discuss whether the procedure should be eased for smaller denominations: $20, $50? What if the cashier knows the guest from previous hotel visits? Be certain that your policy distinguishes between the newer currency (new $10 introduced in January 2001, and new $5 introduced in March 2002) and the older currency (which will be in circulation for many years to come).

5. Some hotels prevent cashiers from knowing their net receipts. Without knowing net receipts, the cashier turns in everything from the day's drawer except the bank. If the drawer is significantly over for the shift, the cashier is none the wiser and is not tempted to steal the amount of the overage. Do you support such a policy? Are there any drawbacks to not allowing cashiers access to their net receipt figures?

## CASE STUDY

## The Missing Front-Desk Cash Deposit

Ibrahim and Wenli are called into the general manager's office on the morning of November 12. Ibrahim's cash deposit from his morning shift on November 11 is missing. Ibrahim tells the GM that he put the deposit into the safe's security drop chute. Wenli was quite busy on the front desk when Ibrahim did this, and afterwards Ibrahim asked Wenli to sign the security sheet as a witness to the money drop. Even though Wenli did not actually see Ibrahim drop the deposit down the chute, she trusted him and gladly signed as a witness, as he had for her on previous occasions when she was cashier and Ibrahim was busy on the front desk.

1. Where did the missing money go? Make a comprehensive list of what person or persons may have taken this money.

2. If you were the front-office manager of this hotel, what extra security steps could you put in place to ensure that this would never happen again?

3. As general manager, would you report this mysterious disappearance to the police?

4. Does the hotel have any options for recovering this missing cash?

## Weblinks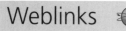

## Chapter 12

# Credit and the City Ledger

## Learning Objectives

After reading this chapter, you will be able to do the following:

1. **Understand the city ledger as it applies to credit cards, other cards, and other city ledger categories.**

2. **Identify the methods used to manage different kinds of credit.**

3. **Understand the mechanics and accounting principles behind postings to and from the city ledger.**

Notwithstanding the discussion of cash in Chapter 11, guests rarely pay with cash. In fact, front-office managers become suspicious when guests indicate that they'll settle that way. They know that skippers leave no incriminating identification. Legitimate guests favour and hotels prefer credit cards. Indeed, credit cards seem to be everyone's favourite method of payment these days. And much like the hotel industry, with its new products and new logos, the credit card industry continues to fashion old offerings into more appealing consumer products. The credit revolution that began during the last half of the twentieth century gains momentum still.

Buying on credit—that is, promising to pay later—is how North America does business. The rest of the world is gradually adopting the idea. Both commercial and retail trade start out as credit transactions. Commercial businesses usually settle their credit purchases by cash, mailing cheques at the end of the month, but even that is changing. Credit card companies have aggressively marketed corporate procurement cards that are used in lieu of cash. MasterCard has BusinessCard,[1] for example, but it is only 1 of an estimated 200 commercial cards. Retail guests, including hotel guests, usually settle their purchases with personal credit cards. With billions of credit card transactions taking place annually, expecting cash at the front desk is out of sync with the realities of the marketplace.

# Review of the City Ledger

Whatever the business, customers who have not yet paid for goods and services already received are called accounts receivable (A/R). Chapter 10 explained that hotels have two types of accounts receivable. Registered guests are called *front-office (transient* or *guest)* accounts receivable. Their debts are tracked on front-office folios.

Those who owe the hotel but are not registered are known as *city* accounts receivable. Their debts are tracked separately by the accounting office.

Accounts receivable records are accumulated in ledgers. The term *ledger* survives although the records are no longer in bound books; they're computerized. Hence, the records of registered guests are grouped together in a front-office (transient or guest) ledger. Likewise, non-registered accounts receivable are grouped in a city ledger. Individual records in the guest ledger are identified by room numbers. City ledger accounts have no room numbers; they are not occupying rooms. Account numbers are used instead.

Most city receivables (accounts receivable that are not registered) start out as front-office receivables (accounts receivable that are registered). A registered guest usually shifts debt from the front office to the back office by using a credit card. The debt is still owed, but the transient guest has left the hotel. Once the guest is no longer registered, the debt becomes part of a city ledger. City ledger accounts receivable include more than credit card companies. Associations, wholesalers, travel agents, individuals, and client companies become city accounts whenever their front-office folios, often master accounts, are transferred to the city ledger for direct billing by mail.

Transferring an account from the front-office ledger to the city ledger is one of the three methods of settling a folio at check-out time. Allowances and cash, the other two methods, were discussed in Chapters 10 and 11. This chapter concludes the unit by viewing the city ledger in its entirety, broadening the discussion beyond city ledger transfers.

# Cards

Credit cards, long the domain of serious shoppers, face potential competition from a recent surge in debit card use.

## Credit Cards

For now, credit card use continues to grow worldwide. Even Europeans, long-time cash traditionalists, have come aboard. Much like the hotel industry has done, credit card companies continue refashioning old offerings into more appealing products. The credit revolution that began during the last half of the twentieth century gains momentum still.

**Kinds of Credit Cards**  Consumer credit cards are growing increasingly alike, but they didn't start out that way. Although the number and variety of credit cards seem endless, consumer cards fall into three general categories. *Bank cards* are the most common, followed by **travel and entertainment cards (T&Es)**. *Private label cards* comprise most of the third category: all others.

The Canadian credit card market is one of the most competitive in the world, with more than 600 institutions issuing Visa, MasterCard, or American Express through 23 principal issuers, including banks, credit unions, caisses populaires, and retailers. They offer a wide variety of products to meet the credit and transaction needs of their customers, whether they are looking for a convenient payment option, low borrowing rates, points programs, insurance coverage, or retail discounts.

The credit card industry is very competitive. Initially, each of the three types of cards was designed for different consumer markets. To some degree, this is still true. However, competition has forced each type of credit card to spread beyond its original

**Exhibit 12-1 ▶**
The use of bank cards in Canada as well as worldwide is on the increase, as shown in this exhibit.

### General Statistics for Canada

| Visa and MasterCard | October 31, 2004 | October 31, 2005 |
| --- | --- | --- |
| Number of cards in circulation (million) | 53.4 | 56.4 |
| Delinquency ratios (90 days and over) | 0.8% | 0.8% |
| Retail sales volume ($ billion) | $168.78 | $190.60 |
| Number of transactions processed (million) | 1664.8 | 1839.7 |
| Average sale ($) | $104.00 | $106.00 |
| Sales and cash advance volume ($ billion) | $192.17 | $216.04 |

### Worldwide Market Share of Major Credit Cards
(Arrows show market share increasing or decreasing)

| | |
| --- | --- |
| Visa | 60.30 ↑ |
| MasterCard | 26.88 ↓ |
| American Express | 11.04 ↑ |
| JCB | 1.29 ↓ |
| Diners Club | 0.4 ↓ |

concept. The differences between bank cards and T&Es blur as banking deregulations allow and competition forces each to take on attributes of the other. No longer are there sharp distinctions. Some bank cards now charge an annual fee, although they were initially offered without charge. T&Es, which traditionally required merchants to wait for reimbursement, have introduced express deposits like the bank cards. Prestige cards with high spending limits and special privileges are offered now by bank cards to the affluent, who were the original customers of the T&E cards. Both are racing to develop smart cards to broaden usage and reduce fraud. The battle has been joined. See Exhibit 12-1, which compares worldwide market share for major credit cards.

**Travel and Entertainment Cards (T&Es)** The best known of the T&E cards are American Express (AmEx) and Diners Club. EnRoute, a card issued by Air Canada, has recently amalgamated with Diners Club, and members can get a Diners Club card that accumulates Aeroplan miles, which are redeemable with Air Canada. Diners Club cards are issued in Canada by Citibank Canada. T&E cards are not part of the banking system; they do not encourage slow payment with high interest. The user is expected to settle in full each month. T&Es are slower than bank cards to reimburse merchants and hotels. This provides another means of earnings, called **float**. If collection is made from cardholders on day 1 and payment to the merchants is delayed until day 11, the credit card company has interest-free use of that money for 10 days. What is aggravating to the merchant waiting for several hundreds or even thousands of dollars is very big money to the T&E working with tens of millions of dollars. Everyone—credit card company, merchant, business user, and consumer—chases the float. Float is one explanation for the increased use of credit cards by businesses. The business has interest-free use of the money for 30 to 60 days, between dates of purchase and payment to the credit card company.

Bank agreements have shut out T&Es from the banking system. MasterCard and Visa prevent member banks from issuing T&E cards even if they want to. AmEx and

Discover (in the United States) have challenged them, and the government's investigation has carried the matter to court. Overseas, where there are no such restrictions, T&E cards are issued by banks.

**Private Label Cards** Gasoline companies (Esso, Shell, etc.) marketed private label cards for many years. Consumers once carried a variety of gas cards as they carry a variety of credit cards today. Billing and payment were handled through the corporate gas companies. The oil embargo of the 1970s changed the retail gasoline industry dramatically and contributed to the disappearance of these private label cards.

Department stores have fared better. They still issue private label cards but have replaced their policy of selling only with company cards by now accepting national credit cards as well.

**New Products** In their continuing quest for market share, credit card issuers have introduced many new products. Two in particular, *affinity cards* and *co-branded cards,* were big hits when first issued.

Affinity cards carry two designations: the name of the affiliated group and that of the credit card company. Almost any organization that offers the credit card company an extensive mailing list can affiliate. Charities, professional organizations, public-service television stations, and environmental groups add their names to the already established national card. The card company gets a list of possible new card users. Affinity cards are supposed to sharpen the group's identity and get members to use the card for the benefit of the organization. Affinity cards failed on two counts. First, banks gave up a portion of their discount fees expecting to recover the costs with higher interest receipts. It didn't happen. Second, card users gave up rewards to benefit the group. That worked for only so long. As the quality of rewards improved, member support declined. Co-branded cards held a different promise, beginning with their availability to the general public. Affinity cards were limited to affiliated groups. Co-branding didn't survive as planned. Major co-branders abandoned their participation because of high costs. For example, Ford Motor Company co-branded with Citibank's card; however, liabilities grew too rapidly. Ford had already paid out $500 million when it exited. Almost as quickly as the boisterous appearance of affinity cards came their quiet demise. But co-branding remained.

Co-branded cards are especially popular with lodging companies. Hilton, Marriott, Starwood—all hotel chains—co-brand with credit card companies. Co-branded cards carry special privileges, such as cheque cashing, room upgrades, and free continental breakfasts. In the longer run, guests build equity in loyalty programs: frequent-flier accounts, frequent-guest programs, or better still, both. Key to co-branding is the value of the reward. The companies are not giving away autos or hotels, just points in loyalty programs. Some chains use the same points to settle complaints (see Chapter 7).

Total points increased substantially during the lodging slump that started in this century. Luring guests with more points soon built liabilities for the lodging industry that approached those of the airlines.

BROADENING THE MARKET New products aren't always as dramatic as affinity and co-branded cards, although they may be introduced with just as much hoopla. Basic cards have morphed into gold cards, platinum cards, titanium cards, and back to blue cards and black cards. Each is presented as a new product with different costs, different privileges, and different rewards.

**How the System Works**   The system works because there is something in it for everyone (see Exhibit 12-2). Credit card *users* (hotel guests) purchase goods and services without cash. Payment may be financed through the credit card or delayed until billing, 20 to 50 days later. Card *issuers* (the banks) profit through a variety of fees, which are discussed next. *Merchants* (the hotels) co-operate in the system, although they foot the entire cost. But they benefit by making sales that might otherwise go elsewhere, and they do so with less risk of loss. Hotels generally have done away with the position of credit manager. *Local banks* (the first step in processing the charges) have no float, but they earn fees for handling the transaction.

**Fees**   Credit card companies charge merchant/hotels discount fees. Bank cards charge at the lower range, 1 to 2 percent of the transaction; T&Es charge at the upper end, 3 to 5 percent. Card fees are no different from other business expenses—they can be negotiated. Large-volume merchants such as hotel chains negotiate smaller discount fees. Competition among rival banks and their independent sales organizations (ISOs) is so keen that even the smallest hotel dickers successfully. Besides, hotels have other banking relationships that give the merchant additional bargaining leverage. Franchise systems have a competitive edge over independents because they combine the volume

**Exhibit 12-2** ▶
The full burden of settlement, 2.56 percent ($100 – $97.44), falls on the merchant/hotel as credit card charges clear the interchange system. Transaction fees, rental equipment fees, and chargeback fees are other costs paid by the merchant. Unless customers are careful money managers, they too will contribute through late fees and interest.

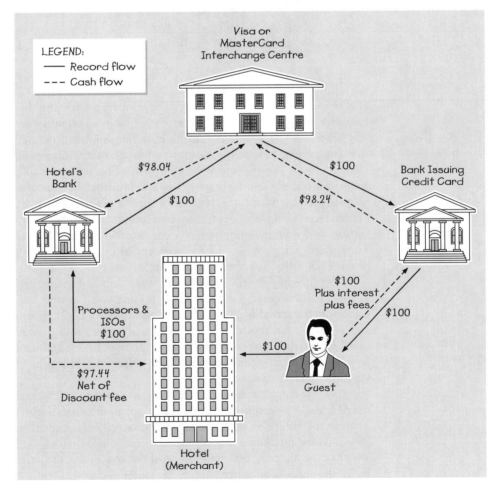

**Exhibit 12-3** ▶

Electronic verification (by swiping the credit card through the horizontal reader) is faster and less costly to the merchant/hotel than is manual input by means of the touch-tone telephone. The cost of buying or renting the equipment is offset in part by savings in reduced discount fees.

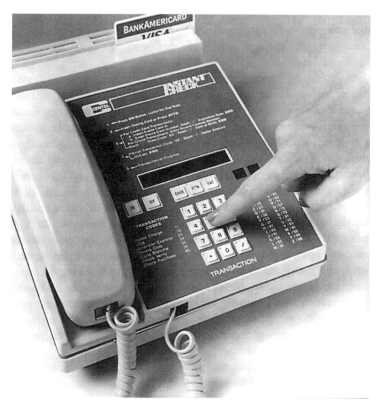

of their memberships. Umbrella organizations have tried to do the same for independents, but administrative costs offset the gains from quantity discounts.

Card type (bank versus T&E) and dollar volume generated are only two of many cost components. Handling, authorization, and settlement procedures add to the merchants' (hotels') costs. Before the credit card business grew so large, banks handled all support services. Costs have now been unbundled. The jobs of selling the merchant and servicing the merchant are handled by agents other than the banks. With these services come fees: setup fees, per-transaction fees, programming fees, statement fees, authorization fees, monthly minimum charges, telecommunication costs, and lease payments. These third-party costs add 2 to 3 percent or more to the discount fees. Effective rates often reach 3 to 5 percent, even for bank cards!

Costs are higher still if credit cards are handled manually. Point-of-sale terminals in food and beverage outlets save processing fees. So does swiping cards through an electronic scanner during registration (see Exhibit 12-3). Waiting until later to manually verify a card that the guest has already taken away incurs extra fees. All "non-mag" alternatives (manual handling, telephones, faxes, and mail) carry higher discount fees. Savings from electronic processing offset somewhat the costs of owning or leasing electronic equipment.

Another fee, a chargeback fee, is levied against the hotel when a charge is dishonoured because of disputes with guests or errors in processing. The fee is an extra insult because the hotel also loses the amount charged, the original sale. Folio charges made by guests for purchases in lobby shops raise similar issues. At best, the hotel pays no less than the discount fee on the value of the concessionaire's charge. If there's a chargeback, the concession purchase hits the hotel again—this time for the full value of the charge. Credit card fees and dishonoured charges must always be part of a concessionaire's lease.

Interest on unpaid balances, late charges, and annual fees are card users' major costs. New, insulting fees are on the horizon. Several issuers charge for inactive accounts or for accounts that fail to make minimum monthly purchases. There's an additional fee if the account is closed. Such unconscionable charges are reminiscent of the lodging industry's failed efforts at collecting for early check-outs or for reservation cancellations less than 72 hours (3 days!) in advance. Neither industry is apt to make friends.

## Other Cards

Despite their placement in a chapter titled "Credit and the City Ledger," neither debit cards nor smart cards are categories of the city ledger. However, they are issued by the same credit card companies, and they do affect both hotels and guests.

**Debit Cards** Debit cards transfer funds electronically (EFT, electronic funds transfer). Money is instantaneously switched from the cardholder's bank account to the merchant/hotel's bank account. Settlement is immediate. With debit cards, there is no debt and hence no accounts receivable. Debit cards are cash settlements, as explained in Chapter 11, but cash settlements without risk of dishonest employees, of overages and shortages (no one makes change), or of bounced cheques.

Use of debit cards climbed—quadrupled between 1995 and 2004—as credit card debt burgeoned. Fear of overextending their credit encouraged consumers to pay immediately (by debit card) rather than delay (by credit card), even though float was lost. Credit card companies unintentionally encouraged the change by reducing grace periods (float time dropped from 29 to 21 days), increasing late fees, and awarding loyalty points for debit card purchases. Debit cards mean fewer written cheques, which are costly for banks to process. Theft is the major negative for debit cards. An impostor can clear out the user's entire bank account. Debit card issuers now cover such losses as they do with credit cards.

As customers shifted toward debit cards, banks began charging them fees. Merchants were already paying fees. Merchant fees are higher if customers sign for the debit charge (about $0.60 per transaction); lower if they punch in PIN numbers (about $0.15). Retailers have sued over the difference.

Debit cards are the first step in the march toward the cashless society that futurists predict. Electronic funds transfer means savings in processing expenses, in time and paper handling, and in accounting costs for merchants, banks, and consumers. Smart cards are the next step.

**Smart Cards** Smart cards were introduced in France during the 1950s, and Europe has maintained its lead in this area since then. Card companies in the United States are working, even co-operating, on smart card development. Progress is slow because a universal system is essential. A hybrid card containing both a magnetic strip and a computer chip may appear during the transition.

Smart cards, the next level of sophistication, are miniature computers scarcely different in size and appearance from a standard credit card. They have an electronic chip instead of the magnetic stripe of present-day cards. That's why they're also called *digital cash* or *chip cards*. Unlike credit cards, smart cards carry a sizable quantity of storage in their microchip databases. The typical card has 8K of memory, roughly 15 pages of typed data. The memory can be accessed by card-reader devices that quickly scan and use information from the card. Smart cards are seen to be the future because they are everything in one. They are credit cards, stored-value cards, identification cards, debit cards, door keys, medical and insurance records, ATM cards, and more, all rolled into one. Smart card use will gain momentum as Internet commerce rises and better methods are needed for paying across the Web. Smart card use will require additional investments in equipment at the merchant/hotel level.

## Other City Ledger Categories

Credit cards are found in every city ledger because credit cards are one of the three methods of settling accounts (see Chapter 10). Depending on its market, hotels may or may not have other city ledger accounts. Charges arise from parties (weddings, for example) or other ballroom rentals (charity dances, for example) that never register even one person. Most city ledger postings come from registered guests who transfer their accounts from front-office folios to back-office city ledgers. For individuals, that means city ledger credit cards. For groups and associations, that means individual city ledger accounts, one of which is master accounts.

**Master Accounts**    Master accounts accumulate charges for groups. As Chapter 10 explained, master accounts are front-office folios. However, the guest is a group or association, not an individual person. Room charges, entertainment, banquets, and meeting room space are just some of the charges that master accounts accumulate. Outside vendors (florists, bands, and audiovisual rentals) are sometimes paid by the hotel and charged to the master account. Chapters 10 and 11 explain how these charges are posted to the front-office folios. Total charges are transferred to the city ledger when the event ends. Billing and collection follow.

Functions that involve hundreds of persons using rooms, rental space, and banquets represent very large sums of money. The hotel wants prompt payment. To ensure this, the master account folio is carefully reviewed by the client (the meeting planner, the association executive, etc.) and by the hotel (the sales manager and the accountant). Errors in master account folios may be substantial, but even meeting managers concede that they are not always in the hotel's favour. Even so, there are four common errors that irritate meeting planners. Attending to these beforehand expedites the billing, settlement, and eventual payment. Preventing the complaint is what good service is all about.

Error 1 is split billing. Meeting planners complain that charges are incorrectly split between master accounts and individual, personal accounts. Charges for group events should appear on the master folio and not on the personal folio of the executive who signs the tab. Front-office employees grow careless despite specific, written instructions from the client.

Error 2 is unauthorized signatures. Meeting and convention groups have many bosses. In addition to the elected board of directors, the officers, and the paid professional staff, there are informal leaders and past officers. Not all of these persons are authorized to sign for charges. Meeting planners complain that unauthorized charges with unauthorized signatures appear on master accounts despite an advanced list of authorized signatures having been provided.

Error 3 is the sequence of posting. The breakfast charge of day 2 of the meeting should not appear on the folio before the dinner of day 1. Picky clients require the entire bill to be reposted to show each event in sequence. Comparisons to the original contract and to the function sheets are facilitated thereby. That pleases the meeting planner, but the hotel could have done it beforehand.

Error 4 is comp rooms. Complimentary rooms are given to the group according to a widely used formula: 1 free room night per 50 paid room nights. Meeting planners complain that hotels deduct the lowest room rates against the free markers instead of the highest room rates. Comp rooms go either to VIPs or to staff members working the convention. Therefore, when making the adjustment, the best rates should be comped, says the client. Specifically, if the group has a secretary in one room and a keynote speaker in another, the hotel should match the one comp room allowed against the speaker's higher room rate, not the staffer's lower room rate.

Although it is best to resolve billing differences while they are still fresh, it may not be possible to do so before the group departs. Agreed-upon items should be resolved and billed promptly without waiting to reach accord on the few differences. Otherwise, a small sum keeps thousands of master account dollars unpaid.

**Groups and Packages** Master accounts are used whenever one account receivable is responsible for the charges of an entire group. Such is the case with single entities such as travelling athletic teams and prepaid tour packages. Names and room numbers of group members are available at the desk. Further identification of the membership is shown on the room rack: with colour on older manual racks; with code on newer computer racks.

The hotel may be told to post every member's charge to the master account. That's rare. Split folios are the more likely design. Major items such as VIP rooms and group meals are posted to the A folio, the master account, for which the entity pays. Personal incidentals are charged to B folios and paid as the individual guests check out. They may be reminded of that arrangement when they arrive. Sometimes the alert comes while they're on the bus, sometimes by computer-generated notices included with the room keys (see Exhibit 12-4).

**Exhibit 12-4** ▶
Key envelopes readied for distribution to an arriving group. Discount coupons, convention/ group information, and reminders about settling personal expenses (B folio charges) may be included along with the key.

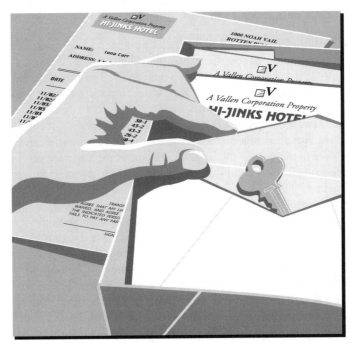

Who pays for what is more clearly understood with tour packages. The package has been marketed and sold with certain services included or not. Services that are not included are posted to the guest's individual folio. Coupons are issued to the guests for those services included in the package. The coupons are colour-coded and dated to limit their use to the particular package. Guests pay for breakfast, drinks, tennis—whatever is part of the prepaid package—with the appropriate coupon. Cashiers in the various hotel departments treat the coupons as part of their turn-in (see Chapter 11).

Coupons are charged to the tour operator's master account, so breakage accrues to the tour operator. That is, the tour operator collects from the guest for the entire tour but pays the hotel only for actual tickets returned to the master account. By not using the services they have purchased, guests create additional profit for the promoter. The hotel also creates additional profits for the promoter if it handles the vouchers carelessly. Vouchers are not just coloured slips of paper that can be lost or thrown away; they are debts the promoter must pay if the hotel can account for them.

In the hotel's own inclusive tour (IT) package, breakages accrue to the hotel. The package is sold to the guest and the money is collected in advance (minus commissions if it goes through a travel agency). If the guest fails to use the coupon, the hotel has gained. Accounting-wise, the hotel distributes the single payment received from the guest among the departments, allocating a portion to room sales, food sales, tennis sales, bar sales, and so on.

**Individual City Ledger Receivables** Hotels have accounts receivable that originate with individuals as well as with groups. The former are not as large in dollar volume as the latter, but in some ways they are more difficult to manage.

**Travel Agencies** Hotels and travel agencies have a strong love–hate relationship. That antipathy springs from the industry's view that travel agents, as third parties in the reservation process, are paid for supplying hotels with the hotels' own customers. Travel agents complain about not getting paid, which lodging's spokespersons deny vehemently. If hotel payments are sporadic, at least they're there.

**The Original City Ledger Accounts** Local individuals and companies were the original non-registered accounts receivable. Hence came the term *city* ledger. Individual accounts still exist, but they have been replaced in the main by the widespread use of credit cards. Hotels hunger for individual city accounts with good credit—payment is made in full without credit card fees.

What accounts there are may not be local and may not originate at the front desk. Standard city accounts include individuals and companies that pre-establish credit in order to use the hotel's facilities. A distant company may send employees to the hotel on a regular basis. A local business might use guest rooms for visitors and public rooms for business meetings and social affairs. Once credit has been established, the authorized user merely signs for the charges. Bills go out monthly, sometimes more frequently.

Airline crews are a good example of the standard city ledger account. They are much sought after by hotels as basic occupancy even though the average daily rate is very low. Layover crews charge rooms to the airline's city account, and once a month the hotel bills. Airline contracts sometimes require the hotel to accommodate stranded travellers as well as crews. Typically, the airline pays for the facilities by giving the passenger a **miscellaneous charge order (MCO)**. The stranded passenger pays with the MCO, which the hotel uses to balance the front-office folio. The account receivable is transferred to the city ledger and the airline is billed. MCOs are also used when the airline acts as a travel agency and books the guest into a prepaid room. The MCO becomes a travel agency voucher, as explained later.

**Banquet Charges** Credit cards have also replaced open-book credit (based solely on a signature) that was once the norm for banquet charges. Party givers and banquet chairpersons once expected to sign for the party, leaving the hotel waiting for collection. Catering managers still give open-book credit in limited cases. When open credit has not been cleared beforehand, collection is arranged in advance with a credit card or cheque. When open credit has been cleared beforehand, a bill is presented and signed at the close of the event. The value of the function is charged to a one-use city ledger account and billed within three days, which follows the billing pattern for speedy check-outs and master accounts.

Pay-as-you-go functions are much riskier affairs. The group may be known, but there is no financial security behind it. Included in this category are school proms, political dinners, charitable fundraisers, and other speculative functions that base payment on ticket sales. A portion of the estimated bill should be collected in advance, and a ticket accounting system should be part of the upfront agreement. The credit department should review the contract and establish the identity and creditworthiness of the responsible individual.

**Late Charges** Late charges are departmental charges (food, beverage, spa) that appear on the folio after the guest has checked out. These postings were late getting into the system either from the point-of-sale terminal or from the front-desk terminal.

Late charges are irritants to both the guest and the hotel. Guests may need to modify expense accounts after the late charge arrives in the mail. Hotels may need to absorb the costs because guests often refuse to pay after the fact. If the charge is small, the hotel might not even bill. The cost of processing and the loss of guest goodwill might be more than the amount sought.

Collections are easier when the folio of the departed guest has been transferred to the city ledger with a credit card. Then the front-office folio is retrieved, updated with the late charge, and transferred to the city ledger along with the earlier folio charges. The process is not even noticeable with express check-outs. Accurate folios arrive when the guest is copied by mail some three days later and the total shown agrees with the amount submitted to the credit card company.

The discrepancy is sharper if the guest settled at the cashier's window with a signed credit card voucher. Then the copy that the guest carries away will be smaller than the amount that the credit card company bills. If the card company does not permit after-the-fact additions to a signed charge slip, the hotel bills the guest directly using the registration card's address. The hotel has a second chance at collection, but that doesn't minimize the guest's anger. Direct billing of late charges is the only option for guests who settle with cash, cheques, or traveller's checks. There is no option at all if there is a corrected or dishonoured charge from a non-registered guest who used the bar or dining room. Non-registered means that the guest's address is not known to the hotel. Credit card companies will not release the cardholder's address nor allow altered charge slips.

LATE CHARGE PROCEDURES Late charges are abbreviated by **LC** (**late charge**) or **AD** (**after departure**). Small late charges—say, $15 and under—are wiped off with an allowance. First, the departed guest's folio is reopened and the charge—now, a late charge—is posted in the regular manner. Immediately, the new balance is zeroed out by means of an allowance (see Chapter 10). This procedure creates a permanent record of the charge.

A separate late charge folio is an alternative approach. All small late charges are posted there rather than individually to each folio. Daily, the total late charges are cleared with one allowance, which is obviously less burdensome for the desk. Either way, management should get a daily allowance report, which is one of the exception reports prepared during the night audit (see Chapter 13).

Notwithstanding these provisions for using allowances on late charges, efforts to collect late charges should be conscientiously pursued. In that case, the late charge could be posted to the guest's closed folio and immediately transferred to the city ledger for billing.

> Increases in assets, including *accounts receivable* and cash, are made with debits.
> Increases in incomes (food, beverage, spa, etc.) are made with credits.
>
> Debit: Accounts Receivable/Guest's Folio
>     Credit: Proper Departmental (food, beverage, spa, etc.) Sale
> *Explanation:* Late-charge income posted to reopened folio.
>
> Decreases in incomes (food, beverage, spa, etc.) are made with debits.
> Decreases in assets, including *accounts receivable* and cash, are made with credits.
>
> Debit: Proper Departmental (food, beverage, spa, etc.) Allowance
>     Credit: Accounts Receivable/Guest's Folio
> *Explanation:* Allowance issued for late charge to zero out the folio balance.

**Delinquent Accounts**   Into the delinquent (or bad debt) division of the city ledger go all receivables that are awaiting final disposition. Such is the case with large, uncollectible late charges that were not treated as allowances. They, and other unrecoverable debts, are eventually written off the books as bad debts.

Returned cheques (bounced cheques) also account for a portion of delinquent receivables. Rather than re-establishing the customer's old records, returned cheques are viewed as new debt and tracked separately. Cheques come back for many reasons. Chief among them are insufficient funds, no such account, account closed, illegible signature, and incorrect date. Since passing bad cheques is a criminal offence in some jurisdictions, hotels should support the police in prosecuting offenders even when restitution is made.

Credit card chargebacks, guests who skip (intentionally leave without paying), and judgmental mistakes in extending open credit comprise the remainder of the delinquent division. For most hotels, credit card chargebacks, skips, and open credit errors represent a negligible operating cost. Hotels that show significant costs in these areas should re-evaluate their credit policies.

**Executive Accounts**   Hotel executives can be city ledger receivables in their own hotel. Management people use the hotel for personal pleasure as well as for house business. Company policy dictates how charges are to be made. House entertainment might be distinguished from personal charges on the **guest cheque** by an "H" (house business) or an "E" (entertainment) added under the signature. Without the "H" symbol, the accounting department bills the person as a regular city account. Many times, though, the billing is only a percentage of the actual menu price, depending on the employment agreement.

**Due Bills**   Hotels have traded room nights for products since the great depression of the 1930s. Swaps with radio and television stations, billboards, newspapers, and magazines involve free rooms for free advertising. Trades with manufacturers for capital goods such as beds, carpets, and televisions are a later development. Evidence of the hotel's obligation to meet its half of the bargain is shown on a contract called a **due bill**. Due bills are also called **trade advertising contracts**, *trade-outs, contra accounts,* or *reciprocal trade agreements*. Temporary accounts receivable are needed in the city ledger when the other party in the swap checks in to take advantage of the "free" facilities.

RATIONALE FOR DUE BILLS   Airlines, theatres, arenas, and the media deal in highly perishable products. So do hotels. There is no means of recapturing an unsold airline seat or an unused television spot for resale on another day. The same is true with the lodging industry. All of these businesses have the same problem: There is no way to inventory the product for resale at a later time. Once the newspaper is printed, that day's advertising space is lost. Once the night has passed, that night's empty hotel room cannot be sold again. Trading the lost inventory for something useful is mutually beneficial when both parties have unsold, perishable products.

The hotel would like to restrict the products it trades to its most profitable item (rooms) and have the occupant pay in cash for the less profitable items (food and beverage). This is understandable from the hotel's point of view. The cost of providing an otherwise empty room is minimal; the cost of food and beverage is high. Moreover, unused food and beverage, unlike unused rooms, can be sold the following day. The advertising media set restrictions, too, making no promise as to where the hotel's ad will appear in print or at what time it will be heard on the airwaves.

Due bills are favoured during periods of low or moderate occupancy and are less popular during busy periods. The oil embargo of the 1970s and the poor economy of the early 1980s brought a rebirth of due bill usage.

PROCESSING THE DUE BILL   Due bill users must present the actual due bill agreement at the time of registration. This permits the guest-service agent to assign the most expensive accommodations. (The hotel's cost of delivering an expensive room is almost the same as delivering an inexpensive one.) The clerk also verifies the expiration date of the agreement. Amounts unused after that date are lost to the due bill holder. When that happens—and it does frequently—the hotel gets the advertising (or whatever), but the media company never gets to use all of its due bill.

The due bill is attached to the registration card and the rate is marked "Due Bill" along with the dollar room charge. A standard guest folio, or sometimes one specially coloured or coded, is used. The actual due bill is filed at the front desk during the guest's stay. After the value of the accommodations used has been recorded on the due bill, it is returned to the holder at check-out.

The transient folio, which was used to accumulate charges during the due bill user's stay, is transferred to the city ledger in the usual manner. However, the city ledger account is treated differently. There is no billing. Instead, the account is charged off against the liability incurred by the contract. At the time of the agreement, a liability was created by the hotel's promise to furnish accommodations to the media or other trader. As hotel accommodations are furnished, that liability is decreased. It is balanced off against the city ledger account that was created from the transfer of the guest folio at the time of check-out.

> Increases in assets, including *prepaid advertising* and cash, are made with debits. Increases in liabilities, including *due bills* and taxes *payable,* are made with credits.
>
> >   Debit: Prepaid Advertising
> >       Credit: Due Bills Payable
> >   *Explanation:* Negotiated a swap of rooms for advertising.
>
> Increases in assets, including accounts receivable and cash, are made with debits. Increases in incomes (*rooms,* food, beverage, spa) are made with credits.
>
> >   Debit: Accounts Receivable/Guest's Folio
> >       Credit: Room Sales
> >   *Explanation:* Due-bill guest occupies accommodations.
>
> Decreases in liabilities, including *due bills payable,* are made with debits. Decreases in assets including *accounts receivable* and cash are made with credits.
>
> >   Debit: Due Bills Payable
> >       Credit: Accounts Receivable/Guest's Folio
> >   *Explanation:* Due-bill guest pays transient folio with a trade-out via the City Ledger.

# Managing Credit

Organizing and processing credit charges through the city ledger, the first segment of this chapter, is but one component of credit. Management must attend to a long list of other functions, including bad debt management, cheque processing, internal procedures, and collections. But first of all, management must create its credit policies.

## Cost–Benefit Decision

There is no perfect credit policy. Any business that extends credit is vulnerable to loss. Each credit decision weighs immediate, determinable benefits against possible, uncertain costs. Recognizing that, the hotel industry has reduced its level of open credit. More reliance is now placed on credit cards and credit investigations. Open credit still has traditional uses—for advances to concessionaires, outlays for tips, payments for cash-on-delivery (COD) packages, and even some convention/banquet sales.

The issue is not black and white—always credit/never credit. Every full-service hotel offers some amount of credit. The question focuses on how much, when, and under what circumstances credit is offered. The answer is not always the same, even for the same credit manager in the same hotel. With different conditions, credit could be severely curtailed, moderately administered, or liberally issued, even to the same customer with the same credit standing (see Exhibit 12-5).

High occupancy, the first item in Exhibit 12-5, permits the hotel to adopt a conservative credit policy. There is no reason to replace low-risk guests with those of uncertain credit standing. When occupancy is high, a bad debt loss is the sum of full rack rate plus administrative costs, not just the marginal cost of providing a room during low occupancy.

Food and beverage sales, which have a high variable cost, are different. Far more caution is needed to justify banquet sales during a low period than room sales during

**Exhibit 12-5** ▶

Factors other than the creditworthiness of the guest explain why credit is tightened and eased over time even for the same guest at the same hotel. Likewise credit may be denied at one property and welcomed at another a short distance away.

| Severely Curtailed | Moderately Administered | Liberally Issued |
|---|---|---|
| High occupancy | – | Low occupancy |
| In-season | – | Off-season |
| No competition | – | Price cutting |
| Established property | – | New hotel |
| Interest rates are high | – | Interest rates are low |
| Reputable hotel | – | Disreputable hotel |
| Item of high variable cost | – | Item of low variable cost |
| Inexperienced lender | – | Low losses from debt recovery |
| Hotel's credit overextended | – | Hotel has good credit rating |

a low period. A banquet bad debt may well cost the hotel two-thirds or more of the bill (food, call-in labour, flowers, special cake, favours, etc.). Room losses are substantially less, both in percentage (about 25 percent marginal cost) and in absolute dollars.

Hotels reduce rates when occupancies are low. This would also be the time for a more liberal credit policy. In fact, the more liberal credit policy might be traded for the lower room rates. Too dismal a circumstance and the hotel will need to give both to get the business. Fighting for market share or competing with better-appointed properties are additional reasons for liberalizing credit (see Exhibit 12-5).

## The Management Function

Establishing and monitoring credit is a broad-based management function coordinated by the credit manager. If there is no credit manager, the controller takes on the task. Some responsibilities are handed off to other managers, who then form a credit committee. The rooms manager assumes an active role in front-office credit, and the sales/catering executives do the same for banquets and group business.

**Extending Credit** Collecting from overdue accounts begins with identifying them. This can be done at the time of registration or earlier. Very few reservations come directly to the hotel as they once did. Pre-screening to verify credit is just not possible, and it's certainly not doable with walk-in guests. Thus, after-the-fact collections depend on procedures in place during registration.

Identification was more reliable when guests had reservations that involved correspondence. Then, the name and address, and perhaps even the company name, was verified by mail. This must now be done at registration with complete name, not just initials; complete address, not just post office box, office building, or city. Scribbled, illegible signatures must be translated. Early suspicions can be confirmed quickly. Postal code directories uncover false addresses. Some hotels have the bell staff record car licence numbers on rooming slips. Telephone calls to the guest's supposed office puts many issues in perspective.

Unheard of a generation ago, guests are expected to announce their method of settlement as they register. Strange as it seems, hotels prefer credit cards with their costly merchant fees over cash or cheques. This shifts some credit issues to the credit card companies and provides the hotel with help from the fraud divisions of the credit card companies.

Credit procedures put stress on the clerk–guest interchange. Specific information must be elicited but done under the customer relations umbrella. Tact in selecting the right words and care in applying voice intonations—often ignored in training programs—must be taught and practised. Many factors, such as a tired guest or a misplaced reservation, exacerbate an already awkward situation. If baggage is missing or light, the clerk will need to press for more complete details. If the guest is nervous or poorly dressed, the clerk may insist on photocopying a driver's licence. The line between information gathering and invasion is a thin one, as is the line between guest understanding and anger. Front-office clerks need to be masters of diplomacy.

Because walk-ins pose additional credit risks, they are flagged with special identifications. **NR (no reservation)**, **OS (off-the-street)**, and **WI (walk-in)** are common abbreviations. The registration cards of walk-ins are not always filed immediately. Some properties have their credit managers inspect them. Credit managers use telephone directories, credit card companies, city directories, colleagues, and direct-dial telephone calls to verify information about questionable guests, be they walk-ins or otherwise.

Suspicious guests can be required to pay in advance—credit card or not. Paid-in-advance guests are usually denied credit throughout the house. Extreme measures like these do not build guest loyalty. Few walk-ins intend to defraud the hotel. The extra caution needed to protect against some should not disintegrate into anti-service for all.

## Managing the Specifics

Credit is an issue for every operating department, but the heaviest burden falls on the front desk. As with all that happens at the front desk, the guest and the staff stand face to face, increasing the tension and hardening the positions. Credit issues must be resolved firmly and yet with courtesy, even though the pressure of time often demands instantaneous decisions. Poorly conceived and poorly implemented credit policies undermine even the best guest-service programs.

Early departure fees were one horrible example that gained momentum during the heady occupancy that closed the 1990s. Guests who left earlier than their original reservation were charged an early departure fee of as much as $50. Try standing across the desk and explaining that fee to an early departure with hundreds of dollars in folio charges. As one would expect, the practice did not survive the steep downturn in occupancy that followed.

**Minimizing Chargebacks**   Hotels work very hard to find and to service customers. Large costs are incurred in marketing and employee training. In light of those efforts and costs, the hotel's failure to collect the bill is beyond understanding. However, that is just what happens with an estimated 50 percent of all chargebacks. Chargebacks are credit card charges disallowed by the card company because (1) the guest refuses to pay, or (2) a procedural error makes the charge unacceptable to the card company.

Most credit card companies allow hotels 30 days to respond to and submit evidence about chargebacks. Hotel credit offices simply fail to answer. Reservation no-shows are the most common chargebacks. Guests guarantee the reservation using a credit card and then refuse to pay the first night when they don't show. With the credit card number and no record of a cancellation number, the hotel has a strong argument, especially if the card company advertises its guarantee of this type of reservation. However, there can be no collection if the credit office fails to complete the inquiry. Of course, not pushing for payment may be more about guest relations than about credit. If that's the case, early check-out fees have no footing at all.

Mistakes in procedure account for another group of chargebacks. Procedural chargebacks originate more with departmental cashiers than with accounting offices. Training programs, often undertaken with help from card companies, concentrate on the do's and don'ts of taking and processing cards.

1. Be aware that every business is assigned a **floor limit,** which is the maximum dollar volume allowed on a single credit card without additional authorization.

2. Insist that employees know that limit, because, once exceeded, all charges, including those below the floor, are voided.

3. Do not split charges on two or more vouchers to avoid the floor limits.

4. Never give a cash refund if an unused advance deposit was made through a credit card charge (or travel agency voucher, for that matter).

5. Bill credit card companies promptly.

6. Refuse to post fictitious items in order to give cash against the credit card.

7. Watch for altered cards, rearranged numbers, or replaced digits that will make a hot card usable. Clues are glue on the card, blurred holograms, colour variations, or misaligned numbers. Compare numbers on the back and front sides. Watch for altered signature panels, which are made tamper-evident by repetitive designs on the panels.

8. Adhere to the recommendations of the credit card companies: Do not place telephone numbers on credit card slips.

9. Question credit card signatures made with a felt-tip pen that could be used to cover an original signature.

10. Compare the signature on the departmental voucher with the signature on the credit card. If still uncertain, compare with the registration card signature.

11. Make certain that the card imprints completely on all copies of the voucher; check the clarity of the signature.

12. Use the proper voucher form if a manual system is still in place. Each company has its own voucher and may not accept its competitors'.

13. Anticipate employee misuse—changed figures or additional charges that permit the employee to pocket some cash.

14. Answer promptly chargeback inquiries from the credit card companies.

15. Instruct employees not to apprehend anyone suspected of using an invalid card, nor to exercise any force in retrieving a card. Since the card remains the property of the credit card company, cardholders agree to surrender it on request. Agents of the hotel should not destroy the card nor publicly humiliate the guests.

16. Carry insurance against false arrest based on incorrect information furnished by the credit card company.

17. Refuse credit cards whose expiration date has passed the last day of the month specified. Watch on some cards for "from" dates; charges before that time will be rejected.

18. Compare the credit card and driver's licence signatures when suspicious of the individual or the card.

19. Teach cashiers that MasterCard uses numbers that begin with 5, Visa numbers begin with 4, and AmEx numbers begin with 3.

20. Maximize recovery by retaining original documents such as signed outlet or room service vouchers.

**Monitoring Credit** For most guests, credit is checked only twice: first on arrival and then on departure. A small number of guests are tracked more closely to make certain that the credit policies of the card company and of the hotel are being followed. Two restrictions are placed on hotel credit card use. Every hotel has a credit limit or floor limit for the premises. The floor limit is the maximum credit the hotel can extend to any one guest without getting prior approval from the credit card company. Obviously, the initial floor limit should be as high as the hotel can negotiate. Just as obvious, that limit is a function of the hotel's average daily rate. If the card is approved at registration, the credit card company guarantees payment up to that floor—actually, a ceiling. In case of default, credit card charges above that ceiling void the entire guarantee, even the amount below the ceiling if prior approval wasn't obtained.

Losses can be substantial if floor limits are breached without prior clearance. However, it is a problem with only a small number of guests, and only if those guests fail to pay. Only then does the hotel turn to the credit card company for reimbursement. The danger is minimized if folio balances are constantly monitored. The job is usually assigned to the swing or graveyard shifts to make certain that an examination takes place at least once daily. In a manual system, the clerk flips through the bucket, scrutinizing each folio by noting the daily charges and the cumulative balance of each account receivable. With a computer, an over limit report, which is an exception report (see Chapter 13), can be screened quickly several times during the day. Whether done manually or electronically, the monitor must project the rate of spending as the folio nears the floor thresholds.

Questionable folios, and even some picked at random, are examined in detail. Is there a credit card for the room? Are the numbers legible? Is the expiration date still valid? Is the balance below the floor? Is an approval number on file? The total charges are examined, but especially the pattern of charges. In a report, the night clerk lists suspicious accounts, which the credit manager examines first thing in the morning.

**Credit Alerts and Skippers** Intentional skippers can be identified by the pattern of things they do. Indeed, the credit manager should develop a standard description much like airlines have done for the typical hijacker. The average skipper is male, 30 to 35 years old, a late walk-in with **light baggage** and vague identification. He is a heavy tipper and a quick new friend of the bartender. The skipper makes no telephone calls that can be used to trace him. His address is usually a well-known one in a large city, but it proves to be false. He writes his name and address poorly and offers no business identification.

Skipper alerts begin with light or worthless luggage. Guests become doubly suspect when they charge their folios with small items, which one normally pays for with cash. Skippers compound the hotel's costs by passing bad cheques or using stolen credit cards. Bad-cheque passers concentrate on weekends or holidays when commercial hotels are understaffed and banks are closed. With ATM machines readily available, fewer and fewer hotels are cashing cheques. Those that do should maintain a cheque-cashing record to alert other shifts of ongoing activities. Then a cheque-cashing report becomes part of the night audit activities.

Skippers and bad-cheque passers frequently work one area before moving on. A telephone or fax network among local hotels does much to identify the culprit even before his or her arrival. Photographs of suspects and identifying information, perhaps from the police, will undoubtedly be displayed someday on computer terminals.

**Exhibit 12-6** ▶
The likelihood of collecting from accounts receivable decreases over time. To minimize bad debts, accounting offices must bill promptly and aggressively pursue unpaid accounts.

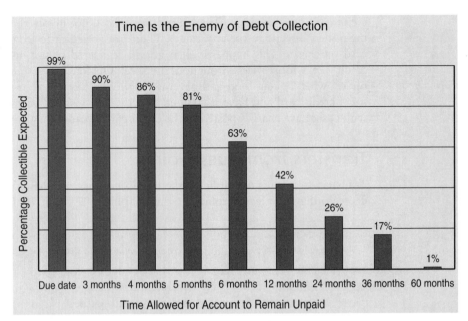

Something needs to be done because crime has moved from the street into the hotel. Frustrating the criminal takes the combined efforts of all employees. Clerks, bellpersons, house police, cashiers, housekeepers, engineers, and room service waiters, too, must watch for and report the telltale signs. Large quantities of blank cheques or money orders, firearms and burglary tools, keys from other hotels, unusual amounts of cash or gems, or just heavy traffic or loitering about a room indicate that serious trouble is brewing.

**Collecting Receivables** Accounts receivable are what the city ledger is all about. Some receivables enter the city ledger directly—credit card charges in the food and beverage outlets, for example. Most receivables come to the back office from the front office as transfers from the guest ledger to the city ledger. Here is accumulated every category of debt: master accounts, travel agency coupons, wholesaler settlements, skippers, credit cards, direct billings, convention and association activities, due bills, delinquent accounts, executive accounts, and banquet charges. How these debts are collected and by whom reflects on the hotel's cash flow and its profit picture. Having gone to the trouble of marketing, servicing, and charging the account, the hotel can be no less diligent in collecting what's due (see Exhibit 12-6).

# Mechanics of the Entry

Some guests, but very few, settle their front-office folios with cash. They are not accounts receivable. Some guests, a somewhat larger number, settle their food and beverage purchases with cash. Neither are they accounts receivable. With those two exceptions, all hotel customers are accounts receivable. Hotels bill and collect these receivables through the city ledger.

Two methods are used to get the information to the city ledger in the first place. Under one system, the one used for registered guests, charges are accumulated on the front-office folio and transferred to the city ledger. In Chapter 10, many pages are assigned to this procedure. The second source of city ledger transactions is purchases by credit card or open credit. The front-office folio is not involved; charges are made from the outlets directly to the city ledger. There are no ledger-to-ledger transfers with credit card purchases. This happens when guests, registered or not, use credit cards or open credit to pay for services throughout the hotel. Obviously, registered guests can use either option when buying food and beverage services. They can charge the folio or they can use a credit card and have it charged directly. Unregistered customers, who do not pay with cash, have charges posted to the credit card because they have no front-office folio.

## Transfers *from* Guest Folios

Transfers *from* the guest folio *to* the city ledger increase the city ledger receivable and decrease the guest ledger folio (see the final line of Exhibit 10-1).

> Increases in assets, including *accounts receivable* and cash, are made with debits.
> Decreases in assets, including *accounts receivable* and cash, are made with credits.
>
>     Debit: Accounts Receivable, City Ledger/Credit Card Company
>         Credit: Accounts Receivable, Guest Ledger (Folio)/Guest Name
>     *Explanation:* Folio settled with a credit card.
> OR
>     Debit: Accounts Receivable, City Ledger/Personal or Company Account
>         Credit: Accounts Receivable, Guest Ledger (Folio)/Guest Name
>     *Explanation:* Folio to be settled by direct billing.

Total debits to the city ledger must equal total credits from the guest ledger both daily and cumulatively. Once the transfer is made, billing takes place from the city ledger. When settlement is received (from an individual, company, organization, or credit card issuer), the debt (the city ledger account receivable) is cleared and the cheque (cash) is deposited. For some receivables, such as an association's master account or a bridal shower, the one-time city ledger account is closed. Other receivables, such as the credit card companies, are continuing records with new charges and new payments continually flowing in and out.

> Increases in assets, including accounts receivable and *cash*, are made with debits.
> Decreases in assets, including *accounts receivable* and cash, are made with credits.
>
>     Debit: Cash
>         Credit: Accounts Receivable, City Ledger/Personal or Credit-Card Co.
>     *Explanation:* Any city-ledger account receivable settled its account

The procedure just described applies to almost every city ledger account. Travel agency records and frequent-guest programs are two exceptions. With bank cards, the merchant/hotel gets an almost instantaneous deposit in its bank account, but that deposit is reduced by the amount of the merchant fees, as it is with T&E cards. Accounting for those fees is similar to accounting for travel agency commissions.

**Travel Agency Records** Accounting for the travel agency commission starts with the reservation. Commissionable reservations are flagged, and that identification is carried onto the registration card and the folio. Computer systems capture and track the travel agency guest more efficiently than manual systems. Whichever system is used, commissionable folios are segregated from non-commissionable folios and immediate attention is given to DNAs (did not arrive). A notice of non-arrival, frequently a post-card, is mailed to the travel agency. This forestalls a claim and the endless correspondence that follows.

**Frequent-Guest Programs** The rationale for frequent-guest programs (FGPs) has been discussed several times throughout the book. The mechanics of the programs are equally clear. Guests earn points toward free room nights and sometimes airline points as well. Each stay is validated electronically or, rarely now, manually. Points are earned in every type and class of hotel within the chain, but are usually cashed in at resort destinations. The resort accepts payment with a FGP coupon and looks to the parent company for reimbursement.

> Increases in assets, including *accounts receivable* and cash, are made with debits.
> Increases in incomes (sales of *room,* food, and beverage) are made with credits.
>
> Debit: Accounts Receivable/Folio/Guest Account      100
>     Credit: Rooms Sales                              100
> *Explanation:* Guest with FGP voucher charges accommodations on the A folio.
> Increases in assets, including *accounts receivable* and cash, are made with debits.
> Decreases in assets, including *accounts receivable* and cash, are made with credits.
>
> Debit: Accounts Receivable/City Ledger/FGP Account      100
>     Credit: Accounts Receivable/Folio/Guest Account          100
> *Explanation:* FGP guest checks out and room charge is transferred to city ledger.

Split folios are used to process the award coupons that frequent guests tender. Onto the B folio are posted all of the incidental charges. The guest is responsible for these and pays them at check-out. The A folio, which contains the room charge, is transferred at check-out to the FGP account, a receivable in the city ledger. The chain is billed either for the full rack rate or at a reduced rate agreed to in the FGP contract. Only rarely is the hotel reimbursed at the rack rate. Rooms have a high profit margin and the parent company knows that. Besides, sales from guest purchases of food and beverage are additional incomes since they are not covered by the voucher. A rooms allowance reduces the amount between the rack rate charged against the guest's award coupon and the rate reimbursed by the parent company. That allowance can be made when the bill is sent to the chain or when payment is received.

> Increases in assets, including accounts receivable and *cash*, are made with debits.
> Decreases in sales, including *allowances,* are made with debits.
> Decreases in assets, including *accounts receivable* and cash, are made with credits.
>
> Debit: Cash                                       40
> Debit: Room Allowances/Frequent Guest Program    60
>     Credit: Accounts Receivable/City Ledger/FGP Account with Chain  100
> *Explanation:* FGP account is settled at rate agreed to in FGP contract.

FGPs are marketing programs, so every hotel of the chain contributes on a per-room basis toward the costs. From the fund come payments for rooms used as well as the sales and administrative expenses. Reimbursement for bad cheques is one such expense. FGPs offer cheque-cashing privileges. Should the cheque bounce, the hotel transfers the unpaid amount to the chain's city ledger account and bills along with the reimbursable room charge.

Under some FGPs, the monthly amount due to the hotel from the chain is offset against the monthly amount due to the chain from the hotel: FGP fees and franchise fees. Others keep the several accounts separate, collecting from the FGP on the normal 30-day cycle of city ledger billing.

## Transfers *to* Guest Folios

Occasionally, though not often, guests with unpaid city ledger accounts return to the hotel. The balance owed is then transferred *from* the city ledger *to* the guest ledger at the front desk. Shifting accounts in that direction is the opposite of all other ledger-to-ledger transfers that have been discussed. When this guest checks out, the total debt (that incurred during the current stay and that transferred *to* from the previous stay) is due. Settlement may simply mean another transfer: that of the new total in the usual manner from the guest ledger back to the city ledger. The most frequent use of these *from* city ledger *to* guest ledger transfers are advance deposits, which are discussed in depth at the close of Chapter 10.

## City Ledger Postings without Transfers

Many guests, whether registered or not, use credit cards to pay for food and beverage services. These credit card charges become part of the departmental cashiers' daily turn-in (see Chapter 11). As such, they go directly to the accounting office, bypassing the front office and bypassing the ledger-to-ledger transfers that have been discussed. How the accounting office processes these credit card charges depends on the type of credit card system in place. Most hotels have replaced the manual slips with electronic capture.

**Manual Charge Slips** If the hotel still uses the manual credit card form, departmental cashiers process each on an imprinter, obtain the guest's signature, and include the signed slips as part of their turn-in. These signed slips are separated by type (MasterCard, Visa, etc.) in the accounting office. Then they are batched and bundled, usually in groups of 100 vouchers. As a total, the bundle is posted to the credit card company's account receivable and forwarded with a **transmittal form**. The accounting entry charges the credit card company and records the income from the departmental outlet:

Increases in assets, including *accounts receivable* and cash, are made with debits. Increases in incomes (sales of *food* and *beverage*) are made with credits.

Debit: Accounts Receivable/City Ledger/Credit Card Company   65
Credit: Food Sales, Beverage Sales, etc.                                          65
*Explanation:* Guest paid for services with a credit card.

**Exhibit 12-7** ▶
Pencil-and-paper forms for credit cards have been replaced almost entirely by electronic terminals (see Exhibit 12-3) that verify the card and record the transaction. Although the charge is transmitted electronically, both the hotel and the guest carry away a receipt that looks like an old-fashioned adding machine tape.

▤**V**

*A Vallen Corporation Property*

HAVE A NICE DAY
TAX INVOICE
AMEX MERCHANT : 5 19-7
BATCH: 000023

ACCOUNT NUMBER
3   0 7 2  00                          AM
DATE-TIME                        EXP. DATE
08DEC   17:55                      09
TRANSACTION TYPE              APPROVAL CODE
SALE                                      3
REFERENCE/INVOICE NO.           TERMINAL
000111                             1 3 994

HOTEL/REST

TOTAL $488.84
TAX INCL
CUSTOMER SIGN BELOW

X  *Jack L Morrow*
CARDHOLDER NAME

MORROW JL

I ACKNOWLEDGE RECEIPT FOR GOODS AND SERVICES AND LIABILITY FOR CHARGES AS RECORDED HEREON AND WILL OBSERVE MY AGREEMENT WITH THE CARD ISSUERS

**Electronic Draft Capture** The communications highway has brought significant changes to the handling of credit card charges. Guests encounter manual charge slips less and less. Instead, the electronic verification of the card's authenticity (swiping the card through the reader) is followed by an electronic printout of the charges. A slip of paper (see Exhibit 12-7) that looks much like the tape of an old-fashioned adding machine is presented for signature. One copy goes to the guest; the second copy remains with the hotel or merchant as part of the cashier's departmental turn-in.

What happens during the processing is less visible, but more important, than what happens with the copies of the charge slips. The charge is captured electronically (EDT, electronic draft capture) by the credit card company. Simultaneously, the status of the card is validated, approval to proceed is granted, and the card's ceiling is cleared. EDT eliminates paper sales drafts and the sorting, postage, and manual posting that batch handling involves. Communicating with the financial institution through an electronic process means quicker access to the funds. Funds could be transferred immediately by EFT or delayed until the records are transmitted overnight to the clearing centre. Either way, funds are accessed more rapidly than through the manual system. Moreover, credit card companies reduce the merchant discount fees when EDT is used.

Speedy electronic data, much of it by laser imaging, represents additional float for the credit card company. The earlier that the charge appears on the customer's monthly statement, the sooner the credit card company is paid. All credit cards have electronic capture by one of several means.

In the early stages, manual-dial telephones and then touch-tone terminals were used to get card authorization. EFT with point-of-sale online processing is the other end of the technology. Swiping the card through the terminal obtains the authorization at registration and interfaces the hotel's computer (PMS) with the credit card computer. Electronic billing and ultimate collection from the card issuer then follows. In between the dial and the online interface options are a series of electronic choices depending on what costs the hotel can absorb or counterbalance through savings. Whether purchased or leased, equipment and software costs must be absorbed, perhaps negotiated as part of the discount fee. Maintenance and repairs must be provided, but by whom and for how much is also at issue. In general, the more automatic the procedure, the higher the costs but the greater the savings in discount fees.

## Summary

Today's travellers prefer credit to cash. In fact, they see credit as their right, not as a privilege granted by the seller. Hotel keepers accommodate this business fact of life but with a keen eye toward credit management. Assigning some credit responsibilities to third parties (the credit card companies, chiefly) reduces some of the hotel industry's credit woes. Credit card companies have the same objectives (increasing sales, decreasing credit losses) as the lodging industry, and despite some operational irritations, work closely with it.

Hotels track and bill their credit guests (accounts receivable) through the city ledger. *City ledger* is an easy way of referring to a group of records that contains information about unregistered persons who owe the hotel for services. Hotels provide rooms, food, beverages, and other services to a variety of city ledger identities. Among them are banquet and convention groups, travel agents, companies, individuals (including the hotel's own executives), and frequent-guest participants. Most city ledger records start out as front-office folios, which become city ledger accounts when the guests check out and transfer the amounts owed to a credit card. Other city accounts come directly into the city ledger from credit card charges in the hotel's various outlets.

Modern electronic communication has replaced much of the paper record keeping that once plagued the front desk. The development of this capability has been undertaken by a variety of third-party intermediaries. Lodging now has numerous credit partners, including national credit card companies and banking institutions. They issue two classes of credit card. Travel and entertainment cards (T&Es) are used heavily by businesses and individuals with better credit ratings. Bank cards are in more widespread use. The two types continue to borrow ideas from one another, so their differences are blurring. They will blur even more if a series of court cases helps the T&Es locate within the banking system.

Credit and credit cards have become essential to and inseparable from the lodging industry's management of credit through the city ledger.

## Questions and Problems

1. Write two dialogues for a training manual that is to be used by guest-service agents at the front desk. Include the questions posed by a room clerk seeking additional credit information and the responses made by a guest. What disposition does the room clerk make when (a)

a walk-in guest arrives with no baggage? (b) a same-day reservation arrives, but no information has been provided previously?

2. Explain how the following transfers should be handled. Be specific, citing the location of the entry, the ledger or ledgers involved, and the debit or credit requirements.

    (a) A transient guest checks out using a national credit card.

    (b) The president and treasurer of a small company check in for a business meeting. The hotel has been carrying the unpaid balance of a charge generated by these officers at their last business meeting about three months ago.

    (c) A couple departs and requests that the balance of the folio be charged to the couple's parents, who are registered in another room. The parents concur.

    (d) An association completes its meeting and the association executive, after reviewing the balance due, requests billing to the group's headquarters.

3. In terms of the front office and of the city ledger, explain the quick check-out system used by numerous hotels.

4. Many older hotels in the area in which your resort is located have suffered for years from a seasonal influx of skippers and room burglary gangs operating with stolen keys. (Few of these old properties have modern locks.) The local hotel association has asked you to draft a plan for a security network that could be implemented before the next season. Prepare the plan, providing details of the procedure by explaining the roles of the individuals or groups involved.

5. In terms of the front office and of the city ledger, explain how a reservation request from a travel agent is processed if (a) the agency has a good credit relationship with the hotel and the guest pays the agency; (b) the agency has no credit rating with the hotel and the guest pays the agency; and (c) the guest makes no payment to the agency.

6. A noticeable squeeze on profits had brought the management team to a brainstorming session. The controller puts one idea forth. Noting the large amount of credit card business that the hotel is doing, the controller suggests that each tip charged to a credit card be reduced by 4.77 percent when paid to the employee. (That amount is the average discount fee the hotel is paying to all credit card companies.) The controller further suggests that an additional 1.1 percent be subtracted, representing the percentage of credit card charges that prove uncollectible. What comments would the food and beverage manager be apt to make? The rooms manager?

## CASE STUDY

### The Receivables Problem

John Stephens is the new chief financial officer of an older 300-room hotel in Regina, Saskatchewan. After acclimatizing to his new position, he has sat down to take a serious look at the way in which the hotel manages its accounts receivables. At present, the hotel invoices its American Express and Diners Club cards once per month, and front-desk clerks are allowed to grant credit to guests and companies that they feel are trustworthy. This has resulted in the hotel's total receivables being much higher than normal for a hotel of its size. As well, the hotel's bad debts to total receivables ratio is quite high.

Stephens hopes to set up a receivables program that works for everyone concerned while protecting the hotel from extensive bad debts. Can you help him with some of the questions he may have?

1. Some experts suggest that no more than 2 percent of accounts receivables should become bad debts. Is it necessarily a

good thing to be under this percentage and is it always a bad thing to be over it? What if the hotel's bad debts were zero—is that a good thing?

2. Is it better to use an outside collection agency to collect bad debts or to handle it internally? Substantiate your answer.

3. Who should make the decision on whether credit is granted? Should it be done by front-desk clerks, since they are the ones dealing directly with guests? If not, what position or positions should be responsible for making this decision? Substantiate your answers.

## Note

1. Trademark names are used throughout the chapter.

## Weblinks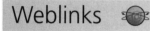

MasterCard in Canada
**www.mastercard.com/canada/**

Visa Canada
**www.visa.ca/en**

Citibank Canada
**www.citibank.com/canada**

American Express Canada
**www.americanexpress.com/canada**

# Part V

# Technology

**CHAPTER 13 ▸ The Night Audit**

**CHAPTER 14 ▸ Property Management System Interfaces**

North America's ever-increasing rate of productivity is due in large measure to the shift from labour-intensive work to electronic equipment. Lodging is a significant participant, although certainly not at the forefront of the movement. New devices are being tested and older ones refined as the industry strives to better serve its clientele and manage its operating costs. Automated elevators, direct-dial telephones, and electronic keys were the forerunners of what will certainly come to be an all-electronic hotel.

Property management systems (PMSs) were among the early efforts. As hotels grew larger, new approaches were needed to offset the increases in billing errors caused by paper-and-pencil folios. The first hotel PMSs borrowed applications from other industries. They failed to meet the lodging industry's unique needs. Vision didn't become reality until suppliers recognized the size of the potential market. Only then did manufacturers invest the research dollars needed to develop hotel-specific software. Although the lodging industry invested very little in research, reliable, inexpensive, and easy-to-use systems gradually emerged. The paper jam disappeared, employee accuracy increased, and management reporting improved. Costs fell so dramatically that even the smallest property replaced the hand-prepared folio with the electronic one.

The first chapter of this final unit examines the PMS in terms of the night audit. Users cannot see into electronic equipment, so glimpses of the old pencil-and-paper audit are also included. These pencil-and-paper segments help explain both the purpose and the procedure of the night audit, as they did in Chapter 10 with folio billing. Night audits uncover and correct errors in guest billing and prepare reports for management's use the following day. Error detection and correction were the main thrust of the pencil-and-paper audits; management reporting is the driving force of the electronic audit.

Property management systems gather, store, and quickly retrieve information. Their ability to handle vast amounts of data has made possible the industry's important frequent-guest programs. Technology is ready now to move beyond the routine posting of room rates and taxes and data manipulation. The next generation of electronic solutions will focus beyond clerical labour savings. What about computerized vacuum cleaners?

Chapter 14 looks at some of the first results of this emerging technology. Among them are call accounting systems, in-room television, on-demand films, safety deposit accessibility, in-room vending, and telecommunications. Guests who once selected hotels on the basis of swimming pools and bath amenities are starting to choose on the basis of sophisticated television-based entertainment and in-room business centres. There soon will be other criteria that we cannot even foresee at this time. And the speed of change will be, indeed, as rapid as it is always forecasted to be. Just a few years ago, the centralized business centre was the ultimate for commercial hotels; today, the equipment is in the guest's own room and the centre is no more.

## Chapter 13

# The Night Audit

## Learning Objectives

After reading this chapter, you will be able to do the following:

1. **Understand the position of the night auditor and the function of the night audit.**

2. **Identify how the property management system (PMS) has become increasingly important in producing accurate transcripts and management reports while saving labour.**

The night audit ends the hotel's day. All records of accounts receivable (A/R) are collected, corrected, and summarized by the night audit crew—in a small hotel, this is no more than a single person. Closing the day's accounting records validates the work of the previous shifts and provides information for the issues of the upcoming day.

What night auditors do and how they do it have changed dramatically since the introduction of **electronic data processing (EDP)** to the front desk. EDP has altered the focus and changed the procedure. Prior to the introduction of computers, the audit concentrated on uncovering errors. There are fewer errors with the property management system (PMS), and finding them is easier, so management reporting has become the new emphasis.

## The Night Auditor

Despite the title, the night auditor is rarely a trained accountant and is an auditor only by the broadest definition. In general terms, an *auditor* is an appraiser-reporter of the accuracy and integrity of records and financial statements. One type of auditing, internal auditing, involves procedural control and an accounting review of operations and records. Internal auditing also reports on the activities of other employees. It is this final definition that best explains the role of the hotel night auditor.

No special knowledge of accounting or even of bookkeeping's debits and credits is required of the night auditor. Having this knowledge is helpful and desirable, but it is sufficient for the auditor to have good arithmetic skills, self-discipline, and a penchant for detailed work. Auditors must be careful, accurate, and reliable. The latter trait is an especially redeeming one because the unattractive working hours make replacements difficult to recruit and almost impossible to find on short notice.

## Work Shift

The audit crew works the graveyard shift, arriving sometime between 11 P.M. and midnight and finishing some eight hours later, at 7 or 8 A.M. Since the audit reconciles records needed to start the new day, night auditors remain on the job until the audit is complete, regardless of the hour.

## General Duties

The audit staff of a large hotel consists of a senior auditor and assistants. A separate night crew handles the usual duties of the desk, freeing the auditors to perform their functions without interruption. In a small hotel, a single auditor relieves the entire desk, filling the jobs of reservationist, room clerk, cashier, telephone operator, and auditor. Whether or not auditors assume these front-office tasks, they must be conversant with them. It is those very duties that the night audit audits.

When the actual tasks are taken on, the night auditor is likely to be the only responsible employee on duty. The auditor assumes the position of night manager whether the title is there or not. The same range of problems faced by the day manager is involved, but to a lesser degree. Emergencies, credit, mechanical breakdowns, accidents, and deaths are some of the situations encountered by the night manager.

Security and incident reports must be filed by the night auditor/manager either alone or co-operatively with the security staff. Without a security contingent, the auditor may be the one who walks security rounds and fire watch.

Few hotels of less than 150 rooms employ a night engineer. Yet management has generally been lax in preparing the night auditor/manager for the problems that arise in this area of responsibility. Fire, plumbing problems, power failures, elevator mishaps, and boiler troubles are matters that may take the auditor's time.

Equally time consuming are guest relations: a noisy party going into the early hours of the morning; the victorious football team shouting in the lobby; a sick guest; visiting conventioneers in the eleventh-floor suite; paid reservations yet to arrive and the hotel 100 percent occupied. Such are the non-accounting matters for which the night auditor might be responsible.

Mature judgment and experience are needed to carry out these non-audit functions. The combination of audit skills, working hours, and responsibility merit a higher salary for the night auditor than for the average guest-service agent, but the spread is not noticeably larger.

# The Audit

The night audit is an audit of accounts receivable, of folios. Cash sales in food, beverage, and other outlets of the hotel are not included in the night audit because they are not posted to folios. Instead, cash sales are audited by the income auditor, sometimes called the day auditor, in conjunction with the general cashier. Folio sales to accounts receivable pass through the night audit to the same income or day audit, which takes place the next morning. There, both types of sales (cash and credit) are combined. From that total comes the daily report to the manager and the ultimate entries in the hotel's sales journal.

## Reconciling Accounts Receivable

Every business authenticates its accounts receivable periodically. Whereas other retailers balance and close their accounts monthly, hotels do the job nightly. The night audit verifies the accuracy and completeness of each guest folio each night.

Hotel auditors lack the luxury of time because hotel keeping is a very transient business. Arrivals and departures keep coming and going without notice at all hours of the day and night. Each new day brings more charges and more credits whether or not the previous day has been reconciled. There is no holding a departing guest until the folio is ready. The night audit must make certain that it always is ready.

The pressure of immediacy is missing with city ledger guests. City ledger guests are not registered, so their billing cycle is more like the accounts receivable of other businesses. Depending on the nature of the original charge, city receivables are billed for the first time 3 days—sometimes 10 days—after the charge is incurred.

## The Closeout Hour

The night audit reviews the records of a single day. Since hotels never close, management selects an arbitrary hour, the **closeout hour** (also called the **close of the day**), to officially end one day and start the next. The actual time selected depends on the operating hours of the lounges, restaurants, and room service of the particular hotel. Each new charge changes the folio, so the audit is prepared when changes are infrequent—in the early morning hours when guests are in bed. Departmental charges before the closeout hour are included in today's records. Departmental charges after the closeout hour are posted to the folio on the following date after the night audit has been completed.

A late closeout hour captures the last of the day's charges, but it puts pressure on the auditing staff, which needs to finish the job before the early departures begin leaving. On the other hand, too early a closeout hour throws all charges of the late evening into the following day, in effect delaying their audit for 24 hours. Standardized stationery forms list midnight as the closeout hour, but the actual time is set by management.

## Posting Room Charges Manually

Posting (recording) room charges is one of the night auditor's major tasks. Before the advent of the PMS, room charges were posted manually. That required each folio to be removed one by one from the cashier's well (see Exhibit 10-3). The room charge and the room tax were recorded in pencil, the column totalled, and the folio returned to the well in room number sequence. Exhibit 13-1 illustrates the results on a manual folio: $60 recorded on the horizontal line labelled "rooms" and $3 for the tax. The $78 and $6.24 posted in Exhibit 10-2 offers a second illustration.

Once the room charge and tax are posted, the night auditor adds the column, which includes the previous day's total. (The second columns of Exhibits 13-1 and 10-2 illustrate the addition.) The new balance is carried forward from the bottom of the column to the top of the column of the following day. In this manner, a cumulative balance is maintained, and the manual folio is ready at any time for the departing guest.

**Exhibit 13-1** ▶
Pencil-and-paper folios (see also Exhibit 10-2) accumulate daily charges in separate columns. Figures in the appropriate day's column are copied onto a transcript sheet for balancing during that night's audit. Column 10/6 has been copied to line 1 of Exhibit 13-10. Note the credit balance of ($19) that opens October 6. (*For ease in reading, all illustrations use small dollar values, which may not seem realistic.*)

**THE CITY HOTEL**
**ANYWHERE, CANADA**                                    #8001

NAME __B. M. Oncampus__
ADDRESS __1 Campus Rd., University City__
ROOM NUMBER __1406__                          RATE __60__
NUMBER IN THE PARTY __1__                      CLERK __ABC__
DATE OF ARRIVAL __10/5__          DATE OF DEPARTURE __10/7__
CHANGES: ROOM NO. _____  TO ROOM NO. _____  NEW RATE _____

| | | | | | | | |
|---|---|---|---|---|---|---|---|
| DATE | 10/5 | 10/6 | 10/7 | | | | |
| BAL. FWD | | (19) | 70 | | | | |
| ROOMS | 60 | 60 | | | | | |
| TAX | 3 | 3 | | | | | |
| FOOD | 10 | 12 | | | | | |
| | | | | | | | |
| BAR | | 6 | | | | | |
| TELEPH | | | | | | | |
| | | | | | | | |
| LAUNDRY | | | | | | | |
| CASH DISBR GARAGE | 8 | 8 | | | | | |
| TRANSFERS | | | | | | | |
| | | | | | | | |
| TOT CHRG | 81 | 70 | | | | | |
| CASH | | | | | | | |
| ALLOWANCES | | | | | | | |
| TRANSFERS | 100 | | | | | | |
| TOT CRDS | 100 | | | | | | |
| BAL DUE | (19) | 70 | | | | | |

Included in the cumulative total are departmental charges other than for the room. These are posted throughout the day by the front-office staff as the charges arrive at the front desk from the operating departments. Exhibit 13-1 shows these as food, bar, and garage. Garage is a cash paid-out made by the hotel to the garage for the guest.

**Manual System Errors** With a manual system, the same values are written repeatedly. Guests' names, room numbers, and dollar values are recorded many times by different individuals on registration cards and folios, vouchers, and control sheets. The night auditor rewrites the figures once more: room rates, departmental charges, credits, and others. Writing, rewriting, and adding columns manually create numerous human errors that PMSs avoid. Point-of-sale (POS) terminals (see Exhibit 13-2) communicate electronically, bypassing the need for written vouchers between the department and the desk.

Additional errors are inherent in the manual system. Poor handwriting is the most obvious one. When handwritten, the numerals 1 and 7, 4 and 9, and 3 and 8 are often confused. Recopying also causes slides and transpositions. **Slides** are misplaced units, which may involve decimals. Saying 53 21 mentally or aloud may result in either 53.21 or 5321 being recorded. **Transpositions** are similar errors, but the digits are reordered—53.21 may become 35.21.

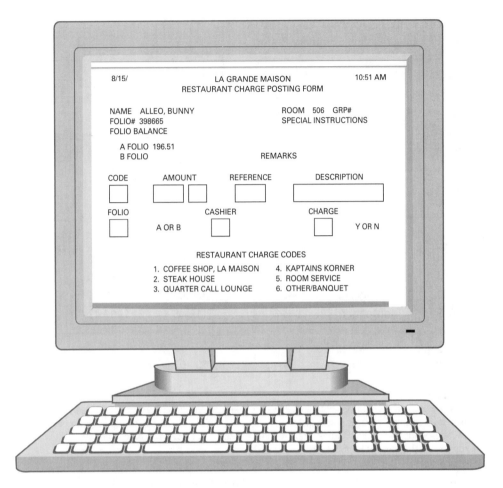

Even simple addition causes problems. The auditor may create errors by incorrectly totalling the folios, the control sheet, or the packets of vouchers. Adding machines help, but there is no guarantee that the figures are accurately entered. Hand audits still require adding-machine tapes to allow comparison between the actual figures and those entered into the calculator.

Subtracting one total from another highlights the error. Errors of addition usually appear as differences of 1 in the unit columns. If the difference in the totals is 1 cent, 10 cents, $1, $10, and so on, the culprit is likely to be an error of addition. If not an error of addition, it might be a slide or transposition. Slides and transpositions are flagged when the difference in the total is evenly divisible by 9. For example, the difference between 53.21 and 35.21 is 18, evenly divisible by 9. Searching for mistakes begins by looking for errors of addition or transpositions and slides.

## Posting Room Charges Electronically

Posting room charges electronically is easier and far faster than posting manually. There are no folios, and there is no bucket or well (see Exhibit 10-3). Time is saved in simply not removing and replacing 100 or 300 or 1000 folios from a cashier's bucket. Room rates are not posted individually, and hundreds of folios are not added up.

| Room # | Name | Folio # | Open Bal | Charges | Credits | Close Bal |
|--------|------|---------|----------|---------|---------|-----------|
| | **THE CITY HOTEL, ANYWHERE, CANADA** | | | | | **Page 1** |
| | 03/16    **Guest Ledger Summary Report** | | | | | |
| 3004 | Huent | 0457 | –0– | 81.30 | .00 | 81.30 |
| 3005 | Wanake | 0398 | 65.72 | 91.44 | .00 | 157.16 |
| 3008 | Lee | 0431 | 132.00 | 101.01 | .00 | 233.01 |
| 3110 | Langden | 0420 | –0– | 99.87 | 100.00 | 0.13– |
| 3111 | Nelston | 0408 | 233.65 | 145.61 | .00 | 379.26 |
| 3117 | O'Harra | 0461 | 789.75 | 121.10 | .00 | 910.85 |
| 6121 | Chiu | 0444 | 32.60- | 99.87 | .00 | 67.27 |
| 6133 | Valex | 0335 | –0– | 165.30 | .00 | 165.30 |
| 7003 | Roberts | 0428 | 336.66 | 109.55 | .00 | 446.21 |
| 7009 | Haittenberg | 0454 | 19.45 | 87.43 | .00 | 106.88 |
| **Totals** | | | **44 651.07** | **18 632.98** | **950.00** | **62 334.05** |

▲

**Exhibit 13-3**
A hard copy (printed copy) of closing folio balances is prepared nightly as part of the PMS audit and left at the desk the following day. The new day's opening balances (last night's closing balances) are then available in case of computer failure. Each column of this computer report corresponds to a column on the hand-prepared transcript. For example, the counterpart of the Charges column of Exhibit 13-3 is column 16, Total Debits, of Exhibit 13-10.

Room charges with the appropriate taxes have been programmed into the computer. Memory knows how much each room is to be billed and how much tax to be added. No math errors here. Activating the audit program brings all of the accounts receivable up to date in memory. Folios containing the new information are printed on demand, illustrated by any of the folio exhibits in Chapter 10.

Computers do crash, so a hard copy, a nightly printout, for emergency backup is part of every night audit (see Exhibit 13-3).

**Room Charges Not Posted by the Auditor** Normally, room charges are posted by the night auditor. Infrequently, and then only because of special circumstances, room and tax are posted by the day crew, not by the night auditor. In two of the instances, the auditor is simply not there at the time the charge is to be posted. The first of these involves guests who arrive and depart on the same day, called day rate, use rate, or part day rate guests. These guests arrive during the day after the previous night's audit has been finished. They depart before the night audit of the following day. Since the folio is opened and closed without any intervening audit, the room charge, which is often less than a full night's rate, must be posted by the day watch.

Extra room charges for late check-outs are the second special case. Brief extensions to the check-out hour are usually accommodated without charge when space allows. Extraordinary delays, or even brief occupancy when demand is high, incur late-departure charges, occasionally as much as a full night's rate. During the heady days of the late

1990s, when hotels thought they could do no wrong, guests were charged another type of penalty. Special room charges were levied on guests who failed to stay through the reservation period. Whatever the reason, excess room charges that occur between shifts of the night audit must be posted and collected by the front-office cashier.

# Revenue Verification

There are two major objectives to the audit. The discussion has already focused on one: reconciling accounts receivable. Each folio needs to be updated nightly so an accurate bill can be presented on demand. By the time the audit begins, hundreds of postings will have been made on guest accounts. Among them are charges for food; beverage; local and long-distance telephone calls; laundry and valet; cash advances; in-room charges for films, safes, and bars; greens fees; saunas; ski tows; and more. Added to the day's list are the room charges and local taxes just completed by the night auditor. The audit must prove the accuracy of all.

Chapter 10 emphasized that every departmental charge has equal debits and credits. Thus, each time a guest buys service, the guest account is charged and the departmental income is recorded.

What takes place individually—one folio being increased and one sale being recorded—has application to the audit. A rule of mathematics—the total is equal to the sum of the parts—plays a fundamental role in balancing the audit. All of the income earned by any one department (say, room service) must equal the total of all individual room service charges posted to guest folios. If each individual room service event increases a guest's folio and simultaneously increases income to the room service department, then the totals of each should agree (that is, be in balance). Since there are hundreds of posting and hundreds of folios, this simple fact is not evident immediately. The night audit reconciles the two by making evident this equality: The total income earned by each department from accounts receivable is the same total charged to guest folios.

The accounting rules apply:

> Increases in assets, including *accounts receivable* and cash, are made with debits. Increases in incomes (sales of rooms, *food*, beverage, etc.) are made with credits.
>
> Debit: Accounts Receivable/Guest's Folio    50
> Credit: Proper Departmental (room, *food*, beverage, spa, etc.) Sale  50
> *Explanation*: Guest charged food in the coffee shop.

# Reconciling Using a Property Management System

The night audit provides the most spectacular demonstration of the PMS in action. Only those who have machine-posted using the NCR (National Cash Register) system or hand-copied pages of transcript sheets can appreciate the savings in time and efficiency. Labour savings, the often touted but seldom delivered advantage of computer installations, is certainly evident in the PMS night audit. Since a minimum crew is always needed, the greatest labour savings occur at the largest hotels.

The computer has altered the mechanics of the audit, its purpose, and its scope. Traditionally, the night audit concentrated on finding and correcting errors—except that the errors were caused by employees operating the system. Initial errors, transmittal errors, posting errors, and errors of addition are inherent in the hand audit. The entire thrust of the hand audit is discovery and repair. The computer audit has no such problems. The information that is input with the departmental POS appears everywhere, and everywhere it appears the same. Of course, there are errors of input, and these are discussed shortly.

## Interfacing Different Systems

There are also problems with the PMS—computer bugs. When the situation becomes very serious, the bug is upgraded to a virus. Viruses or glitches (misplaced decimals is a very simple example) are errors of equipment, not errors of audit. Increases in the number of such incidents can usually be traced to additional interfaces, linkages between equipment pieces of various manufacturers. An interface is a third system used to link two unrelated systems. Hotels have as many as 8 or 10 such linkages. Common links to the property management system are POS terminals and **call accounting systems** (see Chapter 14).

Interface problems are created when systems differently designed by different manufacturers are purchased to be used with an already existing PMS. In addition to POS and call accounting (CA), there might be interfaces for in-room minibars, in-room films, reservation programs, housekeeping room status, and others. Recent efforts by the American Hotel & Lodging Association have focused on developing integration standards.[1] These will ensure the compatibility of different products by different manufacturers and not require the special interface programs that bring grief to many hotel systems.

A second wave of integration is being driven by the large franchise companies. To increase seamless communications, particularly reservations between the parent and the franchisee, several large franchisors are now insisting on a particular PMS for each franchisee.[2] Once in place, last-room availability (see Chapter 4) will be accessible across a wide range of channels, including the Web. Consolidation, so apparent in the hotel business, is a likely outcome of technology standardization. The number of technology vendors has declined from the 100-plus that once competed.

## Verifying Basic Data

The PMS is closed and updated daily at the closeout hour in a process akin to the manual night audit. Although the PMS closeout could be done at any time—as could the manual night audit, for that matter—the quiet hours of the early morning are favoured for both. The PMS shuts down during the closeout. Departmental POS terminals cannot interface with the system. Charges to guest accounts must wait until the audit is complete. Manual audits are not quite as dramatic. With much erasing and rewriting, manual audits can accommodate changes during the process.

**Closing Routine** Updating the PMS requires the night auditor to monitor the progress of the audit rather than perform the work. Room charges and room taxes are posted automatically. It is an internal function that the auditor does not see until the job is complete and the hard copy is printed. In contrast, the auditor actually records the rate and tax during the manual audit (see Exhibit 13-1). A summary printout is prepared immediately, showing the folio balances that open the new day (see Exhibit 13-3). This hard-copy recap enables the hotel to settle guest accounts even if the computer crashes. (The upcoming discussion of the manual audit stresses that the opening balances of the new day are the same as the closing balances of the previous day.)

Departmental verifications of revenues are another part of the audit. Unlike manual audits, discrepancies are unusual. Point-of-sale terminals post the same figure both to the account receivable on the folio and to the revenue of the departmental sale. Rare differences are corrected by comparing departmental incomes reported by the PMS to account receivable records such as registered readings and/or vouchers. Vouchers come into play because POS terminals are not used by every hotel. Even those that have them may operate some departments manually. If so, the manual system of vouchers, control sheets, and folios may be partially in place. Even if this is so, the night audit is simplified tremendously with the PMS. The property management system creates the folios and the spreadsheet electronically and ensures the accuracy of the mathematics.

The night auditor finishes the PMS audit with an end-of-the-day routine much like that of the hand audit. A trial balance of debits and credits is made. Debits are charges to the receivable folios; credits are earnings in the several departments. The day and date are closed and the next day opened. The POS terminals are put back online. Monthly and annual totals are accumulated as part of the reporting process that follows next. The sequence varies at each hotel. At some properties, the routine is pre-programmed; at others, the update proceeds by prompts from the system to which the auditor responds.

Folios of guests who are departing the following day may be printed as part of the audit procedure. Pre-printing folios speeds the check-outs. Copies are filed by room number sequence in the cashier's well and produced without delay when the departing guest appears at the desk. If subsequent charges—breakfast, for example—alter the previous night's balance, the old folio is merely discarded and a new one is printed.

A copy of the pre-printed folio might be left under the guest-room door for use in express check-outs. This wouldn't be necessary if the hotel provides express check-out by means of the TV set.

**Express Check-Out** Express check-out is one of the exciting stories of PMS installations. Standing in line to check out has been the bane of hotel guests, who are always in a hurry. Flexible terminals able to quickly shift from registration to departure status, and vice versa, were one of the first PMS innovations to focus on the problem. This increased the number of front-office stations when demand was greatest. Lines were shortened, but not enough.

Because early output printers were slow, many operations began printing the folios of expected departures during the previous night's audit. From printing them to delivering them to the room wasn't a large conceptual jump, but it created zip-out check-out, also called *speedy check-out, no-wait check-out,* or *VIP check-out.*

Zip-out check-out is only for guests using direct billing or credit cards—but that is almost everyone. At first, guests who wanted the service completed a request card. Later, every departure using a credit card had a folio under the door. If the folio was accurate, the guests left after completing one additional step: They either telephoned an extension to give notice, or they dropped a form with the key in a lobby box (see Exhibit 13-4). The final folio was mailed to the guest within a day or two, and the charges were processed through the credit card company.

Express check-out leaped ahead with the interface of On Command's TV pay-movie system into the hotel's PMS. Delivering folios to the room was necessary no longer. The folio appeared on the TV set any time the guest wanted it. From then on, the procedure

▲
**Exhibit 13-4**
Express check-out uses either the in-room TV screen or the envelope pictured. With zip-out check-out, departing guests bypass long lines at the front-office cashier's position, but still notify the hotel of their departures.

was the same. With a click of the remote control, the guest signalled departure. As with zip-out check-out, the folio followed in the mail, and the credit card charges were processed. An integrated PMS transfers the charges, which have been accumulated in the front-office folio, to the city ledger module.

Another great leap forward was taken when self-check-in/check-out terminals were interfaced with the ever-expanding PMS. At freestanding locations within the lobby, self-check-out terminals present guests with their folios and accept their credit cards to speed them on their way. This completes the PMS cycle, which was started when the guest registered at the same terminal (see Exhibit 8-10). It is another step closer to the fully electronic hotel.

**PMS Posting Errors** Property management systems are not guaranteed to be error free! Staff members make mistakes whether the system is manual or electronic. The PMS provides consistent figures throughout, but those values will be in error if the wrong keys are struck. Human errors are not offset by equipment. Computerized front offices minimize system errors and facilitate error discovery, but they do not create error-free environments.

The night auditor prints a detailed list of transactions as the first step in pinpointing errors. The hard copy itemizes transactions by register keys or by reference codes. Reference codes are illustrated on the folio figures throughout Chapter 10. Departmental cashiers need authority to post charges to someone's folio. A source document, such as a signed departmental voucher, provides that authority. Since most source documents are maintained in numerical sequence, the voucher number becomes the reference code. The POS program doesn't post until the cashier inputs that reference number or code.

A different code is used to validate the identity of the guest who is making the charge. The cashier inputs the guest's room number, which the guest provides, and when prompted enters the first several letters of the guest's surname, which the guest also provides. The charge is processed, but not before the system matches the POS information with the registration data in the file of the PMS. Exhibit 13-2 illustrates the computer screen a dining room cashier uses to post a charge.

Matching the guest-room key card (with its magnetic strip) to the PMS's registration data file is another means of verifying the guest's identity. The guest inserts the key card into a POS and the system verifies the identification. Implementation of this system has already begun, but it may be replaced before it even goes into general use. The smart cards of Chapter 12 suggest that one's own credit card may become the key card for the next generation of electronic locks.

The POS system reduces receivable losses by rejecting invalid postings. The guest may have checked out already, be a paid-in-advance customer with no charges permitted, or have exceeded the credit card floor or other credit ceiling set by the hotel. Late charges are reduced dramatically when POS terminals are in place.

Departing guests sometimes challenge the accuracy of departmental postings. Denying that the charges were ever made, they ask for offsetting allowances from the front desk. Obtaining a copy of the cheque (voucher) signed by the guest to show its accuracy is a slow process with a pencil-and-paper system. It is so time consuming that the front-office cashier simply grants the allowance without further investigation. Until recently, the results were the same with a PMS. Now, disputed charges are being met with proof in a test program introduced at the Boca Raton Resort and Beach Club. The PMS is able to display the protested voucher despite the range of operating departments at the Boca: 84 revenue sources, 23 different voucher forms, and 13 different sizes of paper![3]

## Reports from the Night Auditor

An unlimited number of reports can be generated by the PMS once it captures the information. Data can be arranged and reordered in a variety of ways. The registration card is a good example. From it, several different reports can be generated: geographic origin of guests; membership in groups; credit limits; company affiliations; average length of stay; and rate level preference.

The ease of obtaining reports undoubtedly contributed to the vast numbers that were demanded when PMSs were first introduced. Much of that has shaken out. Management took control and pared the numbers by emphasizing exception reports. One no longer sees piles of reports prepared by the night auditor trashed, unread by the recipient the next day.

Still, the night audit produces a wide range of reports for all departments of the front office. Many of these are day-end summaries, since unit managers use (through display terminals or hard-copy print) the same data several times throughout the day. Some reports are traditional from the days of the pencil-and-paper audit: the balancing of accounts receivable, credit alerts, and statistical reports to the manager.

**Turnkey Systems** In a **turnkey** installation, the buyer merely "turns the key" to activate the system. Everything has been done in advance by the vendor. Nothing is ever quite that easy, but it is unlikely that the hotel industry would be so far along if the burden of development had not shifted from individual hotel companies to industry-wide vendors.

Prior to the turnkey concept, each hotel shopped among manufacturers for its own hardware. Then it developed its own software by employing computer specialists, who at that time knew nothing about the business of keeping a hotel. The large data processing departments that appeared as a result of in-house programming disappeared quickly with the introduction of the turnkey package.

Now systems are purchased off the shelf, shopping among suppliers for an existing system that is close to what the hotel needs. And systems are close to what is needed. Generic programs are much alike because hotels are much alike. The differences in off-the-shelf products diminish as third- and fourth-generation programs are developed. Each generation improves flow and screening, and new or missing functions are being added to remain competitive. Most recently, the push has been toward a Windows/Intel environment.

Turnkey companies now dominate the field. Single suppliers furnish both the hardware and the software. If the supplier specializes in one segment, other vendors supply the missing parts. Responsibility remains with the primary vendor, which puts together the package, gets it up and running, trains the staff, and services the installation—not without some major grief for the hotel, of course. Vendors who adopt the Hospitality Information Technology Integration Standards (**HITIS**) that the AH&LA is encouraging will offer systems that interface with all others who comply with HITIS. Hotels that specify HITIS in their bid solicitations will enjoy reduced risks, lower costs, and savings in installation time. Access to the World Wide Web will also change the hotel's PMS from one with dedicated hardware to one that uses Web technology. As that happens, the front-office workstation will become a general-purpose rather than a specific-purpose screen.

Currently, vendors are modifying their off-the-shelf systems to meet special needs. Just as often, however, hotels modify their special needs to conform to the standardized product. As a result, programs are almost identical among hotels with the same vendor and very similar among hotels with different vendors. Nowhere is this standardization more apparent than in the range of reports prepared nightly by the PMS.

**Kinds of Reports** Reports from the night audit fall into several categories: reservations reports; rooms management reports, including reports of room status; accounting reports; and reports to the manager. Unless management remains selective, an excessive number of reports involving expensive machine time, labour, storage, and paper costs is spewed out nightly. Since a good deal of the information keeps changing, viewing it on screens is just as effective and far more economical. Reporting by exception is another approach to the issue.

**Exception Reports** Exception reports highlight situations that digress from the norm. Reporting everything that is as it should be serves no purpose. Reports by exception alert the reader to problem areas without requiring the time-consuming inspection of normal data. A report on credit limits is a good example. Listing the folio balance of every guest against the credit ceiling is unnecessary. It is unduly long and requires a tedious search to find the important information. An exception report lists only those folios that are at, above, or close to the hotel's limit. The size of the report is reduced and the important data are emphasized.

Some common exception reports are listed here:

*Allowance Report:* identifies who authorized each allowance, who received the allowance, the amount, and the reasons.

*Cashier's Overage and Shortage Report:* pinpoints by stations overages and shortages that exceed predetermined norms.

*Comps Report:* similar to an Allowance Report; identifies who authorized each comp, who received the comp, the amount, and the reasons.

*No Luggage Report:* lists occupied rooms in which there is no luggage; a credit report.

*Room Rate Variance Report:* compares actual rates to standard rate schedule and identifies the authority for granting the variance (not meaningful if the hotel is discounting frequently and deeply).

*Skipper Report:* provides room identification, dollar amount, and purported name and address.

*Write-off Report:* lists daily write-offs, usually late charges, whose account balances are less than a specified amount.

**Downtime Reports** **Downtime** reports, for use when the computer crashes, provide insurance against disaster. Like a great deal of insurance, the reports usually go unused because emergencies rarely materialize. Downtime reports are dumped 24 hours later when the contingency has passed and the backup reports of the following day have been printed.

Basic downtime reports include the following:

*Folio Balance Report:* itemizes in room number sequence the balances due from receivables; comparable to columns 2, 1, 4 and 5, 16, 20, 21 and 22 of a manual transcript (compare Exhibits 13-3 and 13-11).

*Guest-List Report:* alphabetizes registered guests with their room numbers; computer version of a manual **information rack.**

*Room Status Report:* identifies vacant, out-of-order, on-change, and occupied rooms at the beginning of the new day; a computerized room count sheet (see Exhibit 13-12).

*Disk Backup:* not a report, but part of the closing sequence of the auditor's shift; data are replicated onto another disk to be retrieved if a malfunction erases the working disk.

**Credit Reports** The night auditor is the credit manager's first line of defence. In that capacity, the night auditor handles both routine matters and special credit situations.

Mention has already been made of the auditor's responsibility to preprint the folios of expected check-outs. Although not nearly as numerous, folios must also be prepared for guests who remain longer than one week. On the guest's seventh night, the auditor prints the folio (or prepares a new folio if the system is manual) for delivery to the guest the next day.

The night auditor also makes an analysis of guest **account balances.** With a manual system, the auditor scans the last column of the transcript (see Exhibit 13-10, column 21) and itemizes those rooms with balances at or near the hotel's limit. The computer makes the same list. If the audit team has time, additional credit duties may be assigned.

All credit reports are sensitive and may be viewed as exception reports:

*Credit Alert:* list of rooms whose folio charges exceed a given amount in a single day. That amount varies with the class of hotel.

*Cumulative Charges Report:* similar to the credit alert except a cumulative figure for the guest's entire stay.

*Floor Report:* list of guests whose folio balances approach the maximum allowed to the hotel by the credit card company, or the maximum the credit card allows on the guest's own card.

*Three-Day Report:* weekly statements that remain unpaid three days after billing.

**Reservations Reports** Computerizing reservations added a new dimension to the process. The toll-free WATS number globalized the reservation network. Instant confirmation was given for dates that were months away to persons who were kilometres apart. In so doing, reams of information—fodder for reports—was generated.

Information is the power to decide. Reservations managers must know the number of rooms sold and the number available, by type, rate, and accommodations. They must know the number of arrivals, departures, stayovers, cancellations, out of orders, and walk-ins, for a start. This information comes to the reservations department in a variety of reports.

Supplemental information flows from the same database. Which rooms are most popular and at which rates? Do no-show factors vary with the season and the day of the week? If so, by how much? How many rooms in which categories are turnaways? How many reservations were walked? How many in-WATS calls were there? How

**Exhibit 13-5** ▶
A computer display of the room rack lists room availability by room type, location, rate, and status. The clerk's selection (lower left) must agree with previous input of room type requested by the arriving guest. If so, the clerk exits with Y (yes), lower right corner, and the assignment is complete. Compare the PMS display with that of the manual rack, Exhibit 13-7.

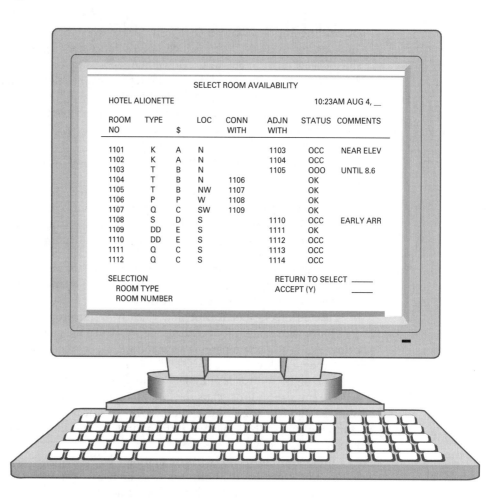

many were initiated by travel agents? Questions of this type illustrate again the dual management–operations capability of the computer.

An alphabetical list of arrivals is an example of the computer in operations. It reduces the number of lost reservations and facilitates the recognition of VIPs. It helps the bell captain schedule a crew. It identifies group affiliation, which improves reservation and billing procedures.

Reservation data can be displayed on a monitor or preserved on hard copy for slower digestion and evaluation. A permanent copy turns the data into a report. Then it serves more as a management tool than an operational one. Although different vendors format reports differently, there is a common grouping for the reservations department, which includes the following:

*Arrivals Report:* alphabetical list of the day's expected arrivals, individually and by groups.

*Cancellation and Change Report:* list of reservation cancellations for the day or reservation changes and cancellations for a later date.

*Central Reservations Report:* analysis of reservations made through the central reservations system, including numbers, kinds, rates, and fees paid.

*Convention (Group) Delegates Report:* compilation of group (and tour) room blocks: the number of rooms booked and the number still available by rate category and name of group. Also called a *Group **Pickup** Report.*

**Exhibit 13-6** ▶
Each function performed by the guest-service agent, Exhibit 13-5, for example, requires a different computer screen, which is called up from this main menu. Two or three masks may be required before the task is completed.

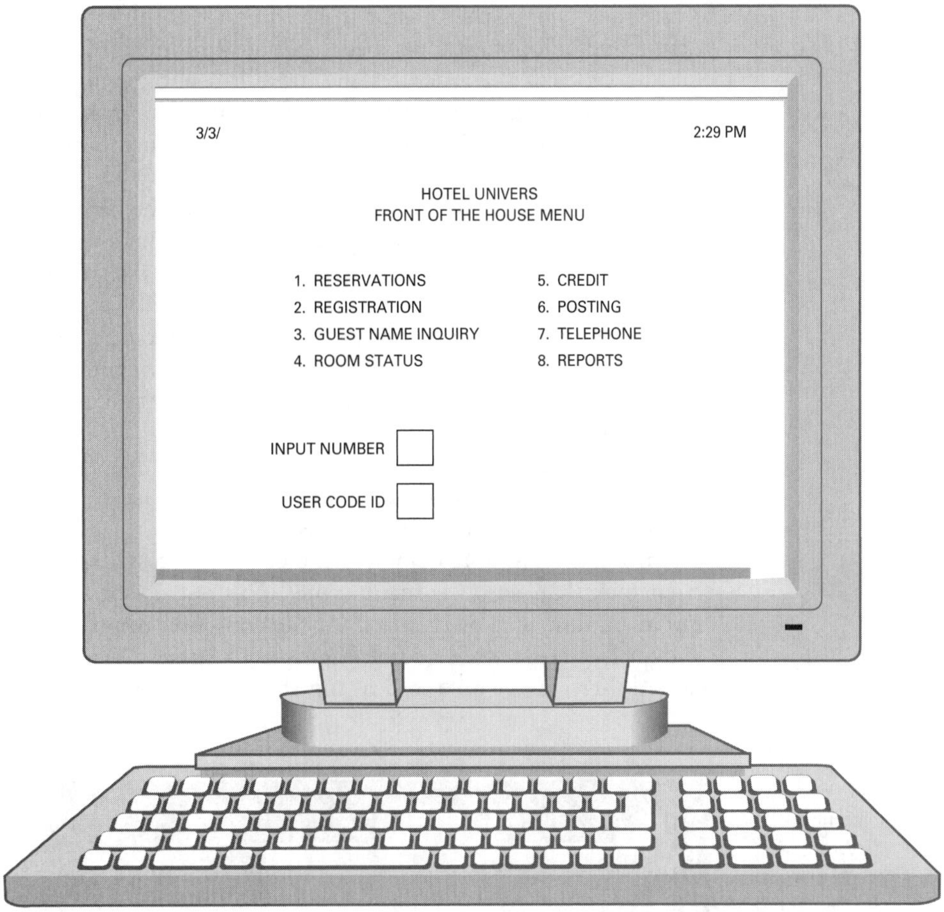

```
3/3/                                                    2:29 PM


                        HOTEL UNIVERS
                     FRONT OF THE HOUSE MENU


              1. RESERVATIONS       5. CREDIT
              2. REGISTRATION       6. POSTING
              3. GUEST NAME INQUIRY 7. TELEPHONE
              4. ROOM STATUS        8. REPORTS



        INPUT NUMBER    [    ]

        USER CODE ID    [    ]
```

*Daily Analysis Report:* one or more reports on the number and percentage of reservations, arrivals, no-shows, walk-ins, and so on, by source (travel agent, housing bureau, etc.) and by type of guest (full rack, corporate rate, etc.).

*Deposit Report:* reservations by deposit status—deposits requested and received, deposits requested and not received, deposits not requested. Could be treated as an exception report.

*Forecast Report:* one of a variety of names (*Extended Arrival Report, Future Availability Report*) for projecting reservations data forward over short or long durations (see Exhibit 6-5).

*Occupancy Report:* projection within the computer's horizon of expected occupancy by category of room.

*Overbooking (Walk) Report:* list of reservations walked, including their identification; the number of walk-ins denied; and the number farmed out to other properties.

*Regrets Report:* report on the number of room requests denied.

**Rooms Management Reports** The PMS has brought major procedural changes to the front office but not to the functions that need doing. Comparisons of the old and the new are best illustrated through the room rack. Unlike manual room racks, which one can see and physically manipulate, computerized racks are in computer memory, viewable only on the monitor screen (see Exhibits 13-5 and 13-6). Whether the clerk turns to one rack type or the other, the information is the same: room rates, location, connecting and adjoining rooms, bed types, and room status.

The computer restructures the data. It separates into different windows what is visible with one glance to the user of the manual rack (see Exhibit 13-7). Separate menus (see Exhibit 13-6) are needed to view what the manual rack identifies as one class of information. With a glance at the manual rack, one sees the rooms vacant and occupied, the rooms out of order and on change, the names of the guests and their city of residence, the number in the party and their company or group affiliation, the rate on the room, and the anticipated check-out date. It doesn't work that way with an electronic system, where separate programs are needed for each function. Room identification (see Exhibit 13-5) is different from guest identification (see Exhibit 13-8).

Far more information is available from the computer rack than from the manual rack (see Exhibit 13-7), but the information has to be manipulated to provide the data. For example, the computerized rack can display all vacant rooms on a given floor. All of the king rooms in the tower or all of the connecting rooms in the lanai building can be listed. Facts that would take many minutes to ascertain, if at all, from the manual rack are flashed onto the screen in seconds.

Information is more complete and can be processed more rapidly with the computerized rack than with the manual one. This is true for the whole, although a greater amount of time may be required for the computer to process a single fact. In a contest to identify a guest whose name begins with either "Mac" or "Mc," for example, the manual user may be able to beat out the computer user.

**Exhibit 13-7** ▶

A manual room rack, circa 1960. With one glance, the guest-service agent determines which rooms are vacant and which occupied; who the occupants are and their home towns; rates paid; arrival and anticipated departure dates. It would take several computer screens to obtain the same information. Colours furnish additional facts: members of a tour group; paid-in-advance; permanent guest; and so on.

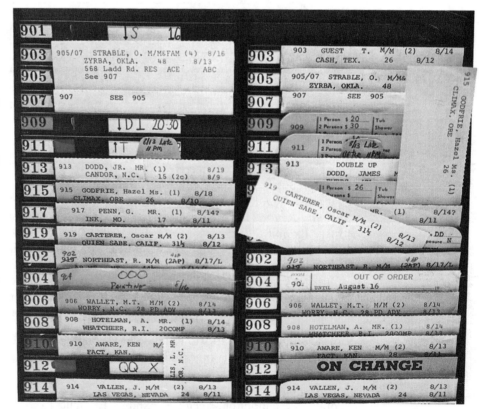

Computer reports for the rooms function include the following:

*Change Report:* identification of room changes, rate changes, and the number in the party.

*Convention Use Report:* summary of the room use by different convention groups in order to justify the number of complimentary rooms.

*Expected-to-Depart Report:* list of anticipated departures. The converse would be a Stayover Report.

*Flag Report:* list of rooms **flagged** for special attention by the desk.

*House Use Report:* list of rooms occupied by hotel personnel.

*Out-of-Order Report:* list of rooms that are out of order or out of inventory, with reasons.

*Pickup Report:* names and room numbers picked up by members of a specific group against its block.

*Rate Analysis Report:* display of distribution of rates by sources—reservations, walk-ins, travel-agency made, reservations system, hotel sales department, packages, **company-made.**

*Room Productivity Report:* evaluation of housekeeping's productivity in total and by individual room attendant.

*VIP Report:* list of distinguished guests and very important persons, including casino high rollers.

**Exhibit 13-8** ▶
Code 3 of Exhibit 13-6 leads to the screen that identifies a particular guest in a particular room. Compare the guest information here with that shown on the room rack slips of Exhibit 13-7.

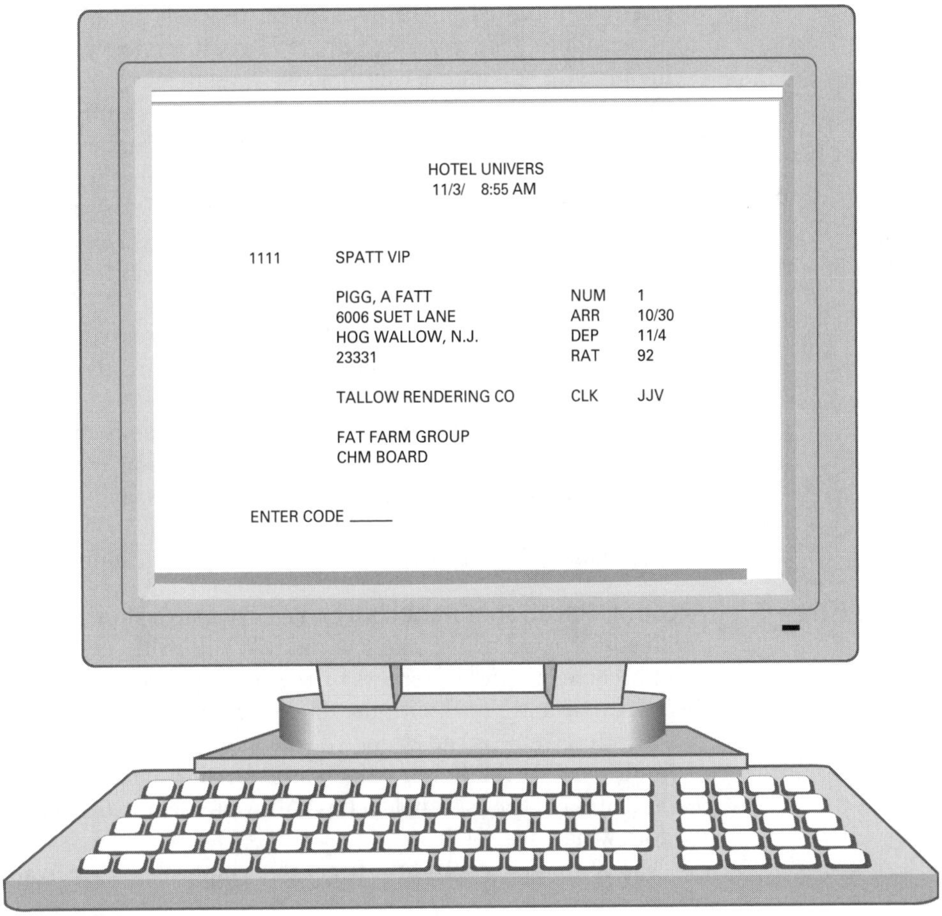

```
                    HOTEL UNIVERS
                    11/3/  8:55 AM


    1111        SPATT VIP

                PIGG, A FATT          NUM    1
                6006 SUET LANE        ARR    10/30
                HOG WALLOW, N.J.      DEP    11/4
                23331                 RAT    92

                TALLOW RENDERING CO   CLK    JJV

                FAT FARM GROUP
                CHM BOARD


    ENTER CODE _____
```

**Rooms Status Reports** Rooms status offers what is probably the best example of an old function with a new face. Whether the hotel uses a manual rack or a computer, room status (on-change, vacant and ready, out-of-order, or occupied rooms) must be communicated between the desk and housekeeping. Clerks need to know which rooms are ready for sale, and housekeeping needs to know which rooms require attention. A room status display on the monitor is called up innumerable times throughout the day by both ends of the communication link.

The communication procedure hasn't changed with the computer. The cashier still puts the room on change as the guest checks out. (This is done electronically if the guest uses the speedy check-out option.) That's how the room clerk learns that a given room will be available soon. On-change status tells housekeeping that the room needs attention. When the room is clean, the housekeeper updates the system, switching the on-change room to ready. Immediately, the desk clerk has the information. The room is sold and the cycle begins anew. The faster the process goes around, the quicker the new guest is settled and the room sale is complete.

Prior to the computer, the cashier–desk–housekeeping link was direct conversation person to person; by means of paper notations; by telephone calls; and, frequently, not at all. The room attendant on the floor wasn't included in the communication loop. Although the critical link, he or she couldn't be reached at all. Today, the room attendant communicates by telephone, not by conversation but as an electronic input device to the computer. Either the room attendant taps in through the telephone or by means of a terminal located in the **linen closet** on each floor. Personal computers are being introduced into guest rooms to upgrade guest service, but they also provide the room attendant with still another terminal.

With access to the computer, the housekeeper's office tracks room attendants as they dial in and out of the system (see Exhibit 13-9). Daily job assignments can also be computer designed. At the start of the shift, each employee gets a hard-copy list of rooms that each is to service. The printout also includes special assignments such as mirrors in the corridors, attention to sick guests, or messages from management to the staff.

In addition to the reports that housekeeping uses to manage the department, room status includes the following:

*Out-of-Order Report:* special focus on out-of-order or out-of-inventory rooms containing dates the rooms went down, expected ready dates, and the causes of each OOO or OOI room.

*Permanent Guest Report:* list of permanent guests by room number and name.

*Room Status List:* room-by-room identification of occupied and vacant rooms, made-up and not-ready rooms, out-of-order rooms, and on-change rooms. (This report is also included among the downtime reports.)

*Sick Guest Report:* list of sick guests by room number and name.

**Accounts Receivable Reports** The PMS prepares electronically the same records that are hand-prepared by the manual audit. What is the very function of the manual night audit becomes a series of reports by the computerized night audit. Both the manual and the electronic audit deal with the day's accounts receivable. A cumulative inventory of accounts receivable is the essence of the audit. The opening balance of receivables, the amount owed to the hotel, is increased by new charges and decreased by payments made that day. The new balance is thus obtained; it becomes the opening balance of the following day's audit.

The computerized audit reflects this emphasis on receivables through a group of related reports:

| HOUSEKEEPER'S ROOM SCHEDULE | | | | | | | 01:53 PM NOV 11 | | | | | |
|---|---|---|---|---|---|---|---|---|---|---|---|---|
| **NAME** | | | | | | **NUMBER** | **DUTY H** | | **MESSAGE SIGNAL OFF** | | | |
| | **NUMBER OF ROOMS ASSIGNED** | | | | | **0** | | | **BEGINNING ROOM NUMBER** | | | |
| **ROOM** | **U-R** | **IN** | **OUT** | **SL** | **HK** | **CO** | **ROOM** | **U-R** | **IN** | **OUT** | **SL** | **HK** | **CO** |
| 1200 | A | 9:35A | 9:49A | SG | OK | SO | 1209 | A | | | SD | D | SO |
| 1201 | A | 9:50A | 10:14A | SS | OK | SO | 1210 | A | 8:44A | 9:02A | SD | OK | SO |
| 1202 | A | 11:50A | 12:12P | SS | OK | SO | 1211 | A | 1:13P | 1:48P | OK | I | OK |
| 1203 | A | 9:20A | 9:35A | SS | OK | SO | 1212 | A | 9:03A | 9:19A | SG | OK | SO |
| 1204 | A | 10:54A | 11:17A | SM | OK | SO | 1213 | A | 1:48 | | OK | 57 | DO |
| 1205 | A | 11:17A | 11:50A | SD | OK | SO | 1214 | A | | | OK | D | DO |
| 1206 | A | 10:31A | 10:54A | SS | OK | SO | 1215 | A | | | OK | D | DO |
| 1207 | A | 10:14A | 10:31A | SS | OK | SO | | | | | | | |
| 1208 | A | 12:12P | 1:13P | OK | OK | OK | | | | | | | |

END DISPLAY

▲
**Exhibit 13-9**
Property management systems track each room attendant, permitting management to monitor productivity and locate the employee if direct communication is required. By the time of this display, 1:53 P.M. (top right), the housekeeper has serviced almost all the rooms.

*Alpha List:* alphabetically lists the entire guest (account receivable) population. Other alpha lists include arrivals and departures.

*City Ledger Transfers:* itemizes all of the accounts transferred to the city ledger that day; a **city ledger journal**.

*Credit Card Report:* reports amounts and identities of credit card charges by both registered and unregistered guests.

*Daily Revenue Report:* analyzes revenue totals from all sources by outlet and means of payment. Comparable to the old machine audit D report (and sometimes called a D report).

*Departmental Sales Journal:* shows the individual transactions of each department (comparable to the vertical columns of a hand transcript, see Exhibit 13-10).

*Guest Ledger Summary:* displays the daily activity for both the A and B folios of individual guest accounts—opening balance, charges and credits, and closing balance (comparable to the horizontal lines of a hand transcript, see Exhibits 13-3 and 13-10).

*Late-Charge Report:* identifies late charges that were transferred to the city ledger that day.

*Posting Report:* displays posting activity by individual POS terminal (comparable to a departmental control sheet).

*Room Revenue (Posting) Report:* displays room, rate, and tax posted at the day's close. Room revenue can be obtained floor by floor, it is comparable to a room count sheet without the taxes also called an occupancy and room revenue report (see Exhibit 13-11).

**Reports to the Manager** The night auditor furnishes information about accounts receivable sales to the income (or day) auditor. The income audit, which includes both cash and accounts receivable sales, casts a wider net than the night audit, which is limited to accounts receivable. Sometimes the income audit and its corresponding report to the manager is delayed, just as the night audit is at times. To offset the delay, the night auditor leaves a preliminary report for the manager. It is abbreviated, of course, because it contains accounts receivable sales only. Still, most hotel sales are accounts receivable sales. Room sales, the hotel's largest revenue source, is sold only on account. There are no cash sales in the rooms department.

**DAILY TRANSCRIPT OF ACCOUNTS RECEIVABLE**    DATE 10/6    19 ____

| 1 ACCOUNT NO. | 2 ROOM NO. | 3 NUMBER OF GUESTS | OPENING BALANCE 4 DEBIT | 5 CREDIT | DEBITS 6 ROOMS | 7 RESTAURANT | 8 BEVERAGES | TELEPHONE 9 LOCAL CALLS | 10 LONG DISTANCE | 11 LAUNDRY | 12 VALET | 13 CASH DISBURSEMENTS | 14 TRANSFERS | 15 ROOM TAX | 16 TOTAL DEBITS | CREDITS 17 CASH RECEIPTS | 18 ALLOWANCES | 19 TRANSFERS | 20 | CLOSING BALANCE 21 DEBIT | 22 CREDIT |
|---|---|---|---|---|---|---|---|---|---|---|---|---|---|---|---|---|---|---|---|---|---|
| 8001 | 1406 | 1 | | 19 — | 60 — | 12 — | 6 — | | | | | 8 — | | 3 — | 70 — | | | | | 70 — | |
| 8811 | 1817 | 2 | 63 60 | | 30 — | 5 — | | | 4 — | | | | | 60 | 39 60 | | | | | 103 20 | |
| 8123 | 1824 | 1 | | | 18 50 | 6 40 | | | | | | 1 — | | 37 | 26 37 | 37 — | | | | | 10 73 |
| 7188 | 1906 | 2 | 21 93 | | 21 56 | | | | | | | | | 43 | 21 99 | | | | | 43 92 | |
| 7913 | 1907 | 2 | 39 96 | | 30 — | | 6 — | | | | | | 47 96 | 60 | 84 56 | | | | | 124 52 | |
| **TOTAL** | 40 | 51 | 768 20 | 153 | 267 6 50 | 52 10 | 61 70 | 7 20 | 18 40 | | | 4 — | 17 — | 47 96 13 53 | 898 39 | 167 50 | 2 10 | | | 1459 02 | 17 03 |

DEPARTURES

| | | | | | | | | | | | | | | | | | | | | | |
|---|---|---|---|---|---|---|---|---|---|---|---|---|---|---|---|---|---|---|---|---|---|
| 8106 | 1616 | 3 | 46 20 | | | 4 40 | | | | | | | | | 4 40 | 50 60 | | | | | |
| 8007 | 1649 | 1 | 18 57 | | | | | | | | | | | | | 18 57 | | 30 | | | | |
| 7992 | 1824 | 2 | 39 96 | | | | 4 — | | 40 | 3 60 | | | | | | | 8 — | | 47 96 | | | |
| **TOTAL** | | | 105 03 | | | 4 40 | 4 — | | 40 | 3 60 | | | | | | 12 40 | 69 17 | 30 | 47 96 | | | |

CITY LEDGER

| **TOTALS** | | | 873 23 | 19 — | 676 50 | 56 50 | 65 70 | 7 60 | 22 — | | | 4 — | 17 — | 47 96 13 53 | 910 79 | 236 67 | 2 40 | 47 96 | | 1459 02 | 17 03 |
|---|---|---|---|---|---|---|---|---|---|---|---|---|---|---|---|---|---|---|---|---|---|

▲

**Exhibit 13-10**

The transcript is a summary of accounts receivable. The vertical daily column of each folio is copied here as a horizontal line. This separates departmental incomes by columns. Column totals are then compared to departmental control sheets to verify account receivable sales.

Two methods of recording the folios are illustrated, *but only one would be used at one time*. Line 1 (the folio of Exhibit 13–1) includes the opening balance of columns 4 minus 5 in the total of column 16. The remaining exhibit illustrates the second method in which column 16 represents only the sum of the day's charges, columns 6 through 15. The cumulative balance of accounts receivable (column 21 minus 22) is the same with both methods. (For ease in reading, all illustrations use small dollar values, which may not seem realistic.)

Exhibit 13-12 illustrates a *night auditor's report to the manager*. Three items are reported: (1) accounts receivable sales in the several departments appear in the upper left. These figures are identical to columns 6 through 16 of the manual transcript (see Exhibit 13-11); (2) a cumulative balance of accounts receivable is at the bottom left of Exhibit 13-12; (3) room statistics and their corresponding ratios, which were introduced in Chapter 1, appear on the right side of this abbreviated night auditor's report. One or all of the values may be changed by the day audit, which could uncover mistakes in any of the sections. There aren't many changes, but new information (cash sales among them) modifies the night auditor's report into the daily report to the manager.

**Room Count, House Count, and Room Income Room count** (the number of rooms sold/occupied), house count (the number of guests/persons registered), and room income (room sales) are computed during the night audit. The three values can be verified by a second calculation, the same kind that results in the cumulative balance of any continuing inventory, including that of accounts receivable. Opening balance plus

**Exhibit 13-11 ▶**
A paper-and-pencil room count sheet is prepared at the closeout hour of each day. It is a snapshot of the room rack at that time. Included are the number of rooms occupied, the number of guests, and the total room revenue. These figures should agree with columns 2, 3, and 6 respectively of the transcript, Exhibit 13-10. The comparable PMS report is the room status list.

| OCCUPANCY AND ROOM REVENUE REPORT | | **Hotel Gary** | | | | | | DAY *Monday* | | DATE *9-18-* | | | | | | | |
|---|---|---|---|---|---|---|---|---|---|---|---|---|---|---|---|---|---|
| | | | | **EAST WING** | | | | | | | | | | | | | |
| ROOM | No Guests | RATE | ROOM | No Guests | RATE | ROOM | No Guests | RATE | ROOM | No Guests | RATE | ROOM | No Guests | RATE | ROOM | No Guests | RATE |
| 3101 | | | 3319 | | | 3615 | | | 3910 | | | 4206 | | | 4501 | | |
| 3102 | | | 3320 | | | 3616 | | | 3912 | | | 4207 | | | 4502 | | |
| 3103 | | | S3322 | 4 | 80 | 3617 | | | 3914 | | | 4208 | | | 4503 | | |
| 3104 | | | 3401 | | | 3618 | | | 3915 | | | 4210 | | | 4504 | | |
| 3105 | | | 3402 | 2 | 66 | 3619 | | | 3916 | | | 4212 | | | 4505 | | |
| 3106 | | | 3403 | 2 | 66 | 3620 | | | 3917 | | | 4214 | | | 4506 | | |
| 3107 | | | 3404 | | | S3622 | | | 3918 | | | 4215 | | | 4507 | | |
| 3108 | | | 3405 | 2 | 68 | 3701 | | | 3919 | | | 4216 | | | 4508 | | |
| 3110 | | | 3406 | | | 3702 | | | 3920 | | | 4217 | | | 4510 | | |
| 3112 | | | 3407 | | | 3703 | | | S3922 | | | 4218 | | | 4512 | | |
| 3114 | | | 3408 | 1 | 58 — | 3704 | | | 4001 | | | 4219 | | | 4514 | | |
| 3115 | | | 3410 | | | 3705 | | | 4002 | | | 4220 | | | 4515 | | |
| 3116 | | | 3412 | 3 | 72 | 3706 | | | 4003 | | | S4222 | | | 4516 | | |
| 3117 | | | 3414 | 1 | 59 50 | 3707 | | | 4004 | | | 4301 | | | 4517 | | |
| 3118 | | | 3415 | 3 | 66 — | 3708 | | | 4005 | | | 4302 | | | 4518 | | |
| 3312 | | | 3606 | 2 | 66 | 3903 | | | S4122 | | | 4418 | | | 4712 | | |
| 3314 | | | 3607 | 2 | 66 | 3904 | | | 4201 | | | 4419 | | | 4714 | | |
| 3315 | | | 3608 | 3 | 71 | 3905 | | | 4202 | | | 4420 | | | 4715 | | |
| 3316 | | | 3610 | 1 | 66 | 3906 | | | 4203 | | | S4422 | | | 4716 | | |
| 3317 | | | 3612 | | | 3907 | | | 4204 | | | | | | 4717 | | |
| 3318 | | | 3614 | | | 3908 | | | 4205 | | | | | | 4718 | | |
| TOTAL | | | TOTAL | 57 | 3,731 00 | TOTAL | | | TOTAL | | | TOTAL | | | TOTAL | | |

additions minus withdrawals equals the closing balance. That formula holds true whether one is counting sheets in housekeeping, bottles of Scotch at the bar, or room count, house count, and room income.

First, arrivals are added to the opening balance. Today's opening balance is yesterday's closing balance. This opening/closing balance idea applies to every running-balance computation. Consider the Scotch. When the bar closes at 2 A.M., there are six bottles of Scotch. Twelve hours later, when the bar reopens, the same six bottles of Scotch are there. The closing balance of one day is the opening balance of the following day. The rule is the same for room statistics. The number of rooms, persons, and dollar income from yesterday's close is increased by today's arrivals and decreased by today's departures. The values determined by the day audit's approach should be the same as those counted by the night audit.

Occasional changes that do not involve arrivals or departures are also added in or subtracted out. These might be room count changes (guest shifts from a three-room suite to a single room), house count changes (a spouse departs from a two-person occupancy with a single folio), or rate changes (previous rate was in error and subsequent nights are charged less). The simple mathematics is illustrated so:

| | Room Count | House Count | Room Income |
|---|---|---|---|
| Opening balance | 840 | 1062 | $174 200 |
| + Arrivals | 316 | 391 | 80 100 |
| = Total | 1156 | 1453 | $254 300 |
| − Departures | 88 | 122 | 16 400 |
| = Total | 1068 | 1331 | $237 900 |
| ± Changes | +6 | −2 | +1730 |
| = Closing balance | 1074 | 1329 | $239 630 |

**THE CITY HOTEL, ANYWHERE, CANADA**                                    Page 1
03/16    Night Auditor's Report

| SALES | | ROOM STATISTICS | |
|---|---|---|---|
| Rooms | $12 900.00 | Total Rooms | 320 |
| Coffee Shop | 1 524.80 | House Use | –0– |
| Steak House | CLOSED | Out of Order | –0– |
| Cap'tn Bar | 896.00 | Complimentary | –0– |
| Telephone | 990.76 | Permanent | 2 |
| Laundry | 100.51 | Room Count | 180 |
| Total Sales | $16 412.07 | Vacant | 140 |
| | | House Count | 210 |

| Other Charges: | |
|---|---|
| Cash Advance | 987.76 |
| Taxes Payable | 540.00 |
| Transfers | 693.15 |
| | $18 632.98 |

| ACCOUNTS RECEIVABLE | | ROOM RATIOS | |
|---|---|---|---|
| Opening Balance | $44 651.07 | % Occupancy | 56.3 |
| Charges | 18 632.98 | % Double Occupancy | 16.7 |
| Total | $63 284.05 | Average Daily Rate | $71.67 |
| Credits | 950.00 | RevPar | $40.31 |
| Closing Balance | $62 334.05 | | |

**Room Statistics** Both the night auditor's report to the manager and the income auditor's daily report to the manager contain statistics. Statistics are merely special ways of
grouping data in an orderly and usable manner. Statistics are the facts expressed in dollars, cents, or numbers. For example, instead of itemizing

| Guest A | Room 597 | $150 |
|---|---|---|
| Guest B | Room 643 | $130 |
| Guest C | Room 842 | $160 |

and so on, one might say that there are 220 guests in 189 rooms paying a total of
$27 198. A great deal of information has been grouped, classified, and presented to
become a statistic.

Taking the next step, these room figures are expressed in ratios, which are more
meaningful than the simple statistic. So, the 189 rooms sold are expressed in relation to the number of rooms available for sale, 270. The result is a percentage of
occupancy, a mathematical expression of how many rooms were sold in relation to
how many could have been sold. The occupancy percentage is a widely quoted figure

## The Hand Transcript

The PMS accumulates a running total of departmental charge sales as each sale takes place. The manual system waits until night to obtain the same totals. Auditors use a *daily transcript of accounts receivable* to distribute folio posting into separate columns. Each column represents the charge sales earned by a particular department. Once separated, the total sales of each department, obtained from the departmental control sheets (see Chapter 10), can be compared to the total sales posted to all folios, obtained from the appropriate column of the transcript. "Once separated" is the operative phrase.

Let's review the steps of the manual audit. The night auditors post all vouchers that arrive before the closeout hour. They record room rates and taxes on each folio. They add the folios and carry the balances forward (see Exhibit 13-1). Next comes the transcript.

Each folio is removed from the well and copied in room-number sequence onto a large spreadsheet, the transcript (Exhibit 13-10). The horizontal lines of the folios (room, food, beverage, spa, etc.) appear as vertical columns on the transcript. This procedure separates the charges of each folio. Doing so allows the capture of the folio totals by departments.

**The Premise** When all folios, including the day's departures, are copied onto the transcript—and that may take several transcript sheets—the night audit is back to the basic premise: Do the totals of the columns, which are the sum of the postings to the individual folios, agree to the charges originating in the departments, as shown on the control sheets?

Although the form of the control sheet differs somewhat in the several departments (in some instances, only the cash register tape is available), the method of proving departmental charges is identical department to department.

Vouchers from the various departments arrive at the desk all during the day. After being posted, each voucher is marked to lessen the chance of duplicating the charge. Next, the cheques (vouchers) are sorted by departments—a job made easier with different colours for each department—and filed into pigeonholes. There they remain for the night auditor, who totals them on an adding machine. The adding machine tape is then attached to the pile of vouchers.

Three different totals are available to the auditor for each department:

1. The total derived from the departmental control sheet. Each time a guest charges a departmental service to the folio, the departmental cashier makes an entry on the control sheet. At the end of the day, this sheet is totalled and forwarded to the night auditor.

2. The total on the adding machine tape of the individual vouchers, which have arrived at the desk one at a time. These are the communicative devices between the departmental cashier and the front-office billing clerk.

3. The total posted to the folio for that department. This total is the sum of the postings made to the folios. The auditor gets that value from the departmental column of the transcript.

If the system is in balance, the departmental control sheet (which records the event) has a total equal to the tape of the vouchers (which communicate the event) and to the sum of the folios (the ultimate record of the event). If the three totals agree, the auditors move to the next department. There, the three comparisons are made again.

and one discussed as early as Chapter 1. Using the illustration, the percen
occupancy is

$$\frac{\text{number of rooms sold (room count)}}{\text{number of rooms available for sale}} = \frac{189}{270} = 70\%$$

A frequent companion to the percentage of occupancy computation is the
daily rate (ADR). Both ratios appear in the night auditor's report to the manage
per occupied room, as this figure is sometimes called, is the income from roo
divided by the number of rooms sold.

$$\frac{\text{room income}}{\text{number of rooms sold (room count)}} = \frac{\$27\ 198}{189} = \$143.90$$

A similar computation, RevPar, once called *sales per available room*, is der
dividing room income by the number of rooms available for sale rather than
actual number of rooms sold.

$$\frac{\text{room income}}{\text{number of rooms available for sale}} = \frac{\$27\ 198}{270} = \$100.73$$

The fourth most frequently cited ratio in the manager's daily report is the p
age of double occupancy. Double occupancy is the relationship of rooms occu
more than one guest to the total number of rooms occupied. That is what the
ing ratio expresses:

$$\frac{\text{number of guests} - \text{number of rooms sold}}{\text{number of rooms sold}} = \frac{220 - 189}{189} = 16.4\%$$

Having finished the audit with the preparation of the night auditor's report to th
ager, the night auditor lays aside the pencils and erasers—or more likely, rubs so
shoulders from working at the keyboard—and, at the end of the shift, goes home t

The following discussion explains the pencil-and-paper audit using a han
script. The content is more historical than contemporary. Readers may choose t
the housekeeping material in Chapter 3 and then skip ahead to the chapter sun

# Reconciling Using a Hand Audit

The purpose of the manual night audit (by hand with pencil and paper) is the s
the purpose of the computerized audit. Each aims to validate folio balanc
accounts receivable, and to verify simultaneously the accurate posting of depart
sales. (Those are charge sales; cash sales do not pass through the night audit.)

Property management systems record the two events simultaneously.
accounts receivable guests buy services (food, beverage, spa, etc.), the PMS r
(posts) the charges on the guest's folio. That posting simultaneously accum
the value of the service with similar sales made to other guests. Not so with p
and-paper systems. When a departmental charge arrives at the front desk by v
a voucher, it is posted to the guest's folio only. There is no means of accumu
all charges made by all guests to that particular department. That must awa
manual night audit.

The manual night audit proves that the total accounts receivable sales in
department (food, beverage, spa, etc.) is the same as the total charged on all folios
work is done with the hand transcript (see Exhibit 13-10).

**The Search** The audit begins in earnest when any one of the values fails to reconcile. If two of the three agree, the search concentrates on the unequal total. There are several likely causes.

Mathematical mistakes account for a very large portion of the errors. The major ones—slides, transpositions, and additions—were explained earlier in the chapter.

A control sheet total larger than the other two totals suggests a voucher (cheque) was lost en route from the department to the desk. It was never posted. Had the voucher been posted and then lost, the voucher total would be the smallest of the three.

Sometimes several columns of the transcript (food and beverage, for example) are smaller than the corresponding control sheets and vouchers, which are in agreement. Most likely a folio was stuck in the well and never appeared on the transcript. Such an omission affects several departments. Simple oversights like this seem less simple in the early morning hours. Then, a cheque omitted from the departmental control sheet or a voucher filed before it was posted means long minutes of searching by the weary auditor.

Vouchers posted to the correct department but to the wrong guest account will not be evident to the auditor. All three totals will agree even though the wrong guest account is charged. This is not so with the reverse situation—when the charge is made to the proper folio but posted to the wrong department. Let's use a food-and-beverage example again. Assume that a restaurant charge appears on the transcript in the beverage column. (The error might originate with the clerk's original folio posting, or the auditors might mistakenly copy from the folio to the wrong transcript column.) The food column total of the transcript would be smaller than the voucher and control sheet totals, which would be in agreement. The total of the beverage column is the clue to the error. That total will be larger than the voucher and control sheet totals by the same difference as the restaurant column was smaller.

One error special to the manual audit is particularly difficult to find. It occurs when the original voucher is incorrectly posted by the desk. The charge is recorded on the folio of a stayover guest but in a previous date's column. That's what would happen if the $6 bar charge in Exhibit 13-1 had been posted in the October 5 (10/5) column instead of in the October 6 (10/6) column. The figure never makes it to the transcript because it doesn't even appear as that day's business. Transcript totals that are smaller than voucher and control sheet totals highlight the problem. Finding it requires the auditor to sort vouchers by room-number sequence and compare each voucher to the transcript column, which is also by room-number sequence. Matching vouchers and transcript entries uncovers the mistake.

Finding and correcting errors is difficult because manual audits have numerous flubs. Mistakes are compounded, so simple column differences are often no clue at all.

It's easy to forget that reconciling the three balances is not the purpose of the audit. Reconciling balances is only a means to the end. As each error is uncovered, the record must be corrected. Either the folio is changed or departmental sales are restated, or both. Making the corrections ensures the guest of an accurate billing and determines the exact revenues of each department. As errors are uncovered, corrections are made and the audit moves to the next department.

**Proving Room Charges** Room charges originate at the front desk. That's different from other departmental charges (food, beverage, spas, etc.), which originate some distance from the desk. Vouchers are not needed to communicate room charges, so there is no departmental control sheet. The room columns of the transcript (income, occupancy, and house count—columns 6, 2, and 3 of Exhibit 13-10) are tested against the room rack, not against vouchers and control sheets.

Basic information that appears on the folios, and thus eventually on the transcript, is identical to that contained in the room rack. Both the rack and the hand-prepared folio have their origins in the same registration card. That duplication enables the auditors to prove the three transcript columns from the room rack. A *room count sheet*, which is a manual version of the computerized *room status list*, is prepared from the room rack (see Exhibit 13-11). This form goes by other names, including *daily rooms report* or *night clerk's report*. From the room count sheet, the auditor obtains a list of occupied rooms, the number of persons in each room, and the rate charged. Grand totals from the room count sheet are compared to grand totals on the transcript, columns 2, 3, and 6.

**Balancing the Transcript's Mathematics** Property management systems monitor their own mathematics, but a manual, pencil-and-paper transcript requires a mathematical check of additions and subtractions. Cross footing, which is adding horizontally across the transcript totals, ensures the mathematical accuracy of all lines of the transcript. A review of the several steps in the manual audit will explain why cross footing works.

*Step 1:* The night auditor posts room charges and taxes to the folios.

*Step 2:* The folios are totalled and the balances carried forward to the next day.

*Step 3:* Folios are copied onto the transcript. Within the figures are errors created by steps 1 and 2 and errors made during the day by the desk cashiers. Among the mathematical errors will be slides and transpositions, inaccurate figures, oversights, duplications, and mistakes in addition and subtraction. The audit is designed to uncover all of these errors.

*Step 4:* The total of each transcript column is proved against other documents, as explained earlier, chiefly control sheets, vouchers, cash sheets, and the room count sheet. Corrections are made on the transcript and on the folio as errors are uncovered. This verification ensures the mathematical accuracy of all departmental columns, which are vertical columns 6 through 19, except column 16 (see Exhibit 13-10).

*Step 5:* The opening balance columns, vertical columns 4 and 5, are now verified. Unlike columns 6 to 15, columns 4 and 5 are not income columns, so there are neither control sheets nor vouchers. The opening balance of each folio is the guest's cumulative debt, carried forward from yesterday. Therefore, the opening balances of today (columns 4 and 5, debit and credit) are compared to the closing balances of yesterday, yesterday's transcript columns 21 and 22.

  The guest goes to bed the previous night owing columns 21 and 22 of yesterday's transcript and awakens the following morning owing the same exact amounts, now reflected in columns 4 and 5 of the new day. If today's opening balance does not agree with yesterday's closing balance—perhaps a folio has been left off today's transcript—a search begins for the discrepancy.

*Step 6:* Cross foot (horizontally add) the totals of columns 6 to 15 to obtain a value. If the transcript is in balance, that value will equal the total of vertical column 16. This can be understood by doing the very same thing on any one horizontal line. Columns 6 to 15 on any horizontal line must equal column 16 of that line. Therefore, cross footing the grand totals of columns 6 to 15 should equal the sum obtained by vertically adding column 16. (The total should equal the sum of its parts.)

  If the sum of all columns does not equal the total of column 16, there is an error on one or more of the horizontal lines, which is, of course, someone's folio.

[That folio was added by the night auditor (step 2) and copied onto the transcript (step 3). Obviously, it was added or copied incorrectly.] Each horizontal line must be cross footed until the mathematical error or errors that contributed to the total error are uncovered. Once uncovered, column 16 of that line will be changed, and since that line represents a folio—the line of figures was copied from the folio—the folio itself must also be corrected.

*Step 7:* Verify the three credits. Previous discussions have stressed the three methods of settling folios: cash, allowances, and transfers. Credit column 17 is the cash settlement and that transcript total is compared to the receipts reported on the cashiers' front-office cash sheets. (Similarly, disbursements on those sheets must agree to the cash disbursement column, column 13 of Exhibit 13-10.)

Column 18, allowances, is compared to the sum of the allowance vouchers granted at the desk that day. Column 19 is the most common credit, since it includes credit card transfers. It is tested against column 14, transfer debits, because transfer credits and debits must always equal. Since most of column 19's transfers (transfers credit) are to the city ledger, balancing with column 14 (transfers debit) requires that the cumulative balance of the city ledger also be reported on the transcript. Exhibit 13-10 shows the equality, but the city ledger is abbreviated at the bottom of the exhibit.

Column 20, which is blank in Exhibit 13-10, is missing on many transcripts. It might be used for advance deposit credits if the hotel's clientele commonly used them, but that's very rare. More likely, it would be used to total credit columns 17, 18, and 19. As such, it would represent the sum of all credits as column 16 represents the sum of the day's debits (charges).

*Step 8:* Cross foot and mathematically balance the entire transcript. First, obtain the net opening balance by subtracting column 5, opening credit balance, from column 4, opening debit balance. To that difference add the total of column 16, which was tested by step 6. These total charges are next reduced by payments (credits), the sum of columns 17, 18, and 19 (or perhaps column 20; see step 7). The result is the net amount owed by accounts receivable.

The transcript is a summary of accounts receivable, a summary of folios. The closing balance represents the total amount that all accounts receivable owe the hotel at the close of the day. It's possible for the hotel to owe one or more guests temporarily, so some lines (folios) will have credit balances, probably as a result of advanced deposits. For two different examples, see column 2 (10/6) of Exhibit 13-1 and the third horizontal line of Exhibit 13-10, column 22.

*Step 9:* Vertical addition is easier to visualize than horizontal cross footing. It's just a more traditional way to do the mathematics. Then the proof, or the formula as it is sometimes called, looks like this (see Exhibit 13-10, line 2):

| | |
|---|---:|
| Opening balance, column 4 minus 5 (debit minus credit) | $63.60 |
| + Charges and services used by guests, column 16 (debits) | 39.60 |
| − Payments made by guests, columns 17 to 19 (credits) | –0– |
| = Closing balance, column 21 minus 22 (debit minus credit) | $103.20 |

The closing balance is the cumulative balance of guests' debt to the hotel and is a debit balance.

The math can also be done by having column 16 represent the running total (see Exhibit 13-10, line 1). Then the formula would look different:

| | |
|---|---:|
| Opening balance, column 4 minus 5 (debit minus credit) | $19.00CR |
| + Charges and services used by guests, columns 6 to 15 (debits) | 89.00DR |
| = Total, column 16 (cumulative debit balance before payments of the day) | 70.00DR |
| – Payments made by guests, column 17 to 19 (credits) | –0– |
| = Closing balance, column 21 minus 22 (debit minus credit) | 70.00 |

The result of the two approaches is the same. The difference is the handling of column 16. Some auditors use column 16 to reflect only the day's debits, as the first formula illustrates. Other auditors use column 16 to reflect the cumulative balance, including the balances of yesterday, the second illustration. Whichever is selected reflects the procedure used on the folios because the transcript is a copy of the folios.

## Summary

Accounts receivable, what guests owe the hotel, grow larger or smaller as guests buy new services or pay down debt. Hotels verify the balances of these accounts receivable (front-office folios) nightly. That procedure is known as the night audit. The audit provides a snapshot of values at the closeout hour—midnight, more or less—of each hotel's day.

Since every accounting transaction has equal debits and credits, each service purchased or debt payment made has an offsetting record. The offset is an equal and opposite entry. Two things happen if, for example, a guest charges a bar drink to the folio. The guest owes more and the bar earned more. An audit focusing on the accuracy of the guest's debt (account receivable) must obviously consider the value of the bar charge. The night audit is designed to prove that each transaction was recorded on a guest folio and that each folio entry is accounted for by some transaction.

Cash sales in the various outlets (restaurants, lounges, and gift shops, for example) do not affect accounts receivable. Only charge sales appear on folios. Cash sales are combined with charge sales by the income (or day) auditors, and the total is reported on the daily report to the manager. Night auditors report charge sales, but only charge sales, in the night auditor's report to the manager.

Hotels maintain a cumulative value of receivables, tracking them just as they inventory other assets—cans of peas, for example. The opening balance of accounts receivable is increased by guest purchases and decreased by guest payments. This closing balance becomes the start of the next day's computation. Thus comes a rolling balance of receivables: some days larger, some days smaller.

Computerized property management systems (PMSs) have replaced manual paper-and-pencil night audits. The result has been improved speed and accuracy both at the desk and during the audit, but especially when posting nightly room charges. Property management systems have done the job so well that additional tasks have been added to what started out as a bookkeeping system. Other technological linkups are being added as the industry adopts a standardized system, Hospitality Information Technology Integration Standards (HITIS). Chapter 14 enlarges on the increasing capacity of the PMS and hints of robotics yet to come.

## Questions and Problems

1. Explain how the three backup reports discussed in the section "Downtime Reports" would be used in the event of a computer malfunction.

2. A guest checks in at 4:30 A.M. on Tuesday, January 8. Under hotel policy, the guest is to be charged for the room night of Monday, January 7. The closeout hour of Monday, January 7, was 12:30 A.M. (on January 8) and the room charge postings were handled automatically by the PMS at approximately 3 A.M. that morning. The room rate is $72 and the tax is 5 percent; no other charges were incurred. Sketch a computer-prepared folio as it would appear when the guest departs on Wednesday, January 9, at 10 A.M. Identify each posting by day and hour and briefly explain who made which posting.

3. **Given**

| | |
|---|---|
| Rooms occupied | 440 |
| Rooms vacant | 160 |
| Total rooms sales | $32 330 |
| House count | 500 |

**Required**

| | |
|---|---|
| The percentage of occupancy | _____ |
| The percentage of double occupancy | _____ |
| ADR | _____ |
| RevPar | _____ |

4. Use Exhibits 13-3 and 13-10, and identify your answers by room numbers.

   (a) Which guests, if any, arrived today?

   (b) Which guests, if any, had advance deposits?

   (c) Which guests, if any, checked out today?

   (d) Which guests, if any, used credit cards at departure?

   (e) Which guests, if any, had amounts due from the hotel?

5. The discussion on reservations reports cites a central reservations report that includes fees. Explain who pays what fees and to whom. About how much might those fees be? (Refer to earlier chapters if necessary.)

6. Is the following transcript in balance? If not, what error or errors might account for the discrepancy? What percentage of sales tax is being charged in this community?

| | |
|---|---|
| Allowances | $ 100.00 |
| Telephone | 670.70 |
| Transfers to | 395.05 |
| Rooms | 9072.00 |
| Cash advance | 444.25 |
| Debit transfer | 395.50 |
| Beverage | 1920.00 |
| Credit card charges | 14 482.07 |
| Cash | 10 071.22 |
| Closing balance | 3670.41 |
| Opening balance | 48 341.50 |
| Rooms tax | 725.76 |
| Food | 3000.10 |
| Closing balance | 43 007.33 |
| Opening balance | 185.00 |
| Total charges | $64 384.81 |

## CASE STUDY

### Working the Night Audit

Jim began his first solo night audit shift with a combination of excitement and anxiety in the 200-room hotel where he had started his hotel career after graduating from a well-known travel and tourism program. He had begun on the front desk, and being a night auditor was the next logical career step as he eyed the future position of front-office manager, either at this property or at one of the chain's other hotels.

On this particular night, the hotel was overbooked. During his night audit training, Jim had learned that this was a common occurrence at this particular hotel, as the front-office manager pushed for 100 percent occupancy each night. In fact, on some nights the hotel ran over 100 percent occupancy as it sold some guaranteed reservations to walk-ins and later collected payment for no-show guarantees, even though their rooms had been sold. Although, the hotel had had some complaints from walked guests whose guaranteed reservations were not held, the general manager seemed to support this position of overbooking and bragged to his peers and superiors about running over 100 percent occupancy.

At 2 A.M., with all of the rooms in the hotel occupied and two guaranteed reservations still to come, Jim felt somewhat confident that he would not have to walk anyone. The evening shift had done a diligent quality check on these reservations; they were not VIPs or regulars, and they had been made many months previously.

Suddenly, the lobby doors opened and in walked an overbooked night auditor's worst nightmare: a newlywed couple with a guaranteed reservation. Jim pondered his next step.

1. Do you agree with the overbooking policy at this hotel? How would you change or refine it?

2. If you were Jim, who would you talk to about your feelings out of concern for yourself and for the hotel's guests?

3. How would you change the information-gathering process in accepting a reservation so that Jim and the other front-office staff would know that a reservation was for newlyweds?

## Notes

1. The AH&LA has been developing integration standards in co-operation with several large chains, notably Holiday and Microsoft. Vendors who adopt the Hospitality Information Technology Integration Standards (HITIS) offer systems that interface with all others who comply with HITIS. Hotels that specify HITIS in their bid solicitations will enjoy reduced risks, lower costs, and savings in installation time. The first set of standards is the interface between POS and PMS.

2. Cendant Corporation is installing chain-mandated property management systems free of charge in all franchise properties because it believes that 60 percent of hotels at the mid-tier or lower levels operate with only racks, cigar boxes, and cash registers. *Lodging Hospitality,* June 1998, pp. 26, 28. (Because the authors concur, this edition of *Check-in, Check-out* continues to include sections on the hand-prepared folio and audit.)

3. *CKC Report,* May 1988, p. 14.

## Weblinks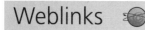

American Hotel & Lodging Association
**www.ahla.com**
InterContinental Hotels Group
**www.ihgplc.com**

Cendant Corporation
**www.cendant.com**

# Chapter 14 Property Management System Interfaces

## Learning Objectives

After reading this chapter, you will be able to do the following:

1. **Understand the history, application, and recent developments of integrated call accounting systems.**

2. **Identify the changes in room-locking devices and categories of locking systems.**

3. **Understand the operation of and uses for other common guest and property management system interfaces.**

From wireless hand-held terminals and ASP software at the front desk to high-speed Internet access and improved smart-card door lock security in the guest room, the industry is experiencing nothing less than a revolution in lodging technology applications. Successful managers are necessarily adding another skill to their laundry list of tasks and abilities. Along with customer service, resource management, industry and company public relations, employee relations, and the like, today's managers also need to be techno-savvy users and investors.

The hospitality industry is maturing in its use of and investment in technology. What used to be considered "technology for the sake of technology" has changed over the last few years. As revenues are negatively affected by stiff competition and increasing use of the Internet, energy and related operating costs continue to rise, and profits are squeezed at every property, hotel operators need to make the most out of every dollar invested in technology.

As such, industry experts are generally advising managers to maximize their existing technologies before looking and investing elsewhere. This advice is especially appropriate for novice managers who have unrealized potential residing on their existing software applications. Talking with current providers about enhanced capabilities related to their property management, call accounting, energy management, electronic locking, and other interfaced systems is an important first step toward saving money and maximizing efficiencies.

Additional recommendations suggest that any new technological application must ultimately affect the guest. Technologies visible to the guest or those that provide a higher level of service should top any list when investment dollars are scarce. In addition to affecting the guest experience, new applications should enhance revenues or boost bottom-line profits. And stand-alone applications are out of favour—new technologies must interface with existing applications and provide some level of synergy to their current use.

This chapter offers a look at some of the major categories of software and hardware applications found at almost any hotel in North America.

# Integrated Call Accounting Systems

Not so many years ago, hotel operators viewed guest room telephones as profit centres. The in-room telephone was a convenience for which the guest was expected to pay. In order to stay in touch with the office, home, family, and friends, the guest depended on the in-room guest telephone.

Today, with close to 65 percent of all business travellers carrying a laptop computer, the in-room telephone is more than just something to talk through. Unfortunately, many hoteliers have not understood this subtle change in its role, so not all hotel guests are getting what they need inside the room. What they need is a connectivity solution—what they get is an old-fashioned telecommunications solution. We are witnessing that change in purpose and product across the industry today.

With the prevalence of wide-range cellular phones and discounted long-distance calling cards, hotels are lucky if the guest even touches the in-room telephone. They'll use it to call another in-house department, another guest room, or maybe even a toll-free access number, but certainly they are not using the in-room telephone to the extent (and profitability) of yesteryear.

To understand the dynamics of in-house PBX and guest room telephone departments today, let's take a look at the evolution of the guest room telephone.

Telephones have been used in hotel rooms since the first were installed in New York City's Netherland Hotel in 1894.[1] Initially, they were manual systems requiring hotel operators to physically connect incoming analog signals via a PBX switchboard system. In 1930, the New Yorker hotel employed 92 manual switchboard telephone operators. That was expensive labour, but full-service hotels correctly viewed the telephone department as a crucial service, and the labour cost was usually offset by telephone department profits.

Years later, manual telephone switchboards gave way to automated call accounting systems, which not only route calls automatically, but identify long-distance and access charges for outgoing calls and interface the entire system with the hotel's property management system (PMS). Automated call accounting systems (CAS) allow a hotel like the New Yorker (today, it is the Ramada Inn & Plaza New Yorker Hotel) to reduce its telephone operator workforce from a high of 92 in 1930 to just 9 operators today.

## Communications Architecture

The CAS, energy management system (EMS), and electronic locking system (ELS) are the three most common interfaces that operate in conjunction with the PMS. Although such systems can readily stand alone, the synergies gained through an interface with the PMS are so great that almost all hotels (especially larger properties) have such interfaces. In-room movies or entertainment, self-check-in and self-check-out systems, in-room safes, and in-room minibar or beverage units are additional examples of PMS interfaces.

In most cases, each of these interfaced systems stands alone with its own processing capabilities. The interface or connection between the stand-alone system (for example, the

EMS) and the PMS provides an uninterrupted flow of guest information. An EMS interface, for example, allows the front-desk PMS to monitor room activity, shut off heating systems and non-essential lighting in unoccupied rooms, and adjust water temperatures as a function of occupancy. Although the EMS is a complete system with its own input, output, and processing, it functions better with a communication interface to the PMS.

**Uniform Connectivity** The history of interface connectivity is one of hit and miss, trial and error. In the 1970s, there were close to 100 vendors of PMSs and numerous manufacturers of point-of-sale (POS) systems, CASs, back-office accounting systems, and guest history databases.

There are plenty of horror stories about hotel operators who spent thousands of dollars on software programming to get one system to electronically interface with another. Many times, however, the hotel was left with a dysfunctional system. Downtime would be common, the interface would slow the processing speed of each system, and valuable data would be lost between the source system and the PMS. This last problem was the worst of all, because hotel revenue (say, from a CAS) was forever lost between systems!

The problem of incompatible interfaces is gradually being eradicated with today's state-of-the-art technologies. Practically every PMS has the capacity to interface with almost every auxiliary system. Indeed, if a property has a stand-alone system that has never been previously interfaced to any brand of PMS, the PMS vendor will often provide free interface software programming. This is a marketing approach many PMS vendors use to enable them to add another system to their list of compatible products. This has been so successful that there are few PMS system–auxiliary system incompatibilities anymore.

New properties have the best of all worlds. Technology managers can choose various interface systems (CAS, EMS, etc.) based on the beneficial synergy each may offer (price, support, guest history, or some other operational feature) without being overly concerned about the interface compatibility between systems.

**Standardization** The lodging industry, unlike other industries, has had less success bringing standardization to market. The problem is that standardization is only as strong as the number of vendors who comply voluntarily. In fact, since 1994, three separate attempts have been made to bring standardization to the lodging industry. In 1994, the Integrating Technology Consortium (ITC) was created. In 1996, Microsoft started the Windows Hospitality Interface Standards (WHIS) initiative. And in 1997, the American Hotel & Lodging Association (AH&LA) convened the Hospitality Industry Technology Interface Standards (HITIS) committee.

Once HITIS is fully introduced, it will become the standard for industry purchases of technological hardware and software. By joining the voluntary consortium, vendors will be entitled to promote their products as complying with industry standards. That's a powerful message because hoteliers who purchase non-complying products would be at risk.

**Data Browsing** Standardization may reach the industry from an unusual direction; it may be market driven. The increasing consolidation of major chains, which we noted in Chapter 1, has accelerated the standardization of PMSs. How long this trend will continue is hard to know, but the results are already evident. In terms of technological capacity, the hospitality industry is quite mature. Hundreds of millions of dollars have been invested year after year to ensure that individual and chain properties are wired. They have successfully automated every stage from check-in to check-out. That's the problem—too much "data" but not enough "information."

The successful competitor of the future will be the chain that strategically uses guest history information (generated by the PMS and its interfaces) and turns it into worthwhile and marketable information. To that end, a standardization of PMS systems makes good sense. Chains have an easier time browsing warehoused data (corporate data browsers are usually Internet-based) when each property in the organization stores information in a like manner—standardization.

Cendant, the world's largest franchising organization (Amerihost Inns, Days Inn, Fairfield, Howard Johnson, Knights Inn, Ramada, Super 8, Travelodge, Villager Lodge, and Wingate Inns), implemented a $75 million standardization program across all properties several years ago. The new standardized property management system—at no charge to the individual franchisees—replaced more than 60 different PMS systems in use chain-wide at that time.

Once the standardized systems are installed, the parent organization will uniformly be able to

- ensure that all revenues are reported accurately;
- browse data at the property, regional, national, and international levels;
- display like-rooms inventory screens and last-room availability information to central reservationists
- create central databases for warehousing such programs as guest history, frequent-guest and frequent-flier programs, corporate and group activity, and travel agent accounts.

## A Brief History of Hotel Telephone Service

Until the mid-1980s, Bell Canada held a monopoly on hotel public branch exchange (PBX) systems. At that time a hotel was forced to rent PBXs and phones from Bell at a high monthly rate, and the hotel never owned the equipment. In the mid-1980s, government deregulation of telecommunications started to change this. Companies such as Mitel offered better technology than Bell. A hotel could install a Mitel system, which could be financed over a five-year period, and the monthly cost would be less than the monthly rental of the Bell system. At the end of the five years, the hotel owned the system. This new system provided direct dial from guest rooms, and the technology allowed for room status update by room attendants to the front desk by simply dialling codes through the phone. A printer behind the front desk provided updated room status information.

In Canada, telephones have always been a cost centre for the hotel. Adding a surcharge to long-distance calls or charging for local calls does not come close to offsetting the cost of the telephone infrastructure.

**Historical Billing Procedures** Before automation, the hotel's operator, who dialled the local call, completed the guest's telephone request. Long-distance numbers were passed on to the telephone company operator, who dialled that connection. The front office posted to the guest folio from a voucher forwarded by the hotel's telephone operator. Local calls were billed at a fixed amount per call. The telephone company called in long-distance charges after the call was completed.

**Long-Distance Billing** Semi-automation came first to long-distance billing. The first development allowed guests to bypass the hotel operator and dial the telephone company's long-distance operator directly. This system also allowed the telephone company to send room charges directly to the hotel by way of Teletype.

**HOBIC** HOBIC (**Hotel Outward Bound Information Centre**) is an acronym for the telephone company's long-distance network. Even today, HOBIC is the system that guests encounter when they use Bell's traditional service. HOBIC, the workhorse of the precomputerized system is still an option for certain hotels (see Exhibits 14-1 and 14-2).

With HOBIC, the guest direct-dials long-distance calls from the room telephone. The first digit dialled, 8, tells the system that long distance is going through. Digit 1, or digit 0 to get the operator, follows; then comes the number to be called. Zero-digit operator intercepts are for person-to-person calls, third-party calls, credit card calls, and collect calls. The distinction between digit 1 and digit 0 is critical. It dictated the strategy of Bell following deregulation. The pursuit of that strategy accounted in large measure for the appearance of the alternative operator services (AOS).

**WATS** Like the entire telecommunications industry, **wide area telephone** (also sometimes transmission) **service (WATS)** has changed since its introduction. The original concept of a flat monthly fee, for which the user could talk indefinitely at any time, has been modified. Charges are now based on increments of time. Rates vary according to the time of day and the day of week. Hundreds of companies have gone into the resale of WATS lines. They buy long-distance lines from Bell at quantity discounts and resell to customers at a lower charge than that of the common carriers.

**Exhibit 14-1 ▶**
When purchasing PBX systems, hotels look for a system life cycle of 8 to 12 years. Therefore, successful vendors (like those shown here) have a history of providing support, software interfaces, and upgrades to current platforms for years and years.

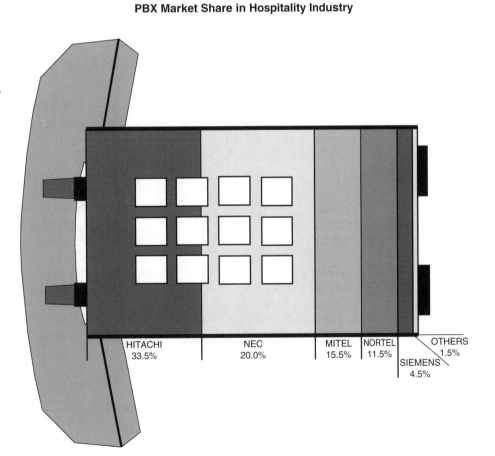

**PBX Market Share in Hospitality Industry**

HITACHI 33.5%   NEC 20.0%   MITEL 15.5%   NORTEL 11.5%   SIEMENS 4.5%   OTHERS 1.5%

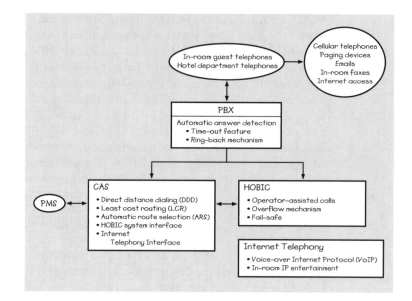

▲
**Exhibit 14-2**
A graphical representation of the call accounting system. Note the increasing role of Internet telephony, in-room faxes, emails, and Internet access.

By the way, the automatic answer-detection function offers two distinct possibilities. The time-out feature (found in older systems) cannot detect when the placed call connects, and it begins charging automatically in 30 to 60 seconds after a standard grace period (usually), even if the placed call is still ringing. In more sophisticated systems, the ring-back mechanism only begins charging after the placed call has actually been answered.

**In-WATS** (incoming toll-free 1-800 or 1-888 numbers) has a critical role in the development of central reservation offices, as explained in Chapter 4. It has become quite fashionable to substitute catchy phrases for traditional telephone numbers in an attempt to retain the number in the user's memory (see Exhibit 14-3).

**Exhibit 14-3** ▶
Here is a baker's dozen of some of the more creative toll-free numbers found in the hospitality industry. Replacing telephone numbers with catchy words and phrases makes the chains' phone numbers more memorable and hopefully creates a higher level of repeat business.

| Company Name | Phone 1-800- |
|---|---|
| Clarion Hotels | Clarion |
| Club Med | Club Med |
| Colonial Williamsburg | History |
| Embassy Suites | Embassy |
| Harrah's (Atlantic City) | 2 Harrah |
| Hilton Hotels | Hiltons |
| Marriott Hotels & Resorts | USA WKND |
| National Car Rental | Car Rent |
| Nikko Hotels International | Nikko US |
| Omni Hotels | The Omni |
| Ramada Hotels | 2 Ramada |
| Renaissance Hotels | Hotels 1 |
| Southwest Airlines | I Fly SWA |

| | ROOM | PLACE CALLED | | | NUMBER | TIME | MIN | TYP | CLASS | RATE |
|---|---|---|---|---|---|---|---|---|---|---|
| A 2-22 | 103 | LOS ANGELES | CA | 213 | 555-7784 | 2245 | 6 | 1 | S | 1.51 |
| A 2-22 | 104 | HUNTITNBCH | CA | 714 | 555-7711 | 1317 | 3 | 1 | K | 1.36 |
| A 2-22 | 107 | WICHITA | KS | 316 | 555-5020 | 0747 | 2 | 1 | B | .43 |
| A 2-22 | 107 | VAN NUYS | CA | 213 | 555-7487 | 0916 | 2 | 1 | K | .97 |
| A 2-22 | 107 | LEWISTON | ME | 207 | 555-6141 | 1628 | 12 | 1 | K | 6.13 |
| A 2-22 | 107 | CHICAGO | IL | 312 | 555-5134 | 1832 | 7 | 1 | S | 1.96 |
| A 2-22 | 107 | CANOGAPARK | CA | 213 | 555-4815 | 1935 | 14 | 1 | S | 3.39 |
| A 2-22 | 108 | PHOENIX | AZ | 602 | 555-4958 | 0810 | 2 | 1 | K | .97 |
| A 2-22 | 111 | ROOPVILLE | GA | 404 | 555-4422 | 0806 | 3 | 1 | K | 1.52 |
| A 2-22 | 111 | NO HOLLYWD | CA | 213 | 555-9540 | 0908 | 1 | 1 | K | .58 |
| A 2-22 | 114 | GREELEY | CO | 303 | 555-5876 | 1750 | 38 | 1 | S | 9.91 |
| A 2-22 | 117 | STPETERSBG | FL | 813 | 555-1411 | 1620 | 4 | 1 | K | 2.21 |
| A 2-22 | 118 | OCILLA | GA | 912 | 555-7464 | 1238 | 1 | 1 | K | .64 |
| A 2-22 | 118 | HUNTITNBCH | CA | 714 | 555-7243 | 1801 | 5 | 1 | S | 1.28 |
| A 2-22 | 125 | CANOGAPARK | CA | 213 | 555-4815 | 1114 | 8 | 1 | K | 3.31 |
| A 2-22 | 125 | CODY | WY | 307 | 555-2245 | 1131 | 5 | 1 | K | 2.34 |
| A 2-22 | 202 | DRAPER | UT | 801 | 555-5093 | 1745 | 3 | 1 | S | .85 |
| A 2-22 | 203 | BOULDER | CO | 303 | 555-1181 | 0902 | 7 | 1 | K | 3.20 |
| A 2-22 | 203 | LONG BEACH | CA | 213 | 555-8832 | 1747 | 8 | 1 | S | 1.98 |
| A 2-22 | 206 | BAMMEL | TX | 713 | 555-7580 | 0811 | 7 | 1 | K | 3.28 |
| A 2-22 | 206 | GREELEY | CO | 303 | 555-7067 | 1723 | 10 | 1 | S | 2.69 |
| A 2-22 | 209 | FORD CITY | PA | 412 | 555-9600 | 1656 | 12 | 1 | K | 4.56 |
| A 2-22 | 210 | LITTLETON | CO | 303 | 555-9999 | 1331 | 2 | 1 | K | 1.05 |

* * * N24 * * *

▲
**Exhibit 14-4**
Printout of long-distance charges generated by the call accounting system. Although this printout was produced in numerical room order, it could just as easily have been printed in chronological order beginning with the first call of the day. Note the shift (A, B, or C), the date, and the room number from which the call was placed. Additionally, this printout (sometimes called an on-the-fly call record) shows location and number called, time of day the call was placed, and duration of the call. The system then evaluates the type and class of call to determine the charge assessed the guest. Also note the 555 exchange used to mask actual telephone numbers—you've probably heard it used in television and movies.

**Out-WATS** has a critical role in call accounting system profitability. Hotels that route guests' long-distance calls over WATS lines may save substantially over normal long-distance costs. These savings may be returned to the guest or are more likely converted into additional hotel profit (see Exhibit 14-4).

## More Recent Developments in Canada

Frustrated hoteliers have been calling for a more cost-effective telephone system. In the past the choice was between direct-dial telephone and fax. Greedy hoteliers caused themselves problems after deregulation by charging exorbitant rates to hotel guests. In many cases, to avoid these charges guests started making calls at less cost on their cellphones. Instead of making more money, hoteliers have seen telephone revenues shrink drastically.

The modern hotelier has to provide Internet, email, cellphones, calling cards, and more. Guest demand for telecommunication services will only continue to increase and be a greater factor in how guests choose where to stay.

Companies such as Conopco and Leduc, Alberta-based OPCOM Hospitality Solutions have been providing some answers. They do it by providing highly responsive call centres across Canada to manage hotel calls and services. The systems share revenue on all operator-assisted calls, provide automated and live operator-assisted calls, and ensure that guest calls for operator assistance are answered promptly. Both of these providers have competitive long-distance rates.

Halifax-based Pacrim Hospitality, a company that owns or manages 35 properties across Canada, recently spent $400 000 on a telephone system for its 323-room Sheraton Calgary. Pacrim uses the Lucent GuestWorks software system, which processes calls and handles messaging. Lucent's latest version allows guests to use Direct Inward Dial (DID) numbers and receive **outside calls** directly to their rooms without intervention from a hotel attendant.

Looking ahead, high-speed wireless promises to further erode telephone revenues. Technology analysts predict in the next few years that full integration of voice, video, and data will become standard in guest rooms. Internet Protocol (IP) telephony promises internal communication, high-speed Internet access, and long-distance calls at a cost much lower than traditional phone lines.

**Emergency 911 Calls**  Another telephone-related issue is the risk caused to the hotel from in-house emergency 911 calls. Many 911 calls that pass through the hotel's PBX systems are routed over normal telephone trunk lines to the public safety answering point (PSAP) assigned to that jurisdiction. If the caller is unable to talk to the PSAP operator, or cannot remember the room number from which he or she is calling, valuable time is lost in the emergency response. That's because the PSAP will only see the name and physical address of the hotel, not the number of the room from which the call is being made. Upon arrival, there may be hundreds of rooms to choose from. Indeed, even if the front desk is able to look up which room made the 911 call, chances are the hotel will not be aware of the emergency until vehicles are pulling up out front. Again, valuable time will be lost.

In this age of increasing technological sophistication, only those hotels boasting a PBX system equipped with enhanced 911 capabilities are safe from potential litigation. With enhanced 911 capabilities, not only will the PSAP be given the guest's room number but the hotel front office and/or security staff will also be alerted to the emergency (see Exhibit 14-5). In many cases, faster hotel staff response time can make a significant difference in the guest's well-being.

**Mandatory and Voluntary System Upgrades**  The hotel industry has begun providing increasing varieties of telephone services to appeal to guests. Sometimes the law mandates such telephone services (as with volume-control features). In other cases, it is as much a marketing decision as anything else. For example, dual lines to data ports may serve corporate hotel guests' needs, but they may represent an unnecessary investment for leisure guests.

**Cordless and Battery-Operated Telephones**  In an effort to differentiate their lodging product, a number of hotel chains (especially extended-stay and all-suite brands) are introducing cordless guest room telephones. During their visit, guests expect all of the comforts of home, including walk-around, cordless freedom when talking on the telephone.

**Exhibit 14-5 ▶**

Feature phones, such as this one from Teledex Corporation, offer safety, convenience, and revenue-generating options to the hotel: Safety because they clearly display the emergency button (especially attractive to hotels with large international markets); convenience because common guest services, marked with appropriate icons, are available at the touch of a button; revenue-generating because some hotels lease telephone buttons to local merchants (proximate restaurants, exercise clubs, and dry-cleaning, for example).

The problem with cordless telephones, however, has been twofold. They are battery-operated, and so the battery needs to be replaced every so often (about every four years). The replacement of the battery is not the time-consuming element. Rather, when the battery is replaced, the telephone requires reprogramming of information. Today's newest telephones feature an on-board computer chip that keeps phone information stored even when the battery wears down.

The other problem with cordless telephones is "crosstalk" and "channel-hopping." You may have experienced similar interference at home if you own more than one cordless telephone. Imagine how exacerbated the problem could be in a hotel with hundreds of cordless guest room telephones operating in a relatively narrow transmission space. Several telecommunications companies have successfully adopted digital spread spectrum technology to avoid such interference. Today, cordless telephones are the latest amenity for new properties and those undergoing extensive guest room renovations!

**Supplemental Guest Services** Some of the most exciting new innovations come in the form of supplemental guest services. Supplemental or *auxiliary* guest services are clearly designed with the guest in mind. They have a positive impact on the perception of quality service by providing the guest with some of the comforts of home or office. Examples of supplemental guest services—commonly viewed as additions to the CAS—include electronic voice messaging, automated attendant services, and automated wake-up systems.

**Electronic Voice Messaging** Guest telephone messages have historically been a cumbersome affair. Some callers wish to leave lengthy messages, operator-transcribed return telephone numbers are often incorrect, and the growing number of international travellers adds a non-English-speaking component to many of the calls. Today's hotels have answered most of these issues with the introduction of electronic voice messaging.

Electronic voice messaging or voice mailboxes are quite similar to the standard answering machine found in a person's home. However, rather than servicing one incoming telephone line, electronic mailbox systems may be capable of handling thousands of extensions. Mailboxes are usually designed to handle hotel executive office extensions as well as guest room telephone lines.

Many systems allow newly arrived hotel guests a chance to record their own personalized messages. This is an especially powerful feature in an international market. Guests can leave customized messages in whichever language they speak, and the hotel does not need to translate their incoming messages.

Furthermore, these systems also allow various hotel departments to prerecord messages. A guest can call the main dining room mailbox and learn the special entree of the night or the hours of operation. Another mailbox might be reserved for use by the concierge staff to promote certain activities in the hotel or across town. The possibilities of such a service are endless.

**Automated Attendant Services** Automated attendant services actually relieve the PBX department from answering the telephone at all. Instead, the caller is asked to select from a series of choices and to press the corresponding telephone digit accordingly.

Automated attendant systems are gaining popularity across the world. Most high-volume telephone centres sport some form of this service. In the hospitality industry, however, there are some guest-service purists who believe that automated attendant systems are too impersonal and mechanical to find a home in such a customer-oriented business. Although these detractors raise a good point, let's remember that practically every national central reservation office currently operates some type of automated attendant system.

**Automated Wake-Up Systems** Automated wake-up systems are consistent with other auxiliary guest services because they both save labour and provide higher levels of customer service. Not only do automated wake-up systems remove the front desk from the repetitive early morning task of phoning each guest room and waking the occupant, they also offer a number of unique features.

Although some automated wake-up systems still require front-desk employees to enter the room number and time of the wake-up call, most systems allow guests to directly input the wake-up time themselves. In addition, most systems produce reports identifying which rooms were called, the time of the calls, and the guest's wake-up status. Wake-up status—call was answered, call was not answered the first time but was eventually answered during one of the routine system call-backs, or phone was never answered—is an important tool for addressing potential guest complaints.

Automated wake-up systems also serve as a unique marketing medium because the groggy guest makes for a wonderful captive audience. In this regard, hotels not only inform guests about the day's weather conditions, they also describe the breakfast specials in the dining room. Some automated wake-up systems even provide an option for guests to design their own personalized wake-up calls!

**Telephone Department Revenues** Telephone system upgrades, cordless guest room phones, and the addition of second or third lines in each room are expensive enhancements for any hotel. But when such investment is made for a department experiencing shrinking revenues, the costs seem even more extravagant. Yet that is exactly what has happened to telephone revenues over the past 10 years.

Historically, telephone department revenues consistently contributed to almost every hotel's bottom line. Representing 3 to 5 percent of gross revenues for the average hotel, any investment in telecommunications paid for itself over time. However, changing guest room telephone use patterns have negatively affected these historical revenues. Here is a broad look at the reasons behind shrinking telephone department revenues and some ideas toward enhancing future profitability.

**Deteriorating Revenues** The average guest room telephone call used to be two to five minutes in duration. Today, with Internet access, email, modem transmissions, and the like, the average corporate phone call lasts 45 to 90 minutes. And with Marriott estimating that 76 percent of all corporate guests carry laptop computers, the problem will only worsen.

The result of this new lifestyle is a growing need for increased hotel telephone capacity. Where one phone line per room was the norm 10 years ago, the trend is to two or even three lines for each guest room (hotels that offer in-room fax machines often provide three separate lines for each room). That is an expensive enhancement.

Guest dialling patterns may be the single biggest culprit causing the deterioration of telephone department revenues. Where guests historically used 0+ dialling to place their calling card or operator-assisted long-distance calls, today that traffic is routed over toll-free lines (no revenue).

This change in dialling patterns has had another negative impact on hotel telephone department bottom lines: increased investment in local trunk lines. Historical trunk configurations no longer serve the modern hotel. Few outgoing calls are long distance, so many long-distance trunks sit idle while toll-free calls are routed through the local telephone company. Because of this new demand for local trunk lines, hotels have experienced increasing trunk congestion and guest dissatisfaction. Guests who simply cannot get a line out of the hotel are forced to wait and try again. And remember, the average corporate telephone call—primarily due to modem use—ranges from 45 to 90 minutes in length! As a result, hotels have found themselves investing in more and more local trunk lines.

**Excessive and Fraudulent Telephone Charges** There are two additional factors not to be overlooked when understanding the deterioration of telephone department revenues. One is the increased use of personal cellular phones. With the introduction of one-rate or no-roaming-fee plans, most corporate guests choose this convenient form of communication when travelling. This goes hand in hand with the second factor leading to reduced guest room telephone usage—the perception that hotel telephone fees are exorbitant.

One guest vacationing at a major resort in Vancouver decided to place a few in-room telephone calls to his home office in Toronto. He called to check his email, chatted a time or two with his boss, and stayed in touch with his secretary. In total, he made seven separate in-room telephone calls to Toronto. The seven calls totalled just 15 minutes. What would you expect to pay for 15 minutes of long-distance calls? Well, upon check-out, this guest was shocked to see his telephone usage totalling $167.00. A mistake? A clerical error? Unfortunately, no. As one expert aptly noted, guest room telephone charges seem to be on par with $8 minibar sodas!

Wyndham International (which has one hotel in Canada, the Wyndham Bristol Place in Toronto) is one chain that understands the average guest's perception that hotels can be unscrupulous when it comes to setting telephone call rates. Wyndham now offers free unlimited local and long-distance calls and free high-speed Internet access to members of its ByRequest guest-recognition program (see Exhibit 14-6).

**Exhibit 14-6** ▶
Taking advantage of least-cost routing technologies affords hotels the unique opportunity of reducing long-distance call costs. Most hotels turn these lower costs into greater profits for their telephone department. Wyndham Hotels & Resorts, however, may have a better idea. Wyndham believes that in an age of increasing scrutiny of corporate travel costs, free local and long-distance calls, high-speed Internet access, faxes, and copies may go a long way toward attracting and retaining valuable customers.

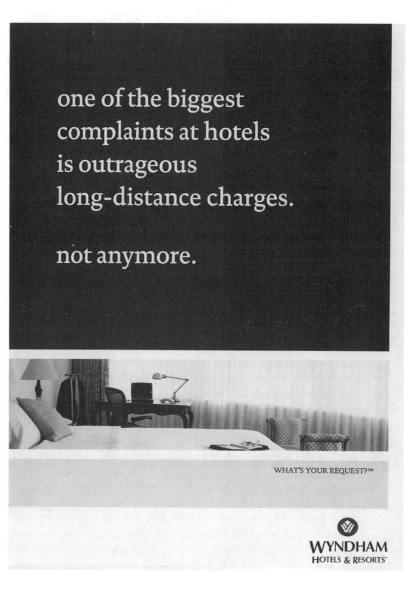

So, who can blame guests for using toll-free calling cards to avoid excessive long-distance charges? Indeed, there is now a company that even helps guests avoid the $1 access fee charged by many hotels for toll-free calls. The company, Kallback, has a unique solution to avoiding such charges: Call its toll-free number but only let the phone ring once, then hang up. Moments later, Kallback's computer will ring you back and enter you into its system—free of any access charge. And you'll see no charge from the hotel for the interrupted single ring. Neat idea!

**A Few Ideas for Enhancing Telephone Department Revenues** The answer to continuing deterioration of telephone revenues is not to simply raise long-distance rates. This was the culprit in the first place. Rather, consider implementing extended call pricing on toll-free, 0+, and local calls. This will generate revenue from those guests who dial a local access number, log on to the Internet, and use their computer for hours on end. Give them a generous period at no charge (say, one hour), but then levy a per-minute fee after that. Of course, such charges are only as good as your in-house disclosure program. Be fair and inform guests about your extended call pricing.

Many other new venues for generating telecommunications revenues are gaining popularity. Certainly, hotels profit from incoming and outgoing fax services, but other options should be considered as well. For example, there is a growing expectation that hotels be able to provide corporate guests with cellular phones for use during their visit. In addition, wireless pagers are also an option. In fact, a number of hotels now provide integrated service from guest room to cellular telephone—after the guest room phone rings for the guest a predetermined number of times, the caller is provided the option of leaving a message or ringing through to the guest's cellular line. Now that's first-class service!

This service is especially worthwhile overseas. Although most corporate guests carry domestic cellular telephones when travelling in Canada, few use their cellular telephones on overseas trips. The idea of renting local cellular service at overseas hotels is catching on and may someday be an expected amenity at higher-end international properties.

**Feature Phones** Today's in-room guest telephones can perform a multitude of functions not generally associated with telephones. These feature phones have met with outstanding approval from hotel guests. Feature phones offer one-button speed dialling to in-house departments or local merchants, who pay for the convenience of a captive audience (see Exhibit 14-5). In addition, they usually offer a hold button and call-waiting function. Such phones are commonly found with a built-in speakerphone, alarm clock, and even an AM/FM radio.

Telephones of a higher (and more expensive) class are commonly called *hard-wired multipurpose phones*. These phones may cost the property $500 or more per unit but are easily justified from an energy-savings standpoint. Hard-wired telephones are available that can regulate temperature levels in the room; control as many as six remote lighting fixtures; turn the television set on, change the channels, and adjust the volume; open and close the curtains; and even change the room status to "do not disturb."

Many hard-wired telephones require the guest to activate the room by inserting a key card in a specially designed slot. When the room is unoccupied, the system automatically disengages most lights, the television, and even heating and air conditioning units, thereby saving the hotel wasted utility costs.

**Internet Protocol Telephony** Aside from generating new methods to raise telephone department revenues, another way to increase net profits is to simply reduce variable costs. Voice-over Internet Protocol (VoIP) offers this approach, to literally reduce variable long-distance and Internet access costs to zero.

We have all heard stories of people making free long-distance telephone calls over the Internet. The technology, however, has not been well accepted by the public. Fraught with problems such as low-quality voice transmissions, poor caller security, and the like, this technology is not popular with individual users. Hotels, however, can use this technology to gain advantage in two ways: They can save money on in-house departmental telephone and Internet use (telephone calls made by employees working on hotel business) and save money on guest room telephone use as well.

What this means for hoteliers is huge cost savings that can either be passed on to guests or used to increase telephone department profits. This technology also integrates email, fax, pagers, and voice mail, allowing hotel guests (and employees) to receive multiple message types over one connection.

Of course, the downside is the initial investment, which represents a large capital outlay for hotels facing lean earnings projections. Still, most major telecommunications companies—Mitel, Nortel, 3Com, Cisco Systems, NEC, and Siemens, to name a few (see Exhibit 14-1)—have been introducing new telephone systems that are VoIP-compatible. According to many experts, it is only a matter of time before most major hotels have this technology in place.

# Guest Room Locking Systems

Without question, today's guest demands far more safety and security than ever before in history. Certain guest markets (for example, corporate female travellers) place hotel security near the very top of their list when selecting a chain or independent property. And guests are not alone in their quest for enhanced security.

Major chains have taken guest security to heart in recent years. A number of chains recommend, and some (such as Hilton Hotels, with its 100 percent electronic locking system compliance in all hotels) require, that electronic security devices be installed in all new construction. Indeed, even the Canadian Automobile Association (CAA) includes guest security protection as part of its property rating system!

Although security involves surveillance, intrusion detection, fire prevention, employee screening, and numerous other concerns, initial efforts have been directed toward lock and key security. It's here that some of the electronic smart switches hold the greatest promise.

## The Room Key Revolution

In recent years, the historical tasks of maintaining key security, tracking lost guest room keys, managing the distribution of master keys, rekeying locks, and inventorying several keys for each of hundreds of rooms have given way to a simple electronic interface. You see, with smart switches, there are no keys to track. The key is disposable or renewable, and each guest gets a new key and a new key combination. With traditional keys, the types that are still used in homes, key loss is staggering. Estimates put the number at one key per room each month. Many hotels have four or five lost keys per day. Lock replacement for Holiday Inns, for example, was pegged at $1 million annually.

Not so many years ago, there was a strong black market for stolen hotel keys (up to $1000 for a master key), and many hotel employees knew about it. Forced entry into guest rooms was almost unknown, because access through stolen, duplicated, or master key blanks was so easy. One group of blitzers (6- to 10-person units) "did" nearly 200 rooms in Anaheim, California, in one morning. And *Los Angeles Magazine* reported the capture of a person who had master keys for 17 hotels.

Those kinds of statistics, and the potential liability they represented, made hoteliers quickly convert to the smart switch electronic locking system (ELS) technology. The first magnetic strip ELS was invented in 1976 by Tor Sornes working for VingCard and installed in North America in 1979 at the Westin Peachtree Plaza hotel in Atlanta, Georgia. The latest locking systems are called RFID (Radio Frequency Identifier) and require no contact, working similar to the remote key fob that unlocks your car.

**Levels of Access** Control of keys begins with an understanding of the type and number of keys available. Most key systems comprise four or five levels of access. Although modern ELSs have changed the format of that access, the terminology and the service performed by each level remain roughly the same as the traditional locking systems of yesteryear.

For the most part, each level of the hierarchy exceeds the level below it. The guest room key level (and the fail-safe level) can access only one room. The next level, the room attendant or housekeeping level, can access an entire wing of rooms. The third level, the general manager or master level, can access the entire hotel property. And the final level, the emergency or E-key level, can access the entire property even when the guest room deadbolt has been activated (see additional discussion related to the deadbolt later in this section).

Although the levels of hierarchy are much the same with both ELS and standard hardware locking systems, ELSs add a new dimension of security. The electronic key card is designed to override and invalidate previous key card combination codes.

For example, Daniel Adams checks into Room 1111 on Monday evening. On Tuesday morning, Adams checks out of the hotel. Because the ELS key card is disposable, he keeps the card as a souvenir for his daughter. Later in the morning, Adams realizes that he has left his wallet hidden in the room. Retrieving the key card from his pocket, Adams is able to enter the room and find his wallet. That's because the hotel front desk has not yet rented Room 1111 to a new guest.

Later in the morning, a room attendant inserts his or her housekeeping key card and enters Room 1111. Although he or she accessed the room after Adams, inserting a housekeeping card in the lock does not invalidate the guest's (Adams') card. That's because the room attendant's card is on a separate level of the hierarchy. At this point, Adams could still access the room. Still later in the day, Room 1111 is rented to Elizabeth Brown. Her insertion of the new guest-level key card into the lock electronically invalidates Adams' card. In fact, Brown's card is designed to invalidate all guest-level key cards with lower code sequences than her own. Similarly, Brown's card can only be overridden with a higher-coded card inserted by the next new guest to check in to Room 1111.

**Microfitted versus Hard-Wired ELS** The Adams/Brown scenario above is generally true for all hotels using microfitted ELSs. It is probably not as true for hotels using more sophisticated hard-wired ELSs. The difference between microfitted and hard-wired is the manner in which the key control centre (the front desk's ELS computer and key card encoder) communicates with each room. With microfitted ELSs, the only way the room lock communicates with the key control centre is through the key card. When an arriving guest inserts a newly written key card, the lock at the guest room door is told to accept this key and any code higher, but to reject all previous key codes.

Microfitted electronic locks are popular because they are less expensive than hard-wired systems. Primarily, they are used in hotel retrofit situations where hard-wiring an existing hotel would make little sense. Refer to "Categories of Locking Systems" later in this chapter.

With a hard-wired ELS, Mr. Adams would likely not have been able to access his room after he checked out. That's because the key control centre is in constant communication with each guest room door lock. After all, there is physical hardware (the hard wire) connecting each guest room door lock to the key control centre (in some cases, locks may use infrared technology to form continual communication without the presence of a hard wire). And because the key control centre is interfaced with the PMS, most guest room keys are invalidated at the time of check-out. At check-out, guests who perhaps left luggage in their room usually have their key codes extended for a brief period of time. Likewise, should Mr. Adams have found his key card invalidated at the guest room door, he needed simply to return to the front desk. The front-desk guest-service representative would have handed him a new temporary or single-access key card. With a temporary key card, he would have been given, say, 15 minutes to return to his room, open the door, and retrieve whatever he had left behind (his wallet).

Hard-wired ELSs are the standard in new hotel construction. That's because so much technology now interfaces with the guest room. And much of this new technology uses the electronic lock's hard-wired feature to connect with the front-desk PMS. Such interfaces as energy management systems, guest room minibars, and in-room safes commonly use hard-wired technology to improve their functionality.

**Online Locking Systems** The trend in coming years will be toward increased integration between other hotel systems and the PMS through the hard-wired ELS. As communication from other systems travels to the PMS via the ELS hard-wire, the system becomes known as an online locking system. Any hard-wired (or those using infrared, radio waves, or pager technology) ELS can be converted to an online system. For many properties, the enhanced capabilities of an online ELS more than compensate for the added cost.

Probably the most valuable enhancement in terms of the hotel's bottom line lies with energy management. Tying EMSs to the guest room door lock allows the system to monitor when the guest is in the room. Certainly, when the room is occupied, all air conditioning, lighting, television, and related functions must be operational. But the moment that the guest leaves the room, many systems can be shut down or reset to an unoccupied energy-savings status. Integrating the EMS through the ELS to the PMS saves the average hotel $10 000 per month or better. A more thorough discussion of the integration of the EMS is provided later in this chapter.

Other benefits of online systems include increased guest-related information. For example, every time a guest enters a certain area (say, the health club), the door-lock card reader automatically sends a record of who accessed the area, the time, and date. This log can provide management with valuable information about the movement of guests in and around the hotel. Online systems also aid housekeeping efficiencies by alerting room attendants when guests depart their rooms. Hotel security is enhanced as well, because the system can warn management when a guest room door has been left open or if there has been forced entry. Management can also track the minute-by-minute whereabouts of all employees who use an electronic key card to access guest rooms and other secured locks.

**Exhibit 14-7 ▶**
Even traditional mechanical locks have improved with technology. This one can easily be rekeyed. Using a special control key, the interchangeable core is quickly removed and replaced with a new one.

**The Guest Room Key Level** The single guest key, which fits a standard lock and deadbolt (see Exhibit 14-7), an electronic lock (see Exhibit 14-8), or a non-electronic lock (see Exhibit 14-9), gives the guest access to the room. In some hotels, the same key that fits the guest room door may also unlock connecting doors between rooms (when such access is warranted), open spa or health club facilities, and even open lobby entrance doors. With electronic locking systems, a single key card can be programmed to open an almost unlimited variety of doors. A meeting planner who wishes to leave a welcoming gift in the rooms of arriving guests, for example, would probably be given one key programmed to access all arriving rooms. The key would have an expiration time on it, so the meeting planner could leave gifts between, say, 2 and 4 P.M., but it would become invalid as guests began arriving after 4 P.M.

Once inside the room, virtually all types of hotel locks (traditional, electronic, or non-electronic) provide guests with deadbolts for added security. However, locking the door from inside sometimes trips a signal, which tells the room attendant that the room is occupied. In this age of enhanced security and concern for potential litigation, such signal devices may be outdated. You see, signal systems of all types—do not disturb signs, lock signals, light systems, room service trays left in the corridor, signals on latches, and message notes on the door—tell the thief as well as the room attendant whether the room is occupied.

**The Fail-Safe Key Level** The second level in the key distribution hierarchy is only found with ELSs. The fail-safe level provides a pre-established option for use during computer

**Exhibit 14-8** ▶

Some guests prefer traditional-looking room keys (possibly, they feel more secure than with a simple plastic key card). Those shown here have a reprogrammable magnetic strip embedded in them. They are really just a variation of the key card. Other, more creative variations are displayed in Exhibit 14-13.

downtime. Most hotels create at least two fail-safe keys for each guest room. Once created, management secures fail-safe keys until they are needed.

When the host ELS computer is down (inoperative), either because of a power outage or a hardware/software operations problem, the hotel resorts to the use of fail-safe keys. Just like a new guest key card, fail-safe keys invalidate previous guest-level key cards. Yet fail-safe keys do not alter the normal sequence of guest-level key codes. They temporarily interrupt the stream of codes, but once the ELS computer is operational again, the new guest-level key card will invalidate the fail-safe key and everything will be back to normal.

Hotels create two fail-safe keys to gain plenty of time. Two fail-safe keys are good for two new sequences. That's at least two days of fail-safe operation. Once the ELS computer comes back online, front-office management will create new backup fail-safe keys, always keeping at least two such keys in storage for another down period.

**The Room Attendant or Pass Key Level** The next level in the key hierarchy is the room attendant level, also known as the housekeeping level, the **pass key** level, the sub master level, the section level, or even the area key level. Each room attendant–level key controls the room attendant's section of the floor, usually 12 to 18 rooms. Since the pass

▲
**Exhibit 14-9**
Non-electronic locking systems use mechanical hardware. As a result, they are less costly than ELSs and require no batteries, electrical connections, or dedicated computers (see Exhibit 14-13). Yet the code of non-electronic locks can still be changed with each new guest key.

key fits no other subset, both the hotel and the individual room attendant are protected. Well-trained employees of every department refuse guests' requests to be admitted to rooms. Pass keys are used for this purpose only after proper authorization is obtained from the desk.

Room attendants must not permit guests without identification—that is, a room key—to enter open rooms where they are working. Similarly, rooms must not be left unlocked if the room attendant is called away before the room is completed. Obviously, then, the room attendant's own keys should not be hung on the cart or left in the door. That's why a plastic ELS key card hung around the room attendant's neck proves both secure and convenient.

**The Master Key Level** The **master key** or general manager level may be next in the key hierarchy. However, depending on the design of the hotel, there are a number of key hierarchy possibilities between the room attendant level and the master level. For example, some properties may wish to create an inspector-level or floor-level key. This level would exceed the room attendant's key (which opens something like 12 to 18 rooms) by opening all rooms on a given floor or section (probably 60 to 100 rooms). One vendor, SAFLOK, currently offers an ELS with 14 separate levels of hierarchy!

Another possibility is an executive housekeeping–level key that would probably open every room in the hotel. The difference between the executive housekeeping level and the general manager or master level is that the executive housekeeper is restricted from access to certain high-security areas. Although the general manager level will access all locks in the hotel, the executive housekeeper may be denied access to such areas as the accounting office, the food and beverage department, and other administrative offices.

**The Emergency Key** The highest level in the hierarchy is the **emergency key** or **E-key** (sometimes called the grand master). Like the general manager–level key, the E-key can access every lock in the hotel. The difference is that the emergency key can access all rooms regardless of lock status. In other words, even when the guest has activated the deadbolt from inside the room, the E-key can still gain access. During periods of extreme emergency—for example, a guest has taken ill and cannot answer the door, or the fire department needs to enter a guest room—the E-key can literally be the difference between life and death!

**Enhanced ELS Security** The loss of guests' personal belongings from their rooms can be traced to three causes: outsiders (intruders), insiders (employees), and the guests themselves. The smart-switch locks of modern technology have affected primarily the outsiders. However, there have been important spin-offs protecting the hotel from insiders and even from guests. Careless guests lose, misplace, forget, and accuse. Dishonest guests manipulate their hotel stays to bring claims against the property or against their own insurance companies.

The director of research and security for the AH&LA maintains that 30 percent of employees are honest, 30 percent are dishonest, and 40 percent must be protected from themselves—as opportunists, they will take advantage of weaknesses in the system.

**ELS Identification Database** ELSs provide the best line of defence against unethical guests, employees, and even outsiders. That is because the ELS is a smart switch capable of communicating critical information to management.

Many a manager has dealt with an upset guest accusing a hotel employee of theft. In some cases, guests are correct about the employee who has wronged them; in other instances, guests are incorrect. Maybe the "stolen" wristwatch was merely misplaced, lost, or never packed in their luggage in the first place.

Answers to such questions and accusations are ready and waiting inside the microprocessor of the ELS. Hotel management need merely download the information to a hand-held computer (or, in the case of a hard-wired ELS, the front-desk computer can access the information) to learn which key cards have accessed the guest's room during the period in question. Most systems hold at least the last dozen key card entries—other systems hold substantially more. In many cases, the ELS key card–access database provides enough information to solve the "crime."

**Distribution Control** Control must be established over the numbers of employees who have legitimate access to keys. That includes all front-office and uniformed services personnel, the housekeeping staff, and the maintenance crews—well over half of all employees in the hotel. Control must be established on the distribution of keys to the vast number of guests who make legitimate demands for access to their rooms.

An earlier discussion pointed out what the room attendants and the housekeeping department must and must not do with keys on the guest room floors. Good key security invariably focuses on the front desk. Clerks must never issue keys without verifying the guest's identity, a procedure that takes but seconds. Still, in the pressure of the rush hours, many keys are issued with abandon. Almost anyone can request a key and get it (see Exhibit 14-10).

**Automatic Deadbolt Locks** In spite of highly publicized guest room break-ins, some percentage of hotel guests forget to engage the deadbolt lock upon entering the guest room. They leave themselves substantially more vulnerable than when the deadbolt has been activated. To answer this problem, a number of ELS vendors have begun offering automatic deadbolt locks.

Although automatic deadbolt locks have been on the market since the early 1990s, they were initially plagued with problems. Probably the biggest single issue was the noise associated with the automatic deadbolt. Guests felt trapped after hearing a loud click and thud as the deadbolt was engaged and seated. Additionally, there were stories of guests being locked in their rooms because the deadbolt automatically engaged but then malfunctioned and would not disengage. Today's automatic deadbolt systems are quieter and more reliable.

Without the deadbolt in place, burglars easily use spreaders to separate the door latch from the frame. It takes little effort to spread the frame enough to open the door when just the latch is seated. It takes substantially more effort, and usually breaks the frame, to spread it wide enough when the one-inch deadbolt has been engaged.

▲
**Exhibit 14-10**
This photo says it all. Protection from litigation aside, electronic locking systems are so much simpler than managing the inventory of thousands of keys required with a traditional locking approach. And just imagine the nightmare for the maintenance and engineering department should a traditional master key become lost or stolen and the entire hotel have to be rekeyed. With a hard-wired electronic locking system, rekeying for a lost master is a matter of a few simple keystrokes to invalidate the missing master key, create new masters in its place, and never disturb the existing guest-level keys in the process.

Therefore, it is in everyone's best interest—the guests', the hotel's, and the hotel's insurance company's—to automatically engage deadbolts for those guests who forget or don't understand the importance of this protective feature.

## Categories of Locking Systems

There are three categories of guest room door locks available in the marketplace. The most basic of these locks is the standard mechanical keyed door lock found in older lodging properties and personal residences. Next in line in terms of sophistication is the non-electronic locking system door lock. Non-electronic locking systems offer many of the positive attributes found in ELS locks but cost substantially less. ELSs are the third type of door lock available. ELSs come in both microfitted and hard-wired systems.

**Traditional Mechanical Locks** Although the handwriting is on the wall, mechanical locks are still widely used. They are more appropriate for the small property, which can track the history of the individual room lock. Rekeying mechanical locks can be done only by going from door to door and only by keeping good records. That's not feasible with large hotels, which favour smart switches and their remote rekeying capability.

**Changing Mechanical Locks** Changing locks originally meant just that: moving the entire lock from one room to another. With new technology, the method of rotating mechanical locks has changed.

One system uses a removable lock core. With a twist, a control key removes the whole pin–tumbler combination, allowing it to be used in some other housing. The key core is replaced with a different core requiring a different room key. The lock housing remains intact. It is a rapid and effective means of rotating locks for either emergency situations or periodic replacements (see Exhibit 14-7).

The other innovation, changeable tumblers, is even simpler. The change is made in the tumblers without removing the core. The key, not the tumbler, is replaced (see Exhibit 14-11).

Rekeying time is less than one minute for both the guest key and the master key, according to the manufacturer. Keys are not discarded; they are reused. A removable, coloured room number disk snaps in and out of the key, which permits the key to be used in other rooms. Changing disk colours distinguishes previously used keys from the combination currently in use.

**Exhibit 14-11** ▼
Rekeying this deadbolt lock is done externally by changing the key. Making the change requires a master key along with the old and new guest room keys.

**Non-electronic Locking Systems** Non-electronic locking systems are really just sophisticated mechanical locks. However, because a card is used instead of a key, there is often confusion between electronic and non-electronic locking systems. Non-electronic locks use a snap-off card with holes in the plastic (see Exhibit 14-9). According to one manufacturer, 4 billion combinations are possible. Both sides of the card have the same configuration. The door opens when the configuration of holes on the guest card, inserted from the corridor, coincides with the configuration on the control card, which is inserted from the room side.

One variation employs a separate cylinder lock for access by employees and management. Changes can be made in the cylinder lock for the room attendant, master, and E-keys without altering guest-card entry.

The whole system is like all of the other mechanical systems. Someone needs to come to the door and change the card. The change could be done by the bellperson each and every time a new guest is roomed. The bellperson, who gains access through the cylinder lock, breaks off the card parts and completes the rekeying. Rekeying need not be done with each guest, provided the previous guest returns the key(s) at check-out.

**Benefits of Non-electronic Locking Systems** There are several reasons why a hotel might select a non-electronic locking system. First, when compared to standard mechanical locks, non-electronic locking systems are superior. Their rapid rekeying feature is foremost on the list of advantages over the traditional keyed lock.

In addition, non-electronic locking systems offer many of the security advantages associated with electronic locking systems. Similar to an ELS, a new guest key card inserted in the lock will invalidate the previous guest's card. Indeed, hotel managers who select non-electronic locking systems can provide a strong defence in court that their hotels are providing reasonable care and proper levels of guest security. However, the biggest reason that newly constructed properties choose non-electronic locking systems is cost—they are significantly less expensive than even the least costly ELSs.

**Electronic Locking Systems** Although ELSs are the best of all guest room door-locking systems, they are expensive. Average costs are in the neighbourhood of $150 to $350 per door plus the cost of the dedicated computer processor, one or more key-writing terminals, an audit trail interrogator, a printer, software, and programming. Yet most newly constructed properties have ELSs. The price only seems high until you analyze the alternatives.

Electronic locks save direct expenses in two ways: labour and key cost. They also provide less direct monetary savings in terms of lower insurance premiums, reduced liability risk, happier guests, and less property theft. In terms of direct expenses, let's look at the experience of San Diego Marriott Hotel and Marina.

This property was originally constructed with a standard mechanical locking system in all 682 rooms. Today, this property has retrofitted an ELS in its original rooms, and here's why. Guests were constantly losing or misplacing room keys. According to the property's chief engineer, it was not uncommon for the Marriott to rekey up to 40 rooms per day! Each lost room key required the maintenance person to rekey the lock, make four copies of the key, and log in each one. Key blanks cost $2 each (compared to electronic key cards, which cost only about $0.10 each). However, the real expense was not key blanks; it was labour. The maintenance department spent upward of 30 hours per week rekeying door locks. Today, that same property spends less than three hours per week maintaining its electronic locks.

**Power Sources** The system is energized either by a hard-wire hook-up using utility power or by a battery power pack on the door. The hard-wire installations have more capability, but they are far more costly. Each door must be cabled to the console at the front desk (there are also systems that use radio waves, paging, and infrared technology to communicate with the front desk). This proves too expensive for retrofits, which tend toward the microfitted electronic systems.

Hard-wire installations need to provide for power failures, which make the locks inoperative. One seldom-used option is a battery pack on each door. The batteries have a life of one to three years. Large, centralized power packs are generally used, unless the hotel has emergency generators that back up the entire hotel during power failures.

**The Control Centre** The control centre is at the front desk, where the key is issued as part of the registration process (see Exhibit 14-12). What happens there depends on whether the system is hard-wired or microfitted.

**Exhibit 14-12 ▶**
Combination codes for individual room key cards are processed at the main ELS console located at the front office. Each guest receives a disposable key card (other options are available as displayed in Exhibits 14-8 and 14-13).

Notice the key-read/write hardware (lower centre of photo) through which a blank key card is encoded for the new guest. Notice also the sample door lock (at far left of photo and another in the back right corner) with which the front-desk receptionist can demonstrate the functions of the guest room door lock.

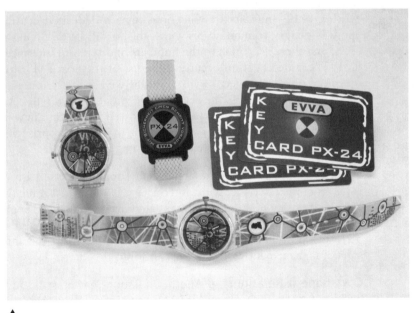

▲
**Exhibit 14-13**
Electronic locking systems are flexible in terms of where (or on what) the magnetic strip is attached. Creative companies have left the key card behind as they seek new innovations. Shown here are TESA's new programmable watches, which eliminate the need to carry a key card. Another company (Sphinx Dialock) has introduced programmable clips, which conveniently hook to the guest's pocket or belt. Another variation requires carrying nothing at all; the guest simply enters a custom-designed PIN number to access the guest room (see Exhibit 14-14).

If the system is hard-wired, the code in the card that is processed at the time of registration is forwarded over the wires (or radio waves) to the lock in the door. Hard-wiring makes the door code and the console code at the desk one and the same. A self-correcting feature verifies the accuracy of the key card, saving the guest from a duplicate trip to the desk because the card doesn't work.

As previously discussed in the scenario with Adams and Brown, microfitted ELSs communicate with the desk by way of the key card. Physically inserting the key card in the lock updates the code sequence in the door lock with the code sequence maintained at the front-desk control centre.

# Other Common Interfaces

As the hotel industry continues its trek and investment toward fully automated and fully integrated properties, a number of decisions face management. Depending on the size, type, age, and market of the property, certain applications and potential interfaces become more or less necessary. Whenever management seeks to enhance its current system, it must ask itself a series of questions.

**Exhibit 14-14**
Keyless locks have recently gained a foothold in the hospitality industry. Active guests who engage in water sports and other recreational activities often misplace their key cards. Additionally, those hotels that check guests in from remote locations or kiosk front desks can simply provide the guest a four- or six-digit number without the added hassle of physically delivering them a key. This Onity Keypad Lock offers access with both a key card and a combination code.

▼

## Prior to the Investment in New Automation

Although the questions below are designed around the concept of interfaced systems, they are appropriate for any hotel investment. Management should ask the questions and analyze the answers before making investments.

**Degradation**  Management should first ask: Will the interfaced system degrade my existing PMS? Interfaced applications have a dedicated **central processing unit** that "polls"—that is, communicates with—the host PMS. Still, interfaces act as "phantom" users, and there are limits to the numbers and types of interfaces appropriate for each PMS. When degradation occurs, the speed of the host PMS slows down. This slower operating time may affect service levels as well as guest and employee satisfaction.

It is critical to assess the degree of degradation that will occur prior to performing the interface. If the PMS is appreciably slowed, significant new hardware and software investment may be necessary. Management should apprise itself of this additional potential cost well in advance of performing the interface.

**Synergy**  Another question management should ask itself is: What is the synergistic value from the interface? Most interfaces provide added value (synergy) to the existing PMS. For example, rather than manually turning on guest room telephones and tracking, pricing, and posting calls, the electronic interface between the CAS and the PMS performs those functions automatically. However, if there is little or no synergy to be gained, management would be wise to forgo the interface.

**Cost–Benefit Relationship**  Another question that must be addressed asks: Is there a positive cost–benefit relationship? Management needs to clearly understand the purpose of the interface, the value added from this new application, and the cost of installing the system. If long-term employee and/or guest benefits are something less than the investment required, management might reconsider the venture.

There is currently a trend to automate everything in sight. Rather than analyzing the cost–benefit relationship, many properties merely follow the industry trend. Yet the reasons for interfacing applications are different for each property. If management cannot answer the cost–benefit question, it should not make the investment.

**Matching Technology to Guest Expectations** Another key factor to consider before jumping into an investment in technology is: How will this new automation affect the guest's experience? (see Exhibit 14-15). Today's sophisticated travellers are receiving more and more from their hotels in the way of technological toys, gadgets, and services. Therefore, when prioritizing their computer applications "wish list," hotels should consider the guests' expectations as well as management's needs.

Corporate hotels are competing on many fronts these days. "Location, location, location" has been augmented by a number of other factors, and a hotel's technological sophistication has become a major selling point for today's frequent business travellers. Indeed, some lodging chains have designed their entire product around the technologically savvy business traveller. Chains like Matrix eSuites Hotels and InternetInns.com offer

**Exhibit 14-15 ▶**

A survey of 2500 frequent travellers conducted by *Lodging Hospitality* and sponsored by ESPN shares some insight about guest preferences. Before investing in guest-operated interfaces, the hotel needs to understand how much value the guests place on the module in question. For example, a hotel would be far better advised to install individualized climate controls (84 percent of frequent travellers said individualized climate controls were either somewhat important or very important) as opposed to in-room fax machines (just 23 percent of frequent travellers said an in-room fax machine was either somewhat important or very important).

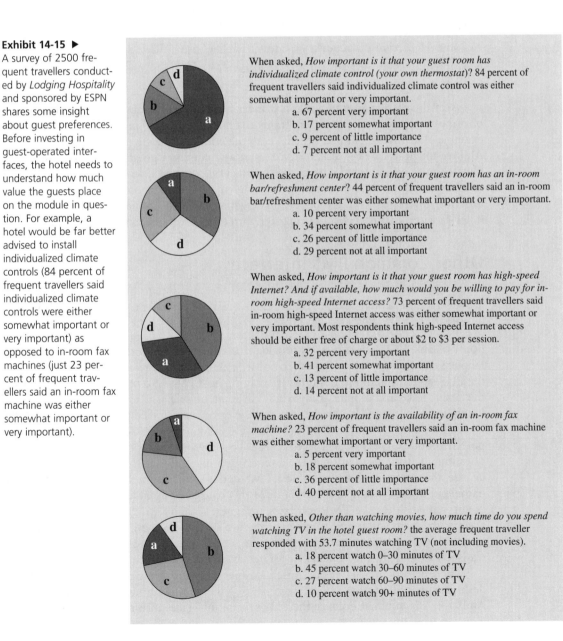

When asked, *How important is it that your guest room has individualized climate control (your own thermostat)?* 84 percent of frequent travellers said individualized climate control was either somewhat important or very important.
    a. 67 percent very important
    b. 17 percent somewhat important
    c. 9 percent of little importance
    d. 7 percent not at all important

When asked, *How important is it that your guest room has an in-room bar/refreshment center?* 44 percent of frequent travellers said an in-room bar/refreshment center was either somewhat important or very important.
    a. 10 percent very important
    b. 34 percent somewhat important
    c. 26 percent of little importance
    d. 29 percent not at all important

When asked, *How important is it that your guest room has high-speed Internet? And if available, how much would you be willing to pay for in-room high-speed Internet access?* 73 percent of frequent travellers said in-room high-speed Internet access was either somewhat important or very important. Most respondents think high-speed Internet access should be either free of charge or about $2 to $3 per session.
    a. 32 percent very important
    b. 41 percent somewhat important
    c. 13 percent of little importance
    d. 14 percent not at all important

When asked, *How important is the availability of an in-room fax machine?* 23 percent of frequent travellers said an in-room fax machine was either somewhat important or very important.
    a. 5 percent very important
    b. 18 percent somewhat important
    c. 36 percent of little importance
    d. 40 percent not at all important

When asked, *Other than watching movies, how much time do you spend watching TV in the hotel guest room?* the average frequent traveller responded with 53.7 minutes watching TV (not including movies).
    a. 18 percent watch 0–30 minutes of TV
    b. 45 percent watch 30–60 minutes of TV
    c. 27 percent watch 60–90 minutes of TV
    d. 10 percent watch 90+ minutes of TV

a variety of standard amenities with a technological slant, including high-speed Internet access, in-room computers, ergonomic workstations, and wireless technology.

To understand why this has become such a valuable market, listen to these surprising statistics developed in part by the Hospitality Sales and Marketing Association International (HSMAI):

- Business travellers are more likely than leisure travellers to have a wireless device (PDA, laptop, wireless phone).
- Mobile phones are increasingly being used to wirelessly access the Internet.
- Smaller devices are favoured for wireless access on the go; mobile phones and PDAs are far more commonly used in airports and hotels than are laptop computers.
- Some 91 percent of frequent business travellers use a mobile phone.
- Some 88 percent of frequent business travellers use a laptop computer.
- Some 41 percent of frequent business travellers use a PDA.
- Some 48 percent of frequent business travellers use high-speed Internet connections in the hotel guest room.

Armed with this information, no wonder hotels are re-examining their technological priorities and adopting certain programs that fit their guests' needs. Probably the best example of an investment that benefits both the hotel and the guest is wireless technology. An investment in wireless technology does more than allow guests to access the Internet. Hotels can gain substantial synergy by implementing their own wireless applications, such as PMS (for check-in and check-out functions in remote locations), POS (for hand-held ordering in restaurants and lounges), managerial modules (so managers can check vital hotel data and emails without having to return to their offices), and so on.

## Other Common PMS Interfaces

Aside from the call accounting and electronic locking systems already discussed, there are several other common PMS interfaces. A fully automated property might also boast an integrated POS, EMS, and guest-operated interfaces.

**Point of Sale (POS)**    POS systems provide true synergy to the hotel operation in terms of labour savings, lower transcription error rates, and reduced late charges. That is because the POS system communicates directly with the host PMS. No matter how distant from the front desk, a computer located at the point of sale (for example, in restaurants, lounges, gift shops, and health club centres) is electronically linked to the front-office PMS.

A POS system removes the hotel from the labour-intensive, error-ridden, manually posted room charge process of yesteryear. The interface poses electronically the same questions that the non-automated system asked manually. Before accepting the room charge, the system polls the front-desk PMS and asks: Is the guest registered under that name and in that room? Is the amount of this charge acceptable to the guest's current credit status? After the PMS validates the guest's ability to charge, the POS system accepts the transaction and transmits the data directly to the guest folio. At the POS terminal, the cashier merely inputs the guest name, guest room number, amount of transaction, and cheque voucher or reference code number (see Exhibit 13-2).

There are no late charges because a cashier forgot to bring the cheque to the front desk. There are no errors of fact from posting the wrong amount to the wrong room. And labour is minimal because the POS system interfaces directly with the PMS.

**Energy Management Systems (EMSs)** Energy management is another common interface to the PMS. By effectively controlling energy (for example, heating, air conditioning, lights, and power to run equipment), the hotel can provide a full level of services and comfort to the guest while effectively minimizing utility-related costs. An EMS conserves electricity, gas, and water by electronically monitoring the property's mechanical equipment.

An EMS saves money in three ways. First, it conserves overall energy use by turning down or shutting off non-essential equipment. Second, it prevents premium charges on utility bills by shedding energy loads during otherwise peak demand periods. Third, it enhances the useful life of equipment by duty-cycling machines on and off.

**Guest Room Consumption** Although some 19 percent of the energy used in full-service properties is used in guest rooms (see Exhibit 14-16), guest room consumption increases to as much as 80 percent in limited-service properties. An EMS/PMS interface can provide substantial savings in terms of guest room energy use. As discussed earlier in this chapter, such interfaces often function around hard-wired ELSs. That's because the hotel already has a physical (hard-wired) connection between every guest room and the front desk; the EMS simply adds a new dimension to electronic equipment already functioning.

**Exhibit 14-16** ▶
Breakdown of energy consumption in a full-service, 300-room hotel. A small effort in reducing HVAC, water, and electrical usage can produce significant annual savings. Even without an automated energy management system, properties can benefit by implementing a voluntary compliance program. Guests can be reminded to turn off lights and the television when exiting the room, hang up towels that are wet but not dirty, and turn off water when brushing their teeth.

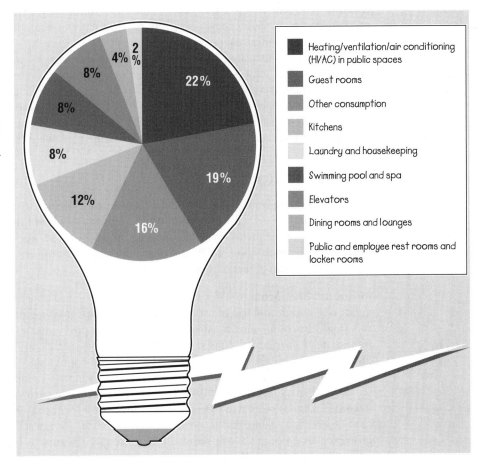

Through an EMS, the PMS reduces energy consumption in unoccupied rooms. Depending on the time of day, the temperature, and forecasted room demand, the EMS may decide to curtail heating and cooling by a few degrees, or it may substantially reduce energy consumption by closing everything down. Even in occupied rooms, the EMS may override the in-room thermostat by a few degrees when faced with peak-demand energy use. The industry generally views a few degrees warmer or colder than the desired temperature as a fair trade—a minimal impact on guest comfort in order for the hotel to substantially save on energy costs. Peak-demand periods usually abate within a few minutes, after which time the EMS ceases the override and the guest's room temperature returns to the desired level.

Through the use of computer algorithms, the EMS may actually control the PMS by determining which rooms should be sold and which rooms should remain unoccupied. A guest checking into a 60-percent-occupied house may be routed (through the room availability screen of the PMS) to a well-occupied floor. This would leave other floors or wings of the hotel totally empty. In such cases, the computer could then shut down hallway ventilation systems, turn off every other ceiling light in the hallway, and reduce the temperature at the remote water heater(s).

An EMS interface might also incorporate in-room occupancy sensors. Tied to the ELS, these sensors use either infrared heat-sensing technology or ultrasonic motion detection equipment to register occupancy in the guest room. A door that has been opened from the inside (without using a key card to gain access) probably indicates that the occupant has left the guest room. This information is validated against the occupancy sensor technology, and if the room is truly unoccupied the EMS reduces or turns off non-essential energy consumption.

Some less-sophisticated in-room occupancy sensors are not connected to the door lock and merely sense body heat (infrared detection) or body movement (ultrasonic motion detection) without verification. Such equipment works fine except in those instances where a heavy sleeper pulls the blankets up over his head. In these situations, neither heat nor movement registers the room as occupied. The guest may be surprised to wake up and find the TV set turned off and the room temperature somewhat less than comfortable.

## The Wired Room

In addition to the integrated applications discussed in the preceding section, today's wired rooms provide a number of additional guest-operated interfaces. The following section provides a brief overview of the more popular guest-operated interfaces. Included here are in-room safes, in-room beverage or minibar systems, fire-safety systems, and in-room entertainment systems.

**In-Room Safes** Modern safes boast two features viewed as essential by today's managers: size and automatic-override features. In terms of size, smaller is better—but not too small! In-room safes must be large enough to provide safekeeping for most common articles carried by guests, yet they should be small enough to be concealed in attractive case goods with finishes that match the room's decor. In terms of size, the safe should be just large enough to secure a guest's laptop computer or briefcase.

Digital safes (see Exhibit 14-17) are superior to key card or traditional lock and key safes. Digital safes work best because there is no secondary element (the key or key card) to be lost. Some safes work with a swipe of the guest's personal credit card. However, that doesn't work so well when the guest wants to lock up the credit card before going down to the pool.

▲
**Exhibit 14-17**
In-room safes reduce guest losses as well as guest demands on front-desk personnel to open safe-deposit boxes. Although in-room safes are sometimes provided as a complimentary amenity, many hotels charge between $1 and $5 or more per day for this guest-operated convenience. Digital safes, similar to the one shown, allow guests to program their own unique combination codes.

Digital safes use a code programmed by each new guest. Everyone has a few digits stored in their brains: birthdates, bank PIN codes, and so on. With a simple "code and close" safe, the guest places the secured items inside and shuts the door, enters a unique PIN code, punches the "close" button, and walks away. It is as simple as that. By the way, some of the newest products on the market feature biometrics (electronic fingerprint readers) rather than digital codes!

Automatic override is another feature of a digital safe. Guests can conceivably forget their code combination—perhaps their spouse programmed it and then left, or perhaps they thought they had entered one code but pushed the wrong buttons by mistake. Should this occur, hotel management has the ability to open the safe by overriding the current combination code. Usually, such an override requires two inputs: some type of hand-held unit, key, or device as well as a secure override access code. Most digital in-room safes maintain an override audit trail.

Electronic safes may be hard-wired to an interfaced central processing unit. If the PMS is interfaced, daily charges are posted automatically to the electronic folio. Manual systems charge guests for the use of the safe in a number of creative ways. Some ask the housekeeping attendant to document whether the safe was used. Another approach is simply to ask the guest at check-in or check-out. Other properties charge a fee for the safe—usually $1 to $5 per day—whether it was used or not (obviously, this approach causes a few guest complaints at check-out). A recent growing trend is to charge all guests a small "fee" for the use of the guest room safe, in-room coffee, and free local phone calls.

Of course, the hotel can provide the safe without charge, as it does other amenities. Charging came about because vendors developed quick payback schemes by which management could justify installing in-room safes.

Other than direct cost recovery, there are economic arguments for not charging. The safes reduce the number of thefts, and that should reduce the cost of insurance. Traffic at safety-deposit boxes falls dramatically, reducing front-office labour costs. Fewer claims mean even larger savings in security and management time. Investigations, guest relations, reports, police inquiries, and correspondence may represent days of lost work. Legal fees, court costs, settlements, and more management time must be factored in if the case goes to trial. Thus, a safe reduces losses, which reduces costs.

Evidence suggests that safes do reduce theft. Electronic door locks do battle with external theft, and in-room safes do battle with internal theft. Experts say that internal theft by employees is usually an impulsive act caused by temptation (laptop computers are proving to be one of the most tempting items). The safe reduces employee opportunity. It also undermines guest moves to defraud the hotel or the insurance company.

**In-Room Minibars** In-room beverage, minibar, or vending systems may be automatically interfaced to the PMS, semi-automatically interfaced (with a hand-held microprocessor), or fully manual in design (see Exhibit 14-18). Both manual and semi-automated minibars rely on a guest honour system. At the time of check-out,

**Exhibit 14-18** ▶
Electronic in-room mini-bar systems can easily support 75 to 100 items. By design, some sections remain at room temperature (nuts and candy) while other sections (soda and champagne) are refrigerated. A new trend offers healthier snacks and personal toiletries in addition to the obligatory liquor and soda.

front-desk clerks ask departing guests if they used the minibar in the last 24 hours. Although some departing guests will invariably fleece the hotel, minibar profits are significant enough to cover a sizable number of losses.

Minibars are extremely convenient—that's their attraction. Guests are often willing to pay a premium for the convenience of having snacks and drinks available in the room. As a result, some hotels have realized rapid payback (sometimes in less than 12 months) from their in-room minibar systems.

With semi-automated minibars, changes in inventory are recorded on a hand-held microprocessor by the room attendant or minibar employee. The microprocessor is capable of storing inventory information from a number of guest rooms before being downloaded via the telephone directly into the PMS interface (see Exhibit 14-19).

Some delay in installing honour bars was caused by several jurisdictions. Without control of consumption by minors, liquor was not permitted in the rooms. Automatically interfaced minibars have changed that: The system can be turned off at certain hours or whenever children are registered.

Interfaced minibars brought additional benefits: eliminating the frequent late charges of the honour system, for one. Automatically interfaced minibars use fibre optic sensors to identify when a product has been removed for consumption. These sensors are often programmed with a slight delay to allow for those guests who wish to handle, look at, and then possibly return the product to the refrigerator. Once the product has been removed for a period of time, the sensor alerts the interface, which then charges the guest folio for the minibar item. Not only does this minimize cheating and late charges, it also produces a restocking report that simplifies the job of the minibar employee. There is no longer any reason for the minibar employee to enter and

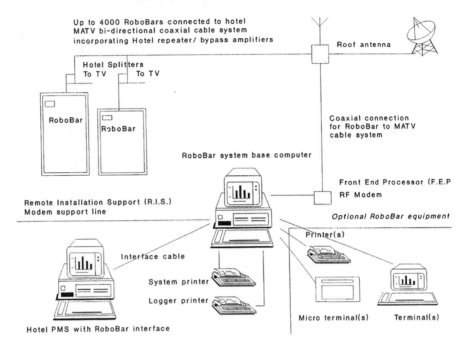

**Exhibit 14-19 ▶**
Advanced systems, such as this one from RoboBar, deliver in-room amenities with maximum efficiency. There are several notable features: Purchases are posted to the folio electronically as the guest removes the product, bars can be locked remotely to comply with local liquor laws, and restocking reports are prepared automatically, so there's no need for a physical count.

check every guest room, but rather only those from which an item was removed.

Aside from the recent technological advances in minibars, there has been a revolution of purpose as well. Gone are the days when minibars were stocked exclusively with liquor and stale snacks. The new purpose has minibars stocking a multitude of items ranging from healthier snacks and beverages to indispensable products such as toiletry items. Imagine the relief of the guest who doesn't discover until morning that he has forgotten his razor, and finds one conveniently located in the minibar (that's far better than walking downstairs to the front desk in pyjamas).

Even the pricing of minibar products has become somewhat more user friendly in recent years. A grand opening special at Nikko Hotel in Hanoi included the entire original contents of the in-room minibar free of charge. Who knows, the future may see more hotel minibar promotions and creative uses (even complimentary continental breakfast) in years to come.

**In-Room Entertainment Systems** In-room movie or entertainment systems hold a great deal of promise for the years to come. Recent trends suggest continued investments in guest room televisions. The rule of thumb is to provide guests with in-room televisions equal to or surpassing the size and quality of the sets they have at home. Therefore, as home electronics grow more high-tech, so must guest room electronics. One mid-sized chain now provides 42-inch flat-panel plasma televisions in all of its luxury and upscale rooms!

Another trend is to increase the number of cable channels available to the average guest. Guests grow frustrated channel-surfing through the few (10 or so) channels found at many hotels. They expect to find 40 or 50 channels (again, similar to what they might have at home), so hotels are complying by providing greater viewing

selection. The three most popularly viewed cable channels in hotel rooms are HBO, Showtime, and Disney.

The availability of in-room movies, for which most hotels charge (using the electronic folio), is another popular amenity (see Exhibit 14-20). DVD viewing is another. Some hotels charge, and some do not; some rent films via electronic vending machines, and some supply them gratis on the concierge floors

Most hotels in Canada have Sony PlayStations available in all of their rooms. Some hotels, such as the Crowne Plaza in Moncton, New Brunswick, feature "Kids Suites," rooms that have various activities for children. Sony has recently released a LocationFree® player pack, which provides television any time, anywhere on alternative devices including PlayStations. These are currently available in wireless hot spots such as Fredericton, New Brunswick, and Toronto, Ontario, in Canada as well as more than 200 cities in North America.

Although not exactly entertainment, the proceedings taking place in the conference area of the hotel can be viewed on the TV in some hotels. Other TV channels offer airline schedules; news, sports, and stock market reports; local restaurant guides; the guest folio; weather reports; advertising; and personal messages left for the guest.

When some capabilities of the telephone and personal computer are added, television broadens its service offerings. Express check-out and room status are two common functions. A room service menu can be viewed (changes are easier to make and less costly than with printed menus) and orders can be placed. Other orders can also be placed: a morning wake-up call; a reservation in a dining room that hasn't opened; goods from shops in the hotel (or mall merchants, if the hotel is so located). Even airline tickets can be ordered. With a remote printer at the front desk—eventually, perhaps, in the guest room—tickets can also be picked up.

The trend by the big three lodging pay-per-view companies—SpectraVision, LodgeNet Entertainment, and On Command Video—has changed in recent years. Where a signed pay-per-view contract once guaranteed the hotel a free TV set in every room, today's contracts provide more information technology without the free sets.

Less sophisticated hotels can still get the free TV sets, but more advanced properties are opting to buy the sets themselves in order to have the pay-per-view company include a wider range of differentiated services in the contract.

**Fire-Safety Systems** Although fire-safety systems are not truly guest-operated devices, they do monitor and detect activities occurring in the guest room. Like most interfaced functions, fire-safety systems began as stand-alone devices. An example is a single smoke detector in the corridor. Change came quickly after several widely publicized fires occurred. In quick response, many municipalities passed retrofit legislation. The emphasis was toward interfacing fire technology and the PMS, using the hard wires of the call accounting or locking systems, or through wireless broadcasting. Some jurisdictions mandated hard-wiring—integrating the control panels and the room communication systems.

Hard-wired systems tie each room sensor to a fire-control panel on the premises. In-room smoke detectors and sprinkler-head sensors can also be included to provide an early warning network. An annunciator on the panel pinpoints the source of the smoke or fire. The interfaced system then does several things automatically:

- It releases the magnetic locks that hold open the fire doors.
- It adjusts the ventilation and air-handling systems to minimize the spread of fire and externally vent smoke as necessary.
- It automatically notifies guests in their rooms through the activation of horns or speakers, it may dial each guest room telephone and play a pre-recorded message, and it notifies the local fire department. On arrival at the scene, the fire department takes control of the speakers and announces specific instructions.
- It automatically overrides all affected elevators and returns them to the ground floor.

Codes require evacuation routes in corridors and rooms to be clearly marked. In-room signage now identifies that route and the closest exit. Lighted, phosphorescent signs in the corridors at crawling height have gained popularity since their introduction in the Far East over a decade ago.

Instead of ignoring the reality of the danger, which had been the stance for a long time, hotel companies have begun to communicate their concerns. Written booklets and evacuation instructions have been prepared. With electronic systems, audio instructions are also being offered. Other emergency systems use the music channels or the television speakers. The voice comes through even if the switch is off. Special hard-wired systems and in-room sprinklers are legislated in several places that have experienced especially deadly fires, such as Las Vegas, Toronto, and San Juan.

A message that is recorded tends to be more calming and informative than a live one made during the excitement of an emergency. Several hotels have asked the local fire marshal to tape this message.

**The Electronic Concierge** In an effort to provide guests with additional information while easing the strain on the concierge desk (or eliminating the position altogether), hotels have heartily embraced electronic concierge technology. Through either the guest room television, a dedicated kiosk or a computer terminal in the lobby, or even a phone-based system (where guests interact by pushing the appropriate phone buttons), guests receive answers to questions about local attractions, restaurants, museums, shows, and so on. Some of the more sophisticated systems even provide maps (which can be printed at the front desk or concierge desk, if warranted) and recommended routes.

Hotels are not the only venue that supports electronic concierge systems. They are also commonly found at bus depots, airline terminals, city halls, and other public or quasi-public buildings. Hotels, however, benefit tremendously from this new technology, which is usually installed free of charge. Whether the electronic service replaces or merely supplements a live concierge desk, the guest saves time and gains an overview of community attractions from the information available through the electronic concierge.

However, the guest is not always provided a full and accurate picture. You see, electronic concierge services are provided by businesses that profit from advertising included at the site. Large communication companies often fund the investment necessary to start such services. To be listed at the site, local merchants pay rates ranging from $100 to $1000 per month. Not all merchants choose to participate, and that's where the picture becomes muddled. Asking the concierge desk where the nearest Italian restaurant is located may point you to a lovely place right next door. The electronic concierge, however, will highlight only those Italian restaurants that pay a monthly fee. As such, the guest may drive kilometres out of the way seeking the closest Italian restaurant, having been provided with something less than full disclosure.

# Summary

The lodging industry lagged behind most other businesses in terms of adopting computer automation in the 1970s. As a result, most hotel operations avoided the first generations of computer development, choosing instead to wait for the faster, cheaper, more perfected systems that were soon to follow. The waiting is over, and hospitality computer applications have gained acceptance at a dizzying rate. Today, technology prevails across all spectrums of the lodging industry.

Few properties operate without a computerized call accounting system (CAS). The CAS performs many tasks that historically belonged to the hotel telephone operator: It identifies when a guest call is made, the originating room, the duration, the destination, and the cost of the call. Once the long-distance carrier cost of the call is determined, most properties add a profit margin to help defray CAS equipment costs and to make a reasonable return on investment for the hotel. Some chains, however, choose to make no profit on either long-distance or local guest phone calls. Functioning in concert with the CAS are sophisticated guest room telephones. These feature telephones are actually capable of serving as a remote control for a number of in-room services. Pressing a few buttons on the phone may close the drapes, dim the lights, adjust the temperature, or lower the television volume.

Another common technological interface found in hotels is the electronic locking system (ELS). Few newly constructed hotels are built without some form of locking system technology. This technology may include non-electronic locking systems that use specially encoded keys, but more often than not it will be an ELS. The ELS may be microfitted (that is, battery operated) or hard-wired. Though more expensive, hard-wired systems can feature a number of enhancements. Since each hard-wired lock is actually wired directly to the front desk, the hotel can integrate fire safety, occupancy sensors, and energy management components directly through the door lock.

In addition to the CAS and the ELS, a number of guest-room or guest-service interfaces are also available in full-service, technologically sophisticated properties. Common guest-service interfaces include point-of-sale and energy management systems. In the guest room, there may be electronic safe, minibar, entertainment, fire-safety, and concierge system interfaces.

# Questions and Problems

1. The relationship of the telephone and hotel industries has changed significantly since the 1960s. List three major pieces of legislation, court rulings, findings by the Canadian Radio-television and Telecommunications Commission (CRTC), or decisions by members of either industry that caused or contributed to the changes. How did each alter the way in which the hotel's telephone department operates?

2. Undoubtedly, some PMS vendors will comply with the new HITIS standards and others will not. What are the advantages and disadvantages to a hotel manager who purchases software from a vendor in compliance?

3. Most hotel operations charge a premium for the convenience of placing long-distance phone calls directly from the room. This premium may range from 10 to 25 percent above the actual cost of the call. Other prop-erties charge as much as 10 times the cost of the call. Assuming that the hotel announces its surcharge with a notice, discuss the fairness of charging the guest such a premium. Is it ethical to charge a small premium (say, 10 to 25 percent)? Is it ethical to charge a large premium (say, 10 times the cost)? At what point does the hotel overstep the limits of "fairness"?

4. Identify by name the levels of keys that comprise the locking systems of most hotels. Explain who has access to which keys and what purpose is served by each level. How does the system work if the mechanical lock and key are replaced by the computer and computer key card?

5. Be creative and imagine the hotel room of the future. Describe several guest-operated interfaces or devices that might be available in your fictitious hotel room of tomorrow.

# CASE STUDY

## The New Property Management System (PMS)

Lew Blum had been hired as a director of operations for a group of six privately owned, non-franchised properties in Nova Scotia. As Blum looked forward to the challenges of his new position, he listened with interest as the owner pontificated about the new PMS system that had been installed at one of the hotels. The owner's long-range vision was to computerize all of the properties, as he understood what some of the advantages of computerization might be.

When Blum set out on his first visit to each of the properties, he chose to visit the computerized property first. It was with some surprise and dismay that he discovered the guest-service agents checking in guests on a manual basis and still using the old semi-automated electronic system that had disappeared in the late 1980s in most of the chain hotels with which this hotel competed.

In his first meeting with the general manager (GM) of this property, Blum asked about the computer system that the owner had bragged about and reportedly spent $30 000 on. The GM stated that the hotel had a number of older long-term employees on the desk who were minimally computer literate and fought the introduction of the new system. The front-office manager (FOM), who had come from a computerized chain property, had been a champion for the new PMS; however, he had left the hotel a month ago. The GM said that with the loss of the FOM, it made sense to go back to the semi-automated system with which most of the clerks were familiar and proficient. The $30 000 PMS was now neatly stored in the basement of the hotel.

Blum pondered what to do next!

1. In your opinion, what steps should have been taken at this hotel before introducing the new PMS?

2. What should Blum do now?

3. What could the GM have done when the FOM left the employ of the hotel?

## Note

1. Donald E. Lundberg, *Inside Innkeeping* (Dubuque, IA: William C. Brown Company, Publishers, 1956), p. 91.

## Weblinks

Canadian Radio-television and Telecommunications Commission (CRTC)
**www.crtc.gc.ca**

AT&T
**www.attcanada.com**

Bell Canada
**www.bell.ca**

Mitel
**www.mitel.com**

SpectraVision and On Command
**www.spectravision.com**

# Bibliography

Abbot, P. *Front Office: Procedures, Special Skills and Management*. Oxford: Butterworth-Heinemann, 1991.

*The ABCs of Travel*. New York: Public Transportation and Travel Division, Ziff-Davis Publishing Co., 1972.

Abramson, Susan, and Stuchin, Marcie. *The Boutique Hotel*. Weimar, TX: Culinary and Hospitality Industry Publications Service, 2001.

Anolik, Alexander. *Travel, Tourism and Hospitality Law*. Elmsford, NY: National Publishers of the Black Hills, Inc., 1988.

Arthur, Roland, and Gladwell, Derek. *The Hotel Assistant Manager*, 3rd ed. London: Barrie & Rockliff, 1975.

Astroff, Milton, and Abbey, James. *Convention Sales and Services*, 5th ed. Cranbury, NJ: Waterbury Press, 1998.

Axler, Bruce. *Focus on . . . Security for Hotels, Motels, and Restaurants*. Indianapolis, IN: ITT Educational Publishing, 1974.

———. *Room Care for Hotels and Motels*. Indianapolis, IN: ITT Educational Publishing, 1974.

Baird, C., and Carla, L. *Front Office Assignment*. London: Pitman Publishing Ltd., 1988.

Baker, Sue, Bradley, Pam, and Huyton, Jeremy. *Principles of Hotel Front Office Operations*, 2nd ed. London: Cassell PLC, 1996.

Barba, Stephen. "Operating the Traditional American Plan Resort," in *The Practices of Hospitality Management*, editors Pizam, Lewis, and Manning. Westport, CT: AVI Publishing Co., Inc., 1982.

Bardi, James A. *Hotel Front Office Management*, 2nd ed. New York: John Wiley & Sons, Inc., 1996.

Barth, Stephen. *Hospitality Law: Managing Legal Issues in the Hospitality Industry*. New York: John Wiley & Sons, 2001.

Baum, Tom, and Mudambi, Ram. *Economic and Management Methods for Tourism and Hospitality Research*. New York: John Wiley & Sons, 1999.

*Be Our Guest, Perfecting the Art of Customer Service*. Lake Buena Vista, FL: Disney Institute [no date].

Beavis, J.R.S., and Medlik, S. *A Manual of Hotel Reception*, 3rd ed. London: William Heinemann Ltd., 1981.

Berman, Shelley. *A Hotel Is a Place . . . .* Los Angeles: Price/Stern/Sloan Publishers, Inc., 1972.

Boomer, Lucius. *Hotel Management*. New York: Harper & Row, 1938.

Borsenik, Frank. *The Management of Maintenance and Engineering Systems in the Hospitality Industry*, 4th ed. New York: John Wiley & Sons, Inc., 1997.

Braham, Bruce. *Computer Systems in the Hotel and Catering Industry*. London: Cassell Educational Ltd., 1988.

———. *Hotel Front Office*, 2nd ed. Gloucestershire, England: Stanley Thornes, 1993.

Brotherton, Bob (Ed.). *The Handbook of Contemporary Hospitality Management Research*. New York: John Wiley & Sons, 1999.

Browning, Marjorie. *Night Audit Procedure*. Columbus, OH: The Christopher Inn, March 1, 1969.

Bryson, McDowell, and Ziminski, Adele. *The Concierge: Key to Hospitality*. New York: John Wiley & Sons, Inc., 1992.

Bucher, A.F. *101 Tips on Check Cashing*. New York: Ahrens Publishing Co., Inc., circa 1930.

Burstein, Harvey. *Hotel Security Management*. New York: Praeger Publishers, Inc., 1975.

Buzby, Walter J. *Hotel and Motel Security Management*. Los Angeles: Security World Publishing Co., 1976.

Cabot, Anthony. *Casino Gaming Policy, Economics and Regulation*. Las Vegas, NV: UNLV International Gaming Institute, 1996.

Casado, Matt. *Housekeeping Management*. New York: John Wiley & Sons, 2000.

Chandler, Raymond. *Trouble Is My Business*. New York: Ballantine Books, Inc., 1972.

*Check and Credit-Card Fraud Prevention Manual*. New York: The Atlantic Institute, Atcom Publishing, 1984.

Collins, Galen, and Malik, Tarun. *Hospitality Information Technology: Learning How to Use It*, 3rd ed. Dubuque, IA: Kendall/Hunt Publishing Company, 1997.

*Convention Liaison Council Manual*, 6th ed. Washington, DC: Convention Liaison Council, 1994.

Cournoyer, Norman, Marshall, Anthony, and Morris, Karen. *Hotel, Restaurant and Travel Law: A Preventive Approach*, 5th ed. Albany, NY: Delmar, 1999.

*The Credit Card Industry*. National Education Program of Discover Card. Riverwoods, IL: Novus Network Services, 1996.

Dahl, J.O. *Bellman and Elevator Operator*. Revised by Crete Dahl. Stamford, CT: The Dahls, 1993.

———. *Room Clerk's Manual*. Revised by Crete Dahl. Stamford, CT: The Dahls, 1993.

DeFranco, Agnes, and Noriega, Pender. *Cost Control in the Hospitality Industry*. Upper Saddle River, NJ: Prentice-Hall, 1999.

Dervaes, C. *The Travel Dictionary*. Tampa, FL: Solitaire Publishing, 1992.

Deveau, Jack, and Penraat, Jaap. *The Efficient Room Clerk*. New York: Learning Information, Inc., 1968.

DeVeau, Linsley, and DeVeau, Patricia. *Front Office Management and Operations*. Upper Saddle River, NJ: Prentice Hall, 1996.

*Directory of Hotel and Motel Companies*, 66th ed. Waldorf, MD: American Hotel & Motel Association, 1997.

Dittmer, Paul. *Dimensions of the Hospitality Industry: An Introduction*, 3rd ed. New York: John Wiley & Sons, 2001.

Dix, Colin, and Baird, Chris. *Front Office Operations*, 3rd ed. London: Pitman Publishing Ltd., 1988.

Drury, Tony, and Ferrier, Charles. *Credit Cards*. London: Butterworth, 1984.

Dukas, Peter. *Hotel Front Office Management and Operations*, 3rd ed. Dubuque, IA: William C. Brown Company, Publishers, 1970.

Dunn, David. "Front Office Accounting Machines in Hotels," unpublished master's thesis, Cornell University, Ithaca, NY, June 1965.

Dunseath, M., and Ransom, J. *The Hotel Bookkeeper Receptionist*. London: Barrie & Rockliff, 1967.

Ellis, Raymond. *Hotel/Motel Security Management*. East Lansing, MI: Educational Institute, 1986.

Fidel, John. *Hotel Data Systems*, rev. ed. Albuquerque, NM: September 1972.

Ford, Robert, and Heaton, Cherrill. *Managing the Guest Experience in Hospitality*. Albany, NY: Delmar, 2000.

Foster, Dennis. *The Business of Hospitality: Back Office Operations and Administration*. Peoria, IL: Glencoe Publishing Co., 1992.

———. *Rooms at the Inn: Front Office Operations and Administration*. Peoria, IL: Glencoe Publishing Co., 1992.

*Front Office and Reservations*. Burlingame, CA: Hyatt Corporation, 1978.

*Front Office Courtesy Pays*. Small Business Administration. Washington, DC: U.S. Government Printing Office, 1956.

*Front Office Manual*. New York: New Yorker Hotel, 1931.

*Front Office Manual: Franchise Division*. Sheraton Hotels & Inns, Worldwide [no date].

*Front Office Operations Manual (of the) Hotel McCurdy, Evansville, Indiana*. Research Bureau of the American Hotel Association, April 1923.

*Front Office Selling*. East Lansing, MI: Educational Institute of the American Hotel & Motel Association [no date].

*Front Office Selling "Tips."* New York: Hotel Sales Management Association, 1960.

Gathje, Curtis. *At the Plaza: An Illustrated History of the World's Most Famous Hotel*. New York: St. Martin's Press, 2000.

Gatiss, Gordon. *Total Quality Management*. London: Cassell PLC, 1996.

Giroux, Sharon. *Hosting the Disabled: Crossing the Communication Barrier*. Albany, NY: Delmar Publishers, 1994 (video).

Godowski, S. *Microcomputers in the Hotel and Catering Industry*. London: William Heinemann Ltd., 1988.

Goldblatt, Joe. *Special Events*. New York: John Wiley & Sons, 2002.

Gomes, Albert. *Hospitality in Transition*. Houston, TX: Pannell Kerr Foster, 1985.

Goodwin, John, and Gaston, Jolie. *Hotel, Hospitality and Tourism Law*, 5th ed. Scottsdale, AZ: Gorsuch Scarisbrick, Publishers, 1997.

Gray, William S., and Liguore, Salvatore C. *Hotel and Motel Management and Operations*, 3rd ed. Upper Saddle River, NJ: Prentice Hall, 1994.

*Guest Relations Training for Front Office Cashiers*. Boston: Sheraton Corporation of America, 1961.

*A Guide to Terminology in the Leisure Time Industries*. Philadelphia: Laventhol & Horwath, [no date].

Hall, Orrin, *Motel-Hotel Front Office Procedures*. Hollywood Beach, FL: circa 1971.

Hall, S.S.J. *Quality Assurance in the Hospitality Industry*. Milwaukee, WI: ASQC Quality Press, 1990.

Hamilton, Francis. *Hotel Front Office Management*. Miami, FL: 1947.

Haszonics, Joseph. *Front Office Operation*. New York: ITT Educational Services, Inc., 1971.

Heldenbrand, H. V. *Front Office Psychology*. Evanston, IL: John Wiley & Sons, Inc., 1944. Republished by American Hotel Register Company, Chicago, circa 1982.

Herzog, Lawrence. "On the Line." *Hotelier*. Toronto, ON: Kostuch Publications, March/April 2003 (pp. 45–47).

Hilton, Conrad. *Be My Guest*. Englewood Cliffs, NJ: Prentice Hall, 1957.

Hitz, Ralph. *Standard Practice Manuals for Hotel Operation, I, Front Service Division*, 2nd ed. New York: Harper & Row, 1936.

*A Hospitality Guide to the Americans with Disabilities Act*. Horsham, PA: LPR Publications, 1999.

*Hotel and Travel Index*. Secaucus, NJ: Cahners Travel Group, Quarterly.

*The Hotelman Looks at the Business of Meetings*. St. Paul, MN: 3M Business Press, 1968.

Hsu, Cathy, and Powers, Tom. *Marketing Hospitality*, 3rd ed. New York: John Wiley & Sons, 2001.

Hubbart, Roy. *The Hubbart Formula for Evaluating Rate Structures of Hotel Rooms*. New York: American Hotel & Motel Association, 1952.

*Hyatt Travel Futures Project Report on Business Travelers*. New York: prepared for Hyatt Hotels and Resorts by Research & Forecasts, Inc., December 1988.

*Implications of Microcomputers in Small and Medium Hotel and Catering Firms*. Prepared for the Hotel and Catering Industry Training Board by the Department of Hotel, Catering, and Tourism Management, University of Surrey, Guildford, Surrey, England, November 1980.

Ingold, Anthony, McMahon-Beattie, Una, and Yeoman, Ian (Eds.). *Yield Management*, 2nd ed. Washington, D.C.: Continuum, 2001.

Ismail, Ahmed. *Front Office Operations & Management*. Albany, NY: Delmar, 2001.

———. *Hotel Sales & Operations*. Albany, NY: Delmar, 1999.

Iverson, Kathleen. *Managing Human Resources in the Hospitality Industry: An Experiential Approach*, 1st ed. Upper Saddle River, NJ: Prentice Hall, 2001.

Iverson, Kathleen M. *Introduction to Hospitality Management*. New York: Van Nostrand Reinhold, 1989.

Jones, Christine, and Paul, Val. *Accommodations Management*. London: Botsford Academic and Education, 1985.

Kaplan, Michael. *The New Hotel, International and Resort Designs*. Weimer, TX: Culinary and Hospitality Industry Publications Services, 2002.

Kasavana, Michael, and Brooks, Richard. *Managing Front Office Operations*, 5th ed. East Lansing, MI: Educational Institute, 1998.

Kasavana, Michael, and Cahill, John. *Hospitality Industry Computer Systems*, 3rd ed. East Lansing, MI: Educational Institute, 1997.

Kasavana, Michael, and Cahill, John J. *Managing Technology in the Hospitality Indusustry*, 4th ed. Orlando, FL: Educational Institute of the American Hotel & Lodging Industry, 2003.

Kline, Sheryl, and Sullivan, William. *Hotel Front Office Simulation*. New York: John Wiley & Sons, 2002.

Lawrence, Janet. *Room Sales and Reception Management*. Boston: The Innkeeping Institute of America, 1970.

Leask, Anna, and Yeoman, Ian. *Heritage Visitor Attractions: An Operations Management Perspective*. London: Cassell Academic, 1999.

Lefler, Janet, and Calanese, Salvatore. *The Correct Cashier*. New York: Ahrens Publishing Co., Inc., 1960.

Link Hospitality Consultants, Ltd. *Canadian Job Strategy: Hotel Front Office Specialist*. Calgary, AB: Southern Alberta Institute of Technology, 1986.

Lundberg, Donald. *Front Office Human Relations*. Distributed by NU:PAK, San Marcos, CA, 1970.

Martin, Robert, and Jones, Tom. *Professional Management of Housekeeping Operations*, 3rd ed. New York: John Wiley & Sons, Inc., 1998.

*MasterCard International Frequent Business Traveler Study*. Presented at the American Hotel & Motel Association Annual Meeting, November 14, 1983.

Medlik, S. *The Business of Hotels*. London: William Heinemann Ltd., 1980.

———. *Dictionary of Travel*. Oxford: Butterworth-Heinemann, 1993.

———. *Profile of the Hotel and Catering Industry*, 2nd ed. London: William Heinemann Ltd., 1978.

Meek, Howard B. *A Theory of Room Rates*. Ithaca, NY: Cornell University, Department of Hotel Administration, June 1938.

*A Meeting Planner's Guide to Master Account Billing*. Developed by the Insurance Conference Planners, and published by The Educational Institute of the American Hotel & Motel Association, May 1980.

Metelka, Charles J. *The Dictionary of Hospitality, Travel and Tourism*, 3rd ed. Albany, NY: Delmar Publishers, Inc., 1989.

Michael, Angie. *Best Impressions in Hospitality*. Albany, NY: Delmar, 2000.

Ministry of Tourism. *The Front Desk Business*. Toronto, ON: Ontario Ministry of Tourism, 1978.

Moreo, Patrick, Sammons, Gail, and Dougan, James. *Front Office Operations and Night Audit Work Book*, 4th ed. Upper Saddle River, NJ: Prentice Hall, 1996.

Nebel, Eddystone. *Managing Hotels Effectively: Lessons from Outstanding General Managers*. New York: John Wiley & Sons, 1991.

O'Connor, Peter. *Using Computers in Hospitality and Tourism*. London: Cassell PLC, 1995.

Ogilvie, A.W.T. *Lecture Outline in Front Office*. American Hotel Association, 1923.

Paananen, Donna. *Selling Out: A How-to Manual on Reservations Management*. East Lansing, MI: Educational Institute, 1985.

Paige, Grace, and Paige, Jane. *The Hotel Receptionist*, 3rd ed. London: Holt, Rinehart and Winston, 1988.

———. *Hotel Front Desk Personnel*, rev. ed. New York: Van Nostrand Reinhold Co., Inc., 1988.

Pfeiffer, W., Voegele, M., and Wolley, G. *The Correct Service Department for Hotels, Motor Hotels, Motels and Resorts*. New York: Ahrens Publishing Co., Inc., 1962.

Picot, Derek. *Hotel Reservations*. Jersey City, NJ: Parkwest Publications, 1997.

Powers, Tom, and Barrows, Clayton. *Introduction to the Hospitality Industry*, New York: John Wiley & Sons, 2003.

Poynter, James. *Foreign Independent Tours*. Albany, NY: Delmar Publishers, 1989.

———. *Mystery Shopping*. Dubuque, IA: Kendall/Hunt Publishing, 1996.

*Property Management and Point of Sale Systems: Guide to Selection*. New York: American Hotel & Motel Association.

Raleigh, Lori, and Roginsky, Rachel (Eds.). *Hotel Investments: Issues & Perspectives*, 2nd ed. Orlando, FL: Educational Institute of the American Hotel & Lodging Industry, 1999.

Ransley, Josef, and Ingram, Hadyn (Eds.). *Developing Hospitality Properties and Facilities*. London: Butterworth-Heinemann, 2000.

*Relieving Reservation Headaches*. East Lansing, MI: Educational Institute of the American Hotel & Motel Association, 1979.

Renner, Peter. *Basic Hotel Front Office Procedures*, 3rd ed. New York: Van Nostrand Reinhold Co., Inc., 1993.

"Resale in the Lodging Industry: A Bell System Perspective." American Hotel & Motel Association, Mid-year Meeting, Nashville, TN, April 1982.

"Room Clerk, The Man Up Front." *Motel/Motor Inn Journal*, 1977.

Roper, A. J. *Hotel Consortia and Structures: An Analyses of the Emergence of Hotel Consortia as Transorganizational Forms*. Oxford University [no date].

Rosenzweig, Stan. *Hotel/Motel Telephone Systems: Opportunities Through Deregulation*. East Lansing, MI: Educational Institute of the American Hotel & Motel Association, 1982.

Ross, Bruce. "Hotel Reservation Systems Present and Future." Unpublished master's monograph, Cornell University, Ithaca, NY, May 1977.

Rushmore, Stephen. *Hotel Investments: A Guide for Lenders and Owners*. New York: Warren, Gorham & Lamont, Inc., 1990.

Rushmore, Stephen, and Baum, Erich. *Hotels & Motels: Valuations and Market Studies*. Addison, IL: Appraisal Institute, 2001.

Rutes, Walter, Penner, Richard, and Adams, Lawrence. *Hotel Design, Planning, and Development*. New York: W. W. Norton, 2001.

Rutherford, Denney. *Hotel Management and Operations*, 3rd ed. New York: John Wiley & Sons, 2001.

Saunders, K.C. *Head Hall Porter*. London: Catering Education Research Institute, 1980.

Saunders, K.C., and Pullen, R. *An Occupational Study of Room Maids in Hotels*. Middlesex, England: Middlesex Polytechnic, 1987.

Scatchard, Bill. *Upsetting the Applecart: A Common Sense Approach to Successful Hotel Operations for the '90s*. Box 19156, Tampa, FL 33686; 1994.

Schneider, Madelin, and Georgina Tucker. *The Professional Housekeeper*. New York: Van Nostrand Reinhold Co., Inc., 1989.

Self, Robert. *Long Distance for Less*. New York: Telecom Library, Inc., 1982.

Shaw, Margaret, and Morris, Susan. *Hospitality Sales: A Marketing Approach*. New York: John Wiley & Sons, 1999.

Sherry, John. *How to Exclude and Eject Undesirable Guests*. Stamford, CT: The Dahls, 1943.

Sicherman, Irving. *The Investment in the Lodging Business*. Scranton, PA: Sicherman, 1977.

*Starting and Managing a Small Motel*. Small Business Administration. Washington, DC: U.S. Government Printing Office, 1963.

*The State of Technology in the Lodging Industry*. New York: American Hotel & Motel Association, 1980.

Stiel, Holly. *Ultimate Service: The Complete Handbook to the World of the Concierge*. Upper Saddle River, NJ: Prentice Hall, 1994.

Stutts, Alan, and Borsenik, Frank. *Maintenance Handbook for Hotels, Motels and Resorts*, 4th ed. New York: John Wiley & Sons, Inc., 1997.

*Successful Credit and Collection Techniques*. East Lansing, MI: Educational Institute of the American Hotel & Motel Association, 1981.

Tarbet, J.R. *A Handbook of Hotel Front Office Procedure*. Pullman, WA: Student Book Corporation, circa 1955.

Taylor, Derek, and Thomason, Richard. *Profitable Hotel Reception*. Elmsford, NY: Pergamon Press, Inc., 1982.

*Trends in the Hotel-Motel Business*. New York: Pannell Kerr Forster & Co., various years.

*Uniform-Service Training*. Boston: Sheraton Corporation of America, 1960.

*Uniform System of Accounts for the Lodging Industry*, 9th ed. New York: Hotel Association of New York City, 1996.

Vallen, Jerome, and Abbey, James. *The Art and Science of Hospitality Management*. East Lansing, MI: Educational Institute, 1987.

Van Hoof, H., McDonald, M., Yu, L., and Vallen, G. *A Host of Opportunities: An Introduction to Hospitality Management*. Chicago: Richard D. Irwin, Inc., 1996.

VanStrien, Kimberly, et al. *Front Office Management and Operations*. Upper Saddle River, NJ: Prentice Hall, 1998.

Walker, Terri, and Miller, Richard. *The 2000 Hotel & Lodging Market Research Handbook*, 3rd ed. Norcross, GA: Richard K. Miller, 1999.

Weissinger, Suzanne S. *Hotel/Motel Operations*. Cincinnati, OH: South-Western Publishing Co., 1989.

White, Paul, and Beckley, Helen. *Hotel Reception*, 4th ed. London: Edward Arnold (Publishers) Ltd., 1982.

Wingenter, Tom, et al. *The Relationship of Lodging Prices to Occupancy: A Study of Accommodations in Northern Wisconsin*. Madison, WI: University of Wisconsin Cooperative Extension Service, 1982–83.

Wittemann, Ad. *Hotel Room Clerk*. Las Vegas, NV: Camelot Consultants, 1986.

Wolosz, Joe. *Hotel & Motel Sales, Marketing & Promotion: Strategies to Impact Revenue & Increase Occupancy for Smaller Lodging Properties*. San Francisco, CA: Infinite Corridor Publishers, 1997.

Woods, Robert, Heck, William, and Sciarini, Michael. *Turnover and Diversity in the Lodging Industry*. New York: American Hotel Foundation, 1998.

Woods, Robert, and King, Judith. *Managing for Quality in the Hospitality Industry*. East Lansing, MI: Educational Institute, 1996.

*Yellowstone Park Company Cashier Training Program*. Yellowstone: Yellowstone Park Co., 1978.

Yeoman, Ian, and Ingold, Anthony. *Yield Management*. London: Cassell PLC, 1997.

Yu, Lawrence. *The International Hospitality Business: Management and Operations*. Binghamton, NY: Haworth Hospitality Press, 1999.

# Glossary

Words in *italic* in each definition are themselves defined elsewhere in the Glossary. (Words not listed might be found in the Index.) cf. means "compare."

**account balance** The difference between the *debit* and *credit* values of the *guest bill*.

**account card** See *guest bill*.

**account receivable** A company, organization, or individual, *registered* or not, who has an outstanding bill with the hotel.

**accounts receivable ledger** The aggregate of individual *account receivable* records.

**ADA** See *Americans with Disabilities Act*.

**adjoining rooms** Rooms that abut along the corridor but do not connect through private doors; cf. *connecting rooms*.

**ADR** See *average daily rate*.

**advance deposit** A deposit furnished by the guest on a room *reservation* that the hotel is holding.

**affiliated hotel** One of a chain, *franchise,* or *referral* system, the membership of which provides special advantages, particularly a national reservation system.

**A folio** See *master account*.

**after departure (AD)** A *late charge*.

**allowance** A reduction to the folio, as an adjustment either for unsatisfactory service or for a posting error. Also called a *rebate*.

**amenities** Literally any extra product or service found in the hotel. A swimming pool, concierge desk, health spa, and so on are all technically known as amenities. However, this term has primarily come to be used for in-room guest products. Such complimentary in-room items as soap, shampoo, suntan lotion, mouthwash, and the like are most commonly considered amenities.

**amenity creep** The proliferation of all guest products and services when hotels compete by offering more extensive amenities; originally referred to in-room amenities or toiletries only.

**American plan (AP)** A method of quoting room rates where the charge includes room and three meals.

**Americans with Disabilities Act (ADA)** Established in 1990, the ADA prohibits discrimination against any guest or employee because of his or her disability.

**available rooms** The number of guest rooms the hotel has for sale—either the total in the hotel or the number unoccupied on a given day.

**average daily rate (ADR)** The average daily rate paid by guests; computed by dividing room revenue by the number of rooms occupied. More recently called sales per occupied room.

**back to back** (1) A sequence of consecutive *group* departures and arrivals usually arranged by tour operators so that rooms are never vacant; (2) a floor plan design that brings the piping of adjacent baths into a common shaft.

**bank** Coins and small bills given to the cashier for making change.

**bank cards** Credit cards issued by banks, usually for a smaller fee than that charged by *travel and entertainment cards*.

**bed and breakfast (B&B)** Lodging and breakfast offered in a domestic setting by families in their own homes; less frequently, the Continental plan.

**bell captain** The supervisor of the bellpersons and other uniformed service personnel.

**bellstand** The bellperson's desk located in the lobby close to and visible from the front desk.

**B folio** The second folio (the individual's folio) used with a *master account*.

**blanket reservation** A *block* of rooms held for a particular *group*, with individual members requesting assignments from that block.

**block** (1) A restriction placed in a pocket of the *room rack* to limit the clerk's discretion in assigning the room; (2) a number of rooms reserved for one *group*.

**book** To sell hotel space, either to a person or to a *group* needing a *block* of rooms.

**bottom line** The final line of a profit-and-loss statement: either net profit or net loss.

**box** A reservation term that allows no *reservations* from either side of the boxed dates to spill through.

**bucket** See *cashier's well*.

**California length** An extra-long bed, about 2 m to 2.1 m instead of the usual 1.9 m.

**call accounting system (CAS)** A computerized program that prices and records telephone calls on the guest's electronic folio through a *property management system (PMS)* interface.

**cancellation** A guest's request to the hotel to void a *reservation* previously made.

**cancellation number** A coded number provided by the hotel or *central reservations office* to a guest who cancels a *reservation*.

**cash advance** See *cash paid-outs*.

**cash disbursement** See *cash paid-outs*.

**cashier's report** The cash *turn-in* form completed by a departmental cashier at the close of the *watch*.

**cashier's well** The file that holds the guest folios, often recessed in the countertop; also known as tub, bucket, or *pit*.

**cash paid-outs** Monies disbursed for guests, either advances or loans, and charged to their accounts like other departmental services.

**casualty factor** The number of *reservations* of a *group* (*cancellations* plus *no-shows*) that fail to appear.

**central processing unit (CPU)** The hardware/*software* nucleus of the computer that performs and monitors the essential functions.

**central reservations office (CRO)** A private or chain-operated office that accepts and processes *reservations* on behalf of its membership.

**central reservations system (CRS)** The sophisticated hardware and *software* used by a *central reservations office* to accurately track and manage *reservations* requests for member properties.

**chargeback** Credit card charges refused by the credit card company for one reason or another.

**check-out hour** The time by which guests must vacate rooms or be charged for an additional day.

**city accounts receivable** See *city ledger*.

**city ledger** An *accounts receivable ledger* of non-registered guests.

**city ledger journal** The form used to record transactions that affect the *city ledger*.

**close of the day** An arbitrary hour that management designates to separate the records of one day from those of the next.

**closeout hour** Also called *close of the day*.

**commercial hotel** A transient hotel catering to a business clientele.

**commercial rate** A reduced room *rate* given to business people to promote occupancy.

**commissionable** An indication that the hotel will pay *travel agents* the standard fee for business placed.

**comp** Short for "complimentary" accommodations—and occasionally food and beverage—furnished without charge.

**company-made (reservation)** A *reservation* guaranteed by the arriving guest's company.

**concession** A hotel tenant (concessionaire) whose facilities and services are indistinguishable from those owned and operated by the hotel.

**concierge** (1) A European position, increasingly found in North American hotels, responsible for handling guests' needs, particularly those relating to out-of-hotel services; (2) designation of the sleeping floor where these services are offered.

**condominium** A multi-unit dwelling wherein each owner maintains separate title to the unit while sharing ownership rights and responsibilities for the public space.

**conference centre** A property that caters to small business meetings, corporate retreats, and conferences. Generally considered smaller in size and more personable in nature than a convention property.

**confirmed reservation** The hotel's acknowledgment, usually in writing, to the guest's *reservation* request.

**connecting rooms** *Adjoining rooms* with direct, private access, making use of the corridor unnecessary.

**continental breakfast** A small meal including some combination of the following: bread, rolls, sweet rolls, juice, and coffee.

Often set up in bulk by the innkeeper or host; continental breakfasts are usually self-service.

**corner (room)** An *outside room* on a corner of the building having two exposures.

**cot** See *rollaway bed*.

**credit** An accounting term that indicates a decrease in the *account receivable*; the opposite of *debit*.

**daybed** Similar to a *studio bed* except that it is an addition to the hotel room rather than a basic furnishing.

**day rate** A reduced charge for occupancy of less than overnight; used when the *party* arrives and departs on the same day. Also *part-day rate*.

**dead room change** A physical change of rooms made by the hotel in the guest's absence so no tip is earned by the *last* bellperson.

**debit** An accounting term that indicates an increase in the *account receivable*; the opposite of *credit*.

**deluxe** A designation implying the best accommodations; unreliable unless part of an official rating system.

**departure** Check-out.

**did not stay (DNS)** Means the guest left almost immediately after *registering*.

**difference returnable** See *exchange*.

**double** (1) A bed approximately 1.35 m by 1.9 m; (2) the rate charged for two persons occupying one room; (3) a room with a double bed.

**double occupancy** (1) Room occupancy by two persons; (2) a ratio relating the number of rooms double occupied to the number of rooms sold.

**downtime** That time span during which the computer is inoperative because of malfunction or pre-emptive operations.

**due back** See *exchange*.

**due bank** See *exchange*.

**due bill** See *trade advertising contract*.

**early arrival** A guest who arrives a day or two earlier than the *reservation* calls for.

**economy class** See *tourist class*.

**electronic data processing (EDP)** A data handling system that relies on electronic (computer) equipment.

**emergency key (E-key)** One key that opens all guest rooms, including those locked from within, even those with the room key still in the lock.

**European plan (EP)** A method of quoting room rates where the charge includes room accommodations only.

**exchange** The excess of cash *turn-in* over *net receipts*; the difference is returnable (due back) to the front-office cashier; also called *due back*, *due bank*, or *difference* returnable.

**executive room** See *studio*.

**exposure** The direction (north, south, east, or west) or view (ocean, mountain) in which the guest room faces.

**express check-in** Mechanical or electronic methods of check-in that expedite arrival and eliminate the need to stop at the desk.

**express check-out** Mechanical or electronic methods of check-out that expedite *departure* and eliminate the need to stop at the desk.

**family plan** A special room rate that allows children to occupy their parent's room at no additional charge.

**family room** (1) Two double beds; (2) a room with two such beds capable of accommodating four persons; see quad.

**FAM trip** Familiarization trip taken by travel agents at little or no cost to acquaint themselves with *properties* and destinations.

**fenced rates** One of several tools used by the reservations department to maximize room revenues under *yield management* systems, including non-refundable, prepaid *reservations* and *reservations* not subject to change.

**first class** A designation for medium-priced accommodations with corresponding facilities and services.

**flag** A device for calling the room clerk's attention to a particular room in the *room rack*.

**flat rate** (1) See *run-of-the-house rate*; (2) same price for *single* or *double occupancy*.

**float** The free use of outstanding funds during the period that cheques and credit card charges are in transition for payment.

**floor (release) limit** The maximum amount of charges permitted to a credit card user at a given *property* without clearance; the limit is established for the property, not for the user.

**forecast** A future projection of estimated business volume.

**forfeited deposit** A deposit reservation kept by the hotel when a *no-show* fails to cancel the reservation; also called a lost deposit.

**franchise** (1) An independently owned hotel or motel that appears to be part of a chain and pays a fee for that right and for the right to participate in the chain's advertising and reservations systems; (2) the chain's right (its franchise) to sell such permission, or the permission itself, or both.

**franchisee** One who buys a *franchise*.

**franchisor** One who sells a *franchise*.

**front** The next bellperson eligible for a *rooming* assignment or other errand apt to produce a *gratuity*; cf. *last*.

**front office** A broad term that includes the physical front desk as well as the duties and functions involved in the sale and service of guest rooms.

**front of the house** (1) The area of the hotel visible to guests in contrast to the back of the house, which is not in the public view; (2) all of the functions that are part of the *front office*.

**full house** Means 100 percent *occupancy*, all guest rooms sold.

**full service** Means that a complete line of services and departments are provided, in contrast to a *limited-service* hotel or motel.

**general manager (GM)** The hotel's chief executive.

**global distribution system (GDS)** The hardware, *software*, and computer lines over which travel agents, airlines, online subscription networks, and others access *central reservations systems* and individual *property management systems*.

**gratuity** A tip given to an employee by a guest, sometimes willingly and sometimes automatically added to the charges.

**graveyard** A work shift beginning about midnight.

**greens fee** A charge for the use of the golf course.

**group** A number of persons with whom the hotel deals (reservation, billing, etc.) as if they were one party.

**guaranteed rate** The assurance of a fixed rate regardless of *occupancy*, often given in consideration of a large number of *room nights* per year pledged by a company.

**guest account** See *guest bill*.

**guest bill** An accounting statement used to record and display the charges and payments made by registered guests (*accounts receivable*) during their hotel stay. Different formats are used for hand-prepared bills and bills prepared by *property management systems*; also known as folio or *account card*.

**guest cheque** The bill presented to patrons of the dining rooms and bars and, when signed, often used as the departmental voucher.

**guest history** A record of the guest's visits, including rooms assigned, rates paid, special needs, credit rating, and personal information; used to provide better guest service and better marketing approaches.

**guest night** The stay of one guest for one night; also called *room night* or bed night.

**guest-service area** See *front office*.

**handicapped room** A guest room furnished with devices and built large enough to accommodate guests with physical handicaps.

**hide-a-bed** See *sofa bed*.

**HITIS** An acronym for Hospitality Industry Technology Integration Standards, which are computer interface standards developed to facilitate the interface of computer systems from various vendors onto the hotel's *property management system*.

**HOBIC** An acronym for Hotel Outward Bound Information Centre, the telephone company's long-distance hotel network.

**holdover** See *overstay*.

**Hollywood bed** *Twin* beds joined by a common headboard.

**hospitality suite (room)** A facility used for entertaining, usually at conventions, trade shows, and similar meetings.

**hostel** An inexpensive but supervised facility with limited services catering to young travellers on foot or bicycle.

**hotelier** Innkeeper or hotel keeper, originally from the French.

**hotel manager** Hotel executive responsible for the front of the house, including *front office*, housekeeping, and uniformed services; sometimes called rooms manager or house manager.

**house bank** See *bank*.

**housekeeper's report** A report on the status of guest rooms, prepared by the linen room and used by the front desk to verify the accuracy of the *room rack*.

**housing bureau** A citywide reservations office, usually run by the convention bureau, for assigning *reservation* requests to participating hotels during a citywide convention.

**Hubbart room rate formula** A basis for determining room rates developed by Roy Hubbart and distributed by the American Hotel & Lodging Association.

**imprest petty cash** A technique for controlling petty cash disbursements by which a special, small cash fund is used for minor cash payments and periodically reimbursed.

**incentive (group, guest, tour, or trip)** Persons who have won a hotel stay (usually with transportation included) as a reward for meeting and excelling their sales quotas or other company-established standards.

**inclusive tour** The hotel's move into the lucrative group market. Combines housing, food, and entertainment but no transportation and usually packaged as a two- or three-night stay.

**independent** A *property* with no chain or *franchise* affiliation, although one proprietor might own several such properties.

**information rack** An alphabetic listing of registered guests with a room number cross-reference.

**in-house** On the premises, such as an in-house laundry.

**in-season rate** A *resort hotel's* maximum rate, charged when the demand is heaviest, as it is during the middle of the summer or winter; cf. *off-season rate*.

**inside room** A guest room that faces an inner courtyard or light court enclosed by three or four sides of the building.

**International Association of Travel Agents (IATA)** A professional affiliation that both lobbies on behalf of the travel industry and identifies/verifies legitimate travel agents to other vendors.

**in-WATS** See *wide area telephone service*.

**junior suite** One large room, sometimes with a half partition, furnished as both a *parlour* and a bedroom.

**king** An extra-long, extra-wide *double* bed at least 2 m by 2 m.

**lanai** A Hawaiian term for "veranda"; a room with a porch or balcony usually overlooking gardens or water.

**last** The designation for the bellperson who most recently completed a *front*.

**last-room availability** A sophisticated reservations system that provides real-time access between the chain's *central reservations system* and the hotel's *in-house property management system*.

**late arrival** A guest with a *reservation* who expects to arrive after the cutoff hour and so notifies the hotel.

**late charge (LC)** A departmental charge that arrives at the front desk for billing after the guest has checked out.

**late check-out** A departing guest who remains beyond the *check-out hour* with permission of the desk and thus without charge.

**ledger** A group of folios.

**light baggage** Insufficient luggage in quantity or quality on which to extend credit; the guest pays in advance.

**limited service** A hotel or motel that provides little or no services other than the room; a budget hotel (motel); cf. *full service*.

**linen closet** A storage closet for linens and other housekeeping supplies usually located conveniently along the corridor for the use of the housekeeping staff.

**lost and found** An area, usually under the housekeeper's jurisdiction, for the control and storage of lost-and-found items.

**maitre d'hotel** The headwaiter.

**master account** One folio prepared for a *group* (convention, company, tour) on which all group charges are accumulated. Sometimes called the *A folio*.

**master key** One key controlling several *pass keys* and opening all of the guests rooms on one floor; also called a floor key.

**miscellaneous charge order (MCO)** An airline voucher authorizing the sale of services to the guest named on the form, with payment due from the airline.

**modified American plan (MAP)** A method of quoting room rates in which the charge includes breakfast and dinner as well as the room.

**mom-and-pop** A small, family-owned business with limited capitalization in which the family, rather than paid employees, furnishes the bulk of the labour.

**moment of truth** A popular term describing the interaction between a guest and a staff member, when all of the advertising and representations made by the hotel come down to the quality of the service delivered at that moment.

**net receipts** The difference between cash taken in and *cash paid-outs*.

**night audit** A daily reconciliation, which is completed during the *graveyard* shift, of both *accounts receivable* and income from the *operating departments*.

**night auditor** The person or persons responsible for the *night audit*.

**no reservation (NR)** See *walk-in*.

**no-show** A *reservation* that fails to arrive.

**occupancy (percentage of occupancy, occupancy percentage)** A ratio relating the number of rooms sold *(room count)* to the number of rooms available for sale.

**occupied** (1) A room that is sold or taken and is not available for sale; (2) someone is physically in the room at this time.

**ocean view** Other than a front room, but with some view of the ocean.

**off-season rate** A reduced room rate charged by *resort hotels* when demand is lowest; cf. *in-season rate*.

**off the street (OS)** See *walk-in*.

**on change** The status of a room recently vacated but not yet available for new occupants.

**online (computer)** Computer facilities hooked directly to input and output devices for instantaneous communication.

**operating departments** Those divisions of the hotel directly involved with the service of the guest, in contrast to support divisions such as personnel and accounting.

**out of inventory (OOI)** A significant problem has removed this room from availability. Although *out of order (OOO)* rooms are usually available in only a matter of hours, OOI rooms may be unavailable for days or weeks.

**out of order (OOO)** The room is not available for sale because of some planned or unexpected temporary shutdown of facilities.

**outside call** A telephone call that enters the switchboard from outside the hotel; a call that terminates outside the hotel.

**outside laundry (valet)** A non-hotel laundry or valet service contracted by the hotel in order to offer a full line of services.

**outside room** A room on the perimeter of the building facing outward with an *exposure* more desirable than that of an *inside room*.

**out-WATS** See *wide area telephone service*.

**over or short** A discrepancy between the cash on hand and the amount that should be on hand.

**override** (1) Extra commission above a standard percentage to encourage or reward quantity bookings; (2) the process by which the operator bypasses certain limits built into the computer program.

**overstay** A guest who remains beyond the expiration of the anticipated stay.

**package** A number of services (transportation, room, food, entertainment) normally purchased separately but put together and marketed at a reduced price made possible by volume and *breakage*.

**paid in advance** A room charge that is collected prior to occupancy, which is the usual procedure when a guest has *light baggage*; with some motels, it is standard procedure for every guest.

**parlour** The living room portion of a *suite*.

**part-day rate (guest)** See *day rate*.

**party** *Front-office* term that references either the individual guest ("Who's the party in Room 100?") or several members of the group ("When will your party arrive?").

**pass key** (1) A sub *master key* capable of opening all locks within a limited, single set of 12 to 18 rooms, but no other; (2) a guest key for access to public space (spa, pool).

**penthouse** Accommodations, most always *suites*, located on the top floor of the hotel, theoretically on the roof.

**percentage of occupancy** See *occupancy*.

**permanent guest** A resident of long-term duration whose stay may or may not be formalized with a lease.

**petty cash** See *imprest petty cash*.

**pickup** (1) The procedure used with NCR front-office posting machines to accumulate the folio balance by entering the previous balance into the machine before posting the new charges; (2) the figure so entered.

**pit** See *cashier's well*.

**plan** The basis on which room rate charges are made; see *American plan* and *European plan*.

**point-of-sale (POS) terminal** An electronic "cash register" providing *online* communications to the *property management system* from a remote sales location, in contrast to an input device at the *front office*.

**porte cochère** The covered entryway that provides shelter for those entering and leaving a hotel; French: coach gate [port-ko-shâr].

**preassign** *Reservations* are assigned to specific rooms that are *blocked* before the guests arrive; cf. *preregistration*.

**prereg(istration)** Registration is done by the hotel before the guest arrives, although the actual *registration card* is not completed; used with groups and tours to reduce *front-office* congestion, since individual guests need not then approach the desk; cf. *preassign*.

**property** Another way to reference a hotel, includes physical facilities and personnel.

**property management system (PMS)** A hotel's, that is a *property's*, basic computer installation designed for a variety of functions in both the back office and the *front office*.

**quad** Accommodations for four persons.

**quality assurance (QA)** A managerial and operational approach that enlists employee support in delivering a consistently high level of service.

**quality circle (QO)** A group of persons from different but related departments who meet on a regular basis for dialogue and problem resolution as part of a *quality assurance* program.

**quality management (QM)** See *total quality management* and *quality assurance*.

**quality of the reservation** Differentiates *reservations* on how likely they are to be honoured by the guest: *paid-in-advance reservation* vs. guaranteed reservation vs. 6 P.M. cutoff hour, etc.

**queen** An extra-long, extra-wide *double* bed, about 2 m to 2.1 m long by 1.5 m wide; see *California length*; see *king*.

**quote** To state the cost of an item, room rates in particular.

**rate cutting** A reduction in rate that attracts business away from competitors rather than create new customers or new markets.

**real estate investment trust (REIT)** A form of real estate ownership (public corporation) that became popular during the real estate recovery of the mid-1990s because of its income tax advantages.

**rebate** See *allowance*.

**referral** A *central reservation system* operated by *independent* properties in contrast to that operated by chains and *franchisors* for their *affiliated hotels*.

**registered, not assigned (RNA)** The guest has *registered*, but is awaiting assignment to a specific room until space becomes available; see *on change*.

**register(ing), registration** (1) Indication (completing and signing the *registration card*) by a new arrival of intent to become a guest; (2) register: the name for a book that served at one time as the registration record.

**registration card** A form completed during *registration* to provide the hotel with information about the guest, including name and address, and to provide the guest with information about the hotel, including legal issues.

**rep(resentative)** Short for hotel representative: An agent under contract, rather than an employee under salary, who represents the hotel in distant cities or for special activities, chiefly marketing activities, but sometimes gaming related.

**reservation** A mutual agreement between the guest and the hotel, the former to take accommodations on a given date for a given period of time and the latter to furnish the same.

**residential hotel** A hotel catering to long-stay guests who have made the *property* their home and residence; see also *permanent guest*.

**resort hotel** A hotel that caters to vacationing guests by providing recreational and entertainment facilities.

**RevPar** Short for revenue per available room, a ratio of room revenue to the number of *available rooms*.

**rollaway bed** A portable utility bed approximately 0.75 m by 1.8 m; also called a *cot*.

**room count** The number of occupied rooms.

**rooming (a guest)** The entire procedure during which the desk greets, *registers*, and assigns new arrivals, and the bell staff accompanies them to their rooms (rooms them).

**rooming slip** A form issued by the desk during the *rooming* procedure to the bellperson for guest identification, and left by the bellperson with the guest to give the guest an opportunity to verify name, rate, and room number.

**room night** See *guest night*.

**room rack** A piece of *front-office* equipment, largely replaced by the *property management system*, in which each guest room is represented by a metal pocket with colours and symbols to aid the room clerk in identifying the accommodations.

**room service** Food and beverage service provided in the privacy of the guest room by a designated (room service) waiter or waitress.

**rooms ledger** All of the *guest bills* owed by registered guests (*accounts receivable*) and maintained in the *front office*, in contrast to the group of *city ledger* bills (non-registered guests) maintained in the accounting or back office.

**run-of-the-house rate** A special *group* rate, generally the midpoint of the rack rate with a single, flat price applying to any room, *suites* excepted, on a best-available basis.

**safety deposit boxes** Individual sections of the vault where guests store valuables and cashiers keep house *banks*.

**segmentation** The proliferation of many hotel types as the lodging industry attempts to target its facilities to smaller and smaller market niches (segments).

**sell and report** *Wholesalers*, tour operators, *reps*, airlines, and *central reservation systems* free sell rooms, periodically reporting the sale to the hotel; also called status control.

**sell up** Convincing the arriving guest to take a higher priced room than was planned or reserved.

**service charge** A percentage (usually from 10 to 20 percent) added to the bill for distribution to service employees in lieu of direct tipping.

**service elevators** Back elevators for use by employees (room service, housekeeping, maintenance, etc.) on hotel business and not readily visible to the guests.

**single** (1) A bed approximately 0.9 m by 1.9 m; (2) a room with accommodations for one; (3) occupancy by one person; (4) the rate charged for one person.

**size** The capacity of the hotel as measured by the number of guest rooms.

**skipper** A guest who departs surreptitiously, leaving an unpaid bill.

**slide** The transcription error caused by a misplaced decimal, as when 36.20 is written as 3.62.

**sofa bed** A sofa with a fixed back and arms that unfolds into a standard *single* or *double* bed; also called a *hide-a-bed*.

**software** The programs and routines that give instructions to the computer.

**special attention (SPATT)** A label assigned to important guests designated for special treatment; see *very important person*.

**spread rate** Assignment of *group* members or conventioneers using the standard rate distribution, although prices might be less than rack rates; cf. *run-of-the-house rate*.

**star reservation** Indicates the arrival of a *very important person*.

**studio** (1) A bed approximately 0.9 m wide by 1.9 m long without a headboard or footboard that serves as a sofa during the day; (2) the room containing such a bed; cf. *sofa bed*.

**suite** A series of *connecting rooms* with one or more bedrooms and a *parlour*; very large suites occasionally include additional rooms such as dining rooms; see *hospitality suite*.

**swing** The work shift between the day *watch* and the *graveyard* shift; usually starts between 3 and 4 P.M.

**timeshare** (1) A method of acquiring vacation accommodations by which each occupant purchases the right to use the facility (room or apartment) for a specified period; partial ownership of the real estate, which was not possible initially, has broadened the market; (2) term for users who share computer facilities.

**total quality management (TQM)** A way to continuously improve performance at every level of operation, in every functional area of an organization, using all available human and capital resources. See also *quality assurance*.

**tour group** See *package*.

**tourist class** A designation for *limited-service* hotels whose accommodations frequently lack private baths; also called *economy class*.

**trade advertising contract** An agreement by which hotel accommodations are swapped for advertising space or broadcast time; also called a *due bill*.

**transient accounts receivable** An accounts receivable ledger of registered guests.

**transient guest** A short-term guest.

**transient ledger** See *rooms ledger*.

**transmittal form** The form provided by national credit card companies for recording and remitting non-electronic credit card charges accumulated by the hotel.

**transposition** A transcription error caused by reordering the sequence of digits, as when 389 is written as 398.

**travel and entertainment card (T&E)** A credit card issued by a proprietary company other than a retailer for which the user pays an annual fee; cf. *bank card*.

**turn-in** The sum deposited with the general cashier by the departmental cashier at the close of each shift.

**turnkey** A facility (computer, *franchise*, entire hotel) so complete that it is ready for use at the turn of a key.

**twin** (1) A bed approximately 1 m wide by 1.9 m long to sleep a single occupant; (2) a room with two such beds, *twins*.

**twins** Two *twin* beds.

**type** The kind of market toward which the hotel is directed, traditionally: *commercial*, *residential*, and *resort*.

**understay** A guest who leaves before the expiration of the anticipated stay.

**unoccupied** (1) An unsold room; (2) a room that is *occupied* but temporarily vacant, the guest is out.

**U-owe-me** See *exchange*.

**upgrade** Move a *reservation* or a currently registered guest to a better accommodation or class of service.

**vacancy** The hotel is not fully *occupied*, so there are rooms available for sale.

**very important person (VIP)** A *reservation* or guest who warrants *special attention* and handling.

**walk (a guest)** To turn away guests holding confirmed *reservations* due to a lack of available rooms.

**walk-in (WI)** A guest without a *reservation* who requests and receives accommodations.

**watch** Another term for the work shift.

**wholesaler** An entrepreneur who conceives, finances, and services *group* and *package* tours that he or she promotes (often through travel agents) to the general public.

**wide area telephone service (WATS)** Long-distance telephone lines provided at special rates—even wholesale—to large users; separate charges are levied for incoming and outgoing WATS lines.

**yield** The product of *occupancy* times *average daily rate.*

**yield management** (1) Controlling room rates and restricting occupancy in order to maximize gross revenue (*yield*) from all sources; (2) a computerized program using artificial intelligence.

# Exhibits Credits

## Chapter 1

Exhibit 1-1 (page 4): Courtesy of the Trump Organization.

Exhibit 1-2 (page 6): Statistics provided by the Hotel Association of Canada.

Exhibit 1-5 (page 14): Courtesy of Canada Select.

Exhibit 1-6 (page 17): Reprinted with permission from A-1 Lakeview Bed and Breakfast at Porter's Lake, Nova Scotia.

Exhibit 1-10 (page 24): Courtesy of Barton Creek Resort, Austin, Texas.

Exhibit 1-11 (page 27): Adapted from Statistics Canada website http://www40.statcan.ca/l01/cst01/arts38a.htm (Last Modified 2006-08-31).

Exhibit 1-12 (page 28): Adapted from Statistics Canada website http://www40.statcan.ca/l01/cst01/arts40a.htm (Last Modified 2006-09-01).

Exhibit 1-16 (page 34): Courtesy of Las Vegas Convention and Visitors Authority, Las Vegas, Nevada.

Exhibit 1-17 (page 36): Courtesy of the Hotel Association of Canada.

## Chapter 2

Exhibit 2-2 (page 54): Courtesy of the Wynfrey, Birmingham, Alabama.

Exhibit 2-4 (page 60): Courtesy of the Fairmont Royal York, Toronto, Ontario.

Exhibit 2-5 (page 62): Courtesy of the Fairmont Royal York, Toronto, Ontario.

Exhibit 2-6 (page 64): Courtesy of Jerome B. Temple and *Lodging* magazine.

Exhibit 2-7 (page 65): Courtesy of Grand Hyatt Washington, Washington, D.C.

Exhibit 2-8 (page 66): Courtesy of Delta Hotels & Resorts, Toronto, Ontario, Canada.

Exhibit 2-10 (page 67): Courtesy of Wilcox International, Inc., Division of American Hotel Register Co., Northbrook, Illinois.

Exhibit 2-13 (page 70): Courtesy of the Sofitel Chicago Water Tower Hotel, Chicago, Illinois.

Exhibit 2-14 (page 70): Courtesy of the Mirage Hotel, Las Vegas, Nevada.

Exhibit 2-15 (page 71): Courtesy of Candlewood Hotel Company, Wichita, Kansas.

## Chapter 3

Exhibit 3-1 (page 83): Courtesy of Smith Travel Research.

Exhibit 3-2 (page 84): Reproduced with permission from *The Rooms Chronicle* (Volume 2, No 5, Sept/Oct 1994), NMRG Publishing, PO Box 2036, Niagara University, NY 14109.

Exhibit 3-3 (page 85): Courtesy of Delta/Fairmont Hotels.

Exhibit 3-4 (page 87): Courtesy of InterContinental Hotels.

Exhibit 3-5 (page 89): Courtesy of InterContinental Hotels.

Exhibit 3-6 (page 93): Courtesy of Delta/Fairmont Hotels.

Exhibit 3-7 (page 94): Courtesy of Delta/Fairmont Hotels.

Exhibit 3-8 (page 95): *The Professional Housekeeper* 4e Schneider, Copyright © 1999; "Reprinted with permission from John Wiley & Sons, Inc."

Exhibit 3-9 (page 96): Courtesy of American Hotel & Lodging Association.

Exhibit 3-10 (page 97): Courtesy of Delta/Fairmont Hotels.

Exhibit 3-11 (page 98): Courtesy of Delta/Fairmont Hotels.

Exhibit 3-12 (page 99): Courtesy of American Hotel & Lodging Association.

Exhibit 3-13 (page 99): Courtesy of Delta/Fairmont Hotels.

## Chapter 4

Exhibit 4-1 (page 108): *Hotel and Motel Management Magazine*.

Exhibit 4-2 (page 109): Courtesy of Fairmont Hotels.

Exhibit 4-4 (page 115): *Hotel and Motel Management Magazine*.

Exhibit 4-5 (page 116): Adapted from Statistics Canada website http://www40.statcan.ca/l01/cst01/comm09a.htm (Last Modified: 2005-02-18).

Exhibit 4-6(a) (page 117): Courtesy of Fairmont Hotels.

Exhibit 4-6(b) (page 118): Courtesy of Fairmont Hotels.

Exhibit 4-7 (page 119): *Lodging Magazine's* Lodging Trends/Pegasus Report.

Exhibit 4-8 (page 120): Courtesy of Fairmont Hotels and Resorts.

Exhibit 4-10(a) (page 130): Courtesy of TravelCLICK.

Exhibit 4-10(b) (page 131): Courtesy of TravelCLICK.

## Chapter 5

Exhibit 5-1(a) (page 140): Courtesy of Cyber Tigers, Inc. Chicago, Illinois.

Exhibit 5-1(b) (page 141): Courtesy of Cyber Tigers, Inc. Chicago, Illinois.

Exhibit 5-6 (page 153): Courtesy of IACB International Association of Convention Bureaus, Washington, D.C.

Exhibit 5-7 (page 153): Courtesy of IACB International

Association of Convention Bureaus, Washington, D.C.

Exhibit 5-8(a) (page 154): Courtesy of the Metro Toronto Convention Centre, Toronto, Ontario, Canada.

Exhibit 5-8(b) (page 155): Courtesy of the Metro Toronto Convention Centre, Toronto, Ontario, Canada.

Exhibit 5-9 (page 161): Courtesy of the Metro Toronto Convention Centre, Toronto, Ontario, Canada.

Exhibit 5-11 (page 166): Courtesy of Jennifer Brown, CMP; Strategic Site Specialist, Meeting Sites Resource, Newport Beach, California.

## Chapter 6

Exhibit 6-1 (page 171): Courtesy of AmeriSuites Incorporated, Patterson, New Jersey and Multi-Systems, Inc., Phoenix, Arizona.

Exhibit 6-5 (page 180): Courtesy of Geac Computers, Inc., Tustin, California.

## Chapter 8

Exhibit 8-2 (page 235): Courtesy of the Wedgewood Hotel, Vancouver, British Columbia, Canada.

Exhibit 8-3 (page 237): Courtesy of Fairmont Hotels and Resorts.

Exhibit 8-7 (page 248): Courtesy of Hayman Island Resort, North Queensland, Australia.

Exhibit 8-10 (page 255): Courtesy of Multi-Systems, Incorporated, Phoenix, Arizona.

Exhibit 8-11 (page 258): Courtesy of The Fairmont Hotel and Tower, San Francisco, California.

Exhibit 8-12 (page 259): Adapted from "Highly Effective Bell Staff Enhances Your Property's Image." *Hotel & Resort Industry,* May 1988, pp. 84–89.

Exhibit 8-14 (page 264): Courtesy of Hilton Niagara Falls, Niagara Falls, Ontario.

## Chapter 9

Exhibit 9-1 (page 269): Courtesy of the Canadian Tourism Commission.

Exhibit 9-3 (page 273): Courtesy of the Hotel Association of Canada.

Exhibit 9-4 (page 274): Courtesy of the Hotel Association of Canada.

Exhibit 9-6 (page 276): Reprinted with permission from Evelyne Lesage and the Bear Trail Couples Resort.

Exhibit 9-7 (page 280): Courtesy of priceline.com, Stamford, Connecticut.

Exhibit 9-11(a) (page 290): Courtesy of the American Hotel & Motel Association, Washington, D.C.

Exhibit 9-11(b) (page 291): Courtesy of the American Hotel & Motel Association, Washington, D.C.

Exhibit 9-13 (page 295): Courtesy of Laventhol & Horwath, Philadelphia.

Exhibit 9-15 (page 298): Courtesy of the Hospitality Sales and Marketing Association International, New York.

## Chapter 10

Exhibit 10-4 (page 311): Courtesy of Daytona Beach Hotel Resort, Daytona Beach, Florida.

Exhibit 10-5 (page 315): Courtesy of the Radisson Hotel Ottawa Centre, Ottawa, Ontario, Canada.

Exhibit 10-7 (page 318): Courtesy of the Stouffer Westchester Hotel, White Plains, New York.

Exhibit 10-8 (page 319): Courtesy of the Hawaii Prince Hotel, Honolulu, Hawaii.

Exhibit 10-9 (page 322): Courtesy of Kayco Systems, Lake Elsinore, California.

Exhibit 10-11 (page 326): Courtesy of the Hotel Macdonald, Edmonton, Alberta, Canada.

Exhibit 10-12 (page 329): Courtesy of the Sydney Renaissance Hotel, Sydney, New South Wales, Australia.

## Chapter 11

Exhibit 11-1 (page 336): Courtesy of Mr. Payroll Corporation, Fort Worth, Texas.

Exhibit 11-2 (page 341): Courtesy of Kayco Systems, Lake Elsinore, California.

Exhibit 11-7 (page 349): Courtesy of Kayco Systems, Lake Elsinore, California.

Exhibit 11-8 (page 352): © HER MAJESTY THE QUEEN IN RIGHT OF CANADA as represented by the Royal Mounted Police (RCMP). Reprinted with the permission of the RCMP.

Exhibit 11-9 (page 353): © HER MAJESTY THE QUEEN IN RIGHT OF CANADA as represented by the Royal Mounted Police (RCMP). Reprinted with the permission of the RCMP.

Exhibit 11-10 (page 354): Courtesy of Angstrom Technologies, Erlanger, Kentucky.

Exhibit 11-11 (page 354): © HER MAJESTY THE QUEEN IN RIGHT OF CANADA as represented by the Royal Mounted Police (RCMP). Reprinted with the permission of the RCMP.

## Chapter 12

Exhibit 12-1 (page 363): Courtesy Canadian Bankers Association and the Nilson Report.

Exhibit 12-3 (page 366): Courtesy of Centel Transaction Services, Las Vegas, Nevada.

## Chapter 13

Exhibit 13-10 (page 408): Courtesy of American Hotel Register Co., Northbrook, Illinois.

## Chapter 14

Exhibit 14-1 (page 423): *Hotel & Motel Management,* January 15, 2001.

Exhibit 14-4 (page 425): Courtesy of Centel, Las Vegas, Nevada.

Exhibit 14-5 (page 427): Courtesy of Teledex Corporation, San Jose, California.

Exhibit 14-6 (page 430): Courtesy of Wyndham Hotels & Resorts, Dallas, Texas.

Exhibit 14-7 (page 434): Courtesy of Schlage Lock Company, San Francisco, California.

Exhibit 14-8 (page 435): Courtesy of ILCO Unican, Inc., Montreal, Quebec.

Exhibit 14-9 (page 436): Courtesy of CORKEY Control Systems, Hayward, California.

Exhibit 14-11 (page 439): Courtesy of Winfield Locks, Inc., Costa Mesa, California.

Exhibit 14-12 (page 441): Courtesy of ILCO Unican, Inc., Montreal, Quebec, Canada.

Exhibit 14-13 (page 441): Courtesy of TESA Entry Systems, Norcross, Georgia.

Exhibit 14-14 (page 442): Courtesy of Onity, Inc. Norcross, Georgia.

Exhibit 14-15 (page 443): *Lodging Hospitality Magazine.*

Exhibit 14-17 (page 447): Courtesy of Elsafe of Nevada and Elsafe International, Vanvikan, Norway.

Exhibit 14-18 (page 448): Courtesy of Minibar North America, Inc., Bethesda, Maryland.

Exhibit 14-19 (page 449): Courtesy of Minibar North America, Inc., Bethesda, Maryland.

Exhibit 14-20 (page 450): Courtesy of SpectraVision, Richardson, Texas.

# Index